INTERNATIONAL LIBRARY OF GROUP ANALYSIS 22

The Social Unconscious
Selected Papers

Earl Hopper

Foreword by Malcolm Pines

Jessica Kingsley Publishers
London and Philadelphia

For permission to reprint the text contained in this book I wish to thank the following co-authors and publishers:

1. 'Some effects of supervisory style: a sociological analysis', published in 1965 by *The British Journal of Sociology XVI*, 3, 189–203. 2. 'A Sociological View of Large Groups' (written with Mrs Anne Weyman) published in 1975 in L. Kreeger (ed) *The Large Group: Dynamics and Therapy in London* by Constable and Company Limited. Reprinted in 1994 in London by Karnac Books (Ltd). 3. 'Report on the Large Group' (written with Dr Lionel Kreeger) published in 1980 in C. Garland (ed) *Proceedings of the Survivor Syndrome Workshop (1979). Group Analysis*, Special Edition, November, 67–81. 4. 'Overview' (written with Mrs Caroline Garland) published in 1980 in C. Garland (ed) *Proceedings of the Survivor Syndrome Workshop (1979). Group Analysis*, Special Edition, November, 93–97. 5. 'The Problem of Context in Group Analytic Psychotherapy: A Clinical Illustration and a Brief Theoretical Discussion', published in 1985 in M. Pines (ed) *Bion and Group Psychotherapy*, in London by Routledge and Kegan Paul. 6. 'The social unconscious in clinical work', published in 1996 in *Group 20*, 1, 7–42. 7. 'On the nature of hope in psychoanalysis and group analysis', published in 2001 in the *British Journal of Psychotherapy 18*, 2, 205–226.

First published in the United Kingdom in 2003
by Jessica Kingsley Publishers Ltd
116 Pentonville Road
London N1 9JB, England
and
325 Chestnut Street
Philadelphia, PA 19106, USA

www.jkp.com

Library of Congress Cataloging in Publication Data
A CIP catalog record for this book is available from the Library of Congress

British Library Cataloguing in Publication Data
A CIP catalogue record for this book is available from the British Library

ISBN 1 84310 088 6

Printed and Bound in Great Britain by Athenaeum Press,
Gateshead, Tyne and Wear

The Social Unconscious offers a carefully composed selection of the author's group analytic contributions. Their composition amounts to what could be described as a continuous crescendo, starting from 'A Sociological View of Large Groups' to the paper on 'The Social Unconscious in Clinical Work', culminating in Earl Hopper's profound thought on countertransference in groups and the nature of hope in group analysis. To absorb them certainly does make a demand on the reader, although a very rewarding one as the complexities of sociology, group analysis and psychoanalysis are put in mutually enriching perspectives, a thing not usually done in clinical papers today. Reading becomes sheer pleasure when Earl Hopper, as a practising analyst, occasionally unbuttons his academic shirt, showing his passionate concern for those who share the group analytic circle as subjects and citizens.

— Dieter Nitzgen,
Psychoanalyst and Group Analyst, Germany

Earl Hopper's writing contributes a penetrating and unique view of pathology rooted in society as well as in the individual psyche. From the clinical perspective, he advances our knowledge of the social unconscious pointed to by S.H. Foulkes, and augments the better-known individual unconscious brought into clinical practice by Freud.

— Dennis Brown,
Psychoanalyst and Group Analyst, UK

Contents

List of Tables and Figures

Foreword

Earl Hopper's mastery of the theories and facts of formal sociology is evident in the early papers of this collection. We can follow his evolution to mastery of the different but related theories and facts of group analysis and psychoanalysis in the later papers. He does not jettison ideas and perspectives, but continues to integrate the old with the new in ways that are both conservative and innovative.

When I read the proposal for the publication of this selection of papers, I suggested that readers would appreciate a more personal note, an introduction to the person of the author. I am pleased that my suggestion was accepted. In his Acknowledgements, he has paid generous tribute to his mentors and teachers. In fact, we should all acknowledge such indebtedness, especially if we proclaim the primacy of social factors, and if we regard personal creativity as part of social and cultural processes.

Earl Hopper weaves a fascinating and complex tapestry from the threads of the social and of the individual. Although explicit in the papers on aggression and social constraints, and on the large group, this group analytical perspective is brought out most fully in the papers on context and countertransference processes.

'Wounded Bird' discloses the depths to which the author plunges into his own subjectivity in following the group's unconscious dynamics. He does this in a way that exemplifies Keats' 'negative capability', the quality possessed by a person who is 'capable of being in uncertainties, mysteries, doubts, without any irritable reaching after facts and reasons'. Hopper held his grip on his uncertainties, mysteries and doubts until he felt able to reach a deeper understanding of the communications in his group, which he then expressed with passion. We can see the response that his intervention brought about.

This book concludes with a paper on hope, which Hopper understands as the exercise of the transcendent imagination within a particular social, cultural and political context. He draws ideas from various fields of knowledge that are essential to our work as psychoanalysts and group analysts. Hopper has understood my own papers on hope in connection with healing, wholeness and coherency (Pines 1998), and has built upon these views.

To my mind this selection of papers on the social unconscious demonstrates a dynamic tension within Hopper: the social scientist, hungry for overarching theories and scientific facts; the psychoanalyst, aware of the depths and complexities of each person's unique mentality; and the group analyst, striving to bring these disciplines into productive coherency. I see this dynamic tension as a continuing source of creativity, involving a relentless struggle to resolve internal and external conflicts.

Earl Hopper and I have had an interwoven and productive but at times difficult relationship. Together we launched the International Library of Group Psychotherapy and Group Process published by Routledge, which was the series previous to this present International Library of Group Analysis. Without his energy and drive the series would not have appeared, and I am glad to acknowledge his part in it. He wrote the Introduction to my own Collected Papers, and he has repaid my compliment to him by asking me to write this Foreword. However, I am the senior colleague who owned the print to which Hopper refers, and with which he identified, in 'Wounded Bird'. I admired this print, arranged its framing and hung it in the apartment in which Hopper and I both worked.

Earl Hopper has had a distinguished career as a sociologist, psychoanalyst and group analyst. He is a valued colleague and teacher in England, the United States and elsewhere. He has not flinched from the perilous work that is required in order to integrate sociology, psychoanalysis and group analysis. Hopper's personal qualities of combative determination and optimism have helped him to cope with the turmoil that is always present at the boundaries. We have benefited from his commitment to the 'work', and can look forward to the publication of further books.

Reference

Pines, M. (1998) 'Psychic Development and the Group Analytic Situation'. In M. Pines (ed) *Circular Reflections*. London: Jessica Kingsley Publishers.

Acknowledgements

The publication of a selection of my papers on the social unconscious reflects my attempts to integrate personal, social and intellectual diversity and contrariety. It gives me the opportunity to acknowledge the help and encouragement that I have received from friends and colleagues, many of whom taught me more than I realized at the time. Some of my mentors are now dead. Since they were unable to wait, I have to comfort myself with the old adage 'Better late than never'. I would also like to record some aspects of my transitions from St Louis to London, and from sociology to group analysis and psychoanalysis.

When I was an undergraduate at Washington University in St Louis, I wanted to become a psychoanalyst. Although I was fascinated by anthropology, sociology and social psychology, I thought that being a psychoanalyst offered a better opportunity for more satisfying work. At that time in the United States, in order to become a psychoanalyst it was necessary first to become a psychiatrist. As I prepared to go to Harvard Medical School, I was persuaded by Mrs Katherine Draper, my High School sociology teacher, to stay in St Louis, and to do post-graduate work in the Department of Sociology. Katherine was the only daughter of a well-known general practitioner, and the first feminist I had met. I wish that I could convey how liberating it was to have heard a High School teacher in St Louis during the 1950s argue that Afro-Americans, who were then called 'Negroes', should be able to eat at the same restaurants as Whites, and that socialism was not sinful.

While studying at Washington University, I was deeply influenced by Professor Jules Henry, who was a psychoanalytically informed anthropologist whose work was in the field of personality and culture. I was also influenced by Professor Alvin Gouldner, who was preoccupied with the problems of conflict and consensus in sociology, but especially by Professor Robert Hamblin, who kindled my interest in the study of small groups, and Professor Joseph Kahl who taught social stratification. These sociologists were all interested in social systems as well as in personality, and taught their subjects in such a way that I was unaware that the study of one might preclude the study of the other.

In 1961 I became friends with Eric Dunning, who is currently a Professor of Sociology at the University of Leicester, while he was studying sociology in St Louis. Eric introduced me to Professor Ilya Neustadt and his colleague Professor Norbert Elias, who invited me to be an Assistant Lecturer in Sociology at the University of Leicester. Needing a break from The Civil Rights Movement, I accepted the position with pleasure. In 1962 my wife and daughter and I arrived in Southampton on the SS Rotterdam thinking that after 'doing Europe' for a year or so, we would return to the United States. However, in 1967, after a further four years as an Assistant Lecturer at Cambridge University, where I was deeply influenced by the work of Professor David Lockwood on social cohesion, I came to the London School of Economics, where I was a Lecturer in Sociology until 1982.

I am especially indebted to Norbert Elias, both professionally and personally. I always learned from my 'conversations' with him. Norbert was very fond of ending heated debates by saying, 'Well, my Dear, we must agree to disagree'. When I came to London and felt that I needed personal therapy, I discussed this with Norbert. He referred me to Mrs Ilse Seglow, a Founder Member of the British Association of Psychotherapists. Norbert told me that Ilse was also a group analyst. She had been an actress, had studied sociology in Frankfurt during the 1930's, and was very interested in social issues.

In due course, I became more and more interested in clinical work, and became a student at the Association. Ilse became my training therapist. I wish that she had been more of a psychoanalyst and less of a therapist who worked according to her own unique lights and voices, but my therapy and collaboration with Ilse were very important to me.[1]

At a Conference of the International Association of Group Psychotherapy in 1968 in Vienna, I observed that in debate with Dr Eric Berne, the founder of transactional analysis, Malcolm Pines, who at that time worked at the Cassell Hospital with Dr Tom Maine, one of the founders of the therapeutic community movement, was fearless in expressing his own psychoanalytical views, and seemed able to be both a psychoanalyst and a group analyst without a personal sense of conflict; Ilse suggested that I seek supervision from Malcolm for my first training case. Later Malcolm consulted to the therapeutic community at the Atkinson Morley Hospital, and in 1971, thanks to a Fellowship from the Nuffield Foundation, I worked at the Hospital as an Honorary Psychotherapist and Research Officer, mainly in order to have more intensive clinical experience within a hospital setting.

Ilse then encouraged me to ask Dr Walter Schindler for supervision. Walter was analyzed by Stekel, and like Malcolm worked with both individuals and groups, albeit from a different point of view, more influenced by the pioneers in group psychotherapy in Germany. The patient whom I brought to supervision was mute, but by default I learned a great deal from Walter's clinical seminars and personal reminiscences about psychoanalysis in pre-war Berlin and in post-war London, and about his several discussions with Freud and constant debates with Foulkes. I qualified as a psychotherapist in 1971.

Ilse also encouraged me to enroll in the first Introductory Course offered by the new Institute of Group Analysis. She recommended that I join a group conducted by Dr Robin Skynner. She said that Robin was not reluctant to model a certain 'manliness' within a milieu in which most of the males in our profession were concerned with being good enough mothers. Personally, I found him to be the 'Norman Mailer' of group analysis, but I was deeply impressed by the sincerity of his efforts to locate symptoms within the crucible of the family, and to treat people within this natural unit, at least in so far as it was possible to do so. At the time, his work was radical and creative in its attempts to bring together insights from adjacent disciplines. However, I never really understood his continuing attacks on psychoanalysis, and assumed that more personal issues were involved.

Ilse co-conducted a group with Mr Harold Kaye for five years. Harold was one of the founders of the Institute of Group Analysis, and deeply influenced by Jungian analysis and by his work with Foulkes. After I was in group analysis with Ilse and Harold, he supervised my first group.

Ilse and Harold introduced me to Dr S. H. Foulkes. I learned that although several pioneers began to work with people in groups for the purpose of providing psychotherapy, Foulkes sought to understand the social unconscious. Acknowledging the influence of Norbert's ideas, he stressed the importance of the sociality of human nature. He was the first to outline the theory and practice of group analysis as a form of psychoanalytic therapy, and as a modification to the classical psychoanalytical model of personality and human development. I had several informal discussions with Foulkes, who invited me to become interested in the Group Analytic Society, and to meet some of his colleagues.

I was fortunate to have further supervision for my groups from Foulkes within the context of what he called a 'slow-open' counter-transference workshop. Among the members of this workshop were several psychoanalysts from abroad, including Dr Bill Blomfield from Melbourne. Bill also believed that group analysis and psychoanalysis should not be distinct disciplines. I corresponded with Bill after he returned to Melbourne, and was always impressed by his willingness to consider new ideas, and by his struggles to integrate them with what he already knew but sensed was inadequate. I qualified as a group analyst in 1974.

My work with Dr Margaret Christie-Brown was very important to me. We co-conducted a once-weekly psychotherapy group from 1971 to 1985. We devoted many hours to the discussion of our patients and the complexities of group process, and especially of our countertransference to the group and to one another. I am confident that the group benefited from our commitment to them and to the work. I wonder how many group analysts have been able to sustain this kind of relationship in private practice for so long a period of time.

I had frequent discussions with Patrick de Maré, who provided medical cover for therapists associated with the London Centre for Psychotherapy. I read the early drafts of *Perspectives in Group Psychotherapy* (1972), and he listened to my attempts to integrate the work of Marx, Durkheim and Freud. Pat had begun his passion for large groups, but I was rather skeptical about their therapeutic value. I felt that they were very unstable, and might suddenly deteriorate into either a horde, mob, or mass, and I did not wish to participate in a 'massification process'. This was the first time that I used this concept to refer to the process through which the members of a group lose their individual identities and tend to function as though they were one grandiose person. I was pleased that Pat (1972, p.8) acknowledged our discussions.

Pat suggested that I ask Dr Lionel Kreeger for further supervision for a new patient whom I had accepted for psychoanalysis. He said that Lionel was the closest I would ever get to a Kleinian psychoanalyst who was committed to the practice of group analysis. I had noticed Lionel during the scientific meetings of the Group Analytic Society, and assumed that he was a Kleinian psychoanalyst, because he was always silent. Lionel accepted me into supervision. Again I learned that a psychoanalyst was able to be a group analyst, and vice versa, and to draw on insights and experiences from both professions, although it was commonly believed that such integration was impossible. I learned in particular about the value of holding and containing, and about the functions of projective identification.

Lionel also introduced me to Mr James Home. Jim and I did not work together clinically, but we had regular meetings to discuss my work, and various philosophical and religious questions that we believed were at the heart of psychoanalysis and group analysis. We were both interested in Blake's work, and in *The Tempest*. Later, we co-conducted a reading seminar for the students at the Institute of Group Analysis. We introduced at least one cohort of group analysts to the work of Malinowski. However, Jim drew the line at Marx and Engels.

My colleagues and their ideas made it possible for me to develop my identity as a psychotherapist and group analyst without having to jettison sociology and social psychology. However, through my work with Lionel and Jim I realized that I really wanted a full psychoanalysis, and to become a psychoanalyst. It seems that I had never really given up my original goal, if becoming a psychoanalyst can be called a 'goal'.

Lionel referred me to Dr Adam Limentani, who became my training psychoanalyst at the Institute of Psycho-Analysis. Although Adam was deeply ambivalent towards group analysis as a form of treatment, I am confident that slowly he grew to respect the contributions that group analysis might make to psychoanalysis. I used to say to him that no matter how much they were in touch with primitive psychic life, psychoanalysts who did not have clinical and training experience in groups were unable to recognize group-specific phenomena, such as 'basic assumptions'. In turn, he would stress that without analytical experience, I would never be able to move beyond the mere description of 'basic assumptions', and to feel their roots within psychotic anxieties, and even if it were possible to get in touch with psychotic anxieties within groups, this only proved that groups were not suitable for clinical work. We were never able to agree about the unconscious meanings of my continuing interests in both group analysis and psychoanalysis, partly because I refused to accept that they were of necessity separate disciplines, and, therefore, that this issue could not be understood merely in terms of splitting either the maternal object or the parental couple. If a 'person' was a product of both the 'organism' and the 'society', how could group analysis be distinct from psychoanalysis, at least theoretically?

My supervisors for training in psychoanalysis at the Institute of Psycho-Analysis were Miss Pearl King and Mr Tom Hayley. Although they did not practice group analysis, they understood its basic theory. Pearl had been influenced by Dr John Rickman, and written influential papers on collective psychopathology; Tom had trained as an anthropologist, and understood completely my interest in the social unconscious and in the study of personality and culture. I qualified as a psychoanalyst in 1982, when I also left the London School of Economics for full-time private practice, but continued to lecture and teach in various universities and training programs in psychoanalysis and group analysis.

Dr Clifford Yorke was my first consultant on the Membership Course. I was influenced by Cliff's papers on drug addiction. While working with him I learned that he had been Malcolm's Senior Registrar at the Cassell Hospital. My second consultant on the Course was Dr Harold Stewart. My psychoanalytical perspective is virtually identical to the one outlined by Harold in 'Types of transference interpretation: an object-relations view' (1987), and 'Interpretation and other agents for psychic change' (1990). I qualified as a full member of the Institute in 1986.

Throughout my training I was struck by how much the group analytical perspective had permeated British Object Relations thinking, and vice versa, although this was barely recognized or acknowledged. All group analysts who were psychoanalysts were members of the Group of Independent Psychoanalysts. No group analysts were members of the Klein Group or the Group of Contemporary Freudians. This is still the case. Of course, such differentiations and splits may be more a matter of the politics of the mental health professions in London than they are of substantive intellectual issues.

Looking back, it would be hard to overstate how important the Survivor Syndrome Workshop was for me. Held in 1979, this Workshop was the first event to be sponsored by the Institute of Group Analysis and the Group Analytic Society (London) in which the models of lectures, seminars, application groups and large and small theme-centered experiential groups were used in order to explore the unconscious aspects of learning about a particular topic and how these are expressed in parallel processes at every social, organizational and personal 'level'. The organizing committee of the Workshop consisted of Caroline Garland, Celia Read and myself under the chairmanship of Meg Sharpe. Caroline and I were able to write together; Meg modeled the importance of dynamic administration and containment in organizational work; and Celia had introduced me to my wife. I remember well that I left the last part of the Workshop in order to be with my wife during the birth of my daughter Catherine. This experience of creativity in the midst of despair and annihilation has remained a source of inspiration for me.

When first published, the bibliographies of these papers in *The Social Unconscious: Selected Papers* were virtually exhaustive. I have since learned from Hanna Biran (1997), Mark Ettin (2001), Yolanda Gampel (1996), Gordon Lawrence (1998, 2000), Dieter Nitzgen (2001), Janine Puget (1991) and Gerhard Wilke (2001), to name only a few members of an extensive network of scholars and clinicians who share an interest in the social unconscious. Especially important is the work of Dennis Brown and Louis Zinkin (1994), Farhad Dalal (1998), Franco Di Maria and his colleagues (1994), Claudio Neri (1998) and Tom Ormay (2001). Claudio, Dennis and Tom are attempting to integrate psychoanalysis and group analysis, a project with which I identify.

In the first note to each Chapter of *The Social Unconscious: Selected Papers* I have cited those colleagues who have given me the benefit of their substantive and editorial criticisms. My patients have been my most important teachers. One of my current therapeutic groups started in 1969, and it is probably the first slow-open twice-weekly group in private practice in the United Kingdom, and possibly in the world. The support and friendship of Lionel Kreeger and Estela Welldon in England, and Marsha Block, David and Jill Scharff and Saul Scheidlinger in the United States, have been very important to me, particularly during the 1980's when I wrote these papers. My wife Cicely and my daughters Catherine, Rachel, and Pauline, have given me the time and space both to think and to write. I would never have prepared this manuscript for publication without the loyalty and dedication of my personal assistant Céline Stakol.

References

Biran, H. (1997) 'Myths, memories and roles – how they live again in the group process.' *Free Associations 41*, 7, 1, 31–49.

Brown, D. and Zinkin, L. (1994) *The Psyche and the Social World*. London: Routledge.

Dalal, F. (1998) *Taking the Group Seriously*. London: Jessica Kingsley Publishers.

de Maré, P. (1972) *Perspectives in Group Psychotherapy*. London: Allen and Unwin.

Di Maria, F. and Lavanco, G. (1994) *Nel Nome Del Gruppo*. Palermo: Arke.

Ettin, M. (2001) 'The deep structure of group life: unconscious dimensions.' *Group 25*, 4, 253–298.

Gampel, Y. (1996) 'The Interminal Uncanny'. In L. Rangell and R. Moses-Hrushovski (eds) *Psychanalysis at the Political Border*. Madison, CT: International Universities Press.

Lawrence, W. G. (ed) (1998) *Social Dreaming @ Work*. London: Karnac Books.

Lawrence, W. G. (2000) *Tongued With Fire: Groups in Experience*. London: Karnac Books.

Neri, C. (1998) *Group*. London: Jessica Kingsley Publishers.

Nitzgen, D. (2001) 'Training in democracy, democracy in training: notes on group analysis and democracy.' *Group Analysis 34*, 3, 331–349.

Ormay, T. (2001) 'The social unconscious.' *Special Issue of Group Analysis 34*, 1, 5–8.

Puget, J. (1991) 'The social context: searching for a hypothesis.' *Free Associations 21*, 2, 1, 21–33.

Stewart, H. (1987) 'Types of transference interpretation: an object-relations view.' In *Psychic Experience and Problems of Technique*. London: Routledge.

Stewart, H. (1990) 'Interpretation and other agents for psychic change.' *The International Review of Psycho-Analysis 71*, 61–70.

Wilke, G. (2001) *How to be a Good Enough GP*. Oxon: Radcliffe Medical Press Ltd.

Note

1   In 1973, along with others, I helped Ilse found the new London Centre for Psychotherapy. From the start, the Centre was always intended to be 'left wing' in its training and treatment policies, and we always tried to provide psychotherapy for those who could not afford to pay for it elsewhere, and many of us accepted at least one patient without charge. We were also committed to the development of 'applied analysis'. One of the reasons why the London Centre for Psychotherapy separated from the British Association of Psychotherapists was that Ilse insisted that group analysis should be part of the training experience for all psychotherapists, and should be one of the therapeutic modalities available at the new Centre. In fact, 'theme-centered' group experience was a feature of training programs at the Centre until 1998, when this was dropped in the Centre's attempt to gain admission into the British Confederation of Psychotherapists. Thus, in a sense, the Centre and the Association have become re-united, at least in their orientations and personnel.

For my daughter
Catherine Isabel

To see a World in a grain of sand,
And a Heaven in a wild flower,
Hold Infinity in the palm of you hand,
And Eternity in an hour.

William Blake (1757–1827)

Preface

Terrorists have destroyed the Twin Towers of the World Trade Center and parts of the Pentagon. The 'Western Coalition', which is a euphemism for the United States, continues to bomb Afghanistan. Military action against Iraq and various other societies who are said to harbor terrorist organizations is imminent. The war between Israel and the Palestinians has escalated sharply, and the conflicts on which it is based are seemingly without resolution. Popular support for extreme right-wing movements has increased. Clearly, our political leaders, sociologists, group analysts and psychoanalysts would all benefit from authentic dialogue, as, in turn, would our patients.

I am reminded of a lecture in 1991 by a senior Kleinian psychoanalyst entitled 'On the Psychoanalysis of the War in the Gulf' at a Special Event sponsored by the Institute of Group Analysis (London). She argued that this military violence could be explained by an eruption of the forces of innate malign envy, based on the so-called 'death instinct', combined with the unbridled greed of Americans for beef and 'cheap gasoline'. I was the Respondent to her lecture. I will quote at length from an edited transcript of a recording of my necessarily extemporaneous remarks:

> I prefer an object relations orientation that is informed by a tradition in sociological thinking that social facts can only be explained adequately in terms of other social facts. Social facts cannot be explained in terms of psychic facts, especially when it is believed that psychic facts come mainly from organismic facts. Although social facts are completely intertwined with psychic facts, we need to examine the relationships among these realms or levels or components of human reality, and not mix them together indiscriminately.
>
> Let us consider some particularly complex social facts which structure the personalities of the people who are constrained by them: the Middle East consists of a number of countries whose boundaries have been drawn in the sand with a stick. What have military men and politicians done to this region of the earth with so many natural resources covered by sand? We should examine the institutionalized forms of gender identity throughout the Middle East. What are the implications of the term "The Muslim Brotherhood"? There are enormous differences between the unbounded and

uncontrolled power of men, and the limited and highly circumscribed power of women. I want to understand more about the role of mother in these societies. We must also examine kinship units as a source of power. It is not by chance that the people around Saddam Hussein are basically from the same "family". Major discrepancies exist between power based on wealth, and power based on international investment in manufacturing and modern technology. Such inequalities are associated with political instability, paranoia and a tendency towards violence.

War cannot be explained in terms of the so-called death instinct, envy and greed. In fact, if we accept your Kleinian psychoanalytical view of human nature we would have to explain why we are not at war all the time.

We must reconsider the concept of the social unconscious. This has never been more important.

What I said then, I would say today. However, the concept of the social unconscious is not only important politically. It is also important in our theoretical and clinical work. The 'social unconscious' provides a bridge from sociology to group analysis and to contemporary psychoanalysis, which share a syndrome of assumptions about human nature (Hopper 2002), for example:

1. In the beginning there is no such thing as an infant but only a mother/infant couple within a social context; thus, the mother/infant couple can be described as two bodies/one mind.

2. An ego of adaptation precedes an ego of agency, which is emergent, and based on social relations mediated through communications, ultimately through language.

3. As a complement to 'body-ego' we need 'society-ego' or 'other-ego' or 'we-go' (Klein, G. 1976, p.178) which are equally primary and develop in parallel.

4. External constraints are not only a matter of inhibition and restraint, but also a matter of creative facilitation and enablement.

5. Psychic facts are preceded by both social and organismic facts; thus, the first emotion is not innate malign envy based on the so-called 'death instinct', and the first psychic act is not a projection of the anxiety inherent in it; on the contrary, psychic life begins with processes of internalization.

6. Although external objects are impregnated with projections, they can be internalized in their pristine form.

7. Although envy is ubiquitous, it should be understood as a defense against the fear of annihilation; thus, helplessness and shame are closer to the heart of the human condition than are envy and guilt.

8. 'Unintegration' precedes 'integration', but 'disintegration' follows trauma, especially breaks in attachments and impingements to the safety shield.

9. Trauma and traumatogenic processes are central to the study and treatment of psycho-pathology, which is not to deny the importance of unconscious fantasies.

10. Persons and groups are open systems; thus, groups are always open to the personalities of their participants, and vice versa, from conception to death.

It is essential to take a 'wider', sociological view of society in groups in persons which is not opposed to a 'deeper', psychoanalytical view of persons in groups in society. Actually, the very use of 'wider' and 'deeper' is misleading, in that a sociological view should not lack depth, and a psychoanalytical perspective should not be insensitive to context. People and groups must always be located within their foundation matrices. It is necessary to think in terms of 'horizontal depth'. Within the infinite context of time and space, the self belongs mostly to others, who may have lived far away and long ago. One's own unconscious experience may be held by an 'other', and an other's unconscious experience may be held by one's self. Such experience may even become institutionalized within groups and more complex social systems. The development and maintenance of personal autonomy can only be understood within the context of social, cultural and political constraints.

Although Winnicott (1967) referred to the 'location' of cultural experience, the concept of location of both experience and autonomy (which can be traced to the work of German and Austrian psychoanalysts during the 1930s, for example Bernfeld (1929)) has been central to the theory and method of Group Analysis from its very inception (Foulkes 1964). So, too, the study of trauma and traumatogenic processes. Psychoanalysis and group analysis should be completely intertwined. This is why I am always both a psychoanalyst and a group analyst, whether I am working with one person, a couch and a chair, or with several people, a table and a collection of chairs.

The papers that I have selected for *The Social Unconscious* were written between 1964 and 1985. After they were presented at various workshops and conferences, all but one were published in diverse journals between 1965 and 2001. However, most of this material is now difficult to find, especially in the United States. It is, therefore, very satisfying to have these papers together in one 'space'. It is also convenient for further work. However, in order to make the book more coherent I have eliminated a few redundant paragraphs from the original versions of what can now be taken as 'chapters' of both a journey and a book.

Chapter 1, 'Some Effects of Supervisory Style: A Sociological Analysis', focuses on the etiology of aggressive feelings and aggression. I develop a series of hypotheses that link aggression to aggressive feelings on the basis of frustration, threats to self-esteem, normative orientations to authority, and normative orientations to the expression of feelings in general and aggressive feelings in particular. Although I did not know it at the time, this was one of the first studies in England of the social unconscious.

Chapter 2, 'A Sociological View of Large Groups', was written with Anne Weyman and developed from previous work with Eric Dunning on the topic of industrialization and convergence. We emphasize that although all groups are social systems, not all social systems are groups. Thus, the dynamics of groups should not be inferred to be those of societies and intermediate social formations, as though they were all isomorphic. It is always important to locate groups within their various environments, to which they are 'open' by definition.

Chapter 3, the 'Report on the Large Group' of the Survivor Syndrome Workshop, was written with Lionel Kreeger. We define 'equivalence', and connect it with projective identification, on the one hand, and the 'social unconscious' on the other. We also illustrate these processes with data from our experience of the Group. Chapter 4, the 'Overview' of the Survivor Syndrome Workshop, was written with Caroline Garland. We describe various processes that occurred in the workshop as a whole, and connect them with more general issues.

Chapter 5, 'The Problem of Context in Group-Analytic Psychotherapy', is concerned with the effects of social, cultural and political facts and forces within the environment of the Group on various aspects of processes within the Group. I was concerned with the emergence of anti-Semitism throughout

Europe, but I was shocked to experience this from my patients. Before this paper was published, my practice consisted mostly of non-Jews; after it was published, only Jews were referred to me. Curiously, I started again to have non-Jewish patients in my practice only after it became more widely known that I worked extensively with survivors of the Shoah. My new patients told me that they thought that if I could share the suffering of Shoah survivors, then they could trust me not to withdraw from their pain.

Chapter 6, 'The Social Unconscious in Clinical Work', was first drafted in 1984 but not published until a decade later. Here I give less attention to anti-Semitism and more to processes such as homophobia, gender, terrorism and social violence, and rapid social change. The 'paradigm' of dichotomized time and space is similar to the famous Johari Window, but this concrete figure is merely a way of picturing the constraints of context. The study of the social unconscious and the study of context go together, especially because the personalities of the members of a group constitute one of the group's environments or contexts.

Chapter 7, 'Wounded Bird: A Study of the Social Unconscious and Countertransference', was first drafted in 1985, but has not been published before. I focus on the constraints of the social unconscious on my countertransference in one of my twice-weekly groups. Although I have presented 'Wounded Bird' at several small meetings of senior colleagues, I have not published it before now because the experiences described in the paper were still too raw. Also, I no longer work with the transference and countertransference in a way that requires that I function as a so-called 'blank screen'. London is like a village, especially the sections of it from which my clients are drawn. Over the years I have learned that it is not helpful to pretend that my patients have no outside information about me, and that the information that they do have is fantasy and gossip. It is more helpful to recognize and to accept their information, to be curious about the meanings that such information has for us, and sometimes even to discuss it.

After I wrote 'Wounded Bird', my work took a different direction, as seen in *The Fourth Basic Assumption in the Unconscious Life of Groups* (Hopper 2003). However, I returned to the topic of the social unconscious in connection with the dimensions of time and space in clinical work in my Presidential Lecture in 1998 in London at the Thirteenth Congress of the International Association of Group Psychotherapy. The conference was called 'Annihilation Survival Re-Creation', and my lecture was entitled 'On the Nature of Hope'. I developed the lecture into a trilogy of papers, the first of which, 'On the

Nature of Hope in Psychoanalysis and Group Analysis', is the last chapter in *The Social Unconscious: Selected Papers*.

Unfortunately, in the past couple of years or so, the study of the social unconscious has become fashionable. The concept has begun to be absorbed into the intellectual ideology of group analysis. Therefore, I will conclude this Preface with my Hopper (2001) 'Response' to the Special Edition of *Group Analysis* on the social unconscious:

> were it not for the limitations of the traditional psychoanalytical concept of the unconscious (and non-conscious) mind, or the mind of which we are unconscious, it would not be necessary to give the topic of the social unconscious, or the social constraints on the mind of which we are unconscious, quite so much polemical attention. We must not underestimate how narcissistically wounded people can be by the discovery that their 'free will' is limited by their social and cultural circumstances, which are not merely a matter of their economic well being. We must not throw out the proverbial baby of psychoanalysis with the bath water of its excesses and resistances. I am continually surprised by the current tendency of group analysts to forget and to ignore a century's work concerning the unconscious constraints of the body on the mind, and on unconscious impulses, anxieties, fantasies, and protective defenses, and their vicissitudes, as part of normal personal and group functioning, and of personal and collective pathology. I am alarmed that nowadays leading group analysts have adopted what almost a half century ago [sociologists] called an 'over-socialized conception' of mankind, which neglects such phenomena as aggression and conflict, not to mention lust. (p.187)

References

Bernfeld, S. (1929) 'Der soziale Ort und seine Bedeutung für Neurose, Verwahrlosung und Pädagogik.' *Imago XV*, 2, 17–24.

Foulkes, S.H. (1964) *Therapeutic Group Analysis*. London: Allen and Unwin.

Hopper, E. (2001) 'A response to papers on the social unconscious.' *Group Analysis 34*, 1, 187–190.

Hopper, E. (2002) 'The social unconscious: A post-Foulkesian perspective.' Letter to the Editor. *Group Analysis 35*, 2, 333–335.

Hopper, E. (2003) *The Fourth Basic Assumption in the Unconscious Life of Groups.* London: Jessica Kingsley Publishers.

Klein, G. S. (1976) *Psychoanalytic Theory: An Exploration of Essentials*. New York: International Universities Press.

Winnicott, D.W. (1967) 'The location of cultural experience.' *International Journal of Psycho-Analysis 48*, 3, 368–372.

CHAPTER 1

Some Effects of Supervisory Style

A Sociological Analysis[1]

Introduction

This study is based on a replication, in an English factory and under controlled structural conditions, of an American laboratory investigation of some effects of supervisory styles. Its main objectives are to expand the analytical system used in the American investigation and to formulate certain generalizations which apply to a variety of group situations. I therefore regard it as an effort primarily in general sociology and only secondarily in industrial sociology.

Statement of the problem

In reviewing the literature on supervisory behavior and some of its effects, Day and Hamblin (1964) found that, in both field and laboratory studies, the strength of the relationships between supervisory styles and the dependent variables, productivity, job satisfaction, and morale, varied considerably.[2] They attempted to bring together these previous findings by suggesting a set of hypotheses based on a modified version of the frustration–aggression hypothesis (Miller 1941) and by introducing a new variable, the self-esteem of the worker.

Day and Hamblin conceptualized two continua of supervisory styles. One ranged from 'close' to 'anomic', the other from 'punitive' to 'non-punitive'.[3] For the purposes of their experiment, they operationalized 'close' and 'general' supervision – the latter being on the continuum of 'close' to 'anomic' supervision – and punitive and non-punitive supervision:

1. Close supervision. 'For purposes of measurement this is conceptualized as one end of the continuum that describes the degree to which a supervision specifies the roles of the subordinates and checks up to see that they comply with the [role definitions].'

2. General supervision. 'This involves a moderate number of specifications and check-ups, at least enough to let the workers know what they are supposed to do.'

3. Punitive supervision. This is a supervisory style in which 'a supervisor enforces work specifications or rules by aggressing against those subordinates who depart from or violate the rules'.

4. Non-punitive supervision. This refers to a slightly 'distant' or disinterested posture characterized by the absence of either rewards or punishments.[4]

Productivity was conceptualized by the two authors as potentially aggressive behavior. And, in a carefully controlled laboratory experiment, they tested the following hypotheses:

1. Close and/or punitive styles of supervision will be experienced as frustrating by the workers.

2. When the workers are frustrated there will be an 'increase in the amount of verbal aggression towards the supervisor, a decrease in productivity, an increase in dissatisfaction with the work situation, (and) an increase in verbal aggression toward co-workers'.

3. But these forms of aggression will be less frequent, less intense, or possibly absent when the workers' self-esteem is high.

In other words they hypothesized that any form of supervision which frustrated the workers would cause them to behave aggressively;[5] but the degree to which a given form of supervision would be experienced as frustrating depended on self-esteem.[6] The hypotheses were confirmed with the exception of those involving displaced aggression and the one stressing the importance of self-esteem under conditions of punitive supervision.

In a previous work on aggression, Hamblin had made a notable and comprehensive statement on the several stages in the frustration–aggression sequence (Hamblin *et al.* 1963). It is, therefore, somewhat surprising that in their experimental study Day and Hamblin include aggressive feelings ('instigation to aggression') among the other indices of aggression itself, rather than treating it as the principal intervening variable between frustration and the occurrence of aggression. It is possible, however, to utilize parts of Hamblin's statements on the frustration–aggression hypothesis for making further refinements in our understanding of the effects of supervisory behavior.

First, one can usefully expand their analytical system. By omitting the intervening variable from the sequence 'frustration – aggressive feelings – aggression' Day and Hamblin appear to suggest that variations in aggressive behavior are controlled only by the intensity of the frustrating agent and by the self-esteem of the workers. I think, however, that workers may feel aggressive yet neither verbalize nor act out their feelings. Aggressive feelings probably become relevant for the group in so far as they erupt into manifest aggression, and this they may do only under special conditions. Further, although any form of supervision has a frustration potential, whether or not it becomes frustrating depends on how the workers perceive it. Along with individual variations in self-esteem, workers in a group may define supervisory behavior differently in different situations. Moreover, variations in structural conditions, which may influence these sequences and which Day and Hamblin have not controlled, may have caused spurious relationships to appear. In short, it is crucial to specify some of the structural variables which affect the applicability of their psychological hypothesis.

Second, it would be prudent to examine the extent to which Day and Hamblin's findings should be generalized. In order to proceed with rigor and economy, they conceptualized the work group as being constrained only by those factors which they explicitly regarded as part of the task structure.[7] Although this aided them in discovering patterns of covariation among their experimental variables, it made their generalizations to real industrial work groups highly indiscriminate. If one does wish to generalize from an experimental situation, one must first consider certain 'givens', i.e. basic structural constraints by which the laboratory sample differs from most real work groups.[8]

A consideration of Day and Hamblin's laboratory sample[9] suggests that it was undifferentiated with respect to variations in social class and previous work experience. Nor did it allow them to ask such questions as: Why have the women come to work? Are they mothers? Have they returned to a job previously left at marriage? Is this their first job? What do their husbands do? Where are their children? What are their wages? In other words, what are the structural conditions under which the psychological hypothesis becomes relevant for sociological study?

It is true that Day and Hamblin's findings do not differ markedly from those of some American studies which have used working class samples in industrial settings. (Katz, Maccoby and Morse 1950; Katz *et al.* 1951).[10] But in most cases important structural variables, such as mobility opportunities, normative expectations of authority and the expression of emotions, or combinations of these, have not been controlled (Collins, Dalton and Roy 1946; Dubin 1956; Dubin *et al.* 1965; Roy 1952a). And although variations in the social composition of an American sample may not be important, certainly inferences to other societies are hardly justified. The apparent consistency of American findings, therefore, does not eliminate the need for structural analysis of work groups, particularly in other countries.

In sum, such a study as that by Day and Hamblin must be viewed as an advance, but decidedly an inconclusive one. I have nonetheless made use of it as a starting point for my own investigation.

Supervisory styles and normative expectations

It is a general principle that frustration is directly related to incongruity between expectations and experience of a given event in a specific context.[11] It follows that close and/or punitive supervision will not be frustrating unless it violates the subordinates' normative expectations. To understand, then, the effects of variations in supervisory styles – that is, to account for their frustrating quality – it is necessary to know the subordinates' normative expectations of authority. It is also relevant to know under what conditions these expectations vary.

Normative expectations of authority influence the way in which a supervisory style will be perceived. By normative expectations of authority I here refer to that degree of asymmetry in the authority relationship between subordinates and their supervisor which is deemed acceptable and appropriate by the actors involved: in short, how they think that power should be distributed and exercised in a specific situation. This can be considered either from the viewpoint of the subordinates or that of their supervisor. They need not agree, and to the extent that their assessments differ, the chances of conflict will be higher. In this discussion, however, I am primarily concerned with the viewpoint of the subordinates (Kornhauser, Dubin and Ross 1954).

Within the context of the occupational role in the industrial work groups, it is, then, useful to know how receptive the subordinates think they ought to be to a given form of supervision. In this connection, one can think of a continuum which ranges from complete 'receptivity' to complete 'rejectivity'. At one extreme the subordinates are willing to tolerate a large amount of supervisory control; at the other, they normatively reject any encroachments on their attempt to maximize their own control over their work roles.[12]

Between these extremes there is a range of norms of conditional and negotiable acceptance of supervisory control. Norms in this range rule that subordinates should be receptive as long as certain of their conditions are met. Their acceptance hinges on a delicate bargain which has been formally and informally struck and maintained between the subordinates and the supervisor. These norms demand explicitly or tacitly that the supervisor perform his tasks in such a manner that the subordinates can maximize the types of satisfactions they want most from the system, with respect, for example, to advancement, money, rest periods, the length of the working week, and, indeed, with respect to such a crucial matter as the supervisory style itself. The maintenance of the bargain will depend on a number of contingencies. If aspirations should rise out of proportion to earnings, if earnings themselves should fall, or if the supervisor's behavior were not helpful in enabling the subordinates to maintain their self-esteem, they might become less receptive to his authority.[13]

Normative expectations of authority need not be constant for all situations in which a person might participate in a subordinate role. In studying how normatively receptive the subordinates are to a given supervisory experience it is necessary, therefore, to specify the context of the task, the completion of which requires supervision. It is true that the evidence on this problem is not wholly conclusive. Some studies suggest that being a subordinate in an occupational role has an all-pervasive consequence such that the occupant is constrained to take analogous subordinate roles whenever superordinates or their surrogates are present.[14]

But there is sufficient evidence from other studies to indicate that this is not always the case. A person might take a subordinate role in a work group, for example, but refuse it in a local political group (Erbe 1964; Lane 1959a). Or a foreman in a factory might refuse to perform a similar role in a group which forms spontaneously in response to a street corner accident. A person who is a leader in the classroom may be a follower on the athletic field. More precisely, experiments on leadership confirm that the same person is rarely both a task and a popular leader, particularly in the same situation (Bales

1950). In the discussion which follows, the context to be taken as given will be the work group in an industrial setting.

Normative expectations of authority, however, are not affected by the context of task situation alone. They are also products of previous life experience both in occupational and non-occupational roles, particularly in so far as they have determined or have been affected by the subordinates' social class situation. One of the most important sources of variation in normative expectations of authority would, therefore, be the social class of the subordinate.[15]

I hypothesize that middle class subordinates will be less receptive to close and/or punitive supervision than their working class counterparts, and, hence, will be more easily and frequently frustrated by these supervisory styles. I shall now indicate how my analysis of the relevant literature has led me to formulate this hypothesis.

If one postulates that the subordinates' satisfaction with the authority system and their position in it is a direct function of their social class and the task context, and if, further, one takes the evidence regarding their degree of satisfaction with the first two dimensions as a pointer to their likely expectations of authority, then the following paradigm provides a useful framework for the systematic interpretation of that evidence:

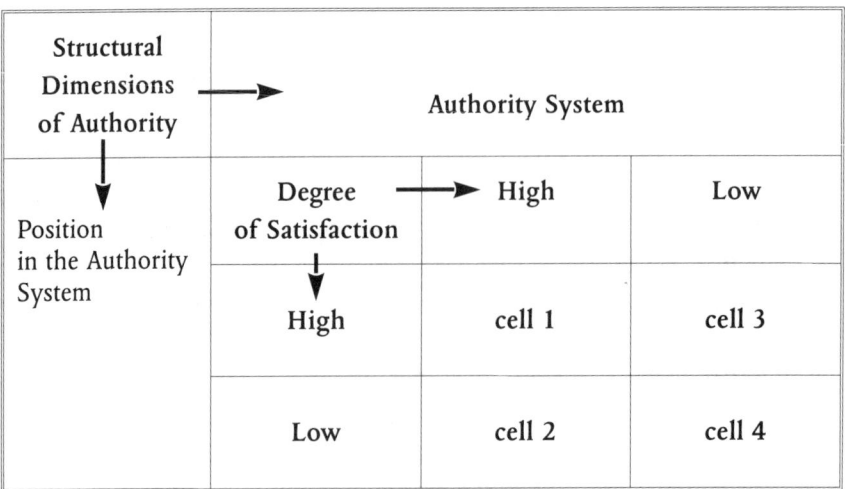

Figure 1.1: Degree of satisfaction with authority system and position in the authority system

Cell 1 – which refers to a high degree of satisfaction with both the authority system and position in it – is likely to represent those subordinates who accept and conform completely to their subordinate roles. These subordinates enter the system fully recognizing that their rewards will be commensurate with their position and worth. They think of themselves as requiring supervision, and they consider it the supervisor's duty to exercise authority. Their main source of satisfaction from the supervisory relationship is the honor which accrues from association with a person of higher status. One can call this a 'traditional' orientation to work, particularly likely to exist in a society with a rigid status system, and one can hypothesize that it is inversely related to susceptibility to frustration from supervisory behavior; and, further, that the working class in England is more likely than the middle class to be characterized by its vestiges.

As economic opportunities increase, however, and the rigidity of traditional status systems slowly gives way, workers who once believed their stations to be permanent and legitimate begin to regard them as legitimate only in so far as they need not be permanent. This development has several implications. A growing number of workers will begin their careers in cell 4 – which refers to low satisfaction with both the authority system and their position in it – and they will thereby increase the pressure on 'traditional' workers to follow suit. An increasing number of 'traditionally' oriented workers are likely, then, to move from cell 1 to cell 4. More workers with better than average education may enter the system in cell 2 – which refers to high satisfaction with the authority system and low satisfaction with the position in it; but many of the working class subordinates in cell 2 are likely to find themselves in cell 4 before the end of their careers. By whatever route subordinates do enter cell 4, however, they are likely to be normatively receptive to supervisory authority – though less so than the subordinates in cell 1; but why this should be the case might be traced to the following considerations.[16]

Essentially the same pressures that cause the traditional workers, those who are in cell 1, to become disenchanted with the system and their position, also affect the 'modern' workers, the subordinates who have arrived in cell 4. One can ask these subordinates: what do you expect from work? Why do you come to work? Their consistent responses to these questions are revealing. Subsistence is a pressing concern for them and they are expected to obtain gainful employment as soon as possible. Their life experience at home and in school does not prepare them for jobs which offer other than economic rewards. Working class occupations increasingly require little skill, and even this can be learned in a short time on the job. 'Responsibility' has been removed to supervisory roles or else to the 'machines' with their highly skilled engineers. 'Dignity' ceases to depend on having a high degree of control over one's work role. These subordinates are likely to be relatively unconcerned with the social prerogatives of their occupational roles, e.g. meeting new people, developing potentials, taking responsibility, being creative, working in a friendly atmosphere, getting the approval of line officers.

But having rejected the system and their own place in it, they redefine their attachment to the system and make an instrumental adjustment to their place within it. They will use the system for their own purposes and will endure its discomforts as long as their own terms can be met. As long as they can obtain what they consider to be a just reward for their efforts, they will co-operate more or less with their supervisor and will remain within the system.[17]

Their positions will, in a sense, become 'ritualized', but not in the same way as in the case, for example, of a bank clerk. Their tasks are so obviously menial and far removed from the decision-making behavior of management that they become ritualized in the sense of 'rigid' and 'repetitive' rather than 'sacred'. But, in effect, a type of 'sanctity' characterizes their work routines, which reduces their cognitive involvement with the tasks. Events at work are kept separate from those at home to a much higher degree than in the middle class. And as long as the supervisor does not interfere in their routine or break his bargain, they are likely to be relatively less concerned with what he does.

The working class subordinate, then, whether he be 'traditional' and, hence, completely receptive to supervisory authority, or 'modern' and, hence, conditionally receptive, is likely to be less frustrated by close and/or punitive supervision than his middle class counterpart. On the one hand he will take his supervisory experience as appropriate to his status, and on the other he will insulate himself against it.

I shall now refer to those subordinates who are mobility oriented. They are typical members of cell 2, which represents high satisfaction with the system and low satisfaction with the position in it. This cell includes middle class subordinates and also some of the 'modern' aspiring workers. These subordinates are likely to be more concerned with supervisory behavior than those in cell 1 and cell 4; they are likely to be quite sensitive to and easily frustrated by it.

There are important differences in the orientations of the different classes to social mobility. The middle class cultural system emphasizes the possibility of individual mobility, success through achievement, perseverance in the face of blocks, the reality of egalitarianism, and advancement as more desirable than security.[18] This is contrasted with working class normative systems which encourage collective rather than individual mobility, particularly in the sense of maintaining a collective bargaining instrument even if it is to be used for individual improvement.[19]

Middle class occupational tasks require a wide range of diffuse skills, particularly those ambiguous social skills which make some people more suitable than others for front office work. And though they are not always concerned with the manipulation of ideas and people rather than of things, they nevertheless may provide, even in the case of fairly routine clerical work, a feeling of involvement with the management process.[20] It is true that as lower white-collar tasks become more and more automated and require less skill, they will be increasingly difficult to distinguish from working class ones. This development may encourage an orientation to work which in some respects resembles that of working class members of cell 4.[21] But at the same time it has highlighted the importance of some of the traditional distinctions between the working and middle class occupations. At present there is still too great a difference between the mobility opportunity objectively available to blue- and white-collar workers to have eliminated the differences in their respective expectations of the work experience.

The middle class employee is likely to assume that the system he enters works essentially in his favor and that he can better his own position by working within its rules; and in this way both he and the firm will benefit. A member of cell 2 will probably feel a sense of heightened competition with co-workers for the favoritism of his superordinate. His ties with other subordinates are tenuous, particularly with those who are also anxious to advance. He may aspire to his supervisor's job. And as long as he does not overconform to the middle class achievement norm and thereby become an 'eager beaver', he will probably receive and become dependent upon the praise of his supervisor. He is, therefore, likely to experience his relationship to his supervisor in a highly personal way. Since this relationship is most important in determining his future advancement in the firm, he is probably quite concerned with, sensitive to, and easily frustrated by supervisory behavior, and normatively rejective of an excess of it.

Aspiring subordinates, however, are more often than not unsuccessful in satisfying their aspirations. This is true not only of the middle class striver but also of those aspiring manual workers who have internalized some of the middle class orientations discussed above and who wish to cross the manual–non-manual line. When it appears to either the working class or middle class striver that he will be unable to rise above his present unsatisfactory achievement level, there are a number of alternative forms of instrumental adjustment available to him (Chinoy 1952, 1955; Clinard 1964; Guest 1954; Lane 1959b; Merton 1957). Both classes of subordinates probably begin their adjustment by vicariously channeling their former personal mobility aspirations into the achievement of their children. But the working class striver is then likely to adjust in the direction of cell 4, a situation characterized by opting out of the system. The middle class striver is more likely to move to cell 3, one of 'ritualism' in the sense in which Merton used the term, and which is characterized by low satisfaction with the system and high satisfaction with the position in it.

The middle class subordinates in cell 3 take their job requirements as though they were the ends of the dominant system, thereby identifying their personal occupational goals with what are means for those who are dominant in the system. Even though they are essentially dissatisfied with the system, the manifest acceptance of the ritualist's own place within it results in a tacit confirmation of the existing authority structure. This type of subordinate is one of the main sources of support for the system, providing strength and stability. As long as the firm does not meet with externally caused crises or does not require a large dose of innovation from within, they will be highly valued employees. But they will be very much concerned with the manner in which they are supervised. Like members of cell 2, they are likely to be normatively rejective of and easily frustrated by close and/or punitive supervision.

In sum, the same degree of 'closeness' and/or 'punitiveness' in supervision will probably be less frustrating to the working class employee, most likely to be in cells 1 or 4, than to his middle class counterpart, most likely to be in cells 2 or 3.

Self-esteem

Given that normative expectations of authority are a basic structural control, it is reasonable to hypothesize that variations in subordinates' self-esteem should influence their experience of supervisory behavior as more or less frustrating. But in contrast to Day and Hamblin's treatment of this variable, I do not consider it to be a constant and personal quality which remains fixed regardless of changes in the social context. I think it can vary from high to low in different situations. Nor is a given degree of self-esteem important in controlling frustration unless one feels that one ought to be more highly esteemed by others in a given situation than one actually is. One can define this variable, as Day and Hamblin do, as 'the personal estimation of the degree to which one's presentation of self is creditable and successful'; but one should add, within the constraints of a given social context.

A person can have different amounts of self-esteem in different contexts. When self-esteem is low, one's self image will be more vulnerable to the threats of supervisory behavior. But the relevance of self-esteem is determined by whether the work situation is deemed important. Since task performance in working class occupational roles neither requires much self-esteem nor offers scope for its development, even 'traditional' workers probably do not depend highly on the work role to support their self image. [22] Middle class occupational roles, however, often require a certain amount of self-esteem as well as providing greater opportunities for its development.[23] Most recruits to such jobs are already normatively oriented to the importance of work for their self image.

I would therefore hypothesize that a scale for self-esteem administered to workers on the job would show that working class subordinates have a lower range of self-esteem and less variation within that range than do their middle class counterparts. Although in general the higher the self-esteem, the less threatening and, therefore, the less frustrating the supervisory behavior to the subordinates, when the workers accept a low level of self-esteem as appropriate for themselves in a given context, minor variations around that level will not be inversely related to the ease with which they become frustrated.[24] In other words, the importance of the psychological variable, self-esteem, is likely to be determined by the sociological variable, the constraints of the normative expectations of authority.

Aggression: interactional and normative controls

According to the substantial evidence which supports the frustration –aggression law, aggressive feelings always follow frustration. In the same way that frustration does not always follow a potentially frustrating experience, however, aggression probably does not necessarily follow the arousal of aggressive feelings. Both interactional and normative variables are likely to control the latter sequence.

In the first instance one should note the structure of the task itself. If a worker is dependent on his supervisor for scarce knowledge, skills, or goods, then it is only prudent for him to inhibit the aggressive feelings which the supervisor's behavior may induce (Argyle, Gardner and Cioffi 1957; Goldthorpe 1959). Method of payment is another variable which may determine the likelihood and pattern with which production is used as an aggressive weapon. If subordinates are paid on a piece-work basis, for example, then their productivity variations cut with a two-edged blade. Frustration under piece-work conditions may not erupt into lowered productivity as quickly as it might under other methods of payment, although evidence suggests that workers do frequently subordinate their wage considerations to other needs.[25]

In general, then, I would hypothesize that to the extent to which the supervisor is not directly involved in the task and that his subordinates do not directly need him, his subordinates' aggressive feelings will more easily and frequently erupt into aggressive behavior.

Possibly even more important are the subordinates' conceptions of 'propriety' or 'good manners' on their own part. This is not just a consciously manipulated set of constraints on aggressive feelings, for it reflects the totality of constraining experiences which surrounds the subordinates in both their work roles and extra-work lives. 'Manners', in other words, may refer not only to controlling one's temper with a boss or supervisor but also with someone who is your 'better'.[26]

Manners of subordinate groups vary with ethnic and social class composition. In general, however, there are national folkways which constrain most of the members of the society. In England, for example, there is an emphasis on self-restraint in all social classes, particularly regarding the interactions between the classes. Inhibiting one's feelings in the presence of outsiders is appropriate behavior, and functions as a useful offensive device in interpersonal conflict. This is apparent from the way in which, for example, industrial bargainings, sporting events, political debates, are conducted. This normative orientation probably inhibits aggressive feelings – which may be equally as intense as, for example, those occurring under similar conditions in America – from becoming manifest aggression.

The degree of suppression of feelings is, thus, another normative variable brought from the total society to the work group. It will, in addition to the interactional requirements of the task and the interactional aspects of the task context, control the strength of the frustration–aggression hypothesis. There will probably be less difference in the amounts of aggression between the two classes of subordinates previously discussed than in the amounts of their aggressive feelings. And in general there may be a minimum of aggression even when aggressive feelings run high.

Summary of propositions

I should like to make explicit the hypotheses implied in the preceding sections. The crucial problem is to expand the analytical system of the psychological variables, frustration, aggressive feelings, aggression, and self-esteem, by including the structural variables, normative expectations of authority and the normative expression of emotions:

1. Close and/or punitive supervision are not frustrating in themselves but will become frustrating when they violate the subordinates' normative expectations of authority.

2. The less traditional and the more conditional the subordinates' normative expectations of authority, the smaller the range of deviation from their conception of ideal supervisory behavior which they can tolerate without becoming frustrated. And given conditional receptivity, it is more likely that supervisory behavior itself will be included in the subordinate–supervisor bargain. The greater the inclusion of supervisory behavior, the less the subordinates will allow the supervisor to behave closely and/or punitively without themselves becoming frustrated.

3. Middle class subordinates are more likely than their working class counterparts to find a given degree of punitive and/or close supervision frustrating. When working class subordinates are frustrated, they are likely to define their frustration as a group grievance; consequently, the resulting malaise may be more widespread than in the case of middle class subordinates where individual variations are likely to be more important.

4. If the subordinates deem their work roles important to their self images, then the higher their self-esteem within the task context, the more they can tolerate violations of their ideal conception of

supervisory propriety over and above the limits of sensitivity already established by their normative expectations of authority.

5.   The middle class subordinates' self images are more likely than those of their working class counterparts to depend on their work roles. Consequently variations in self-esteem will influence the frustration of the middle class subordinates more than they will that of the working class.

6.   The greater the frustration, the greater the aggressive feelings towards the supervisor and/or his surrogates, as well as towards the task and productivity; also, the greater the frustration, the more likely that aggressive feelings will be displaced onto the co-workers.

7.   Assuming at least that the subordinates do not require special goods or services from their supervisor and that they are not working on any form of piece-work payment, then the degree to which their normative orientation to the expression of emotions is suppressive will determine the degree to which they manifest their aggressive feelings in aggressive behavior, such as in heightened verbal aggression, increased verbalization of dissatisfaction with the job, or lowered productivity.

8.   The working class and middle class subordinates in England are both likely to have a suppressive normative orientation to the expression of emotions, such that no differences may be found between the two classes in respect of the degree to which they manifest their aggressive feelings in aggressive behavior – even though the strength of their feelings may differ.

References

Argyle, M., Gardner, G. and Cioffi, F. (1957) 'The measurement of supervisory methods.' *Human Relations 10*, 4, 295–313.

Argyris, C. (1957) *Personality and Organization.* New York: Harper & Brothers.

Baldamus, W. (1961) *Efficiency and Effort.* London: Tavistock Publications.

Bales, R. F. (1950) *Interaction Process Analysis.* Reading, Mass: Addison-Wesley.

Behrend, H. (1957) 'The effort bargain.' *Industrial and Labor Relations Review 4*, July, 18–32.

Berger, B. B. (1960) *Working Class Suburb: A Study of Auto Workers in Suburbia.* Berkeley: The University of California Press.

Bottomore, T. B. (1963) 'Social Satisfaction in Voluntary Organisations.' In D. Glass (ed) *Social Mobility in Britain.* London: Routledge and Kegan Paul Ltd.

Chinoy, E. (1952) 'The traditions of opportunity and the aspirations of automobile workers.' *American Journal of Sociology 57*, 5, 453–9.

Chinoy, E. (1955) *Automobile Workers and the American Dream.* New York: Doubleday & Co.

Clinard, M. B. (ed) (1964) *Anomie and Deviant Behaviour.* New York: The Free Press.

Collins, O., Dalton, M. and Roy, D. (1946) 'Restriction of output and social clearage in industry.' *Applied Anthropology 5*, Summer, 1–14.

Day, R. C. and Hamblin, R. L. (1964) 'Some effects of close and punitive styles of supervision.' *American Journal of Sociology 69*, 5, 499–510.

Dennis, N, Henriques, F. and Slaughter, C. (1956) *Coal in our Life.* London: Eyre and Spottiswoode.

Dennis, N. Henriques, F. and Slaughter, C. (1960) *Tradition and Change.* Oxford: Oxford University Press.

Dubin, R. (1956) 'Industrial workers' world: A study of the "central life interests" of industrial workers.' *Social Problems 3*, January, 131–142.

Dubin, R., Homans, C., Mann, F. C. and Miller, D. C. (1965) *Leadership and Productivity.* San Francisco: Chandler Publishing Co.

Erbe, W. (1964) 'Social involvement and political activity: A replication and elaboration.' *American Sociological Review 29*, 2, April, 198–216.

Glass, D. V. (ed) (1963) [1954] *Social Mobility in Britain.* London: Routledge and Kegan Paul Ltd. (Original work published 1954.)

Goffman, E. (1959) *The Presentation of Self in Everyday Life.* New York: Doubleday & Co.

Goldthorpe, J. H. (1959) 'Technical organization as a factor in supervisor–worker conflict.' *British Journal of Sociology 10*, 3, 133–163.

Goldthorpe, J. H. and Lockwood, D. (1963) 'Affluence and the British class structure.' *The Sociological Review 11*, 2, July, 143–164.

Gorer, G. (1948) *The Americans.* London: Cresset Press Ltd.

Gorer, G. (1955) *Exploring English Character.* London: Cresset Press Ltd.

Gouldner, A. W. (1955) *Wildcat Strike: A Study of an Unofficial Strike.* London: Routledge and Kegan Paul Ltd.

Guest, R. H. (1954) 'Work careers and aspirations of mass production workers.' *American Sociological Review 19*, 2, April, 155–163.

Hamblin, R. L., Bridger, D., Day, R. and Yancey, W. (1963) 'Interference–aggression law.' *Sociometry 26*, 2, 190–216.

Hamblin, R. L. (1964) 'Punitive and non-punitive supervision.' *Social Problems 11*, 4, 345–359.

Hyman, H. H. (1954) 'The Value Systems of Different Classes: A Social Psychological Contribution to the Analysis of Stratification.' In R. Bendix and S. Lipset (eds) *Class, Status and Power.* London: Routledge and Kegan Paul Ltd.

Inkeles, A. (1960) 'Industrial man: The relation of status to experience, perception and value.' *American Journal of Sociology LXVI*, July, 1–31.

Kahl, J. H. (1953) 'Educational and occupational aspirations of "common man" boys.' *Harvard Educational Review 23*, 2, 186–203.

Katz, D., Maccoby, N. and Morse, N. C. (1950) *Productivity Supervision and Morale in an Office Situation.* Part I. Michigan: Survey Research Center.

Katz, D., Maccoby, N., Gurin, S. and Floor, L. G. (1951) *Productivity Supervision and Morale among Railroad Workers*. Ann Arbor, Michigan: Survey Research Center.

Knupfer, G. (1947) 'Portrait of an underdog.' *Public Opinion Quarterly XI*, 2, 103–14.

Kornhauser A., Dubin, R. and Ross. A. M. (1954) 'Problems and Viewpoints.' In A. Kornhauser, R. Dubin and A. M. Ross (eds) *Industrial Conflict*. New York: McGrath-Hill Book Company.

Lane, R. E. (1959a) *Political Life: Why People Get Involved in Politics*. Glencoe, IL: The Free Press.

Lane, R. E. (1959b) 'Status anxiety and the fear of equals.' *American Political Science Review 53*, 1, March, 35–51.

Lipset, S. M.and Bendix, R. (1959) *Social Mobility in Industrial Society*. London: Heinemann.

Lipset, S. M., Bendix, R. and Malm, F. T. (1955) 'Job plans and entry into the labour market.' *Social Forces 33*, March, 224–32.

Lockwood, D. (1958) *The Blackcoated Worker*. London: Allen and Unwin.

Martin, F. M. (1963a) [1954] 'Some Subjective Aspects of Social Stratification.' In D. V. Glass (ed) *Social Mobility in Britain*. London: Routledge and Kegan Paul Ltd. (Original work published 1954.)

Martin, F. M. (1963b) [1954] 'An Inquiry into Parents' Preferences in Secondary Education.' In D. V.Glass (ed) *Social Mobility in Britain*. London: Routledge and Kegan Paul Ltd (Original work published 1954.)

Merton, R. K. (ed) (1957) 'Social structure and anomie.' In *Social Theory and Social Structure*. Glencoe, Ill : The Free Press.

Miller, N. E. (1941) 'The frustration–aggression hypothesis.' *American Psychological Review XLVIII*, 337–42.

Orwell, G. (2001) [1937] *The Road to Wigan Pier*. London: Penguin Books. (Original work published 1937.)

Pear, T. H. (1955) *English Social Differences*. London: Allen and Unwin.

Roy, D. F (1952a) 'Quota restriction and goldbricking in a machine shop.' *American Journal of Sociology 57*, March, 427–442.

Roy, D. F. (1952b) 'Restriction of output in a piece work machine shop.' *American Journal of Sociology 57*, March, 443–459.

Roy, D. F. (1953) 'Work satisfaction and social reward in quota achievement: An analysis of piece work incentives.' *American Sociological Review 18*, 2, 507–514.

Stacey, M. A.(1960) *Tradition and Change: A Study of Banbury*. Oxford: Oxford University Press.

Stone, R. C. (1952) 'Mobility factors: How they affect workers' attitudes and conduct towards incentive systems.' *American Sociological Review 17*, February, 58–64.

Strodtbeck, F., James, R. and Hawkins, C. (1961) 'Social Status in Jury Deliberations.' In E. Maccoby, T. Newcomb and E. Hartley (eds) *Reading in Social Psychology*. New York: Henry Holt, 379–387.

Tannenbaum, R. and Massarik, F. (1950) 'Participation by subordinates in the managerial decision-making process.' *The Canadian Journal of Economics and Political Science 16*, 3, 408–18.

Treanton, J. R. and Reynaud, J. D. (1963–4) 'Industrial Sociology 1951–62: A French report and bibliography.' *Current Sociology XII*, 2.

Whyte, W. F. (1955) *Money and Motivation*. New York: Harper and Bros.

Wolf, K. H. (ed) (1950) *The Sociology of Georg Simmel*. Glencoe, Ill: The Free Press.

Notes

1   This chapter was first published as 'Some effects of supervisory style: A sociological analysis' in 1965 in *The British Journal of Sociology XVI*, 3, 189–203 . I am indebted to my former colleagues in the Department of Sociology at the University of Leicester and to my colleagues at Cambridge University for helpful comments on an earlier draft of this article.

2   I refer to this study in the course of my article, and shall omit further references to it. For my replication I was able to use a mimeographed version of it. I should also refer here to an earlier participant observation study of a work group in a cement factory in Midwestern United States in which Hamblin himself found that productivity, job satisfaction, and morale were negatively related to punitive as opposed to nonpunitive supervision.

3   I would suggest two modifications to this conceptualization. The situation which they referred to as 'anomic supervision' should in effect be called 'no supervision'. 'Anomic supervision' could refer, for example, to that situation in which the supervisor is uncertain of his supervisory role or in which his supervision had lost its regulating power. Again, the opposite extreme of 'punitive supervision' is 'rewarding supervision'. This refers to the reinforcing of this desired behavior by rewarding the subordinates when they comply with the rules, by the use, for example, of bonuses.

4   Despite some of the limitations of these definitions, I have used them as convenient pointers for the discussion which follows.

5   The effects of punitive and close supervision may be the same because both are frustrating, although punitive supervision involves the intentional use of aggression to gain the compliance of subordinates.

6   On the basis of Goffman's (1959) work they argued that the higher the subordinates' self-esteem, the less concerned they would be to preserve their 'fronts', and hence, the greater their ability to withstand supervisory behavior which threatened their self images without becoming frustrated.

7   Of course it is difficult to delineate the work situation from other aspects of the community. For one significant attempt, however, see a study of miners in a Yorkshire village (Dennis, Henriques and Slaughter 1956) and a study of automobile workers in an American suburb (Berger 1960).

8   Many laboratory sociologists think that their experiments are conducted in a 'neutral context'. They fail to understand that a laboratory is a very special type of context, but very different from most of those to which one would want to apply laboratory findings. For example, subjects may well be more objective in a laboratory experiment, a point some sociologists claim in support of their generalizations from these experiments; but I would argue that this itself is an indication that the laboratory is a special source of constraints.

9   Twenty-four groups of four women each were recruited from undergraduate classes and dormitories at Washington University. They were all between the ages of 17 and 19 and were either freshmen or sophomores.

10   For the most recent and comprehensive bibliography of relevant studies, see Treanton and Reynaud (1963–64).

11   One can distinguish two types of expectations: realistic or anticipatory and normative.
       It may be assumed that there will be a minimum of incongruity between actual super-
       visory experience and anticipations of supervisory experience in most work groups
       most of the time. In other words, assuming 'stability' to be usual, there will be high
       congruity between actual supervisory experience and anticipations, and also norma-
       tive expectations. When past experience has been inadequate or inconsistent, how-
       ever, subordinates are unable to form their anticipations with confidence. Particularly
       under such conditions, frustration will probably be strongly related to incongruity be-
       tween experience and normative expectations. This is probably the case in many labo-
       ratory experiments, as well as in industrial situations undergoing change, for example,
       with respect to management turnover, physical plant alterations, or new production
       methods. In this study I shall be concerned with normative expectations.

12   This is why it may be unwise to use the term 'authority' when referring to both work-
       ers and, say, middle management in the same organization: if authority is rejected then
       it is no longer authority in the sense that sociologists usually the term, i.e. as legiti-
       mated power.

13   For an earlier and preliminary statement of this problem, see Gouldner's (1955) re-
       marks on the 'indulgency pattern' in *Wildcat Strike: A Study of an Unofficial Strike.*

14   An illuminating though value-loaded illustration of this phenomenon is to be found in
       George Orwell's (1937) *The Road to Wigan Pier.* A more reliable source is Strodtbeck,
       James and Hawkins (1961). See also Bottomore (1963).

15   It is an empirical problem whether social class would be as important in this respect in
       America as in England. The middle classes in both countries exhibit important similar-
       ities in their normative orientations towards mobility, in their egalitarian ideology, and
       emphasis on success by achievement. But the working class in America may be more
       like the American middle class than like the English working class. It is possible that
       the recent history of economic expansion in America has produced an egalitarian
       mythology as a national rather than as a class characteristic. The facts of a relatively
       rapid ethnic group assimilation, social and geographical mobility over great social and
       geographical distances, and a relatively unselective educational system may have
       reduced class differences in normative orientations to work. The American middle
       class and the English working class may, therefore, represent two extremes in the
       degree of sensitivity to supervisory authority.

16   I shall discuss the subordinates in cell 2, whether they remain in it or move to cell 4 in
       the course of their careers, when I come to discuss middle class subordinates.

17   Perhaps Marx's discussion of the 'cash nexus', however polemical in tone, may be rele-
       vant in the context. One should also refer to Georg Simmel's brilliant analysis of the
       relationships of a complex monetary system, personality, and position (Wolf 1950).
       On 'economic behaviour' specifically, see Behrend (1957) and Baldamus (1961). For
       a general consideration of money as a motivator, see Whyte (1955).

18   Both American and British data are relevant here. For American data see Hyman
       (1954); Knupfer (1947); and Lipset and Bendix (1959). The English data are more
       sparse: Dennis, Henriques and Slaughter (1960); Glass (1963[1954]); Martin (1963a
       [1954], 1963b [1954]); and Stacey (1960). It has long been known that middle class
       adolescents are more likely than their working class counterparts to seek opportuni-
       ties for advancement rather than security, for example, Kahl (1953) and Lipset, Bendix
       and Malm (1955).

19   See Goldthorpe and Lockwood (1963). They discuss 'collectivistic' and 'individualis-
       tic' orientations of workers. One aspect of the former is the perception of one's own

interests as being bound up with those of cohorts but cut off from and against those of the superordinate. The interesting point is made that the 'new workers' may be collectively oriented for individual improvement, as might be the lower middle class, as the character of their occupations changes.

20   This is of course too simplified a statement. For a detailed structural analysis of some aspects of this matter, see Lockwood (1958) and Tannenbaum and Massarik (1950).

21   An interesting case in this respect is the bank strike in England. On the one hand the clerks' concern for negotiating instruments for 'wage considerations' resembles that of a traditional union of manual workers. On the other hand, the degree to which bank clerks still try to distinguish themselves from manual workers in dress, voting, budgeting, house furnishings, and so on has not been lessened.

22   For a more detailed discussion see Argyris (1957). Although he recognizes that when workers are disengaged from their occupational roles many of the frustrating features of these roles are not felt as such, he fails, I think, to stress the widespread pattern of disengagement and in fact, therefore, treats it as unusual rather than normal.

23   For a discussion of international similarities in class differentials with respect to involvement in and satisfaction with the occupational role, see Inkeles (1960) and Tannenbaum and Massarik (1950). I have observed workers showing more ego concern in tea-breaks than they do on the job, even when they are being 'bawled out' for some mistake.

24   At least the strength of such a relationship will be controlled by normative receptivity to supervisory authority.

25   A particularly interesting situation would be a piece-work system combined with a structured dependence on the supervisor for parts or services. For early studies of conditions affecting restriction of output and the role of payment schemes, see Roy (1952b, 1953) and Stone (1952) .

26   This also applies to remaining aloof from irritations caused by your 'underlings', but this is less relevant to the present paper. For an informative but not very sociological discussion of English manners see Pear (1955) and for a similar discussion of American manners, see Gorer (1948, 1955).

CHAPTER 2

A Sociological View of Large Groups[1]

with Anne Weyman

This article has several purposes: to introduce certain elements of the socio-logical perspective which may clarify the nature, or ontological status, of social phenomena and processes, to isolate several properties of large groups as distinct from their members, to provide concepts for the denotation of these properties and to discuss their interrelationships.

What is sociology and the sociological perspective?

Sociology is the scientific[2] study of social systems which results in public, communicable, systematic, reliable and valid knowledge about them.

The application of a systems perspective to the study of human collectivi-ties is not an imposition of order upon chaos. Evidence shows that human collectivities possess systemic properties and the development of the concept 'system' is part of an attempt to understand them. It enables us to see beyond the ostensibly random activities of individuals and to discover patterns of social order and conflict.

A system exists if a set of elements within an environment relate to one another in such a way that changes in them can be predicted without reference to that environment. The actual relationships among the elements of a system and between the system and its environment are always problem-atic. Perfect systems do not exist in the social world; their imperfections often constitute their most interesting and relevant properties, especially in connection with social change.

Although this definition is formulated in a highly abstract way, it may be applied to any empirical reality which has systemic properties, regardless of its size or complexity. For example, it might be used to study a dyadic relationship, a small group, a formal organization, an economy or a society. Sociology would have little to contribute to the understanding of large groups if they were not social systems.

A social system is a specific kind of system. The term 'social' refers to two interrelated properties of human collectivities, the recognition of which is axiomatic to sociology. The first of these essential properties is that human beings cannot exist except within a society of some kind, no matter how simple, and that society cannot exist without human beings. Human organisms might be born and survive for a while in the wild, but would not be recognized as human beings. They would not be able to speak, reason or feel in the way that human beings do; they would not have the needs and responses acquired through socialization, not only in infancy, but also throughout life.[3] The dichotomy between society and the individual is an abstraction. This does not mean that society and the individual are in complete harmony but that, although social constraints on some human beings may derive from external coercion and force, society is maintained primarily through internal volition.[4] Social forces require a high degree of participation from both those who force and those who are forced.

The second essential property to which the term social refers is that much of society is made up of emotional or mental phenomena. These exist in the mind and are a product of interactions between human beings. The existence and maintenance of all social phenomena, except in so far as they rely on material inventions like technology, are an expression of meaningful 'human action' (as distinct from behavior) based on a body of shared understandings and a common intellectual and emotional discourse.

It follows that the understanding of social phenomena demands the recognition that the essence of the social is that it is human and the essence of the human is that it is social.[5] Thus, the properties of any social system cannot be distinguished fully from the properties of the human beings who are its members. However, the properties of social phenomena also transcend the properties of the members of social systems and their actions. Therefore, the properties of social systems may be studied independently of the individuals within them and the properties of individuals may be studied independently of their social context, within reason. For example, it is possible to study the structure of authority within a particular group without taking into account the personalities of its members. It is known that groups of a certain size faced with certain types of tasks tend to develop specific kinds of authority structure, despite the existence of a variety of personality characteristics amongst their members. Similarly, it is possible to study an individual's personal styles concerning authority without taking account of the basic authority structures to which he has been exposed and in which he will have to participate. Although these essential aspects of his social context are important, they may be less important in the first instance than knowledge about many of his other personality characteristics such as how frightened he is of helplessness and dependency.

The study of any problem requires the choice of its boundaries. These are set by the resources available and the kind of solution sought. However, if all the elements of the system are not taken into account, by definition, the solution to the problem will be partial. Sociologists are particularly aware of the partial nature of such explanations, and stress the importance of the context within which the boundary is drawn. For example, they argue that although interaction between individuals in a group can be understood, to an extent, by considering processes within the group, the group exists in a social environment which cannot be ignored completely. It is impossible to consider everything at once, but it is essential to realize that every study involves a choice to concentrate on certain aspects and not others.

This stress on the social context of all interaction is often ignored. Many people are unable to see that to find explanations for human action it is necessary to go beyond the individual.[6] However, their 'individualism' is misleading. Human action is affected by social phenomena, and it must be recognized that when the consequences of social phenomena are identifiable and hence 'real', the phenomena themselves are real.[7]

The sociological perspective is based on the acknowledgement of the social as real and that it affects human action. The concept 'social system' is a particularly valuable tool for this work. It enables us to establish the systemic properties of social forms and to analyze the various relationships among them and their effects on individuals' actions. Furthermore, we can examine the relationship of any particular system to its environment. The categories obtained from the analysis of one system can be used to compare different types of social system, whether these are different societies or parts of any one society. Thus, our knowledge of the social system 'society' can help to extend our knowledge of the social system 'large group'. It can do so in two ways: first, by disclosing similarities and differences in structure, and, second, by clarifying the nature of the interaction between them. This latter process is extremely important because society is the environment in which the large group exists and hence forms its social context, the vital focus of the socio-logical perspective.

Elements of the social system

The elements of a social system are those roles, relationships and norms which are primarily concerned with the attempted solution of fundamental problems. We will first consider the concept of a fundamental problem and then will examine the notions of roles, relationships and norms.

Fundamental problems

The term fundamental problem describes any problem which people must attempt to solve if they are to survive. There are two kinds of fundamental problem. The first arises from the nature of the human organism[8], and the second from the structure of any organization through which people attempt to solve the first type of problem.[9]

Although it is possible to have different forms of social organization within which people attempt to solve organism-specific problems, once a particular form of social organization exists, it presents fundamental problems of its own. These problems are in a sense derivative from organismic ones, but they are nonetheless constraining. For example, if people did not have to eat to live, they would not have an economy, but because they have an economy they are almost as much constrained by the development and main-tenance of its particular form as they are by their need to eat. Equally, the solution of the organism-specific problem of co-ordination requires that leaders be selected and trained. The provision of suitable succession demands that this must be a continuous process. However, it may be accomplished in various ways, two of the most familiar being hereditary succession and election. Both assure succession, but each presents the society with an additional set of fundamental problems which must be dealt with if the arrangement is to work.

The idea that fundamental problems can be related to particular institu-tions leads us to the concept of sub-system. Each sub-system is related to activities which are concerned primarily with a specific fundamental problem. Such sub-systems are not always easily distinguished empirically, especially in the case of simple societies. However, they can always be distinguished analytically no matter how simple the society under consideration. Thus, in the case of the social system 'society', the elements of the system are equivalent to the sub-systems which are themselves related to particular problems.

Many sociologists have tried to classify fundamental problems as a basis for the comparison of all social systems.[10] However, such schemes have proved of little help in efforts to understand actual social systems. The difficulty is not their level of abstraction, but their lack of theoretical and logical justification. They are primarily *ad hoc* lists which seem adequate only because they are so general. Such schemes may facilitate the presentation of data but should not be held in too much esteem by those in search of conceptual order. In fact, sociologists are only able to indicate that there are fundamental problems and to suggest which of these are shown by current evidence to be universal. These insights can be used in constructing testable propositions.

Although the list of problems which have been treated in this way pertains to societies, any social system which has sufficient social stability for it to have recognizable boundaries and, therefore, which is identifiable as a social system, contains sets of activities which are concerned with their attempted solution. However, some social systems are specialized. They depend on other social systems in their environment for the attempted solution of one or more of their own problems. For example, one organization may rely on another to provide it with already socialized human beings. Equally, a large group may specialize in the maintenance and production of core values and may depend on other agencies for everything else. However, a specialized social system of any kind is likely to have some arrangements which contribute to its own maintenance, if only to provide for the receipt and distribution of goods and services it receives from other systems.

So far, we have concentrated on those similarities among people which are the result of the human condition and which enable us to analyze society into its constituent sub-systems, such as the educational sub-system or the economic sub-system. We must now look at the actual activities which go on within social systems. To do so we must return to the notions of roles, relationships and norms.

Roles, relationships and norms: social structure

When we say that social phenomena are structured we mean that in all relationships people do not just meet as people. Instead, they meet as the incumbents of various roles which are attached to certain positions. There are many varied roles and positions in a society and people occupy and act in more than one. All social action involves positions and roles and comprises two interrelated components of social structure which we shall call interaction patterns and normative patterns (Gouldner and Gouldner 1963). Interaction patterns are the actual affiliations and relationships between people, and normative patterns are the rules which specify the form and content which these interactions should take. Consider, for example, the social structure of the relationships between a subordinate and his boss: the boss usually initiates verbal interaction, and has control over the basic framework of the relationship; the normative patterns pertaining to this relationship concern the manner in which orders should be given, received and accepted or rejected. The interaction and normative patterns of this relationship may not concur: although the boss may usually initiate the verbal exchange, both he and his subordinate may share the norm that they should be equal in their initiation of verbal exchanges.

Five types of interaction patterns are particularly important: the exchange of goods and services, co-operation towards a common goal, voluntary conformity to social norms, involuntary conformity resulting from coercion, and the struggle which follows from conflict (Nisbett 1970). Any particular interaction may contain more than one of these types of pattern. For example, marriage may be seen as an exchange of goods and services, co-operation towards a common goal (happiness, social prestige) or conformity to the norm that people ought to get married. In this case, the interaction could be considered in terms of any of the categories, depending on your attitude to marriage.

The causal connections between interaction patterns and normative patterns are always problematic. When a new behavior pattern is established coercion may be required to impose it; if those who coerce have control over the socialization process, they can ensure that future generations will accept the pattern as 'natural'. Thus, an interaction pattern based on differences in power may impose a normative pattern which reinforces it. Although the interaction pattern is usually primary, under some conditions the normative patterns may initiate or preclude certain interaction patterns. For example, if it is felt that people should not express their feelings readily then they will not necessarily behave aggressively even though they may feel aggressive, and this will influence the way others behave towards them.

'Social structure' is not a sub-system of the society. It is a term which refers to the interaction and normative patterns which pervade an entire social system, and occur in endless forms throughout it. As a consequence of the fact that all social phenomena are structured, people in different positions tend to have different views, interests and attitudes. In any structured relationship there are differences of interest which engender different views (Lieberman 1970).[11]

Differentiation need not always involve stratification.[12] However, when a relationship is characterized by an unequal distribution of rewards, it will almost always involve a conflict of interest. Even though the norms may say that the differences are just, such conflicts will reduce the possibility of co-operation.

The term 'social stratification' describes the fact that social positions are hierarchically ordered so that some people own more than others, some have more political power and some have more social status. An individual's positions in all these hierarchies are likely to be congruent, but discrepancies do exist. A poorly paid profession such as the clergy may have high social status, whereas a bookmaker who earns large amounts may have low status. Status is a more problematic basis for a hierarchy than the other two dimensions because it is more of a social construct, and different groups in society may differ violently in their assessment of the social prestige of different occupations (Young and Willmott 1956). The more concrete basis of economic and political stratification is reflected in the fact that it is unusual for those without economic power to have political power. It may appear that a politician without economic power may nonetheless have political power. However, he is constrained by the economic power of others, and can further their interests without being rich himself.

Various types of structural arrangements are possible in all social systems ranging from societies to large or small groups. The sociologist attempts to understand these variations. Dimensions of comparison are required for this task and we will now discuss some of them.

Some important dimensions of social systems

It is surprising how much information is offered by locating a social system on a number of fundamental dimensions such as:

Complexity

Societies vary in their degree of complexity with respect to the differentiation and specialization of their parts. Differentiation and specialization refer to the number of more or less empirically discrete elements with distinct boundaries within a social system which relate to the attempted solution of its various fundamental problems. Thus, the ease with which sub-systems can be identified empirically and the degree to which they are concerned primarily with one fundamental problem, and with that problem alone, is a function of the social system's complexity. A continuum from 'ideal complexity' to 'ideal simplicity' can be envisaged. A society may become more or less complex, and this increasing or decreasing complexity may be manifest in either the interaction system or the normative system, but usually in both.

As societies become more complex, their sub-systems come to consist of specific roles which are combined in distinct structural units. Less complex societies have more diffuse roles which are less distinctly grouped. A specific role requires action, thought and feelings from its holder which are circumscribed and bounded, and does not require a full personal involvement. A relationship between two such roles is like two billiard balls touching. For example, a bank manager and his client have a highly specific relationship. On the other hand, a role characterized by diffuseness requires a full personal involvement in its tasks. Even though the tasks themselves may be clearly defined, they are usually exceedingly complex, and it is difficult to formulate standards for assessing their performance. A relationship which is structurally diffuse may be compared to two warm wet sponges pressed together. A good teacher and his pupil, a therapist and his patient, a parent and his child, and siblings all have diffuse relationships.

Social systems that are complex will have sub-systems which are primarily made up of structural units in the form of sets of specific roles, but they will also contain some structural patterns which are more diffuse. Less complex societies will consist primarily of structural units which contain diffuse roles, but they will also have some specific roles. Thus, increasing and decreasing complexity does not necessarily occur evenly throughout a society. Indeed, some problems may be more effectively dealt with by diffuse rather than specific relationships. Socialization and education are two processes which fall into this category.[13]

Cohesion

Cohesion in general refers to the degree to which the elements of a system are interdependent. The degree to which change in one element produces change in the rest of the system is an index of its degree of cohesion. Again systems can be placed on a continuum from 'ideal cohesion' to 'ideal incohesion'. No known system is ideally cohesive but some approach this state.

The term 'social cohesion' refers to the degree to which actions in a system are constrained by the existing patterns of affiliation and norms so that the activities of its members can continue. The extent to which people are interdependent within their affiliations for the provision and receipt of services can be referred to as the degree to which their interaction patterns are 'integrated'.[14] The extent to which they share common norms, and, hence, have similar views of what form these ties should take, can be referred to as the degree to which their normative patterns are 'solidary'. Thus, just as social structure is composed of both interactive and normative patterns, so social cohesion consists of both integration and solidarity. This distinction is useful for comparing social systems. Two systems may be equally cohesive, but in one case this may be mainly due to integration of the interaction networks, whereas in the other it may depend mainly on the solidarity of the normative networks. For example, the cohesion of a business enterprise depends mainly on the integration of its interaction networks, whereas that of a large group depends on the solidarity of its normative networks.

Closure

Closure refers to the degree to which an element in a system is influenced by any elements in the system's environment. No known system is totally closed but some approach this state. By definition, no system can be totally open. If a social form is believed to approach this state, the concept 'system' cannot be applied to it. Its boundaries must be redefined to include the relevant aspects of what was previously considered to be its environment. Societies are perhaps among the most open of all known systems, but even they are fairly closed.

Just as all systems have environments, so any system is itself an environment with respect to its constituent elements. When considering any one element in a system or its relationships with other elements, it is therefore crucial to keep in mind the effects of all the remaining elements in the system.

This can be seen as a problem in controlling the environment of the constituent elements. It may also be useful to specify the type of environment in question. Although often somewhat arbitrary, a distinction should be made between the natural, social and psychological environments. Some social systems may be relatively closed with respect to one but relatively open with respect to another.

Dynamism

Dynamism refers to the amount and rate of interactions within the relationships which comprise the constituent elements of social systems, among these elements and between them and the environment. If no interactions occur within the system, it is 'ideally static'. No known social system is ideally static but some approach this state.[15] Interaction processes may manifest various kinds of pattern, e.g. cyclical, and the amount and rate usually vary in accordance with particular events, such as a breaking of rules by a member of a large group or the departure of a member of a small group. It is important to recognize that interactions can range from slight gestures to hitting someone. High levels of dynamism need not always involve an increased amount of verbal communication.

Stability

Stability refers to the degree to which the social structure of a system does not change. Few systems are ideally stable, and few can maintain high levels of instability without changing in such important ways as to involve redefinition of their boundaries. The location of a system in a continuum of stability–instability may be partly independent of its location on a continuum of dynamism–stasis'. For example, a system may be characterized by a repetitive change cycle in which the structure of the system fluctuates between two states at given time intervals. Such a system would be highly dynamic, but may still be characterized by a stable equilibrium. Indeed, it is possible that a pattern of cyclical change of this kind may function to maintain a system's stability.[16] The stability of any system's equilibrium is, however, problematic, on account of influences which emanate both from the environment and from within the system itself, e.g., the discovery and utilization of new sources of energy, or such internal phenomena as rapid changes in the amount of goods available for distribution, or changes in people's perceptions of what is socially just.

Some sets of dimensions

The position of a social system on any one of the above five dimensions tends to be related to its position on any other. Although these relationships are sufficiently imperfect to permit each dimension to be conceptualized as independent of the others, they tend to constitute a syndrome. With reference to society, two syndromes are particularly interesting. They have been called 'simple' and 'complex'.[17] We will now examine the way in which some of the dimensions of these syndromes interrelate.

Complexity and social cohesion

The social cohesion of 'simple' societies (those with a relatively low degree of differentiation and specialization) tends to be based to a large extent on normative solidarity. The norms in such societies are likely to have an altruistic content, largely because relations among their members are characterized by diffuseness and emotional involvement. The simple structure of their interaction systems provides a basis only for relatively low degrees of interdependence, and there are relatively few opportunities for conflict either with respect to goods and services or with respect to power and authority differentials. Where such differentials exist, for example in slightly less simple societies, they are not likely to be marked by sufficient social distance to be conducive to deep-rooted tensions and conflicts. Simple societies, therefore, have little need for differentiated agencies which specialize in co-ordinating activities in the society. Nor is there a great need for specialized management of conflict and tension. We do not claim that simple societies are completely tension and conflict free, but merely suggest that they contain relatively few 'axes of tension' compared with their more complex counterparts. Therefore, when morale, an index of solidarity, is high, the members do not require a high degree of direction in order for co-operation to occur.

In contrast, the social cohesion of complex societies is based on the integration of their interaction systems. As a consequence of a higher degree of differentiation, they are likely to be co-ordinated primarily through the purposive activities of specialized and bureaucratically organized central agencies. The tendency towards specialized, centralized, and bureaucratized co-ordination in such societies results from the size and complexity of their organizational tasks. It stems also from their highly differentiated interaction systems whose role specificity and impersonal nature tend to produce a relatively low degree of consensus on norms and values. Furthermore, when consensus exists it is usually restricted to those norms and values with an egoistic content which encourage people to be more aware of their differences than their similarities.[18] Thus, like their more simple counterparts, complex societies may also manifest high degrees of social cohesion, but when they do, it tends to derive from the deliberate action of central agencies, both at the societal and sub-system levels, and not from the solidarity produced by their normative systems.[19]

As a society becomes more complex, there is also a greater likelihood that groups with conflicting interests and values will emerge. Tension and conflict between such groups tend to be endemic in complex societies, and constitute a pressure on the specialized agencies of central co-ordination to manage tension and conflict. Such agencies come increasingly to perform a regulative function with respect to norms and values; that is, they attempt to use their central position and the various resources at their disposal in order to maintain a reasonable balance between expectations and real possibilities. In addition, owing to their greater specialization and differentiation of parts, complex societies tend to develop large numbers of relatively autonomous nuclei which are potential loci of centrifugal pressure. Such nuclei are capable of becoming self-sufficient with respect to their own co-ordination and the satisfaction of all their fundamental problems. At the same time, the high degree of interdependence among the various parts in such a system implies that the cost incurred through the loss of any one unit would be high. As a result, a further premium is placed upon the centralization of control in order to combat the potentially fissiparous tendencies of such autonomous nuclei and to maintain the integrity of the system as a whole (Gouldner 1959).

Complexity and openness

Complex systems tend to be closed to their natural environments. First, they are likely to have specialized and differentiated institutions for dealing with nature. Second, they are likely to have relatively powerful technologies, although this does not derive from their level of complexity alone. However, members of complex societies are often surprised and humiliated by the powerlessness of their organizations and technology in the face of natural disasters. They are often less able to cope with such natural intrusions than members of simple societies who have never become so dependent on specialized personnel, whose simple technology is more in equilibrium with their natural environment, and whose mode of life does not insulate them from the natural world. They are more open to it and, at the same time, more adaptable.

Although complex societies are ostensibly open to their social environment because their social cohesion derives from the integration of their interaction systems, in fact they are relatively closed to it. They are able to impose their own internal patterns of specialization, differentiation and interdependence on their relationships with the social environment. The development of such relationships can occur with relatively little effect on the system as a whole. Social intrusions may occur but their speed and depth are regulated by the existing interaction and normative patterns. In contrast, although simple societies are ostensibly closed because their cohesion derives from their normative solidarity and an essential element of this solidarity is the social definition of who is 'us' and 'them', in fact, they are relatively open, especially when they exist in relative isolation and are self-sufficient economically. Consequently, they are more vulnerable to vagaries in their social environment than complex societies are. When confronted with a social intrusion or even a threat of one, their systematic response is likely to be rejecting, especially as any accommodation will tend to require major structural change.

Complex systems tend to be closed to their psychological environment. This environment, in contrast with the social and natural environments, exists within the social and territorial boundaries of the social system. The patterns of interaction and normative regulation of societies requires only a limited participation by their members in any particular act except for those involved in certain special processes such as socialization. Individuals are constrained both normatively and through a system of sanctions to participate in collective activities in a bounded way. Authority and power tend to be invested in certain echelons of organizations, and the conduct of both collective and personal affairs is subject to mainly impersonal regulations. Paradoxically, complex societies permit their members a great display of personal idiosyncrasies and refrain from a high degree of social regulation of much of their everyday life; as long as their members fulfill the expectations embodied in specific roles, what they do and feel elsewhere is of little consequence. However, as the fulfillment of specific roles is so totally important to the cohesion and functioning of a complex society, those in power strive to maintain highly organized sets of sanctions to ensure that these are fulfilled in a consistent and reliable manner.[20]

In contrast, simple societies are more open to their members. Although authority is apparently vested in office, it is almost impossible for members to see a person and his office as separate entities. People in such societies tend to relate to each other in terms of who they are rather than what they do. Consequently, as fulfillment of office occurs simultaneously with everyday activities and personal idiosyncrasies are dangerous, simple societies regulate the daily routine of their members to a far greater extent than complex societies do.

Complexity and instability

Change within a social system may be the result of internal or external factors. Hence, the stability or instability of a society is related to both its degree of internal dynamism and its degree of openness to its various environments.

In our discussion of cohesion and complexity, we pointed out that complex societies contain many structures which serve as axes of tension and which are potential sources of structural change. Hence, the pressure for such change within complex societies is likely to be continuous. In contrast, simple societies contain fewer axes of tension, and their potential for endogenously generated change is small. However, the actual relationship between endogenous sources of social change and change itself is problematic and complex; it is subject to many factors which are beyond the scope of this discussion. For example, complex societies usually possess highly developed technologies which enable their rulers to regulate endogenous sources of change. Nonetheless, if all sources of social change were endogenous, complex societies would tend to be relatively dynamic and unstable and simple societies static and stable.

The stability or instability of a society also depends on its degree of openness to its environments.[21] Closure to any environment is likely to be a source of stability.[22] Complex societies tend to be closed to all their environments; only a very major environmental change is likely to affect them.[23] However, if such a change occurs, its effects may be considerable. Simple societies are more open to their environments and, hence, are more easily affected by changes in them. Thus, if all sources of social change were exogenous, complex societies would be more static and stable than simple ones. The overall stability or instability of a society depends on both sources of change, and the actual mixture in any society at any time is an empirical question.

We will now examine the concept 'group' from a social systems point of view, and then consider those groups which might be called 'large'. Our aim is to show what groups have in common with all social systems and what distinguishes them as a special type of social system.

Groups as social systems

In a sense, all human collectivities with more than merely logical status, such as 'people with black hair', are groups. As such they will have many properties in common, and many propositions about social organization will apply to them. However, this is too narrow an approach. The use of the term 'group' as a substitute for 'social system' reduces the validity of the concept 'group' to denote a particular type of social system which differs from others in important respects, and hence will have certain organization-specific problems. Whereas all groups are social systems, not all social systems are groups. This is obvious if a group is compared with an industrial society. However, the difference is not just a question of size and complexity; groups differ from simple societies too. In fact, a group is a social system with definite properties of its own, which we will now consider.

A group is concerned with solving only a limited number of fundamental problems. Although its members must strive to solve all their fundamental problems, they will not necessarily do so within the context of the group. Indeed, if they try to do so, either they will fail or the structure of the group will be modified to such an extent that it will cease to be a group. As a result of its limited aims, a group must exist within the context of a larger social system on which it depends for the solution of those problems with which it is not concerned directly. Hence, a group is different from a society, however simple.

Furthermore, the limitation of its aims makes a group a relatively transitory system, no matter how long it has been established. Permanence requires institutionalization. There are two reasons why this process does not occur in groups. First, the existence and boundaries of a group are often more important to its members than to non-members. Institutionalization requires that non-members believe that the group's existence and boundaries should be maintained. Second, any one member of the group may believe that his membership will be of limited duration; the permanence of the collectivity beyond this time may be relatively unimportant to him. This is obviously true of a therapy group and, for example, it is increasingly true of industrial work groups. Thus, there is little pressure for institutionalization either from within or from outside the group. Hence, a group differs from an organization because it is not institutionalized.

A group is very open to the personality systems of its members. It is also part of their identity. Groups are characterized by intimate face-to-face interaction, and are fundamental to the formation and maintenance of the social nature of their individual members. As a result, a sense of being part of a whole develops; the individual becomes part of 'we'.[24] However, the potential for such internalization is also related to stages in an individual's development. Groups which are entered into late in life may never be internalized fully by their members.

It is important to recognize that the degree to which a collectivity can be institutionalized or internalized does not depend on its size. Although many collectivities which are highly institutionalized and internalized are large, such as a church or a student body at a university, many large groups are transitory. For example, a crowd or an audience is not institutionalized and can be only superficially internalized by its members. In fact, except in unusual circumstances, these collectivities are probably not internalized at all. Similarly, some highly institutionalized collectivities are small, such as a family, and many are of moderate size, such as a university department or a surgical ward. In general, groups are highly internalized but not institutionalized. Families are the prototype of all groups, but in the sociological sense of the concept, as they are an institutionalized sub-system of the society, they are not really groups.

On the basis of a social systems perspective groups can be located on certain of the dimensions discussed above. In this way we can establish the syndrome of properties by which a social system can be denoted as a group. A social system constitutes a group to the extent that: it has a relatively simple organizational structure; it is relatively open with respect to its natural, psychological and social environments; and it is relatively unstable with respect to its boundaries.

Our treatment of groups may be contrasted with that offered by Cartwright and Zander (1953) who define groups as a set of people with the following characteristics: they have frequent interaction and are defined by themselves and by others as members of the group; they share norms concerning matters of common interest and participate in a system of interlocking roles; they identify with one another as a result of having internalized the same model objects or ideals in their superegos; they find participation rewarding and pursue promotively interdependent goals; they have a collective perception of their unity and act in a unitary manner towards the environment.

This definition is propositional. It states that to the extent to which a set of people have these properties, they form a group. Although these properties tend to form a syndrome, the nature and determinants of their interdependence is problematic. Evidence suggests that the degree to which people are in frequent interaction is the basis of group formation. This is especially so if their interactions are demarcated in time and place in a regular and consistent manner such that the visibility of the boundaries between members and non-members is high. Shared norms arise from these patterns of interaction, and participation in a system of interlocking roles arises from frequent interaction (Homans 1950). Mutual identification, for example among siblings, on the basis of a commonly held model, for instance the mother or the father or both, is probably essential to the capacity of any person to enter and participate in a group;[25] it is problematic whether all members of a group have introjected a particular object which is unique to them as members of that particular group. This may emerge in time but it is not essential for all phases of group activity. The remaining properties are also not essential, but are likely to emerge under certain conditions. Further, although it is significant that a group is the only social system which can plausibly be considered as sets of people, in fact Cartwright and Zander's (1953) approach is misleading because it implies that all social systems are groups.[26]

Groups are not all the same, and types of groups should be distinguished; propositions which apply to some may not apply to others. However, the actual classification of groups is difficult. Cartwright and Zander point out that many different classificatory schemes have been proposed. A common procedure has been to select a few properties and to define 'types' of group on the basis of whether these properties are present or absent. Among the properties most often employed are: size (number of members), amount of physical interaction among members, degree of intimacy, level of solidarity, locus of control of group activities, extent of formalization of rules governing relations among members and tendency of members to react to one another as individual persons or as occupants of roles. Although it would be possible to construct a large number of types of group by combining these properties in various ways, usually only dichotomies have resulted: formal and informal, primary and secondary, small–large, *gemeinschaft–gesellschaft*,[27] autonomous–dependent, temporary–permanent, consensual–symbiotic. Sometimes a rather different procedure has been advocated in which groups are classified according to their objectives or social settings. Accordingly, they are said to be work groups, therapy groups, social groups, committees, clubs, gangs, teams, co-ordinating groups, religious groups, and the like.

This sort of procedure is not satisfactory. Although the typologies which result may be useful for certain purposes, they are essentially *ad hoc*, and the organizational variation within each type is so great as to equal, if not exceed, the variation between types. Such distinctions are helpful only in that they permit further specification of categories based on organizational properties. Indeed, as Cartwright and Zander use such a wide definition of groups, they include categories such as *gemeinschaft* and *gesellschaft* which apply to societies but not really to groups.

Present knowledge does not permit us to propose a classificatory schema for groups. In any case, such schema depend on the purpose to which they are to be put. However, two things are certain: although size may be important, indeed given our definition of groups it may be more important than any other property, it may not be very useful for purposes of classification; and therapy groups should not be taken as typical of groups in general.

Large groups

In this section we will attempt to point out the special features of large groups. Although the number of people in a large group may approximate to the number of people in an organization, the distinction between these two types of social systems is based on differences in their interaction and normative systems. Indeed, according to our approach, large groups have essentially the same kinds of interaction and normative systems as small groups and quite different interaction and normative systems from those of organizations. If there is a significant difference between large and small groups, then the problem of locating the transition point from small to large is crucial.

A growing body of literature and unpublished discussion from psycho-therapy suggests that large groups are not very different from small groups. Some psychotherapists report that, to their great surprise, groups of 50 to 75 evince many of the characteristics of groups of less than 10. However, others suggest that when a group exceeds 16, members experience the group and their participation in it in a new way and begin to behave differently.[28] An alternative opinion puts this figure between 5 and 7. For example, the panchayat or council of an Indian village has 5 members, and some Englishmen say that an ideal dinner party consists of 5 to 7 people (Berelson

and Steiner 1964). However, with such a small number of people the personalities of guests play a part, as does the food, and, as those who give dinner
parties know to their cost, there is no golden rule for success. Ten people who
already know each other may be a better number than six who do not. These
examples only serve to illustrate the need for empirical research into the
effects of size on group processes and, unfortunately, little exists.

In principle, many different disciplines might offer insight into the effect
of size on groups, but in practice they do not. Ethnology has tended to deal
with behavior which is either irrelevant to humans or too far removed from
its human counterpart to be isomorphic; the fact that rats become aggressive
when their population density reaches a certain point adds little to our
knowledge of the effects of size on groups. Anthropologists who have
studied group-like social systems, such as tribes and bands, have concentrated
on the effects of variation in size on the development of new organizational
forms and the disintegration of simpler collectivities, and are concerned with
numbers in the thousands. Psychology and social psychology have
emphasized the study of small groups. Studies of the effects of variation in
size are available, but with few exceptions the range has been from 2 to 12.
Valuable exceptions are those studies of learning behavior which show that
once a group exceeds 15, the decrease in personal participation is so great
that members might just as well attend lectures of 400 (Boocock 1966).
There is an extensive sociological literature which discusses the effect of size
on the interaction and normative patterns of social organizations. Although
this information does not derive from studies of large groups, we will review
the most relevant literature, together with findings from social psychology,
and use them to examine the problem of the transition from small to large.

Any discussion of the effects of variation in size must begin with Simmel
(Wolff 1950). An important contribution is his analysis of dyadic and triadic
relationships. Simmel saw the dyadic relationship as elemental to all forms of
social organization, and examined its effects on the two people involved. He
stressed that the most extreme human feelings are experienced within a dyad;
no other relationship contains the same feelings of love, hate, freedom,
isolation, jealousy, understanding, devotion or betrayal. Once he established
the nature of the dyad, Simmel discussed what happens to the structure of the
dyad and to the two people involved when a third is introduced. He argued
that these effects are disproportionately great; the addition of one person to
the dyad is likely to be more important than the addition of one to any other
group.[29]

Simmel extrapolated his argument to consider the effects of size in general. He pointed out that the effects of changes in size are not linear, either for one collectivity or for the relationship between clearly demarcated parts of a social system. For example, he commented that an army of 10,000 can control a population of 1 million more easily than one person can control 100, or 100 can control 10,000. Even though in each case the ratios are the same, the absolute size of the controlling force is important. Thus, size alone can be an independent factor.

It is worth recalling the very early experiments of Asch (1952) on conformity. They contain some information about the effects of size and illustrate the importance of the dyadic relationship. Asch showed that if a person had one close affiliate and confidant in a group, then virtually no matter how many members exert pressure on him to conform, he will be able to resist and follow his own judgement. Although in general the larger the group the greater the pressure to conform, once membership reaches 50, any further increase in size has a negligible effect. Thus, the number 50 may be the point at which a small group becomes large. However, other studies suggest different transition points; and the transition point may vary according to the type of process being observed.

On the basis of numerous experimental studies, Bales and Borgatta (1955) showed that as a group increases in size from 2 or 3 up to 15 or 20, the 'active' members tend to dominate interaction and 'passive' members inhibit their participation, and the group's discussion becomes less exploratory and adventurous, the group's atmosphere becomes less intimate and members' actions more anonymous, and generally members feel less satisfied. Unresolved differences amongst members become more acceptable. For most of these tendencies the transition occurred in the membership range 5–7.[30]

The experiments also showed that in general as the group gets larger, members show less tension, but its release is more obvious. Feelings of solidarity are expressed more openly and readily, but agreement decreases. Although opinions are less sought after and given, more ideas and information are forthcoming.

Many of these trends were interpreted as the result of two interrelated factors. As size increases, the time available for talking to each member decreases; and each person is confronted with an exponentially larger number of persons. Each member is under pressure to maintain a more or less adequate relationship with each other member. Thus, as size increases, each member has more relationships to maintain and less time to do so.

A central issue in sociological studies has been the relationship between size and the complexity of social organization. With respect to groups, Bales and Borgatta (1957) found that a slight increase in complexity was associated with an increase in size from 2 or 3 to 15 or 20. For example, greater demands are made on the leader; the leader becomes more differentiated from the rest of the group; the group becomes more tolerant of direction by the leader; proceedings become more centralized; the group takes longer to make value judgements; sub-groups tend to form and the rules and procedures of the group become more formalized. Once again, the most obvious transition occurred when the group reached a membership of between 5 and 7.

Some sociologists have argued that within an industrial economy, the efficient use of resources in large-scale industrial organizations requires specialization and differentiation of work. As a result, problems of communication and co-ordination arise, and create a tendency towards complexity, formalization, hierarchy, and other elements of bureaucracy. This proposition is, however, the subject of debate. Most sociologists accept that increase in size leads to greater complexity and its consequences, but the more important issue is the range of sizes within which this relationship operates, and the various other internal and external conditions which might regulate it (Blau 1965; Blau and Schoenherr 1971; Gerth and Mills 1958 [1946]; Michels 1962). Another finding is that the larger the organization, the more likely it is that an informal organization will emerge which may conflict with the formal one.

The material that derives from organizations is in principle applicable to groups, and it is reasonable to assume that as groups get larger they will exhibit some tendency towards complexity. We have commented above that some people who work with large therapy groups suggest that as groups increase from 10 to 100 they do not show such tendencies. This inconsistency requires resolution. There are several possible explanations. These groups may not exhibit such changes because their members are primarily concerned with conformity to the unspoken expectations of those who have power and authority over the members and on whom the members depend. Alternatively, as those groups exist within a more formal organization, such as a hospital, there are no organizational positions or labels which can be applied to such changes; without concepts to describe informal complexity, it may go unnoticed.[31]

As groups have little formal structure, it is easy to overlook the development of an informal structure, and to assume that groups tend to be the same no matter how big they are. Simmel postulated that dyads are the elemental structures of all groups. We would supplement this view by suggesting that dyads and triads form the elemental structures of small groups and, at a certain size, small groups form the elemental structures of large groups.[32] The size at which this differentiation occurs must be established empirically; it may vary from group to group according to their purposes. Equally, it may vary for different processes within the same group. Within large groups, small groups may be less stable than their own component dyads or triads, but again this is an empirical question. Interactions in large groups will be among individuals who represent not only themselves but their sub-groups as well. It follows that the upper limit of a large group may be equal to the square of the upper limit of a small group. However, as the upper limit of a small group still eludes us, this proposition is of limited value.

If we accept that an increase in the size of a group creates the conditions for increased complexity, it must be recognized that increased complexity presents its own problems. For example, it is harder to balance individual and collective needs and, hence, there is pressure towards formalization. Many people prefer the relatively more impersonal and anonymous relationships of large groups. In large therapy groups, such people may be able to defend themselves against the types of feelings they might experience in a small group, in which case their preference for a large therapy group might be a 'resistance'.

It is consistent with our earlier analysis of complex and simple societies to postulate that increased complexity is likely to favor the development of egoistic normative patterns at the expense of altruistic ones. Consequently, large groups are often preoccupied with the time-consuming task of maintaining their solidarity. Participation in the collective pursuit of this aim may provide an experience which enables members to realize that their own identities are intertwined with that of the group. In maintaining the boundaries of a large group, the members are able to maintain their own personal boundaries, and at the same time the realization that much of the self is intertwined with significant collectivities provides a greater awareness of that part of the self which is unique. Of course, participation in small groups also provides opportunities for this experience. However, large groups may be better sources of it because of their greater chaos and potential for schism.

Groups and their environments

We stated previously that the sociological perspective is contextual. A fuller understanding of the structure and process of any group, and especially large groups, requires that their environments be taken into account.[33] An understanding and knowledge of the societal and institutional context of large groups is one of the most important contributions which sociology has to offer. This can be illustrated by some examples.

Israel is a country in which systematic efforts to use large groups for psychotherapy have been made. Springmann (1974) uses a technique which derives from Bion and Ezriel's work on small groups; interpretations are made in terms of the group's collective transference to the conductor. His evidence suggests that this is more effective than most psychotherapists would have thought possible. This may be explained sociologically in terms of certain features of Israeli society. In Israel, the population is very young. Age cohorts are not only a demographic category, but are an important structural form. They mediate between individuals and national institutions, and are the basis of peer group culture, which is an important source of social control and continued socialization throughout the life cycle; they create and maintain standards concerning what constitutes an Israeli citizen. Israeli culture defines its citizens as members of a large group, the paradigm of which is an extended family or tribe in which geographical and political boundaries coincide with religious boundaries. It has been a matter of policy that peer groups should assist in the assimilation of the children of immigrants. Even the army takes account of this social fact. Although it is highly disciplined, relationships between officers and ranks are informal. Such informality is possible because of the high degree of mutual identification throughout the hierarchy.

This kind of societal context creates a special type of personality structure. Selves are not rigorously distinguished from others. 'Individuality' is less highly valued. It is interesting that the most common forename in Israel is 'Israel', which indicates the extent to which individuals are likely to identify with the collectivity. We do not suggest that Israel is without egoistic norms and is one happy family, but it does provide a situation in which participation in large groups is less likely to be experienced as a threat to personal identity or as a deprivation of an intimate relationship with another person. Consequently, interpretation of collective transference in terms of the group as a whole will inevitably have an impact on each participant.

All communications within groups should be understood in the light of the authority structures of the surrounding society. The authority of senior psychotherapists in large therapeutic groups within British hospitals and the bases of their power to control patients' lives derives primarily from the authority and power structure of the hospital and the stratification of British society. The performance and contribution of these psychotherapists within a group may be a secondary influence. Interpretations of transference phenomena which ignore this reality can be misleading; e.g. the suppression by patients of aggressive feelings may derive from their correct assessment of the consequences of expressing them.

Similarly, symptoms classified as neurotic might be normative for a particular social class or ethnic group. For example, the degree to which patients openly complain and express their feelings about those who are responsible for their treatment is a cultural variable. Some ethnic groups whose members often fight with knives may interpret any facial wounds, however slight, as a sign of defeat. Intense concern about minor facial scars may be a source of misunderstanding; a member of such a group may see them as signifying a loss of status, and seek plastic surgery to restore his former status, whereas the hospital might see him as neurotic and in need of psychotherapy (MacGregor 1960).

So far, we have stressed the ways in which the environment of large groups influences structures and processes within the group. However, large groups may also affect structures and processes in their environment. These effects are likely to be indirect. People from different positions in structures of authority and power usually meet in role-specific situations and consequently engage one another with narrow segments of themselves. This often generates mutual fantasies and facilitates the formation of stereotypes based on positions and functions rather than more realistic mutual understanding of the various views and interests which of necessity are contained within large organizations. In such circumstances, decisions and actions are not taken on the basis of rational assessments of the resources and constraints which characterize all positions in the organization.

When large groups from various segments and echelons of an organization come together regularly outside the formal context of their organizational roles to discuss matters of mutual interest, communication with the organization is facilitated. Such sharing of views and feelings may help the organization to run more smoothly and enable members to understand that the formal structure of the organization is not immutable. However, if change is to occur with a minimum of tension and conflict, members must be aware of the scope and limitations of their power to initiate change and of their own irrational attachments to certain types of procedure. Discussion of goals and strategies with people from all parts of the organization may help members to understand the systematic nature of their organization and help them realize that all change is likely to have unanticipated consequences. The use of large groups for such purposes has been called 'sociotherapy' (Edelson 1970).

Although the term 'sociotherapy' has pejorative connotations for those involved in the promotion of social change, in fact, large groups have been used in this way outside formal organizations. In Chile, for example, the revolution aimed at participatory democracy. Early reports indicated that for some tasks very few decisions were made at the top. Money and materials for rebuilding houses were allocated by central government but how these resources should have been used was left to the neighborhood. Decisions were not made on a village basis. The endogenous informal organization was used instead. Early every morning a meeting of a large group from a neighborhood decided how the work was to be done. The size of the group varied from day to day, and the personnel also changed. So far little is known about this experiment, but undoubtedly those concerned with large groups in formal organizations would benefit from studies of it. Equally, the use of large groups within a community would benefit from more research into large groups in organizations.

References

Asch, S. E. (1952) *Social Psychology*. Englewood Cliffs: Prentice Hall.

Bales, R. F. and Borgatta, E. F. (1955) 'Size of Group as a Factor in the Interaction Profile.' In P. Hare, E. F. Borgatta and R. F. Bales (eds) *Small Groups: Studies in Social Interaction*. Glencoe, Ill: The Free Press.

Bales, R. F. and Borgatta, E. F. (1957) 'Structure and Dynamics of Small Groups: A Review of Four Variables.' In J. B. Gittler (ed) *Review of Sociology: Analysis of a Decade*. New York: Wiley.

Berelson, B. and Steiner, G. A. (1964) *Human Behavior*. New York: Harcourt, Brace and World.

Blau, P. M. (1965) *Bureaucracy in Modern Society*. New York: Random House.

Blau, P. M. and Schoenherr, R. A. (1971) *The Structure of Organisations*. New York: Basic Books.

Boocock, S. S. (1966) 'Towards a sociology of learning.' *Sociology of Education 39*, 1, 1–45.

Caplow, T. (1968) *Two Against One: Coalitions in Triads*. Englewood Cliffs: Prentice-Hall.

Cartwright, D. and Zander A. (1953) *Group Dynamics*. New York: Row Peterson.

Cohen, P. S. (1968) *Modern Social Theory*. London: Heinemann.

Cooley, C. H. (1909) *Social Organisation.* New York: Scribners.

Durkheim, E. (1947) [1893] *The Division of Labour in Society.* Translated by G. Simpson. Glencoe, IL: The Free Press.

Edelson, M. (1970) *Sociotherapy and Psychotherapy.* London: The University of Chicago Press.

Evans-Pritchard, E. E. (1940) *The Nuer.* Oxford: Oxford University Press.

Gerth, H. H. and Wright Mills, C. (eds) (1958) [1946] *From Max Weber: Essays in Sociology.* New York: Oxford University Press. (Original work published 1946.)

Gouldner, A. W. (1959) 'Autonomy and Reciprocity in Functional Theory.' In L. Gross (ed) *Symposium on Sociological Theory.* New York: Row Peterson.

Gouldner, A. W. and Gouldner, H. P. (1963) *Modern Society: An Introduction to the Study of Human Interaction.* London: Harcourt, Brace and World.

Harlow, H . F. and Harlow, M. (1962) 'Social deprivation in monkeys.' *Scientific American 207,* 5, 136–146.

Homans, G. C. (1950) *The Human Group.* New York: Harcourt, Brace.

Hopper, E. (1965) 'Some effects of supervisory style: A sociological analysis.' *The British Journal of Sociology XVI,* 3, 189–205.

Hopper, E. (1973) 'Relative Deprivation, Occupational Status, and Occupation "Situs": The Theoretical and Empirical Application of a Neglected Concept.' In M. Warner (ed) *The Sociology of the Workplace.* London: Allen and Unwin.

Hopper, E. (1994) [1975] 'A Sociological View of Large Groups.' In L. Kreeger (ed) *The Large Group: Dynamics and Therapy.* London: Karnac (Books) Ltd. (Original work published 1975.)

Lieberman, S. (1970) 'The Effects of Changes in Roles on the Attitudes of Role Occupants.' In N. J. Smelser and W. T. Smelser (eds) *Personality and Social Systems.* New York: Wiley.

Lockwood, D. (1964) 'Social Integration and System Integration.' In G. K. Zollschan and W. Hirsch (eds) *Explorations in Social Change.* London: Houghton Mifflin.

MacGregor, F .C. (1960) *Social Science in Nursing.* New York: Russell Sage.

Michels, R. (1962) *Political Parties.* New York: Collier-Macmillan.

Nisbett, R. A. (1970) *The Social Bond.* New York: Alfred Knopf.

Parsons, T. (1951) *The Social System.* London: Routledge and Kegan Paul.

Springmann, R. R. (1974) 'The application of interpretations in large groups.' *International Journal of Group Psychotherapy 24,* 3, 333–342.

Tonnies, F. (1963) [1887] *Community and Society.* Translated and edited by C. P. Loomis. New York: Harper and Row.

Wolff, K. (ed) (1950) *The Sociology of Georg Simmel.* New York: The Free Press.

Young, M. and Willmott, P. (1956) 'Social grading by manual workers.' *British Journal of Sociology 7,* 4, 337–345.

Notes

1   This chapter was first published as 'A Sociological View of Large Groups' in L. Kreeger
        (ed) *The Large Group: Dynamics and Therapy* in 1975 by Constable and Company Ltd
        and reprinted in 1994 in London by Karnac (Books) Ltd.

2   The debate about the nature of social science is a continuing one. Science is both a
        body of knowledge and a way of knowing, a source of new knowledge and a method
        of validating what we 'know' about the world. Any particular science consists of a set
        of theories which form its basic paradigm. New knowledge is obtained by using the
        hypothetico-deductive method to test and extrapolate this paradigm. Sometimes new
        findings challenge the theories to such an extent that they have to be replaced or
        altered. The origin of the hypothesis that is being tested is not important, although it
        will usually be derived from the existing theories available to the scientist. In the social
        sciences this creates special problems because not only is the 'scientist' part of his
        subject matter, but also he has definite views about it; and his own views may influence
        his formulation of an hypothesis, and his interpretation of evidence. Ideally this
        should not matter as his work can be subjected to critical scrutiny by other scientists,
        but they may have the same values, and so the basic assumptions which underlie his
        work may not be challenged.

3   It is worth remembering that the first 'men' appeared in a breeding group, some mem-
        bers of which were undoubtedly apes, and that some animals such as monkeys can
        only really be 'monkeys' if they are brought up with other monkeys (Harlow and
        Harlow 1962).

4   The concept of internal volition is itself problematic. If a man needs to earn and he
        knows that another has control of the means of his livelihood and that there is no
        chance of his changing this situation, is his 'acceptance' of it 'internal volition'? Some
        sociologists answer this question by arguing that what people have to do becomes
        what they want to do. (However, we would ask under what conditions the internaliza-
        tion of the status quo occurs.)

5   The first of these two properties has been ignored by those whose training has been
        primarily in social sciences and the second by those who are psychologists. The first
        group tend to reify social phenomena and to have an over-socialized concept of man,
        whereas the second are usually resistant to any perspective which denies the primacy
        of human action and the view that action derives mainly from the organism.

6   They think that to do so is to admit helplessness with respect to control over one's im-
        mediate situation and alternatives for action. This may help to account for the resis-
        tance to sociological insight among those people who experience a lack of personal
        control as frightening. Some may use it as an excuse for avoiding the effort of isolating
        what can be changed in the existing situation from what cannot.

7   It is surprising that whereas intelligent people have no difficulty in accepting the exis-
        tence of invisible forces and phenomena in the explanation of the physical and natural
        universe, even when subatomic particles are no longer expressed in terms other than
        'energy', they refuse to accept that such phenomena as social classes or groups exist
        and are real in the sense that they are more than an aggregate of their personnel.

8   Problems specific to the organism are primary since they must be solved before people
        can seek solutions to all other problems. Hence they are universal. Examples of such
        fundamental problems are socialization, education, economic activity, social
        co-ordination, and conflict and tension management.
                It can be argued that this last problem would not exist in an ideal social system,
        and that even though such a system has never existed, it is not a theoretical impossibil-

ity. If the socialization process were complete, so that all could participate fully in any form of social organization, and if the co-ordination of activity benefited all equally so that some groups were not excluded from achieving certain goals, many sources of tension might be removed. However, the need for tension management may be due mainly to the existence of exploitation and inequality as a property of particular forms of social organization and as organisation-specific.

This is not to ignore the classical debate within both sociology and psychology concerning the natural character of aggressive feelings and aggression. We prefer the view that aggressive feelings are a function of frustration. In so far as frustration is fundamental to the human condition, so too are aggressive feelings. Nonetheless, many psychologists have not given sufficient attention to the various social conditions which regulate this process.

9   Problems specific to organization are numerous. Ordinarily, they are not universal because no particular organizational form is necessarily universal. However, as all human life must take place within a society, certain organizational problems always occur. We will mention only two of the most obvious and important.

Legitimate reproduction: Infants must be given a legitimate status and a position in the social system. Widespread use of contraception indicates that even the desire for children is a social product and that reproduction is too important to be left to organismic factors alone.

The development and maintenance of core values: These help people to come to terms with their social and non-social environments. These environments are difficult to control, and the introduction of general principles which create order out of chaos may make them more predictable and provide guidelines for dealing with them. These values tend to be very general but form the basis for the derivation of specific norms. They are oriented to the solution of specific tasks, and require specific institutions for their development and maintenance.

10   Perhaps Parsons's (1951) is the best known scheme, with its categories of goal attainment, adaptation, integration and latent pattern maintenance.

11   Lieberman (1970) has shown that workers who are promoted to foremen become more favorable to the management, but that if they return to the shop floor, their old attitudes return too.

12   For example, people in the same class but in different sections of the labor market, such as managers in financial institutions and their counterparts in manufacturing industry, differ in many of their personal and interpersonal characteristics, such as their feelings of powerlessness with respect to their control of society (Hopper 1973).

13   Societies which have tried to replace the family with other institutions have often returned to more traditional family structures. This has been so in Russia and in the case of some of the Israeli kibbutzim.

14   The degree to which interaction patterns are integrated may be viewed at several levels of analysis. For example, one can refer to the degree to which a person's many roles are integrated. At another level, one can refer to the degree to which the institutions of a society are integrated with other institutions.

15   Even an inorganic system like a building, which seems to be in a state of 'static equilibrium', is open to environmental influences which can make it disintegrate in time.

16   The annual change cycle of the Nuer in which they accommodate to seasonal climatic changes through structural changes in their society is an example of this type of fluctuation (Evans-Pritchard 1940).

17   The dimension 'simple–complex' has often been viewed as a developmental sequence, and any change towards complexity has been called 'development', and changes towards simplicity, 'regression'. However, this treatment is based on an organismic analogy and must be used with great caution. Social systems are not organisms and do not evince natural laws of growth or determination. Hence, the term 'stages or phases of development' may be used as a description, but does not denote an inevitable evolutionary process (Cohen 1968). A more serious difficulty is that 'development' has been used to connote adulthood, which is felt to be better and more mature, and 'regression' to connote childhood which is worse and more immature. However, simplicity or complexity should not be interpreted in this way.

18   Interestingly enough, the lack of solidarity produced by a system of egoistic norms may actually contribute to the cohesion of a society with an organically integrated interaction system, e.g., through the constraints of universal norms of achievement and norms of affective neutrality which facilitate bureaucratization. Such latent processes and, to a lesser extent, those connected with altruistic norms which give rise, for example, to nationalistic sentiments, are also likely to play their part in the cohesion of complex societies. But they tend to be much less important than is the case in their relatively simple, mechanically organized counterparts, and perhaps are of importance only under conditions of severe crisis for the whole society, such as a war.

19   This view is consistent with the distinction between system integration and social integration introduced by Lockwood (1964).

20   The careful regulation of part of life and the lack of regulation elsewhere may be a source of distress to the individual who only knows how to behave in a narrow range of circumstances. Traditional and simple societies have less of this 'freedom' and less of the anxiety that goes with it.

21   Once again the present systems approach treats the personalities of members of the system as its psychological environment.

22   Closure can, however, prevent the absorption of useful phenomena such as new knowledge.

23   Awareness of vulnerability to any kind of environment may stimulate actions which attempt to increase the degree of closure.

24   Our approach to groups is similar to Cooley's (1909) discussion of 'primary' groups. However, we regard his notion of a 'secondary' group, which includes any social form other than a primary group, to be a residual category of little explanatory value, especially as some of these collectivities, such as a church or even a nation, can become highly internalized despite their high degree of institutionalization. In simple societies, there are very few collectivities which can be internalized. For example, there may only be kinship units and the tribe. In complex societies there are many, ranging from simple family units to the nation. Which collectivity is identified by the individual as 'we' at any time depends on various factors. For example, in war the nation may become more prominent than the family, and in inter-school athletic competitions the school team becomes more important than the house team.

25   This is why the family is such an important prototype for all groups.

26   The plausibility of considering groups as sets of people is related to the fact that groups are very open to their psychological environment. Hence, psychologies of various kinds have more to offer to the understanding of groups than of societal social systems, as evidenced by such banal phrases as the 'sane society'.

27   Tonnies (1963 [1887]) introduced this dichotomy to distinguish 'community' from
      'society'. Many other dichotomies have also been introduced, e.g., Durkheim's (1947
      [1893]) mechanical and organic solidarity.

28   In support of this view, Pierre Turquet points out that each player in a chess game has
      16 men, and he considers that this may be the largest number of people that an indi-
      vidual can keep consciously in mind at one time (Address to the British Association of
      Psychotherapists Training Course in Group Psychotherapy, 1972).

29   A review of the empirical evidence for Simmel's work is given in Caplow (1968).

30   They believe that the number of individuals a group member can take into account at
      one time is between five and seven. However, the number varies with age.

31   Equally it is possible that psychotherapists do not wish to see the changes.

32   We would argue that no dyad can exist without a social context which contains at least
      one other person. No two people can maintain a relationship without the shared sym-
      bols of the group, which has a prior existence. It may be misleading to call any social
      form 'elemental'. However, it is consistent with the sociological perspective that the
      most elemental form is the triad.

33   We do not intend to enter the debate about specific therapeutic techniques which in-
      volve only the interpretation of transference phenomena and exclude external material
      from their interpretations.

CHAPTER 3

'Report on the Large Group' of the Survivor Syndrome Workshop (1979)[1]

with Lionel Kreeger

The background

The organizing committee of the Survivor Syndrome Workshop planned a series of three sessions of the Large Group as an opportunity for participants to integrate their responses to various aspects of massive social trauma, and in particular to survivors and the 'survivor syndrome'. It was assumed that since participants were drawn from different nations, ethnic groups, professions, age groups and backgrounds and that since Large Groups tend to provoke regression with marked tendencies towards paranoid/schizoid phenomena, participants would have the opportunity to experience, clarify, and, perhaps, to work through – in conditions of comparative safety – the phenomena of persecution, stereotyping and scapegoating; victimization and rescuing; surviving; and mourning in connection with the loss of 'objects' ranging from people to segments of society and culture. In other words, the Large Group was intended as a hologram for the dynamics of the Workshop as a whole.

Celia Read and Caroline Garland, who were members of the Committee, had proposed the Workshop partly on the basis of their own experiences in a large group, which was part of the Introductory Course offered by the Institute of Group Analysis during 1975/6. They participated in a particularly dramatic incident concerning a young German woman who spoke of her loneliness and need to mourn, which led to their discussing the potential which large groups offered for the particular tasks of the Workshop. In fact as long ago as 1967, in various lectures and conversations, de Maré had suggested that large groups might have therapeutic potential for survivors of concentration camps; and at about the same time, Dr Robin Skynner mentioned that large groups might be used therapeutically for people whose problem seemed related to large group phenomena, such as adolescents who had difficulties with gangs.

However novel it may be, at least in certain settings such as universities, using an experiential group or the experiential aspects of a task group of whatever size for an essentially didactic purpose is not a new idea. The theoretical rationale for doing so within the Group-Analytic Society and the Institute of Group Analysis can be traced to conversations with the late Harold Kaye. For example, during 1970, Hopper participated in one of Kaye's training groups in which the members observed that the social and psychological dynamics of a group tended to manifest unconsciously the central intellectual and emotional themes of the substantive issues under discussion, and, in particular, those aspects of themes which are absent from conscious discussion because they have been repressed or split off and denied, and are thus subjected to the vicissitudes of projection and projective identification, as well as to introjection and introjective identification. Kaye termed this phenomenon 'equivalence'.[2] We agreed to think about equivalence in order to be better able to use it for pedagogic and therapeutic purposes.

Thus, the Committee decided that the task of the Large Group should be primarily experiential, as opposed to the other sub-structures of the Workshop, where the task would be either primarily informative and didactic or theme-centered. The proceedings were to be unstructured except for duration – one and a half hours; the membership was to include all the participants, staff and resource people on an equal basis. Apart from the role of participant only two further roles were to be differentiated, 'co-conductor' and 'reporter'. The ecology was to be one large group with individual chairs arranged in one circle, but, if necessary, in concentric circles.

Initially the Committee had planned for only one conductor and one alternate. When Pat de Maré declined their invitation to be the conductor, Lionel Kreeger accepted and Earl Hopper agreed to be an alternate. However, as the Committee became more aware of the nature of the task, they began to feel that it might be better if the Large Group were co-conducted. Around this time, Kreeger became seriously ill but, after considerable deliberation, agreed not to withdraw, provided he had a co-conductor. Hopper agreed to be the co-conductor. However, shortly thereafter Hopper learned that his wife was expecting their first child on the weekend of the Workshop. In the hope that alternative co-conductors could be found at the last minute, the Committee agreed that Kreeger and Hopper would co-conduct the Large Group, and Caroline Garland would act as the reporter.

The proceedings of three sessions of the Large Group

The brief account which follows is based on what might be termed our 're-membered perceptions'. However, the third session is taken from Garland's written notes, with our occasional additions. The problems of objectivity and of scope are discussed subsequently.

The first session

Apart from the co-conductors and the reporter, virtually everyone was late; participants, including staff, drifted in over a period of about fifteen minutes. After waiting a couple of minutes, Kreeger initiated verbal communication by saying, 'Well, it's a little after 11 o'clock, time to start.' His remark was met with silence. After about five minutes or so, which felt like a quarter of an hour, the silence was punctuated by occasional remarks about the chairs and the room in general. Participants shifted their chairs in order to sit in the outer circles and closest to the door; as usual, later arrivals were forced into the center. Many engaged in conversation about the room and the chairs.

After the Group got settled, Kreeger attempted to facilitate discussion by acknowledging his own anxiety and personal sense of chaos, especially about feeling de-skilled or inadequately skilled for the tasks at hand; in evidence he stated that he'd dropped two breakfast trays that morning. This was met with further silence. Eventually, a man from Holland expressed his bewilderment at what he was doing in such a workshop and in the Large Group; he wondered what the organizers of the Workshop wanted from the participants, who the organizers were, and what the Institute of Group Analysis was? Hopper answered by asking, in effect, 'Do you usually come to workshops where you know so little about the organizers?' The issue was more or less dropped.

The second quarter of this session was characterized by attempts to identify various sub-groups, to distinguish among them, to define who was a survivor and who was not, who was 'really' a survivor and who an imposter, who were the persecutors and were are the victims, and, ultimately, who were the Jews and who were not, more or less on the presumption that all Jews are survivors or all survivors are Jews. Participants accused the staff of prejudice and narrow-mindedness, as though the staff were responsible for the fact that Jews were receiving so much attention, especially in the light of the current problems presented by the 'boat people'. The participants were preoccupied with who the staff were and what they were like. One commented that on the basis of the administrative inefficiency of the Institute of Group Analysis, she began the Workshop thinking that the staff must be non-Jewish and anti-Semitic, but she now felt that they must be Jewish, parochial and chauvinistic. Another commented that non-Jews had a 'lot to worry about' on this Workshop.

The third phase was initiated by statements the apparent intention of which was to dissolve the incipient sub-groups, e.g. 'we are all survivors'. However, it soon became clear that this move towards solidarity and integration was half-hearted; the roles of 'Jew' and 'survivor' were highly coveted because participants believed that they would attract the most benevolent attention. A participant of Anglo-Polish descent made a particularly strong statement that not only was he a survivor, but Jews were not the only survivors – they did not have a monopoly on surviving. Although he did not comment upon it, Hopper felt that a murmur of anxiety and restlessness rippled through the Group, but Kreeger did not share this observation.

At this point, a woman who had identified herself by 'My name is X and I am a doctor', described an experience that she had early in the morning on the way to the Workshop (apparently she had not spent the previous night in residence). She saw an automobile accident where one car bumped into the rear of another, and clearly someone was hurt; although she was a doctor, she stood by as an observer, not quite knowing whether she wanted to get involved, whether there was anything for her to do, whether she should come to the Workshop. When eventually she thought that enough people had gathered around and everything was under control, she continued on to the Workshop. However, she was still concerned whether she should have gone to their aid, and involved herself in this clash between two individuals and two cars. She felt preoccupied with such questions as, if she had entered the situation, which car would she have entered and who would she have helped first? Hopper brought this back to the Group by suggesting that the communication might pertain to emergent sub-groups and their potential clash, the two co-conductors and, indeed, to the issue whether one particular sub-group or person in the Large Group might get run over by another. Again, the Group attempted to sort out who was a survivor. Many were irritated with the man who claimed that although he was not a Jew, he was nonetheless a survivor. There followed a long silence and a sense of apprehension.

The last quarter of the session began with attempts to break the silence. For example, Rabbi S. Herman, a member of the Resource Staff, said that he felt that we were like Jews getting into the box cars about to be driven to Auschwitz, and the next 48 hours would offer us such an experience. A participant began to shout that he was himself a survivor of Auschwitz, and in his opinion this remark was a devaluation of the experience of having been a real survivor; being in this Workshop was nothing like the real thing. Many sympathized with his point of view. Once again the Group lapsed into a longish silence during which several participants, including at least one member of staff, seemed to have fallen asleep.

The silence was interrupted by occasional attempts to discuss social trauma. Eventually, Hopper said that he was not learning anything new and in his opinion the communications were truisms and platitudes; he also emphasized that he was not feeling much except mild boredom. Within a few moments a lengthy discussion ensued, concerning various aspects of the issue of trust. Are we safe enough to have illusions and fantasies? Is it possible to enter through empathy and imagination the inner-worlds of survivors and the worlds from which they survived? Can we trust one another? Can we heal some of the differences and the distinctions among us sufficiently to be able to have a decent workshop? Can we actually do enough over two days? The tone in which these important questions were asked conveyed a sense of optimism.

A participant asked if we were safe enough to be depressed, and if depression wasn't all that we could have? Isn't mourning all that we can do? At this point, the man from Holland who in the beginning of the session said how pessimistic he was about the prospects of the Workshop, said that he had changed his mind; although the task was enormous, although he didn't know if we would be able to accomplish much, and although he was apprehensive, he was hopeful and prepared to do his best. Several participants agreed.

The second session

Almost everyone was late, again including staff. Hopper waited for Kreeger to begin, but when he noticed that Kreeger was going to remain silent, he said, 'Well, it's now 9:30, time to start', which is what Kreeger always says when he starts a large group. Kreeger then said, 'Well, it's now 9:32, but who's counting?', but he did not utter another word for an hour and a half. It seemed that about 25 minutes passed before verbal communication continued, although in fact the silence lasted only a few minutes. However, the striking feature of the session was its mood, rather than its verbal content.

As the committee had anticipated, both participants and staff were fatigued. The first half hour consisted of ugly, irritable bickering and attacks upon everything: the Workshop, the organization, the organizers, the participants, and especially the Large Group itself. Why are we here? This is a waste of time. We want to be asleep. We want to be talking with one another. We want to be having a drink. We want to be back in our Small Groups. The mood was unbelievably despairing. The words 'horrible' and 'repellent' come to mind. The Group was fragmented into various pairs who seemed to be gossiping to one another. Many were agitated and restless, but many were asleep, including at least two members of staff. The co-conductors were silent; although they did not say so, they were shocked by the extent to which the participants brought to this session only the bad bits, deep depression and a sense of persecution, especially because they had heard that so far the participants were having a good experience, and they were especially distressed at the behavior of the staff.

Neither Professor (A.) nor Rabbi (B.) was able to attend the session. Another member of the Resource Staff seemed to encourage a manic mood; he began to chat and laugh with his neighbor, a child analyst. When he was asked by Harold Behr, a member of staff, why he was fidgeting, he laughed in a tone which implied that the answer to this question was self-evident, and said that he was trying to stay awake. He seemed irritated with the proceedings.

Although Hopper felt apprehensive about speaking before Kreeger, once he realized that Kreeger was going to remain silent he intervened by saying that the Group's mood and behavior reminded him of Bettelheim's (1979) observation that in the concentration camps, prisoners would often make a 'storm in a teacup'.[3] What felt like a reflective silence followed.

An analyst who had been working in Israel began a long, heated and very complicated attack: the organizers of the Workshop were useless; large groups were an utter waste of time; she was ashamed to be there; she felt persecuted by the lack of understanding shown by the participants; and, above all, she was appalled by their lack of political awareness and commitment. It was extremely difficult to understand the substance of her communication, but the main themes pertained to 'shame' and 'politics'; basically, we should be ashamed of our lack of political commitment. The mood of the Group prevented the co-conductors from offering what might have been an enabling interpretation concerning feelings of helplessness, impotence and shame among Jews, females and especially Jewish females. People did not know what to do; they were very tired, and they were really unable to understand her. Finally, Hopper confronted her with a description of this impasse. Then, many told her that she was being intrusive and persecuting, and they were feeling utterly helpless against her constant haranguing and verbal flagellation. An Israeli woman, originally from Holland, said to her: 'You are persecuting us. It is as though you are a German who is persecuting us'. Suddenly, she seemed to realize that the Group was not rejecting the substance of her communication as much as her mood, and she became silent.

A member of staff, Dr Malcolm Pines, then initiated a discussion of how persecuting borderline patients could be. The Group quickly resonated to this theme, led by another member of staff, Dr Colin James. A participant commented that the Group had been animated by the tremendous anger which they had just experienced. Gradually, the discussion shifted to survivors. They are persecuting in treatment situations; they project into the therapist feelings of which they are unconscious and which are almost always unbelievably painful; the therapist has to be very careful with his countertransference and general affective responses, because he will have feelings that he is not used to having towards patients.

Following another silence, Pines suggested that the real survivors on the Workshop were withholding their experiences from the Group and that, however unlikely it may seem, the Group could learn from them, at least in the present situation. A real survivor, who in the first group had said that, by making an analogy between the large group experience and the Holocaust, participants were devaluing the experience of being a survivor, jumped up from his chair and began attacking all the participants, the organizers and the co-conductors for deserting the woman who had been talking so long. He argued that we had failed to realize that in the present context she was the victim and needed to be rescued, and we were ignoring her in the same way society had ignored survivors of the Holocaust. Hopper commented that participants were trying to find someone who would save them from their sense of persecution; in so far as attempts to turn the experience into a discussion of borderline patients and countertransference problems had not worked, the call for help from real survivors had been met by a real survivor attempting to become a real savior. This was a manifestation of an unconscious attempt at metamorphosis from victim to savior in response to the Group's unconscious demands to be rescued from their despair.

This comment was followed eventually by grudging and sporadic efforts at discussion. Dr Shamai Davidson expressed openly his disapproval of using a large group as a modality for either didactic or therapeutic experiences concerning topics of the present kind. Several participants agreed. Hopper commented that the Group were attempting to make the co-conductors and the organizing committee feel utterly useless and helpless, and to frustrate their aims and demolish their hopes, which was undoubtedly a way of communicating to them what the Group imagined it must have been like to have been in a concentration camp, as well as a way of trying to control them because they were deemed responsible for the Group's predicaments. This was followed by silence and then a further effort at discussion. Although the session ended on a note of fragmentation and despair, during these final few moments Hopper sensed a slight increase in solidarity, but Kreeger did not share this perception.

The interval between the second and the third sessions

Strictly speaking, intervals between sessions and other contextual events are not part of the proceedings. However, certain material may constitute an exception to this general rule.

After the second session many participants formed into couples and small groups in order to find something to eat and drink, and to be together a while. This lasted until the early morning and, for some, throughout the night. Of course, others went straight to bed, which in the circumstances was equally noteworthy.

Hopper left the Workshop before breakfast, on hearing that his wife had started labor and was in hospital. During a general discussion after breakfast Pines agreed to substitute. The staff said that they all felt utterly despondent about the outcome of the Workshop; some, including Kreeger, wondered if large groups should be dropped from the Institute's model for workshops.

Kreeger and Pines were prepared to jettison their non-directive interpretative roles, and to provide a more didactic experience.

The consensus was that at the start of the morning lecture Pines would announce that Hopper had left in order to be with his wife who had gone into labor. However, Pines was five minutes late. During this time, the lecturer, Rabbi S. Herman, had begun to establish rapport with his audience through informal chat and eye contact. Finally, after introducing himself, Herman began his lecture. When Pines came in, he sensed that it would be inappropriate to break the strong rapport which had already been established. By the time the lecture was over, it had become completely inappropriate to give the reason for Hopper's absence, because Herman had referred to the recent death of his own child, and the audience were deeply moved, many in tears.

As the staff prepared to enter the third and final session, they felt completely lacking in confidence, and inadequate for their task. Although they were aware that the participants had had a powerful cathartic experience in Herman's lecture, some were puzzled about the nature of this response. It may be relevant to note that of the few participants who are known to have felt this way, several were or had been patients of one of the co-conductors.

The third session

The participants were more punctual than during the previous two sessions; however, during the first five minutes they continued to come in, find chairs and get settled. Pines was a couple of minutes late. He was followed shortly by Kreeger – the first time he had ever been late for a large group. The participants continued to chatter in an amicable but subdued manner. Pines announced that Hopper was absent, gave the reasons why, and said that he would be taking his place as co-conductor. It seemed that very few people heard him.

Kreeger remained silent throughout the Group. Pines was more active. Initial remarks concerned the change in mood which followed Herman's lecture. Participants felt that they had had a cathartic experience. They felt good about it, and hoped that they could maintain these feelings for the remaining hours of the Workshop.

The thin, intense man who in the first session was hostile to using large groups in this way, commented that the proceedings had been dominated by the Nazi Holocaust, and this had produced in him a succession of reactions, starting with frustration and irritation but moving towards the conviction that he had learned something important both about himself and, unexpectedly, about the nature of social trauma; he thought that this change was facilitated by Herman's lecture.

Participants began to share their own predominantly similar reactions. Although not everyone was pleased that the Nazi Holocaust was the predominant concern, many felt that they had learned about the basic issues and their own reactions to them. Someone commented that she now understood how the Nazi Holocaust could be used as a paradigm for social trauma in general. Pines commented that the Large Group seemed to have 'come together' in that it had something of its own to offer – it was no longer being used merely as a container for the shit of the Workshop.

As a woman was speaking, a slight commotion began on the other side of the room. A small, frail, elderly lady (known by many to have worked with children who survived the Holocaust) was complaining that she could not hear clearly. She was helped forward through the ranks of chairs to the center of the Group. As she was re-seated, a young German who was also in the back of the room claimed that he too wanted to be at the heart of matters, and made his way to the inner circle. While people watched silently and expectantly, several others, one by one, picked their way through the chairs from the periphery to the center, until it was virtually full. Eventually, everyone seemed to be seated where they felt comfortable. They had formed a group within a group. Pines looked around with a smile, and observed that about eight Jews and four non-Jews were in the center, a proportion which seemed 'about right'.

The woman who had been speaking when the change of seating began now spoke up fiercely about having been interrupted. Others resonated to her comment, and said that in this context it was significant to speak out against what was felt to be wrong or unjust. However, the ability actually to change one's position, to shift one's thinking or feeling, as demonstrated by the physical movement within the Group, was seen to be equally important. One member of staff, Mrs Liesel Hearst, spoke of the paralyzing effect that a system can have upon those who operate within it; for instance at the end of such a workshop she would normally have sat with her group at lunchtime, feeling that to share a meal together would be an appropriate way to end an experience of this kind; but today she found that she was unable to withstand the pressure from other staff members who felt that they should eat as a staff group. (In fact, it had been difficult throughout the Workshop to keep the staff together; Hopper was constantly trying to get them to stay in their roles, which in this context meant maintaining distance from other participants, and during one staff meeting, he was referred to as an SS officer.) She wondered why she had been unable to defy them. She was annoyed with herself that she had not done so. A German woman took up this theme: she said that she had a Jewish father and a Christian mother (a 'mixling'); as a child during the war she too had found it difficult to act when she most wanted to, but that the Nazi Holocaust was over; we had to look to the future and even to the present; what do we do with our anger and frustration from before if we do not use it to act now, and, in particular, to stop and to prevent such horrors.

During the ensuing comments about the fact that people had to make choices, a participant distinguished the 'Jews' from the 'aggressors'. He was jumped on for this, and although he acknowledged it to be a slip of the tongue, he was felt to have reflected a distinction that existed in the minds of many: Jews are victims, non-Jews are persecutors; victims are Jews, persecutors are non-Jews. The German who moved into the inner circle expressed his pleasure that the slip had been recognized, and that such 'labeling' had been diagnosed as false; he said that he moved into the center because he had to confront those who he felt were labeling him with a black star as a German aggressor, in the same way that Jews had been made to wear yellow stars.

Rabbi (B.) spoke for a while to the effect that what counted was one's status as a human being, making reference to Einstein. Eventually, Pines expressed his conviction that the Large Group was not the place for political speeches, and went on to say that the crucial issue was to face the fact that each person contained both victim and aggressor within himself – at least potentially. For us, therapists who were working with survivors or who were contemplating doing so, the problem was that such patients were capable of turning us into persecutors. He spoke of his own shame at having once struck a patient who he felt had goaded him unendurably until he became what the patient felt him to be.

Yet, it seemed impossible to get away from the split between Jew and non-Jew, as opposed to victim and persecutor. Someone expressed his feeling that the Jews in the Group might become persecutors. Others spoke of certain events in the Workshop that had been experienced as persecuting, such as a personal sense of panic during the psychodrama seminar when the light went out after the nuclear attack. So this was what it would feel like! But, someone added, the lights had been out since the beginning of the Workshop; was it safe enough yet to explore some of the splits which had occurred? Someone expressed the belief that only now were we able to look at the Holocaust both within and without, in effect for the first time. What were we to do with what we saw? Was this to be a political party or a therapeutic group? Perhaps the horror of last night's Large Group was necessary, because we cannot forge unity without going through Hell, and we cannot deal with the persecutor in our patients before we have dealt with him (or her) in ourselves. At the moment there was still a split: the Jews were carrying the victimized part of all of us, and the non-Jews, the persecuting. Thus, it was necessary to deal with the Holocaust and what it stood for. We knew what we had to do, but we did not know how to do it. We had to face the fact that however clearly we may have seen the task, it could not have been accomplished by 5 p.m. that afternoon.

Participants returned to the theme of bringing 'opposites' together. For example, a Catholic member of staff referred to the psychodrama seminar: as a result of the first explosion, she had been mortally wounded, and had been tended by Rabbi Herman who, as a result of the second explosion had himself been killed; they felt that they had ascended to heaven together, finding no distinction between a Catholic and a Jewish death, or a Catholic and a Jewish heaven. The question was asked whether a messiah might emerge from such a marriage of opposites. The suspicion was that he would be a Jewish messiah! Many participants then confessed that they had felt a mixture of admiration and envy of Herman's 'brilliant' lecture. Such envy was thought to be an important element in anti-Semitism. Herman responded to all this with a plea for openness. He said that if we are willing to let ourselves be as 'open' and 'receptive' as, possible, we may be able to create enough 'space' for something to happen.

In the silence that followed, Mrs Meg Sharpe, the convenor of the organizing committee, spoke: she had felt both persecuted and persecuting over the business of arranging the Workshop, but now some sort of a truce may have been negotiated; perhaps it was symbolized by her having shared her ice cream with Rabbi (B.) on the way to this session of the Large Group.

The session ended silently.

Brief interpretative remarks

The Large Group was used as a container for primitive social and psychological processes, especially for those feelings and fantasies connected with persecution which participants had repressed, or split off from their more conscious, central, cognitive and emotional experiences within other substructures of the Workshop. Thus, it may be the case that the brief, interpretative remarks which follow pertain to the central themes of the Workshop as a whole. In so far as the Workshop was used as a container for similarly unconscious processes within present society, these remarks may also pertain to certain current events within the context of the Workshop, such as the growth of the National Front and its related activities. Whether such inferences are justifiable will be discussed briefly below.

Before the first session

Participants experienced a collapse of their contextual social matrix. They were isolated from their everyday worlds through the process of registering and entering their simple, spartan rooms, set within a somewhat brutal concrete building, with wire mesh and metal fixtures, telephones that were often out of order, inadequate sound insulation, etc.[4] Although the efficiency of this operation was less than 'Germanic', by Friday morning participants evinced a general sense of dependency, perhaps encouraged by the long queues for breakfast. They seemed mildly dazed and confused, especially about the ecology of the Workshop.

The first session

From the beginning, the co-conductors sensed that participants wanted to be soothed, nourished and protected, although most of them would have denied it. Kreeger tried to facilitate discussion by sharing his own anxiety with them, but participants quickly recognized that fundamentally there is no escape from the large group experience. As is typical of large groups, both primitive anxieties inherent in strong regressive tendencies and processes of defense against them were manifest immediately. Participants demanded, on the one hand, that social distinctions be maintained so as to provide a sense of order, and, on the other, that such distinctions be resolved in order to provide a sense of unity and completeness. In other words, they began to search for security in the form of 'masculine/paternal', hierarchy and organization, and in the form of their eternal alternative – 'feminine/maternal' massification and social homogeneity. Of course, the dilemma is that each defense is a source of a particular type of anxiety which in turn requires the other defense.

The attack upon social distinctions was a reflection of the general wish to merge with the maternal object, primarily as a defense against their envy of the staff, and as a way of competing with others, who they feared might be given more or be safer than themselves. At one level, this can be understood as an attack upon linking (Bion 1959) and, at another, upon the maternal object itself. As this preliminary stage, participants refused to acknowledge the existence of enemies within themselves or even within the Group. Of course, some participants had identified the staff and the Institute of Group Analysis as their enemy, but it is interesting that they attacked the administrative staff rather than the Workshop staff, who might yet have proved to be of help.

As the anxiety of the participants increased, so too did their suspiciousness of the staff and their confusion about the meaning and purpose of the Workshop and of the Large Group in particular. Frustration and rage were abundant; not only did participants seem to envy the staff their opportunity to remain outside the experience – an opportunity which was entirely imagined – but they also seemed to fear that they would be persecutors, in a sense like SS officers. A collective tendency towards the paranoid/schizoid position began to crystallize, as manifest in splitting, projection and the formation of sub-groups, followed by stereotyping and the preliminary phases of scapegoating. Fight/flight activity occurred, but when it became too intense, participants looked outside the Group for objects towards whom they might vent their feelings, as shown in the anecdote about the car accident.

This lengthy communication, which the participants listened to in silence and with obvious interest, warrants particular attention. As might be expected among so many members of the helping professions, the accident may have expressed the prevalence of rescue fantasies and genuine reparative wishes, which were more easily mobilized for survivors of a car accident than for survivors of the Holocaust.

Yet the communication may also have been characterized by 'dream work', especially condensing. Among the several meanings which it may have contained are the following: an unconscious wish, with attendant anxiety and guilt, for an anal primal scene between the co-conductors; an unconscious fear that such a scene would occur, and that as a result a monster would be produced who would get out of control and devour the participants; an unconscious wish, again with attendant fear, anxiety and guilt, that the participants would witness battles between the co-conductors and the other sub-groups, such that proceedings would stop; an unconscious fear that such an accident and/or battles would occur, but that proceedings would not stop, and that instead participants would be helpless witnesses of such scenes. Among additional aspects of the communications are that some participants may have envied the relationships of people outside the Group, even if they were in an automobile accident, in preference to the relationships which they imagined to be imminent within the Group; yet their envy of such relationships outside of the Workshop may have been so intense that it was expressed in the wish that outsiders would have the same sort of accident that they imagined that the insiders were about to witness and possibly to experience. In any case, it was only with extreme reluctance that participants returned to a consideration of intra-group processes.

Participants were frightened to enter into any fantasy activity or world of illusion, where enemies might reside. This would have required some empathy and identification with an experience of Holocaust of any kind. For example, some of the Group seemed to experience the analogy between certain aspects of the Large Group and Jews being transported to Auschwitz as an evil, seductive invitation to participate in a concrete reenactment of the real thing. The consensus was to flee from the illusory experience and to avoid facing the anxieties inherent in their fantasy that a Holocaust was imminent.

The response might have been different if instead of so direct an analogy a version of the following interpretation had been offered: 'I feel that the Group is beginning to experience this Workshop as though they were Jews about to be taken to Auschwitz, and, thus, the considerable fear and anxiety which is present pertains to the fantasy that what happened to them is going to happen to us. This fantasy has to be dealt with before we can use the Group to learn more about the experience.' However, for reasons which will become clear below, it is important to recall that it was Rabbi Herman who offered this analogy and the real survivor of Auschwitz who led the flight from the fantasy. (It is likely that if the co-conductors had made what in retrospect might seem to have been an appropriate and timely intervention, these crucial actions might not have occurred.)

Slowly the participants began to recognize their anxiety and defenses. By the end of the session, they developed a tentative working alliance (or a collective form of masochism, as the case may be). They expressed a degree of open-mindedness and preparedness to go through the experience of the Workshop despite having complaints about its organization, and suspicions whether the staff could contain the feelings aroused by the topic.

The second session

Manic defenses were prevalent during dinner and during the seminars which followed, especially in the psychodrama seminar, where heterosexual and homosexual flirtations occurred. However, in the second session these defenses were overwhelmed by depressive anxieties of exceptional strength and depth. Participants wallowed in what some would call a pure culture of death (Bettelheim 1979), others, a collective sense of aphanasis or anxiety concerning impending annihilation (Jones 1977 [1948]) and still others, a shared realization that a totally good object does not exist (Segal 1975 [1964]). In any case, without wanting to open a discussion of this aspect of metapsychology, it was possible to distinguish two interdependent moods: one, of utter emptiness, despair and meaninglessness unrelieved by any source of nourishment or warmth; the other, of helpless, suppressed rage primarily towards the staff, but also towards the Group itself.

In response to the rage, participants did not resort to splitting, projection, and sub-grouping. (Of course, they continued to define the staff as a special sub-group, but compared to the multiple sub-grouping which characterized the first session, this new sense of 'us and them' marked a significant development from an aggregate to a group.) Nor did the participants look outside for targets towards whom they could displace their feelings. Nor, with the exception of the one woman who had recently worked in Israel, did they attack the co-conductors and other members of the staff directly. Instead, participants attacked themselves individually and collectively, as seen in their intense irritability and frustration, followed by boredom and restlessness, fatigue, despondency and a sense of depersonalization. They oscillated between agitated and schizoid forms of depression, as is typical of large groups when participants are frightened to express their anger towards those in power, and when their regression is so great that they have confused themselves with their objects (Hopper 1977; Springmann 1976). Is it possible that participants had come to identify unconsciously with prisoners in the death and concentration camps? Is it possible that in the same way that prisoners could not express their rage, helplessness, and despair without risking death, participants were unable to express their feelings directly? Were the staff seen as analogous to those leaders of the Jewish community who were responsible for negotiations with the Nazis and/or who helped to maintain a collective denial until it was too late?

Under these circumstances it is not surprising that projective identification was the main defense against such feelings. Participants used this process to control those they deemed responsible for their predicament, i.e. the staff in general and the co-conductors in particular. This defense was especially efficient in that it also served as an offensive attack, because once the co-conductors and the staff became aware of the projection they had no alternative but to experience the feelings involved. The force of the projection was so strong that it became difficult for them to remain faithful to their tasks. For example, was it really appropriate for members of staff to have initiated the general discussion of borderline pathology and countertransference problems? Were they using this issue in order to avoid their own feelings towards the participants and, perhaps in particular, the co-conductors?

Another example of how difficult it was to stay in role is offered by the polarization in mood and style which occurred between the co-conductors. Whereas Kreeger allowed himself to be used as a container, and thus to absorb the projected sense of death and helplessness in the face of an inevitable calamity, Hopper felt determined to stay alive in his professional role in the face of difficult demands from colleagues and participants. It was as though Kreeger and Hopper were enacting the complementary father/son role-set described in the 'survivor literature', for example, Elie Wiesel's (1981 [1960]) *Night*, in which a father dies in his son's arms shortly before freedom. This view may be elaborated by a number of further observations. Kreeger's recent illness may have led him to a greater sensitivity to anxieties concerning senseless death and destruction; and Hopper's awareness of the impending birth of his child may have augmented his need to master such anxieties and to convert them into the creation and maintenance of hope. Equally, the relationship between Kreeger and Hopper may have been the target of the Group's envious attack, also expressed through projective identification; in this respect, the attack may have been a continuation of the themes which were expressed in the first session in connection with the car accident and the co-conductors, the staff in general, and the internal workings of the Institute. Of course, participants in co-conducted groups usually want to separate their co-conductors, and to cut one off from the other, and vice versa. Also Kreeger and Hopper may have perceived that the Group was attacking their relationship in terms of their own fantasies about the Group as an object through which their working relationship was mediated. Obviously, it is difficult to assess precisely the importance to be given to each of these factors and to various combinations of them.

The interval between the second and the third sessions

It is likely that the drinking, eating and sexual activity which are reported to have occurred among a few participants after the second session and throughout the night served as a manic defense against feelings of despair. Participants wanted to escape from the experience of the Large Group, and to be rescued from the Workshop. As a defense against this despair, they began an unconscious search for a messiah.[5] Of course, participants in residential Workshops are prone to enact fantasies of incest with attendant risks of discovery and punishment, and perhaps this is more marked when many have professional and social relationships with one another, and especially when some have clinical relationships with the staff of the Workshop.

Rabbi Herman's lecture on Saturday was not only a useful presentation of important information, it was also a moving and masterly performance. It helped to create a sense of purpose and commitment to the task. However, it is possible that with the unconscious amplification of the process by many of the staff, Herman was colluding unconsciously with the participants. Many must have shared his awareness that Saturday morning was a Jewish Sabbath, a time for sermons rather than for scientific lectures. Furthermore, many already knew that Hopper had gone to be with his wife during labor. Undoubtedly Herman must have been deeply affected by a birth under such circumstances. In the hope that he might be able to alleviate their despair, with which he had great empathy, he gave the participants something very special. Thus some may have thought that they had found a Savior in Herman himself. In the fantasy that he would guide them and protect them, they entered the third and last session of the Large Group.

The third session

Although the staff were anxious and the co-conductors uncertain about what they would encounter, the participants expressed from the start their pleasure in having achieved something – perhaps only having come through a shared regression, but believing that they had also acquired insight. The session was marked by an absence of tension and sub-grouping associated with flight/fight activity and paranoid anxiety. The participants were able to express their positive feelings, and to give to the staff a sense of appreciation for the Workshop, although at this point they did not go so far as to express positive feelings about the Large Group. It is possible that this sense of solidarity and high degree of integration was a manifestation of a deep but comparatively benign regression, characterized by loss of individual autonomy and a feeling of having merged into a large homogeneous unity. Participants may have enacted their sense of being at one with the many, of being a part of a larger whole, by showing their deep concern for the elderly woman's comfort and ability to participate: as a Jewish refugee from Germany who was intimately involved with survivors, and as a personification of the maternal object the group had subjectively become, she was perfect for attempts at reparation.

Within this maternal matrix, participants enacted the central theme of the session, and what they hoped would be the main outcome of the Workshop: they formed a group within a group. This was not a case of sub-grouping as a reflection of splitting and projection. It was an attempt to create a more pure and innocent, yet amplified, version of themselves, in the same way that the action of a play within a play contains the condensed clues or code to the central message of the larger play.[6] In contrast to the destructive, empty despair of the 'storm in a teacup' of the second session, participants now enacted a pregnant woman, through the formation of an inner group. They demonstrated their conviction that they had heard through their ears and seen through their eyes the various messages of the Workshop, that they had been impregnated by them, and that they were now ready to give birth to a child as a symbol of hope for the future and of their own creative potential as they were themselves a symbol of the creativity of the relationship between the co-conductors and among relationships the staff in general (Jones 1914).

Of course, this action contained a number of highly condensed meanings, again as in a dream. The following are several of the many unconscious wishes which may have been expressed: to bring Germans and Jews together in the hope that the Holocaust was finished, forgiven and would be no more; to give something back to Herman in gratitude for his lecture and as a replacement for his own loss; and to give something back to Kreeger in reparation for their fantasy destruction of Hopper.

It is also possible that some participants may have identified with Hopper's wife on the basis of their envy of the experience of giving birth, especially because she was outside the Workshop and had escaped its more painful feelings – more painful than, and perhaps painful in a different way, from childbirth. They may also have been attempting to regulate their anxiety about a birth about which they had no knowledge except that it was imminent; in this connection, the birth in question may have been the fantasy birth of a messiah within the Group rather than the real birth of Hopper's child.

Several parallel processes followed this dreamlike phase of the session. Participants acknowledged and accepted the limitations on work which are of necessity imposed by the structure of a workshop, but expressed their commitment to carry on work of this kind. Non-Jews, both German and non-German, explored tentatively the problem of the 'return of the repressed', that is, their fears that Jews would now become what they had themselves repressed and projected into Jews, and that Jews would now retaliate for what had been done to them. Feelings of guilt were acknowledged. In this connection both Jewish and non-Jewish participants began to explore in an apparently sincere way the fact that victims and persecutors exist in each of us, and how difficult and pervasive were problems with authority in general.

Perhaps a workshop of this kind can end only with a defensive posture. How else can people cope with such phenomena and their aftermath – not only in reality but even in an 'as if' experience? Yet it is appropriate to wonder about the change from the chaotic and despondent session on Friday to the more positive and cohesive session on Saturday morning. Did it result from Herman's having met the participants' dependency needs through his moving address? Did he produce an overt mourning process? Perhaps participants worked through something important during the interval between the two sessions.

Yet, in closing, it is possible to suggest that the Group may have ended on a manic, inappropriately triumphant note. For example, some participants thought that perhaps the awful group the night before had been necessary – Hell before Heaven and chaos before order; they even seemed grateful for the experience of having survived a collective regression into the illusion of concentration and death camps. In retrospect the attempts to bring various polarized opposites together were inevitably oversimplified, and may have been used by many participants as a way of avoiding having to recognize the despair which attends the irreconcilable and the unforgivable. To some extent this may be typical of large groups, no matter what their topic – the imagery of sexualized pairing, which was accompanied by the unconscious wish for a messiah, served as a defense against depressive anxieties. Some participants may have believed that the Messiah had come in the form of Rabbi Herman. Earlier in the session Rabbi (B.) may also have been affected by these underlying group processes. Did the Group create the role of savior in such a way that the two Rabbis in the Workshop were unconsciously, but ineluctably drawn towards it? There is evidence for both points of view.

Problems concerning objectivity and scope

A number of factors may have limited the objectivity of these accounts of the proceedings, and the scope of these interpretative remarks. Hopper was absent from the third session, and although Kreeger was present, the nature of his involvement was such that his memory was selective. They therefore used Garland's notes for their account of the third session, but it remained difficult for them to remark interpretatively on a session from which they were absent, whether literally or figuratively, without offering a mechanical application of theory to events in a manner which is even more *ad hoc* than is usual in this type of work.

It was also difficult for the co-conductors to disregard a variety of intrusions from the contemporary and local context of the Group and the Workshop. Some participants were past or present patients of some of the staff and of the co-conductors; some of the participants and staff were candidates at the Institute of Group Analysis, and some, including members of staff, were not; some were professional colleagues in other settings, and some were close friends; and some were rivals and some worked in rival organizations. At times, prior knowledge of individuals and their relationships drew the attention of the co-conductors from the Group as a whole and from the more common effects of its central action upon the participants.

Moreover as a defensive strategy against anxiety resulting from powerful and strange work experiences, people tend to cling to what they already know. Since their perceptions become overly governed by an excessive degree of previously formulated hypotheses and assumptions, and, hence, expectations, it is more and more difficult for them to learn anything new. It is possible that although many of the participants in the Workshop were able to overcome this problem, the co-conductors themselves did not escape these constraints.

One aspect of this more general problem is that, inevitably, this report was prepared after the Workshop and particularly the Large Group itself. Many of the feelings and fantasies which arose in response to these experiences remained unclear and inadequately worked through, especially among the staff, the co-conductors and the organizing committee, within the local and contemporary context of their personal and professional relationships, especially, but not only, within the Group Analytic Society, the Institute of

Group Analysis and the Group Analytic Practice. It is possible that in the same way that the constraints of unconscious processes which stemmed from events within the larger context of the Workshop were manifest within the Workshop and in particular the Large Group, the constraints of processes arising from these latter events were manifest in the work of preparing this report and to some extent the volume in which it appears, as well as in personal and professional relationships within the organizations involved. (See Hopper and Garland (1980), a version of which is reprinted as Chapter 4 of this book.)

Nevertheless, we have learned once again to appreciate that it is of therapeutic and didactic value for patients and students to recognize that their therapists and teachers have survived their unconscious, pre-conscious and even conscious attacks. Thus, in case there should be any doubts, we would like to serve notice that we have survived, and that the Large Group was not a calamity.

References

Bettelheim, B. (1979) *Surviving and Other Essays*. London: Thames and Hudson Ltd.

Bion, W. R. (1959) 'Attacks on linking.' *International Journal of Psycho-Analysis 40*, 5, 308–315.

Hopper, E. (1977) 'Correspondence.' *Group Analysis 10*, 3, 9–11.

Hopper, E. and Garland, C. (1980) 'Overview.' In C. Garland (ed) 'Proceedings of the Survivor Syndrome Workshop (1979).' *Group Analysis,* Special Edition, November, 93–97.

Jones, E. (1951) [1914] 'The Madonna's Conception Through the Ear.' *Essays in Applied Psycho-Analysis 2*. London: The Hogarth Press, 266–357. (Original work published 1914.)

Jones, E. (ed) (1977) [1948] 'Fear, Guilt and Hate.' *Papers on Psychoanalysis*. London: Maresfield Reprints. (Original work published 1948.)

Pawelczynska, C. A. (1979) *Values and Violence in Auschwitz: A Sociological Analysis*. Berkeley: University of California Press.

Sager, C. J. and Kaplan, H. S. (eds) (1972) *Progress in Group and Family Therapy*. New York: Brunner/Mazel.

Segal, H. (1975) [1964] *Introduction to the Work of Melanie Klein*. London: The Hogarth Press. (Original work published 1964.)

Shakespeare, W. (1998) *The Tempest* (The Oxford Shakespeare). Oxford: Oxford University Press.

Springmann, R. (1976) 'Fragmentation in large groups.' *Group Analysis 3.* December, 185–188.

Werfel, F. (1997) [1983] *The Forty Days of Musa Dagh*. New York: Carrol and Graf Publishers. (Original work published 1983.)

Wiesel, E. (1981) [1960] *Night*. London: Penguin (Books), (Original work published in 1960.)

Notes

1   This chapter was first published in C. Garland (ed) (1980) 'Proceedings of the Survivor Syndrome Workshop (1979).' *Group Analysis*, Special Edition, November, 93–97.

2   On occasion, Kaye spoke of 'Dr Foulkes' Theory of Equivalence'. Hopper used to think that Kaye was reluctant to take credit for an idea which was so embryonic in form, especially in so far as it may have developed in conversations with Foulkes. He was not surprised to read in *Group Analysis* (May 1975) a letter from Werner Beck stating that Kaye used the term 'equivalence theory' in a workshop in Altaussee during 1973, and a reply from Foulkes that the phenomenon to which Beck referred was one with which all group analysts were very familiar, that he never heard Kaye use the term, and by implication saw no value in it. Unfortunately, Beck's example was misleading, although it is possible that Kaye used the term in the way described. In fact, 'equivalence' refers to a particular process, based on very primitive inter-psychic processes, one function of which is to communicate that which has been made unconscious because of the anxiety and splitting involved. The term was not meant to refer to more or less straightforward repetitions or displacements, but to processes through which certain aspects of both the historical and the contemporary context of a group might be brought into it, and in turn how the intra-group processes might be taken into the future. Nonetheless, it must be said that Kaye did not describe this phenomenon systematically, nor did he extend his thinking on the issue, at least publicly, before he died. Sometimes he referred to Ruth Cohen's work, for example 'Style and Spirit of the Theme-Centred Interactional Method' (Sager and Kaplan 1972), but he was really more concerned with the unconscious, dynamic aspects of how a group creates and maintains a theme. Kreeger recalls several conversations with Kaye about equivalence and feels that it is possible but unlikely that Foulkes did not remember discussing it with Kaye. This process will be discussed in 'Overview' of the Survivor Syndrome Workshop, a version of which is reprinted as Chapter 4 of this book.

3   Was Bettelheim aware of the profundity of his observation? Certainly Shakespeare understood the social and psychological implications of using a tempest as a metaphor for the social and psychological aspects of regression, disintegration, depression and reintegration.

4   In this connection it is worth noting the intake processes of concentration camps and their intended and unintended effects. Similarly, in reference to the regression which followed the loss of a complete village (Werfel 1983).

5   The alternative of going immediately to sleep may also be seen as a defensive strategy, but perhaps members were fairly certain that the Messiah would not come that night. It is also possible that some people may have been exhausted, and others hungry and thirsty. Nevertheless, this latter activity is reminiscent of the romantic unions which are reported to have developed in certain concentration camps, and which sometimes gave rise to pregnancy and childbirth (Pawelczynska 1979). Is it possible that such unions can be understood in terms of the wish to be rescued through the creation of a messiah as reflected in basic assumption pairing as a defense against despair? Otherwise they would be difficult to explain, especially since starving prisoners lost their sexual desires, and since romantic unions could only be conducted with the protection of collaborators under conditions of the utmost secrecy, for if discovered the couple would bring the most severe punishment to all concerned – death would be a release.

6   For example, consider the play within the third act of *The Tempest*: a celebration of personal maturity, marriage, fertility and social cohesion in general, offering a microcosm of the central action of the larger play: personal and social integration.

CHAPTER 4

'Overview' of the Survivor Syndrome Workshop (1979)[1]

with Caroline Garland

It is a necessary, though by no means an inevitable, sequel to a workshop such as this, that one should at some point draw back and ask what happened, and what has been learned as a result of what happened. That point is of course reached by different participants at different times. We hope that the publication of our own view of events will not inhibit others from continuing to work with the material themselves, or from reacting to and commenting upon our speculations. They are brief, and will do no more than touch on the two main areas in which we felt learning occurred: that of the subject matter – survival, and that of the context – the Workshop itself.

Firstly, the content. Here the Workshop perhaps provided a more profound view of what it means to be a survivor (particularly for those of us in Britain who have had relatively little first-hand experience of major traumata). There is a popular sense in which 'survival' is a romantic notion, conveying the impression of 'bloody but unbowed'. The implication is that it is an active condition; one did not become a survivor by turning one's face to the wall. Psychotherapists are familiar with another version: to have survived a psychically adverse environment, moreover to be engaged in the active task of spinning such rough straw into something which, if not gold, is at least very much more workable than might have been the case, permits the patient to entertain the notion of himself as the survivor of a hostile personal world. More specific trauma – the early loss of a parent, a divorce, a war – can augment the sense of survival still further.

Neither of these meanings, none of these associations, begin to approximate to the nature of the survival of which we talked at the Workshop. Survival of a concentration camp, of 'events beyond the imagination of mankind'[2] cannot be encompassed by a literary or romantic framework. The word must be reforged for the condition, just as dawning comprehension of the enormity of what was survived obliged the Western world to reforge its beliefs about civilization, progress, and what, if anything, might be meant by human nature.

As well, perhaps, we learned something of the nature of the Holocaust itself. This workshop, intended as a discussion of the kind of life that is lived by the few that may remain alive after any major disaster, and the ways in which the quality of that life might be improved, found itself talking and thinking almost solely about the Holocaust and its survivors. How and why did it happen that all possible catastrophes, past, present or future, were virtually ignored in favor of this one? A related question is why a Workshop entitled 'Death and Dying' (held in the same building for a comparable cost approximately six months later) should have been so well attended, whereas a workshop on survival – on the face of it a subject with more intrinsic future – should have been belatedly and sparsely attended. The answers to these questions may equally be related.

Undoubtedly our straightforward lack of experience as conference administrators contributed to some extent. However, in our view a more significant factor was that the domination of the proceedings by the Holocaust could have been predicted, given the bias of the precirculated papers and the choice of two of the three main speakers. The organizing committee must at some level have known this; and given the proportion of participants that were Jews, and even survivors themselves, the majority of participants must have known it too. One may suggest therefore that those who came, came knowing that they would be talking about the Holocaust; and that many of those who stayed away did so in order to avoid having to do so. In this sense, the focus of the Workshop's topic had been accurately gauged by most who had encountered its publicity.

To turn away altogether, or to stay and be overwhelmed; they may be the only responses available to the majority of us when faced with the Holocaust. For in the very special sense in which we are all its heirs, living in its aftermath, we have each of us, at some level or another, to deal with it. We inhabit the same moral community as not only its victims, but also its perpetrators; there is between us all a consciousness of kind. To turn away altogether is infinitely the greater temptation.

Thus Dr Davidson's deceptively simple phrase, 'what happened really happened' is salutary; it reminds us, after a moment's pause, of the extent to which most of us are capable of denying the appalling, inconceivable truth: *what happened really happened.*

And yet when for a time we cease to deny its reality and turn to face the Holocaust, what happens then? We suggest that a partial answer to that question lies in the events of the Workshop itself. There are some categories of event that can be comprehended by working from the lesser to the greater example: to move towns is to understand something of the quality of the refugee experience. Yet that is not so in this instance. To comprehend one's survival of, for example, an earthquake, is still not to approach an understanding of the prolonged and systematic assault by the machinery of death upon one's substance and coherence as a human being. There is an irreversible quality to the sequence: even, we suggest, the Japanese experience of the sudden total devastation of Hiroshima leaves untouched the blackest, most depraved parts of the totalitarian nightmare realized by the Nazis. For this generation to look at survival at all is a commitment to beginning with the Holocaust: the grammar and vocabulary of catastrophe was, for us, created in the camps. To comprehend it is to be able to speak something of the language of all disaster, and know something of the constructions underlying all survival.

We are suggesting, therefore, that to cast even a sidelong glance at the Holocaust via the contemplation of 'survival of disaster' is instantly to come within its gravitational pull. There is then no way of avoiding being drawn for a time into that densest and most profound of black holes, from which nothing, not light itself, escapes.

This part of the 'pull' of the subject is inherent in its nature – yet, since we ourselves are not merely inert matter, we must also look at the nature of what is being pulled, those who voluntarily place themselves within that gravitational field. It may well be impossible to distinguish the genuinely reparative motive from the manic, or to diagnose with certainty whether it is that, through an interest in working with survivors, one set of defenses is being substituted for another; but we must at least mention these possibilities in order to acknowledge the inevitable profundity and complexity of motivation in this area.

Such an issue leads inevitably to the third area of learning concerning the Workshop's subject matter: the task for the therapist. Its magnitude became very clear during the Workshop, articulated with greatest force, though by different members in different ways, during the Large Groups. The therapist is being asked to bear, and to share, what is essentially unbearable and unshareable. To tolerate these demands he must have recognized, acknowledged and to some extent become reconciled with what is unbearable and unshareable within himself, the victim of whom he is ashamed and the perpetrator for whom he feels guilt.

Nowhere is this better expressed than by the philosopher Alan Montefiore who is reported (Garland 1980) to have said that as modern psychology, above all perhaps psychoanalysis, has served to remind us in its own particular language, and as art and religion have in their own diverse ways always known – there are sufficient elements of aggression and self-destruction, of sadism and masochism, hidden away in each one of us, not, of course, to turn us into conscious or active sadists or masochists, but to enable us to participate at some level of refused, inarticulate, unwilling, but nevertheless insistent imagination in the realized fantasies of those for whom the internal or external pressures of life have brought these elements into conscious and active play. The unimaginable belongs to that part of my own darkest imagination – or, at least, that imagination which, whether it be 'mine' or not, I may have to recognize as within me – to which my whole conscious, 'normally' sensitive being refuses the very right of existence.

The process of recognition of, and reconciliation with, these elements must be actively sustained by the therapist if he is to listen – and to hear what he is told – without fear, without desire, and without loss of the integrity of his own sense of self.

This was the task facing the Workshop as a whole, as it was the task facing each of its members. The potency of the dilemma as revealed through the three sessions of the Large Group, thesis, antithesis and synthesis respectively, may well, we acknowledge, have been expressed sequentially and with greater clarity than it could have been for any individual member.

At this point, we turn from the subject matter of the Workshop to the context within which it was discussed. First, we feel confirmed in our belief in the value of the group experience within a workshop, and of the way it may be used for essentially pedagogical purposes. When the topic under consideration is likely to arouse strong and conflicting emotions, as is almost always the case in the study of people and their social systems, lectures and seminars are usefully supplemented with opportunities for experiential learning. The social structuring of more traditional pedagogical techniques does not allow for the expression of feelings; they must be either suppressed, or subjected to various kinds of unconscious psychological defense, in which case they become a source of interference with cognitive processes. However, through the use of various combinations of small and large groups, it is possible to express and to try to understand those feelings and fantasies which are taboo within more conventional learning structures.

For example, small theme-centered groups are particularly helpful for the assimilation of information which has been acquired through lectures, and for the application of cognitive themes to more immediate and personal concerns. Large groups, on the other hand, are an exceptionally powerful but as yet undeveloped device for containing intense and destructive impulses so that other types of learning may occur effectively within the other sub-structures of the Workshop. Participation in a large group involves the experience of chaotic and confusing feelings, not only during the early stages, when they might be expected, but also subsequently at apparently random moments. They are all the more difficult to tolerate because not everyone is aware that almost invariably such feelings can be clarified and even worked through within this setting. However, in order for an experience of this kind to be valuable, people must be fully willing to participate, and thus to risk, and perhaps to sacrifice a sense of objectivity – at least temporarily. It is often difficult to sustain the knowledge that what seems at the time to be a loss of objectivity is often only the loss of a sense of certainty about the boundaries of social and psychological reality (which is in itself difficult and disturbing enough).

It may well be productive to prepare people for the vicissitudes of a large group, and for how they may be affected by it. This may be particularly true in the case of staff, because when they are asked to take the same roles as other members of a workshop they inevitably lose the protection afforded by their professional roles and relationships. Status and expertise in other areas, however closely related they may be to the topic in question, will not in themselves prevent the occurrence of potential side-effects of the creative use of regressive phenomena. Nonetheless, the tolerance of uncertainty and the willingness to negotiate the definitions of social and psychological reality – sometimes silently but always in a spirit of mutuality – are essential for psychotherapeutic work, perhaps particularly with survivors.

So far we have been describing the facilitating value of the group experience in a workshop such as this, but we would like to go further. Groups also provide a setting in which the phenomenon of equivalence may occur. Through this phenomenon it may be possible to recognize certain kinds of information which it is difficult to communicate through formal pedagogical means, particularly those means which emphasize cognitive content through the use of predominantly hierarchical, one-way relationships between the teacher and the taught. As mentioned in the Report on the Large Group (Chapter 3 of this book), equivalence is the name coined by the late Harold Kaye for the phenomenon in which various unconscious feelings and fantasies associated with the topic under discussion are manifested, through projective and introjective processes, within the social and psychological dynamics of the group (for example, the formation of a small group within the large group). The more projective and introjective processes predominate, the more likely it is that equivalence will occur. It is therefore a function of at least three factors: the extent to which the feelings and fantasies are unconscious and the psychological defenses involved are primitive; the severity of the anxiety and guilt associated with these feelings and fantasies; and the extent to which the members of the group are regressed. The larger the group, the deeper, stronger and more florid are regressive phenomena. Thus it is predictable that when topics as painful and profound as survival are discussed within a large group, the predominant mode of communication is likely to involve projection, and introjection and equivalence is likely to occur.

It is possible that Bion (1961) was referring to one aspect of this phenomenon when he wrote:

> In work group activity time is intrinsic. In basic assumption activity it has no place. Basic assumption group functions are active before even a group comes together in a room, and continue after the group has dispersed. There is neither development nor decay in basic assumption functions, and in this respect they differ totally from those of the work group... (p.172)

In other words, although the boundaries of a work group can be located in terms of time and (although Bion does not say so) social space, the work group may contain within it the actions and the imagery related to those feelings and fantasies which are part of the basic assumption group, and which have originated elsewhere – also in terms of both time and social space. Furthermore, although the work group ends at a clearly defined point, the basic assumption group may continue indefinitely, and affect processes and interactions which extend far beyond the Workshop itself.

Some of the material associated with particular basic assumption processes manifested within the Large Group was described in the Report on the Large Group (Chapter 3 of this book) where the authors explored the relationship between events within the Large Group and its immediate context. However, equally, other events were brought into the Group which had originated, in terms of time, at moments extending from the distant past to the more immediate present; and in terms of social space, both at home and abroad. Thus those members of the Workshop who had survived concentration camps were able to convey the experience of despair felt by people under conditions of utter helplessness and exposure to persecution; this communication was augmented and amplified by those who had had considerable therapeutic experience with survivors; and it resonated among those who were able to engage in intuitive and empathic acts of imagination. In this way, material was made available which was fundamental to the understanding of what it means to be a survivor and hence crucial to effective work with survivors and their children; and by implication to the understanding of the experience of concentration camps in particular and social trauma in general.

We should also mention that just as information about the nature of survival was made available to the Workshop as a whole, so possibly did the Workshop also contain the information about ourselves and our personal and professional lives and relationships which led us to hold a conference such as this, and which governs the uses we will make of it – both those which we hope have been creative and truly reparative, and those which have been in the defensive service of our individual and collective psychopathologies.

Clearly, however, recognition of the phenomenon of equivalence is not enough. There is a further stage, in which learning must move beyond its implicit or 'equivalent' form, and become explicit; be fed back into the cognitive activity of a workshop in order to attain its potential effectiveness. We are aware that this stage was reached by very few, if any, during this Workshop itself, whether staff or members. Perhaps it is only now, a year later, that we may hope that we and others have reached the point at which we can achieve a fuller understanding of the difficult and painful material manifested in the Workshop through the modality of equivalence.

What can one say in summary about the value of such an experience? Perhaps that question can only be answered on a personal level, as it has been by the many who spoke during the Workshop itself and the many who have contributed to this volume. We hope that its publication will stimulate many more to recollection, response and reaction.

On a purely practical level first, an attempt is being made, through the London School of Economics, to match survivors of various social trauma (including refugees) with selected samples of the indigenous population, in order to learn more about the long-term social and psychological effects of massive social trauma. Second, we have had enough feedback from Workshop members to feel that there could be considerable value in establishing a focal point for a network of those who work in any capacity with survivors. As well as providing literature and reference material, such a network might offer support and supervision on a regular basis. Answers to the enclosed questionnaire will help us to determine the need for such provision.

Finally, however, the Workshop has clarified for some of us the lessons for the present that have been made explicit by this exploration of the past. To acknowledge the refused, inarticulate, unwilling, but nevertheless insistent imagination within ourselves is to become aware of the permanent existence of those for whom the internal or external pressures of life may, as events continue to show, bring those elements into active play. A clear-sighted vigilance against the growth of totalitarian attitudes in any form, however embryonic, is therefore not only morally desirable, but it is also from our professional point of view a form of prevention that is infinitely preferable to cure.

References

Bion, W. R. (1961) *Experiences in Groups and Other Papers*. London: Tavistock Publications.

Garland, C. (1980) *Personal Communication*.

Hopper, E. and Garland, C. (1980) 'Overview.' In C. Garland (ed) 'Proceedings of the Survivor Syndrome Workshop (1979).' *Group Analysis*, Special Edition, November, 93–97.

The Times (1945) 'The Captives of Belsen: Internment Camp Horrors.' 19 April, p.4.

Notes

1   This chapter was first published in C. Garland (ed) (1980) 'Proceedings of the Survivor Syndrome Workshop' (1979). *Group Analysis*, Special Edition, November, 93–97.

2   *The Times* (1945) 'The Captives of Belsen: Internment Camp Horrors.' 19 April, p.4.

CHAPTER 5

The Problem of Context
in Group-Analytic Psychotherapy

A Clinical Illustration
and a Brief Theoretical Discussion[1]

My purpose is to discuss certain aspects of the 'problem of context', primarily in order to indicate a distinguishing feature of group-analytic psychotherapy as developed by S. H. Foulkes (1948),[2] namely: the clinical application of the axiom that the nature of the human is social, and of the social, human, at all stages of life and at all phases of history. After defining the concept of context, I will state the problem in formal terms, and illustrate it with a brief clinical vignette, which includes my interpretation and its effects. I will also mention certain theoretical aspects of the problem, in particular those which suggest a limitation inherent in the approach of W. R. Bion (1961).

Introduction

The concept of 'context'

'Context' refers to those parts of a text which precede and/or follow a particular passage, and which are sufficient in number to enable a person to determine the meaning or meanings which the author intended. In the first instance, I would like to draw attention to the etymology of the word 'context'.

The prefix con- is related to cum, meaning 'together', 'together with', 'in combination' and 'in union', and further, 'altogether', 'completely', and 'intensive' or 'in depth'. It is closely related to such words as 'community', 'communion', and 'common', and reminiscent of the word 'religion', deriving from the Latin *religare*, meaning 'to bind again', 'to connect', 'to bring together in entirety', 'to make whole', etc., and connoting 'being bound together through oath' or 'being part of an unaltered whole'.

This line of association should not be surprising. The stem word 'text' can be traced to *texto, texare, texui, textum*, etc. meaning to weave: thus, fabric or tissue, woven material. A 'text' is woven from words. Later, *textus* was used to refer to the Gospel precisely as it was written in all its authoritative glory.

These connotations are infinitely suggestive, but especially intriguing is the implicit idea (or perhaps metaphor) to the effect that a thread and its properties will always be governed by their location within a larger whole, in this instance a fabric or textile. So, too, is the implication that logically the etiological chain for any dependent variable will always start with 'God', who will always be the hypothetical author of any definitive text concerning the Beginning, or the hypothetical weaver who has created the textile. In other words, in all schemes of thought the context of the context will always be some form of the Holy.

It follows by definition that properties of both material and nonmaterial phenomena are characteristic only of wholes that are located within contexts, which are woven together from their constituent elements. Properties of contexts are, therefore, emergent and irreducible to the properties of any of their elements. With respect to persons, the true Oedipus complex could be seen as an emergent phenomenon; and with respect to social formation, structures of authority or group morale would be in this category.

The meaning of the word 'context' is also related to the meaning of the word 'understand'. In order to understand an event it is necessary to locate it within an abstract category of such events, and then to relate this category to at least one other such category, the existence and qualities of which are less puzzling.

The problem of context

One type of event is a communication. Holding aside a variety of problems in the philosophy of science, especially concerning the topic of hermeneutics, let us consider the phenomenon of transference as an event in communication between two or more people. A transference refers to an unconscious repetition or replication in the present, in a more or less crystallized or fossilized way, of impulse, pain, defense, and internal and external object relationships as they have occurred in the personal past, usually in infancy but including those of childhood and even of adolescence. As such, a transference contains a coded account of its own social and psychological etiology. 'Theory' offers a set of rules according to which the code of a transference can be deciphered or interpreted, usually by one of the parties within the relationship.

It follows that in order to understand a transference, it must be contextualized, that is, related to other categories of events that are thought by certain people to have a particular relationship to it, a relationship that may be delineated in terms of time and social psychological space. The contextualization of the collective transference of a group, for example to its conductor, is especially difficult. After all, the boundaries of a group are not identical with those of its members, and the principle of apperception leads relentlessly back towards the Beginning and into the Womb. Thus, typically, but somewhat curiously, the contextualization of the collective transference is limited to two categories of events: those which are socially near and comparatively recent in the group's history (which means comparatively late in the life cycles of the group members); and those which are socially distant and pre-historical (which means during the early infancies of the group members, when it is assumed that, in so far as biological constraints predominate, idiosyncratic variation in experience will tend to be minimal, and the content of unconscious fantasy, universal). However, this approach is both too narrow and too shallow, which brings us to what is problematic about the phenomenon of context.

A 'problem' is neither more nor less than a question or a set of questions that are hard to answer, and I would like to ask a few of them. In attempting to contextualize a transference is it possible and is it therapeutically useful to explore a full range of events on the dimensions of time and social psychological space? How far from the so-called 'here and now' should we go? The later phases of life? The structure and function of social institutions, not only now but also in a person's past? Should we take account of events which occurred even before a person was born, and were located in another country? (Of course, a transference contains information about what people anticipate and what they may strive to make happen, a point which did not go unnoticed by D. M. Thomas (1981), in *The White Hotel*, but I will not discuss here the notion of precognition, and will limit my enquiry to replication.)

My answer to each of these questions is, on balance, yes, but very much on balance. I do not confine my attempts to contextualize a transference only to the infantile unconscious, but try to explore a fuller range of events on the dimensions of time and social psychological space. In this connection, it is worth recalling Bion's cryptic remark that the 'basic assumption group knows no time', and although he did not quite say so, knows no space (1961).[3] Actually, this is much more sociological than his few statements about social institutions and society, and about the existence of social facts, and may be the basis for a dynamic social psychology of group processes within their societal context. It offers a point of convergence between the sociological and psychoanalytical points of view, and is reminiscent of the basic approach of Foulkes (1984), as refined by de Maré (1972) and Pines (1978).[4] Certainly, it was the starting point for my own thinking about the application of the problem of context to clinical work. A brief outline of what I think is my clinical technique follows.

Some aspects of technique

Before turning to a clinical illustration of my tentative but affirmative answer to the questions with which I have defined the problem of context, I would like first to describe a few central aspects of how I think I usually conduct groups who meet for psychotherapy. My groups meet for forty weeks per year, and the sessions last for one and a half hours. On a few occasions per year I allow them to meet without me, but at the usual time and place. The groups consist of from seven to nine patients, usually four men and five women, ranging from around twenty-five to sixty-five years of age, representing a cross-section of neurotic and personality disorders, not including more than one really difficult patient or more than one of a really distinctive type, such as an addict, criminal, a depressive, a paranoid, etc. During the last few years, I have tended to see my group patients individually for at least a few months before they enter the group; this is in keeping with the evidence concerning favorable outcomes, but I work this way primarily because I enjoy it. By and large the patients are a cross-section of the urban and suburban middle class, with a slight bias towards the professional upper middle class and the helping professions in general. Jews are not overrepresented, as they are in most studies of the patient population in the urban areas of North America. The average length of stay is about four to five years, which seems to surprise people who do not know much about group-analytic therapy, including our most severe critics within psychiatry and psychoanalysis, who assume that patients stay in treatment for a matter of months, if not a few weekends. In any case, I have what we call 'slow-open' groups; they go on as long as I do, but new patients come in when old patients go out.

Ordinarily, I speak after about twenty to thirty minutes, but I have no general rule. Sometimes I start the group, and sometimes I remain silent all the way through. Usually, I try to sense the common group tension (Ezriel 1950, 1957), which almost always involves basic assumption patterns (Bion 1961), and then to interpret this collective transference from the group to the object or objects in question – usually, but not always, to myself. Afterwards I try to help the group discover what each person has contributed to it as well as how each is affected by it. However, and this is important because it distinguishes the way I work from the approach of those who follow what they take to be the conventional 'Tavi' model, I may talk first to a particular person or to the partners in a sub group, depending on how they may be dramatizing or personifying the general theme. I often talk to individual members of the group, not only because they have come to me as patients and not as students of group dynamics, but also because I perceive them in terms of their location within the group matrix, so that talking to one person is not necessarily in conflict or at odds with the concern of the group as a whole (Foulkes 1948). I also try to be alert to the recapitulations within the group process of each individual's early family life (Schindler 1951).

Several groups may go by before we (the group and I) have made anything like a comprehensive interpretation, and there are always an indefinite number of loose ends. Although I am obliged to see my patients essentially as patients, I do regard the group, and even use the group, as my co-conductors. I value their capacity collectively to be holding and containing.

I rarely go beyond interpretations and 'interpretative actions'. I assume that this encourages the development of 'psychic muscle', as well as the capacity for reflection. Although I break rules more often than I abide by them, I try to communicate in an intelligent and organized way. I think of myself as a fairly spontaneous and warm type of therapist.

I am not particularly concerned about my own transparency. Patients see what they see, and they make whatever use of it they wish and can. However, I do not favor self-disclosure. At certain times judicious self-disclosure may be necessary and helpful, but usually it is a therapeutic burden.

In my attempts to understand what my patients are asking me to understand, I allow myself to be guided by certain aspects of counter-transference, which can be used as though it were litmus paper in a chemistry experiment. Although one's countertransference can be a source of difficulty, it may also be a source of information about the transference – an issue to be discussed further below.

A brief clinical vignette

This session is from a group who were meeting in my consulting room at home one autumn in the early 1980s. In its conscious and unconscious themes, the material is fairly typical, not only of this particular group but also of my other groups.[5] It is necessary to trade the accuracy of a recording for the communication of a mood, and to remember that this passage is taken out of context.

1. I took a seat, the group continued to complain about the weather, it was cold and damp – 'It's not the cold, but the damp' – and the rain beat against the window panes of my consulting room, which is in the attic of my house. Someone said, 'Still, mustn't complain, it could be worse.' The group drew closer together around our center table. I felt that their sense of solidarity increased – not unlike what happens at the beginning of the telling of a ghost story or at the beginning of any ritualized story-telling event. It is not for nothing that so many stories start with storms.

    I thought to myself that nothing changes: 'It's not the cold, but the damp', and 'Still, mustn't complain' were the first words I heard when I came to England over twenty years ago. The weather in the late autumn was seldom different – for that matter the summer isn't either – and rarely had I heard a group discuss the weather, although they probably do talk about it while waiting for me to come into the room. So, my antennae went out immediately.

2. The discussion shifted to a critical appreciation of my house and consulting suite. They remarked upon its late Victorian style – 'or is it Edwardian?', the way I had converted it, especially the alterations to the staircase, the general mixture of old and new (brick, pine and glass combined with high ceilings, old moldings, large architraves, etc.) and, turning to the room itself, the colors ('buttermilk, oatmeal, and earth clay', as one patient put it, 'colors of trendy architects and feminist earth-mothers'), the two austere double-glazed windows set into the eaves, and the 'director's chairs' from Habitat (which members of the group set up for themselves when they come in after the other seats are taken). They neglected to mention those items of furniture which pertain to my work as a psychoanalyst: the two comfortable chairs, for

which there is some competition, and the couch, which comes apart into three seats for group work.

I was feeling very uncomfortable, too closely examined, as though they were inspecting my private parts and parts of my private life. After all, they had been coming to my house once a week for eight years. Why suddenly should they have become so preoccupied, ostensibly with my room? Why should they have cut themselves off from our history?

3.   They returned to the weather outside, reassuring themselves that it was dry and warm inside. A woman said that the staircase on the side of the house, which they had to use in order to reach the suite, was too exposed – cold, wet, windy, dark, not at all safe, and she wondered why I had not enclosed it, since they had been complaining about it for as long as she had been in the group (over five years). Another said that this was obviously because my family and I didn't have to use it (which was probably correct). The group's non-complainer said, 'Still, it's nice inside'.

I was thinking about my house as a symbol of mother's body, my own body and of my own mind; about passages into and out of mother's body as well as my own; how often one overlooks the importance of the material surroundings of a group – perhaps as one kind of transitional object; how early the Oedipus complex really begins; how ubiquitous and deep are the problems concerning the boundaries between the inside and outside of persons and groups, etc. I was also reminded of a lunch-time discussion I was having a few days previously at the London School of Economics about the history and scope of the literary usage of a ship as a symbol for society and for the state.

4.   The group came back to the consulting room. An older man spoke about the cost of housing and conversion work nowadays, and supposed that the Habitat chairs must have cost about £5 when I bought them, whereas they were now closer to £20. Another man said that everything goes up but his income. This remark was met with silence (partly, I suspected, because he is impotent; and I detected what the author of *Brideshead Revisited* might have called a 'bat-squeak' of anxiety). He then apologized for messing up the carpet with his wet, muddy shoes (which he did all the time anyway, for he really was an archetype of a mess), and the group echoed that the carpet would be dry by the time the group was over, and the mud could be swept up. Another man asked me what did I expect, for surely this sort of damage was what the estate agents would call normal wear and tear, and was probably taken into account in my fees, which was why I put them up every year.

I was feeling annoyed at the mess, and mildly guilty about the fees for 'psychic conversion work' – but I was also thinking that I was pleased with my house and consulting room. I was tempted to interpret certain aspects of their desires to intrude and to spoil in connection with their envy of me and of my relationships with my family and my house, combined with their fear and feelings of guilt, and to show them how this was being manifested in various forms of splitting and projection. However, since I was vaguely aware that I wanted to punish them rather than understand them, I remained silent until I could sort my responses. I have learned that in this frame of mind it is best not to trot out the death rattles of correct interpretations, but to be silent in order to give myself space for reflection, not to defend myself from my patients by putting some theory between us. For example, I did not want to fall back on a ritualized interpretation which involved, for example, feelings of envy, fight–flight patterns, preoccupations with 'mother's body', smearing attacks with faeces, etc.

5. The comment about fees prompted a young artist (who had never taken a conventional job in his life, because he had inherited several houses in London and an estate in the country, and of whom in this respect I was myself envious) to offer to paint a mural on my wall (which was in part a continuation of the desire to smear my walls with faeces), but he thought that I was not the kind of person to spend money on art – at least not from an unknown artist. This was followed by a phase of pairing between two young females and him, and between the two females. The communication concerned the problems of careers and marriage nowadays, and their jealousy and envy of his young, anorexic wife who is also from an extremely wealthy family.

Eventually, one of the two women said to me in a flirtatious way that my wife probably worked in the media – but didn't really have to – and that she was undoubtedly a kept woman – which the patient wouldn't mind being herself except that not only did she need a wife rather than a husband, but she also wanted a baby. There is probably at least one such woman in all the groups that we conduct nowadays; she sounded as though she were taken from the notes for Margaret Drabble's next book. In any case, I had to struggle against my desire to become embroiled with her, a type for whom I am an easy mark. I caught myself, remained silent, and realized that I had begun to feel a bit bored, almost a little depressed – although depressed is too strong a term. I sensed that I wanted this flirtatious female to excite me. I was aware that the artist's insult had a grain of truth in it, and that I was hurt by it, but that this alone would not account for my feelings. I continued to monitor my feelings, but I was somewhat perplexed, and a little disturbed. I remained silent, not because I had nothing to say, but because I could not identify the mood of the group.

6.   My silence was rewarded. The painter commented that Prince Charles and Lady Di were going to live near his house in the country. Someone commented that Lady Di was pregnant, and another said that her tits would be enormous. The older woman said that Charles was very nice, more like the Queen, whereas Anne was a real cow, more like her father. Several joined in to say how marvelous the wedding was, and one said that she had heard that even the psychoanalysts had watched it on the telly in Helsinki last summer (she was right). The group began to discuss the pros and cons of royalty: the painter felt that although it cost the taxpayers quite a lot, it was one way to maintain these old country houses; others were concerned with snobbery, and felt that the funds for the Royal Family were being 'sucked right out of their pockets'.

   Intellectually, I could follow the themes of gender confusion, preoccupation with my personal and family life, especially during the summer break, my family and the Royal Family and my fees and taxes, not to mention the basic assumption of pairing projected into the aristocracy, sexuality as a manic defense against depression, etc. In fact, I was tempted to call attention to their depression, but I decided to contain their projections for a while longer, mainly because I did not know how to account for their intensity. Also, I had begun to feel somewhat sluggish. I thought to myself that Bion would turn out to be right in all respects, that I had nothing of my own to offer, and that I was out of the group – I was uncertain whether I was being kept out or just felt out of it. I also felt lonely and isolated.

7.   After a very brief silence, a girl with the same name as a young female member of the Royal Family, who is usually silent and self-contained, began to cry. (Everyone seemed surprised but me; after all, they had been laughing and pairing in a manic way while I was feeling sad.) Let us call her Elizabeth. She had learned that the house in which she and her husband and daughter of two had their small flat was riddled with wet rot and dry rot and God knows what. The place was virtually diseased. The wet rot was mainly in the basement flats and in the joists below the ground floor flats, and the dry rot ran up one wall all the way to the roof timbers, and her flat had both. The insurance wouldn't cover it. Given the complex pattern of ownership among the freeholder, the leaseholder, several sub-tenants, the banks and the

building societies who held long-term mortgages – it was a real mess. She and her husband would have to go further into debt and borrow from her parents, who were retired and whose savings had not kept pace with inflation, and in any case they needed their savings because her mother's cancer was worse, and their expenses were greater. She and her husband agreed to negotiate with the freeholders and insurance company on behalf of all the tenants, gratis. When pressed about why, she said that it was because they didn't trust anyone else to do it, and they couldn't afford to pay anyone. She added that it might even lead to paid work; she didn't want to be a typist, her husband refused to drive a mini-cab, and they didn't want to emigrate.

The group knew that Elizabeth's husband had lost his job a year ago, and had set up a small financial services company that he operated from this flat, which was prohibited by their lease. She worked as a part-time secretary for him, but before she became pregnant she was about to become a stockbroker.

I was aware that I was being asked to provide psychotherapy free of charge, but I was fairly certain that the group were not more than preconscious of this. I was also aware that the group continued to be preoccupied with houses, and the problem of gender identity. Elizabeth was caught up in a defensive identification with me. Clearly, she needed some personal attention, but I waited to see if someone in the group would give it to her.

The group were moved by her desperate situation, and through their gestures and noises of involvement and understanding, they gave the impression that they could empathize with it. She went on to say that the freehold was owned by Hasidic Jews through a maze of interlocking companies, and that they were being distinctly unhelpful. They were prepared to buy back the leases at 'current valuation' (which must have been at about a quarter of what they had cost). Several flats were owned by rich Arabs who used them to house their servants, and they were hard to contact. One flat was owned by a nice Iranian couple who had got out of Iran a few years ago, and who had put all their savings into their flat. The other English couples were also broke, and in one case the husband had just lost his job.

I began to feel drowsy, which usually means that I am defending myself against the experience of being hated by people who are not fully aware of their feelings, and against my desire to confront and attack in response to my own hurt and, I suppose, fear. I was unable to concentrate on the details of how her life seemed to be collapsing around her, and realized that the group seemed more compassionate than I. They began to share similar experiences with Elizabeth. This is an example of how a group can function as co-therapist, but in retrospect I believe that it was primarily a continuation of their attempts to make me feel excluded while at the same time to make themselves feel that they had something of great, exclusive value, an issue to which I will return.

8. · In our field details are everything, but it is necessary now to condense this report. In the ensuing discussion, I noticed three related themes, the first of which was the malady of the building itself. An entire house could be eaten away by rot. From the inside. You wouldn't even know that it was there until the house fell down. Timber could be turned to fungus. Like a dried-up leaf in which only a few stems held it all together. A debate developed about the origins of rot: whether wet rot comes before dry rot, or vice versa; was it best to keep it under control and live with it? Or would it be better to tear the whole thing down and start again, which would be painful in the short run, but better in the long run. It was necessary first to stop all the leaks (from the roof, from the plumbing, rising damp, penetrating damp, etc.), but 'dry' was not enough, 'well-ventilated' was also important. Be careful about modern building materials – they do not breathe.

I was aware that the group were concerned with the design faults of the female body. They were also deeply affected by what they imagined was the disintegration of the body of Elizabeth's mother. Also apparent were the problems of gender identity and its connection with Elizabeth's marriage to a man who was perceived as 'wet'.

The second theme concerned the type of people involved. Wasn't it ironic about the Arabs and the Jews? The Arabs were all over London. But the Jews had in fact survived. They owned all the property. They always came off best. Typical. Also the architects and lawyers. They always get their fees. Social parasites and prostitutes living off the misery of ordinary people. The group knew that I had been working with survivors of social trauma, and had been involved in bringing the Survivor Syndrome to public attention. It was reasonable to suppose that the group believed that I was a Jew. I had become familiar with the apparently universal usage of 'Jew' as a highly condensed symbol of femininity and perversion in men.

The third theme was that things were not what they used to be. It was impossible to trust anyone in London today. Hasidic Jews were frightening in their black clothes and hats, and they ought to try harder to fit in. If they wanted to live in England then they ought to act like English people. Someone remarked on the hairstyle of Hasidic Jews.

I sensed that I was being asked to explain this custom, but I remained impassive. I thought that this last remark might, at the very least, have been a veiled reference to my own change of hairstyle a few months ago from long to very short. The interrelatedness of these last few themes was striking, in a way that ordinarily I find intellectually stimulating.

At this point I intervened. However, before I report what I said, I would like to write more about what I was feeling and about how I used this knowledge in order to formulate a particular interpretation of the group's collective transference to me.

An interlude: reflections upon technique and theory

The session was almost over. I was still silent. I said to myself that although silence was not always rewarded, it was seldom wrong or destructive, and that on such an occasion self-containment was especially important. This gave me space for reflection.

I had considered various interpretations concerning sexual and aggressive impulses and fantasies, paranoid–schizoid and depressive anxieties, personal and collective defenses – including the three basic assumption patterns and combinations of them, etc. I had discarded them, not because they would have been incorrect, but because somehow they would have been restrictive rather than enabling; they might even have been collusive. I decided that the group had been asking me to understand them; I felt the strong pull to reassure them that I did. After all, this was group-analytic therapy. It occurred to me that even this was a subtle defense on my part, and that it was probably stopping me from really understanding.

I tried, therefore, to review what I had been feeling rather than thinking. As the collective transference of the group towards me developed, I felt anxious, somewhat de-personalized, excluded, lonely, isolated and a bit drowsy, more-or-less in that order. Specifically, I had come to feel in my countertransference that the members of the group were full, that I was empty, and that I was being kept out of their lives, relationships, and bountiful stores of all good things. In other words, I had come to be envious of the group, especially of their sense of cohesion and exclusiveness, based partly on their sense of being English and of belonging to England. I had a sense of myself as an American Jew who only *lived* in England, and as a sociologist who had subsequently become a psychotherapist, group analyst, and most recently a psychoanalyst, but who had not become a 'Doctor'.[6]

Yet, I was familiar with these feelings of an outsider, a marginal man. They are the product of my early life experiences, and of a mixture of old and new experiences in the sense that I remain influenced by the old and on occasions am prone to provoke the new. In any case, I felt that I had come to terms with these matters, at least more than my personal responses in this session would suggest. Whatever I might think and feel in my personal life, I did not feel this way 'usually' and 'really' towards this group of patients.

I concluded that my countertransference was not primarily pathological but an important source of data concerning the nature of the collective transference. Whether or not I was feeling envious of the group on my own behalf, I was holding envious feelings that the members of the group had unconsciously denied, split off, and projected into me. They had succeeded in making me feel towards them what they had been feeling towards me.

I would like now to discuss certain aspects of envy, and to make explicit certain of my beliefs. First of all, feelings of envy are always painful. They involve a sense of emptiness and the loss of all sense of value. They diminish the capacity to hope and be hopeful. However, as is the case for all feelings, the object of envy should be distinguished from its aims, defenses, origins and functions:

1. In this instance, I was the *object* of the group's envious feelings, as were my possessions, ranging from the group itself to aspects of my body, personality and situation. Of course, people may not be fully conscious of the objects of their feelings, and their objects may be merely the last in a long series of objects which are associated unconsciously over time and space. For example, the group were not aware that they were feeling envious of me and my possessions, and that they were re-living earlier feelings (which they may have continued to feel) towards the members of their families of orientation (not to mention still earlier part objects).

2. Their *aim* was to spoil the pleasure, power, and security which I was perceived to be deriving from the possessions and qualities that they were attributing to me.[7]

3. Their main *defense* was projective identification, its intensity having been amplified because it had been used collectively. No defense is really efficient, but with respect to envy, projective identification both facilitates its aim, and offers a further degree of relief from the pain involved. The object is spoiled by evoking the same feelings

which prompted the defense, thereby making the object less enviable; at the same time, parts of the self are disavowed or disowned, and unwanted feelings are evacuated. An attempt is also made to communicate and to ask for understanding, especially concerning those anxieties which are linked to envy both developmentally and etiologically.[8]

4. Although envy appears in early infancy, its etiological *origins* are subject to debate. Is it the purest manifestation of the death instinct, and, in turn, does it evoke the first mental representation? Is it rooted within the social psychology of the mother–infant relationship which is itself part of a larger social and cultural network? If determined by both instinctual *and* environmental factors, what weight should be assigned to each, and what is the nature of their interaction? Is it useful to distinguish actual envy from potential envy from so-called predispositions towards envy? Is it important to consider circumstances which characterize later phases of life-trajectories? Do factors which account for the origins of envy differ from those which contribute to its maintenance, and with respect to the latter, might such factors vary over time? It is impossible to answer such questions here, but they indicate the scope and complexity of this issue (Hopper 1981,1982).

5. Preoccupation with the origins of envy detracts from a consideration of its *functions*, especially those which are benign. Since envy involves pain, rage and the desire to spoil, it is difficult to imagine that it might function in the service of maturation and growth. For example, envy might be essential for the development of the capacity for competition, rivalry, self-determination and autonomy, all of which are important for the fulfillment of a variety of achievement orientations, especially with respect to goals associated with a society's system of stratification. Envy might serve as a defense against the anxiety inherent in feelings of personal and social powerlessness or helplessness, aphanisis or annihilation anxiety, confusion and other forms of 'nameless dread'; it helps to shift attention from such feelings themselves to their source, and from their source within physical sensations to one within the external world. As such, it might stimulate the desire to understand, to master and even to change the external world. After all, the desire to change the world may be essential for the survival of the

species, and since it may sometimes be necessary to be destructive
in order to be constructive, it is wrong to assess envy in terms of
the value that particular interest groups assign to its objects.

I would now like to make explicit several aspects of the above considerations,
but these are more a matter of personal opinion than of clinical fact or theory.
I believe that in so far as a therapist is able to understand and to convey that a
meaningful communication has in fact occurred between his patient(s) and
himself, it is possible to break vicious and malign circles of internal and
external relationships of a certain kind, especially those involving envious
retaliation, and to establish a sense of safety sufficient to permit self-
containment, reflection, and, ultimately, more effective action. However, this
is especially difficult when feelings such as envy have been communicated
through projective identification, and interpretations of a transference that
has been made manifest in this way may easily become persecuting rather
than helpful.

Thus, it is reasonable to wonder how I had been able to conclude with
confidence that the feelings that I experienced within my countertransference were not primarily my own, but the denied, split-off and
projected feelings of my patients? In other words, how could I have been sure
that I was not prejudiced, not to say 'paranoid', or at any rate not more so than
usual? It is impossible to answer such questions here, but, basically, I had to
trust my own trained and experienced intuition. After all, projective identification is based upon processes which can be used in the service of empathy,
without which it would be impossible to do analytical work. It will always be
difficult to distinguish certain types of transference from approximately
accurate perceptions, and extremely difficult to distinguish certain types of
countertransference which facilitate communication from those which
impede it. Communications of this sort will always involve complex
processes of reciprocity and complementarity – of asymmetrical mutuality,
and it will always be impossible to know with certainty where projective
identification ends and introjective identification begins. Psychic reality is
always inter-personal, and, thus, the truth of statements about psychic facts is
always negotiable. In other words, the politics of knowledge in the human
sciences are inevitable, especially at this very basic level of perception,
definition and construction of psychic and social facts concerning an inter-
personal relationship in which the participants are also the negotiants.[9]

An interpretation, which is one type of explanation or hypothesis, is
always part of a larger theory, which will always involve assumptions and

various other untestable axioms. Thus, interpretations always have moral and political implications, especially when they concern elemental feelings which occur early on in life, and which raise questions concerning the boundaries of physical, social and psychological realms. Interpretations of these phenomena will always be controversial, and will always require acts of faith in the tenets of one school of thought rather than another. For example, those which emphasize instinctual origins rather than social facts imply that human nature cannot be changed, and that social institutions cannot be changed because they are based on human nature. Thus, the existing distributions of economic status and political power, whether within a society or a particular organization, are always seen as natural, especially because they are correlated inevitably with age, sex, and other ascribed characteristics, such as 'natural talent'. It follows from this point of view that whereas expressions of discontent are rooted in pathology, attempts to maintain the existing order are based on health.

In contrast, it could be argued that such explanations are nothing more than heuristic devices for the closure of theoretical systems, for the neutralization of recalcitrance. Theories of instincts do not explain phenomena.[10] They merely rename them. They turn us away from wondering about object relations throughout life, and lead us back to the so-called environmental constraints of the intra-uterine world, and, ultimately, to the zygote. Where will this end? Is the density of cilia in the fallopian tubes more relevant than the structure of the education system? Why not explore more fully the implications of Freud's ironic truism that out of this world people do not fall? For example, with respect to feelings of envy, surely it is as important to consider the effects of a mother's ability and capacity to provide good-enough mothering, and the constraints upon her of the stratification system of an industrial society, as it is to cite the effects of the so called 'death instinct'. Her child may be as helpless in the face of social constraints as biological ones, but social arrangements are not made in heaven.

Clearly, I am making a plea for the development of a more sociologically informed theory of object relations, one which requires an inter-personal model of the mind and a recognition of social facts. Organisms, persons and groups are not the same order of phenomena. Statements about one do not necessarily apply to the others, although they must be consistent. Psychic facts presuppose the prior and simultaneous existence of social facts as well as of organic facts. In other words, organisms, persons and groups must be viewed as open systems. This means that the personalities of the members of a group are elements of the context of a group, while at the same time a group itself is part of the context of the personalities of its members. It also means that the structure and process of a group express hologramatically the configurations of its societal context. Although basic personality pattern and character structure may be established during infancy, important elements of intra-personal and inter-personal functioning continue to emerge and to develop throughout life, which is governed by both the structure of the organism and the structure of the society. It would be impossible to derive this perspective from the Platonist epistemology which Bion acquired on his journey into the Cave, where many of his disciples remain, and thereby risk the entombment of group psychotherapy – not to mention psychoanalysis itself.

To return to my main theme: I wondered whether an attempt to clarify the group's envious hatred and their defensive projective identifications should be followed by a statement that connected their collective transference with those events which are supposed to be the original source of envy and potential envy within us all? Or, that they were using their envy as a defense against other feelings that were even more painful, such as helplessness, and thus were passive and inactive with regard to their attempts to understand and even to change the sources of these feelings within their contemporary worlds? In other words, I asked myself specific forms of the more general questions with which I defined initially the problem of context. In answer, on this occasion, as a matter of judgement and emphasis, I would contextualize the collective transference in terms of the 'far-away-there' and 'now', and in terms of the 'far-away-there' and 'then'. More precisely, I would focus upon the unconscious effects of social facts that operated during the infancies of these patients and during their daily lives as adults.

The clinical vignette continued: the interpretation

Finally, I broke my silence. Unfortunately, I made an interpretative speech. However, I would not want this mistake, which was based on my anxiety, to overshadow the essence of the matter, namely, a particular contextualization, not a particular aspect of technique.

I said that to feel helpless when one is helpless is not necessarily a bad thing.[11] In fact, it may be the first step towards finding a good, constructive and realistic solution. If you can tolerate the anxiety of it all, you may have some time to think, and you may be able to avoid making things worse.

Yet, I went on, I suspect that you may not be fully aware of what is really making you feel so helpless. Most of you know that you will be able to cope with dry rot and wet rot and all the difficulties that go along with it, and I suspect that most of you have been hearing what has been said in terms of disturbing desires and fears about everything that comes to your mind in connection with such words as 'wet' and 'dry', feelings which may have already begun to give us some trouble when you were talking about the rain and the mud, the painting, the Royal Family and the Royal Baby, husbands and wives, males and females, etc., and I guess that you are almost aware of what this has to do with me and us here ! But many of you have been denying (the defense) how frightened, helpless, and confused you feel (the feeling of pain against which they were trying to defend themselves) about the state of the nation, and in particular about the battles between the 'wets' and the 'drys' in Mrs Thatcher's Cabinet (a source in the 'there' and 'now' of the painful feelings).[12]

I will go even further, I continued. Some of you may be feeling something like what the Germans felt in the 1930s, when – like now – everything was so topsy-turvy, and nobody knew who was who. These conditions make your feelings of fear, helplessness, and confusion even worse, but they may also be leading you to deal with these feelings by looking for scapegoats (in this instance scapegoating is a form of instrumental adjustment to the painful feelings and to the sources of the feelings).[13] You are very ready to blame Jews, professionals, and so on, including me – and maybe even especially me – an American Jewish professional who you think will be safe from all this because you think I have two jobs as well as two countries. In other words, you are scapegoating me because you envy me, and you envy me because you think I am free from the painful feelings of help-lessness that many of you are experiencing as a result of social forces which seem to you to be beyond your control, in the same way that you tend to scapegoat Jews and others whom you also envy – outside the group – and for the same reasons. We seem to be recreating before our very eyes the same sort of problems that are going on in our society. And they are not so different from what has happened at other times and at other places.

Following a brief silence, I went on to say that it was curious that although the group knew that I would understand their feelings about this type of thing, they seemed to feel too ashamed to talk about them openly, almost as though they had fallen into a state of 'group disgrace' (Weber 1947). I said that this may have had something to do with their fear that if they lost their jobs they would not be able to afford my fees, and that they would lose their contact with me and the group. Although many had owed me money in the past, it seemed that they had become reluctant to discuss this openly with me now. I suggested that perhaps they felt that I would go back to America soon, and reject them, but also that I was responsible for their economic insecurity (although in fact every one of the patients in this group was better off economically than they were when they started treatment – as I have often observed to be the case).

Finally, by way of concluding my interpretative lecture (I emphasize again that this was very poor technique) I said that precisely because all this is so painful and confusing, you would like to throw me off the scent. You would like me to lose my sense of smell. You want me to direct your attention to the *infantile* origins of your envious feelings, the ones against which most of you are fairly well defended at this very moment. You know so much about psychoanalysis nowadays that you want to explain everything away in terms of your mothers and fathers when you were babies. Tits, willies, bums and pooh-poohs! You don't really want to go where it's hottest and smelliest tonight. But if we allow ourselves to be seduced in this way, we would make a mockery out of what we have learned from psychoanalysis.

The aftermath of this interpretative intervention

Following my intervention the group was silent. I found myself thinking that they were probably feeling chastised by my overly long and somewhat fervent comments. Yet, I also sensed that their silence was thoughtful. They seemed to be using the psychic space which my boundary-maintaining (both mine and theirs) intervention had helped to create in order to reflect upon the many implications and meanings of what had transpired.

During the silence I found myself thinking about a public lecture that I had attended recently at the Tavistock Clinic. It was one of a series on the application of psychoanalytical ideas to community issues. The speaker suggested that young black men in Brixton were unable to trust older white men in positions of authority because they had failed to work through the anxieties inherent in the paranoid–schizoid position, and that they were poor and unemployed because they were unable to make healthy introjections of the opportunities available, or in other words, that an unemployment rate in excess of 30 per cent over a decade was due to the experience which the males (but apparently not the females) had at '*the* breast' during their first few months of life. In the discussion, I said (or hope that I said) that unless we can acknowledge the reality of the helplessness that confronts people, we will be unable to help them filter out their accurate perceptions of reality from their fantastic distortions of it; unless we can acknowledge our own feelings of guilt, we will be unable to help our patients find the most effective and efficient forms of instrumental adjustment available to them; and that unless we can help them endure the pain inherent in feeling helpless, we may have to accept that paranoid fantasies and their attendant consequences are, inevitably, the only defensive solution available to them. To explain poverty and unemployment primarily in terms of the character traits of the poor and the unemployed is insulting and presumptuous. It makes a mockery out of what we have learned from psychoanalysis, and it ignores what we have learned from sociology about how social facts affect psychic processes, and vice versa. One does not have to be a political activist to believe that psycho-therapists ought to learn something about the nature of social processes, and to try to understand how our patients are constrained by social events. My remarks were met with silence and hostile embarrassment.

In retrospect, this event may account in part for my having approached my group's communications in the way I did. It may also help to explain why I reacted in the way I have described, and why I spoke for so long – so long that the session had to stop soon after I did. However, the group took up my interpretation in depth and in detail during the next couple of months. The material which followed was characterized by a mixture of themes, but they were preoccupied with issues concerning sexual perversion, the perversion of power, and the social psychology of envy, and, in this connection, with the meaning attributed to 'Jew' and 'Jewishness'. In my experience, this combina-tion is not unusual, but it is often easier for an English group to talk about their sexual perversions and even their most bizarre masturbation fantasies than about the occupations of their fathers or where they went to school. In fact, if a conductor does not consider such matters more or less in the beginning, a group can go on for a very long time without ever knowing what its members do for a living. Why this should be so is a topic in itself, but it offers another example of the unconscious effects of social facts, that are denied.

Later that evening, while I was dictating my notes about the group process and the contributions of the various patients to it, I found myself ruminating that given the impossibility of ever giving a so-called 'complete interpretation', would it have been better to have gone directly to the usual 'there' and 'then' origins of envy, rather than to the etiology that I had chosen, or, in other words, would giving emphasis to the infantile origins of their feelings have been less defensive and more helpful than looking at the social constraints inherent in their adult lives? I am still uncertain about the answers to this question, and I am still without rules concerning interpretative contextualizations of the transference. More importantly, I continue to wonder if I gave Elizabeth enough personal attention. Actually, I know that I did not, and that in a group I could not, and I worry about this feature of all forms of group psychotherapy.

References

Bion, W. R. (1961) *Experiences in Groups.* London: Tavistock.

de Maré, P. (1972) *Perspectives in Group Psychotherapy.* London: Allen and Unwin.

Ezriel, H. (1950) 'A psycho-analytic approach to group treatment.' *British Journal of Medical Psychology 23,* 1, 59–74.

Ezriel, H. (1957) 'The role of transference in psycho-analytic and other approaches to group treatment.' *Acta Psychotherapeutica, supplementum 7,* 101–116.

Foulkes, S. H. (1984) [1948] *Introduction to Group Analytic Psychotherapy.* London: Maresfield. (Original work published 1948).

Fromm, E. (1970) *The Crisis of Psycho-Analysis.* Harmondsworth: Penguin.

Fromm, E. (1980) *Beyond the Chains of Illusion.* London: Abacus.

Hopper, E. (1981) *Social Mobility: A Study of Social Control and Insatiability.* Oxford: Basil Blackwell Publisher Ltd.

Hopper, E. (1982) 'A Comment on Professor Jahoda's "The Individual and the Group".' In M. Pines and L. Rafaelsen (eds) *The Individual and the Group: Boundaries and Interrelations.* New York/London: Plenum Press.

Pines, M. (1978) 'Contributions of S. H. Foulkes to Group Analytic Therapy.' In L. R. Wolberg, M. H. Aronson and D. R. Wolberg (eds) *Group Therapy.* New York: Stratton.

Schindler, W. (1951) 'Family patterns in group formations and therapy.' *International Journal of Group Psychotherapy 1,* 1, 100–105.

Spillius, E. (1983) 'Developments from the work of Melanie Klein.' *The British Psycho-Analytical Society Bulletin,* January, 17–35.

Thomas, D. M. (1981) *The White Hotel.* London: Victor Gollancz.

Weber, M. (1947) *The Theory of Social and Economic Organization.* T. Parsons (ed) New York: Oxford University Press.

Zinkin, L. (1979) 'The collective and the personal.' *Journal of Analytical Psychology 24,* 3, 227–250.

Notes

1   This chapter was published as 'The Problem of Context in Group-Analytic Psycho-
        therapy: A Clinical Illustration and Brief Theoretical Discussion' in 1985 in M. Pines
        (ed) *W. R. Bion and Group Psychotherapy.* London: Routledge and Kegan Paul. Previous
        versions were published as 'Group analysis: the problem of context' in 1982 in *Group
        Analysis XV,* 2, 136–157, and in the *International Journal of Group Psychotherapy 34,* 2,
        173–200.

2   The use of 'analysis' or 'group-analysis' or 'group-analytic psychotherapy' or
        'group-analytic therapy' is often a matter of the politics and sociology of the profes-
        sion, and not a theoretical or technical problem. Many in the helping professions need
        to emphasize 'analysis' in order to assert their power over those who are not psychoan-
        alysts or to assert some kind of identity for themselves within a jungle of confusing
        professional labels. However, when compared to psychoanalysis proper, group analy-
        sis is 'therapy', especially when practiced by those who do not have a psychoanalytic
        perspective; yet, when compared to encounter groups and such like, it is much more
        akin to 'analysis'.

3   This remark is somewhat typical of Bion in that after countless hours of reflection I am
        still not certain whether it is banal or an insight of genius. Many in London have re-
        sponded to his utterances as though they are from the Buddha, thereby underestimat-
        ing their own creative insights as readers of his text. In this, he is not dissimilar from
        Foulkes, whose work on the 'matrix' has had the same effects. Perhaps this is an aspect
        of a kind of genius in our profession.

4   Although this is not a theoretical paper, it is worth calling attention in this connection
        to the 'collective unconscious' and the 'social unconscious', both highly ambiguous
        but perhaps overly neglected concepts. Modern London Jungians have begun to re-
        work Jung's concept of the 'collective unconscious' with its foundations in
        phylogenesis, the inheritance of ascribed characteristics, and such notions as the 'con-
        sciousness of race' (and it is unfortunate that space does not permit a further discussion
        of such topics as the phylogenetic aspects of the source and development of the
        'superego' according to classical Freudian thought) – all of which were, of course, en-
        tirely consistent with some of Freud's central themes (Zinkin 1979). In so doing, they
        have come close to what Fromm meant by the social unconscious (Fromm 1970,
        1980). Although Foulkes was interested in the clinical application of these notions, he
        was unable to transcend the ambiguities inherent in them. It would be helpful, there-
        fore, to differentiate at least three aspects of the social unconscious: that the impulses
        and attendant fantasies of which people are likely to be unconscious are governed by
        cultural beliefs, values and norms; that as a result, specifically, of their fear of feelings
        of isolation, shame and helplessness, people are likely to become, and to remain, un-
        conscious of those social arrangements which govern their power to control their own
        and other people's life chances; and that societies and their constituent social group-
        ings have ways of ensuring that people remain unaware of their non-conscious
        impulses and fantasies. However, it would be misleading to use the term 'mechanism
        of defense' to refer to social processes; for example, although the institution of educa-
        tion is an important agency of socialization, it should not be regarded as a society's
        'mechanism of defense' any more than as an ego-based creative activity, which is pre-
        cisely why it is so misleading to think about groups as though they were persons.

5   Typicality and topicality are always danger signals, but I am satisfied that in this in-
        stance I was not looking a gift horse in the mouth except in so far as the group wanted
        to help me prepare this article. Material which seems typical and topical may alert one

      to the unconscious constraints of social facts, but it may indicate that one is eliciting the material.

6   I suppose that even a doctor is not a 'Doctor', and certainly a Ph.D. does not entitle one to be a 'Doctor'. One day I shall ask my mother what a 'Doctor' is, but I suspect that not even by a 'Doctor' would a doctor be a 'Doctor'.

7   It is worth noting that I was in fact deriving these goods from these possessions and qualities, but not to the extent believed. I was better off than some of them, but worse off than others.

8   'Projective identification' is, of course, one of the cornerstones of modern Kleinian Theory, a judicious review of which can be found in Spillius (1983), who locates Bion within this development.

9   The only justification for the institutionalized arrogance of those psychoanalysts who work only on the basis of projective identification, and who neglect the problem of their own introjective identification, is that if they were not always right they would have to become their patients' patients.

10   Closed ideologies based on simplistic theories of instincts are especially noxious and self-defeating when they characterize forms of psychoanalysis and the therapies derived from them, ultimately because they imply that people cannot really change anyway, at least not very much, a view that must be unacceptable to those who contract to offer help. Of course, adherents to such systems of thought always allow for one degree of freedom, namely, approved actions based on reflective insight which has been acquired in a particular way in association with approved members of the 'school'. This goes far beyond the altogether reasonable view that the untrained must be trained by the fully trained, and that important actions must be based on thought. Instead, it functions as an institutionalized form of protection of persons and their local interests, and may lead to the ossification and demise of what could otherwise be a continuing and vital source of ideas.

11   I realized that I had written this sentence in my book (Hopper 1981), thus illustrating how one can use thoughts and words as a security blanket.

12   This very pregnant sentence refers to what may well be the essence of a group experience. I have referred, on the one hand, to what is virtually protomental, and, on the other, to social factors which constrain the lives of adults. Thus, it could be left to the group to respond to my interpretation in whatever ways they wished. In this sense, a good interpretation should have the quality of an 'image' in a good play or novel; however, in so far as it comes from the conductor, it should reflect back to the group the image which they have created. In fact, I should have stopped with this sentence, and waited to see how the group responded. Readers from outside the United Kingdom may not know that the slang 'wet' has many and various connotations, but in this context it refers to those who are 'soft liberals', economically and politically, for instance those who might favor higher and more progressive income taxes combined with greater government expenditures to help the poor and particular industries, whereas 'dry' refers to the 'hard-liners', the pure 'monetarists', etc.

13   It is worth noting that an 'instrumental adjustment' is more than simply a defense. It is a form of action which affects others, and which can also be assessed in terms of its effectiveness and efficiency. Since an action will almost always involve the actions of others, it becomes an interaction, which is a feature of a group process (Hopper 1981).

CHAPTER 6

The Social Unconscious
in Clinical Work[1]

The central theme of this chapter concerns the unconscious constraints of social systems on individuals and their internal worlds, and, at the same time, the effects that unconscious fantasies, actions, thoughts and feelings have on social systems. This field of knowledge is usually known as 'The Individual and the Group'. Group analysis or psychoanalytical group therapy is based on this field of knowledge. An analyst who is unaware of the effects of social facts and social forces will not be sensitive to the unconscious recreation of them within the therapeutic situation. He will not be able to provide a space for patients to imagine how their identities have been formed at particular historical and political junctures, and how this continues to affect them throughout their lives.

The unconscious constraints of social facts and social forces: the concept of the social unconscious

The study of groups is always contextual, as is the study of individuals, which is why it is virtually impossible to consider the one without the other. Contexts are infinite in number and variety, as, for example, we have the ecological, the social, the cultural, the psychological, and the physiological. Groups are exceedingly open systems, and, therefore, highly dependent on the provision of 'goods and services' from beyond their own boundaries. Usually, group analysts focus on the psychological context, but here I am concerned with the social context and how a group and its members are affected by it. Many features of the social context are involved: for example, the culturally supported models and analogies that might be used for descriptions of a group, for descriptions of the healing process and the role of the therapist, as well as the structure of referral networks, the education and training systems for therapists, the social welfare institutions, etc. (Hopper (1994 [1975]), a version of which is reprinted as Chapter 2 of this book).

The concept of the social unconscious refers to the existence and constraints of social, cultural and communicational arrangements of which people are unaware: unaware, in so far as these arrangements are not perceived (not 'known'), and if perceived not acknowledged ('denied'), and if acknowledged, not taken as problematic ('given'), and if taken as problematic, not considered with an optimal degree of detachment and objectivity. Although social constraints are sometimes understood in terms of myth, ritual and custom, such constraints are in the realm of the 'unknown' to the same extent as the constraints of instincts and fantasies, especially in societies with high status rigidity (Hopper 1981). However, 'constraint' is not meant to imply only 'restraint', 'inhibition', or 'limitation', but also 'facilitation', 'development' and even the transformation of sensations into feelings.

The concept of the social unconscious may be used to refer to the social and cultural elements and processes that exist within three categories of unconscious phenomena: that of which people are unaware but of which they were formerly aware, for example, the thoughts and feelings denoted by the 'Oedipus complex'; that of which they are unaware but of which they were partly aware, for example, fantasy life that occurred prior to language acquisition; and that of which they are unaware, and of which they were never aware. Information that was and is barely accessible to knowing, and that could not and cannot really be known directly, is called 'archaic', or more helpfully 'the unthought known' (Bollas 1987), although I prefer to think in terms of the 'dynamic non-conscious'.

The social unconscious is not merely a matter of the preconscious, and cannot be reduced to questions of awareness. The social unconscious is 'lawful' in the same sense that the dynamic unconscious operates according to 'primary process'. Structural dilemma and contradictions abound, and some arrangements and cultural patterns preclude others.

It is misleading to assume that people have unconscious minds in the same sense that they have complex brains; it is more appropriate to assume that people are unconscious, pre-conscious and non-conscious of much thought, feeling, fantasy and even sensation. Similarly, social systems do not have 'unconscious minds' or any kinds of mind, and the use of the concept of the social unconscious should not be taken to imply otherwise. After all, social systems are not organisms, and the notion 'group mind' is rather misleading. Nonetheless, whereas we have come to accept the validity and utility of the concept 'unconscious' for phenomena originating in the body, we need a concept like the 'social unconscious' in order to discuss social, cultural and communicational constraints.

It is virtually impossible to learn about some aspects of such constraints, because inevitably we are caught up within them and formed by them. Also, attempts to understand the social unconscious are met with a mixture of personal and social resistance, because feelings of personal and social power-lessness follow from increased insight into social facts and social forces. The appreciation of social causation and the limits it sets on the fundamental notion of free will is a blow to our narcissism and confuses our sense of ourselves as moral beings.

One type of social resistance with which group analysts are especially familiar is 'normative reticence', manifest in socially governed blank stares and silence, the very root of social secrecy, which core groups may use to peripheralise and marginalise the newcomer and the outsider (Hopper 1981). Ideology is the most common form of social resistance. 'Messengers' and 'truth-sayers' about the social unconscious are usually regarded as 'diffi-cult', 'adolescent', 'rebellious', 'bad-mannered', 'paranoid' even, which reflects a labeling process by those in power which is the first line of social defense and control.

Within the tradition of group analysis, Foulkes (1964) awarded special importance to the recognition and analysis of social forces at both inter-personal and trans-personal levels, and it is assumed that from the beginning of life the psyche is both organic and social. He wrote:

> '...the group-analytic situation, while dealing with the unconscious in the Freudian sense, brings into operation and perspective a totally different area of which the individual is equally unaware. Moreover, the individual is as much compelled by these colossal forces as by his own id and defends himself against their recognition without being aware of it, but in quite different ways and modes. One might speak of a social or interpersonal unconscious.' (p.258)[2]

Foulkes and Anthony's (1984) concept of matrix was intended to convey both inhibition and facilitation, as well as 'mold', and 'foundation matrix' meant that people and groups are rooted within species, societies, cultures and systems of communications (de Maré 1972). The seminal work of Moreno (1934) suggests that psychodrama and group analysis have common origins.

It may be helpful to present here three examples of the unconscious effects of social and cultural facts and forces from non-clinical settings. I will confine my examples to the unconscious effects of stratification systems on ambition, which is usually considered only in terms of the Oedipus complex. I will present further examples as I develop my argument, but I have discussed such phenomena at length in Hopper (1981) and Hopper and Osborn (1975).

In an unpublished study of the social class background of mothers who used child guidance clinics in the National Health Service, I found that although the expectation was that the mothers should have been working class, that is, married to men in manual work and be in manual work themselves, in fact they came from lower middle class backgrounds, and were very capable of utilizing the system. The problems of the children could then be understood in terms of family patterns within the lower middle class, involving mothers and fathers who had themselves experienced inconsistent definitions of their class and status by the system of education and stratification, partly because they were socially mobile. The mothers were often employed as secretaries for men who were in more powerful positions than their husbands. They put enormous pressure on their children to achieve more and more. The Oedipus complex of their sons included the male employers of the mothers, and collusion between mothers and sons to denigrate the authority of the father was commonplace, and frequently associated with latent homosexuality and difficulty in making a satisfactory identification with fathers.

There are many other sources of the normative limitations to ambition. I remember putting one of my daughters to bed when she was about five years old. In a very seductive and manipulative way she began to cry a little, and said, 'You know, Daddy, I am very sad, because I have just realized that I will never be queen'. In the United States I would have understood this communication in terms of a fairy tale, and realized that she was communicating her struggle to renounce her Oedipal wishes. However, how should I have understood such a communication in England, where there is a queen, where the renunciation of Oedipal wishes involves acquiescence in a particular system of social stratification, based on ascribed rather than achieved characteristics, and on the inheritance of privilege in an especially rigid and particular way? In England little girls who want to be queens must wait for a prince, who may actually come. My daughter had to realize that not only would she never be my wife, but also that she would never be a queen, and all that this involved, unless she married a prince. What would she have to give up in order to marry a prince? Whatever the comparative strengths and weaknesses of American society and culture, people are brought up with the conviction that there is nothing they cannot be, provided they want it badly enough and are prepared to achieve it, which carries its own problems of culturally supported omnipotence, grandiosity and insatiability.

Another example of the constraints of social facts on intra-psychic life and inter-personal processes is the effects of normative orientations to authority with regard to how frustrated people become under conditions of close and punitive supervision at work, and the effects of normative orientations with respect to the expression of feelings on how aggressive they become when they have been frustrated (Hopper 1965, a version of which is reprinted as Chapter 1 of this book). In a study of frustration and aggression and its effects on productivity among female workers in machine tool factories in England, I found that middle class women were less receptive than their working class counterparts to the exercise of close and punitive supervision, and, therefore, were more likely to become frustrated and to feel aggressive in response to this style of supervision. However, they were also more likely than their working class counterparts to suppress their aggressive feelings, and, therefore, more likely to displace their aggressive feelings into lowered productivity, even when this resulted in lower income for their work. In other words, social and cultural facts must be taken into account in attempts to understand the nature of aggressive feelings and of aggression.

The unconscious repetition of social situations: the concept of equivalence

In various kinds of social system, people tend unconsciously to recreate situations (in terms of actions, fantasies, object relations and affects) that have occurred at another time and space, such that the new or later situation may be taken as 'equivalent' to the old or previous one (Hopper and Kreeger 1980, a version of which is reprinted as Chapter 3 of this book). Although 'equivalence' is based on the social unconscious, it is analogous to a person's creation of symptoms or dreams in terms of unconscious fantasies emanating from the biologically based unconscious mind or id, at least from the point of view of traditional psychoanalysis.

The situations that people are most likely to recreate are those in which they have been traumatized, because the anxieties connected with the trauma as well as the perceptions of the trauma itself are usually subjected to denial and other forms of primal protections (Kinston and Cohen 1986), such as encapsulations and disassociations. Therefore, people need to recreate traumatic situations in the service of expulsion and attack, and mastery and control, and, above all, in an attempt to communicate non-verbal and ineffable experience. These processes are associated with the repetition compulsion and traumatophilia.

Equivalence occurs through forms of externalization and internalization, especially projective and introjective identification. Equivalence can be seen as a kind of group-transference of an unconsciously perceived situation in its social context to its present situation.[3] This is likely to occur when people have regressed, as they do in groups, especially in large groups. Enactments occur before the traumatic situation can be re-experienced (which is why the provision of a space safe for acting-in is so important in all forms of psycho-therapy).

An example of equivalence was described by Hopper and Kreeger (1980) a version of which is reprinted as Chapter 3 of this book, in their 'Report on the Large Group' of the Survivor Syndrome Workshop. They suggested that the participants in the workshop recreated what they had imagined unconsciously had been the concentration camp experience, including psychic numbing and identification with the aggressors.

In sum, people are affected profoundly by social and cultural facts and forces, and such constraints are largely unconscious at all phases of 'life tra-jectories' (Hopper 1981). Situations characterized by extreme helplessness are especially likely to be repeated.

Before illustrating the clinical application of these concepts of the social unconscious and of equivalence and this hypothesis about the repetition of traumatic situations, I will introduce a more general orientation or frame of reference to clinical work, which I regard as 'group-analytical'.

A general frame of reference for clinical work

Although my clinical work and theoretical approach to psychoanalytical group therapy owe more to Foulkes and his colleagues than to Bion and his, especially in connection with the importance that I attach to the sociality of human nature, I always begin with Bion's (1961) remark in *Experiences in Groups* to the effect that the basic assumption group knows no time and knows no space,[4] which is as relevant to the boundaries of the psycho-analytical dyad as it is to therapeutic groups and to social systems of any kind. On the basis of this utterance, I would construct a paradigm of the realms of clinical work in terms of time and space for patient and therapist.

| | | Space | |
		Here	There
Time	Now	1	2
	Then	3	4

Figure 6.1 Paradigm: Realms of clinical work in terms of time and space for patient and therapist.

The dimension of time can be dichotomized into 'Now' and 'Then', and the dimension of space into 'Here' and 'There'. Thus, this paradigm consists of four cells : 'Here and Now', 'Here and Then', 'There and Now', and 'There and Then'. Communications between the analyst and the patient can be considered in terms of each of these four cells

Cell One: Here and Now

The 'Here and Now' is denoted by a communication such as the patient saying, 'I do not want to lie on the couch, because I want to see your face', and the analyst responding, 'You are frightened that if we take our eyes off each other, we will not exist for each other, and you will be alone and unprotected, and I will turn my mind elsewhere'. We have been taught to give special emphasis to the communications between analyst and patient within the 'Here and Now'. From the point of view of the ascendant paradigm in psychoanalysis, at least in London, we are taught that although traditionally the prudent analyst worked from surface to depth, that is, he went from where it is coolest to where it is hottest, it would be better to proceed as quickly as possible to where it is hottest; and it is asserted that it is hottest in the 'Here and Now', in the sense that affect is strongest within this particular juncture of time and space.

Although traditionally the transference was understood in terms of defense and resistance to insight, and as a source of interference with helpful reconstructive work, currently the 'transference' refers to the total relationship between analyst and patient, and not to an inappropriate repetition of past experience as a specific strand within this total relationship (Joseph, B. 1989). By definition, therefore, work within the transference is work within the 'Here and Now', and it is asserted that this should take precedence over all other elements of therapeutic work, and some would argue that this constitutes the entire scope of therapeutic work. In any case, the very nature of unconscious fantasy distorts the perception and introjection of objects in their 'true' state, and, therefore, personal history cannot be told with any degree of objectivity. From the point of view of existential psychotherapy, we are taught that there is nothing available but the 'Here and Now', and it is inevitable that reconstruction will be based on retrospective projection. In other words, whether the relationship between patient and analyst should be understood entirely in terms of the transference, or whether entirely in terms of its existential reality, it is essential to work within the 'Here and Now'.

These points are both truisms and unnecessarily restrictive. They are as defensive in their own way as the original view to the effect that reconstruction is not only possible but curative in itself, based on the catharsis and the 'Eureka!' theories of the value of discovering buried, historical, personal truths. Apart from the fact that it not always hotter in the 'Here and Now', the basic concept of the 'Here and Now' should not be confused with the idea of the 'ahistorical present', which is based on the entirely untenable assumption that it is possible to have an ahistorical situation comprising of individuals. It may be possible to have an ahistorical situation composed of 'organisms' in a limited biological sense of the term, but individuals and their situations are always in the historical present by definition. In my view, the analysis of the transference is the primary task of therapeutic work; however, whereas the transference consists of much less than the total relationship between analyst and patient, the analysis of the transference must include a great deal more than merely the 'Here and Now'.

Cell Two: There and Now

The 'There and Now' is denoted by a communication such as the patient saying, 'My wife does not understand me, and is not really interested in my point of view', and the analyst responding, 'Perhaps she would understand more and be more interested in your point of view if you spoke to her as a wife and not as your business partner whom, she seems to feel, you would prefer to spend your evenings with'. 'There and Now' refers to what is happening between the patient and his 'significant others', a wife or a partner, peers, or people who are at the social nodules in his inter-personal network. In many ways, this is the stuff of conscious material, but this is also where we meet the social unconscious.

Cell Three: Here and Then

The 'Here and Then' is denoted by a communication such as the exchange that I have quoted above, 'I do not want to lie on the couch...' followed by the response '...I will turn my mind elsewhere' but extended by the analyst's adding the sentence, '...as you felt when your mother read her book while she fed you'. The 'Here and Then' includes the work of reconstruction, in that traditionally we try to connect what is taking place in the 'Here and Now' with what has happened in the person's early life. We can go back and back and back, to the then and then and then. Therefore, the 'Here and Then' refers to the trajectory of the patient's interpersonal world, starting in the womb, if not before. From the point of view of the patient and the analyst, however, the treatment relationship, the entry of the analyst into the patient's life, is a recent event. Thus, I would include the treatment relationship within the 'Here and Then', because it refers to what happened between analyst and patient a 'moment before', and then the 'moment before that', and the 'moment before that' within the history of the treatment relationship. 'Yesterday' or even 'earlier in the session' is part of the 'Here and Then'.

Cell Four: There and Then

We all work in the 'Here and Now', and we try to connect these phenomena with the 'Here and Then' and the 'There and Now', and vice versa. For example, we try to help a patient understand that he is relating to us in the same way that he related to a parent at an earlier phase of life, and this is how, for example, he seems to relate to his wife or partner. These three cells constitute the three angles of the classical therapeutic triangle. However, I would like us now to consider a fourth angle, in effect to try to square the therapeutic triangle.

The 'There and Then' is denoted by a communication such as the patient saying, 'I feel that my mother could not concentrate on me', within the context of repeating his complaints that when he was a little boy during the war, his mother was always preoccupied with other matters and other people, always listening to the radio and making telephone calls to her mother, and the analyst responding, 'She may have been preoccupied with the news that her cousins were caught in the Warsaw Ghetto, and felt that she was lucky to be alive and to have you, as well as that she was very helpless and guilty about them'. The 'There and Then' refers to the patient's earlier experience of social facts within his broader social context, especially but not exclusively as mediated through his relationships within the 'Here and Then', such as his family and other early primary groups.

Let us consider another example. Members of that generation born between 1945 and 1949 in countries involved in World War II are often helped by realizing that they have in common a particular pattern of experience over which they had virtually no control. After the war there was an atmosphere of hope and optimism based on the conviction that the world had been made safe for democracy by husbands, fathers and men in general who were returning from battle. Yet, millions of children were then born into the new working class suburbs in which they went from birth to 'latency' without having seen their fathers more than occasionally, perhaps on weekends. The decision to build so much marvelous housing did not take account of the fact that the lives of those who moved into these white suburbs of detached homes with gardens would be utterly and irrevocably changed, if not destroyed, because Father's work remained many miles away. Moreover, one part of the extended family moved, but other parts stayed put, thereby creating millions of isolated housewives without support from their mothers, sisters and friends, and without traditional shops and services. The changes in the society and culture that were brought about by the fulfillment of the necessary requirements for new cars and roads were of a magnitude comparable only to the introduction of the horse into the lives of the Plains Indians a few thousand years ago. Many members of the generation of post-war baby boomers whose fathers were experienced as intrusive 'part-objects', because that is really what they tended to be, continue to experience males in authority in more or less the same way. At present it seems to be exceedingly difficult in many countries involved in World War II to maintain a connection between power and authority, clear boundaries of gender roles and a consensus about the nature of perversion and its normative status.

Although we are taught that in good clinical work we should avoid discussions of material that could be categorized as 'There and Then', because it is an attempt to escape from more pressing, immediate anxieties – a collusive defensive maneuver – I have come to disagree. The interpretation of the transference within the 'Here and Now' is not complete without reference to the 'There and Then'. Malan's (1979) notion of the 'therapeutic triangle' must be changed to the 'therapeutic square'. We must be able to help a patient put together the pieces of both his social and psychic communities. Of course, we should not try to make a complete interpretation all at once, but build it over a period of months, if not years.

How do we think about material located in the 'Now and There' and 'Then and There', in cells two and four of Paradigm 6.1? To be more precise: How do we think about this material in ways that are useful clinically, in ways that are likely to foster maturation on the part of our patients? In order to begin to answer these questions I would propose a second paradigm of realms of clinical work in terms of two dichotomies. The first is whether the patient is consciously preoccupied with political and social topics (for example, discourse about the conflict in what used to be called Yugoslavia or in the EU), or with apolitical and asocial topics (for example, discourse about what happened in the family, what the patient is feeling, the nature of his sexuality, and so on). The second dichotomy is whether the therapist's interventions are derived from those theories, hypotheses, concepts and data that emphasize external social facts (for example, the structure of authority and power relationships within which the patient works and is unconsciously constrained) or internal psychic facts (such as the unconscious Oedipus complex). It is important to remember that in terms of the social unconscious a person may be as unaware of external social facts as he is of internal psychic facts.

		Therapist's intervention emphasizes the constraints of:	
		Internal Realities	**External Realities**
Patient's Preoccupations	**Asocial and Apolitical**	1	2
	Social and Political	3	4

Figure 6.2 Paradigm: Realms of clinical work in terms of patient's preoccupations with political and social phenomena, and of therapist's emphasis on internal or external reality.

This paradigm has four cells, in terms of whether the content of the patient's material is consciously political and social or apolitical and asocial, and whether the therapist's concerns emphasize the constraints of the patient's internal psychic world or those of his external social world. Communications between analyst and patient can be considered in terms of each of these four cells:

Cell One: The patient's material is consciously apolitical and asocial, and the analyst emphasizes the patient's internal world

This cell is denoted by a communication such as a patient's reporting a dream about being lost in a large house containing many rooms, wandering from room to room and becoming increasingly more frantic as he searches for his analyst. The analyst interprets in terms of the patient's search for a part of his father that will help him negotiate his independence from the influence of his mother's mind, if not from her very body, and, therefore, help him with his identification as an adult male. The analyst also interprets in terms of how these unconscious fantasies and infantile relationships are repeated within the transference. However, the analyst does not draw attention to such connotations of 'large house' as 'wealth', 'privilege' and 'social location'.

Cell Two: The patient's material is apolitical and asocial, and the analyst emphasizes the patient's external world.

This cell is denoted by a communication such as a patient's talking about his relationship with his father when he was a boy, and how this is related to what he thinks and feels about his analyst in that very session, and the analyst's interpreting how the patient's relationship to the analyst is unconsciously affected by the structure of authority in the patient's work situation; or, a patient's discussing her desirous cravings for a male child, and the analyst's helping her to understand that this is based not only on envy and its vicissitudes in connection with aspects of her very early relationship to her mother's body and subsequently to her relationship to her father and, perhaps, her brothers and their bodies, but also, and perhaps even primarily, on the social fact that in her society there has been limited opportunity for the experience of the expression of her power and mastery and creativity except through the use of her body and its products, and, therefore, that it is hardly surprising that she should wish to have control over a male child.

To help a patient understand that during the first few months of life the difficulties he had at the breast can be traced to difficulties that his mother had in feeding him, because she and her husband were constrained by a terrible recession, her husband was unemployed and felt humiliated and jealous of the new baby, and needed her attention and help almost as much as the patient did, is as liberating as that his mother withdrew from him, because he was hateful towards her due to a surfeit of innate malign envy. In other words, the examination of envy and greed and the impulses to eat and to bite and to chew must be contextualised not only in terms of the body, which is obvious, but also in terms of the family, class and status groups of the society at a certain point in time.

Cell Three: The patient's material is consciously political and social, and the analyst emphasizes the patient's internal world

This cell is denoted by a communication such as a patient's referring to the systematic dismantling of the institutions of the Welfare State, and the analyst's interpreting in terms of the patient's anxiety about losing his mother's attentions when his brother was born, and about how this is repeated within the transference in connection with a forthcoming long weekend when his analyst will have to cancel Friday and Monday sessions.

Cell Four: The patient material is consciously political and social, and the analyst emphasizes the patient's external world

This cell is denoted by a communication such as an upwardly mobile patient's bemoaning his own greed and insatiability for status, and the analyst's interpreting his chronic dissatisfaction with the analysis in terms of: the unconscious effects of his multiple comparative reference groups on the nature of his ambition; the connection between his ambition and his personal, sexual and professional identities; the effects of his serial friendship groups on his inability to form and to anchor his normative expectations for stratification goals (Hopper 1981). This does not prevent the analyst from drawing attention to his patient's conflicting intrapsychic loyalties to his father and mother, and to his attempts to free himself from his collusive engulfment by his mother by denigrating his father who was regarded as merely an uneducated manual worker.

From the point of view of traditional psychoanalysis, the interpretative work in cells two and four is really very problematic, defensive and collusive. However, I believe that it is essential to include this perspective. It is equally defensive and collusive not to discuss social and political facts, and to avoid anxiety about them by turning to more familiar concerns and concepts. I believe that there are ways of creating space for the discussion of social reality and political issues without taking sides, and without advocating particular solutions. An important case in point is that many Shoah survivors had very long analyses in which their Shoah experiences were neglected (Simon 1992).

Clinical illustrations of the unconscious constraints of social and cultural facts in group analysis

I will now illustrate work in the second and fourth cells of the two paradigms presented above – that is, in the 'There and Now' and 'There and Then', the interpretation of intra-psychic processes and conflicts in terms of inter-personal processes that reflect the constraints of past and present social and cultural facts. The concepts of the social unconscious and of equivalence inform my approach. Again, I usually work within the first and third cells of these two paradigms, that is, in the 'Here and Now' and in the 'Here and

Then'. These different sources of explanation of the transference and countertransference are not mutually exclusive. On the contrary.

Clinical illustration (i)

The following clinical vignette is based on several sessions from one of my twice-weekly Groups, meeting during the 1990s.

A forty-year-old woman, who was in the group for about fifteen years, and who I know got a lot from it, eventually made a good relationship with a man, had a baby and left the Group. As one of the first patients in the Group, she had become central to it. None of the women could find a way to take her place. They were so competitive with one another as to who might take her place that they were immobilized. For a while after she left, we were all bereft, but also pleased for her. Slowly the Group mourned the loss. However, they insisted that I continued to be bereft. I felt that this was not really true. I was under some pressure to introduce a 'replacement' patient, who was referred to me by a senior psychoanalyst colleague who had become ill and to whom I felt loyal and indebted. The patient needed help, and I wanted to be of help, and to demonstrate how helpful my Group could be. Therefore, about three months after my original group member left, but before I was convinced that the Group was ready for her, I introduced a new female member. She was an extremely talented, distinguished neurologist. She was also tall, slender and blonde with very big eyes. She was a great threat to the women in the Group, although they expressed their shame at having such feelings, especially given their own achievements as well as their ideology concerning such competition.

One evening an equally distinguished male director of clinical work at a teaching hospital in London, who was lean and handsome and youthful in appearance, told the Group that he had a problem. Thanks to the help he had received from the Group, he could no longer engage in certain sadistic and humiliating sexual behavior with his wife, with whom he worked, and found that instead he was compelled to go to prostitutes. On the way home from the Group he had to pick up a street prostitute, return to her room, almost always in a run-down hotel, and after attempting to have a discussion with her about politics and her own personal life history, make her take off her clothes, which he would denigrate as 'common' and 'vulgar', and then spank her. He traced this change as occurring a few weeks after the new woman had come into the Group.

While he was speaking, I began to think about how 'split' the new female member seemed to be, and how unresponsive she was to the men in the Group, yet how involved she was with me, and, necessarily, I with her, although no words were spoken between us. While my mind was moving towards the obvious connection between the prostitute and the new female member, I also began to think about myself and the prostitute from the point of view of a type of narcissistic identification, and how this might be the basis for certain kinds of perverse behavior. I then began to connect perversions and perverse impulses with an inability and refusal to mourn and with the fear of annihilation, and to think about competition among the women and the difficulty men have in competing with sisters for parental attention, because this requires an acceptance of their own femininity and vulnerability, and that – in effect – life is easier for women. The point was that I had introduced into the Group an 'object' rather than a person, in the sense that it must have felt that I regarded one person as the same as another, if the loss of a person could be managed by my simply bringing in another person, and that the loss of the breast could be managed by substituting a pacifier – or a 'dummy', as it is called in the UK, a word that not only rhymes with 'mummy' (meaning both 'mom' and a dead Egyptian), but means also a mannequin or a ventriloquist's puppet.

My thoughts were interrupted when one woman began to talk with a sense of urgency about her father who seemed to be having what might be described as a depressive breakdown as he approached seventy years of age. However, she wondered if he had Alzheimer's disease (a diagnosis that she, as an accountant, was, perhaps, not qualified to make). She was very sad about this, and wondered what she could do to be of help. A member of the Group who was a psychiatrist said rather abruptly, 'He needs a psychiatrist.' She ignored him completely, and went on to say something like, 'Oh! I wish Earl would see him. He needs somebody like Earl, somebody who is very nice, not like my mother, sisters, cousins and me who never let him finish a sentence. He needs somebody who will listen...' Suddenly the psychiatrist slammed his fist down on the chair, and said, 'He needs a psychiatrist'. He scared the hell out of us. She looked at him, looked at me and went on talking. A few minutes later she turned to him again and said, 'What did you say?' He said, 'It's too fucking late. It's too fucking late, you bitch. I spoke. I said "He needs a psychiatrist", but now I am not going to explain what I meant.' Although the psychiatrist was absolutely correct that her father needed a psychiatrist, a black social worker said, 'Look, you see what I have to cope with. You see what I have to cope with. You see how these psychiatrists behave.' It went on like that. We did not have a chance to focus on this issue.

I found myself continuing to think about the scene before this rather dramatic exchange took place. I was wondering about the need for a vulnerable, sad male to be rescued from an engulfing, manipulating female, and about how the unconscious themes of the Group had remained more or less constant despite the apparent variety of more conscious, secondary process themes of the manifest content of their communications. I shifted to wondering if the woman whose father had become ill might be expressing for the whole Group its feeling that in my silence and perhaps inappropriate introduction of the new member into the Group I had become ill. However, these thoughts remained private. The Group were talking so much and so furiously! I could not have got a word in edgeways unless I had wished to take over the Group. I was able to take a more silent and receptive role than usual – to lead from behind, so to say – while at the same time waiting to see where the Group would take me. As far as I know the Group did not experience my silence as a withdrawal but as active and attentive listening.

Over a period of a couple of weeks the Group was a veritable Tower of Babel. Although an outsider might have thought that it was falling apart, I did not regard the Group as being in a state of 'disarroy' (Turquet 1994 [1975]), because there is a sense in which only a fairly cohesive social system can contain the expression of such conflicting opinions. This particular Group has a disproportionate number of members from the helping professions – as do most twice-weekly groups recognized as suitable for candidates at the Institute of Group Analysis. However, the four members of the Group who were not members of the helping professions, two women and two men, felt left out of the sub-group of professionals, and felt very envious of them. A man said, 'Who the fucking hell are all of you so-called professionals, telling us how to live our lives? None of you works for a living. You don't actually make anything. You don't manufacture anything.' Two women agreed that having escaped from receiving so much formal education, they had lived more interesting lives, and they knew more about feelings and relationships than the female professionals ever would. The Group became preoccupied with questions such as: Who had I been fucking? Who was the mother of this new baby? This was the group's language, not mine, although for the most part I do use their vernacular. Also, over the years, various colleagues have been named as the mothers of my new patients, depending on the publicity such colleagues may be having at the time, and depending on their fields of interest, for example, trauma, female perversions, gender issues, etc. and any new patient is assumed to have the problems associated with the colleague's special interest. There was complete chaos. This was not a mere squabble. The passions were very strong.

I could have intervened in various ways, and one way need not necessarily have excluded another. There is no such thing as a right or a wrong interpretation on the part of a conductor of a group who is experiencing such material. However, I was moving towards making an interpretation that I hoped, based on an understanding of the psychological context of the transference, would elucidate the situation. We had lost a soft, feminine woman, who also exemplified the best work that the Group could do. We were in mourning, but could not acknowledge it. I may have been more concerned with my very ill colleague than with the patient who left, and they may have been more concerned with their perceived loss of my involvement with them, perhaps with a degree of accuracy. While the members of the Group were projecting into me their own inability and refusal to mourn, they were themselves retreating into paranoid–schizoid modes of experience. In response to their experience of failed dependency as a consequence of my bringing a new woman into the Group before they were really ready, they were regressing further into a shared fear of annihilation. At the intra-psychic level this fear was experienced as fission and fragmentation and, at the level of group process, as aggregation, one of the bi-polar forms of incohesion, including sub-grouping. The members of the helping professions were fighting one another for who would be on top of the pile, and the non-professionals were wrestling for social dominance and for control over access to me and the 'objects' for whom I stood. However, both professionals and non-professionals were united in their hatred of the new, successful, professional woman, who was perceived as both an unyielding and intrusive foreign object, and as very needy and vulnerable. She 'carried' split-off parts of me and of themselves, and, therefore, she was regarded as interfering with their perfect communion with the Group as a whole and with me. This process of scapegoating was a consequence of projecting unwanted parts of the whole Group into one particular member, and was based on shared experiences of encapsulated trauma, which involved similar experiences in the early lives of several of the members of the Group. Various members of the Group were leading the processes of aggregation – for example, the man who expressed his perverse impulses and crustacean defenses.[5]

In fact, I did not intervene. Instead, the Group itself began to try very hard to understand the meanings of all this in terms of what I have called the 'Here and Now' and the 'Here and Then', more or less in a traditional manner. They demonstrated considerable maturity in their ability to contain their psychotic anxieties and in their willingness and ability to understand how they had been engaging in defensive and protective maneuverings in order to avoid the experience of the pain associated with such states of mind. However, I felt that their insights were not authentic, that is, they were correct but without appropriate affect. They were too 'intellectual'. They were based on an 'imitative identification' (Gaddini 1992) with me, involving imitation without internalization, suggesting an underlying rage and anxiety about loss and separation from me.

While I was contemplating all this, a woman, who is not a member of the helping professions, intervened quietly and tentatively with a kind of interpretative question. She wondered aloud if the Group was worried about what had been happening in the National Health Service, and about the social unrest that we had been reading about all over Europe in connection with the 'Maastricht Treaty'. The Group became silent and thoughtful. I thought to myself that the only thing wrong with this interpretation was that I had not formulated it myself, which was, of course, one of its best features! Various members of the Group acknowledged the validity and pertinence of this interpretation. They expressed their concerns about being helpless and powerless in response to various social and political problems in Britain and in Europe generally, problems that have been expressed in conflict once again between blacks and whites, Jews and non-Jews, and the native born and immigrants. Within the National Health Service and other institutions of the withering Welfare State, such problems have been expressed between medical and non-medical hospital staff generally, especially between psychiatrists and non-medical managers in hospitals, I suppose because nowadays the demarcations in their skills are less clear-cut, and their respective positions are characterized by status incongruence (Hopper 1981). So many non-medical managers are upwardly mobile and black, and so many psychiatrists are neither. For several weeks the Group was preoccupied with these issues and their anxiety about them. They attempted to become more aware of the unconscious constraints of current social and political developments. The Group even talked about football hooliganism, and had some very interesting things to say about it!

To summarize, the Group shared a fear of annihilation, and evinced processes of aggregation, including sub-grouping. However, their collective and individual transference material in the 'Here and Now' was connected to social constraints in the 'There and Now'. The effects of 'Maastricht' were as unconscious as the effects of various aspects of their experience as infants and children. This was not a matter of the social 'pre-conscious', a simple matter of a lack of awareness of social turmoil in their current society and region of the world. I would argue that the Group recreated a situation that was equivalent to what was happening within their wider social context, precisely because they were unconscious of their feelings of helplessness and powerlessness, and of their feeling confused by social and cultural changes, which they did not understand. Slowly, the Group made connections between the material of the 'Here and Now' and 'There and Now' and what had happened in Europe when most of them were either children or not yet born, or, in other words, to social facts and forces in the 'There and Then'. This was not a defensive respite from the powerful feelings of anxiety about the aggression that had occurred. Nor was it an attempt by the woman whose father had become ill to be helpful to me, at least not primarily. Nor was it an attempt by the Group to avoid mourning the lost female member – at least not primarily. It was an attempt to mourn losses associated with World War II and the subsequent demise of the United Kingdom politically, socially and economically, and to work through anxieties associated with the loss of social order and a sense that the nation could sustain an attitude of hopeful optimism. The Group may even have been working with the unconscious anxieties and preoccupations of their parents. Such issues cannot be reduced to more personal idiosyncratic concerns, which is not to suggest that they are not completely intertwined with more contextual concerns. In fact, I was reminded of Weber's (1947) concepts of group-charisma and group-disgrace, and their association with pride and shame. I emphasized the unconscious constraints of social facts and forces in the 'There and Then' and 'There and Now', because to have interpreted their anxieties and perceptions of my failures and inadequacies primarily as a repetition of their more personal experiences of failed dependency during infancy and childhood within the 'Here and Then' would have been collusive with and defensive against the anxieties of their current social and political situations. However, never to concentrate on the 'Here and Then', or even to give too little emphasis to it, would be equally collusive with and defensive against other anxieties. In fact, many months later, when another female patient left the Group and the Group began to evince processes that were similar to the ones that I have described, the interpretative work was directed almost entirely to the 'Here and Then'.

Clinical illustration (ii)

The following clinical vignette is based on several sessions from another of my twice-weekly Groups. It also illustrates the constraints of social facts and social forces within the 'There and Now', closely connected with events within the 'There and Then'.

The sessions occurred in July 1982, a few weeks before the summer break, when my Groups were meeting in the Group Analytic Practice, near Baker Street Tube Station, not far from Regent's Park, in Central London. Seven or eight Groups were meeting at the same time, from 6 p.m. –7.30 p.m. Before my Groups began I usually had coffee with colleagues in a small room across the corridor from the room in which my Group met. I noticed that people were a bit early, which usually indicates some anxiety. As far as I knew the Group was not going through a difficult period, yet I sensed that they had come early because they wanted the safety of the Group room and the Group situation.

I entered the room promptly at 6 p.m. The Group began with an inordinately long silence. This is not common in my Groups, although when it does happen it is never without meaning, although not always the same meaning. In any case, this silence felt inconsistent with what I had experienced in the previous few sessions. When the silence was broken, there was a great deal of space between words and sentences. People would speak, lapse into silence and start again. It was hard for me to understand their communication, because the sentences were split up and fragmented, the clauses of sentences were not connected in a meaningful way – what Britton (1994) calls the 'language of either/and' – people spoke slowly, using non-sequiturs. There was an absence of eye contact. The members of the Group might have been attempting to imitate or caricature a type of group analyst who does not say very much, keeps his body very still, his arms close to his body or folded, his legs crossed at the ankles, looking down at the table.

Suddenly we became aware of a symphony of tummy rumbles (borygmie). One person's stomach began to rumble, another's made a similar but louder noise, a third's replied in a higher pitch. My own stomach began to thunder. Amidst laughter, this continued for what seemed to be ages, but must have been at most a couple of minutes. These noises continued from time to time during the rest of the Group.

This was a mature Group in which the current members had a lot of experience of one another. They began to say that they were hungry and angry. Someone suggested the Group was anticipating being separated from me and from one another during the forthcoming holiday. Another said, 'Clearly, we are beginning to take in too much air as Mummy pushes us away, and we have a little indigestion.' There is nothing wrong with this type of interpretation, of course, apposite as it is for separation anxiety before holidays. Moreover, we were aware that separation anxiety is very closely associated with fear of annihilation, and, therefore, when it is actually experienced it is very painful. However, I felt that the Group's own interpretation was an attempt to shelter us from something explosive, rather than an exploration of the nature of their hidden feelings. I felt that there was some anxiety about separation and the withdrawal of protection, some personal fission and fragmentation and a vague sense of protective alienation as a response to this kind of anxiety. And, therefore, there was low cohesion as manifest in aggregation, expressed primarily in non-verbal communications, such as gaze avoidance, and in massification, in which the search for safety is expressed in fusion and confusion within the Group, and in the wish, if not compulsion, to communicate in silence – in this case undermined by their interpersonal borygmie. I realized that although I could sense the anxiety and describe the inter-personal defenses, I did not really know why they were so anxious. Therefore, in response to their 'interpretations', I said, 'This does not feel right to me'. After a moment's silence, I continued, 'I wonder if we feel safe enough to find out more about this, and if not, why not?'

The Group lapsed into a thoughtful silence which seemed to go on forever. Finally a woman said, 'Do you know…there's just been an explosion. A bomb has just gone off at the bandstand in Regent's Park where the Queen's Military Band (The Royal Green Jackets) was playing.' The bandstand was less than 1,000 yards from where we were sitting. In fact many of us in the flat had heard the explosion while we were drinking coffee before the Groups started. It sounded as if a big lorry had backfired. None of us had said a word about it. We had continued to drink our coffee. It could be said that this was a denial, given the number of explosions that had occurred in London during the preceding week. Of the nine members of the Group, four said that they had come from Baker Street tube station and had heard the explosion; three had come individually through the park, and each had seen human limbs on the grass, many dead bodies, fire-engines and police cars speeding through the area, and a lot of blood. We were all shocked, but especially those of us who had witnessed this terrible event. Three of us who had not, including myself, felt rather left out. We continued to discuss this horrifying experience, and to offer some comfort to one another, until the Group stopped.

At the next session, forty-eight hours later, a woman of Irish and Welsh background who was upwardly mobile from the working class and whose family, especially her father, were highly politicized, started by talking about her social origins. Not once during her previous four and a half years in the Group had she been able to do this. (Class remains so important, but is rarely discussed. England still has a high degree of status rigidity, and people are ashamed of having lowly social origins. It is easier to learn about a patient's most secret, bizarre masturbation fantasies than about what his father did for a living.) She went on to talk about her violent feelings against the middle class women in the Group, who she felt did not accept her despite the fact that she had gone to university, had done very well and was a qualified social worker.

She was interrupted by a homosexual psychiatrist from abroad. He expressed his strong desire to bomb the Institute of Group Analysis, because he believed that homosexuals were not accepted for training. The patient assumed that he would not be accepted, and he quoted an early book by Foulkes to the effect that homosexuality should be a criterion for exclusion from training. He cried, and he talked about his sadistic impulses, not only towards me, but also towards the entire establishment in which the Group was embedded. This was very much to his benefit, because we were able to shift the issue and his feelings about it from the realm of secrecy to one of privacy, and he was able to begin to test the reality of his concern.

I would suggest that this development in the Group would not have occurred if we had concentrated on separation anxiety in terms of psychotic anxieties originating within the first few months of life, and in terms of a repetition of these anxieties in response to the impending holiday break. In fact, it would have produced 'false self' protections supporting the encapsulation of traumatic experience, as seen in the Group's secrecy and attacks on the coherency of their mother tongue. Perhaps the experience would have been discussed eventually, after we had read the newspapers and watched TV reports, but by then the scarring would have begun. We would never have been able to share the feelings of being right in the middle of such explosive material, and to help one another make sense of this experience.

It does not take a great deal of intelligence and theoretical acumen for analysts to say, 'This does not feel right to me'. It does take a sense of authenticity and a willingness to think laterally or 'horizontally' without feeling that interest in the social context is defensive or superficial. In fact, it may be worth thinking about 'horizontal depth'.

I discussed the effects of this terrible, calamitous event with my colleagues who were conducting Groups in the other rooms in the Practice. I learned that my Group was the only one who brought up this material. All the other groups concentrated on anxieties about the impending holiday, with the exception of one in which there had been a great deal of laughter, and the particular therapist felt that such laughter expressed relief and happy anticipation at having a few weeks without the obligations of therapy, and that this was not a manic defense against depressive anxiety. One of my colleagues assured me that his Group were able to stay 'right with their despairing feelings' about the summer break, and that they had not needed to escape into a discussion of 'distant' events.

Clinical illustrations of the maturation of individuals in group analysis

In group analysis and in all forms of group psychotherapy it is necessary to keep in mind the welfare and development of each individual member of the Group. I would like to focus on certain individuals in the two Groups presented. This requires a model of maturity. A model of maturity is implied in my theory of the unconscious effects of social and cultural constraints. This model is based on modifications to the model of 'genital maturity' in traditional psychoanalysis. Genital maturity emphasizes the capacity to procreate, to love and to relate to other people within the context of a biologically based phase of development denoted by a 'balanced' superego, indicating a satisfactory resolution of the Oedipus complex (Pollack and Ross 1988). This rather simplified version of the classical model has many precursors within western and other traditions of thought and therapy (Rustomjee 1993), and many modifications to it have been suggested by both psychoanalysts and others in the field of human development. For example, many (Brown 1961) have argued that social relationships require more emphasis, because they are the basis of the development of intra-psychic object relations, rather than the other way around. The idea that social and cultural patterns of love and love relationships establish situations that people must negotiate in order to mature, is not central to psychoanalytical thought. Nor is the idea that the

Oedipus complex is resolved in terms of socially structured domestic authority and power, and also in terms of the normative basis of passivity and activity, within the context of the total system of stratification of the wider society (Malinowski 1937). For example, the normal Oedipus complex in the Southern Italian rural family is not normal for a Northern Italian industrial family (Parsons 1957); what is normal in Tel Aviv is not normal for certain kibbutzim (Bettelheim 1969); and, to flog a dead horse, what is normal in Rye, New York, is not normal in University City, Missouri, in Taiwan or Hampstead or Hampstead Garden Suburb. The Oedipus complex is an ideal type for purposes of illustration and theory building. Clinical work requires specific contextualisation, because abnormality can only be understood in terms of normality, which is always defined in terms of the social and cultural context (Joseph, E. 1982).

Another modification of the classical model of maturity is that maturity involves the willingness and ability to work. Of course, to 'work' has many meanings: eating and doing what is necessary in order to eat; defecating in order to avoid indigestion as well as to repay Mother and to give her presents, which may be based on a bargain that has been struck unconsciously in terms of the exchange value of milk and faeces, which itself may be based on the value that Mother has placed on her feeding and that Baby has put on the work involved in good sucking. However, male and female parental power and influence are based on being able to fulfill an occupational role and to derive both primary and secondary pleasures from it. In fact, the identity of an adult is governed by his location within the world of work, as is the antici-patory identity of a child, and certainly, an adolescent. Work occurs in occupational roles that are part of a specific system of economic, status and political stratification that implies specific authority and power structures and a status quo, which says more than that occupational roles exist in complex organizations with authority structures (Richards 1948).[6]

There is, however, yet another theme in the critique of the traditional model of psychological maturity. It was first raised by Erich Fromm (1963) in a little-known paper called 'The Revolutionary Character'. I rather like the title, but I can see that some people might be bothered by the connotations of revolution, and by the even more disturbing fact that the book in which it was published was entitled The Dogma of Christ. Fromm writes:

> 'The Revolutionary Character' is someone who is identified with humanity, and therefore transcends the narrow limits of his own society and who is able therefore to criticize his or any other society. He is not caught in the

parochial culture in which he happens to be born, which is nothing but an accident of time and geography. He is able to look at his environment with the open eyes of a man who is awake and who finds the criteria of judging the accidental and that which is not accidental according to the norms which are in and for the human race. (p.111)

By 'revolutionary character' Fromm really means 'the mature person', rather than a character type or character disorder. He is suggesting a stage of development in which a person can be sufficiently detached to be able to take his social circumstances as problematic, but sufficiently involved to be able to identify with them and to be affected by them and, in turn, to be willing to affect them. To reach a point whereby one can be compassionate, sympathetic and empathetic, yet sufficiently detached to take a situation as problematic, is really a great psychological achievement. An infant cannot do this. Human beings must strive to achieve a sense of balance between involvement and detachment, and such balance indicates that a certain kind of maturity has been reached. Fromm would say: that which is not accidental is that which is rational, or at least which can be explained rationally, according to the laws of science or even of social science. The mature person is one who has been able to transcend the limits of his own particular background, and, therefore, to reflect upon his circumstances, to take them as problematic and to locate them within their historical and contemporary social context. He is able and willing to think about his own psychic life and that of others, his own inter-personal community and that of others, and about his own identity and that of others (Fonagy 1989). He will be aware of the relativity of social and personal ethics, even if ignorant of the language needed to discuss it; and he will have considered the traditional free will/determinism problem, even if he has never learned that the idea that we must try not only to understand reality but also to change it was a Marxist, revolutionary idea. The revolutionary character will be able and willing to take the risks involved in attempting to change the very social circumstances within which he has come to be able to think, to make judgements, to act and to be creative.

An essential feature of increased 'psychic muscle' is the ability to withstand and even to make creative use of social resistance to revolutionary action. The revolutionary character must be able to make the social unconscious conscious, which compliments the traditional idea that maturity requires the substitution of ego for id. Obviously, attacks on authority are not always an expression of unresolved Oedipal struggles, just as attempts by those in authority to maintain the status quo are not always an expression of their sense of responsibility and probity.

We could include this idea of the revolutionary character within 'genital maturity', but it seems to me that the concept of a revolutionary character subsumes the concept of genital maturity. This is the essence of de Maré's (1991) concept of citizenship: 'maturity' implies the willingness and the ability to take the roles associated with the status of 'citizen'. Of course, this is also a group phenomenon in that people cannot take such roles if they have not also ensured that citizenship is available, which is a political process.[7] The willingness and ability to take the roles of citizenship and to ensure that such roles exist within a democratic society can be facilitated through what Foulkes and Anthony (1984) termed 'ego training in action'.

I will now illustrate the clinical relevance of these ideas by describing certain aspects of the behavior and feelings of three members of the Groups presented above. In the first Group, the man who expressed so poignantly his frustrations arising from his work with colleagues, who were members of the medical profession, became more active in the politics of his profession and in his hospital. He initiated a new committee consisting of both medical and non-medical personnel, and it seemed that this committee would do some good work in alleviating the anxious concerns that were interfering with the clinical work in his particular department. This man was an immigrant. He became more proficient in understanding other sub-cultures as well as his own, because he recognized that his own 'world view' (Serrano and Ruiz 1990) was problematic, that is, based on a number of dimensions of his life experience which were not shared by others. It was then possible for him to adopt the folk ways and styles of his colleagues and the new culture within which his work roles and life in general were embedded. In his political activities within his hospital he conducted himself with determination and resolve, but also with dignity and self-control, despite the usual pressures put upon him by his opponents, especially those in authority.

Another personal development can be seen in the self-image and actions of the woman who was so concerned about the welfare of her father. She was able to take the necessary and appropriate steps to arrange proper care for him, which included both medical and non-medical intervention, and in general was able to help her entire family respond constructively to this domestic catastrophe. She acknowledged that when she thought about her vulnerable father, she thought about him as her 'Jewish father', and connected this image with her inability to make relationships with Jewish men, who she felt were 'weak' and 'feminine'. This caused her some sense of confusion because she wanted to please herself as well as her parents who wanted her to marry a Jew. She also acknowledged that she thought of herself as a Jewish boy or specifically as a Jewish son who could feel herself to be a woman only in relation to Christian men. Eventually she may recognize her desire to be mothered by the women whom she perceives to be behind the men in her life, but in the meantime she is in the process of discovering that it is possible to negotiate her own gender identity, although, for reasons of both biology and of sociology, not entirely as she pleases.

A third personal development, or lack of it, is manifest, as discussed in the second vignette, in the case of the homosexual psychiatrist from abroad who wished to become a group analyst. He became convinced that homosexuality was a counter-indication for acceptance for training by the Institute despite assurances and evidence to the contrary. Rather than confront the relevant committees and their perceived policies, he renounced his aspirations. He was unable to make use of the views offered by the other members of the Group and myself that not only was he frightened to be judged and assessed by authorities whom he respected, but he was also terrified to learn more about how he used his homosexuality to defend against psychotic anxieties, and to express his sadomasochistic desires. Following a prolonged period of hatred of another male candidate, he left the Group at short notice. I was unable to communicate to him in a meaningful way that he was repeating his hatred of his 'chosen' little brother, and his conviction that I preferred his brother to him, as would the Institute. I would regard this as an example of a therapeutic failure – mine, and his.

These data illustrate how, by making it possible for Groups to work in the second and fourth cells of the two paradigms that I have described, people were able to take some steps towards becoming what Fromm called a 'revolutionary character'. They became more ready to participate as citizens, and they developed their sense that they could make history as well as be made by it.

Afterthoughts

Rather than draw conclusions in the usual sense, I would emphasize two of the sub-texts of my thesis. The open and honest discussion of traumatic events and their consequences should not be confined to situations that have been defined as 'therapy'. In democratic societies this always presents a dilemma: if space is not provided for working through traumatic events, they will never be worked through; and if space is provided, those in power will have to deal with threats to their authority. Unresolved, this dilemma usually stops those in authority from providing the space for full discussion, and gives rise to situations that require the exercise of managerial power over and over again, because traumatic events tend to be repeated over and over again, not only in societies but also in organizations of various kinds ranging from large industrial firms to child guidance clinics. I am reminded of Winnicott's statement that people in psychoanalytical treatment often get worse before they get better, the clinical observation that very depressed patients often commit suicide just after their depression starts to lift, and the sociological insight that revolutions occur just after there have been dramatic improvements in the standards of living of deprived sections of the population, especially in the lower middle classes. I would prefer to work with such possibilities than to suffer the repetition of catastrophes.

It may not be possible for psychotherapy to help break these vicious circles. I do not suggest that if we could just talk in therapy groups about, for example, the situation in Northern Ireland, terrorism would stop and peace would erupt. However, it must be acknowledged that the study of the social unconscious is neglected in the training of group analysts, and is utterly ignored in the training of psychoanalysts (Hopper 1985, a version of which is reprinted as Chapter 5 of this book). Unless candidates are encouraged to think in these terms, and at least to reflect upon the key debates in the development of psychoanalysis and all forms of group psychotherapy, they can hardly be expected to be sensitive to the questions and problems that I have described. Our training programs reflect the unconscious constraints of social, cultural and political aspects of our profession and of the societies in which it functions. In societies with a high degree of status rigidity and with education systems characterized by premature specialization in either the natural sciences or the arts, the social sciences are defined as peripheral to knowledge, in parallel with categories of people whose qualifications are defined as inferior and marginal. Selection processes in these societies are based on theories of intelligence and mobility that emphasize the importance of the innate as opposed to the environmental, and such processes are repeated in later professional training. However, in all societies physicians are especially at risk. Immigrants and refugees, who may include the socially and geographically mobile, find it easier to learn about social facts and social forces, and to do the intellectual and emotional work that is required in order to explore the trans-cultural aspects of personal identity. Nonetheless, marginality can generate a search for a professional identity that overrides social and cultural diversity and dislocation (Budd and Hopper 1992). Perhaps this is one of the reasons why professional training in psychotherapy is characterized by an unacceptable degree of religiosity.

It is time to consider the prevailing and ascendant definitions of the boundaries of psychoanalysis and group analysis, with their implications for the structure of training programs and patterns of professional identities and affiliations. It is possible to improve our system of professional training, but not if we continue to deny the importance of the social unconscious in both our theories and our clinical work. The Kleinian aphorism may be correct that when it comes to helping patients understand how they are constrained by external social and political events, analysts are no better than any other Tom, Dick or Harriet. But I would argue that they should be, and that some of the social sciences should be an obligatory part of their training, at least as much as – if not more than – the study of biology and physiology. The irony in Freud's aside to Jones 'Out of this world we will not fall', was misplaced. He might just as well have said 'Out of our bodies we will not fall'. Actually, both points of view are essential.

References

Austen, J. (1995) [1811] *Sense and Sensibility.* London: Penguin Books. (Original work published 1811.)

Bellow, S. (1970) *Mr. Sammler's Planet.* London: Weidenfeld and Nicholson.

Bendix, R. (1966) 'A memoir of my father.' *The Canadian Revue of Sociology and Anthropology 2*, 1, 1–27.

Bettelheim, B. (1969) *Children of the Dream.* London: Thames and Hudson.

Bion, W. (1961) *Experiences in Groups.* London: Tavistock.

Bleger, J. (1966) 'Psychoanalysis of the psychoanalytic frame.' *International Journal of Psycho-Analysis 48*, 4, 511–519.

Bollas, C. (1987) *The Shadow of the Object.* London: Free Association Press.

Britton, R. (1994) 'The blindness of the seeing eye: Inverse symmetry as a defence against reality.' *Psychoanalytical Inquiry 14*, 3, 365–378.

Brown, J. (1961) *Freud and the Post-Freudians.* Harmondsworth: Penguin.

Budd, S. and Hopper, E. (1992) 'The reception of psychoanalysis in Great Britain: A sociological approach.' International Association for the History of Psychoanalysis Conference on a Comparative History of the Early Stages of Psychoanalysis in Europe, Brussels, September.

Burman, R. and Roel, G. (1986) Personal communications.

de Maré, P. (1972) *Perspectives Group Psychotherapy.* London: Allen and Unwin.

de Maré, P. (1991) *Koinonia.* London: Karnac Books.

Erikson, E. (1959) *Identity and the Life Cycle.* New York: International University Press.

Fonagy, P. (1989) 'On tolerating mental states.' *Bulletin of The Anna Freud Centre 12*, 91–115.

Foulkes, S. H. (1964) *Therapeutic Group Analysis*. London: Allen and Unwin.

Foulkes, S. H. and Anthony, E. J. (1984) [1957] *Group Psychotherapy: The Psychoanalytic Approach*. London: Karnac. (Original work published 1957.)

Fromm, E. (1962) 'The Social Unconscious'. In *Beyond the Chains of Illusion: My Encounter with Marx and Freud*. New York: Simon and Schuster.

Fromm, E. (1963) 'The Revolutionary Character'. In *The Dogma of Christ*, New York: Holt, Rinehart and Winston.

Fromm, E. (1984) [1930] *The Working Class in Weimar Germany: A Psychological & Sociological Study*, trans. Barbara Weinberger, Cambridge, Mass: Harward University Press. (Original work published 1930.)

Gaddini, E. (1992) *A Psychoanalytic Theory of Infantile Experience*. A. Limentani (ed). London: Routledge.

Hopper, E. (1965) 'Some effects of supervisory style: A sociological analysis.' *British Journal of Sociology XVI*, 3, 189-203

Hopper, E. (1981) *Social Mobility: A Study of Social Control and Insatiability*. Oxford: Basil Blackwell Publisher Ltd.

Hopper, E. (1985) 'The Problem of Context in Group Analytic Psychotherapy: A Clinical Illustration and Brief Theoretical Discussion.' In M. Pines (ed) *Bion and Group Psychotherapy*. London: Routledge and Kegan Paul.

Hopper, E. (1989a). *Psychotic anxieties and society: Fission (fragmentation)/fusion and aggregation/massification*. Royal College of Psychiatry. Cambridge, UK.

Hopper, E. (1989b). 'Aggregation/massification and fission (fragmentation)/fusion: A fourth basic assumption?' For the Eighth International Conference of the International Association of Group Psychotherapy, Amsterdam.

Hopper, E. (1990). 'The Treatment In Groups of People With Borderline and Narcissistic Disturbances.' *Informex Cassettes*. Annual Conference of the AGPA. San Antonio.

Hopper, E. (1991) 'Encapsulation as a defence against the fear of annihilation.' *International Journal of Psycho-Analysis 72*, 4, 607–624.

Hopper, E. (1992) 'A comment on Spillius, E. "Two ways of experiencing envy".' *The British Psycho-Analytical Society Bulletin* December 28, 11, 15-16.

Hopper, E. (1993) 'Hope And Dread In A Group of Child Survivors of The Shoah. Panel on Trauma.' *Informex Cassettes*. Annual Conference of the American Group Psychotherapy Association. San Diego.

Hopper, E. (1994) [1975] 'A Sociological View of Large Groups.' In L. Kreeger (ed) *The Large Group: Dynamics and Therapy*. London: Karnac (Books) Ltd. (Original work published 1975)

Hopper, E. (1994a) 'L'incapsulamento come difesa contro il timore di annientamento.' *Plexus… Lo spazio del gruppo*, September, 103–128.

Hopper, E. (1997) 'Traumatic experience in the unconscious life of groups: A fourth basic assumption.' *Group Analysis 30*, 4, 439–470.

Hopper, E. (2000) 'From objects and subjects to citizens: Group analysis and the study of maturity.' *Group Analysis 33*, 1, 29–34.

Hopper, E. (2001) 'Difficult patients in Group analysis: the personification of (ba) I:A/M.' *Group 25*, 3, 139–171.

Hopper, E. (2003) *The Fourth Basic Assumption in the Unconscious Life of Groups*. London: Jessica Kingsley Publishers. In Press.

Hopper, E. and Kreeger L. (1980) 'Report on the Large Group'. In C. Garland (ed) *Proceedings of the Survivor Syndrome Workshop*. London: Institute of Group Analysis, November, 67-81.

Hopper, E. and Osborn, M. (1975) *Adult Students: Education, Selection and Social Control*. London: Frances Pinter.

Horney, K. (1937) *The Neurotic Personality of our Time*. Norton: New York.

Joseph, B. (1989). 'Transference: the total situation.' *International Journal of Psycho-Analysis 66*, 4, 447–454.

Joseph, E. (1982) 'Normal in psychoanalysis.' *International Journal of Psycho-Analysis 62*, 3, 3–13.

Jung, C. (1951) *On Synchronicity, Collected Works 8*, paragraphs 965–97 and 816–868. London: Routledge and Kegan Paul.

Kaes, R. (1979) 'Introduction a l'analyse transitionelle.' In R. Kaes (ed) *Crise, Rupture et Dépassement*. Paris: Dunod.

Kernberg, O. (1993) 'The couple's constructive and destructive superego functions.' *Journal of the American Psychoanalytic Association 41*, 3, 653–677.

Kinston, W. and Cohen, J. (1986) 'Primal repression: Clinical and theoretical aspects.' *International Journal of Psycho-Analysis 67*, 3, 337–56.

Khaleelee, O. and Miller, E. (1985) 'Beyond the Small Group.' In M. Pines, (ed) *Bion and Group Psychotherapy*. London: Routledge and Kegan Paul.

Klein, E. (1993) Personal communication.

Kohut, H. and Wolf, E. (1978) 'The disorders of the self and their treatment: An outline.' *International Journal of Psycho-Analysis 59*, 4, 414–425.

Koller, P., Marmar, C. and Kanas, N. (1992) 'Psychodynamic group treatment of post-traumatic stress disorder in Vietnam Veterans.' *International Journal of Group Psychotherapy 42*, 2, 225–245.

Koller, P. (1993) 'Contribution. Panel on Trauma.' *Informex Cassettes*. Annual Conference of the AGPA, San Diego.

Kroll, L. (1992) Personal communication.

Lacan, J. (1977) *Ecrits*. Trans. A. Sheridan. London: Tavistock.

Lawrence, G. (1991) 'Won from the void and formless infinite: Experiences of social dreaming.' *Free Associations 2*, 22, 259–294.

Le Roy, J. (1994) 'Group Analysis and Culture.' In D. Brown and L. Zinkin (eds) *The Psyche and The Social World*. London: Routledge.

LeVine, R. (1973) *Culture, Behaviour and Personality*. Chicago: Aldine.

Malan, D. (1979) *Individual Psychotherapy and the Science of Psychodynamics*. London: Butterworths.

Malinowski, B. (1937) *Sex and Repression in a Savage Society*. London : Routledge and Kegan Paul.

Maslow, A. (1954) 'The instinctoid nature of basic needs.' *Journal of Personality 22*, 1, 340–341.

Miles, B. (1993) 'Contribution. Panel on Trauma.' *Informex Cassettes*. Annual Conference of the American Group Psychotherapy Association. San Diego.

Mitchell, S. (1994) *Hope and Dread in Psychoanalysis*. New York: Basic Books.

Moreno, J. (1934) *Who Shall Survive?* Washington, D.C.: Nervous and Mental Disease Publishing Company.

Moreno, J. (1959) [1954–55]'Interpersonal therapy, group psychotherapy and the function of the unconscious.' *Psychodrama 2*. New York: Beacon House (Original work published 1954-55).

Parsons, A. (1957) *Belief, Magic and Anomie*. New York: The Free Press.

Pedder, J. (1988) 'Termination reconsidered.' *International Journal of Psycho-Analysis 69*, 4, 495–505.

Pollack, G. and Ross, J. (1988) *The Oedipus Papers*. New York: International Universities Press.

Puget, J. (1989) 'Groupe analytique et formation.' *Revue de Psychotherapie Psychoanalitique de Groupe 13*, 137–54.

Richards, A. (1948) *Hunger and Work in a Savage Tribe*. Glencoe, Ill: The Free Press.

Roth, P. (1995) [1967] *Portnoy's Complaint*. London: Vintage. (Original work published 1967.)

Rouchy, J. C. (1987) 'Identité culturelle et groupes d'appartenance.' *Revue de Psychotherapie Psychoanalytique de Groupe 9*, 2, 31–41.

Rustomjee, S. (1993) 'Traversing the Psychoanalytic Pathway.' Paper presented at the Third Pacific Rim Regional Congress, Taiwan, September.

Serrano, A. and Ruiz, E. (1990) 'Transferential and Cultural Issues in Group Psychotherapy.' In S. Tuttman (ed) *Psychoanalytic Group: Theory and Therapy*. Madison, Connecticut: International Universities Press.

Sheldrake, R. (1987) *New Science of Life: Hypothesis of Formative Causation*. London: Paladin Books.

Simon, B. (1992) 'Incest – see under Oedipus Complex: The history of an error in psychoanalysis.' *Journal of the American Psychoanalytic Association 40*, 4, 955–988.

Spector-Person, E. (1992) 'Romantic Love: At the Intersection of the Psyche and the Cultural Unconscious.' In T. Shapiro and R. Emde (eds) *Affect: Psychoanalytic Perspective*. New York: International Universities Press.

Spillius, E. (ed) (1988) *Melanie Klein Today*. London: Routledge.

Strindberg, J. A. (1992) [1878] *Miss Julie*. London: Reed Consumer Books. (Original work published 1878.)

Turquet, P. (1994) [1975] 'Threats to Identity in the Large Group.' In L. Kreeger (ed) *The Large Group: Dynamics and Therapy*. London: Karnac (Books) Ltd. (Original work published 1975.)

Tustin, F. (1981) *Autistic States in Children*. London : Routledge and Kegan Paul.

Weber, M. (1947) *The Theory of Social and Economic Organization*. T. Parsons (ed) New York: Oxford University Press.

Winnicott, D. (1965) *The Maturational Process and the Facilitating Environment*. New York: International Universities Press.

Zinkin, L. (1979) 'The collective and the personal.' *Journal of Analytic Psychology 74*, 3, 227–250.

Notes

1   Although drafted in the mid-1980s, this chapter was first published in 1994 as 'Il tempo del cambiamento', in F. di Maria and G. Lavanco (eds) *Nel Nome Del Gruppo*, Palermo: Arke; in 1996 as 'Das gesellschaftliche Unbewußte in der klinischen Arbeit: Reflexionen über die "vollstandige Deutung" und die "Quadratur des therapeutischen Dreiecks" in *Gruppenanalyse 6*,1, 67–113; and in *Mekbatz 2*, 2, 7–75. The first and definitive version in English was published in 1996 as 'The social unconscious in clinical work' in *Group 20*, 1, 7–42. Excerpts were published in 1997 in *The Official Journal of the Japan Association of Group Psychotherapy 13*, 2, 184–187. A slightly revised version was published in 1999 in C. Oakley (ed) *What is a Group? A New Look at Theory in Practice*, London: Rebus Press. Parts of this chapter were developed as a tribute to Pat de Maré and his work in 'From objects and subjects to citizens: Group analysis and the study of maturity' in 2000 in *Group Analysis 33*, 1, 29–34. Excerpts were also published in 2001 as 'The social unconscious: theoretical considerations' in a Special Issue of *Group Analysis 34*, 1, 9–29. This work has benefited from my discussions of it with Anna Aguirregabiria, Dennis Brown, Barbara Elliot, Hans Reijzer, and David and Jill Scharff, and through interaction with live audiences in Berlin, Lisbon, London, Melbourne, Palermo, Stockholm, Sydney, Tel Aviv and Washington, D.C.

2   Although Karen Horney (1937) was the first psychoanalyst to apply the 'social unconscious' to clinical work in a creative and systematic way, the concept was introduced by Fromm (1930, 1962). It has never gained popular usage, perhaps because it has an oxymoronic quality: although suggesting radical intentions, it is based on an organismic analogy that has conservative implications. The ideas that underpin the concept have a long history in the social sciences, and include the work of Durkheim, Weber and especially Marx.

The tradition of Marxist thought is now so politicized that we forget how much we are indebted to it for our understanding of such topics as alienation and the sociality of human nature, and for attempts to integrate 'system' and 'action' perspectives. My own appreciation of the concept of the social unconscious has been influenced by the work of American sociologists such as Merton, Reisman, Gerth and Mills, and of those American anthropologists who developed the field of 'culture and personality' (Le Vine 1973). Of special interest is 'A memoir of my father' by Bendix (1966), an entirely overlooked study of the personification of social forces within the traditions of Frankfurt Sociology. Winnicott (1965) was searching for the concept when he introduced the notion of 'environmental mother', as was Kernberg (1993) in his recent studies of shared superego functions within the couple. Puget (1989), Kaës (1979) and Rouchy (1987) are each attempting to elucidate the concept of the social unconscious, as illustrated most recently by Le Roy (1994). A number of novelists and dramatists have demonstrated their understanding of the social unconscious, as exemplified by *Sense and Sensibility* by Jane Austen (1811), *Portnoy's Complaint* by Phillip Roth (1967) and *Miss Julie* by Strindberg (1878), not to mention Shakespeare in virtually every play he wrote.

The concept of the social unconscious differs from the traditional Jungian concept of the collective unconscious, with its emphasis on the inheritance of acquired characteristics. However, it is similar to more contemporary Jungian views of the 'shared unconscious', which emphasize the interpersonal, the inter-subjective and socialization in general (Zinkin 1979). It is also similar to the 'cultural unconscious' introduced by the American psychoanalyst Ethel Spector-Person (1992) in her recent article 'Romantic Love: at the Intersection of the Psyche and the Cultural Unconscious'.

'Social unconscious', 'shared unconscious' and 'cultural unconscious' are reminiscent of the past debates between American and British anthropologists about the differences between what used to be called American 'cultural' anthropology and British 'social' anthropology. It was said that American social scientists were somehow unable to work with problems of social constraints and power structures, were more interested in problems of personal adjustment and adaptation of individuals to their circumstances, and were unable to recognize that culture develops both within and in response to social and political arrangements, which are themselves not made in heaven. Of course, British anthropologists were only able to make these claims because they focused their attention on tribal societies rather than on Britain itself.

3   In one way or another equivalence has been studied by many in our own and in adjacent fields. Especially pertinent are the studies of social dreaming by Lawrence (1991), and of the social concerns of groups by Khaleelee and Miller (1985). So, too, is the novel *Mr Sammler's Planet* by Bellow (1970). Moreno's (1954-55) discussions of synchronicitous events in terms of inter-subjectivity are helpful. Jung (1951) was attempting to discuss equivalence when he discussed 'synchronicity', but he became preoccupied with the mystical connections between coincidental events. In this tradition, the 'alternative scientist' Sheldrake (1987) describes in terms of 'morphic resonance' what he postulates to be the increased rate at which certain events occur (or recur) following the incidence of a prototype event.

4   This aphorism implies that our interventions will always be political actions that give value to some phenomena and devalue others, and will always reflect our own location within an infinite field of time and space, of which it is impossible ever to be fully conscious, although this is not to suggest that we are free from the obligation to try. It is through disciplined self-reflection upon this matter by which the professional is distinguished from the amateur, no matter how talented and well-meaning the latter may be.

5   Since writing this paper, I (Hopper 1989a, b, 1990, 1991, 1992, 1993, 1994a) have discussed elsewhere my ideas about encapsulation in groups and its basis in processes of aggregation and massification as bi-polar forms of incohesion. This is a fourth basic assumption (Hopper 1997) in the unconscious life of groups and group-like social systems, as manifest in their interaction, normation and communication systems. The characteristics of people who are most likely to become the personifiers of this particular basic assumption group are what Tustin (1981) called 'crustacean' and 'amoeboid' forms of autistic encapsulation as typical bio-psychological protective responses to severe trauma. They are linked to what Kohut and Wolf (1978) termed 'contact avoidance' and 'merger hunger', and to different aspects of what Bleger (1966) termed 'epiloid states' in response to 'ambiguity'. This is the foundation of my work in groups with people who have borderline and narcissistic disorders, and with those who have survived massive social trauma. Groups of victims of trauma of various kinds e.g., war in the Old Yugoslavia (Klein 1993), social collapse in the old USSR (Kroll 1992), earthquakes in Mexico (Burman and Roel 1986), the military dictatorship in Argentina (Puget 1989), concentration camps (Hopper 1993), child sexual abuse (Miles 1993), and the Vietnam war (Koller 1993; Koller, Marmar and Kanas 1992), all evince very similar processes. For a comprehensive statement of my theory of Incohesion: Aggregation/ Massification or (ba) I:A/M and its applications to clinical group analysis, see Hopper (2001) and Hopper (2003).

6   It is necessary at least to mention the work of Maslow (1954) and many others on the stages of life from birth (if not conception) to death, with particular emphasis on maturation throughout the life cycle. Erikson (1959) gave special emphasis to the impor-

tance of social and cultural constraints for the continuing development of the ego. Lacan (1977) stressed that maturation is never complete in that, virtually by definition, it is impossible to fulfill the aphorism that where id was, there shall ego be. Many of these ideas have been discussed in connection with the issue of termination in psychoanalysis (Pedder 1988). The 'Kleinian development' (Spillius 1988) implies that 'maturation' and 'termination' be reconsidered more fundamentally in terms of the stability of depressive position functioning, the security of the internal good object and the capacity to feel gratitude. In emphasizing the constraints of parental character rather than instincts, the inter-personalists have taken up similar themes in their polemic against both classical Freudian and classical Kleinian schools, but are wary of going beyond the confines of the bi-personal field (Mitchell 1994).

7   The idea of 'citizenship' may be contrasted with Turquet's (1975) notion that being an 'individual member' of a group is an indication of maturity. I have discussed this in the context of my theory of Incohesion: Aggregation/Massification or (ba) I:A/M as a fourth basic assumption, and have suggested that 'singletons' are prevalent during states of aggregation, and 'membership individuals' during states of massification. (Since writing this paper, I have developed this idea in Hopper (2000)).

CHAPTER 7

Wounded Bird

A Study of the Social Unconscious and Countertransference in Group Analysis[1]

In this chapter I will illustrate the constraints of the social unconscious with clinical data from one of my groups which met twice a week for the purpose of psychotherapy. However, I will focus on the constraints of various social, cultural, economic and political factors on my countertransference. I will also show how 'getting in touch' with these constraints helped me to free the group from their compulsion to enact their unconscious perceptions of my internal world, and, thus, to think about themselves more deeply and more passionately.

Unless countertransference processes are subjected to continuous scrutiny, various scotomata and personal conflicts and preoccupations are likely to interfere with analytical neutrality, objectivity and the maintenance of free-floating attention. It is, therefore, especially important to illustrate countertransference processes, both as defensive phenomena and as tools for understanding unconscious communication, which is the essence of the inter-subjective nature of psychic reality and our ability to perceive our internal worlds.

Clinical data about countertransference processes are rarely presented.[2] It is often believed that information about an analyst limits his patients' scope for fantasy, and, therefore, their ability to understand communications primarily in terms of unconscious meanings. Also, it is difficult for an analyst to acknowledge that he is not quite as mature as he would wish, or as the idealizations by his favorite patients and students would suggest, especially in public, despite the evidence that sometimes patients benefit from a greater symmetry of authority and power within the analytical space.

Clinical data about the constraints of the social unconscious are also rarely presented.[3] Partly this stems from the fact that clinicians are rarely trained in the social sciences. Although group analysis draws upon sociology and social psychology, group psychotherapy generally and psychoanalytical group therapy in particular do not, which is why it is often assumed, incorrectly, that the constraints of the social unconscious are a matter of the 'pre-conscious', and, therefore, that they are more shallow and superficial than the constraints of the continuing personal, biologically based dynamic unconscious of the mental life of infancy. In fact, these two psychic structures and realms of experience are completely intertwined.

If little is known about the use of countertransference processes, and still less about the constraints of the social unconscious, the constraints of the social unconscious on the countertransference are only barely understood. Virtually nothing has been written about how an analyst uses insights into the origins and maintenance of his social identity in order better to understand his patients.[4] It is likely that he has been taught that an interest in social identity is defensive against anxieties associated with impulses and fantasies that are 'unconscious', in the usual sense of the term. He might need to protect himself against anxieties associated with helplessness and power-lessness to improve the circumstances of his patients, and against feelings of guilt about his comparative well being (Hopper 1985, a version of which is reprinted as Chapter 5 of this book). He might also need to protect himself against the pain of narcissistic injury associated with insights into the many ways in which his freedom to think and to feel is limited, which is especially troublesome to those who base their work on the premise that 'insight' is both liberating and therapeutic. Yet, another reason why this topic has been neglected might be that the constraints of the social unconscious are often studied in connection with the experience of social trauma, which is prevalent among the members of the mental health professions, who wish to avoid their own anxieties of loss, damage and abandonment within the clinical setting. Whatever the reason for these lacunae, it is important to accumulate a body of literature about the origins of countertransference processes within the 'There and Then' and 'There and Now'.

Before turning to the clinical vignette, I would like to indicate several concerns that I have about publishing this material. It is impossible to write about countertransference processes without self-disclosure. However, I have tried to avoid gratuitous and confessional self-disclosure. I have tried to confine myself to information that seems relevant to my main argument. Nonetheless, the material presented here may arouse anxiety that interferes with communication and thought. I do not know how to prevent this, but I would like to emphasize that I am writing about the social unconscious as honestly as possible in an attempt to maximize the dignity afforded to each and every human being.

I will try to capture the truth of my experience as a clinical group analyst, and to make some sense of it. Yet, it must be acknowledged that *in situ* countertransference processes are barely conscious. They are likely to be fleeting, chaotic and volatile. Writing about them gives a false sense of coherence.

I will organize this presentation in phases: the group's communications, including my interpretations and conscious thoughts and feelings, punctuated by my countertransference processes, followed by further material from the group, again punctuated by my countertransference, and so on. There is much that can be said about the material, and much that I could have said but have not. I will not discuss this presentation, but will simply allow it to stand. For emphasis, I will repeat these last two sentences. *There is much that can be said about the material, and much that I could have said but have not. I will not 'discuss' this presentation, but will simply allow it to stand.*

The clinical vignette

1. This twice-weekly heterogeneous group of adults was composed of four men and four women plus myself. The youngest member was twenty-seven years of age, and the eldest was sixty-four years of age. They were all 'middle class'. They had all graduated from universities. Three members of the group were in the mental health professions. The group had been meeting for more than a decade in a room within the premises of a group practice in Central London.

2. Of the eight members of the group, three formed themselves into a con-tra-group. This contra-group became an 'institutionalized' defense against free-floating communication.

    One of the members of the contra-group was a 'Black' man. I use this term in its current sense, not only to convey Afro-Caribbean descent, but also the wish to make a political statement. 'Black' means 'not-white', perhaps in the same way that the assertion of identity may be based on 'not-me' processes. I will call him James.

James was born in an extremely impoverished village in Barbados (in this case a fictitious island). His father was an unskilled, uneducated agricultural worker. His mother and older sisters were the main providers of income and domestic stability. He was the youngest of thirteen children, but another child was born after he came to England when he was fifteen years of age.

He did extremely well at his new fee-paying school, which had a Church connection. This school had brought over many black children from the Islands. It was founded in the early 1800s by a few people whose families had earned their wealth through the slave trade. James said that its ostensible purpose was to give 'boys' a 'better life'. During his initial interview he said that although when he left Barbados he experienced an intense sense of loss, after a fairly brief period of chronic nausea he became psychically numb. As he put it, 'I forgot all about it'.

After acquiring a Master's degree in Sociology, James became a social worker. He worked hard to maintain an identification with people of poverty and of color and with West Indians in particular, while at the same time to enter the professional middle classes in London. He had developed a personal style marked by a curious mixture of ambition and ingratiating submissive-ness. He felt that he had repaid his benefactors handsomely.

Whenever James talked at any length, he began to perspire heavily, and became embarrassed and ashamed. Sometimes he became explosive, and began to stutter and stammer. Other members of the Group would then avert their gaze from him or become politely over-attentive. He would then calm down and try again to speak. If he could not communicate what he had intended, he would miss the next two or three groups.

James usually sat between two women. To me he often seemed to be a baby on their laps or on the Group's lap.

One of the women was a Jewish South African of East European and Russian origins. Around forty years of age, she was an attractive, shapely brunette.[5] If her parents had taken another boat or another route from Russia, she would have been born in an American city or perhaps an English one. As a result of her political activities, she had to leave her country and her family. She came to England in the 1960s in order to read Sociology at a well-known institution of higher education in London. In effect, she reversed the immigration process by repeating the experience of being a refugee. I will call her Sharon.

Although Sharon had been given an intensive initial, diagnostic interview by the senior psychiatrist who referred her to me, her notes contained curiously little information about her recent life. Therefore, I interviewed her again. The middle of three sisters, she stressed that her father always wanted at least one son, and that all three daughters had disappointed him. Sharon's recall of detail from her early life contrasted with her sense of vagueness and blank spaces about her more recent life. She described herself as a 'left-wing feminist'. She said that she was frightened that the psychiatrist and I would denigrate her efforts to forge an independent life, and was reluctant to give us much information. At the same time she wanted help, more from a group than from either a male or a female analyst, towards whom she was ambivalent. I learned that at two years of age, when her mother was pregnant, she had an accident in the kitchen and was very badly scalded on her breasts and upper arms. Her father, a successful businessman, was somehow unavailable, and remained 'out of the picture'.

Sharon was preoccupied – if not obsessed – with James. He was not merely an 'object of interest'. She regarded him as a kind of 'Black Messiah'. She was constantly trying to help him, look after him, give him advice, and so on. When he perspired she was the first to offer him a tissue, in much the same way that certain patients are always the first to offer a tissue to someone who cries. Although she was genuinely interested in him, she often tried to be my co-conductor, offering him warmth and support in parallel with my interpretations. Sometimes, this seemed to be co-operative, but often it seemed to be competitive, in that my interventions were deemed to be cold and unfeeling, and greeted with a raised eyebrow or a change in her posture that was intended to convey her contempt for my comments. However, the more she tried to administer to his needs, the more anxious James became.

The other woman who composed the lap on which James sat was English and upper middle class by birth. She was the eldest of seven children from one father and three mothers. Her own mother committed suicide when she was five years of age, shortly after the birth of a younger brother. Her father was a very successful businessman. Of considerable wealth, she traced her family back to the late 1500s . Archetypically English in appearance and style, she had pale skin and blonde hair. She had come to the group for help with her marriage and with her general sense of boredom. She admired powerful men and felt that she understood them. However, she complained that her husband was a 'weak' man, and very dependent on her, as all of her boyfriends had been. Occasionally, she had affairs with powerful men, but she always returned to her husband, for which she held herself in contempt, recognizing that she was as dependent on him as he was on her. She traveled up to London from Somerset on two evenings a week, usually by train, sometimes staying overnight. This was quite an effort, and reflected her deep and sustained commitment to her therapy and to the Group. I will call her Penelope.

Penelope felt herself to be closer to me than Sharon was. Penelope regarded me as the source of power in the Group. She was very competitive with Sharon, and regarded her with contempt. She was surprised that she felt so competitive with her. However, this was a set of fluid triangles or squares, and the intensity of the component relationships varied over time.

Like Sharon, Penelope was also preoccupied with James. She was particularly interested in his success at work and with his attempts to buy a flat. James was more responsive to Penelope than he was to Sharon.

3. James wanted to train at an Institute of psychotherapy, and was preoccupied with whether as a black he would be accepted. He seemed not to know that the Institute had members of various colors and nationalities. Although the criteria for admissions, the composition of forthcoming panels, etc., had become part of the texture of the Group's discussions, James was unwilling to seek any official information about admissions, except for the few facts available from the Institute's brochure. He was frightened that he would be rejected. However, he felt anxious that he could not be both a student at a prestigious Institute and a black man who was loyal to the memory of his father. To be a qualified social worker was one thing; to be a psychotherapist was another.

Sharon and Penelope were not really interested in James's 'internal' conflicts. Although they knew very little about the Institute's admissions policy and procedures, this did not stop them from proffering advice to James about how he should proceed. They wanted to make certain that he would be accepted for training. They advised him about how to organize his life in order to enable him to fulfill his ambitions. They discussed strategies, and talked about whom they knew who would help him.

James and his two female 'sponsors' seemed virtually to deny that I could help him a very great deal. They treated me as someone who had very little authority and power, except an arbitrary veto of some sort. In fact, the two women immobilized the man emotionally, and blocked his sporadic, half-hearted attempts to identify with me. I seemed to be regarded as an older white man who had power over James, but not one who could identify with him, and who would want to help him to develop and to reach his goals. Similarly, Sharon and Penelope did not seem to know or want to know James as a human being. They regarded him in terms of their own constructions of a young black man.

Sharon and Penelope refused to share James with the other members of the Group, who increasingly felt unacknowledged and unimportant both to me and to the Group as a whole. It seemed impossible to penetrate this Group 'cyst' or 'cell' or 'enclave'. For example, I suggested that members of the Group had become the bystanders or audience of a 'play within a play', which was a metaphor for a fetus as well as a secret. This interpretation seemed to perpetuate the situation rather than to increase the Group's willingness to think about how they had structured themselves.

Although I empathized with James, I was unable to communicate with him in a way that facilitated his continuing individuation and maturation. I got nowhere talking about his anxieties in connection with men in authority, and about how he really wanted to take over these two very attractive women. He was unmoved by my efforts to help him understand that he wanted to make me feel as helpless as he felt himself to be, both 'Here and Now' and 'Here and Then' when he was a child in Barbados. Nor was he impressed by my interpretation that he wanted me to understand how helpless his father had been, both within the family and in the 'There and Then' of his life as a cane cutter. Similarly, I was unable to communicate with Sharon and Penelope in such a way that they were able to let James go.

I wanted us to learn what 'blackness' really meant both socially and personally. I wanted the Group to recover their capacity for free-floating communication and to discuss their many and various problems. However, I was vaguely aware that I wanted this more than good analysis would allow. I was becoming exasperated with the Group's personal and collective defenses. In other words, I wanted to avoid 'our' underlying anxieties.

The Group began to reject me as the one who personified the 'as if' quality which is essential for the therapeutic process, at least with respect to the analysis of the transference. Perhaps I had lost the right balance between involvement and detachment. In any case, I felt somewhat marginalized from the life of the Group as a whole, but in particular from the life of the cell of three, and this feeling persisted for several weeks.

4. One night, as I entered the room, I became aware of an uncharacteristic silence and an atmosphere of secrecy. People avoided looking at one another. No one looked at me. They seemed uncomfortable with one another. I sensed

that they had been talking about me before I came into the room. I wondered if I were becoming paranoid. The silence lasted for about thirty minutes, during which I thought that perhaps the atmosphere of secrecy had begun a few weeks previously.

I tried to focus on my own feelings and fantasies. I felt entrapped and helpless. When I looked at the contra-group of one black man and two white women I saw a penis caught between two white breasts or two white thighs. Then I saw a piece of faeces caught between two white buttocks. Then I became perturbed. I realized that I was using my sophisticated under-standing of the symbolization of part objects in order to cut myself off from the possibility of an authentic experience. I would have to try to stay with my feelings.

I felt frightened and frustrated. I became aware that I was thinking about James as though he were 'Caliban'. I was determined that a Black man in my Group would not be reduced to 'a thing of darkness', even if, paradoxically, he was being used as a beam of light. I became preoccupied with questions: To whom did my images of Caliban in the contra-group 'belong'? Was I carrying these images for someone else or were they my own? Did they refer to parts of the Group as mother? Was Caliban a part of me? I wondered about his homosexuality, maleness and femaleness and masculinity and femininity. I wondered about my own gender and sexual identity. I felt a need to rescue Caliban, to 'spring' him from his tender trap. Was I Prospero? I could not remember for the life of me whether it was Ariel or Caliban who was caught within the cleft of a tree trunk. Who had Prospero sprung? Was the play to which I had referred *The Tempest*? My thoughts shifted to the possibilities of an enactment of an Oedipal configuration by myself, Caliban and the two female protagonists of the contra-group: Caliban was my infantile self; I was my own father; Sharon and Penelope were my mother and/or parts of her; and the other members of the Group were my family. Did 'Penelope' convey associations to water? Could Caliban have fantasies about his own father that were remotely similar to the ones that I had about mine? My God, these thoughts and associations took a lot of learning!

I wondered about my inability to interpret this in such a way that the Group could get in touch with their underlying fantasies and painful anxieties. From time to time the Group had expressed the view that I was pre-occupied with Caliban, and that he was actually my favorite. It had been said that I believed that my success as a therapist would be measured by his success as a patient. I felt that there was at least a grain of truth in this accusation.

Although I was not really preoccupied with Caliban, it was difficult not to focus on him. Yet, somehow I had not allowed myself to know him. I began to wonder about my own 'thing of darkness'. I started to feel very anxious. I was aware that my heart was beating faster.

As I became more aware of my anxiety, a member of the Group began to talk about her wish to become pregnant. A male member talked about his conflicts between being a husband and a baby. Yet another woman talked about her desire to become a psychoanalyst or a psychotherapist, and said that she would have to leave the Group for a full analysis with me. Although she knew that I was not a training psychoanalyst, she assured the Group that one day I would become one, and she would be my first student analysand. The Group discussed this proposition at some length, preferring not to have the facts at their disposal. The woman who wanted to become pregnant said that the woman who wanted to become my analysand wanted to be my unborn baby. I was aware that my own thoughts and feelings and preoccupations were somehow very similar to those of the Group, more so than might ordinarily be the case.

5. At the next session the Group was still fairly silent. I felt that they were frightened of going further. Their communications were desultory and half-hearted. No one seemed willing to respond to what another person said. I wondered whether I was too intellectual, cold, penetrating, critical. It occurred to me that they were frightened of various forthcoming life events, for example, that one of them would be rejected by the Institute, which would be experienced as a castration and as an annihilation of hope carried within the embryonic identity of a candidate. I said that some members of the Group were worried that I could not protect them from such profound disappointments, just as throughout their lives they had been unprotected from various violations of justice. My comments were greeted with silence. It crossed my mind that the Group shared an unconscious fantasy that I was damaged or at least limited as an analyst. I felt frustrated at being unable to rescue Caliban from his internal encapsulations and external entrapments, and the Group from domination by its encapsulated contra-group. Clearly, I was failing to understand what the Group were thinking and feeling and trying to communicate both to me and to one another. I also felt uncertain, vulnerable and de-skilled in my ability to disentangle fantasies from realities, both theirs and mine. Perhaps I had lost my authority. Not so much that I had 'lost' it, as that it had deserted me. As I was trying to clarify my feelings I became aware that it was time to stop.

6. In between sessions I gave myself several hours of quiet time in order to think about what was happening. I thought briefly about the association of silence, secrecy, encapsulated traumatic experience, and encapsulated contra-grouping. I wondered if the Group confused my abstinence and reticence, on the one hand, with their assumptions about my secrecy, and on the other, with self-protectiveness. I began to formulate in my mind how to clarify the main features of these silent communications through projective and introjective identification. Suddenly it occurred to me that some members of the Group had heard that during the past couple of years or so my family and I were having a very hard time coping with an accumulation of traumatic events. I became convinced that the Group had picked up various facts through the grapevine, as it were. I felt disconcerted that my own situation might be impinging into the Group, and that I had not been able to protect them from the burden of having this information about me. I began to wonder how they might have heard, and if they wanted to talk about what had happened, and how I was coping. They must have been worried whether I was able to concentrate on them. Perhaps they were concerned about me. Was Caliban being used as a kind of scapegoat for me? Did the Group experience me as having suffered as much as Caliban? Had I been colluding with this? Had I been using Caliban to carry my traumatized self? The answer to these questions was 'most probably yes'.

I do not want to write about these traumatic events and processes in any detail. Most of the people involved are still alive, and I would like to protect the confidentiality of my family, friends, colleagues and other associates. I will try to convey the essence of my experience through a simple list of events, more or less in sequence:

- My wife had a miscarriage during the fourth month of her pregnancy.

- My second daughter had an extremely difficult birth and suffered severe and permanent neurological impairments.

- I had surgery for a dysplastic melanoma. I became aware of the melanoma about a week before the birth; it was removed about a month after the birth; and the biopsy site was re-excised a few weeks later.

- My daughter who was born during the Survivor Syndrome Workshop in 1979 lost her hearing in one ear as a consequence of mumps.

- We had serious subsidence in our house.
- We had two serious burglaries.
- We were involved in intensive, time-consuming negotiations with insurance companies in order to force them to settle the legitimate claims for compensation for the subsidence and for the burglaries.
- I was extremely disappointed with several senior psychoanalysts and group analysts who failed my legitimate expectations of support from them. With a few notable and much appreciated exceptions, virtually none of my colleagues offered simple expressions of sorrow, such as 'I've heard that you are having a hard time, and I am sorry', preferring instead distancing but intrusive questions, such as 'Have you figured out yet why you had a melanoma?', and accusing but defensive statements, such as 'You have to acknowledge that you seduced the burglars by having too much glass in the doors and windows at the back of your house'.
- My own psychoanalyst was elected President of the International Psycho-Analytical Association and I experienced him as having less 'space' for me.
- I was caught up in very unpleasant political conflicts within the British Psycho-Analytical Society which involved the Group of Independent Psychoanalysts being squeezed into political paralysis, and its leadership insulted and humiliated.
- I was engaged in troubled and troublesome rivalries with my brothers in connection with succession and inheritance.
- My father died suddenly.

My own struggles to cope with these events were influenced by my previous experience of various kinds of trauma at various phases of my life. Obviously, I was aware of the connections between Caliban and my melanoma; my daughter and my melanoma; helplessness and entrapment; the contra-group and an enclave of cells; my patients, my family of origin, my family of procreation and myself; and so on. However, the common denominator of my responses to all the events on my list was my experience of failed dependency. The milk of sociology, group analysis and psychoanalysis could not protect me. Nor could various figures of paternal authority, that is, particular physicians, accountants, lawyers, insurance agents, psychoanalysts and group analysts. I recalled reading the Book of Job. I had the impression that little was written about Job's affiliations to other people, apart from his comforters.

Although I was wounded, I remained resilient; although I was angry, I remained playful. I was drawn to black humor. I was absolutely determined not to give in, and to protect my wife and daughters from the consequences of these misfortunes. We were blessed in having a few friends, some of whom were colleagues, who helped us stay focused and connected. My identity as a psychoanalyst and group analyst became extremely important to me. This was not merely a matter of having work to do. It was a matter of living up to the ethical obligations of my professional roles. I said to myself that if I could make creative use of these traumatic events I would be a better psychoanalyst and group analyst. I rarely missed a session. My work improved. I began to draft papers. I became more involved in the world of committees and councils.

I decided that I would have to talk a little to the Group about my state of mind and my recent life experiences, although I did not know exactly how I would do this. I knew that inevitably a Group enacted the internal world of its conductor, at least from time to time, and I wanted to analyze this point – counterpoint of the Group's music.

7. The next session began in silence. As I started to speak, a member of the Group more or less interrupted me. She said that she was interested in a print on the wall. The print had never been mentioned before. As far as the Group were concerned, it had been on the wall for ever. It was taken for granted. No one had ever commented on it. At first I thought that it was left behind by Harold Kaye (who had been one of my group analysts), but then I remembered that it belonged to a senior member of the Practice with whom I had a difficult relationship. In any case, the Group became preoccupied with this print.

From memory, the print was framed very simply in silver metal, and looked something like this:

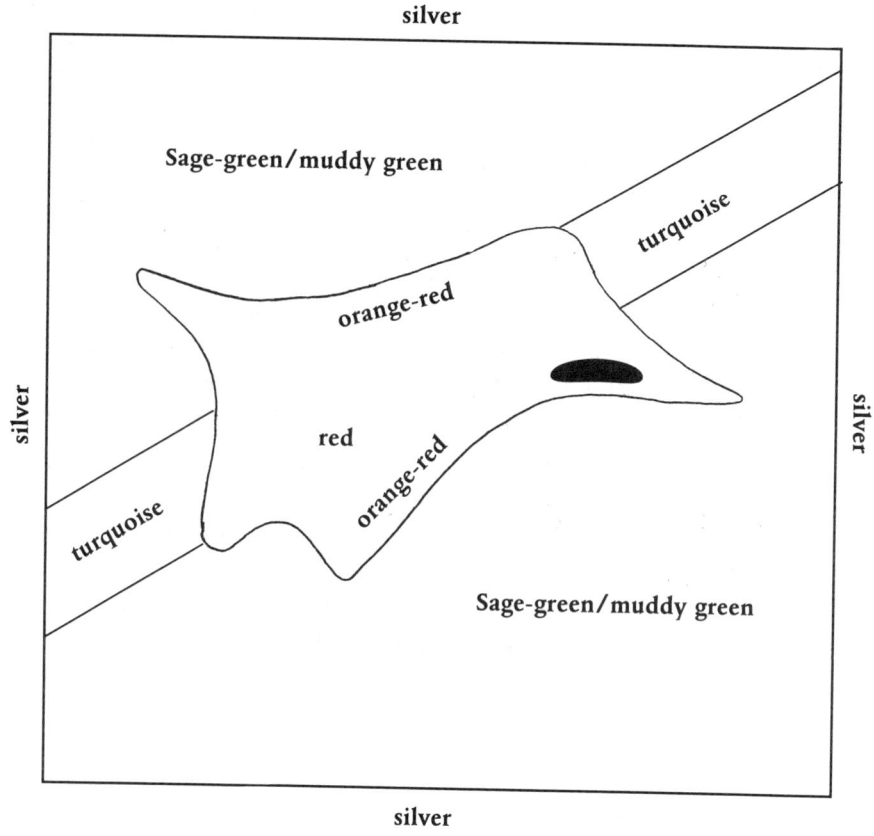

Figure 7.1 An illustration from my memory of the print on the wall.

The shape of the central object was basic, elemental, not dissimilar from those found in some of the works of Klee and various Dutch artists during the 1950s. Its color was red, a good, strong red, fading to an orange-red near its edges. The roundish smudge on the red shape was black. The background material was sage-green. The stripe was turquoise.

The Group talked about the print for at least two sessions. They also talked about other matters, but they always returned to the print. It was like art therapy. The following selection of themes gives some idea of what it meant to them:

- the profile of a man with a big nose and a lot of curly hair
- a dove

- a flying bird

- a spirit

- god's bird

- a wounded bird

- the black dot as Caliban

- the red as X's heat, and the green as Y's envy and jealousy

- a group matrix

- the red as the blood of a uterus and of our explosiveness

- the red as Z's explosiveness

- the meaning of the silver frame

- the turquoise stripe as the split in the group between the people who wanted to become psychotherapists and the rest who were just ordinary patients.

Although I was preoccupied with the possibility that the bird was me and that the black dot on the bird's wing was my own melanoma, this was not in the Group's communications. They tended instead to concentrate on certain messianic themes in connection with a white dove of peace. I interpreted their communications in terms of a manic defense against depressive anxieties, characterized by a somewhat unrealistic and idealized turning to the future in order to avoid the problems of the present. I said that they wanted to avoid recognizing any 'discoloration', and acknowledging their thoughts and feelings about castration, wounding and various fight/flight themes, some of which were connected with the redness and blackness of a wounded bird. I insisted that the Group felt that in one way or another I was a 'wounded bird', and that it was easier and safer to talk about a wounded bird in a picture on the wall than about me. However, for the most part the Group did not take this up, although one woman commented that if by 'wounded' I meant 'sensitive', then, yes, I was a sensitive man. The Group were unable to see that somehow they were preoccupied with my internal world, but at least I was now convinced that this was so.

During the course of our working with this material, I commented that symbolically the Messiah was conceived through Mary's ear by a dove that carried God's word (Jones 1951 [1914]). I said that in some Italian Renaissance paintings words written in Hebrew came out of the dove's little beak. The dove not only announced the conception, but was also God's penis, bringing his seminal words into Mary's ear. This image represented Holy intercourse itself, offering the answer to various 'In the Beginning' questions, such as free will and determinism, creativity, moral responsibility, etc. I did not express myself by stopping the process and saying 'Hey, I want to give you a lecture about biblical symbolism'. I expressed one thought clearly, and when the Group seemed interested, conveyed a bit more of this way of looking at our experience, and, then, in response to some of the Group's comments, said a little more. I (Hopper 1982a) had written a paper on what I called the 'sacred equation', and in retrospect I can see that this paper had stayed with me, and that I must have been continuing to intellectualize my recent experiences with birth. However, my conscious intention was to explore the sexualization of loss and mourning, and how this was manifest in variations on the theme of pairing.

8.   The Group lapsed into reflective silence. The mood was very intimate and tender, but also cautious and protective. I said that our sudden preoccupation with the print suggested that we were dealing with very primitive material. It seemed as though a boil had burst. The Group thought about this comment. They were unanimous that somehow we should take care.

9.   Between sessions, I had a number of thoughts and questions, somewhat overlapping and interlinked. It was fairly clear what a dove meant, but what did a raven or blackbird symbolize? Did 'bird' always refer to the phallus: good ones, bad ones, creative ones, destructive ones, wounded ones, peaceful ones? Might 'bird' also refer to the breast? What color was a 'fagela'? What was the connection between fagela, fag and faggot? Presumably none, because different languages were involved. I searched for the name of the 'depressive position bird', so curiously common in London, black and white with a turquoise stripe on its wings – so beautiful and lively – so unruly and anti-social – so delinquent. Or was this a 'paranoid-schizoid position bird'? I heard the tune and remembered the words of 'Bye-bye, Blackbird'.[6] Were there red-winged blackbirds in England as there were in America? Surely an ordinary gray London pigeon could not be a depressive position bird.

   I remembered my early life in St Louis, where the Missouri and Mississippi Rivers meet. In Hannibal, one hundred miles north of St Louis, Mark Twain wrote *Tom Sawyer* and *Huckleberry Finn*. St Louis was (and still is) regarded as 'Southern' by people from the North, and 'Northern' by people from the South, but as mid-Western by the people who lived there, even if slaves had been sold on the steps of the old Court House. In fact, before World War II most white people had never even shaken hands with a Negro.

However, I was proud that my father was virtually the first businessman in St Louis to employ Negroes on the same terms as whites, that is, all customers had to be served by the salesman whose turn it was, whether he was a Negro or a white man. At first some White customers left the shop when they were greeted by a Negro salesman. How strange it was to remember the word 'Negro', which was so commonplace in the 1940s and 1950s. Nowadays 'Black' or 'Afro-American' would be more acceptable, and 'Negro', insulting. Surely, the Group did not think that they were my slaves or that I was theirs. Or did they?

10. During the next session, the Group shifted their focus from the print to me. They began to comment on what I was wearing. I was shocked to realize that I had put on a red flannel shirt, a black tie and an old sports jacket colored sage-green and light-brown, with a dark-brown and turquoise window-pane overcheck. Although red shirts, black ties and tweed sports jackets were almost conventional in certain American circles of slightly bohemian university students and their professors in Boston and perhaps New York, this style was unusual in England, at least at the time. All the Group joined in, trying to interact with me, play with me, and explore my 'second skin'. I did not enjoy it, but I allowed the Group to use me in this way, and to get to know their version of me. However, although I had become conscious of the connection between the colors of my clothes and the colors of the print, the Group had not.

The connection between skin and skin disturbances, adhesive transferences, and separation and annihilation anxieties crossed my mind. In a vague sort of way I thought about skin and the blackness of the skin of Caliban. How many layers of skin did I have? While their exploration continued I protected myself by thinking about an article that I wanted to write about central masturbation fantasies. I intended to argue that they were coded communications about encapsulated traumatic experiences; that there is an essential connection between screen memories and central masturbation fantasies; and that traumatized societies become preoccupied with perverse myths, fables and stories that lend themselves to the visual imagery of films, paintings, newspaper cartoons and so on, the functions of which are analogous to the functions of masturbation fantasies for traumatized individuals. I was especially interested in the films and paintings that became popular during the late 1920s and 30s in Nazi Germany. Members of traumatized social systems may project various fantasies on to their public walls, canvasses and screens in an attempt to rid themselves of their horrific and perverse preoccupations, which is a way of repeating the fantasy and even the memory of fecal smearing. A public dream on a public canvas might be a collective version of personal fantasies projected on to a dream screen, based on the experience of breast skin and the hallucinated version of it in response to the loss of the 'thing-in-itself'. It was not fortuitous that this idea was developed during the Weimar Republic by psychoanalysts who were about to become refugees from Nazi Germany, for example, Lewin (1946).[7]

Eventually, the Group's exploration of me began to shift from something that seemed helpful to them to something that I felt was perverse. I was relieved that it was time to stop.

11. During the next few days I felt compelled to think about my own responses to the Group and within the Group. I found myself preoccupied with my memories of my father, both good and bad, pleasurable and painful. I remembered my numerous boxing and wrestling lessons. My father used to trap me in complex holds and challenge me to free myself using the special countermaneuvers that he had taught me. It was very important to him that I learned to fight back and to resist any attempts to curtail my freedom. However, one version of this game was very disturbing. After I freed myself he would pretend that he was paralyzed, but could be freed from his paralysis if and only if I touched his foot; however, when I touched his foot, he would trap me again, and I would have to use my newly learned countermaneuvers in order to free myself; then he would pretend again to be paralyzed, and would plead with me to free him from his plight; and again I would rescue him, and again become entrapped. The whole cycle would repeat itself until in despair and exasperation I would beg my mother to stop him torturing me. I must have been a slow learner, but this was a very confusing and perverse game, not least because my mother was not without her own means of entrapment. Over the years I decided that most probably I was being taught what it was like to be a helpless soldier in battle, and a helpless man who after the war had to begin his life again. Even then I had a vague sense that my father envied me the luxury of what he imagined was an indulged childhood safe at home while he was fighting in Germany. Other men his age had stayed at home, and many had done well out of the war.

I found myself 'touching' on various aspects of my father's life: his own secret illegitimacy and adoption by his mother's older brother and his wife, who was hospitalized for an unknown illness, most probably a form of lupus, when he was around twelve years of age, and who was in and out of hospital more or less continuously until she died when he was around twenty-two years of age, not long before he married. How strange that I did not learn about his adoption until I was in my late thirties, shortly after he told me that his adoptive father – my adoptive grandfather – was actually born in the East End of London. He was an 'American-new-world-male', in contrast to the men in my mother's family who were 'European-old-world-males'. He made money in business and lost it all at cards, despite his reputation as one of the best gin rummy players in St Louis. He taught me how to draw and paint, and how to use tools. He was a great leader of our boy scout troop. He taught me how to make a fire with wet wood in the snow. He was an Eagle Scout, and, I think, a Silver Beaver. He was adventurous and highly intelligent, but so self-destructive. He was ashamed of his own social origins and lack of education, and would insist that I was ashamed of him, and refused to believe that I respected him. He felt that by living in Cambridge and London I had rejected him and America. He was proud of my accomplishments as a 'professional', but had amused contempt for my comparative poverty during the many years of my many trainings, which he subsidized with what he called 'care' packages, which were a continuation of American aid to Britain. He was a good father for an adolescent, but a bad father for an infant and child. He was warm and generous and I loved him very much, but he could be cold and cruel. I always had trouble integrating the conflicting traits in his character.

I recalled that my father's Hebrew name was Abraham, my mother's father's Isaac, and that my own Hebrew name is Israel. As a boy I identified with Jacob, who, following his wrestling match with the angel, changed his name to Israel. However, I amalgamated Abraham, Isaac and Jacob/Israel into my 'four' Fathers, and I used to wonder who was the 'fourth' father. What was the real reason for continuing the tradition of circumcision? To free one's self from the weight of female influence and control? To cut the umbilical cord twice, the second time for good measure in order to show who the boss really was? I wondered why such drastic measures were necessary. After all, if my father really was the boss, why did he have to assert his power in such a dramatic way.

Who were the fore-mothers? Actually, there was a 'fourth' mother, but I could not remember who. This was not surprising, because before my brother was born I was an only son and only grandson within the family group of a mother, maternal grandmother, maternal great-grandmother (my maternal grandmother's mother-in-law) two girl cousins, and two aunts, including one by marriage, as well as a 'white nurse' called Granny Coke, and a 'white nanny' called Agnes, and two 'colored' maids called Iris and Crecia. In fact, until my brother was born I was the only boy within the entire so-called extended family, who must have included at least another half-dozen girl cousins and even more nannies and maids. Actually, I had one maternal uncle, but he was ineffectual, and later died in a shooting accident.

My father's adoptive father was a tailor and an amateur handyman who fixed my toys. He also brought his tool box when he came for Sunday lunch. He died a few months after my younger brother was born, and a few months before my father went to war. He lost his father, and I lost mine. Before he left, my father told me that while he was away I was in charge of the family, and if he did not come back, I would be responsible for everyone. My mother and little brother did not agree.

During the war my maternal grandfather was the central figure in this extended family. He owned a delicatessen, and he presided over it. Although he was fluent in several languages, he needed my mother to write letters for him. One of his hobbies was carving and painting flowers on the lids of cigar boxes. Another was reading socialist literature, but he did not talk much about this. He must have realized that St Louis was not Lublin. According to my mother, he had once owned a bookshop in which he sponsored readings by itinerant Yiddish poets and playwrights, and the delicatessen grew out of the bookshop, because my grandmother began to sell sandwiches and drinks to the audiences, who bought more refreshments than books.

I spent many hours in the first booth of the delicatessen with my maternal grandmother who regularly fed me a baked potato the size of one of her breasts with a quarter-pound stick of butter melting on the top, while my great-grandmother (her mother-in-law) played with my hands – in case I should try to push the fork away, and while my grandfather stood at the front counter slicing and bagging loaves of rye bread in less time than it took a few years later with an electric machine. This feat could only be matched by my father who in a few seconds could fillet a smoked forel without breaking a bone or disturbing the flesh. In the other booths people were eating sandwiches with pickled this and pickled that and coleslaw and potato salad, and drinking Coca-Cola or lemon tea, or eating blintzes or cheesecake and lemon tea. These people were always talking and always discussing and always arguing, usually about the war and the Jews, mostly in Yiddish and broken English. Many were losing their relatives, and crying.

Where was my mother? She must have been breastfeeding my brother, who had red hair. What a furry little animal he was. Somehow I always knew that younger siblings were often symbolized by furry little animals like mice and squirrels, not to mention rodents and vermin.

Could I have been aware of all this? Somehow I was, I think. It was obvious that eventually I would become interested in group analysis.

When my father returned from war, he refused to go into such a business. Also, he did not want to be known as the 'son-in-law'. He had been in the retail fur business, and decided to try again. I was angry at him for leaving me in a Jewish garden of temptation. I was even more angry that when he came back from the war he thought that he was still the Head Gardener. However, I needed him to rescue me from the delicatessen. Although later I worked in his fur business one night a week, and on Saturdays and during summer vacations, my mother did everything in her power to dissuade me from going into business with him. Medicine, Law, even Sociology, but not the fur business! How she admired my academic achievements! In fact, I did not want to be trapped in my father's fur business any more than I wanted to be trapped in my mother's delicatessen. I wanted to be an American man, but one who read poetry and novels. I wanted to paint, but pictures of naked women, not flowers on the lids of old cigar boxes.

12. As the next session began, but before anyone else started to speak, I decided to offer an interpretation of the process and its multiple personifications, in terms of vulnerability and entrapment and the absence of good-enough fathers. However, instead of offering my interpretation, I found myself unbuttoning the collar of my role and blurting out:

> What's happening in this Group reminds me of a Bajan village. I feel that I am in a Bajan village where there's poverty and a struggle to eke out a living and to survive – one mother of twelve children – men fucking their brains out all over the village and in the fields of sugar-cane and behind the trees in order to show that they are men, but actually there is nothing that they can do to escape from their despair and depression other than to fuck their brains out. Women having babies at fourteen, fifteen, sixteen. One mother with children and grand-children and great-grandchildren who is very powerful and very hard to get away from. No real father, but a preacher spouting nonsense about how every little thing will be all right in Heaven. Is this what y'all think Caliban's life was like?

My intervention seemed to me to be both bizarre and entirely in touch with the unconscious life of the Group. I said what I said without quite knowing what I was saying or why I was saying it. The sentences formed in my mind and in my mouth, and I trusted myself to say them out loud. If my thoughts and interventions during the preceding few months took an awful lot of learning, this one took an awful lot of unlearning.[8]

I started to go on, but I realized that the Group was stunned. Someone retorted, 'So that's where you've been getting your sun-tan during the holidays'. There was a bit of jokiness. Caliban said that I would make a good preacher. Sharon said that it was probably worse in South Africa. Another man said that it sounded like a pretty good life. The women treated this remark with derision and contempt. However, it dawned on me that each of us was a very long way from home, and that each of us was driven somehow to recreate these 'homes' within the Group. We needed one another in order to do this. None of us could do it on his or her own.

13. I want to convey some of the main developments. I am aware that this may sound like a 'revivalist meeting' when miracles are being recounted. Nonetheless, the changes were dramatic, especially in the general mood of the group.

The members of the encapsulated contra-group began to communicate more freely. James talked about his infancy and childhood in Barbados. Although we had heard quite a lot about his poverty and deprivation, this was usually in the form of a report on the social conditions of the West Indies. We had not really shared his own experience of them. Sharon observed that James had stopped sweating every time he talked to me. He became more relaxed. He claimed that he felt understood, and, in particular, that I had seen the circumstances from which he had come. He felt safer with me. He began to ask me direct questions about admissions to the Institute.

Sharon told a story that I had never heard. Perhaps I had heard many of the main details, but somehow had never put them together into the whole story, either because she did not tell it coherently or we could not really listen or both. She had wanted to leave South Africa a year or so before she actually did, but she was having a love affair with a married man who 'happened' to be either black or colored. She would not give further details about this. He was an active member of a banned political party. Although he had agreed to leave his wife and come to London, at the last moment he changed his mind, by which time she was completely committed to the new plan. She wanted to make him leave his wife. To this end, after she came to London, she adopted a mixed-race child. She regarded the child as 'theirs', but she refused to confirm whether or not her lover was the father of the child. Nonetheless, her lover would not follow her. He said, 'Well, it was your decision. Although I would like to visit you, I don't really want to live with you. My life is here.'

She was not angry with him, because 'That's how men are'. In fact, the Group was holding her together while she was holding on to Caliban who was an amalgamation of everything she had lost but could not mourn. He was both her hope and her despair. It became possible to connect the many meanings of 'blackness', both for her and for us, ranging from parts and 'missing parts' of her own body to perverse, evil deeds and motives, to social and cultural issues of slavery and class, to dirt, to scar tissue, to shame and to things of darkness in general, both hers and ours.

What about Penelope? We had known a bit about her background, but in competition with Sharon she told us more about herself and her family. She said that her family had made their money in the slave-trade. They owned and operated the first slave-trading ships that went from Bristol to Africa and the West Indies, and became fantastically wealthy from the slave trade. She had been brought up in a country house that was built entirely with money earned from the slave-trade. She felt burdened and ashamed of what was, as she put it, 'a black spot on all that I am proud of'. Again, we had much personal and group material to work with for a very long time.

While these stories were unfolding I recalled images from Sylvia Plath's (1981) annihilation anxiety poems. One was about shaking a box of wooden matches and hearing the clatter of live and burnt-out matches, somehow evoking the image of slaves chanting and rowing in unison in the holds of ships. When I first came to England in 1962, I noticed this habit among smokers, especially pipe smokers, and among women in the kitchen who used old-fashioned cooking stoves. The other poem was about the buzz of bees working within a hive conveying a sense of a society without culture, a group-level symbolic equation, and of a society's unconscious anniversary reactions. These were autistic phenomena in response to social trauma.[9] I had shifted from the amoeboid–autistic visual image of the print to an autistic aural sound. Perhaps Margaret Mead was right when she suggested that the aural primal scene was prior to the visual one.

The Group began to explore why they had established a three-person enclave, and why they had suddenly become preoccupied with the print on the wall and then with my clothes and my person. As we discussed the material that was uncovered through the analysis of the defensive nature of these preoccupations, I became more aware of my sadness and my continuing need to work through my own traumatic experiences. My own safety shield had failed me, and not for the first time. However, I consoled myself by thinking that inevitably a slight depression was associated with the development of a strong, independent identity, because growth was always based on giving up one's 'objects', at each and every step of the way. I did not want to be trapped by a social identity any more than I did by the personal projections of my family. My 'delicatessen' could not be reduced to my mother and her body; and my 'fur business' was more than my father and his body. After all, did my self not belong to me?

I thought about the need for a concept of a laminated object and a concept of a laminated ego or self, but I did not take this any further. I also thought about the way snakes shed their skins as they mature. Foulkes (1975) was right when he wrote that group-analytic psychotherapy '…is a form of psychotherapy by the group, of the group, including its conductor' (p.3). In this case, it must be acknowledged that I was helped by the Group to use my countertransference in the service of better communication in order to be of better service to them.[10] I would have to give up my idealizations of psychoanalysis, group analysis and sociology.

A postscript

About a year later I decided that I would try to write about this phase in the life of the Group. I would argue that the benefits of authenticity on the part of the trained and experienced analyst were almost always greater than the harm that might follow from mistakes of emphasis or formulation. It was better to be wrong authentically than right inauthentically. However, had I been wrong?

I decided to examine the print. 'Wounded Bird' was written on the back of it. The print was one of a series by Philip Sutton. I traced him to a village in South Wales. Sutton said that the print was one of a series that he made after a sojourn with his family in southern Australia where he was stimulated by the colors and shapes of the local bird-life. He said that he would never have used a title like 'Wounded Bird', and that it must have been written by the dealer. I learned from a mutual friend that his dealer was his son.

On the basis of this conversation with Sutton, I decided to call the paper 'Wounded Bird'. Immediately upon making this decision, I remembered that in 1962, at the University of Leicester, Norbert Elias called the first lecture in his Introduction to Sociology a 'Bird's Eye View'. I remembered saying to him that this meant 'close to the ground', 'one-eyed' and 'overly magnified', but he insisted that it meant 'over-arching', 'soaring' and 'broad'. I thought that like my grandfather, he could not speak English properly. In retrospect, I realized that 'a bird's eye view' is the only view that is really appropriate for the study of people and groups.

For various reasons I left the Practice where the Group met, and we began to meet in another consulting room. I borrowed 'Wounded Bird', and hung it in the new room for a year or so. From time to time the Group talked about the picture. Eventually, I returned it, and wrote the first draft of this paper from my memory of the experience and the picture itself. When I decided to publish the paper I thought that I should check my memory of the picture; there was, of course, no way that I could check my memory of my experience. However, no one knew where 'Wounded Bird' had gone.

References

Anthony, J. (1993) 'Psychoanalysis and environment.' In G. Pollock and S. Greenspan (eds) *The Course of Life Vol. VI, Late Adulthood.* Madison: International Universities Press.

Balint, M. (1979) [1968] *The Basic Fault. Therapeutic Aspects of Regression.* New York: Brunner/Mazel. (Original work published 1968).

Bettelheim, B. (1969) '"Portnoy's Psychoanalysis: Therapy Notes" found in the files of Dr O. Spielvogel, a New York psychoanalyst.' *Midstream* June/July, 3–10.

Biran, H. (1995) 'Fear of other'. *Palestine–Israel Journal 4,* Autumn, 44–52.

Bloom, L. (1992) 'Psycho-therapy and culture: A critical review.' In L. Bryce Boyer (ed) *The Psycho-Analytical Study of Society 17.* London: The Analytic Press.

Bollas, C. (1992) 'Psychic Genera.' In *Being a Character.* London: Routledge.

Brenman-Pick, I. (1985) 'Working through in the countertransference.' *International Journal of Psycho-Analysis 66,* 2, 157–166.

Brown, D. (1977) 'Drowsiness and the countertransference.' *International Review of Psycho-Analysis 4,* 4, 481–492.

Casement, P. (1990) *Further Learning from the Patient: The Analytic Space and Process.* London: Routledge.

Dalal, F. (1993a) '"Race" and racism – an attempt to organize difference.' *Group Analysis 26,* 3, 277–293.

Dalal, F. (1993b) 'The meaning of boundaries and barriers in the development of cultural identity.' In W. Knauss and U. Keller (eds) *Ninth European Symposium in Group Analysis: 'Boundaries and Barriers'.* Heidelberg: Mattes Verlag.

Davis, F. (1992) 'The cutting edge of racism: An object relations view.' *Bulletin of the British Psychoanalytical Society 28,* 11, 19–29.

Ferenczi, S. and Rank, O. (1986) [1922] *The Development of Psychoanalysis.* Madison: International Universities Press. (Original work published 1922).

Ferenczi, S. (1997) [1932] *Sin simpatia no hay curacion. El Diario clinico de 1932.* Buenos Aires: Amorrortu [Spanish translation of the German edition of the Clinical Diary.]

Foulkes, S. H. (1964) *Therapeutic Group Analysis.* London: Allen and Unwin.

Foulkes, S. H. (1975) *Group Analytic Psychotherapy: Methods and Principles.* London: Gordon and Breech (An Interface Book).

Hartmann, H. (1960) *Psychoanalysis and Moral Values*. New York: International Universities Press.

Hopper, E. (1982a) 'A Comment on Professor M. Jahoda's "Individual and the Group"'. In M. Pines and L. Rafaelsen (eds) *The Proceedings of the Seventh International Congress of Group Psychotherapy*. New York and London: Plenum Press.

Hopper, E. (1982b) 'Group analysis: The problem of context.' *Group Analysis XV*, 2, 136–157.

Hopper, E. (1985) 'The problem of context in group-analytic psychotherapy: A clinical illustration and a brief theoretical discussion.' In M. Pines (ed) *Bion and Group Psychotherapy*. London: Routledge & Kegan Paul.

Hopper, E. (1995) 'A psychoanalytical theory of drug addiction: Unconscious fantasies of homosexuality, compulsions and masturbation within the context of traumatogenic processes.' *International Journal of Psycho-Analysis 76*, 6, 1121–1142.

Hopper, E. (1996) 'The social unconscious in clinical work.' *Group 20*, 1, 7–43.

Jones, E. (1951) [1914] 'The Madonna's Conception Through the Ear.' In *Essays in Applied Psycho-Analysis 2*. London: The Hogarth Press, 266–357. (Original work published 1914).

Kareem, J. and Littlewood, R. (1992) *Intercultural Therapy: Themes, Interpretations and Practice*. Oxford: Blackwell Scientific Publications.

Konig, K. (1995) *Countertransference Analysis*. Northvale, New Jersey: Jason Aronson Inc.

Langs, R.J. (1978) *The Listening Process*. New York: Aronson.

Lewin, B. (1946) 'Sleep, the mouth and the dream screen.' *Psycho-Analytic Quarterly 15*, 2, 1–14.

Limentani, A. (1977) 'Affects and the psychoanalytic situation.' *International Journal of Psycho-Analysis 58*, 2,171–197.

Nabakov, V. (1962) *Pale Fire*. London: Weidenfeld & Nicholson.

Obholzer, A. and Roberts, V. Z. (eds) (1994) *The Unconscious at Work*. London: Routledge.

Plath, S. (1981) *Collected Poems*. T. Hughes (ed) London: Faber & Faber.

Puget, J. (1986) Personal communication concerning what she calls 'overlapping worlds'.

Rance, C. (1989) 'What has group analysis to offer in the context of organisational consultancy?' *Group Analysis 22*, 3, 333–40.

Roth, B. E. (1980) 'Understanding the development of a homogeneous, identity-impaired group through countertransference phenomena.' *International Journal of Group Psychotherapy 30*, 4, 405–426.

Roth, P. (1995) [1967] *Portnoy's Complaint*. London: Vintage. (Original work published 1967).

Schermer, V. (1995) 'Ethnic identity, the sense of self and internalized object relations.' *Mind and Human Interaction 6*,1, 34–43.

Searles, H.F. (1979) *Countertransference and Related Subjects*. New York: International Universities Press.

Skynner, R. (1979) 'Reflections on the family therapist as scapegoat.' *Journal of Family Therapy 1*, 7, 1–19.

Symington, N. (1983) 'The analyst's act of freedom as agent of therapeutic change.' *International Review of Psycho-Analysis 10*, 283-291.

Tubert-Oklander, J. (2002) 'The clinical diary of 1932 and the new psychoanalytic clinic.' Paper read at the International Congress 'Clinical Sandor Ferenczi' Torino, Italy.

Winnicott, D. (1967) 'The location of cultural experience.' *International Journal of Psycho-Analysis 48*, 3, 368–372.

Yalom, I. (1989) *Love's Executioner.* London: Penguin Books Ltd.

Notes

1   For their helpful comments on previous drafts of this Chapter, I am grateful to my brother Saul Hopper and to my colleagues Barbara Elliott, Sheila Ernst, Percival Mars and David and Jill Scharff. As I have written in the Preface to this book, I drafted this chapter in 1985 and 1986, but the present version was written in the late 1990s, as will be seen in some of the citations of recent literature.

2   There are notable exceptions to this. For example: in psychoanalysis, see Brenman-Pick 1985; Brown 1977; Limentani 1977; in group analysis, see Hopper 1985, a version of which is reprinted as Chapter 5 of this book; Konig 1995; Roth 1980; Skynner 1979; and in consultation with organizations, see Obholzer and Roberts 1994; Rance 1989.

3   There are a few notable exceptions to this. For example: in psychoanalysis, see Anthony 1993; Davis 1992; Hopper 1995; in group analysis, see Dalal 1993a, b; Hopper 1985, 1996 (versions of which are reprinted as Chapters 5 and 6 of this book); and in consultation with organizations, see Biran 1995.

4   For example, in 1982, in 'The problem of context in group analysis', I found only one reference, apart from the work of Foulkes (1964), to the social unconscious and countertransference, although I should have cited Bettelheim's (1969) review of Roth's (1967) *Portnoy's Complaint,* in which he suggested that only a non-Jewish analyst could avoid the unconscious complicity that Portnoy demanded. This was still the case in 1985 when I published a revised version of my article (reprinted as Chapter 5 of this book). In 1989, in *Love's Executioner,* Yalom showed that he was sensitive to these issues, but that he did not really work with them. In a discussion of cultural constraints on psychotherapy and psychotherapists, Bloom (1992) could cite only Hartmann's (1960) reference to social reality, and Winnicott's (1967) discussion of the need for the therapist to integrate his understandings of both internal and external constraints. It is interesting that in his valuable discussion of the effects of external reality on intra-psychic life, Anthony (1993) did not mention the countertransference. Notable exceptions to such benign neglect can be found in discussions of countertransference in connection with racism and ethnicity, for example: in England, see Dalal 1993a, b, who cites the articles in the Special Issue of the *Journal of Social Work Practice,* 1988; Davis 1992; Kareem and Littlewood 1992; in Israel, Biran 1995; and in the United States, Schermer 1995.

5   Such a statement might be taken to be politically incorrect, and even offensive, especially to female feminists, but the fact that she looked the way she did was part of the Group process and part of her psychic life, and needs to be stated.

6   I presented some of this material in Melbourne in May 1994. I remembered the name of the black and white bird with the turquoise stripe on its wing when George Christie took me to a game of 'footie' in which The Magpies were playing. He told me that 'black-birding' was the word for bringing convicts in ships to Australia and I wondered if this referred to shipping Africans to other colonies as well. Also, Bill

Blomfield reminded me of the opening lines of Nabakov's *Pale Fire* (1962) which the scriptwriter of *Kolya* must have read.

7   Eventually I did write this paper. Draft number 53 was entitled 'A psychoanalytical theory of drug addiction: Unconscious fantasies of homosexuality, compulsions and masturbation within the context of traumatogenic processes', and published in 1995.

8   My intervention might be understood as an 'inspired interpretation' (Bollas 1992), but I am hesitant to use this notion about my own work. However, 'inspired' may be absolutely accurate. Also relevant is the notion of an 'x-factor' suggested by Symington (1983) as a way of describing a verbal intervention that seems to be a kind of theoretical and semiotic non sequitur.

9   When I looked up the poems, I discovered that my memory was not quite right. 'The Arrival of the Bee-box' did not really contain an image of a box of wooden matches, but an image of the bee-box as a small coffin, and the phrase 'swarmy feeling of African hands'. This poem, combined with 'The Swarm' and 'Wintering', with their continuing line of references to bees, tell us much about the fear of annihilation and its vicissitudes. I had created my own image of a box of wooden matches and an image of an enslaved crew of rowing and chanting Africans on the basis of all of Plath's poems about bees, combined with my knowledge that in the autumn of 1963, a few months after the last of the poems were written, she had gassed herself to death in her kitchen. When I presented some of this material at the Inaugural Workshop in Group Psychotherapy for the Washington School of Psychiatry in June, 1994, Sy Rubenfeld remembered that in a large correctional institution he could tell what the day's atmosphere would be like from the sound of the rhythmic morning marching of the black juvenile inmates/residents.

10   Since writing this paper I have become much more familiar with a line of work in psychoanalysis in which the self-analysis of the countertransference is shared with the reader in the interest of the development of what Tubert-Oklander (2002) calls 'the psychoanalytic clinic', and which has become a central theme in the new 'relational perspective' for example: Ferenczi and Rank 1922; Ferenczi 1932; Balint 1968; Langs 1978; Searles 1979; Puget 1986; Casement 1990; Jacobs 1993a,b; Ogden 1994.

CHAPTER 8

On the Nature of Hope in Psychoanalysis and Group Analysis[1]

Introduction

The title of my article is 'On the Nature of Hope'. 'On' involves an eighteenth century English conceit. It implies that the phenomenon is really too big and too complex for any one author, and, therefore, that he is allowed to be selective. 'Nature' implies, somewhat ironically, that the phenomenon does not belong to religion or magic, but to a realm or domain that permits rational, systematic and skeptical study. Thus, my title implies that in my opinion the phenomenon of hope is finite and contingent, and is a matter for science, to include the psychological and the social sciences. However, I am certain that Hamlet was right when he admonished Horatio that 'There are more things in heaven and earth...than are dreamt of in your philosophy' (Shakespeare, Hamlet, I, v, 166).

After a brief indication of the scope of the topic, I will define 'hope' as it is ordinarily used in English. I will then make several conceptual distinctions that are necessary in order to discuss hope and its vicissitudes. My third task will be to define hope from my own point of view, which is that ultimately hope refers to the ability and willingness to exercise the transcendent imagination within the context of the traumatogenic process. I will focus on the development and maintenance of this human virtue within the context of life trajectories constrained by social, cultural and political factors. Finally, I will discuss some aspects of my view of hope in clinical work. I will not provide a systematic review of the literature, but in future publications I will trace the emergence of my understanding of hope in the context of the development of contemporary object relations theory, and illustrate my argument with clinical vignettes from my practice as a psychoanalyst and group analyst.[2]

Although they did not always agree with one another, and certainly did not always use the word 'hope', in one way or another all the classical analysts discussed the phenomenon of hope, including Freud, Jung, Klein and Balint, and many others. Although Winnicott, Erikson and Fromm considered hope and its vicissitudes in an explicit and focused way, the topic has been ignored by most contemporary psychoanalysts, with a few exceptions, for example, Casement (1985) and Mitchell (1993). Many psychoanalysts agree with Freud (1917) that hope is one of the elements of gratitude, which is a product of the work of mourning, and that giving up unrealistic hopes, or to be more precise, unrealistic goals, while maintaining a hopeful attitude or orientation to life and living, indicates that therapy has been successful, and that termination is in order.

Hope is the very essence of attempts to make creative use of traumatic experience, which always involves reparation, restoration and restitution.[3] For example, the child analyst Anne Alvarez (1992) has written:

> I have looked for a word or concept… (for)… the birth and development of hope in a child who may have been clinically depressed all his life. The nearest I can get is…the 'work of regeneration' or, to paraphrase Daniel Stern and George Herbert, the slow momentous discovery that his shriveled heart can contain greenness. (p.173)

Unfortunately, attempts at re-creation are often inauthentic, and associated with the defensive reenactment of messianic hope.

Although they are not informed by psychoanalysis, even by ego psychology, it is necessary to take account of the work, for example, of Farran, Herth and Popovich (1995), Snyder (1994), Seligman (1991), Vaillant (1993) and many other psychologists and professionals in the field of mental health in the United States, who have virtually defined a new general orientation to psychotherapy. They stress the need to be 'positive' and 'optimistic', and basically to be the 'captain of your own ship'. Of course, they lack what Unamuno (1976) called 'a tragic sense of life', but in this cultural context people who are unable to be masters of their own fate are especially likely to suffer. It must be acknowledged that whereas in the Old World we understand the impossibilities of life, we also have a tendency towards cynicism and resignation. (Nonetheless, the current vogue in the

New World for arranging to have one's own corpse refrigerated in preparation for possible rebirth in the future is not only amusing, but also indicative of how intrapsychic life can never be understood outside the wider social, cultural and political context.)

We have learned from the study of group dynamics that a hopeful attitude towards reaching goals is essential to the maintenance of cohesion and high morale within teams and other kinds of groups. The mobilisation of hope was essential to survival in concentration camps (Dimsdale 1980). Some survivors have reported that maintaining hope was often a group activity, and that isolates did not survive. This seems to be true for many different kinds of social trauma and disasters.

To my knowledge, Pines (1998) is the only group analyst who has discussed hope in clinical work. He connects hope with being affiliated to other people, and with the process of healing, which, in turn, is said to be based on the process of making whole. Pines cites the work of Frank, Menninger, and Yalom, but these authors do not really address the topic of hope as much as recognise its importance.

How a society manages the experience of hope and its frustrations is one of the major themes in sociology, for instance see *The Principle of Hope* by Block (1959). This has been true since the discipline was founded. For example, Durkheim (1951) argued that the absence of hope is the causal factor in 'fatalistic' suicide. Of course, for Durkheim this was a theoretical issue rather than a clinical one; he discussed fatalistic suicide only in a footnote to his more extended consideration of what he termed 'anomic suicide', characterized by a surfeit of unrealistic hope (Hopper 1981).

Virtually all that has been said about hope and re-creation in the fields of psychotherapy, group dynamics, and sociology has already been said within various religious and philosophical traditions. For example, the myth of Pandora and her box continues to fascinate us, especially because one version of the story is that hope was a curse and punishment, and another that it alone offered the possibility of relief from the torments of life. In Greek mythology Elpinor was the God of Hope. Elpistic philosophers believed that nothing maintained and preserved the life of man better than hope itself. The central debates of modern philosophy concern the possibility of ethics without a belief in hope for a life after death. For example, consider the questions raised by Kierkegaard, Nietsche, Sartre and Camus in their essays on existentialism and essentialism.

In the Judeo-Christian tradition, the story of Noah's dove and its olive branch is one of the great foundation myths. In the Jewish tradition, The Talmud, The Mishnah, The Gemara and The Responsa are sources of many insights into the importance of hope in human affairs, and the 'Pirke Abot' or 'Sayings of the Fathers', the earliest part of the Midrash, remains a source of timeless parables and fables about hope. In the Christian tradition, hope is one of the cardinal virtues, along with faith and charity.

The theme of hope and its vicissitudes is ubiquitous in music, ranging from great symphonies, choral music and opera, to folk ballads, popular songs and anthems, whether for a football team or a nation. For example, 'Hatikva' or 'The Hope' is the national anthem of Israel. The first and seventh verses of 'Zdravljica' by France Preseven are used as the national anthem of Slovenia.

Similarly, hope and its vicissitudes are a central theme in western literature, including novels, short stories and poetry. For example, in Dante's (1318) *Divine Comedy* the sign on the gates to Hell read 'Abandon Hope, all ye who enter here' (which was almost certainly mocked by the sign on the gate to Auschwitz which read: 'Work makes you free'). Alexander Pope's (1734) *Essay on Man* is the source of 'Hope springs eternal from the human breast'. 'The Pleasures of Hope' by T. Campbell (1799) was an important philosophical/historical meditation of its day. Prometheus, whether bound or unbound, is a proverbial character. The American poet Emily Dickinson (1996 [1890]) referred to hope as 'the thing with feathers'. *The Waste Land* (1940) and *Four Quartets* (1943) by T. S. Eliot virtually defined the culture of the Anglo-American intelligentsia of the first half of the twentieth century. Harry Hope is the name of the bartender in Eugene O'Neill's (1998 [1940]) *The Iceman Cometh*. In an altogether different vein, and reverting to the poem that he would have been asked to memorize when he was a schoolboy, Woody Allen (1988) entitled one of his notebooks *Without Feathers*; certainly he is sensitive to Freudian readings of this fluttering bird. Set during World War I, *The Regeneration Trilogy* by Pat Barker (1991) is essential reading. Hope is the title of Len Deighton's (1995) cold war trilogy, and Nicholas Mosley (2000 [1990]) called his seminal novel *Hopeful Monsters*, which implies that he thinks that the essence of the twentieth century is an oxymoron.

Hope is both signed and symbolized at every stage in the history of western painting, often contrasted with utter despair or the complete absence of hope.[4] Among my favorite paintings concerned with these themes are Cup of Water and a Rose on a Silver Plate by de Zurbaran, The Good and Evil

Angels by Blake, and The Roofs by Chagall, which balance the abstract with the concrete, and juxtapose the symbols of hope with those of despair.

Inevitably, my article is a personal attempt to make links and connections, both internally and with others. After all, as Rickman (1948) said, '...reactions to guilt – the need to do something about it – may take various forms...including an interest in religion and charitable organizations.' In retrospect, I can see that my current ideas about hope are a continuation of what I have been thinking about for a very long time. For example, as a sociologist I (Hopper 1981) concluded my book on the sources of insatiability with a brief discussion of forms of instrumental adjustment or coping strategies (Freud, A. 1936), some of which involved hopeful resilience, tenacity, and a determination to succeed. As a psychoanalyst, within a discussion of encapsulation as a defense against the fear of annihilation, I (Hopper 1991) considered the positive encapsulation of the good object in order to keep it safe from internal and external dangers: feeling loving and loveable within the context of an internal world of horrific objects was essential to the ability to make creative use of traumatic experience. In my (Hopper 1995) study of the addiction/trauma syndrome I focused on traumatophilia – the love of trauma – as an enactment of traumatic experience in the hope that what can not be symbolized might be communicated through gesture, an idea which has since been elaborated on by others (e.g., Garland 1998) As a group analyst, my (Hopper 1972) early contributions to Group Analysis: International Panel and Correspondence (GAIPAC) were about awe, wonder and hope in connection with the study of freewill and determinism within the context of psychotherapy. My (Hopper 1996) study of the social unconscious in clinical work attempted to show that the possibilities for hopeful resolutions of intrapsychic conflict depended partly on social, cultural and political factors. I returned to this theme in my (Hopper 2000) discussion of citizenship and maturity in a brief note of appreciation of the work of Patrick de Mare. In my (Hopper 1997) Foulkes Lecture on the fourth basic assumption in the unconscious life of groups, I implied that mature hope is possible only when the 'work group' is characterized by authentic cohesion, and not when the group is caught in oscillations between aggregation and massification, the polar forms of incohesion, in response to traumatic experience. I (Hopper 2001) have since emphasized this theme in connection with the treatment in groups of our most difficult patients; following Yalom (1985), I concluded that the primary task of all forms of therapy is to maintain hope, and that where hope does not exist, to instill it.

Nonetheless, in the same way that Yalom did not tell us what hope is, or how to maintain and to instill it, I too have neglected this issue.[5] Thus, my present project.

As I have continued to study the topic of hope, I have learned, unfortunately and to my chagrin, that what I have to say about it is hardly novel. In fact, I am part of an extensive collection – if neither community nor network – of scholars and clinicians who, in their efforts to clarify their thoughts about the topic, have come to very similar conclusions. For example, Charles Rycroft (1979) has actually written that when studying the topic he learned that many others had made the points that he had intended to make.[6] I can only hope that I have organized my ideas in a new way, and have made them applicable to clinical work.

A definition

Before attempting to make these ideas relevant for psychotherapy, it is necessary to say what we mean when we use the word 'hope'. However, any attempt to define hope in a formal way brings to mind the story of the proverbial Russian tourist in Oxford. In the old days, it was always the proverbial American tourist; nowadays it is a Russian, which is, perhaps, significant in its own right. In any case, as the story goes, the Russian was standing on an ancient cobbled pavement, anxiously looking around, clearly lost and late for an appointment, most likely for tea. He stopped a somewhat remote English don who was taking an afternoon stroll, bothering no one. The Russian reached out, tugged on the poor man's sleeve, and pleaded, 'Please, Sir. Please. What is time?' After recovering from this unwelcome intrusion, the don replied, 'I am sorry, but I am not a philosopher'.

I do not identify with this absurd specialization of intellectual life in formal institutions of higher education, but I do know what the poor don meant. Certainly, when I sought a formal definition of 'hope', which, as I will discuss, is closely related to 'time', I turned first to Oxford, but in this case to its Dictionary. First of all, the grammatical forms of the word hope are very complex. The verb for hope and the noun for hope are the same. Moreover, hope can be a proper noun as well as a common noun. It is difficult to get the adjective 'hopeful' and the adverb 'hopefully' absolutely right. For example, consider the following sentence: Hopefully, Hope felt hopeful, and hoped that her hopes would be realized.

The Oxford English Dictionary also suggests some possible speculations on the philology of 'hope', although very little is known about the origins of the word. It seems that 'hope' can be traced via old English, old German and, in turn, old Scandinavian language families to, believe it or not, the word 'help'. The etymology of 'help' takes us to 'helpe'. An 'helpe' was a curved iron bar used to secure the hulls of small Mediterranean sailing boats, and boats that were used on the Sea of Galilee around the time that Jesus was born. (Incidentally, it seems that eight 'helpes' were used for each hull, and that eight people could fit into such a vessel. I am both curious and amused by these data, because eight is the number of people who seem to fit comfortably into a therapeutic group, and this has been discovered independently by many group therapists working in different cultures.)

Although the word 'hope' has various connotations, 'desirous expectation' is the common denominator of them all. In essence, 'hope' conveys an attitude of optimistic trust that the desirous expectation will be satisfied, but tenacity, determination and fortitude are also involved. Hope is a way of feeling, thinking, behaving and relating to the self and others. Hope always refers to the future. The psychologist McDougal (1931) classifies it as a 'prospective emotion'.

Some of the correlates of the relationship between desire and expectation might be categorized according to the following paradigm, based on the cross-tabulation of desire and expectation, each dichotomized into high and low:

		DESIRE	
		HIGH	LOW
EXPECTATION	HIGH	Hope, as manifest in high personal and social morale	Anomie, as personal and social insatiability
	LOW	Manic and greedy rooting and incessant searching for an 'object of desire'	Despair, as manifest in fatalistic resignation

Paradigm 8.1 - Some correlates of states of desire times states of expectation

Many of the maladies of our age can be classified in terms of this paradigm of desire and expectation. For example, when desire and expectation are high, hope, as manifest in high personal and social morale, exists, but when desire and expectation are low, despair, as manifest in fatalistic resignation, is likely to occur. Similarly, when expectation is high and desire low, anomie, as personal and social insatiability, exists, and people are unable to experience any sense of enduring satisfaction, because their expectations are always rising higher than their achievements, which is different from healthy ambition. In contrast, when desire is high and expectation low, manic and greedy rooting and incessant searching for an 'object of desire' is likely to occur, which is not to be confused with a hopeful search for a valued object or state of affairs. I have discussed these personal and social disorders of desire at some length elsewhere (Hopper 1981), and Battegay (1991) has delineated a number of diseases of oral desire. Clearly, hope can be defined in terms of desire and expectation, as can those states of mind characterized by the opposite of hope and the absence of hope. Although the definition of hope provided by the Oxford English Dictionary is indeed a formal and classical one, it is nonetheless relevant for the practice of psychotherapy.

Some conceptual distinctions

Creativity

Hope always implies a belief in the possibility of improvement and of creativity, that is, in the possibility of making something better and something new. However, to be creative is not the same as to create. In many religious traditions it is said that only God can create; man can merely rearrange. Attempts to cross this essential, non-negotiable boundary always leads to tragedy, as seen, for example, in the myths of the Golam, or in Shelley's tale of Frankenstein, which originated around the same time and possibly on the basis of similar motivations, although unconscious. In other words, to be hopeful does not imply omnipotence and omniscience, which may be defensive against the possibilities of being hopeful.

An attitude of mind and associated objects

Hope refers to an attitude towards the objects that a person has cathected. It is important to distinguish hope from the particular objects desired, and from the desired quantity of these objects.

Optimal degree of success

Hope always implies a kind of paradox: on the one hand, that the desirous expectation has not been realized; and on the other, that it has met with some degree of success. This suggests that a hopeful attitude is associated with the experience of an optimal degree of success in reaching those objects that have been valued as goals. This is a very important point, because the classical psychoanalytical idea that hope and despair go together is much too simple. After all, despair can lead to more despair! There are people who have never developed a good object, and there are people whose experience in life has destroyed their good object. Sometimes this destruction is mainly a function of the insecurity with which their good object was held and contained, and sometimes, mainly a function of the horror and terror of their experiences in life. It is, of course, always a mixture of both.

Based on past experience but directed towards the future

Hope is always Janus-faced. Although it is directed towards the future, it is based on past experience. Thus, we can consider the physical, psychological and social causes or sources of hope as desirous expectations of objects to be realized in the future.

Active and passive

Hope can be active or passive. It can involve striving to achieve or to attain an object, or a kind of patient waiting for things to come right or to be put right by others. However, both active and passive forms of hope may be defensive, if not pathological, in that active hope can be counter-passive, and passive hope, counter-active. Passive hope may disguise an inability or refusal to act, and function as an excuse for inactivity. In other words, the relationship between hope and the actions taken to realize desirous expectations is extremely complex.

Mature hope and infantile hope

Over the ages 'mature' hope has been distinguished from 'infantile' hope. Mature hope is regarded as authentic, and even as 'realistic'. In contrast, infantile and childish hope involves excessive idealization, fantasy, wishfulness and either passivity or counter-passivity in the form of omnipotent grandiosity. Infantile hope implies that certain kinds of goals have been

cathected, involving 'pie in the sky', and that narcissistic convictions of enti-
tlement are involved. When infantile hope is thwarted, feelings of bitterness
and denigration are likely to arise. In contrast, when mature hope is thwarted,
feelings of disappointment and vulnerable sorrow are likely to be followed
by the emergence of new hope.

Forms of instrumental adjustment

Hope is different from the forms of instrumental adjustment or coping
strategies that people use when they are unable to reach their goals. For
example, some people may try to change the rules that they believe are the
cause of their present failure, whereas others may change their goals.

The conditions for hope and its goals

Hope must be distinguished from the biological, psychological, social,
cultural and political conditions that govern its development and maintenance, its association with particular goals, and its association with particular
forms of instrumental adjustment. Such conditions range, for example, from
unresolved Oedipal wishes to the structural contradictions in a society's
system of stratification and succession processes.

Conscious and unconscious

People may be conscious or unconscious of their hope and hopefulness. It is
not only hopelessness and dread that may be unconscious. Similarly, people
may be conscious or unconscious of their goals. Unconscious hope, hopefulness and goals involve complex primary processes, such as displacement and
symbolism. We must acknowledge the phenomenon of the 'dreaded wish'.
People may also be conscious or unconscious of the social, cultural and
political constraints on their hope and the objects of it, or in other words of
the constraints of the social unconscious.

Deliverance and redemption

I would like to remind us of some of the essential aspects of the phenomenon
of hope as it is regarded implicitly in the Bible (which is the most important
book on the shelves of therapists of all religious persuasions within all those
societies that have been influenced by the western Judeo-Christian tradition,
although it is essential to recognize other systems of belief, for example,

those of the Muslim world). I have discussed the matter with contemporary theologians of several religious persuasions, and although I am out of my depth, I think that I have it right, basically.

In the Bible hope is for salvation. However, in the Old Testament, salvation refers more to deliverance, and in the New Testament, to redemption, although there is some overlap. In other words, in the Old Testament salvation is oriented to this life on earth, although there is an implicit distinction between waiting hopefully and passively, and searching eagerly and actively. The main goal is deliverance from unhappy circumstances, which ultimately are the will of God. Hope for deliverance 'from' is in effect a prayer for the removal of obstacles to our goals in this life.

In contrast, in the New Testament, salvation is based on a conception of everlasting life in the hereafter, not limited to the individual Christian, but embracing a vision of universal salvation. The meaning of the resurrection is that we too shall rise from the dead and enter into the full inheritance of God's Kingdom. We may entertain this hope because we already know the power of Christ within us. According to this view, hope is one of the four cardinal Christian virtues, along with faith, charity and love, the secular virtues being piety, honor, valor, courtesy, chastity and loyalty.

Salvation is not, however, a goal to be achieved. Deliverance may be an object of hope, and such hope may be supported by faith. Yet, a redeemed person does not actually hope for a life after death. Instead, it is a matter of faith that the continuity of the spirit will overcome all obstacles to desirous expectation, including the ultimate obstacle of death. To anticipate a 'passing' is more palliative than to anticipate an 'end'.

It seems to me that although it is very much a matter of age and phase of life, the phenomenon of hope and our questions about it are more concerned with death and dying than with life and living, that is, with endings, terminations, and apparent impossibilities, than with beginnings, however 'new'. The closer one is to death, the more hope depends on having embraced a conception of life after death, or alternatively on having developed identifications with younger people, for example, one's children and grandchildren, one's students and one's patients, which is different from asking them to realize one's own abandoned hopes. In this sense, hope facilitates a certain kind of boundary crossing, and is the essence of liminality.

Summary

In sum, when we talk of mature, authentic hope, whether active or passive, conscious or unconscious, we are interested in desirous expectations towards objects that are valued as goals that are believed to be realizable and attainable, at least in principle. In mature, authentic hope, despite obstacles and adversity, or perhaps because of them, a certain fortitude, optimistic trust and tenacity will prevail over feelings of despair and bitterness. The development and the maintenance of a hopeful attitude is a characteristic of a mature person, who has the capacity to love, work and play in harmony with others, and who is able and willing to take the role of citizen, that is, of one who is willing and able to try to create the social, cultural and political conditions that are necessary for the development and maintenance of hopeful attitudes, for others as well as for oneself. However, it must be acknowledged that many people fervently believe in the ultimate hope of salvation, whether primarily through deliverance or primarily through redemption, and, therefore, that maturity also involves being at peace with God.

Personal theories

I will now shift from these abstract distinctions to a more personal and clinical level of discussion. I have observed that my most traumatized patients respond to me at two levels, more or less simultaneously, but rarely consciously. Although they listen to me with interest and respect, and some try to enter into dialogue with me about the nature of hope and its vicissitudes, many 'translate' their experience of what I say into the language of their own religious beliefs. For the most part, they have been influenced by the beliefs that prevail in our cultures, and they continue to struggle with these beliefs and their implications for feelings and actions. Some hold religious beliefs that are very personal and idiosyncratic. Sometimes, my patients assign their religious beliefs to other people, such as their putative 'friends', in much the same way that those with a venereal disease seek help for friends rather than themselves. Some patients are ashamed to acknowledge that they continue to have the preoccupations of children and adolescents about the great questions in life concerning the nature of birth, death, and the so-called 'Hereafter', or in other words, as Monty Python would put it, 'The Meaning of Life'; they seem to fear that they can discuss this only in terms that will seem banal to the sophisticated clinician.

Clearly, it is important to help patients discuss these preoccupations, if for no other reason than that they may constitute certain kinds of defense which, from the point of view of traditional psychoanalysis, must be interpreted, not only in general but in the context of the transference and countertransference. However, I have observed that few of us are able to work with religious beliefs with vigor and conviction, very much as few of us are able to tell our very young children that it is not Father Christmas who puts the presents under the Christmas tree. Yet, those of us who work with the victims of profound trauma, especially massive social trauma, welcome the existence of such beliefs as a kind of ally in the therapeutic work. It is important to be able to see things as our patients see them, at least most of the time.

In the beginning, the question for psychoanalysis was, and in a way still is, whether maturity is a matter of the realization of divine inspiration, or a matter of the circumstances of life.[7] However, 'psychoanalysis' and 'group analysis' are different from 'psychoanalyst' and 'group analyst', and both are different from the views of particular psychoanalysts and group analysts. For instance, consistent with the view of hope that Freud (1927) formulated in 'The Future of an Illusion', Schur (1972), Freud's physician and friend, reported that Freud showed great fortitude in the face of a painful and lengthy process of dying from cancer, and confessed that in keeping with his promise to Freud that when the pain became unbearable, it would not be necessary to commit suicide, he administered the fatal dose of morphine. In the course of my work on the topic of hope, I found myself assuming that my colleagues admired the manner in which Freud bore his own death and dying, but at the same time realizing that actually I knew very little about their beliefs. Therefore, I decided to ask a few of them what they thought about hope in connection with death and dying, without actually defining the context of my inquiry. I would like to summarize a few of their replies.

A member of the Group of Independent Psychoanalysts of the British Psychoanalytical Society, who was really more Freudian than Kleinian, told me that he only hoped that he could maintain his curiosity about the process of dying for as long as possible. He implied that there were links between the experience of death and the experience of birth. He believed that how well his patients lived offered some indication of how well he had lived himself. When I asked him about hope he was in his early 80s, ill and facing death.

Another psychoanalyst, who is more Kleinian than Freudian, said: 'Yes, of course, I believe in hope. But only when it is reasonable to do so. After all, a slight depression and a hopeful attitude go together. You must keep your expectations flexible.'

Especially interesting to me was the reply from a Jungian analytical psychologist, who said: 'Absolutely. However, I cannot split off my belief in hope from my belief in the importance of faith and charity. Also, for me, a criterion for successful termination would be a patient's ability to fish his psyche for inspiration during difficult times.' In other words, a belief in hope offers the only solution to the problem of free will and determinism.

All these replies are very different from that of yet another colleague who, having heard that I wanted to talk about death and dying, ran away whenever he saw me coming. They also differ from the implicit response of a colleague who, after several years of suffering a debilitating, terminal illness, took her own life, leaving a farewell letter to the effect that she wished to alleviate her lonely dependence on others. Although she was not a Christian, she professed her belief in the continuity of the spirit.

I also asked colleagues what they thought about referring a patient who said that he was a Christian to a psychoanalyst or group analyst who was not a Christian. I formed the impression that colleagues from a Christian background were inclined to refer Christian patients to Christian colleagues. This went beyond the simple view that they would be able to understand each other better. Instead there was the assumption that the Christian analyst would not view the patient's Christianity as essentially defensive. This was partly a matter of clinical judgement, and partly an unconscious aspect of the referral process concerning with whom one wishes to have clinical children. The referral process may be endogamous to religious groupings, but certainly it contributes to the cohesion of the network of colleagues who do refer to one another.

Many colleagues from all branches of psychoanalysis and from various religious backgrounds were slightly hesitant to answer my question fully. They tended to repudiate the formal views of established religions, which were not to be taken literally, as might children at Sunday School, or at Religion School. Nonetheless, judging from the strong feelings that were aroused by my questions, I have concluded that my colleagues are much more troubled by the phenomenon of hope than they are aware. They last thought about these questions when they were adolescents, and they did not like to be taken back to this turbulent phase of life.

The capacity and willingness to exercise the transcendent imagination within the context of the traumatogenic process

I will now propose a view of hope that is based on contemporary object relations thinking in psychoanalysis and group analysis. My clinical work is informed by this view, which, I suppose, has become a kind of credo.

I believe that the infant is born in a state of primary love for, and harmonious confusion with, his mother, but in a state of great vulnerability and dependency, within a social, cultural and political context which both facilitates the choice of goals and the achievement of them, and presents obstacles to the achievement of objects of desire. Thus, the traumatogenic process is ubiquitous, as are frustration and aggression. However, the extent and intensity of traumatic experience are indeed variable.

Within this context, I would define hope as the willingness and ability to exercise the transcendent imagination in an attempt to overcome obstacles to the fulfillment of desirous expectations. Thus, hope is always associated with resilience, tenacity, fortitude and a degree of realistic optimism, which are forged through the transmuting internalization of good enough relationships with one's primary objects, that is, with the breast as well as the phallus, and with the mother as well as the father, and with siblings as well as parents. On the basis of these virtuous achievements, a person is able to imagine possibilities for making creative use of traumatic experience. Of course, these early internal relationships are developed and maintained throughout life. What might be expected of a healthy infant or child is different from what might be expected of an adult, especially one who is near death.

The ability and willingness to imagine is akin to the 'act of illusion', which is an awkward phrase, but in English there is no verb for the activity of forming an illusion. To 'illude' is more than to think or to form a concept. It is based on symbolization, but it is more complex and comprehensive than symbolization alone. Similarly, it is based on sublimation, but it cannot be reduced to the process of the substitution of one object for another. For me, the act of illusion refers to making an imaginative leap across a chasm of loss, abandonment and damage. It is an attempt to heal a sense of emptiness, of a gap between the expected and the experience of reality. In this sense, an illusion is the product of a positive, constructive activity, and not a protective one, although clearly an illusion can be used defensively, and at some point can be 'illusionary' or even become a delusion.

In the same way that traumatized people may be able to encapsulate the entire traumatogenic process, including both memories and affects, and, thus, protect themselves from the full weight of the fear of annihilation and its associated phenomena, traumatized people may also be able to encapsulate their good experiences and sense of hope for survival and re-creation in order to protect themselves from overwhelming helplessness. Positive encapsulations urge towards repetition and communication in general as much as, if not more than, do negative encapsulations with which we are more familiar. The positive encapsulation of the possibility to imagine alternatives to total helplessness can be dormant for a long, long time, much as the traumatized storyteller remains mute while waiting almost for ever to discover a person to whom he believes that his story can be told.

Envy is indeed the enemy of hope. The desire to spoil the pleasure and creativity of parental intercourse, both within the family and within the mind, is the basic motive for attacking meaning, that is, for stopping oneself from making life meaningful. However, in my view, envy is not an expression of the putative death instinct, but a retaliatory defense against the fear of annihilation associated with the experience of profound helplessness based on the traumatic experience of loss, abandonment and damage. Helplessness precedes envy, and envy is directed towards those objects who are seen as having the ability and wherewithal to be helpful but who are not. Those conditions that mitigate the experience of helplessness and affirm a sense of self-worth and self-esteem are the enemies of envy. In other words, it is possible to minimize the extent and intensity of envy.

The mitigation of envy as a defense against helplessness and its inherent sense of shame depends on the experience of being a member of a community characterized by authentic cohesion involving integration, solidarity and coherence. The transmuting internalization of good enough objects depends on being-in-relationship within the context of a cohesive community, an essential element of which is being-in-dialogue with others. Being in dialogue is the basic condition for being able to tell one's story, not as a repetitive, ruminative substitute for thinking, but as an attempt to make links and to make life meaningful.

Recovery from traumatic experience also requires that relationships within the community are re-established. This depends both on individual members of the community, and on the structure of the community as a whole. For example, rules in the culture govern the ability and willingness of people to conceptualize and think abstractly, and, thus, to symbolize their experience of their internal and external worlds. People tend to be unconscious of these cultural codes and the ways in which they constrain styles of thinking, feeling and even perceiving, and, hence, the way that people can respond to life events. When people are generally powerless, they develop a concrete and operational style of thinking, and they develop forms of child rearing through which they transmit these styles of thinking to their children. In other words, in some sections of our societies, the Chinese water torture quality of everyday life restricts the ability to think about and reflect upon experience.

The ability and willingness to exercise the transcendent imagination depends on the authentic, optimal cohesion of our social groupings, which, in turn, depends on an optimal degree of inequality in power and authority, and on the courage to exercise power and authority with care and responsibility. Without this there can be no safety. This is true for the parent–infant relationship, and it is true for the political life of our organizations and our society. Of course, these realms are interrelated. For example, gender roles and identities are a political matter as well as a biological one, and as a consequence of political action and various social and cultural changes, we have learned that the good father is as important to our mental health as the good mother, and that strength and the capacity to nurture belong to woman and to man.

At the end of the day, however, it is not always possible to put right the consequences of extreme traumatic experience. Various forms of instrumental adjustment are inevitable, and some of these will involve the language of the body, various forms of perversion and addiction. The rates of such painful instrumental adjustments vary – they are more prevalent in traumatized communities, but less prevalent in those communities in which social, cultural and political healing has taken place.

I am convinced that as psychotherapists, we cannot just 'kiss it better', but we can make a difference. For example, the very development of new forms of psychoanalytical and psychodynamic therapy, such as clinical group analysis, including the invention of the large and the median group as a space for the exploration of identity and social life, indicates that we should be hopeful. So, too, does our having learned that, for example, horrific child abuse can be traced to the repetition compulsion, and that this, in turn, can be understood in terms of the desperate attempts of perpetrators to communicate their own traumatic experience. The golden rule of forensic psychotherapy is that the traumatized do unto others as they have been done by, because this is the only way that they can obtain a degree of relief from their own suffering, and in the desperate hope that they will be understood. Most

importantly, we have learned that we can help create with our patients a safe
social–psychological space within which it is possible to dream and to
imagine both the ends and the means for a more satisfactory way of life.

Hope in clinical work

We all agree that psychoanalysis and psychotherapy take place within an
inter-personal matrix, one strand of which is transference and countertransference. Analyst and analysand are challenged to understand how their
present has been caused by their active, perceiving and projecting pasts.
However, building on the work of Foulkes and his colleagues, I (Hopper
1996, a version of which is reprinted as Chapter 6 of this book) have argued
that a more complete understanding of the transference-countertransference
relationship requires the 'location' of this relationship within a matrix of time
and space, defined not only in terms of the 'Here and Now' and the 'Here and
Then', but also the 'There and Now' and even the 'There and Then'. In other
words, in order to enable the analysand to be sufficiently free to construct a
more satisfactory future, it is necessary to extend Malan's (1979) 'therapeutic
triangle' to Hopper's 'therapeutic square'.

Psychoanalysts who have adopted a contemporary object relations perspective have acknowledged that it is important to understand the sociality of
human nature throughout the life cycle, and to explore the constraints of the
social unconscious. For example, David and Jill Scharff (1998) have accepted
my argument that all four cells of the time–space paradigm should be used in
our clinical work, and that we should increase our knowledge of the social
sciences in order to understand how we are influenced by external factors and
forces as well as biological ones. However, the Scharffs have taken issue with
me on a couple of points, and introduced a fundamental extension of my
approach, which is entirely relevant to the present discussion of hope as transcendent imagination. I would like to outline this dialogue.[8]

The Scharffs write:

> Moving on from Winnicott's idea of the potential space between mother
> and infant for creativity and imagination various authors from different
> schools of thought have been writing about the shared experience between
> patient and therapist that leads to growth, [for example]: 'the x factor'
> (Symington), 'genera' (Bollas), 'intersubjectivity' (Stolorow and Atwood),
> 'the co-construction of meaning between patient and analyst' (Gill) and
> 'the analytic third' (Ogden). These concepts all refer to ways of under-
> standing that [the form of] what is created between patient and therapist

[depends on] the particular contributions of personalities and the process unique to these two people… This [third] structure is built from events that happen in the space between the two individuals, not simply within either of them… (p.248)[9]

On the basis of these concerns, and drawing on an essay by Steven Mitchell (1993), the Scharffs insist that we add to my time – space paradigm a 'future dimension', which they call the 'If and When'. The 'If and When' refers to a category of personal and inter-personal mental and emotional experience concerned with the imagination of future possibilities, both for self and other, and for our social and cultural life. In other words, it is necessary to consider the 'If and When' with respect to the 'Here' and the 'There'.

In a discussion of a previous version of Mitchell's article (Hopper 1992), and in subsequent correspondence with the Scharffs, I have argued that their proposed modification is not entirely justifiable. An 'If and When' mode of experience is not a separate aspect of mental and transference organization, because a patient's imagination occurs in the present time, even though it is about the future. Moreover, the structure of the 'If and When' mode of experience is, at least in part, a product of past experience, as is the ability to work within it. This is especially true for people who have been traumatized. For example, it is very difficult for a survivor to imagine future alternatives and to think freely about his past, because the survival of trauma causes a type of suspended memory, a concretisation of mental experience which is at one and the same time both a result of the trauma and a defense against the anxieties associated with it. This actually involves a kind of regression from the mind to the brain and body more generally, that is, from the processes of sociology and psychology to the processes of biology and physiology, and from one kind of scientific discourse to another, which is the basis of Balint's (1968) theory of benign therapeutic regression to a level at which a new beginning might be possible. A negative encapsulation is only a specific instance of the more general issue of social causation. Also, the belief that transcendence is possible in principle, and that others have been able to manage it, may lead to shame and further despair, rather than to a development of the will to overcome. In other words, the ability to transcend is limited, not only within the creative imagination, but also within the external world. We remain half-way between the apes and the angels.

In response, the Scharffs have written to me that

> …the common experience that people (and societies) rewrite history in the light of contemporary experience makes the point that personal and social history is also a matter of current understanding and current importance. The same applies to the future: individuals and societies are constantly revising their visions of the future, which are carried personally and collectively as a current mental and social organization…

This is indeed a very important point. The human condition is such that we do rewrite history in the light of social, cultural and political forces as well as more personal needs, and that we do this both consciously and unconsciously. However, this does not mean that the processes of revision are without contextual constraints. For example, although it may be a matter of degree, revisionist history in democratic societies occurs less frequently and is less acceptable than in totalitarian societies. After all, in times of social crisis, the BBC's World Service remains a valuable source of information on short-wave radios everywhere. Similarly, whereas we are all capable in principle of revising our vision of the future, the capacity to do so is governed by past experience within the complex social, cultural and political context. In both traditional societies and totalitarian ones, the capacity to imagine alternatives for the future may be more limited than it is in modern democratic societies.

In other words, we have an intellectual problem, which is sometimes couched within the context of debates about free will and determinism. Many of us struggled with these issues when we were adolescents. The problem of free will and determinism has beset psychoanalysis from its inception, and it is always associated with one or another of the schismatic movements within psychoanalysis. In a way, the problem is associated with the endless debates about trauma, namely, did the trauma really happen, or was it imagined, or was it a mixture of the two forms of reality, that is, the external and the internal, in which case the issue becomes whether the ultimate cause was the effects of internal, instinctual impulses on fantasy life, as opposed to the constraints of external reality.[10]

Although hope should be regarded as the ability and willingness to exercise the transcendent imagination, which goes beyond regarding hope as desirous expectation, the imagination is limited by past experience, as is our ability to put into effect what we can imagine. Personal, idiosyncratic past experience limits the capacity to symbolize and to transcend the effects of current experience, especially traumatic experience. For example, it is easy enough to focus on the 'Here and Now' and the possibility of transcendence, but in so far as interpretative work is directed towards obstacles to curiosity and the freedom to think and to imagine, it is not so easy to know what should be interpreted in terms of what. In other words, the integration of the perspectives of the biology, sociology, and the philosophy of mind is not only impossible, but also very difficult.

Despite our shared emphasis on object relations thinking, including the importance of understanding the constraints of internal objects, based partly on transmuting internalization of external objects, the Scharffs are primarily existentialist–'action'–object relations thinkers, and I am more of a existen-tialist –'systems'–object relations thinker. However, the Scharffs and I agree clinically. I completely endorse the attempt to ask and to answer the clinical questions: how can we together imagine 'If and When' states of mind, rela-tionships and situations that might be different and perhaps more satisfying?; what can we do to facilitate the development of this mode of experience?; can we think creatively about the future?; can we facilitate the development of situations that are more satisfying for self and others?; can we develop the capacity for taking the role of citizen? I completely endorse the view that the capacity for decision and the willingness to choose depend on becoming free from unconscious constraints of various kinds of bad objects and encapsu-lated traumatic experience. Insight is not a matter of revelation, but a product of hard, painful and disciplined intellectual and emotional work.

And yet, in terms of the theoretical considerations that I have mentioned, it must be acknowledged that people have unequal access to psychotherapy, and training in the provision of psychotherapy is hardly available universally. Moreover, not all people are able to use what psychotherapy is available, or at least use it in a productive way. Despite our best efforts and most fervent hopes, the ubiquitous bad object can be very tenacious indeed, and the per-petuation across the generations of chosen trauma is often intransigent.

Summary and prelude to further work

In this article I have defined hope as desirous expectation, and considered a number of essential conceptual distinctions. I then suggested an alternative definition of hope in terms of the ability and willingness to exercise the tran-scendent imagination with regard to the survival of traumatic experience and attempts to make creative use of this. I have considered several aspects of the emergence of this virtue and its development throughout the life trajectories that are typical of any given societies. I have also considered the application of this perspective to clinical work in terms of the possibilities of forging a clinical team in which therapist and patient seek to understand the obstacles to the exercise of the transcendent imagination.

I have decided not to conclude this article here. In subsequent publications I will illustrate the application of these ideas to clinical work, and trace their emergence within the context of the development of contemporary object relations thinking in psychoanalysis and group analysis.

References

Allen, W. (1988) *Without Feathers.* London: Little Brown.

Alvarez, A. (1992) *Live Company.* London: Taylor Francis.

Balint, M. (1968) *The Basic Fault: Therapeutic Aspects of Regression.* London:Tavistock.

Barker, P. (1991) *The Regeneration Trilogy.* London: Viking.

Battegay, R. (1991) *The Hunger Diseases.* Leviston, NY: Hogrefe & Huber Publishers.

Buchele, B. (2000) 'Life's many pieces: The identity of the group psychotherapist.' *The International Journal of Group Psychotherapy 50,* 4, 419-437.

Block, E. (1959) *Das Prinzip Hoffnung.* Suhrkamp-Verlag, Frankfurt-am-Main.

Bollas, C. (1999) *The Mystery of Things.* London: Routledge.

Campbell, T. (1940) [1799] 'The Pleasures of Hope and other Poems.' In R. Myers (ed) *The Dictionary of English Literature.* (Original work published 1799.)

Casement, P. (1985) *Learning from the Patient.* London: Tavistock.

Dahrendorf, R. (1976) 'Inequality, hope and progress.' Eleanor Rathbone Memorial Lecture: Liverpool University Press.

Dante, A. (1970) [1318] *Divine Comedy* trans. by C. Singleton. Princeton University Press. (Original work published 1318.)

Deighton, L. (1995) *Hope.* London: Harper Collins.

Dickinson, E. (1996) [1890] 'Hope is the thing with feathers.' In *The Selected Poems of Emily Dickinson. Life,* Chapter XXXII, 20. New York: The Modern Library. (Original work published 1890.)

Dietrich, D. and Shabad, P. (1989) *The Problem of Loss and Mourning.* Madison, CT: International Universities Press.

Dimsdale, J. (1980) *Survivors, Victims and Perpetrators: Essays on the Nazi Holocaust.* New York: Hemisphere.

Durkheim, E. (1951) *Suicide.* Glencoe, Illinois: The Free Press.

Eliot, T. S. (1940) *The Waste Land and other Poems.* London: Faber and Faber.

Eliot, T. S. (1943) *Four Quartets: Burnt Norton.* New York: Harcourt, Brace and World.

Farran, C., Herth, A., and Popovich, J. (1995) *Hope and Hopelessness: Critical Clinical Constructs.* Thousand Oaks, CA: Sage.

Freud, A. (1936) *The Ego and the Mechanisms of Defence.* London: The Hogarth Press.

Freud, S. (1917) 'Mourning and Melancholia.' Standard Edition 14, 243–258.

Freud, S. (1927) 'The Future of an Illusion.' Standard Edition 21, 3–56.

Garland, C. (ed) (1998) *Understanding Trauma.* London: Duckworth.

Greenson, R. (1967) *The Technique and Practice of Psychoanalysis*. London: The Hogarth Press.

Haynal, A. (1994) 'Central European Psychoanalysis and its Move Westwards in the 1920's and 30's.' In H. Ehlers and J. Crick (eds) *The Trauma of the Past: Remembering and Working Through*. Lecture Series organized by the Goethe-Institute, London.

Home, J. (1966) 'The concept of the mind.' *International Journal of Psycho-Analysis 47*, 1, 42–49.

Hopper, E. (1971) 'Notes on Stratification, Education and Mobility in Industrial Societies.' In *Readings in the Theory of Educational Systems*. London: Hutchinsons.

Hopper, E. (1972) 'Report and comments on basic principles, changes and trends.' *Group Analysis: International Panel and Correspondence 5*, 2, 91–94.

Hopper, E. (1981) *Social Mobility: A Study of Social Control and Insatiability*. Oxford: Basil Blackwell Publisher Ltd.

Hopper, E. (1991) 'Encapsulation as a defence against the fear of annihilation.' *International Journal of Psycho-Analysis 72*, 4, 607–24.

Hopper, E. (1992) Discussant of *Hope and Dread in Psychoanalysis* by Stephen Mitchell. The Annual Frieda Fromm-Reichmann Lecture. Washington, DC: Washington School of Psychiatry.

Hopper, E. (1995) 'A psychoanalytical theory of drug addiction: Unconscious fantasies of homosexuality, compulsions and masturbation within the context of traumatogenic processes.' *International Journal of Psycho-Analysis 76*, 6, 1121–42.

Hopper, E. (1996) 'The Social Unconscious in Clinical Work.' *Group 20*, 1, 7–42.

Hopper, E. (1997) 'Traumatic Experience in the Unconscious Life Of Groups: A Fourth Basic Assumption.' *Group Analysis 30*, 4, 439–470.

Hopper, E. (1998) 'On the Nature of Hope.' Keynote Lecture. Thirteenth Congress of the International Association of Group Psychotherapy. London, UK. Available on cassette: QED Recording Services Ltd.

Hopper, E. (2000) 'From objects and subjects to citizens: Group analysis and the study of maturity.' *Group Analysis 33*, 1, 29–34.

Hopper, E. (2001) 'Difficult patients in group analysis.' *Group 25*, 3, 139–171.

Kavaler-Adler, S. (1993) *The Compulsion to Create*. London: Routledge.

Malan, D. (1979) *Individual Psychotherapy and the Science of Psychodynamics*. London: Butterworths.

McDougal, W. (1931) *An Introduction to Social Psychology* 22nd edition. London: Methuen.

Mitchell, S. (1993) *Hope and Dread in Psychoanalysis*. New York: Basic Books.

Mosley, N. (2000) [1990] *Hopeful Monsters*. London: Vintage. (Original work published 1990.)

Niederland, W. (1989) 'Trauma, Loss, Restoration, and Creativity.' In D. Dietrich and P. Shabad (eds) *The Problem of Loss and Mourning*. Madison, CT: International Universities Press.

O'Neill, E. (1998) [1940] *The Iceman Cometh*. London: Nick Hern Books Limited. (Original work published 1940.)

Pines, M. (ed) (1998) 'Group Analysis and Healing.' In *Circular Reflections*. London: Jessica Kingsley Publishers Ltd.

Pope, A. (1994) [1734] *An Essay on Man and Other Poems*. New York: Dover. (Original work published in 1734.)

Rickman, J. (1948) 'Guilt and the Dynamics of Psychological Disorder in the Individual.' *Proceedings of the International Conference on Mental Health 3*, 41. London: H K Lewis & Co. Ltd.

Rycroft, C. (1979) 'Steps to an Ecology of Hope.' In R. Fitzgerald (ed) *The Sources of Hope.* Oxford: Pergamon Press.

Rycroft. C. (1985) *Psychoanalysis and Beyond.* London: The Hogarth Press.

Rycroft, C. (1991) 'Faith, Hope and Charity.' *Viewpoints.* London: The Hogarth Press.

Sacks, J. (1997) *The Politics of Hope.* London: Jonathan Cape.

Scharff, D. and Scharff, J. (1998) *Object Relations Individual Therapy.* London: Karnac Books.

Schur, M. (1972) *Freud Living and Dying.* London: The Hogarth Press.

Seligman, M. (1991) *Learned Optimism.* New York: Knopf.

Sklair, L (1998) [1970] *The Sociology of Progress.* London: Routledge. (Original work published 1970.)

Snyder, C. (1994) *The Psychology of Hope.* New York: The Free Press

Unamuno, M. (1976) *A Tragic Sense of Life.* New York: Dover.

Vaillant, G. (1993) *The Wisdom of the Ego.* Cambridge, Mass: Harvard University Press.

Welldon, E. (1997) Twentieth S. H. Foulkes Lecture 'Let the treatment fit the crime: Forensic group psychotherapy.' *Group Analysis 30*, 1, 9–26.

Yalom, I. (1985) *The Theory and Practice of Group Psychotherapy.* New York: Basic Books.

Zetzel, E. (ed) (1958) 'Therapeutic Alliance in the Analysis of Hysteria.' *The Capacity for Emotional Growth.* London: The Hogarth Press.

Notes

1   This chapter was first published in 2001 as 'On the nature of hope in psychoanalysis and group analysis' in the *British Journal of Psychotherapy 18*, 2, 205–226. Previous versions of it were presented in February 2000 at the Weekend Conference of The International Institute of Object Relations Therapy (IIORT) where I received the helpful and stimulating comments of David and Jill Scharff, the Faculty and the students; and in October 2000 at the Slovene Association of Psychotherapists Conference, where I also benefited from the comments of Peter Praper, Franc Peternel and their colleagues and students.

2   Some of this work was presented in my Presidential Lecture 'On the Nature of Hope' at the Thirteenth Congress of the International Association of Group Psychotherapy entitled 'Annihilation, Survival, Re-creation' in 1998 in London. It is available on cassette: QED Recording Services Ltd. I am grateful to Hans Reijzer for his criticisms of previous versions of the lecture and to John Lahr for his stimulating discussions of the topic of hope in contemporary theater.

3   Kavaler-Adler (1993) has provided an excellent review of psychoanalytical discussions of reparation, and has illustrated her own ideas with careful studies of women writers, such as Emily Dickinson and Emily Bronte. In fact, she has entitled one of her chapters 'Emily Bronte I: The Messenger of Hope and the Demon in the Nightwind.' Kavaler-Adler refers to Klein's work on reparation and to Kohut's on restoration, in addition to the work of other authors in the traditions of ego-psychology, object relations and self-psychology. This general theme of attempts to make creative use of the experience of surviving traumatic experience is at least mentioned by several con-

tributors edited by Dietrich and Shabad (1989). Frequent reference is made to the work of Niederland (1989).

4   The following paintings, selected with the help of Mrs Jill Polonsky, are illustrative:

   (a) The Seven Virtues by Francesco Pesellino (about 1455), housed at the Birmingham Museum of Art, Birmingham, Alabama, USA.

   (b) The Annunciation, with St Emidius, by Carlo Crivelli (1486), housed at the National Gallery, London, UK.

   (c) Madonna and Child with SS John the Baptist and Jerome by Parmigianino (1539), housed at the National Gallery, London, UK.

   (d) The Good and Evil Angels by William Blake (1805), housed at the Tate Gallery, London, UK.

   (e) Cup of Water and a Rose on a Silver Plate by Francisco de Zurbaran (1625), housed at the National Gallery, London, UK.

   (f) Hope, replica by George Frederic Watts (1886), housed at the Tate Gallery, London, UK.

   (g) Faa Iheihe by Paul Gauguin (1898), housed at the Tate Gallery, London, UK.

   (h) Hatikva (The Hope) by Salvador Dali (1968), housed at the County Hall, London, UK.

   Similarly, consider the following paintings of the dove and the raven, ranging from images that are like photographs to tho ie that are highly abstract:

   (a) Child with a Dove by Pablo Picasso (1901), housed at the National Gallery, London, UK.

   (b) Wounded Bird by Phillip Sutton (about 1965), housed in a private collection.

   (c) The Roofs by Marc Chagall (1953), Musee d'Art Moderne, Centre Georges Pompidou, Paris, France.

5   It is not without interest that so many authors conclude excellent articles on highly traumatized patients, organizations and societies with spirited assertions that our work challenges us to help transform despair and resignation into hope and re-creation, but do not tell us anything at all about this process and what it might involve (for example, Haynal 1994; Buchele 2000; Welldon 1997).

6   As it happens, Rycroft's argument is very similar to my own. In fact, he refers to my (Hopper 1971) work on the effects of stratification and education on patterns of ambition. In a later version of his article Rycroft (1991) wrote that he should have included this essay in his (Rycroft 1985) collection *Psychoanalysis and Beyond*. I believe that it is not necessary to go beyond psychoanalysis, but it is essential to build on it.

7   This is the same question that has always challenged the social sciences, particularly in connection with the idea of progress. For example, see the work of Sklair (1998), Dahrendorf (1976) and Sacks (1997).

8   The Scharffs also argue that to denote the personal history of the patient we should use the term 'Back Then' rather than 'Here and Then', because 'Here and Then' cannot be extended from the relationship between analyst and analysand to the relationship of the analysand to significant figures in his life prior to the beginning of the treatment relationship, e.g. mother and father during infancy. They also suggest that 'There and Then' be specified to include smaller and more personal groupings, such as the family as distinct from organizations and society itself, and to locate the patient

within them. I am sure that they would also specify the phenomena of the 'There and Now' in a similar way.

These modifications are entirely acceptable. The only problem is to convey with brevity that the 'Here' is merely a space in the life trajectory of the relationship between the patient and the analyst, and in their respective personal life trajectories. The words 'stage' and 'phase' might be more appropriate, but they too convey both time and space simultaneously.

9   Ordinarily I would suggest that the Scharffs should have included Greenson's (1967) 'working alliance' and Zetzel's (1958) 'therapeutic triangle' as strands of the clinical relationship, as well as references to Harold Searles, Edith Jacobson, and even Herbert Rosenfeld. Yet these authors were referring more to a partnership who would work together primarily to understand the effects of the past on the present, and not to what Bollas (1999) calls a clinical 'team' who try to co-construct their view of their present and their vision of a possible future, and, therefore, who might facilitate the transcendence of the present situation and predicament of the analysand, and possibly of the analyst as well.

10   I am reminded of a conversation that I had with the late Jim Home, a psychoanalyst who began to practice as a group analyst around the time that he (1966) wrote 'The concept of the mind'. He was influenced by the work of Rycroft, Lomas and other like-minded psychoanalysts and analytical psychologists. We were having lunch at The Tate, which used to have a great restaurant specializing in very traditional English cooking and classical French wine. We had just taken a rest from viewing an exhibition of Blake's illustrations of the deadly sins, and had begun to discuss sin and virtue, the problem of innate malign envy, Kleinian views on the putative death instinct, issues of free will and determinism and the constraints of biology and of society. Jim and I often discussed these questions. In fact, we would break into such discussions whenever we met. On this occasion, Jim rather suddenly stopped in midstream and said to me, 'You know, Earl, this is our way of saying 'L'Chaim' ('To Life'), rather than 'To Death'. Later, I insisted, 'Jim, it is just one of those things'. With his usual mischievous grin, he replied, 'When you have decided which one, you must promise to tell me'. Shortly thereafter, he suffered several strokes. He died before I had a chance to tell him that 'one' can be 'both', and that 'both' can be 'one', which I suppose he already knew. Jim would have liked my becoming interested in the topic of hope in psychotherapy.

Subject Index

active/passive hope 197
Afghanistan 17
aggregation 143, 145, 147, 160n, 161n, 193
aggression
    interactional and normative controls 20,
        33–5, 36, 47, 130
altruistic norms 52, 63, 70n
ambition, normative limitations 129–30
America *see* United States
analysts/therapists
    internal/external emphasis dichotomy 136–9
    neglect of social sciences in training 154–5,
        163
    recognition of inner victim and persecutor 98
    social identity issues neglected 163
    see also group analysts; psychoanalysts
annihilation anxiety 19, 87, 116, 141, 143,
    145, 147, 183, 188n, 193, 204
anomie 196
anthropology 60
    'cultural' and 'social' 160n
anti-Semitism 20–1, 83
Arabs 112, 113
'archaic' information 127
Auschwitz 76, 86, 192
authority
    group communication and normative
        structures 65
    independent study of social and individual
        aspects 43–4
    supervisory styles and normative expectations
        26–32, 35, 130

basic assumptions 12, 107
    Incohesion: Aggregation/Massification theory
        160n, 161n, 193
    no knowledge of time and space 100–1, 106,
        131–2
benign therapeutic regression 207
Bible 198–9
    Book of Job 173
'bird' symbolism 176
    'depressive position bird' 176
    'Wounded Bird' print 173–7, 184, 185, 213n
'bird's eye view' 184–5
Blacks and blackness 167, 168, 182, 183
    association with 'Caliban' 169

'Negroes' in St Louis 9, 176–7
'not-white' identity 164–5
psychoanalytical explanation of social
    problems rejected 121–2
borygmie (tummy rumbles) 146–7
boss–subordinate relationship, social structure 47
Britain/United Kingdom
    'social' anthropology 160n
    social stratification 65
    state of the nation 120, 144, 145
British Association of Psychotherapists 10, 14n

child abuse 205
Chile, use of large groups in participatory
    democracy 66
Christianity 192, 199, 202
circumcision 179
citizenship 152, 193, 200
closure/openness of social systems 51
    complexity and 53–5
cohesion 50
collective transference
    aspects of technique 107
    contextualization 105, 119
    countertransference as source of data 107–8,
        114–15
    Israel 64
collective unconscious 124n, 159n
complexity of social systems 49
    and 'development' 70n
    and group size 62–3
    and instability 55–6
    and openness 53–5
    and social cohesion 52–3
concentration camps 73, 77, 87, 96, 101, 131
    mobilization of hope 191
    romantic unions 94n
conflict and tension management 52, 53, 68–9n
conformity studies 61
conscious/unconscious hope 198
context
    concept of 103–4
    in group analytic psychotherapy 103–25
    of groups 64–6, 126–7
    problem of 104–6
    and processes of revision 208
    of traumatogenic processes 203–6
coping strategies *see* 'instrumental adjustment'
core values, development and maintenance 69n
countertransference
    distinguishing analyst's feelings from patient's
        projections 117

Author Index

Allen, W. 192
Alvarez, A. 190
Anthony, J. 187n
Argyle, M., Gardner, G. and Cioffi, F. 34
Argyris, C. 41n
Asch, S. E. 61
Austen, J. 159n

Baldamus, W. 40n
Bales, R. F. 27–8
Bales, R. F. and Borgotta, E. F. 61–2
Balint, M. 188n, 207
Barker, P. 192
Battegay, R. 196
Beck, W. 94n
Behr, H. 77
Behrend, H. 40n
Bellow, S. 160n
Bendix, R. 159n
Berelson, B. and Steiner, G. A. 59–60
Berger, B. B. 39n
Berne, E. 10
Bernfeld, S. 19
Bettelheim, B. 77, 87, 94n, 150, 187n
Bion, W. R. 85, 100, 103, 106, 107, 111, 119, 124n, 131–2
Biran, H. 13, 187n
Blake, W. 12, 193, 213n
Blau, P. M. 62
Blau, P. M. and Schoenherr, R. A. 62
Bleger, J. 160n
Block, E. 191
Blomfield, B. 11, 187–8n
Bloom, L. 187n
Bollas, C. 127, 188n, 214n
Boocock, S. S. 60
Bottomore, T. B. 40n
Brenman-Pick, I. 187n
Britton, R. 146
Brown, D. 187n
Brown, D. and Zinkin, L. 13
Brown, J. 149
Buchele, B. 213n
Budd, S. and Hopper, E. 155
Burman, R. and Roel, G. 160n

Campbell, T. 192

Caplow, T. 71n
Cartwright, D. and Zander, A. 57, 58, 59
Casement, P. 188n, 190
Chagall, M. 193, 213n
Chinoy, E. 32
Christie, G. 187n
Christie-Brown, M. 11
Clinard, M. B. 32
Cohen, P. S. 70n
Collins, O., Dalton, M. and Roy, D. 26
Cooley, C. H. 70n
Crivelli, C. 213n

Dahrendorf, R. 213n
Dalal, F. 13, 187n
Dali, S. 213n
Dante, A. 192
Davidson, S. 79
Davis, F. 187n
Day, R. C. and Hamblin, R. L. 23–6, 33
de Maré, P. 11, 73, 106, 129, 152, 193
de Zurbaran, F. 192, 213n
Deighton, L. 192
Dennis, N., Henriques, F. and Slaughter, C. 39n, 40n
Di Maria, F. and Lavanco, G. 13
Dickinson, E. 192
Dietrich, D. and Shabad, P. 213n
Dimsdale, J. 191
Draper, K. 9
Dubin, R. 26
Dubin, R., Homans, C., Mann, F. C. and Miller, D. C. 26
Dunning, E. 9, 20
Durkheim, E. 71n, 191

Edelson, M. 66
Elias, N. 9, 10, 184
Eliot, T. S. 192
Erbe, W. 27
Erikson, E. 160–1n, 190
Ettin, M. 13
Evans-Pritchard, E. E. 69n
Ezriel, H. 107

Farran, C., Herth, A. and Popovich, J. 190
Ferenczi, S. 188n
Ferenczi, S. and Rank, O. 188n
Fonagy, P. 151
Foulkes, S. H. 11, 19, 94n, 103, 106, 107, 124n, 128, 131, 148, 184, 187n, 206
Foulkes, S. H. and Anthony, E. J. 128, 152

Freud, A. 193
Freud, S. 155, 190, 201
Fromm, E. 124n, 150–1, 159n, 190

Gaddini, E. 144
Gampel, Y. 13
Garland, C. 13, 20, 72–3, 74, 92, 98, 193
Gauguin, P. 213n
Gerth, H. H. and Wright Mills, C. 62
Glass, D. V. 40n
Goffman, E. 39n
Goldthorpe, J. H. 34
Goldthorpe, J. H. and Lockwood, D. 40–1n
Gorer, G. 41n
Gouldner, A. W. 9, 40n, 53
Gouldner, A. W. and Gouldner, H. P. 47
Greenson, R. 214n
Guest, R. H. 32

Hamblin, R. L. 9, 39n
Hamblin, R. L., Bridger, D., Day, R. and
    Yancey, W. 24
Harlow, H. F. and Harlow, M. 68n
Hartmann, H. 187n
Hayley, T. 12
Haynal, A. 213n
Hearst, L. 81
Henry, J. 9
Herman, S. 76, 80, 83, 86, 89, 90, 91
Homans, G. C. 58
Home, J. 12, 214n
Hopper, E. 18, 21, 22, 69n, 73–4, 75, 76, 77,
    78, 79, 81–2, 87, 88, 89, 90, 92, 116,
    125n, 127, 128, 129, 130, 131, 139,
    144, 154, 160n, 161n, 163, 176, 187n,
    191, 193, 196, 206, 207, 213n
Hopper, E. and Garland, C. 93
Hopper, E. and Kreeger, L. 130, 131
Hopper, E. and Osborn, M. 129
Horney, K. 159n
Hussein, Saddam 18
Hyman, H. H. 40n

Inkeles, A. 41n

Jacobs, T. 188n
James. C. 78
Jones, E. 87, 90, 175
Joseph, B. 133
Joseph, E. 150
Jung, C. 160n

Kaës, R. 159n
Kahl, J. H. 9, 40n
Kareem, J. and Littlewood, R. 187n
Katz, D., Maccoby, N. and Morse, N. C. 26
Katz, D., Maccoby, N., Gurin, S. and Floor, L. G.
    26
Kavaler-Adler, S. 212n
Kaye, H. 10–11, 73, 94n, 100
Kernberg, O. 159n
Khaleelee, O. and Miller, E. 160n
King, P. 12
Kinston, W. and Cohen, J. 131
Klein, E. 160n
Klein, G. S. 18
Knupfer, G. 40n
Kohut, H. and Wolf, E. 160n
Koller, P. 160n
Koller, P., Marmar, C. and Kanas, N. 160n
Konig, K. 187n
Kornhauser, A., Dubin, R. and Ross, A. M. 26
Kreeger, L. 11, 20, 73–4, 75, 77, 79, 80, 84,
    88, 90, 92
Kroll, L. 160n

Lacan, J. 161n
Lane, R. E. 27, 32
Langs, R. J. 188n
Lawrence, W. G. 13, 160n
Le Roy, J. 159n
Le Vine, R. 159n
Lewin, B. 178
Lieberman, S. 48, 69n
Limentani, A. 12, 187n
Lipset, S. M. and Bendix, R. 40n
Lipset, S. M., Bendix, R. and Malm, F. T. 40n
Lockwood, D. 9, 41n, 70n

MacGregor, F. C. 65
Maine, T. 10
Malan, D. 136, 206
Malinowski, B. 150
Martin, F. M. 40n
Maslow, A. 160n
McDougal, W. 195
Mead, M. 183
Merton, R. K. 32
Michels, R. 62
Miles, B. 160n
Miller, N. E. 23
Mitchell, S. 161n, 190, 207
Montefiore, A. 98

INDICE GENERALE

U.A. 1 LA PERCEZIONE VISIVA

LUCE

Stimolo sensoriale

Occhio

Interpretazione stimolo

Informazioni in memoria

forma chiusa

continuità di direzione

pregnanza (buona forma)

somiglianza (destino comune)

Leggi della GESTALT

esperienza passata

vicinanza

simmetria

ILLUSIONI OTTICHE

PERCEZIONE VISIVA

FORMA

MOVIMENTO

COLORE

SPAZIO

Obiettivi di apprendimento

CONOSCENZE
- I meccanismi della percezione visiva.
- La percezione della forma, del colore, dello spazio, del movimento.
- Le illusioni ottiche e il rapporto figura/sfondo.
- Le leggi della Gestalt Psychologie.

ABILITÀ
- Individuare e spiegare i meccanismi percettivi.
- Riconoscere e costruire immagini ambigue.
- Riconoscere ed applicare le leggi della Gestalt all'interno del campo grafico.

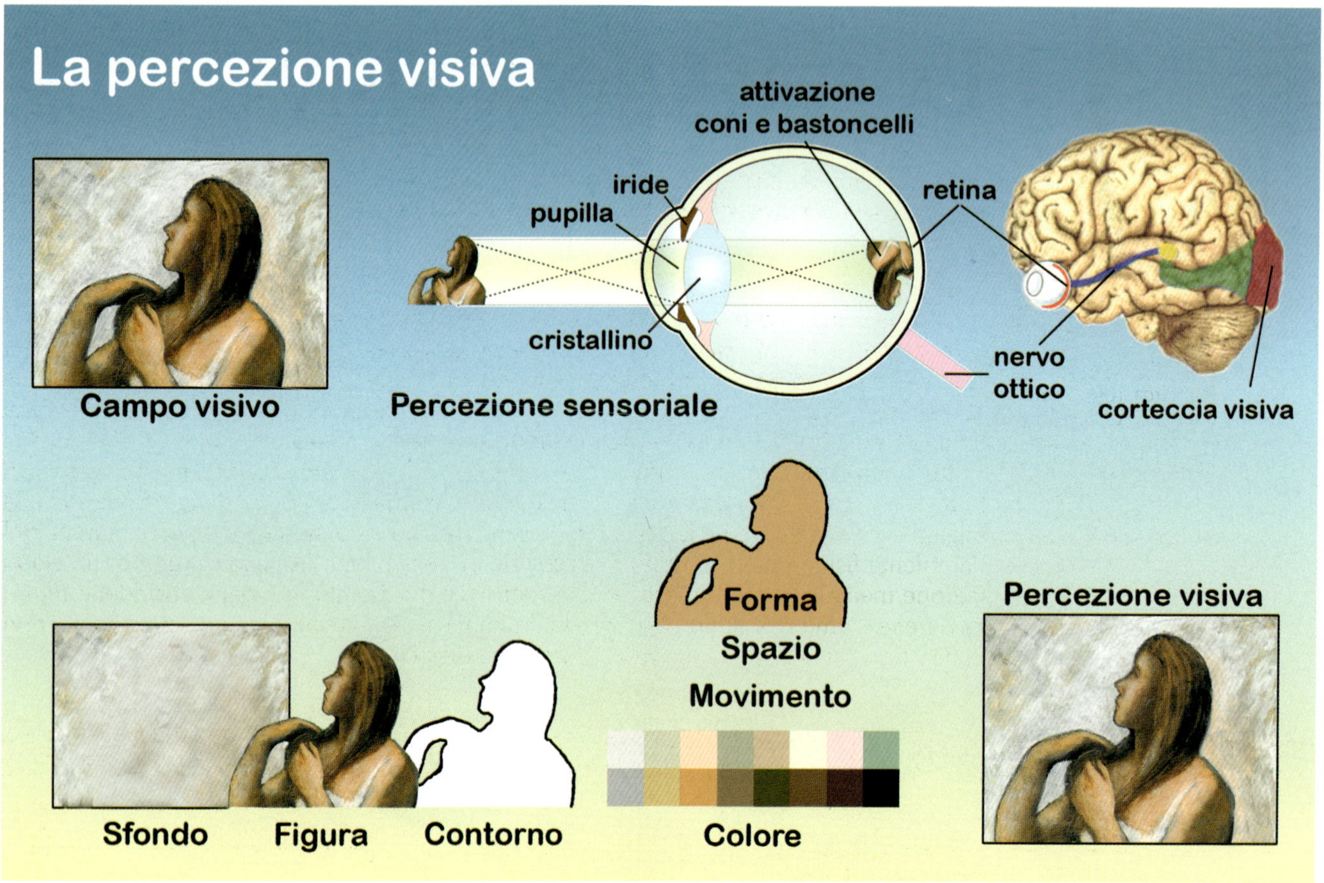

La percezione visiva

Campo visivo

Percezione sensoriale

attivazione coni e bastoncelli

iride

pupilla

retina

cristallino

nervo ottico

corteccia visiva

Sfondo **Figura** **Contorno**

Forma

Spazio

Movimento

Colore

Percezione visiva

1. LA PERCEZIONE

La parola "percezione" deriva dal latino *perceptio*, che indicava l'atto e l'effetto del *percipere*, cioè del percepire, del ricevere. L'italiano **percezione** appartiene soprattutto al linguaggio della filosofia e della psicologia e indica *il processo per cui le sensazioni provenienti dal mondo esterno, ricevute attraverso gli organi di senso, vengono elaborate dalla mente e riconosciute.* Il cosiddetto *mondo fenomenico*, cioè la realtà come ci appare, non è nient'altro che un'interpretazione dei dati che i nostri sistemi percettivi sono in grado di cogliere. A sua volta, il mondo fenomenico che ci costruiamo serve come guida per agire quotidianamente nel mondo fisico reale.

La percezione visiva

Il processo della visione non è affatto semplice e ci pone parecchi problemi: siamo sicuri che ciò che vediamo corrisponda esattamente alla realtà? Come possiamo distinguere le figure dallo sfondo? Come percepiamo i colori e la profondità dello spazio? Come percepiamo gli oggetti in movimento e cosa succede quando siamo noi a muoverci?

Il meccanismo della visione

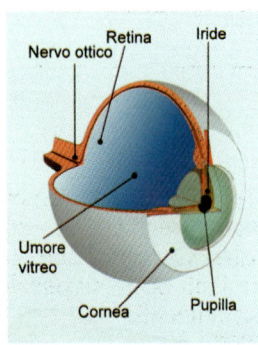

Schema dell'occhio umano.

Retina

Iride

Nervo ottico

Umore vitreo

Cornea

Pupilla

La visione costruisce un **modello** del mondo esterno, a partire dalle configurazioni di luce sulla retina del nostro occhio. Perché si verifichi la visione è quindi necessaria la presenza dei seguenti elementi:

a. *Stimolo distale*, cioè l'evento fornito da un oggetto visibile (una vetrata trasparente e troppo pulita non è visibile);

b. *Luce*, più o meno intensa, che emette radiazioni elettromagnetiche che vengono assorbite o riflesse dalla superficie degli oggetti;

c. *Recettore sensoriale*: cioè l'**occhio**.

La radiazione luminosa visibile provoca nei fotorecettori della retina (coni e bastoncelli) una reazione fotochimica che risponde a particolari variazioni del campo elettromagnetico della luce, cioè a variazioni di intensità (*bastoncelli*) e di intensità e frequenza (*coni*). Sulla retina dell'occhio, quindi, non si "impressiona" alcuna immagine speculare del mondo esterno: l'occhio non è una macchina fotografica!

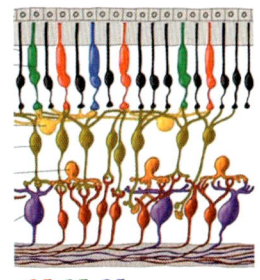

coni
bastoncelli

I bastoncelli (circa 100 milioni in ogni occhio) sono sensibili al bianco e nero anche a bassa intensità luminosa (visione notturna); i coni (circa 6 milioni) sono sensibili alla luce intensa e ai colori.

Successivamente avviene la trasmissione neurale tra la retina e il cervello, mediante il *nervo ottico*, verso la *corteccia visiva* (nel *lobo occipitale*), dove vari tipi di cellule, più o meno complesse, forniscono risposte alle domande sopra formulate. La soglia sensoriale varia in funzione di chi osserva: difetti della vista, attenzione, esercizio, stato emotivo e di salute influiscono sulla visione e, di conseguenza, sulla **percezione visiva** che *è l'interpretazione* rapida e soggettiva **dello stimolo sensoriale, rielaborato e confrontato con le informazioni già presenti e attive nella memoria di ciascuno di noi.**

Le teorie della percezione visiva

Esistono numerose teorie della percezione ed ognuna dà risalto ad aspetti diversi della percezione visiva. Ad esempio, nell'approccio dell'*associazionismo*, l'atto percettivo globale viene scomposto in una serie di sensazioni elementari, mentre per la *teoria della Gestalt* (*forma*, in tedesco) ciò che vediamo è il risultato di un processo innato, che tende ad organizzare gli elementi in un modo comune a tutti gli osservatori. La teoria della Gestalt è attualmente quella più diffusa, anche se recenti teorie sperimentali ne hanno evidenziato alcuni difetti e contraddizioni. Tutte le teorie, comunque, concordano sul fatto che gli oggetti e gli eventi che viviamo come presenti intorno a noi non sono la copia diretta dell'ambiente fisico, ma il risultato di una serie di mediazioni, in quanto frutto di un'elaborazione mentale. Ciò è dimostrato da esperienze di laboratorio e dalle cosiddette *illusioni ottiche*, come possiamo osservare nelle immagini seguenti, dove non esiste corrispondenza tra oggetto reale e oggetto fenomenico (percepito).

ILLUSIONI VISIVE: QUANDO L'OCCHIO CI INGANNA

1. Tracciamo una serie di segmenti uguali, appartenenti a rette parallele tra loro e poste alla stessa distanza.

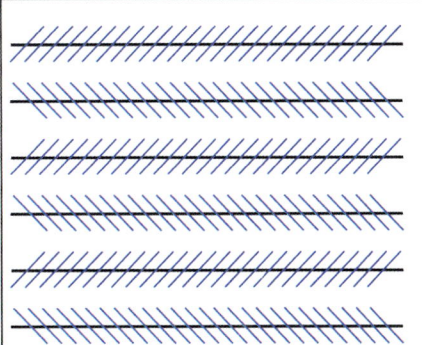

2. Se sovrapponiamo una serie fitta di trattini trasversali e in direzione alternata sulle rette, ecco che abbiamo la sensazione che le linee non siano più né rette né parallele tra loro. (*Illusione di Zöllner, 1860*)

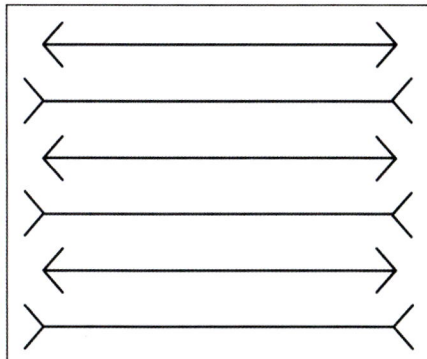

3. Se invece agli estremi dei segmenti poniamo delle frecce in direzione opposta, i segmenti non ci sembreranno più della stessa lunghezza. (*Müller-Lyer, 1889*)

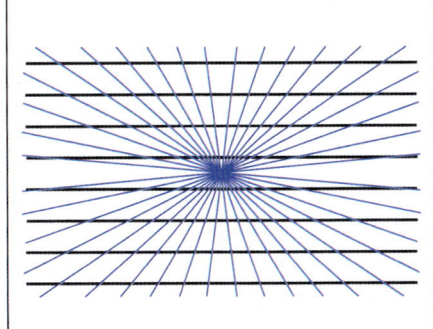

4. Se dal punto centrale tracciamo una serie di segmenti divergenti prospetticamente, le rette sembrano curvarsi verso l'esterno, dando un senso di concavità. (*Hering, 1861*)

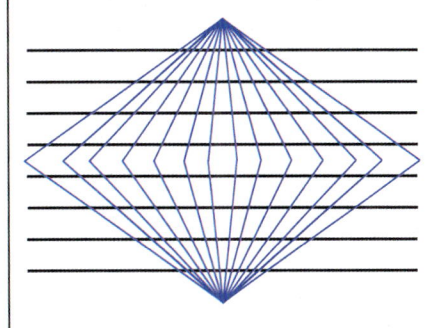

5. Se da due punti esterni tracciamo una serie di segmenti a ventaglio, verso lo spazio centrale, le rette sembrano curvarsi verso l'interno, dando un senso di convessità. (*Wundt, 1898*)

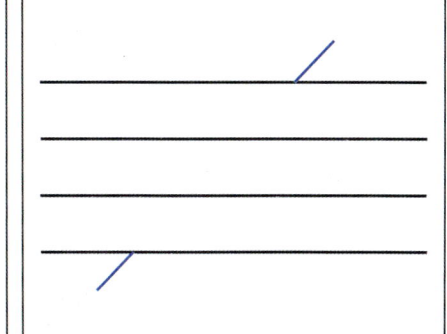

6. Infine, tracciando una retta trasversale che passi sotto i segmenti, percepiamo un'interruzione nella direzione, per cui i terminali della trasversale non ci sembrano allineati. (*Poggendorf, 1860*)

Coppa di Rubin (1915)
Fisicamente la figura è costituita da alcune aree bianche e nere omogenee conti-
gue e collocate sullo stesso
piano. Fenomenicamente
percepiamo una specie di
coppa bianca su sfondo nero uniforme oppure, in al-
ternanza, due visi di profilo
di colore nero su sfondo
bianco.
Le figure hanno carattere
oggettuale, cioè appaiono
come oggetti reali, mentre
gli sfondi hanno carattere di
sostanza, di semplice materiale di supporto alla figura.

Logo aziendale con effetto
di ambivalenza.

La percezione della forma: il rapporto figura/sfondo

Nell'osservare un'immagine percepiamo nitidamente alcuni elementi, in modo meno definito gli altri. Chiameremo *figura* l'immagine percepita, che leggiamo come unità visi-va, e *sfondo* tutto il resto, che si colloca sotto la figura. L'elemento di separazione tra fi-gura e sfondo è la linea di *contorno*, che appartiene alla figura.

Non è possibile leggere figura e sfondo contemporaneamente, poiché la nostra atten-zione può concentrarsi su un'immagine alla volta. La scelta è in parte determinata dalla nostra volontà e dall'esperienza visiva, ma in gran parte dalla conformazione stessa del-l'immagine, per cui siamo portati a soffermarci alternativamente ora sulla figura, ora sullo sfondo.

Perché avvenga la distinzione tra figura e sfondo occorre che, in un campo visivo omo-geneo, esista una discontinuità, cioè che il contrasto sia sufficientemente marcato, altri-menti l'immagine ci apparirà confusa, fino all'indeterminatezza. Tra i fattori che consen-tono di individuare nettamente la figura, i più importanti sono:

- la *nitidezza della forma* della figura rispetto allo sfondo;
- il *contrasto di colore*: percepiamo più facilmente come figura una forma di colore chiaro su sfondo scuro;
- la *differenza di dimensione*: se tra due aree una è più grande e include l'altra, è pro-babile che la più piccola e inclusa sia vista come figura;
- la *posizione delle figure* nello spazio, che può anche determinare la percezione di vi-cinanza o di lontananza per ognuna;
- un *diverso tipo di superficie*: avremo percezioni diverse se, per esempio, come sfon-do c'è una una texture fatta di linee, puntinata oppure perfettamente liscia, piatta ed omogenea.

Le figure ambivalenti

Le cosiddette *figure ambivalenti* (o *ambigue*) esemplificano le difficoltà che si presenta-no in alcuni casi: nel disegno riprodotto *in alto a sinistra*, studiato da **Edgar Rubin**, riu-sciamo a percepire alternativamente come figura la coppa o i due visi di profilo. La nostra preferenza non ricade decisamente su nessuna delle due immagini, in quanto nella nostra mente ambedue sono accettabili in ugual misura.

Altro effetto di ambivalenza è proposto dal cosiddetto **cubo di Necker** (figura *sotto*): fac-ciamo un po' fatica a capire se è diretto verso il basso o verso l'alto, in quanto esistono più interpretazioni possibili.

Il rapporto tra figura e sfondo, usato dagli artisti per stupire e incuriosire, è oggi impie-gato spesso nella grafica pubblicitaria, per attirare l'attenzione dell'osservatore.

Salvador Dalí, *Apparizione del busto di Voltaire*.
Tra le due dame appare il volto sorridente del filosofo francese.

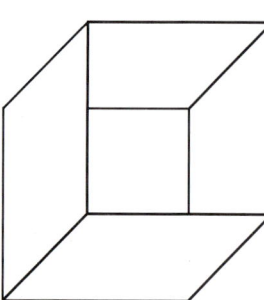

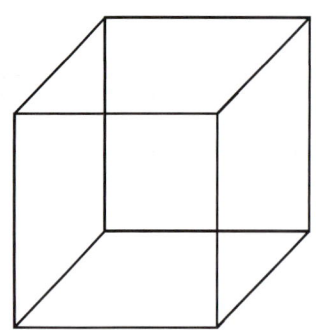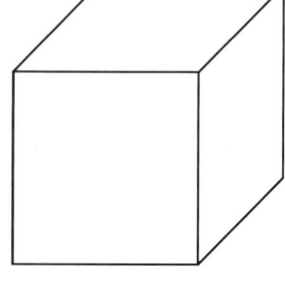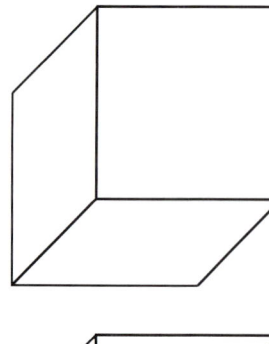

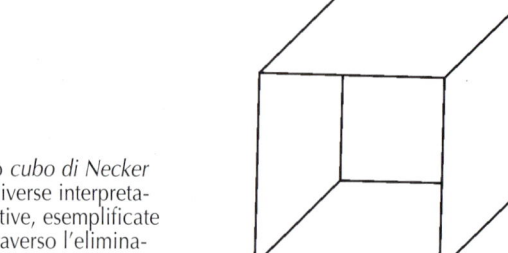

Il cosiddetto *cubo di Necker*
si presta a diverse interpretazioni percettive, esemplificate
a fianco attraverso l'elimina-
zione di alcuni segmenti.

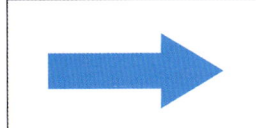

Il rapporto tra figura e sfondo è accentuato (o attenuato) in relazione alla scelta dei colori, fattore assai importante per la leggibilità della segnaletica e della pubblicità.

LA PERCEZIONE DEL COLORE

La *retina* è la parte fotosensibile dell'occhio. Sulla retina ci sono due tipi di recettori, i *coni* e i *bastoncelli*. I coni sono sensibili alla luce forte e a questi si deve la visione dei colori. Ma i coni non reagiscono riconoscendo colore per colore, perché la luce consiste in radiazioni elettromagnetiche di per sé incolori ed invisibili: si attivano invece a seconda dell'energia dei fotoni e sono organizzati in tre gruppi rispettivamente sensibili alle basse, alle medie e alle alte frequenze luminose. Il cervello percepisce quindi i colori dalle letture comparate dei tre gruppi dei coni, filtrandole in base alle esperienze già presenti in memoria.

Se, ad esempio, arrivano sui nostri coni fotoni ad alta energia, questi attiveranno solamente il gruppo sensibile alle alte frequenze luminose e avremo la sensazione di viola, quindi l'oggetto che osserviamo ci apparirà di colore viola. L'occhio può adattarsi rapidamente alle variazioni dell'intensità della luce e distinguere migliaia di sfumature cromatiche.

Tuttavia, secondo la teoria di **Edwin Land** (1909-1991), inventore della macchina fotografica istantanea polaroid, la visione dei colori non è riconducibile ad una sensazione assoluta, ma è il risultato di un confronto simultaneo della quantità di rosso, verde e blu appartenenti ai vari oggetti osservati: quindi, anche al variare delle condizioni di luce (diurna/notturna, interna/esterna, naturale/artificiale) noi vediamo i colori sempre allo stesso modo (*costanza percettiva del colore*).

Fu in seguito a questa teoria che Land perfezionò la pellicola a sviluppo istantaneo, in cui i colori si formano correttamente partendo dai tre colori base, opportunamente filtrati, e registrando la variazione dell'intensità e della frequenza luminosa riflessa dalla superficie degli oggetti.

L'accostamento di colori

Il colore è un elemento fondamentale per la percezione visiva: la visione a colori è più dettagliata rispetto a quella monocromatica e la figura si stacca con maggior chiarezza se è in contrasto cromatico con lo sfondo.

I contrasti e le armonie dei colori sono esposti in modo più dettagliato nella lezione riservata al colore (pag. 93 e seguenti).

È qui sufficiente evidenziare il concetto di relatività del colore: lo stesso colore, infatti, viene percepito in modo diverso se messo in relazione con altri colori, più o meno contrastanti con il primo. Questo fenomeno è importante per accentuare (o diminuire) i livelli di visibilità e di leggibilità del colore, particolarmente importanti, ad esempio, nella segnaletica e nella comunicazione pubblicitaria.

Lo stesso colore verde ci appare diverso al variare dello sfondo in cui è inserito: in certe condizioni si crea un effetto di "contrasto di simultaneità".

La percezione dello spazio

L'assetto ottico ambientale relativo a due punti di vista occupati in successione da un osservatore mobile.

La nostra percezione dello spazio è tridimensionale (basata su larghezza, altezza e profondità). Ciò è dovuto allo schema rappresentativo mentale che ci siamo fatti dello spazio occupato dal nostro corpo: questo spazio è il punto costante di riferimento e confronto tra noi e gli oggetti che ci circondano.

Un oggetto viene percepito nello spazio in quanto ha una posizione nell'ambiente, ed è orientato verso una direzione rispetto a noi e rispetto ad altri oggetti (destra/sinistra, avanti/indietro, alto/basso). L'oggetto cioè si trova ad una certa distanza e ha una certa forma, colore, movimento ecc. Percepire lo spazio significa sostanzialmente percepire i caratteri geometrici delle cose.

Sulla retina dell'occhio, tuttavia, si genera un'immagine bidimensionale: come possiamo allora orientarci nello spazio tridimensionale? Alcuni scienziati sostengono che, nella percezione dello spazio, alla vista si affianca, almeno all'inizio, il senso del tatto.

Il modello contemporaneo della percezione spaziale è però basato sul concetto di "assetto ottico ambientale", per cui una larga parte delle proprietà spaziali delle superfici degli oggetti sono già presenti nella struttura spazio-temporale della luce che arriva all'occhio e noi le interpretiamo in relazione agli angoli solidi che si formano, a partire dal nostro occhio, mentre osserviamo gli oggetti.

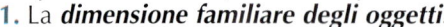

L'esperienza comunque aiuta la percezione mediante alcuni semplici espedienti:

1. La **dimensione familiare degli oggetti**.
   Osservando due oggetti identici ma con dimensioni diverse, quello più grande ci sembrerà più vicino rispetto a quello più piccolo (per la legge della prospettiva lineare).
2. L'**interposizione**.
   Quando un oggetto copre parzialmente un altro, quest'ultimo ci appare ovviamente più lontano e posto dietro l'oggetto che lo copre.
3. **Luce e ombra**.
   L'intensità della luce crea ombre più o meno marcate, che ci aiutano nell'esatta collocazione degli oggetti nello spazio.
4. **Luminosità e contrasto**.
   Oggetti più luminosi e isolati nel campo visivo ci appaiono più vicini, mentre quelli scuri e opachi sembrano più lontani.
5. **Texture**.
   Gli oggetti più lontani presentano una texture di superficie meno nitida e più rada, rispetto a quelli vicini (secondo i principi della cosiddetta prospettiva aerea).

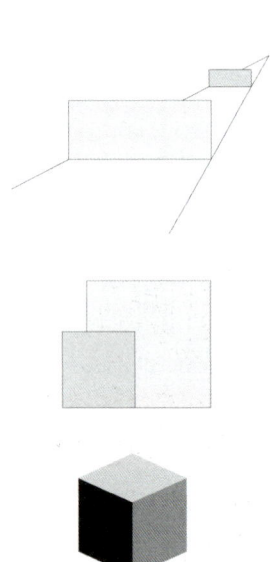

Nella visione binoculare, inoltre, la pur breve distanza tra i due occhi ci consente di percepire l'immagine dello stesso oggetto da punti di vista diversi, per cui il cervello ricompone le due immagini e ci informa con maggior precisione sulle dimensioni e sulla distanza dell'oggetto che osserviamo.

La costanza percettiva dello spazio

La costanza percettiva, in generale, è la tendenza spontanea della percezione a mantenere caratteristiche costanti nel tempo e nello spazio, pur al variare delle situazioni di stimolo sensoriale.

I fenomeni di costanza ci consentono quindi, entro certi limiti, di percepire e riconoscere gli oggetti anche nelle più svariate e sfavorevoli condizioni di osservazione.

Le costanze possono essere di dimensione, forma, colore e luminosità. Per quanto riguarda la percezione dello spazio, ad esempio, una persona alta 180 cm appare conservare la propria grandezza, vicina o lontana che sia, benché le dimensioni della sua immagine nella retina cambino notevolmente: ciò può provocare anche effetti illusori (*vedi figura a sinistra*).

Illusioni in 3D: le figure impossibili

Le immagini di questa pagina sono figure "impossibili", che fingono uno sviluppo nello spazio e sono caratterizzate da due possibilità di interpretazione visiva che si escludono a vicenda. La chiave di lettura è determinata dalla direzione obliqua di osservazione: in *fig. 1*, ad esempio, l'effetto 3D si rovescia a seconda che si osservi l'anello dal basso o dall'alto.

Molte figure impossibili sono basate sul **cuboide**, solido che in assonometria risulta simile al cubo (con 12 spigoli e 8 vertici): la sovrapposizione strategica di alcuni spigoli può determinare configurazioni anomale, possibili nella resa grafica ma non nella realtà tridimensionale (*vedi fig. 2* e *fig. 3*).

Prova a riprodurre o ad inventare una situazione grafica analoga, con tecnica a piacere.

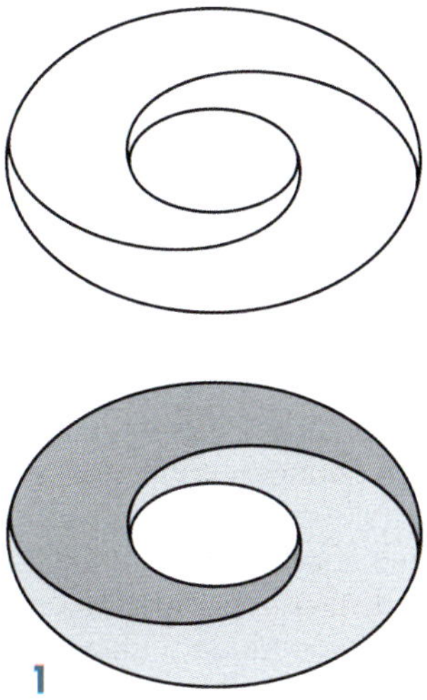

1

2

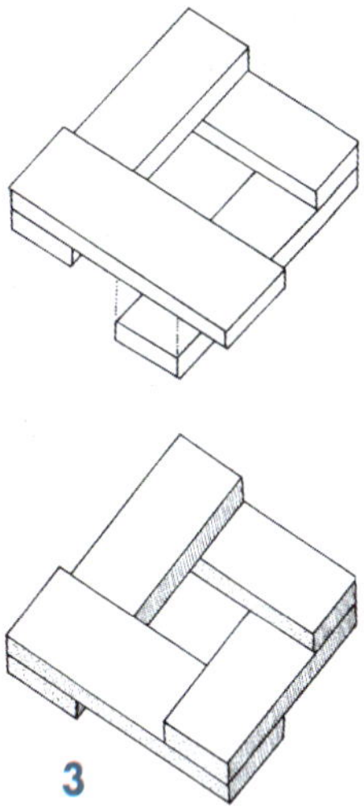

3

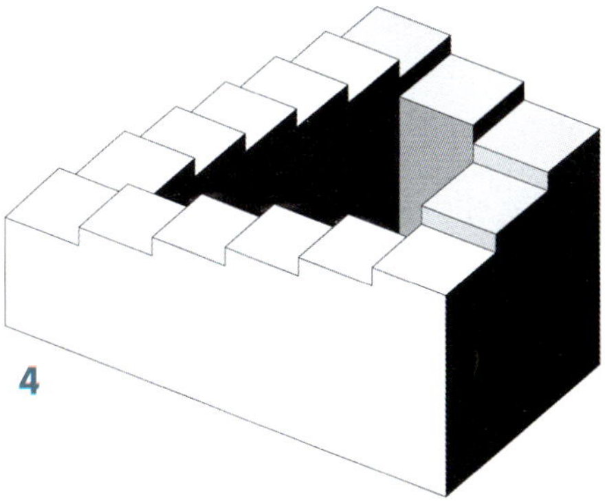

4

Scala senza fine: su questo schema sono basate alcune celebri illustrazioni di Escher.

5

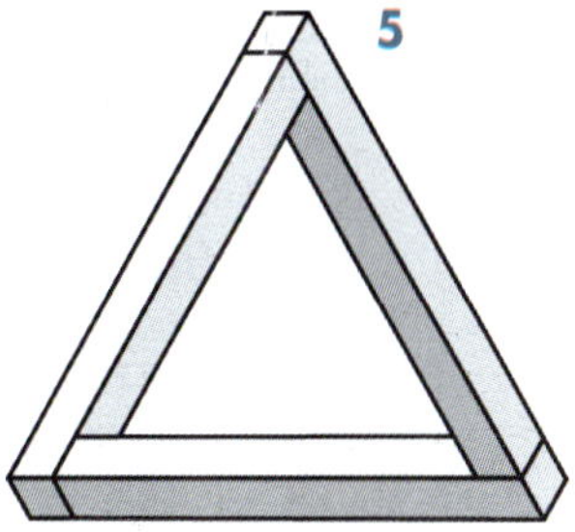

Triangolo di Penrose, altro esempio di figura impossibile.

6

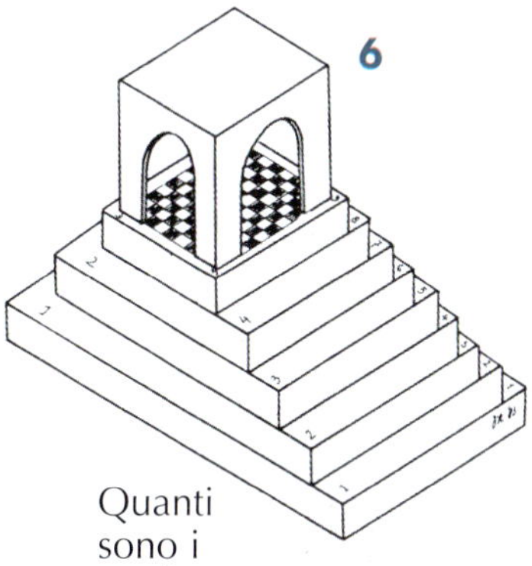

Quanti sono i gradini?

7

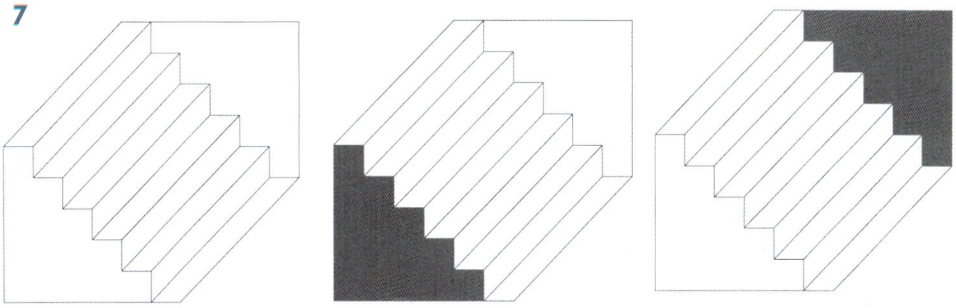

Scala o sottoscala?

8

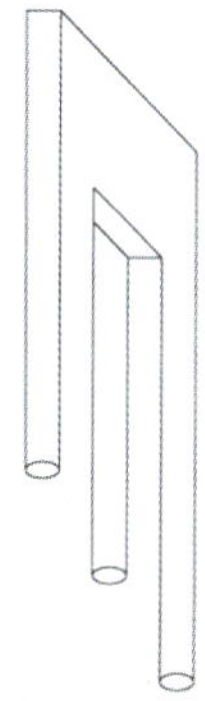

Portale o colonnato?

LA PERCEZIONE DEL MOVIMENTO

La percezione visiva del movimento avviene quando si verifica una modificazione temporale nello stato di stimolazione della retina. Il movimento di un oggetto ha una forte influenza nell'identificazione dell'oggetto stesso rispetto allo sfondo e agli altri oggetti: percepiamo infatti lo spostamento dei suoi margini, che diventano *cineticamente attivi* rispetto a quelli degli oggetti che restano fermi.

La modificazione temporale, però, non deve essere né troppo lenta né troppo rapida, perché esistono una soglia inferiore e una superiore di velocità per la percezione del movimento.

L'occhio può seguire una palla da tennis che viaggia a quasi 100 km l'ora e a parecchi metri di distanza ma, a causa del fenomeno della **persistenza dell'immagine sulla retina** a velocità eccessiva si creano delle scie oppure si verifica l'**effetto stroboscopio**, che è alla base dell'invenzione del cinema e della televisione. Infatti, riproducendo disegni o fotografie facendoli scorrere davanti all'occhio alla velocità di 24 fotogrammi al secondo, l'uomo percepisce le immagini in movimento fluido, come nella realtà.

Un altro tipo di movimento oculare caratteristico è quello che si verifica quando ci spostiamo con rapido movimento trasversale rispetto a ciò che ci sta dinanzi (variazione di parallasse, cioè dell'angolo in funzione del tempo): ad esempio, quando guardiamo un paesaggio da un treno in corsa, se il nostro sguardo si fissa su un punto del paesaggio gli occhi ruotano per mantenere fisso questo punto, con un movimento di inseguimento che compensa lo spostamento. Tuttavia, dopo qualche istante, l'angolo di rotazione degli occhi diviene eccessivo e allora lo sguardo viene riportato su un altro punto del paesaggio, con un effetto di scia.

Nell'arte (e nella comunicazione visiva in genere) per rappresentare il movimento in un'immagine fissa si ricorre ad artifici grafici (ripetizione di una porzione di immagine, effetto scia o colori sfumati) o a composizioni con equilibrio instabile e forti linee di direzione: basti osservare come il movimento è visualizzato in alcune composizioni futuriste, nell'arte cinetica o anche nei più comuni fumetti. Oggi molti artisti usano già strumenti computerizzati e interattivi per creare opere e installazioni video in continua mutazione, che spesso interagiscono con il comportamento del visitatore.

Marcel Duchamp con i suoi dischi ottici che, fatti ruotare, creano la percezione di immagini tridimensionali (effetto stereocinetico).

Istruzioni per l'uso dei dischi ottici:
"Far girare lentamente i dischi ottici Rotorelief *sul piatto di un fonografo. L'immagine in rilievo apparirà subito. Per ottenere il massimo rilievo guardare con un occhio solo, attraverso il visore allegato tenuto a una certa distanza. Dato che il perno del piatto disturba la collocazione dei dischi ottici, impilare qualche disco di musica fino alla completa sparizione della punta."*

Sulla scorta degli studi sulla percezione ottica del movimento e sulla persistenza dell'immagine sulla retina, si possono produrre dischi ottici semplici ma dagli effetti stupefacenti.

Vittorio Corona, *Il corridore*, 1923. Olio su tela, 70x50 cm. Collezione Gattuso, Palermo.

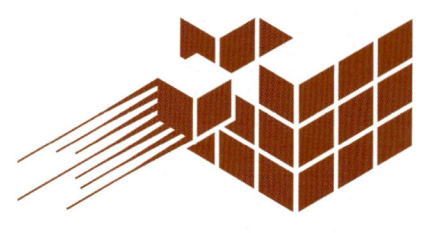

Esempi di marchi aziendali con visualizzazione del movimento.

Nel *triangolo di Kanizsa* vediamo più di quanto non ci sia nello stimolo fisico

2. LE TEORIE DELLA PERCEZIONE

Nei primi decenni del Novecento è stata formalizzata, tra le altre, la **teoria della psicologia della forma** (*Gestalt Psychologie* o *Scuola di Berlino*), destinata ad avere grande importanza, in particolare nel **campo della grafica e della comunicazione visiva**.

Secondo gli studiosi della *Gestalt Psychologie* (tra cui ricordiamo **Max Wertheimer**, **Kurt Koffka**, **Wolfgang Köhler** e l'italiano **Gaetano Kanizsa**) occorre studiare quanto avviene nel mondo fenomenico dell'individuo, cioè studiare ciò che appare e non ciò che avviene nel mondo della realtà.

In qualche caso, infatti, può capitare che non esista corrispondenza tra l'oggetto percepito e l'oggetto reale. Ad esempio:

1. Caso in cui *vediamo più di quanto ci sia nello stimolo fisico*, come accade con il cosiddetto triangolo di Kanizsa (*fig. a fianco in alto*);

2. Caso in cui *si percepisce meno di quanto ci sia nello stimolo fisico*, come accade con la coppa di Rubin (*vedi pag. 8*);

3. Caso in cui *vediamo in maniera distorta ciò che è fisicamente presente nello stimolo* (illusioni visive di *pag. 7*);

Ecco allora che la *configurazione armonica delle forme*, cioè il risultato finale di ciò che vediamo, non è semplicemente dato dalla somma delle sue parti reali, ma dipende da come queste sono disposte nel campo visivo.

LE LEGGI DELLA GESTALT

Le interazioni nel campo visivo sono governate dalla legge della **semplicità** e della **massima omogeneità**, per cui le forze percettive che lo costituiscono si organizzano nel modo più semplice, più regolare, più simmetrico che le circostanze consentano. Nell'esperienza visiva si osserva soltanto l'esito di questo processo organizzativo. Su questa base **Max Wertheimer** nel 1923 ha indicato una serie di *fattori elementari di unificazione* della configurazione, diventati vere e proprie leggi, che spiegano i fenomeni della percezione visiva e ci possono guidare nella realizzazione di una comunicazione grafica equilibrata ed efficace, che sia cioè gradevole e correttamente percepita dall'osservatore. I principali fattori di unificazione citati da Wertheimer sono:

1. La **vicinanza** (o *maggiore densità*)
2. La **somiglianza** (o *minore disomogeneità*)
3. La **continuità di direzione** (o *della curva passante*)
4. La **chiusura**
5. La **pregnanza** (o *buona forma*)
6. L'**esperienza passata**
7. La **simmetria**

Vediamo di analizzare singolarmente queste leggi.

Il risultato finale (*sotto*) non corrisponde alla somma dei suoi componenti (*sopra*), ma dipende dalla loro configurazione.

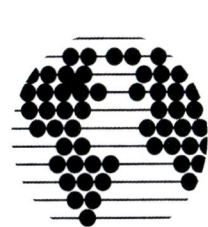
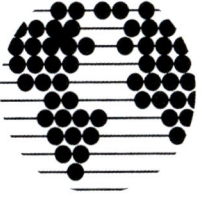

1. Legge della vicinanza (o della maggiore densità)

In un'immagine, anche complessa, tendiamo ad unificare le parti che si trovano a minor distanza tra loro. Per questo motivo, modificando la figura di partenza che è indefinita (*fig. 1a*), la minor distanza tra le mele rosse ci fa cogliere, per vicinanza, la presenza di colonne verticali (*fig. 1b*) o di righe orizzontali (*fig. 1c*).

In questo marchio aziendale, per la legge della vicinanza, i punti disegnano le forme dei continenti

1a

1b
1c
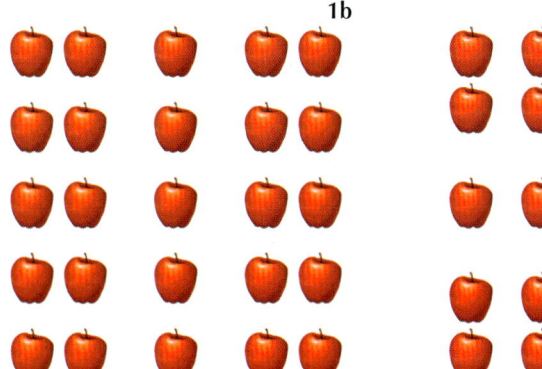

Per quanto riguarda il rapporto **figura-sfondo**, nell'immagine di *fig. 1a* può essere percepita alternativamente come "figura" la croce bianca su sfondo nero, oppure la croce nera su sfondo bianco. Nella *fig. 1b* prevale in genere la croce bianca su sfondo nero e nella *fig. 1c* prevale invece la croce nera su sfondo bianco.

Il fattore vicinanza, infatti, agisce quando una figura ci appare organizzata, unificata e separata dallo sfondo in quanto gli elementi più vicini tra loro, a parità di altre condizioni, vengono percepiti come appartenenti alla stessa unità.

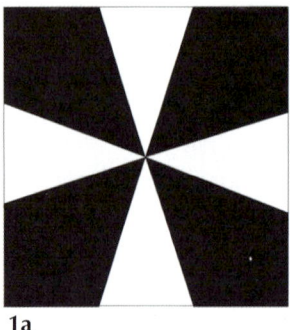  

1a 1b 1c

2. Legge della somiglianza (o della minor disomogeneità)

In un'immagine, anche se discontinua e internamente differenziata, tendiamo a percepire come *configurazione* gli elementi simili tra loro per forma, colore o dimensioni. Questo significa che gli elementi simili tra loro saranno percepiti come parti di una stessa forma. Gli elementi simili (alternativamente mele e pere) ci paiono distribuiti in righe orizzontali nella *fig. 2a*, in colonne verticali nella *fig. 2b*. In *fig. 2c*, invece, percepiamo un triangolo di pere inserito dentro un quadrato di mele.

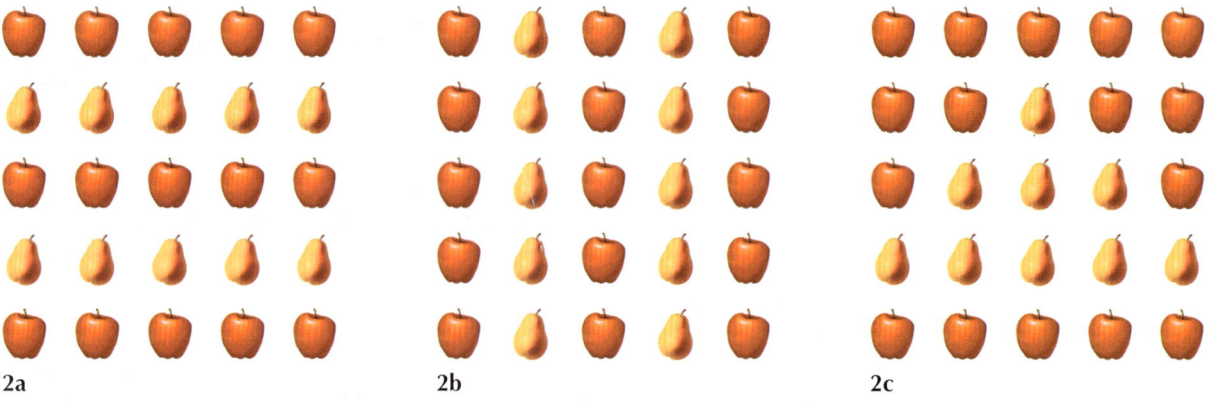

2a 2b 2c

Un caso particolare di unificazione per somiglianza è quello chiamato della *somiglianza di comportamento*, oppure del **destino comune**.

Le parti del campo che si muovono insieme (o in modo simile) tendono a costituirsi come unità. Ad esempio, le sei mele (3 gialle e 3 rosse) della *fig. 3a* appaiono raggruppate spontaneamente in due colonne verticali, grazie ai fattori della vicinanza e della somiglianza. Se però cominciano a muoversi in maniera solidale la mela centrale gialla e le due mele esterne della colonna rossa (e solo quelle) la struttura si modificherebbe: al posto delle due colonne, avremmo due "triangoli" di cui possiamo vedere solo i vertici, uno in movimento e l'altro fermo.

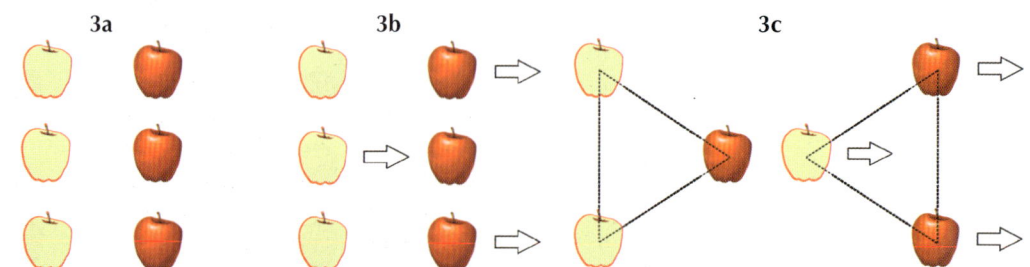

3a 3b 3c

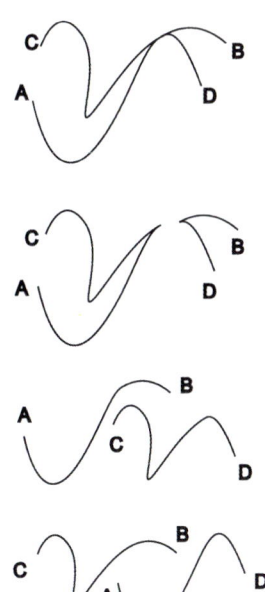

3. Legge della continuità di direzione (o della curva passante)

Gli elementi del campo visivo vengono riuniti in forme in base alla loro continuità di direzione. Infatti il sistema visivo sembra voler evitare bruschi cambiamenti di direzione, e preferire, nel caso di un incrocio tra segmenti, la continuità dei medesimi. Per questo nella *fig. 1a* vediamo due rette che si intersecano, anziché due spezzate che si toccano in un vertice.

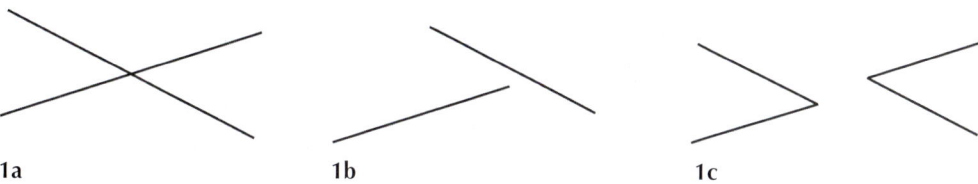

1a   1b   1c

Anche le linee curve tendono a mantenere il proprio andamento dopo l'incrocio: secondo il principio della continuità di direzione, si tende a percepire una linea AB incontrarsi con una linea CD, piuttosto che AC e BD. In questo caso particolare, tuttavia, è possibile considerare anche l'andamento CB e AD, considerando le due linee curve (*fig. a lato*).

4. Legge della chiusura

Se una configurazione tende a chiudersi, la percepiamo più facilmente.

I semicerchi della *fig. 2* potrebbero organizzarsi in due modi: dalla parte della convessità (formando così tre X) oppure dalla parte della concavità (formando così tre cerchi, incompleti). Il principio della chiusura vince sul principio di vicinanza, che vorrebbe invece il costituirsi delle tre X.

È più facile però vedere la configurazione ad X se si esamina la figura partendo da destra e muovendo lo sguardo verso sinistra; al contrario, si vede meglio la configurazione ad O se si parte dalla parte sinistra e si scorre verso destra, perché l'elemento non incluso nell'organizzazione (il "resto") rimane alla fine.

2
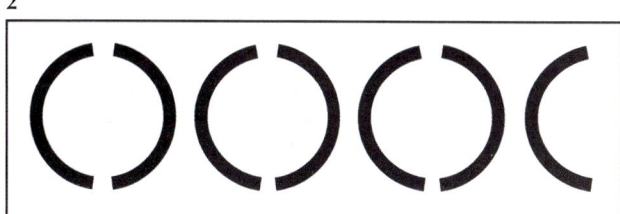

3

Osserviamo un altro esempio di chiusura-vicinanza: nella *fig. 3* gli elementi in alto si raggruppano secondo i principi di vicinanza e di somiglianza, mentre quelli in basso si completano (e si chiudono) sotto le superfici rettangolari bianche. I margini delle figure nere vengono "rubati" dai rettangoli bianchi, lasciando loro la possibilità di continuare di sotto e riunirsi in due esagoni.

5. Legge della pregnanza (o della buona forma)

È sicuramente la legge più importante: ciò che viene percepito contiene una forma organizzata che è la migliore possibile e la più significativa. Nella maggior parte dei casi, la "buona forma" è quella semplice, equilibrata, regolare e simmetrica.

Le *figure 4a* e *4b*, a lato, per il principio di chiusura formano due figure distinte, con una forma propria e ben definita. Se si avvicinano le due figure (come indicato dalla configurazione in *fig. 7c*), esse si trasformano in due nuove configurazioni e diventa più difficile individuare le due configurazioni di partenza.

4
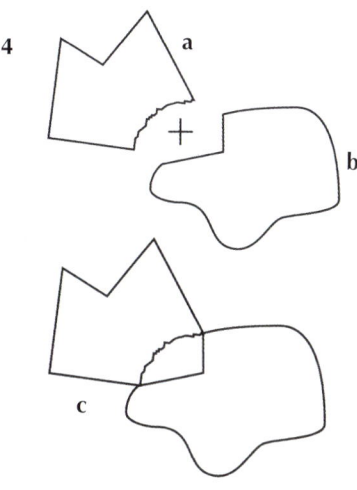

Altri esempi di pregnanza della forma sono evidenziati dalle figure seguenti.

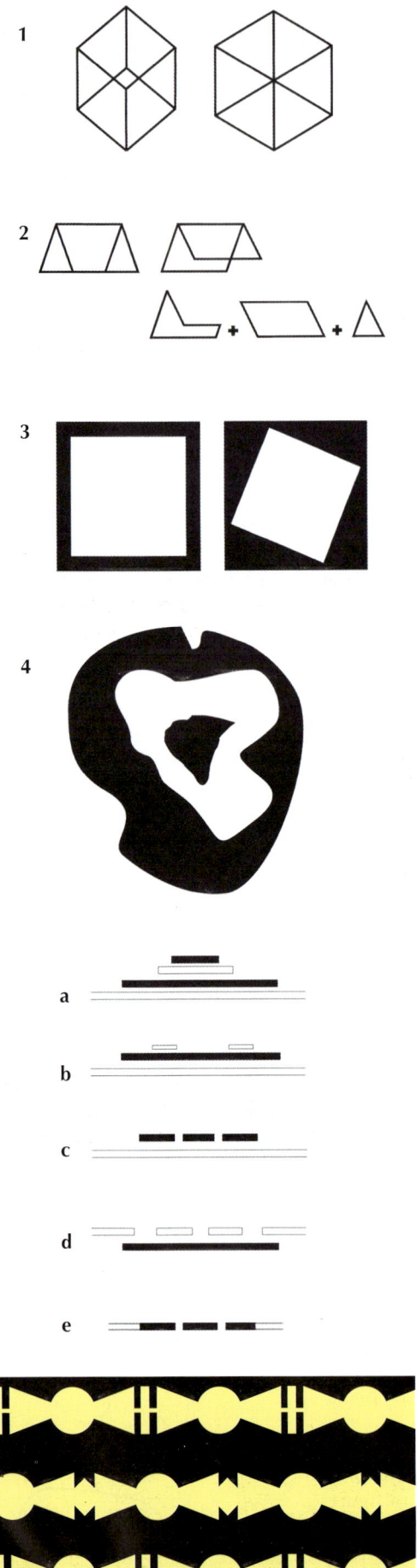

Fig. 1 Le figure geometriche regolari, con alta simmetria, sono esempi di pregnanza. Qui a sinistra si vede chiaramente un cubo, mentre la figura di destra, anch'essa rappresentazione tridimensionale di un cubo, è più difficile da vedere in terza dimensione: essa ci appare come un esagono diviso a spicchi dalle sue diagonali.

Fig. 2 Nella configurazione a sinistra compaiono figure regolari e uguali: ciò la obbliga a "rimanere" nel piano; la configurazione a destra viene invece vista in terza dimensione: se infatti fosse vista piana, sarebbe il risultato di tre parti irregolari. Vederla in 3D semplifica il risultato finale: abbiamo due rettangoli che delimitano un angolo di spazio.

Fig. 3 Tra le due configurazioni non c'è differenza: entrambe sono cornici nere su sfondo bianco. Mentre il disegno di sinistra viene facilmente visto come cornice (ed il bianco appartiene allo sfondo), quello di destra viene più facilmente visto come formato da due quadrati sovrapposti, uno nero (sotto) ed uno bianco (sopra): la zona bianca inclinata non sembra appartenere allo sfondo. La differenza tra le due configurazioni dipende dal *principio della buona forma*: la superficie nera di sinistra viene vista come cornice (ed il bianco è lo sfondo) perché questa è la soluzione più economica data la regolarità della superficie nera, che ha sempre la stessa larghezza. La superficie nera di destra non ha la stessa larghezza: invece di vedere l'irregolarità della cornice, si è portati a visualizzare due quadrati sovrapposti, regolari.

Fig. 4 Per lo stesso motivo, la configurazione a sinistra, ripresa da un'incisione di **Jean Arp** (1887-1966), può essere vista nei diversi modi seguenti:
a. una piramide di sagome bianche e nere alternate;
b. una "ciambella" bianca posta sopra una macchia nera, su sfondo bianco;
c. una "ciambella" nera, con una piccola sagoma nera al centro del buco, posta sopra uno sfondo bianco;
d. un piano bianco, bucato in due punti, che lascia intravedere uno sfondo nero;
e. un solo piano, interrotto da vari intarsi bianchi e neri.
La soluzione più semplice è in realtà la prima: nonostante implichi la partecipazione di un maggior numero di piani rispetto alle altre, grazie anche al principio di chiusura, si riescono ad evitare interruzioni di superficie.

6. Legge dell'esperienza passata

L'esperienza è un fattore empirico: risulta infatti abbastanza intuitivo il fatto che elementi, che, per le nostre esperienze passate, sono abitualmente associati tra di loro, tendano a essere uniti in forme e configurazioni proprie.

7. Legge della simmetria

Anche la simmetria, trasmettendo un senso di ordine e regolarità, favorisce la percezione di configurazioni equilibrate, come possiamo osservare in molteplici esempi nell'arte e nella comunicazione visiva. Ad esempio, nella *fig. 5* percepiamo come figura le parti in giallo perché regolari e simmetriche, rispetto alla parte in nero, che percepiamo come sfondo.

Esempio di figura anomala in un marchio aziendale: leggiamo chiaramente un quadrato bianco all'interno.

Figure complete, incomplete e completamento amodale

Capita sovente, nella realtà e nelle immagini che osserviamo, che le figure non siano complete e ben separate dallo sfondo; anzi, il più delle volte sono incomplete, magari perché coperte da qualche altra immagine o elemento di disturbo.

In questo caso la percezione avviene mediante un completamento "***amodale***", anche senza attivazione di alcun "modo" tradizionale della percezione. Osserviamo, ad esempio la *fig. 1*: vediamo tre triangoli isosceli bianchi sormontati da un rettangolo nero. Ma se "togliamo" il rettangolo (*fig. 2*) vediamo che solo il primo è un triangolo, ma il nostro cervello completa l'immagine nella direzione più regolare e logica, anche senza alcuna giustificazione nella stimolazione retinica.

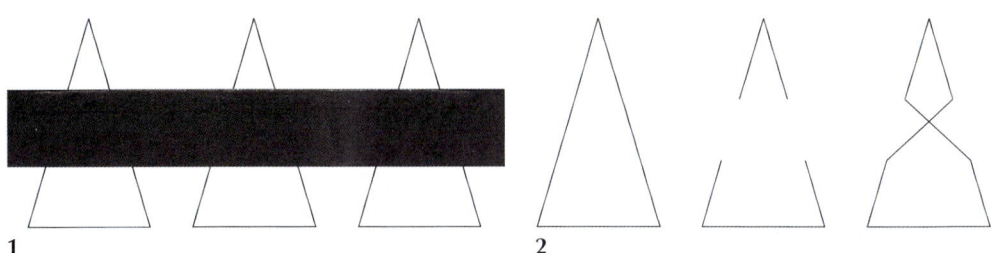

Superfici anomale

In alcuni casi siamo portati a completare le immagini "inventandoci" margini inesistenti, che definiscono superfici anomale, come già visto nel triangolo di Kanizsa di *pag. 15*. Percepiamo infatti nella *fig. 3* a sinistra un quadrato bianco sopra quattro ottagoni e in quella di destra un altro quadrato chiuso fra croci e rombi. Nella *fig. 4*, invece, appare un triangolo anomalo che fa sembrare più lunga la linea verticale di sinistra e più corta quella di destra, creando anche un'illusione ottica.

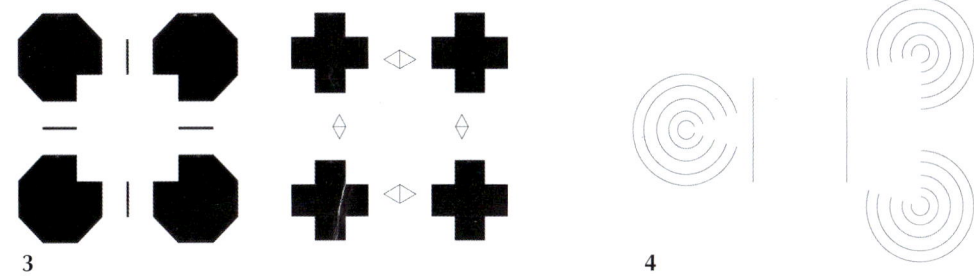

Mascheramento

Il fenomeno del mascheramento avviene quando la percezione di una figura o di un oggetto è resa difficile o impossibile per la presenza di altri elementi nel campo, benché all'oggetto non venga tolto fisicamente nulla. Osserviamo nelle figure sottostanti alcuni tipi di mascheramento, spesso usati anche dai grafici nella realizzazione di marchi e logotipi.

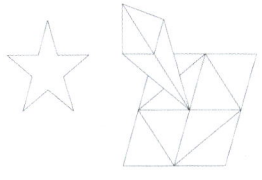

Mascheramento mediante ripetizione della figura.

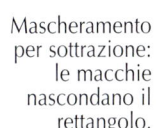

Mascheramento simultaneo: dove si nasconde la stella nell'immagine a fianco?

Mascheramento per progressivo addensamento della texture lineare.

Mascheramento per sottrazione: le macchie nascondano il rettangolo.

Dopo aver letto le pagine inerenti i fenomeni della percezione e studiato le leggi della Gestalt, prova a rispondere alle seguenti domande. Se non ti senti sicuro, torna a rileggere il testo.

1. Percepiamo figure come ambivalenti quando non riusciamo a determinare con certezza quale sia la figura e quale sia lo sfondo.

☐ VERO

☐ FALSO

2. La percezione del colore avviene per mezzo dei:

☐ coni

☐ bastoncelli

3. Le figure sotto riprodotte sono alcune ambigue ed altre impossibili. Indica con la lettera A (ambigua) oppure I (impossibile) la categoria a cui appartiene ogni immagine, spiegandone il motivo.

....

4. Analizza le illustrazioni riportate di seguito, individua a quale tra le leggi della Gestalt possono essere ricondotte, motivando la risposta con una breve descrizione.

....

5. Osserva la figura del marchio a lato e spiega con quali modalità il grafico è riuscito a rendere il senso del volume e dello spazio.

....

....

....

....

....

U.A. 2 — LA COMUNICAZIONE

Obiettivi di apprendimento

CONOSCENZE
- Comunicazione verbale e non verbale.
- Il segno e la comunicazione.
- Il processo comunicativo.
- Le funzioni della comunicazione.

ABILITÀ
- Leggere e interpretare messaggi verbali e non verbali.
- Riconoscere gli elementi del processo comunicativo.
- Individuare, in diversi messaggi, le funzioni della comunicazione.

21

1. NON POSSIAMO NON COMUNICARE...

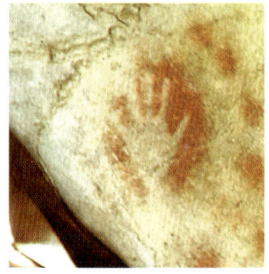

Le impronte lasciate dagli uomini preistorici sulle pareti delle grotte sono una delle prime forme di comunicazione.

Il principio fondamentale di ogni processo di comunicazione è che *"l'uomo non può fare a meno di comunicare"* (**Paul Watzlawick**, *Pragmatica della comunicazione umana*, 1967).

Comunicare è per noi una necessità inderogabile: anche quando ci impuntiamo a non proferire parola e a non ascoltare un interlocutore sgradito, il nostro atteggiamento parla per noi ed esprime esattamente il nostro stato d'animo.

Detto ciò, esistono altri "assiomi" che gli studiosi di comunicazione hanno formulato e che possiamo senz'altro condividere, con un po' di ragionamento.

Ad esempio:

a. Ogni comunicazione presenta un aspetto di **contenuto** e uno di **relazione**, in modo che il secondo classifica il primo. Il contenuto è quello che uno dice e l'aspetto di relazione consiste nel modo in cui lo dice: c'è modo e modo di chiedere aiuto a un compagno per un compito scolastico...

b. L'uomo comunica sia con il **linguaggio analogico** (che comunica per somiglianza) sia con quello **digitale** (numerico e verbale): quello numerico è più preciso ma freddo e formale, mentre quello analogico ha più a che fare con le emozioni e quindi con il linguaggio non verbale.

Comunicazione verbale e non verbale

Nella vita di ogni giorno noi non comunichiamo soltanto il contenuto espresso dalle parole, ma trasmettiamo informazioni, emozioni e passioni anche attraverso il timbro e la cadenza della voce, le posizioni del corpo, i gesti e lo sguardo. È un chiaro esempio di un vero e proprio **linguaggio non verbale**, cioè un modo di comunicare che non ha necessariamente bisogno di parole.

Alcune tipiche espressioni della mimica facciale e della gestualità della fotomodella Claudia Schiffer.

I principali tipi di linguaggio non verbale sono:

1. il **linguaggio visivo**, cioè quello delle immagini, che percepiamo con gli occhi;

2. il **linguaggio uditivo** e **olfattivo**, legato al suono e agli odori, percepiti rispettivamente con orecchie e naso;

3. il **linguaggio cinesico**, legato al movimento (dal greco kinesis), ai gesti e agli atteggiamenti del corpo.

Il linguaggio non verbale comunica mediante un sistema analogico, cioè per somiglianza, fino ad arrivare a costruire un vero e proprio linguaggio del corpo.

Il linguaggio del corpo

Tra i principali elementi del linguaggio del corpo ricordiamo:

1. L'atteggiamento, cioè la postura e le sue modificazioni;

2. La mimica facciale, cioè l'espressione del volto con i suoi segnali;

3. Lo sguardo, importante veicolo di comunicazione;

4. La gestualità, cioè i movimenti delle mani e delle braccia anche nell'eseguire azioni (*cinesica*);

5. La distanza fisica, cioè la gestione dello spazio intorno a sé e in relazione all'altro (*prossemica*);

6. Il tono della voce, cioè non tanto quel che si dice, ma come lo si dice: la velocità dell'eloquio, il volume della voce, il ritmo ed eventuali espressioni sonore prive di contenuto verbale (riso, sbuffi, sospiri, ecc.).

Numerosi psicologi hanno studiato le variazioni di significato del linguaggio del corpo, che cambia presso popoli e culture diversi.

A questo vanno aggiunti anche l'abbigliamento, il trucco e l'ostentazione di segni e simboli di appartenenza a gruppi, tribù, associazioni, partiti politici, ecc.

A noi basta sapere che, nella comunicazione interpersonale, il linguaggio del corpo ha enorme valore poiché, se ben utilizzato, è assai più efficace e coinvolgente delle sole parole.

Modi e mezzi del comunicare: la comunicazione non verbale *(lavoro di gruppo)*

Eseguite una ricerca su alcune forme di comunicazione non verbale, da quelle usate nell'antichità a quelle in uso ai giorni nostri.

Realizzate poi un cartellone riassuntivo che illustri alcuni esempi di queste forme particolari di linguaggio. Provate a comporre una frase o un messaggio usando i diversi sistemi.

Le immagini di questa pagina forniscono indicazioni e suggerimenti operativi.

1. I geroglifici egizi

2. Le bandierine navali

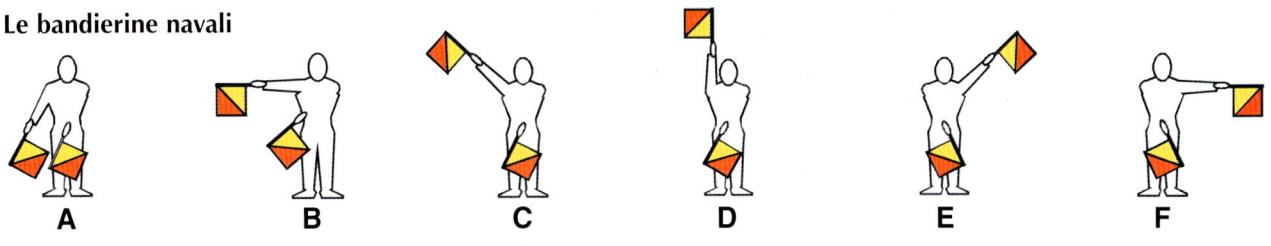

3. I logo del telefonino

4. L'alfabeto manuale per audiolesi

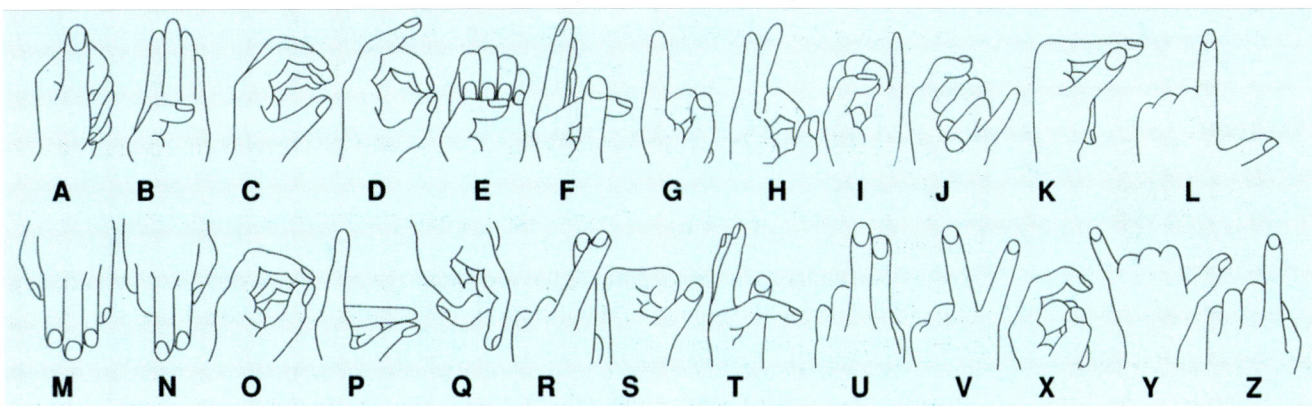

5. Icone e clip-art del computer

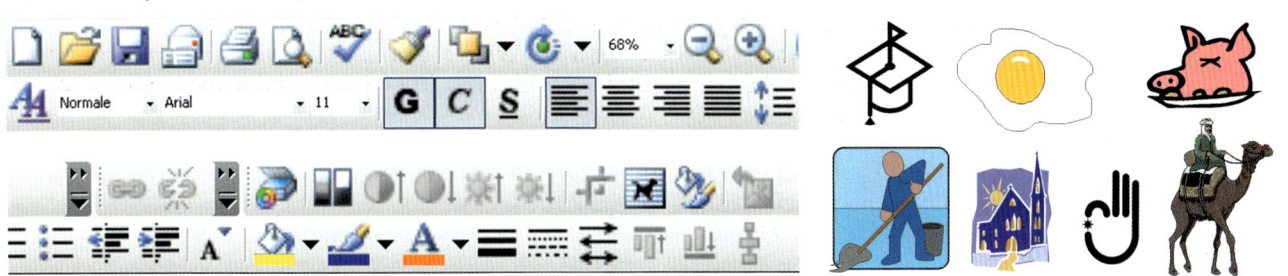

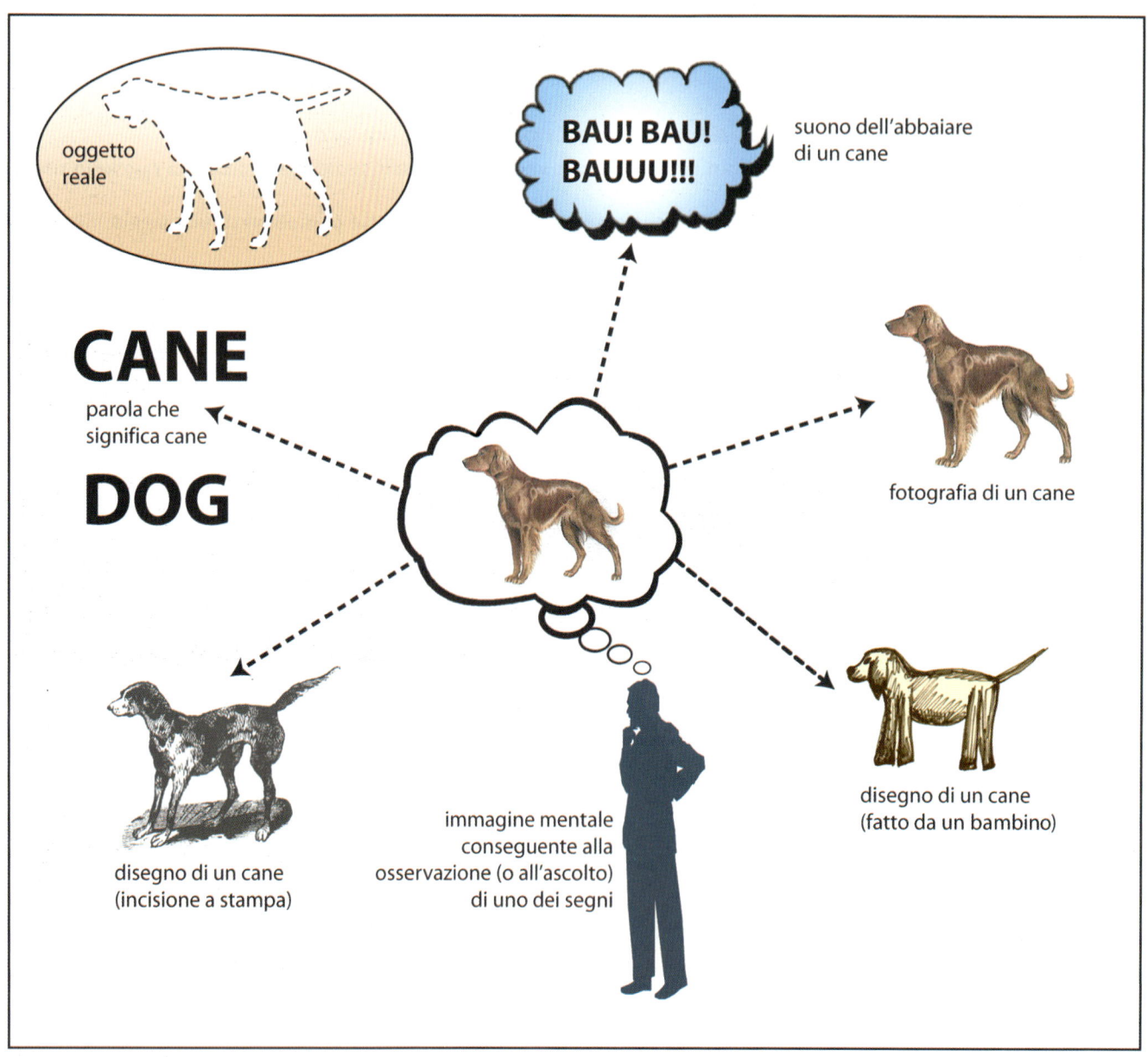

oggetto reale

BAU! BAU! BAUUU!!!
suono dell'abbaiare di un cane

CANE
parola che significa cane

DOG

fotografia di un cane

disegno di un cane (fatto da un bambino)

disegno di un cane (incisione a stampa)

immagine mentale conseguente alla osservazione (o all'ascolto) di uno dei segni

Rappresentazione schematica delle possibili modalità di espressione del segno "cane".

2. L'IMPERO DEI SEGNI

IL SEGNO

Il segno non è una cosa, ma un concetto teorico che indica una realtà complessa, fondamentale all'interno del processo della comunicazione. Questa definizione potrebbe sembrare difficile, ma risulta più comprensibile se facciamo un esempio.

Tutti sappiamo che cos'è un cane, anzi molti di noi ne hanno uno e ci giocano spesso. Non c'è bisogno di averlo davanti che scodinzola e abbaia: pensiamo al cane anche solo guardando una sua fotografia, oppure un disegno fatto da un compagno o un'illustrazione su un libro, ma anche semplicemente ascoltandolo abbaiare in cortile o per strada oppure ancora leggendo su questo libro la parola di quattro lettere che lo indica nella lingua italiana.

Ciascuno di questi segni può rappresentare il "cane", cioè l'animale reale che scodinzola e abbaia, perché ne basta uno per costruirne l'immagine mentale, cioè quello che dovrebbe venirci in mente ascoltando o vedendo uno dei segni. Ognuno si fa poi la propria immagine mentale di un certo "cane", diverso per razza, colore, dimensioni, età: questi particolari vanno quindi definiti meglio per comunicare con precisione un messaggio nel processo di comunicazione.

Nello schema in alto sono rappresentati alcuni segni che indicano l'oggetto "cane", cioè l'animale vero.

LA SEMIOTICA, SCIENZA DEI SEGNI

L'uomo è portato, per sua natura, a cercare di conferire significato a tutto ciò che lo circonda. In secondo luogo, sente l'esigenza di comunicare ad altri le proprie idee, utilizzando una serie di strumenti che definiscono un **linguaggio**.

Esistono vari tipi di linguaggio, ciascuno dei quali si serve di **segni**, che costituiscono un **sistema**.

La **semiotica** (o **semiologia**) è la scienza che studia questi sistemi, per poter dare significato ad ogni oggetto od evento creando, interpretando e comunicando "**segni**" (o **semi**, dal greco semeion, nella terminologia usata dai semiologi).

Come già detto il **segno**, elemento base della comunicazione, **sta** sempre **per qualcosa**, ossia **rappresenta un oggetto** o un evento e può presentarsi in forma di parola, immagine, suono, odore e sapore, atteggiamenti e gesti.

Questi segni, uniti fra loro e regolati da precise norme, costituiscono il **linguaggio della comunicazione**. Abbiamo visto che il linguaggio può essere verbale e non verbale: **la comunicazione visiva si occupa**, in prevalenza, dei linguaggi non verbali, soprattutto **del linguaggio visuale**.

A
ideogramma

A
lettera greca

A
latina maiuscola

A (at)
"chiocciola"

pittogramma

trasformazione
in ideogramma

fonogrammi che indicano il suono A
nel greco antico

La **rappresentazione visiva** dello stesso segno è **varia** ed è soggetta ad un continuo **processo di evoluzione** e di aggiornamento: basti osservare, ad esempio, la figura riprodotta *sopra*, che illustra lo sviluppo del carattere latino A, dal pittogramma al moderno carattere fonetico A, con le relative varietà di rappresentazione.

La **semiotica** parte comunque dal presupposto che tutto può diventare segno, ma solo a partire dal momento in cui noi gli diamo un significato. Esistono diversi modelli applicativi della semiotica, soprattutto per la linguistica.

Ferdinand de Saussure (1857-1913), ad esempio, definì "**segno**" ciò che è composto di due proprietà imprescindibili:

- un **significante**, ovvero la forma materiale che questo segno assume;
- un **significato**, ovvero il concetto che rappresenta, contenuto del messaggio.

Successivamente, alle due proprietà si aggiunse il cosiddetto **referente**, cioè l'oggetto concreto cui si riferisce il segno. Questa triade costituisce la base di ogni tipo di comunicazione e va accuratamente definita.

Ad esempio, se nel reparto elettrodomestici di un ipermercato vediamo un cartello con la scritta "BATTERIE" (*significante*) sappiamo dove rifornirci di pile (*significato*) per il nostro walkman. Si dice allora che il rapporto tra significante e significato crea un processo di significazione. Il referente del segno è la pila.

Un altro esempio: davanti a un semaforo rosso (*significante*) noi sappiamo che dobbiamo fermarci (*significato*). Il referente, in questo caso, è il semaforo stesso.

Non sempre ad un significante corrisponde lo stesso significato: se il cartello "BATTERIE" è esposto nel reparto casalinghi, la massaia immagina pentole da cucina; se invece è posizionato nel reparto degli strumenti musicali il musicista andrà in cerca di piatti e tamburi. Analogamente, il significato "fermarsi", anziché dal semaforo può essere suggerito dal cartello stradale "STOP", annesso alle righe bianche tracciate sull'asfalto.

Starà quindi a noi, per una efficace comunicazione visiva, decidere quale significante e quale significato abbinare al referente per una corretta significazione.

Il "segno" secondo il linguista ginevrino Ferdinand de Saussure.

L'impronta digitale è il classico esempio di indizio.

TIPI DI SEGNO

Nella comunicazione visiva troviamo segni di tipo diverso. Possiamo anzitutto distinguere tra segni naturali e segni artificiali.

I **segni naturali**, presenti nell'ambiente reale, sono quelli che richiamano l'attenzione su qualche fenomeno di cui non conosciamo la causa (**sintomi**), come la febbre o il mal di pancia per un'eventuale influenza, o il fumo, che può farci pensare tanto a un incendio quanto a un falò o ai segnali di fumo degli indiani; oppure quelli che più espressamente sono **indici** di un fatto o di un'azione, ad esempio le **tracce** di un animale sulla sabbia o gli **indizi** polizieschi, come le impronte digitali.

Esistono poi numerosi **segni artificiali**, cioè intenzionalmente creati dall'uomo. Tra questi possiamo distinguere i **segni produttivi omosostanziali** (cioè della stessa sostanza) divisi in **intrinseci** (parte dell'oggetto per il tutto), **traslativi** (riproduzione di un colore o di un aspetto della materia) ed **ostensivi** (l'oggetto reale preso e mostrato come segno).

Segni produttivi eterosostanziali proiettivi sono invece, ad esempio, le rappresentazioni grafiche in prospettiva e **caratterizzanti** sono gli ideogrammi (disegni stilizzati che rappresentano un'idea) o le strisce per la zebra, che indicano immediatamente l'animale.

Assai spesso produciamo e usiamo anche **segni artificiali sostitutivi**, mettendo al posto dell'oggetto **simboli linguistici** (parole e definizioni verbali), **indici vettori** (dito o freccia che indica una direzione), **segni visivi astratti** (segnali stradali, bandiere ecc.), **emblemi**, **stemmi** e **simboli araldici**.

Questa classificazione, ricavata dal *Trattato di semiotica generale* di **Umberto Eco**, non è l'unica possibile e si presta ad ulteriori ampliamenti e modificazioni. È comunque utile ed importante riflettere sulla grande varietà di segni che ci circondano, per poterli meglio distinguere, interpretare e conoscere. Successivamente, saremo anche in grado di produrre segni con sempre maggior consapevolezza, per una comunicazione corretta e più agevole.

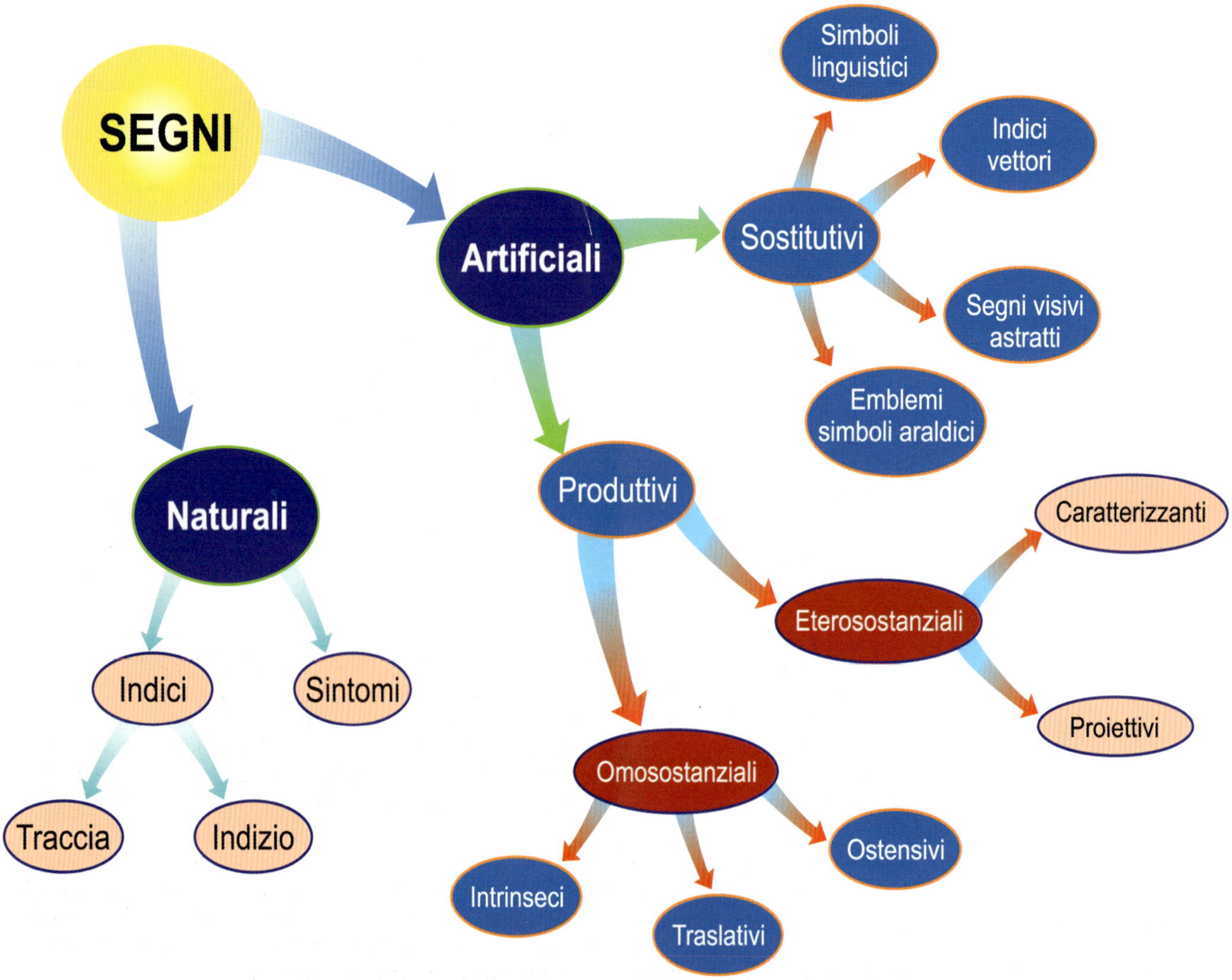

SEGNI

Artificiali

Sostitutivi

Simboli linguistici

Indici vettori

Segni visivi astratti

Emblemi simboli araldici

Produttivi

Caratterizzanti

Eterosostanziali

Proiettivi

Omosostanziali

Intrinseci

Traslativi

Ostensivi

Naturali

Indici

Sintomi

Traccia

Indizio

I cinque cerchi colorati sono simbolo delle olimpiadi.

IL SEGNO VISIVO: ICONA, INDICE, SIMBOLO

Dovendo lavorare con le immagini, risulta più semplice ricondurre i segni a tre tipologie fondamentali:

- **Icona**
- **Indice**
- **Simbolo**

Questo modello di classificazione, elaborato dal filosofo americano **Charles S. Peirce** (1839-1914), si basa sul tipo di rapporto che i segni intrattengono con il referente.

Per **icona** si intende un'immagine che **comunica per somiglianza**, come una fotografia, un quadro con un ritratto o un paesaggio simili al reale: in greco *eikon* significa proprio 'immagine'.

L'**indice** invece **comunica per connessione** o **per orientamento**, suggerisce indicazioni di comportamento, secondo un rapporto causa-effetto: ad esempio, se vedo un lampo nel cielo capisco che è in arrivo un temporale e corro a ripararmi, oppure, se vedo uscire del vapore da una pentola so che non devo metterci la mano perché mi scotterei ecc. Questi segni spesso si riferiscono a un oggetto in virtù di un rapporto fisico diretto con esso e comprendono tutti i segni naturali e i sintomi fisici.

Per **simbolo** si intende un'immagine che **comunica per convenzione**, cioè assume significato e rimanda a un preciso oggetto o evento (il *referente* del simbolo) non per somiglianza ma solo perché così è stato arbitrariamente stabilito. È quello che capita alle lettere dell'alfabeto con cui formiamo le parole o per i numeri che usiamo per fare i conti.

Accade anche con i colori del semaforo, i cartelli stradali o i segnali indicatori per la sicurezza negli edifici, che sono stabiliti e accettati a livello internazionale e solo per questo assumono significato.

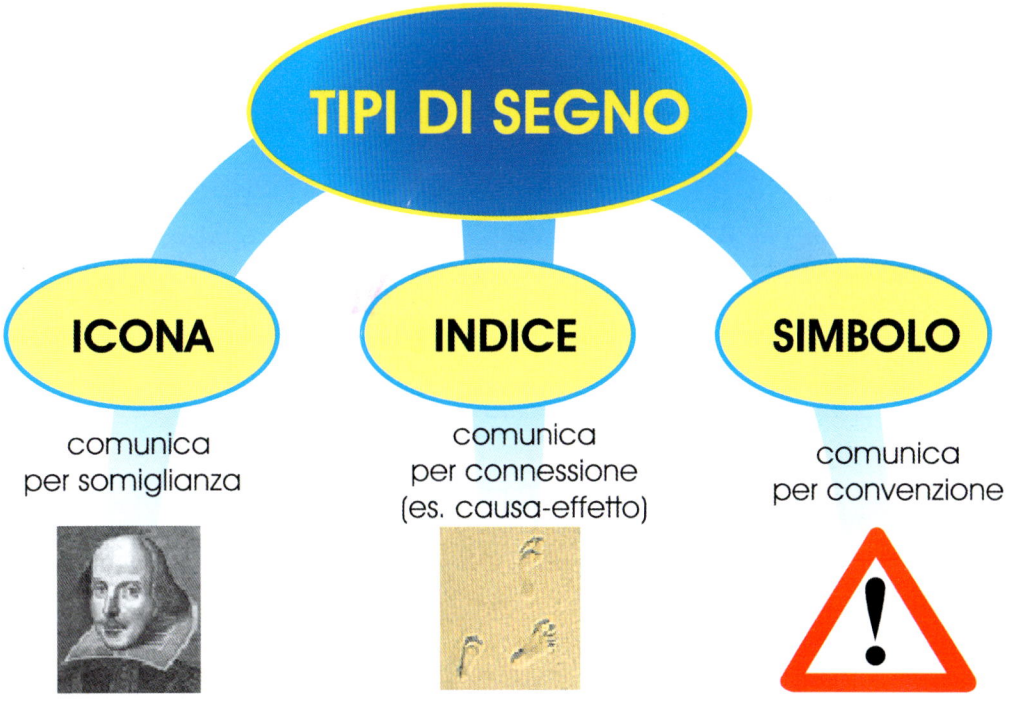

La grammatica del vedere

È relativamente facile individuare, nei messaggi visivi, questi tipi di segno.

Talvolta in un solo messaggio possono essere presenti diverse tipologie di segno: ad esempio, il segnale indicatore dell'uscita di sicurezza (un omino stilizzato che corre verso una porta aperta indicata da una freccia) è certo un *indice* di comportamento, ma possiede anche valore di *simbolo* stabilito e accettato a livello internazionale; inoltre mantiene una pur minima somiglianza con la figura umana e quindi può essere anche considerato un'*icona*.

Come le parole, scritte o pronunciate, anche le immagini si inseriscono nel complesso meccanismo della comunicazione, utilizzando elementi specifici, una propria grammatica, un'adeguata sintassi compositiva e rispondendo a precise leggi, suggerite dagli studiosi dei fenomeni della percezione, della semiologia e della comunicazione visiva, che sono da conoscere e da applicare correttamente e consapevolmente.

Il segnale dell'uscita di sicurezza nasce dall'unione delle tre tipologie di segno.

1. Individuare e spiegare il significante e il significato di un segno

Spiega, di ogni immagine sottostante, in che cosa consistono il significante e il significato.
Indica poi il referente del segno.

⚠️	**Il significante è:** *pannello di lamiera di forma triangolare colorato in bianco, rosso e nero.* **Il significato è:** *attenzione perché c'è un pericolo generico sulla strada* **Il referente è:** *il cartello stradale*
(icona della Madonna con Bambino)	**Il significante è:** .... **Il significato è:** .... **Il referente è:** ....
(fotografia di nube / eruzione)	**Il significante è:** .... **Il significato è:** .... **Il referente è:** ....
(ritratto di Cristoforo Colombo)	**Il significante è:** .... **Il significato è:** .... **Il referente è:** ....

2. Individua icone, indici, simboli

Indica, nelle figure sottostanti, le tipologie del segno, specificando le motivazioni della scelta.

☒ Icona ☐ Indice ☐ Simbolo perché somiglia a un vero albero	☐ Icona ☐ Indice ☐ Simbolo perché	☐ Icona ☐ Indice ☐ Simbolo perché	☐ Icona ☐ Indice ☐ Simbolo perché ....

1. Disegnare segni iconici, segni indice e segni simbolo

Seguendo gli esempi suggeriti disegna a mano libera, nelle colonne sottostanti, icone, indici e simboli grafici. Usa la tecnica che preferisci.

ICONE	INDICI	SIMBOLI
es: ritratto, disegno a fumetti, modello in scala di un oggetto o di un edificio, gesti e atteggiamenti imitativi ecc.	es: segni naturali (fumo, lampo, arcobaleno), impronte, orme, strumenti di misura, cartellino segnaposto, marchio di fabbrica ecc.	es: lettere dell'alfabeto, segno di punteggiatura, numeri , semaforo e segnali stradali, codice Morse, bandiere ecc.

I CONTENUTI DEL "SEGNO"

Denotazione, Connotazione, Evocazione

Ogni segno (icona, indice o simbolo) contiene in sé ulteriori elementi di specificazione, così definiti:

■ Denotazione

Si intende il significato fondamentale di un termine: è la immediata definizione, quasi da dizionario, di ciò che si vede. Ad esempio, se vedo un'automobile, la denotazione è data dalla definizione stessa di auto: *"veicolo a quattro ruote per il trasporto di passeggeri e bagagli"*;

■ Connotazione

Consiste in un'ulteriore precisazione, un allargamento della definizione, anche in rapporto con altri elementi analoghi: tipo, marca, modello, funzione ed effettivo utilizzo (in auto posso viaggiare, fermarmi a riposare, cercare un po' di *privacy*, ecc.);

■ Evocazione

Nasce per libera associazione di idee ed è quasi sempre soggettiva.

L'immagine, in osservatori diversi, può suscitare emozioni e sensazioni diverse: l'auto può essere vista come emblema positivo del progresso tecnico e sociale, oppure come fattore negativo di inquinamento ambientale, oppure vissuta come *status-symbol*, cioè indice di prestigio e ricchezza ecc.

Anche questi elementi sono attentamente da studiare e conoscere, soprattutto se vogliamo costruire messaggi visivi di tipo pubblicitario, indirizzati a un certo pubblico per invogliarlo ad acquistare un prodotto determinato.

Le immagini denotano un segno zodiacale, una bandiera, un fulmine, un'impronta fossile, una poltrona, un'automobile, eppure quando le osserviamo richiamano alla nostra mente molte altre impressioni e pensieri.

Analizzare un'immagine secondo la tipologia e i contenuti del segno

Dopo aver osservato le immagini di questa pagina e letto la relativa spiegazione esprimi verbalmente, confrontandoti con i compagni e il docente, il contenuto del segno nelle foto riportate alla pagina precedente, specificando le motivazioni delle tue scelte.

• **Il segno è**
☐ naturale
☒ artificiale

• **Il segno è da considerare come**
☐ Icona
☐ Indice
☒ Simbolo (usa parole e numeri)

• **Denotazione**
Calendario

• **Connotazione**
Pannello in lamiera con quattro serie di numeri e parole (in materiale plastico) da comporre in modo da formare la data

• **Evocazione**
Ricorda il tempo che passa in modo elegante e funzionale, data la buona visibilità

Raffaello Sanzio, *Madonna del Belvedere* o *Madonna del Prato*, 1506.

• **Il segno è**
☐ naturale
☒ artificiale

• **Il segno è da considerare come**
☒ Icona
☐ Indice
☐ Simbolo (usa parole e numeri)

• **Denotazione**

....

• **Connotazione**

....
....
....

• **Evocazione**

....
....
....

PORTFOLIO

Progettare un pittogramma per un ambiente della scuola

Obiettivo dell'attività: applicare conoscenze e abilità acquisite per creare un pittogramma.

Il pittogramma consiste in un elemento grafico che rappresenta un luogo fisico o un'attività che vi si svolge. Va eseguito privilegiando la forma geometrica semplice, stilizzata ma riconoscibile, a tinta piatta, con un massimo di due colori contrastanti, per aumentarne la visibilità.
Per la sua riconoscibilità non deve essere indispensabile la scritta.

• Osserva e commenta gli esempi di pittogrammi riportati in questa pagina.

• Progetta un pittogramma per un ambiente della scuola applicando la seguente procedura:
  – predisponi un foglio da disegno grande, liscio, diviso in 2 parti;
  – nella parte a sinistra, traccia alcuni schizzi del pittogramma e perfeziona il modello del disegno scelto tra i vari schizzi;
  – nella parte a destra, realizza il disegno geometrico del pittogramma e coloralo con tecnica libera.

EMITTENTE

DESTINATARIO

I tre elementi fondamentali del processo comunicativo.

3. IL PROCESSO COMUNICATIVO

I fattori della comunicazione

Segni e simboli sono da collocare all'interno di un messaggio, a sua volta inserito in un più complesso sistema di comunicazione.

Numerosi sono gli studiosi che hanno teorizzato modelli del processo di comunicazione: per analogia con il testo narrativo, assumiamo come riferimento il modello proposto dal linguista **Roman Jakobson**, aggiornato poi da altri.

In esso i fattori principali della comunicazione sono *emittente*, *messaggio* e *destinatario*.

■ Emittente
È colui che produce l'atto della comunicazione, cioè l'autore del messaggio.

■ Messaggio
È formato dall'insieme di segni, necessari per creare la comunicazione, che, raggruppati secondo precise regole, formano un insieme logico che si riferisce ad un'idea di oggetti concreti o astratti.

■ Destinatario
È colui al quale il messaggio viene indirizzato e di cui diviene lettore e interprete.

La comunicazione avviene sempre in un preciso *contesto*, veicolata da qualcosa che stabilisca il *contatto* e da un preciso *codice* di comunicazione.

■ Contesto
Il contesto, o ambiente, è il "mondo" (fisico, culturale, relazionale) all'interno del quale avviene l'atto comunicativo.

■ Contatto
È il veicolo o **canale** di trasmissione del messaggio.

■ Codice
È il sistema di regole e segni dai significati condivisi, più o meno arbitrari, attraverso il quale le nostre idee si trasformano in parole, suoni, immagini.

Tra mittente e messaggio avviene quindi un processo di **codifica** del messaggio (trasformazione in segni del contenuto comunicativo); a sua volta, il ricevente deve attuare un processo di **decodifica** del messaggio, per poterlo comprendere nella sua completezza. Talvolta nel processo comunicativo si inseriscono anche elementi di **filtro culturale** e di **disturbo** o **rumore**, che rendono più difficoltosa la ricezione del messaggio. Inoltre, il destinatario può inviare una **retrocomunicazione** (*feedback*) al mittente: in tal caso il processo è completo.

Schema generale del processo di comunicazione.
E = emittente
D = destinatario

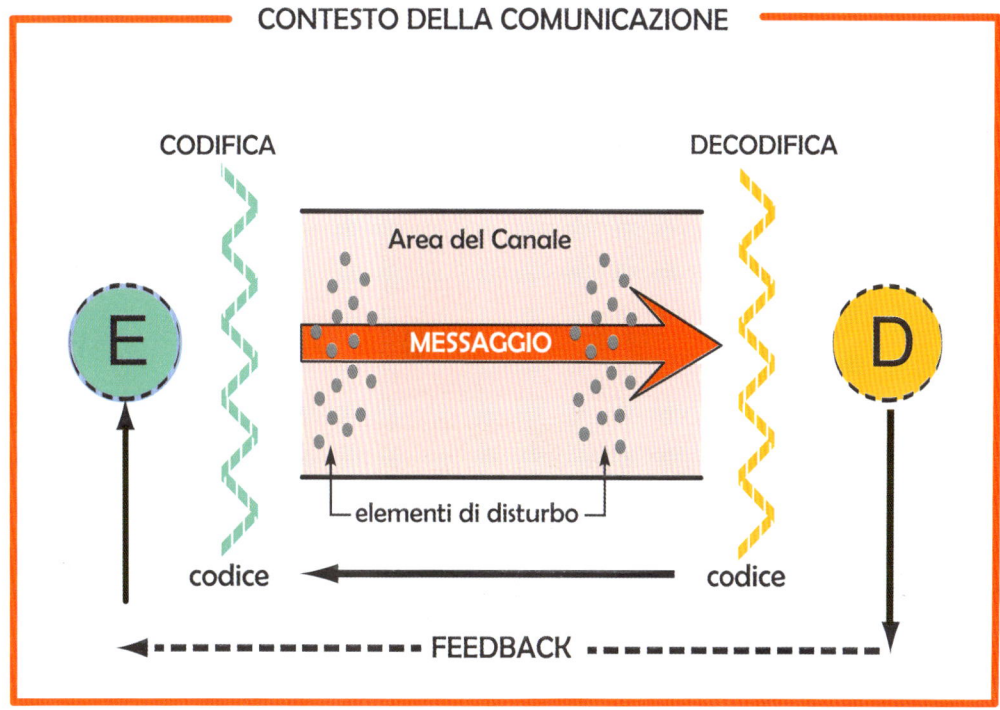

CONTESTO DELLA COMUNICAZIONE

CODIFICA — DECODIFICA

Area del Canale

MESSAGGIO

elementi di disturbo

codice — codice

FEEDBACK

Esempi di comunicazioni visive (e multimediali)

Dopo aver osservato e letto gli esempi proposti (*figg. 1 e 2*), esegui la descrizione del processo comunicativo delle situazioni visualizzate nelle *figure 3 e 4*, indicandone gli elementi principali (*Messaggio - Emittente - Ricevente - Contesto - Canale - Codice ed eventuali elementi di disturbo e di feedback*).

1. Il *messaggio* è quanto viene detto e mostrato dall'insegnante (*mittente*) agli studenti (*destinatari*) presenti nell'aula (*contesto*). Il *codice* è verbale e visuale e il *contatto* è diretto e personale, data la presenza del docente. La *codifica* e la successiva *decodifica* del messaggio dipendono dalla professionalità del docente e dal livello di attenzione degli studenti, che talvolta creano elementi di *disturbo* (*rumore*).

2. Il *messaggio* è il film proiettato sullo schermo: il film è creato da un regista (*mittente*) e cerca di trasmette agli spettatori (*destinatari*) presenti nella sala (*contesto*) emozioni e divertimento. Il *codice* è verbale e visuale e il *contatto* è creato dal proiettore. La *codifica* e la successiva *decodifica* del messaggio dipendono dalla professionalità del regista e dall'attenzione degli spettatori, che talvolta creano momenti di *disturbo* (*rumore*).

3. Manifesto pubblicitario affisso su un cartellone lungo una strada periferica di città.

4. Il critico d'arte Bernard Berenson, in visita alla Galleria Borghese di Roma, davanti alla statua di Paolina Borghese del Canova. Foto di **David Seymour**, 1955.

4. LE FUNZIONI DELLA COMUNICAZIONE VISIVA

Ai singoli fattori della comunicazione visiva possiamo far corrispondere altrettante funzioni comunicative, sempre compresenti, anche se di volta in volta solo una (o due) risulta predominanti.

In analogia con la linguistica, le funzioni della comunicazione sono le seguenti:

1. Funzione espressiva/emotiva

È propria dell'*emittente* che esprime ("*getta fuori*", in latino) il messaggio, comunicando le sue emozioni al destinatario. Grande importanza per questa funzione è svolta dal linguaggio non verbale, cioè dal linguaggio del corpo (*cinesica*) e dalla gestione dello spazio e della distanza (*prossemica*), come già visto a *pag. 22*.

J.P. Laffont-Sygma, concetto di **Oliviero Toscani**, *Comunicazione Benetton*, 1992.
Il fotografo, in questa immagine di sfruttamento del lavoro dei bambini esprime e suscita in noi emozioni di sdegno e compassione: è la funzione espressiva ed emotiva della comunicazione.

2. Funzione poetica/estetica

È inerente a come il messaggio viene costruito, nei suoi aspetti qualitativi: l'equilibrio compositivo di un quadro, l'armonia delle forme e dei colori.

Sol LeWitt, *Bands of Equal Width of Color* (Linee di uguale spessore a colori), 2000.
Nelle opere d'arte, soprattutto nei quadri astratti, la funzione poetica ed estetica è svolta dalla scelta compositiva, dalle forme e dai colori usati dall'artista.

3. Funzione conativa o retorica

Riguarda il *destinatario*, perché il messaggio può essere un ordine, una seduzione, un obbligo, che lo inducono ad assumere un certo comportamento. È molto frequente nei messaggi pubblicitari.

4. Funzione informativa o referenziale

È inerente al contesto, al referente del segno, e avviene quando ci si riferisce a qualcosa, si parla o si informa di qualcosa o si descrive un avvenimento.

Non fatevi spennare

L'immagine di un'oca, con l'invito a non farsi "spennare" fa parte della propaganda per un piumino d'oca dal costo contenuto: un modo ironico, basato sul doppio senso, con funzione retorica.

5. Funzione fática

Avviene quando usiamo segni per mantenere e sottolineare il contatto comunicativo; ad esempio, all'interno di un immagine, molti sono i punti e gli elementi diversi che ci possono indurre ad osservarla a lungo, soffermando lo sguardo.

Le immagini riportate sui cataloghi tecnici e sui manuali d'uso di apparecchiature meccaniche o elettroniche svolgono una prevalente funzione informativa-referenziale e devono quindi essere chiare e leggibili, ad esempio quelle che spiegano come cambiare guscio a un telefono cellulare.

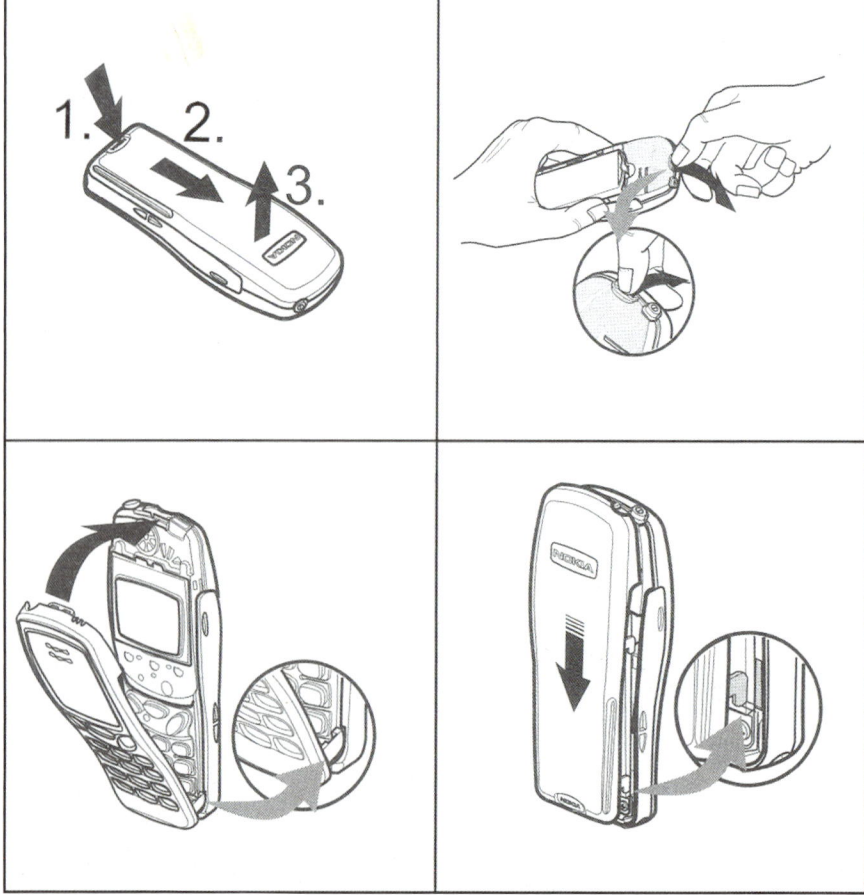

6. Funzione metalinguistica

Si ha quando usiamo segni per spiegare, interpretare e commentare altri segni, cioè facciamo comunicazione sulla comunicazione: si riferisce, chiaramente, al codice.

Ad esempio, le regole grammaticali e sintattiche di una lingua svolgono una funzione metalinguistica.

Salvador Dalí, *Natura morta animata,* 1956.
Le sorprendenti immagini surreali dell'artista spagnolo ci fanno soffermare, a più riprese, su dettagli e particolari che a prima vista ci sfuggono. Questi elementi svolgono una funzione fàtica, di contatto con il quadro. In particolare attira la nostra attenzione il fatto che, paradossalmente, gli oggetti della "natura morta" si mettono in movimento: la straordinaria abilità tecnica dell'artista crea immagini iperrealistiche, quasi si trattasse di effetti cinematografici realizzati attraverso la grafica digitale.

Pieter Bruegel il Vecchio, *La parabola dei ciechi,* 1568. Napoli, Museo Nazionale di Capodimonte. I segni sovrapposti alle immagini per spiegarne alcuni aspetti compositivi hanno funzione metalinguistica.

Le funzioni prevalenti nella comunicazione visiva

Non tutte le funzioni sono sempre evidenti all'interno del processo di comunicazione; anzi, nella maggior parte dei casi solo una o due si notano immediatamente e prendono il sopravvento sulle altre; si tratta di una caratteristica fondamentale della comunicazione, soprattutto per quella pubblicitaria. Osserviamo l'esempio *sotto*, tratto da una campagna pubblicitaria per propagandare la pasta italiana negli Stati Uniti.

Funzione metalinguistica

Viene svolta dalle parole scritte sugli spaghetti, ciascuna corrispondente a un certo tipo di pasta.

Funzione estetica

L'immagine è elegante e ben strutturata: la cravatta fatta di spaghetti ha una forma fluida e si inserisce perfettamente sotto il collo della camicia.

Funzione conativa

L'immagine invita a provare una tra le numerose varietà di paste alimentari prodotte in Italia.

Funzione referenziale-informativa

Numerosissime sono le varietà di paste alimentari italiane, i cui nomi sono scritti sugli spaghetti.

Funzione espressiva

L'immagine incuriosisce perché percepiamo subito che non è possibile usare gli spaghetti come cravatta.

Il rapporto tra gli elementi del processo comunicativo e le funzioni della comunicazione è riassunto in questo schema.

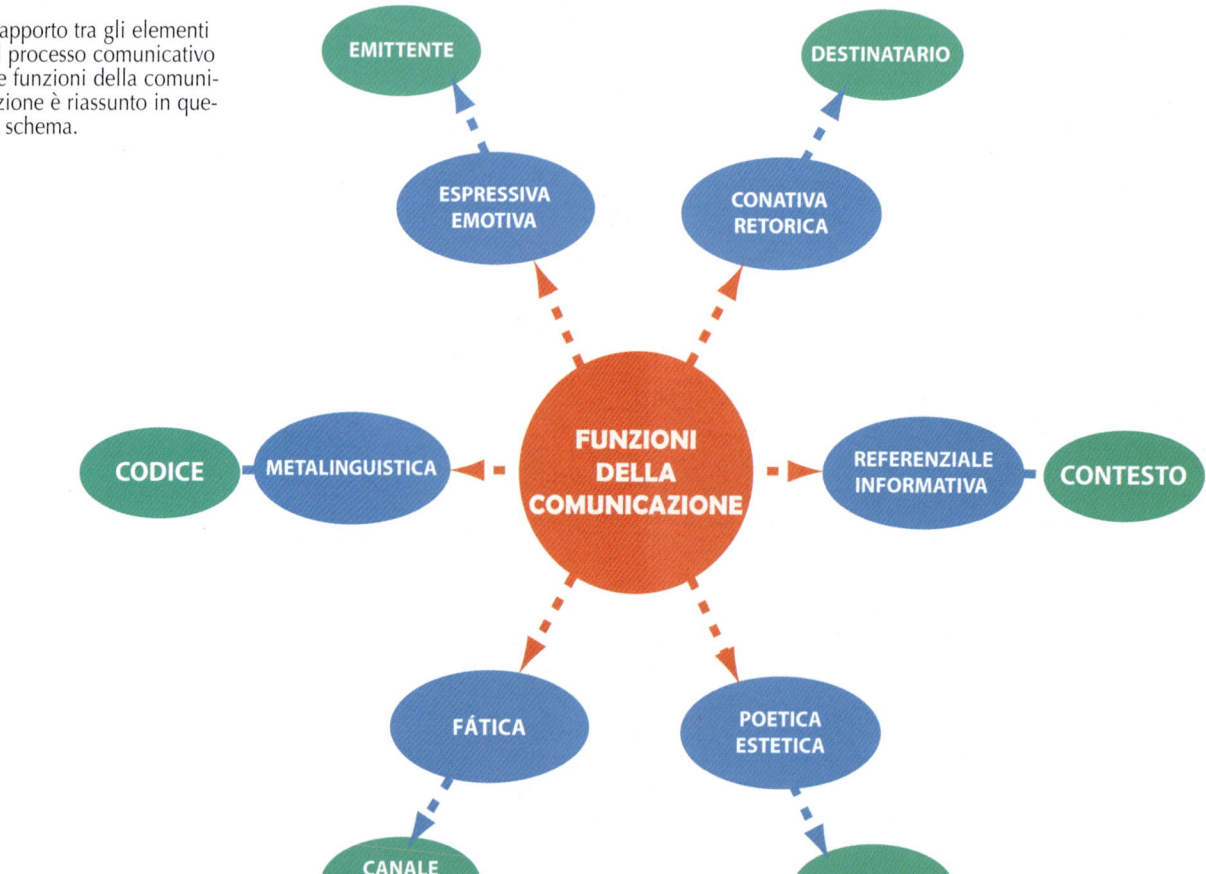

UN ESEMPIO DI LETTURA SEMIOLOGICA GLOBALE DELL'IMMAGINE

A livello di **denotazione** osserviamo l'immagine di un ragazzo che tiene con la mano sinistra una tazza con acqua e sapone e con la destra una cannuccia entro cui soffia, formando una bolla di sapone. La **connotazione** ci suggerisce che il ragazzo è vestito in modo semplice ed è in piedi, dietro un muretto.
Il gioco **evoca** innocenza, serenità e allegria.

Il **segno** è **artificiale** in quanto realizzato da un artista, ed **iconico**, poiché è ben riconoscibile l'immagine di un ragazzo che gioca con le bolle di sapone.

Il **significante** è la tela su cui il pittore ha steso i colori ad olio che formano l'immagine.
Il **significato** allude a innocenti giochi da ragazzi.
Il **referente** del dipinto è il ragazzo che Manet ha osservato per eseguire il ritratto.

Le **funzioni prevalenti** sono quella **espressiva** (gioia e serenità) e quella **estetica**, tipica delle opere d'arte.

Édouard Manet (1832-1883), *Bolle di sapone*, 1867. Olio su tela, Museo Gulbenkian, Lisbona.

L'**emittente** è l'artista e **destinatario** è l'acquirente del quadro (Manet non poteva sapere che sarebbe finito in un museo). Il **contesto** è quello dell'ambiente artistico francese e del mercato dell'arte del XIX secolo, il **messaggio** è di tipo realistico, semplice e di facile comprensione. Il **codice** usato è quello artistico, con attento uso del colore e delle forme in una composizione ben equilibrata, piacevole da guardare nell'insieme e nei dettagli (**contatto**).

Scheda riassuntiva della lettura semiologica di un'immagine

Scegli un'immagine a tuo piacimento e, seguendo la traccia proposta dalla scheda riportata sotto, esegui una lettura semiologica completa, basata sulla conoscenza di tutto ciò che hai studiato in precedenza. Incolla l'immagine al centro del foglio e disponi il testo esplicativo intorno ad essa, sull'esempio della scheda della pagina precedente.

1. Il segno è (naturale/artificiale) perché...	
2. Il significante è costituito da...	
3. Mentre il significato è..	
4. Referente del segno è...	
5. Il tipo di segno è (icona/indice/simbolo) perché...	
6. I contenuti del segno, a livello di denotazione, sono...	
a livello di connotazione...	
a livello di evocazione...	
7. Nella comunicazione si possono individuare i seguenti elementi:	
EMITTENTE	
DESTINATARIO	
CONTESTO	
MESSAGGIO	
CONTATTO	
CODICE	
8. Le funzioni prevalenti di questa comunicazione, tra le seguenti, sono:	Poiché…
ESPRESSIVA – EMOTIVA	
CONATIVA – RETORICA	
REFERENZIALE – INFORMATIVA	
POETICA – ESTETICA	
FATICA	
METALINGUISTICA	

LA COMUNICAZIONE VISIVA E MULTIMEDIALE

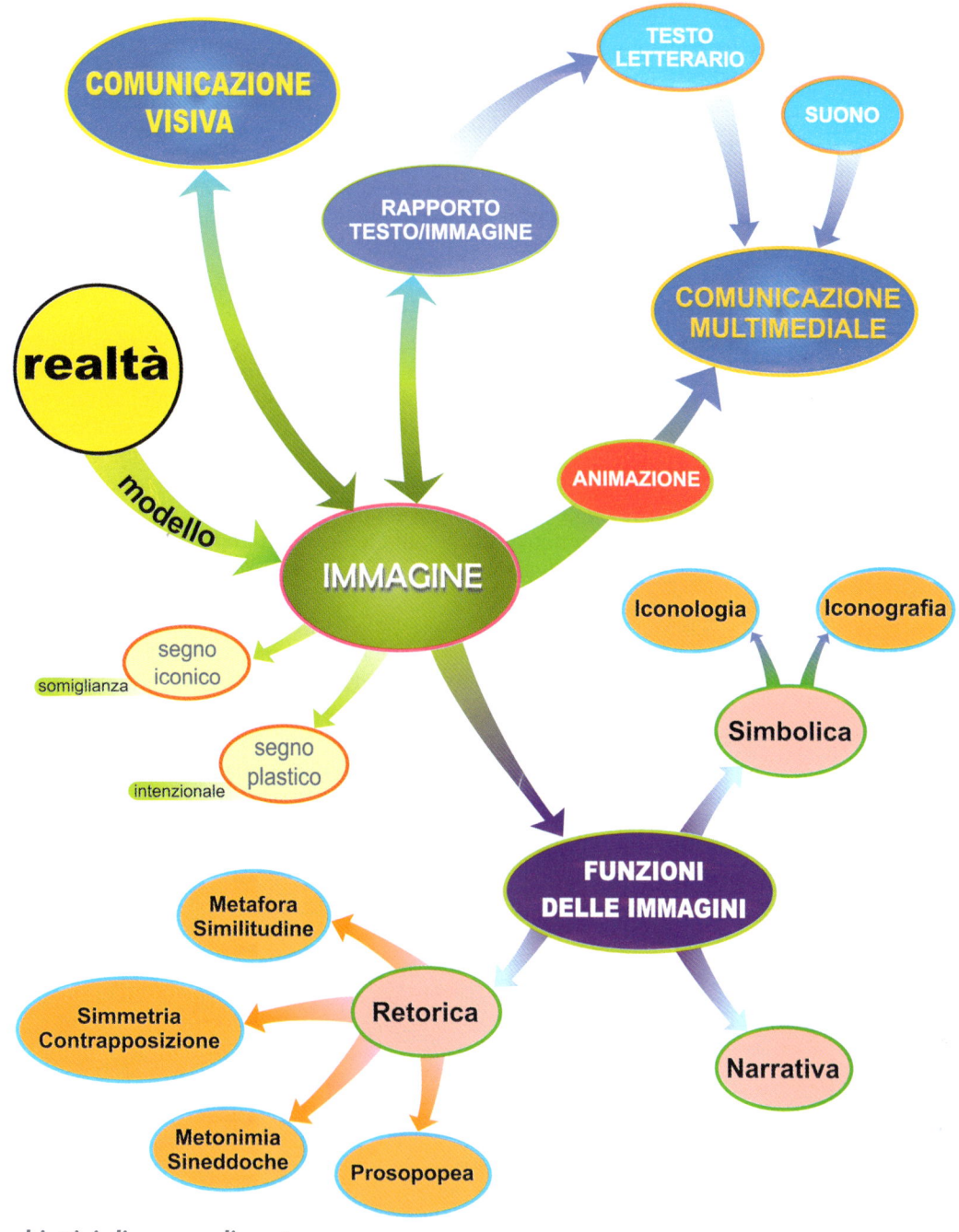

Obiettivi di apprendimento

CONOSCENZE
- Il rapporto immagine-comunicazione.
- La retorica visuale.
- Iconografia e iconologia.
- La comunicazione multimediale.

ABILITÀ
- Leggere e interpretare i contenuti dei messaggi visivi, rapportandoli ai contesti in cui sono stati prodotti.
- Utilizzare criticamente immagini di tipo diverso.
- Riconoscere e visualizzare le metafore visive, cogliendo il valore simbolico di oggetti, di forme del mondo naturale, ecc.
- Individuare e classificare simboli e metafore utilizzate nel campo dell'arte e della pubblicità.

1. IMMAGINI COME MODELLO DELLA REALTÀ

Immagini e realtà

Per quanto somigliante, un'immagine non può essere uguale alla realtà sensoriale: ad esempio, anche la più fedele delle fotografie non potrà mai sostituire un paesaggio reale. Ogni **immagine** è quindi un **modello della realtà**, una sua rappresentazione che si rapporta ad essa non solo e non tanto per la **somiglianza** (grado di *iconicità*) quanto per la proprietà di descrivere, sostituire, interpretare, tradurre la realtà stessa.

Un quadro di un pittore dell'*Espressionismo*, ad esempio, che volutamente deforma le figure e usa colori falsati, spesso esprime meglio la realtà drammatica di un momento politico o sociale particolare, piuttosto che un'opera di un artista della *Pop Art* o dell'*Iperrealismo*, che usano figure molto più vicine alla nostra realtà visiva quotidiana ma meno coinvolgenti emotivamente.

Il segno iconico e il segno plastico

Nella comunicazione visiva il **segno iconico**, riconoscibile per somiglianza con l'oggetto che rappresenta, spesso si trasforma in **segno plastico**, volutamente prodotto ed inserito dal mittente nel messaggio con un preciso contenuto culturale, se non addirittura ideologico. Ciò avviene regolarmente nell'opera d'arte (pensiamo alla simbologia religiosa) ma anche nella pubblicità, mediante procedimenti che associano segni iconici a segni linguistici in una precisa composizione, basata su un nuovo rapporto denotazione-connotazione, che va oltre a ciò che riusciamo a capire a prima vista.

Il segno plastico si articola usando gli elementi del linguaggio visivo (*colore, forma, luce, volume, composizione, texture* ecc.) e varia in relazione alle capacità espressive dell'autore.

Ad esempio, in uno dei manifesti pubblicitari che il fotografo **Oliviero Toscani** ha elaborato per le campagne della catena d'abbigliamento *Benetton*, riconosciamo immediatamente due persone ammanettate per i polsi. Tuttavia, osservando con maggior attenzione, l'immagine, di per sé facilmente comprensibile, può rivelare significati diversi, legati non solo al segno iconico (foto di due persone ammanettate) ma al contenuto culturale e simbolico che l'autore vuole trasmettere mediante l'uso espressivo dell'immagine fotografica, per cui siamo in presenza di un segno plastico.

Anzitutto dal colore delle mani si intuisce che un uomo è bianco e l'altro è nero, ma non si capisce se sono due persone in arresto o se uno dei due è un poliziotto (il bianco o il nero?) e chi è il buono e chi il cattivo?

Non lo sappiamo con certezza, perché il fotografo ha isolato il dettaglio delle mani e dall'abbigliamento non si capisce come può essere il resto dell'immagine: la scelta dell'inquadratura è quindi voluta, per creare maggior curiosità nello spettatore, anche perché il manifesto affisso sui muri misurava 3x4 metri di dimensione. L'immagine, negli USA, ha suscitato le proteste di alcuni gruppi politici, che vi hanno visto un intento razzista. Voi cosa ne pensate?

Identificare il grado di iconicità delle immagini

La graduatoria sotto riportata indica il livello di *iconicità*, cioè di *somiglianza dell'immagine alla realtà* fisica rappresentata. Vale per le immagini fisse e parte dall'oggetto reale per arrivare alle immagini schematiche, con minor livello di realismo, fino all'astrazione e al simbolismo delle parole.
È importante, ai fini della comunicazione visiva, riuscire a capire quale sia il grado di iconicità che dobbiamo raggiungere in relazione allo scopo della comunicazione (descrittiva, informativa o artistico espressiva).
Per esercizio, realizza un cartellone con lo stesso schema e immagini diverse, che puoi trovare su giornali, riviste o in internet.

Grado di iconicità	Tipo di rappresentazione	Esempio	Descrizione dell'esempio
10	Immagine naturale		Qualsiasi fenomeno percettivo della realtà realizzato mediante la visione
9	Modello tridimensionale in scala		Può essere una scultura o un modello plastico
8	Fotografia a colori		Una stampa a colori di una foto a colori tradizionale o digitale
7	Fotografia in bianco e nero		Una stampa di una foto in bianco e nero
6	Pittura realista		Un ritratto, un paesaggio o una natura morta molto simile all'originale
5	Rappresentazione figurativa non realista		Rappresentazione non realistica ma con immagini riconoscibili
4	Pittogramma		Cartello indicante un servizio o un'indicazione mediante un' immagine semplificata
3	Schema motivato		Grafici, diagrammi o cartine geografiche
2	Schema arbitrario		Cartello stradale o simbolo convenzionale
1	Rappresentazione non figurativa		Quadro astratto

2. IMMAGINE/COMUNICAZIONE NEL TESTO VISIVO E NARRATIVO

Dai cantastorie a internet

Un tempo, vecchi cantastorie andavano da un paesino all'altro a raccontare di mirabolanti avvenimenti, di tragiche vicende passionali, di grandi battaglie e avventurose imprese.

I fatti che narravano erano spesso illustrati da cartelloni dai vivaci colori e talvolta si accompagnavano anche con strumenti musicali.

La potenza evocativa della parola veniva quindi ulteriormente amplificata dall'uso delle immagini, che attiravano l'attenzione del pubblico, e sottolineata da suoni, ritmi e melodie che creavano un'atmosfera ancor più coinvolgente.

Allora forse si era un po' più ingenui, sicuramente meno informati e tecnologicamente meno evoluti: oggi, la stessa funzione è svolta dai mezzi di comunicazione di massa (*mass-media*, in inglese), televisione, cinema, internet ecc.

La forza delle immagini e il potere delle parole

Ciò che è rimasto invariato è il rapporto tra parola e immagine, una sintesi, una fusione, una convivenza che potenzia fortemente l'efficacia della comunicazione.

Quando entriamo in un museo e osserviamo un'opera, per quanto evidente possa essere il soggetto di un quadro o di una scultura, quasi istintivamente siamo portati a trovare conferma nella lettura del titolo sull'apposito cartellino. Viceversa, quando parliamo a un normale telefono, spesso rafforziamo istintivamente le nostre parole con gesti e movimenti vari, benché il nostro interlocutore non possa vederci.

Tra la lettura di un testo scritto e quella di un'immagine esistono ovvie differenze: ad esempio, l'alfabeto che compone le parole e la loro pronuncia sono una "convenzione", cioè un elemento prefissato e accettato da tutti (almeno da quelli che usano l'alfabeto occidentale e parlano una certa lingua), mentre un'immagine può essere quasi sempre percepita e capita da chiunque, in ogni parte del mondo.

Tuttavia, se analizziamo con attenzione il testo narrativo e il testo visivo, li possiamo mettere in relazione e scopriremo, senza grandi sforzi, che esistono precisi rapporti, soprattutto nell'ambito della comunicazione.

Quando le immagini raccontano una storia

Le analogie tra testo narrativo e testo visivo si possono spingere al limite della completa sostituzione della parola da parte dell'immagine anche in un contesto prettamente narrativo.

Infatti, oltre ad illustrare qualche episodio particolare di un racconto o di un romanzo con una singola immagine, possiamo usare una sequenza di immagini per raccontare un'intera storia.

Fin dall'antichità, quando la stragrande maggioranza della popolazione era del tutto analfabeta, si usava ricorrere alle immagini non solo come ornamento di case e palazzi ma soprattutto per comunicare valori e insegnamenti.

Ricordiamo, ad esempio, la *Colonna Traiana*, sulla cui superficie si snoda a spirale un lungo nastro con un bassorilievo che visualizza le imprese dell'imperatore romano Traiano contro i Daci.

Pensiamo alle pitture murali e ai mosaici medievali, alle grandi vetrate istoriate (così chiamate proprio perché raccontano una storia) nelle cattedrali gotiche, ai cicli di affreschi di Giotto ad Assisi (in cui si narrano episodi della vita di San Francesco) e a quelli di tanti altri artisti più o meno conosciuti.

Benché analfabeta, l'osservatore restava estasiato di fronte a tali meraviglie ed era in grado di seguire la storia e trarne i dovuti ammaestramenti, anche senza commenti scritti e parlati.

Oggi abbiamo il cinema (un tempo muto e in bianco e nero), la televisione e i videogiochi, che ci coinvolgono maggiormente ma che spesso ci impediscono di riflettere sul significato della storia, privilegiando le immagini incalzanti e spettacolari.

A livello di possibilità di riflessione può funzionare meglio un buon fumetto, con poche didascalie e dialoghi ridotti al minimo: il tratto dei migliori disegnatori sa comunicare sinteticamente la psicologia dei personaggi e illustrare lo sviluppo della storia, sollecitando il nostro cervello ad un atteggiamento più attivo e partecipe.

In questa pagina possiamo osservare alcuni esempi dell'uso delle immagini per raccontare una storia.

Si tratta di tre scene tratte dall'*Arazzo di Bayeux*, un drappo di 70 m di lunghezza voluto dal duca Guglielmo di Normandia per celebrare la spedizione normanna che nel 1066 conquistò il Regno d'Inghilterra, sconfiggendo gli Anglosassoni nella celebre battaglia di Hastings.

Prova a cercare altri esempi analoghi e a mettere per scritto la narrazione rappresentata.

Arazzo di Bayeux, 1066, Cattedrale di Bayeux. Artigiani costruiscono le navi della flotta normanna.

I Normanni attraversano la Manica.

Una scena della Battaglia di Hastings: i cavalieri normanni sono rappresentati con la cotta di maglia blu, quelli inglesi con la cotta di maglia rossa.

3. LINGUAGGIO NATURALE (SCRITTO/ORALE) E LINGUAGGIO VISIVO

Se leggiamo su una guida turistica la descrizione del giardino di una villa rinascimentale, riceviamo informazioni organizzate da precise regole grammaticali e sintattiche e dalla scelta di verbi, nomi e aggettivi: l'abilità dello scrittore ci trasmette, in poche righe, la descrizione di ciò che andremo a vedere, invogliandoci alla visita.

Osservando però una fotografia dello stesso giardino o, meglio ancora, andandoci di persona ecco che l'immagine ci trasmette una molteplicità di stimoli: non abbiamo più bisogno della guida, oppure ricorriamo ad essa solo per chiarire alcuni dettagli storico-artistici.

Ma vediamo schematicamente, in una sorta di contrapposizione, quali sono le specificità dei due linguaggi.

Settignano (Firenze), Giardino di Villa Gamberaia

"[...] la parte del giardino costruita su una enorme terrazza che si affaccia sulla città di Firenze è la più spettacolare, con gli stagni che riflettono il cielo. I venti leggeri fanno frusciare le piante di gerani nei larghi vasi di terracotta, risvegliano i profumi degli alberi d'arancio e delle rose e fanno tremare le alte siepi di bosso come pareti animate." Guida T.C.I.

Linguaggio naturale (scritto/orale)	Linguaggio visivo
È quasi sempre sintetico nelle descrizioni, ma può dare diverse informazioni.	Si presta a molteplici osservazioni, dell'insieme e dei dettagli.
Risponde ad un'organizzazione grammaticale e sintattica della frase (soggetto, predicato, oggetto) e sequenziale del testo, frase dopo frase.	Risponde alle regole del linguaggio visivo e si presta ad una lettura complessiva simultanea, anche se alcuni particolari attirano più di altri.
È aniconico, cioè non assomiglia alla realtà, perché usa simboli (lettere dell'alfabeto, numeri, parole).	È iconico, cioè somiglia alla realtà (almeno la fotografia e la pittura realistica).
Presuppone impegno e concentrazione da parte del lettore.	In molti casi è fruibile con immediatezza e senza sforzo.
Può esprimere relazioni spaziali e temporali.	Esprime, in prevalenza, relazioni spaziali. Solo cinema e televisione (immagini in movimento) possono esprimere relazioni di tempo.
Prevede, in genere, un significato determinato, legato alla comprensione del concetto espresso dallo scrittore.	Può presentare molteplicità di interpretazioni, in relazione allo spettatore.

ANALISI COMPARATA TRA

TESTO NARRATIVO	TESTO VISIVO
Identificazione dell'opera Può essere un racconto, una poesia, un romanzo, un testo teatrale, un articolo di giornale.	Immagine artistica, illustrazione, pubblicità; può essere un quadro, un disegno, una fotografia, un video ecc.
Contesto e genesi dell'opera Si tratta di un passo o di un'opera completa? Precedenti stesure, correzioni e ripensamenti. Accolta con favore o stroncata dai critici?	Osserviamo il supporto: è una tela, un manifesto, una pagina di rivista? Analizziamo schizzi, disegni preparatori, ripensamenti durante la realizzazione dell'opera. Accolta con favore o stroncata dai critici?
Soggetto/Argomento Idea centrale, trama. Analisi del titolo, se è più o meno pertinente.	Immagine astratta o figurativa? Può essere un ritratto, un paesaggio, una natura morta, ecc.
Periodo di esecuzione Data di stesura e pubblicazione Contesto storico/sociale dell'autore; appartenenza a una scuola o movimento, avvenimenti biografici e loro interazione con l'opera.	Anno di realizzazione. Contesto storico/sociale dell'artista; appartenenza a una scuola o movimento, avvenimenti biografici e loro interazione con l'opera.
Analisi strutturale Impressione preliminare. Livello di comprensione del testo. Costruzione del periodo, andamento della narrazione, conclusione definita o aperta ecc.	Prima impressione; comprensibilità più o meno immediata dell'immagine. Possibilità di doppie interpretazioni. Percorso dello sguardo, individuazione di linee di forza, piani di profondità, senso della prospettiva.
Analisi dell'inquadratura Parla l'autore, un narratore o un personaggio? Osservazione dei vari punti di vista sui fatti narrati. Discorso diretto o indiretto?	Composizione dell'immagine, collocazione dei personaggi, angolo di osservazione suggerito dall'artista, illuminazione della scena.
Analisi della raffigurazione Individuazione dei temi principali e secondari. Modalità di esposizione: realismo, ironia, oggettività, fantasia ecc.	Modalità di raffigurazione: naturalistica o astratta, realistica o caricaturale ecc.
Riferimenti culturali Ambientazione o riferimenti a fatti e personaggi di altre epoche, a miti e leggende, a realtà sociali particolari...	Indicazioni visive (costumi, architetture, ambienti) di altre epoche e culture, o dello stato sociale dei personaggi.
Espressività emotiva Descrizione dei sentimenti e della psicologia dei personaggi, del rapporto con gli altri protagonisti. Personaggio portavoce dell'autore? Volontà espressiva dell'autore: testimoniare, educare, commuovere, incitare, ...	Aspetto fisico, abbigliamento, acconciatura, gestualità e atteggiamento dei personaggi. Espressione del volto. Volontà espressiva dell'artista: testimoniare un fatto storico o religioso, commuovere, educare.
Rapporto tra il dichiarato e il suggerito Descrizione esplicita/implicita dei fatti. Denotazione e connotazione. Realtà e simbolismo.	Descrizione esplicita/implicita dei fatti. Denotazione e connotazione. Uso di segni iconografici e loro significato.
Analisi tecnico-stilistica Uso di figure retoriche: sineddoche, metonimia, metafora ecc. Uso di registri linguistici e stili diversi. Grammatica e sintassi.	Uso di figure retoriche visuali: allegorie, metafore, metonimia, ecc. Tecniche grafico-plastiche o multimediali. Elementi del linguaggio visuale: linea, colore, ritmo.
Impressioni conclusive Qual è la vera particolarità? Giudizio personale motivato sul valore dell'opera.	Qual è la vera particolarità? Giudizio personale motivato sul valore dell'opera.

4. COMUNICARE CON LE IMMAGINI

Un biscotto come una spiga di grano... naturale, essenziale, leggero...

L'arte della persuasione

La retorica, o arte del persuadere, è la più antica forma di studio della comunicazione. Da tempi remoti l'uomo è stato affascinato dalle grandi capacità comunicative che alcuni individui mostravano nell'ottenere effetti di persuasione su di un pubblico di ascoltatori. Ne è nata una vera disciplina, la **retorica**, che è *l'arte di parlare bene e in modo persuasivo*. Oltre all'aspetto estetico e formale, essa prevede una funzione di convincimento: l'avvocato usa la retorica per difendere o accusare in un processo, il venditore per convincere un cliente ad acquistare i suoi prodotti, un uomo politico per farsi eleggere ecc.

Altrettanto possiamo dire della retorica visiva, cioè dell'uso particolare delle immagini, nella comunicazione visuale, che utilizza forme retoriche proprio come nel linguaggio scritto o parlato, oppure in collaborazione con esso.

Per essere efficace, la retorica deve sapersi adattare alle persone cui si rivolge, mettersi in sintonia con loro e successivamente comunicare il proprio messaggio: è quindi importante saper scegliere le parole giuste e, di conseguenza, le immagini più appropriate e coinvolgenti.

Il successo di grandi artisti, nei secoli passati, oltre che dall'abilità tecnica, è stato spesso determinato dall'originalità della forma espressiva e della composizione delle immagini.

I meccanismi della retorica

Il meccanismo principale della retorica è la **sostituzione**: consiste nel sostituire una parola, un oggetto, un personaggio con un altro elemento riconoscibile dallo spettatore (o dall'ascoltatore), in modo da rendere curioso e interessante il messaggio senza stravolgerne il referente, cioè l'argomento stesso della comunicazione.

L'esempio più diffuso di applicazione quotidiana della retorica visiva avviene certamente nella **pubblicità**, almeno in quella più strutturata: quasi sempre l'oggetto da propagandare è affiancato (e talvolta sostituito) da immagini che generano attrazione, curiosità, desiderio e, in alcune occasioni, anche sconcerto o repulsione, ma sempre e comunque coinvolgono il destinatario.

Pubblicità di un casco per ciclisti che, specchiato simmetricamente, diventa una curiosa metafora visiva dei polmoni umani. Lo stesso casco, con colori diversi, moltiplicato e ridimensionato, crea l'immagine di un falò fiammeggiante.
Al di là delle metafore più banali, alcuni creativi pubblicitari riescono a realizzare metafore visive di grande suggestione e assai coinvolgenti, che risultano quindi più facili da ricordare rispetto alle altre.

1. Metafora e similitudine

Si applica una **metafora**, o una similitudine, quando **si associano o si sostituiscono in un oggetto** (o in una persona) **caratteristiche proprie di un altro**, senza perdere, ed anzi arricchendo, il significato originale: dire che un atleta è forte come un toro è una metafora che rende molto bene l'idea della forza senza far apparire come un animale il soggetto in questione. Le due cose che entrano in paragone sono di natura diversa, pur mantenendo qualcosa in comune.

Un altro esempio: quando disegniamo la caricatura di una persona esagerandone certi aspetti o alcuni tratti animaleschi, realizziamo un metafora visiva che, se ben costruita, non risulta certo offensiva.

Nelle metafore e nelle similitudini esiste quindi un elemento da comparare e un altro che è il termine del paragone.

La differenza tra metafora e similitudine consiste nella presenza o meno di entrambi gli elementi: nella similitudine si vedono entrambi e la lettura è più semplice ed immediata, mentre nella metafora è presente solo il termine del paragone, da cui il lettore estrae le caratteristiche, le qualità da associare al soggetto del paragone, creando una catena di significati.

Ad esempio, se nell'immagine pubblicitaria di un cosmetico affianco al prodotto l'immagine di un fiore, anziché quello del viso di una donna, creo una metafora visiva che associa agli effetti del prodotto sul viso di una donna le qualità del fiore: freschezza, bellezza, delicatezza e giovinezza.

La metafora non sempre è di lettura immediata: qualcuno apprezzerà magari l'immagine pubblicitaria ma non coglierà la metafora fiore=donna. Molte metafore, poi, presuppongono la conoscenza precisa di un certo contesto sociale e culturale, diversamente non sono significative.

Un letto a banana? La *metafora*, sottolineata anche dal testo "scivolate nel sonno" (come su una buccia di banana, appunto) pubblicizza una set di lenzuola con decori a soggetto.

La donna come un fiore: una delle *metafore* più diffuse nella pubblicità rivolta al pubblico femminile.

La *similitudine* tra la forma della pera e quella degli occhiali "a goccia" è alla base di questa idea pubblicitaria. La presenza di entrambi i termini di paragone agevola notevolmente la lettura e la comprensione dell'immagine.

Una poltrona di patate... Una fantasiosa *metafora* visiva di Armando Testa, grande creativo di pubblicità e artista allo stesso tempo.

2. Metonìmia e sineddoche

Sono figure retoriche abbastanza frequenti, perché più semplici da costruire e soprattutto più immediate da comprendere, rispetto alla metafora. Nella **metonìmia** infatti si sostituisce all'immagine dell'oggetto **un'altra immagine che però mantiene uno stretto rapporto logico e naturale** con esso.

Tipico esempio di metonimia avviene nella rappresentazione del rapporto causa-effetto, di un attrezzo che rappresenta un lavoro, di un contenitore al posto del contenuto, di un prodotto per il produttore, di un luogo di produzione per il prodotto stesso, o anche con la sostituzione di un oggetto all'altro.

La **sineddoche** è una forma particolare di metonimia, perché **indica la parte di un oggetto per il tutto**: per un'agenzia di viaggi, ad esempio, l'immagine della torre Eiffel rappresenta l'intera città di Parigi.

3. Simmetria e contrapposizione

Sono figure retoriche facilmente applicabili all'immagine, poiché si esprimono, nel campo visivo, mediante accostamenti, contrapposizioni e sovrapposizioni di immagini o con variazione di colori e di luci.

Si combinano spesso con le metafore e le metonimie, creando giochi visivi assai gradevoli e largamente impiegati nella comunicazione pubblicitaria.

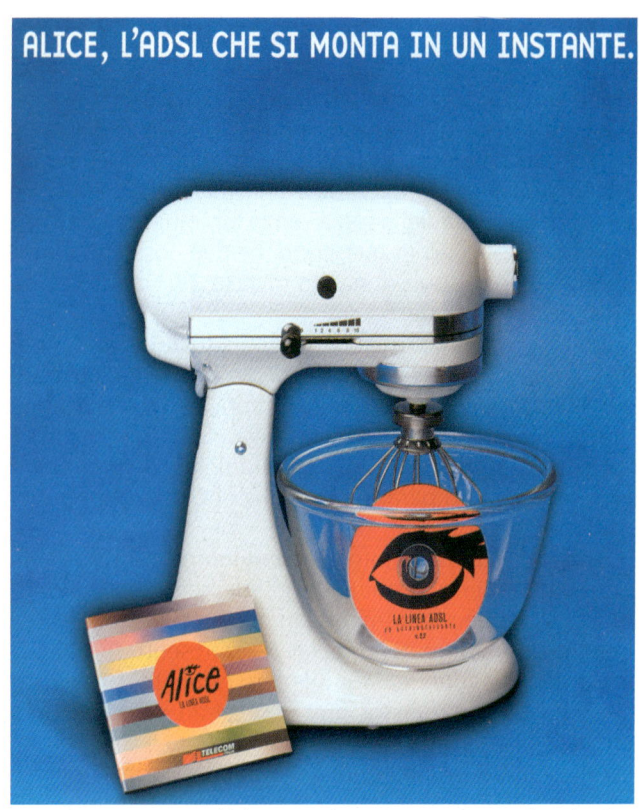

In questa immagine pubblicitaria c'è un *metonimia* paradossale che gioca sulla polisemia del verbo "si monta": si fa la panna montata rapidamente, come si installa ("monta", in gergo informatico) il modem per il collegamento adsl. L'immagine colpisce e attira l'attenzione, nella sua provocatoria essenzialità.

Sotto, due esempi della stessa campagna pubblicitaria di un'azienda che produce indumenti per neonati e future mamme, che utilizza simpatiche immagini simmetriche e in contrapposizione tra loro. Possiamo osservare il perfetto equilibrio delle immagini, la predominanza di colori freddi da una parte (pinguino, polo sud, sci) e caldi dall'altra (canguro, Australia, marsupio).
La presenza degli animali, raffigurati in modo speculare agli umani, introduce anche una forma di gradevole prosopopea.

4. Altre forme retoriche

Altre forme retoriche sono usate in alcune circostanze particolari. Ad esempio la **prosopopea** o **personificazione**, che consiste nel far parlare una cosa o un essere che normalmente non lo fa, come certi animali delle fiabe o gli oggetti (che dovrebbero essere inanimati) dei cartoni animati.

Pensiamo, a questo proposito, anche alla diffusione di *gadget*, di oggetti *portafortuna* o di *mascotte* di manifestazioni sportive ecc.

Assai frequenti sono le **immagini allusive** ed **ironiche**, che coinvolgono lo spettatore in una complicità di interpretazione certe volte maliziosa e spiritosa, ma che non sempre sono capite e apprezzate da tutti, perché si rivolgono ad un pubblico selezionato.

Quando poi si vuole enfatizzare un aspetto particolare o sottolineare temi caricaturali si ricorre spesso anche all'*iperbole*, altra figura retorica che, esagerando i termini, ben si presta all'immagine artistica e pubblicitaria.

Ad un livello più complesso, possiamo considerare figure retoriche anche la **scelta** deliberata **del tipo di inquadratura e dell'illuminazione**: lo stesso oggetto può essere fotografato da punti di vista diversi, presentandone un dettaglio in bella evidenza o creando un alone di sfumato mistero, illuminandolo fortemente o facendolo emergere lentamente dall'ombra.

Sono scelte stilistiche, proprie di ogni artista, che contribuiscono a trasmettere emozioni in modo forse meno evidente ma sicuramente suggestivo e coinvolgente.

Dosso Dossi, *Allegoria della Fortuna*, 1535. Olio su tela, 178x216,5 cm. Los Angeles, Museo Getty.
Le figure retoriche sono molto comuni anche nell'arte, dalle allegorie del Rinascimento alle fantasie surrealiste del XX secolo. Non sempre però sono di facile interpretazione, se non si possiedono specifiche conoscenze iconologiche. Questo quadro, ad esempio, mostra numerosi elementi legati alla raffigurazione della "fortuna" (la cornucopia, il velo, la sfera trasparente, i biglietti della lotteria, il vaso-urna per l'estrazione ecc.) significativi solo se già ne conosciamo la valenza.

Prosopopea: acconciature alla moda per… una mela e un'arancia.

Immagini ironiche: una curiosa somiglianza tra persone e animali, seguendo il detto *"Tale cane, tale padrone"*.

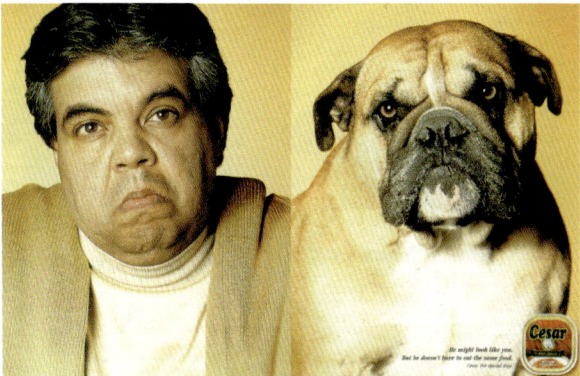

LE PROSOPOPEE VISIVE DELLA CAMPAGNA ESSELUNGA

Tra le campagne pubblicitarie più riuscite è certo da annoverare quella della catena di supermercati Esselunga, in cui vari tipi di alimenti impersonano figure celebri in spiritose prosopopee.

Rapanello Sanzio

Riccardo Cuor di Melone

Re Salamone

TutanPanem

Alavino

Porro Seduto

John Lemon

Aglioween

Antonno e Cleopasta

L'Avocado

Aglio e Olio

Ponzio Pelato

Vincent Van Coc

Mapoleone

Piero della Franpesca

Fico della Mirandola

Raccogliere e classificare immagini con figure della retorica visiva

Obiettivo dell'attività: classificare per tipologia immagini che applicano figure retoriche.

Elabora un cartellone, seguendo lo schema riportato in questa pagina, su cui incollare alcune immagini (pubblicitarie e non) in cui compaiono figure della retorica visiva. Classificale per tipologia ed esprimi un breve commento sull'efficacia del messaggio, in riferimento alla comprensibilità ed originalità delle figure retoriche utilizzate.

METAFORA	SIMILITUDINE

METONIMIA	SINEDDOCHE
	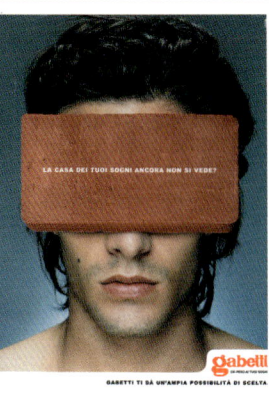
SIMMETRIA	CONTRAPPOSIZIONE

PROSOPOPEA	IPERBOLE

Primavera.

Estate.

Autunno.

Inverno.

Vittorio Amedeo Rapous, *Allegoria delle stagioni*, 1765. Olio su tela. Collezione privata.

La rappresentazione iconografica

L'immagine può richiamare una forma naturale, la figura umana o un oggetto: in questo caso è iconica, cioè realistica. Può invece essere stilizzata o addirittura astratta, quando non vi riconosciamo forme reali, come succede in buona parte dell'arte del XX secolo. L'*iconografia* (*descrizione delle immagini*, in greco) si occupa di catalogare repertori di immagini e temi corrispondenti a un soggetto riconoscibile. Esistono numerosi campi di applicazione dell'iconografia: da un oggetto presente in un quadro, ad esempio, possiamo distinguere un personaggio da un altro, soprattutto in campo mitologico e religioso, e risalire a chi ha prodotto quell'immagine.

Significato del messaggio

Il messaggio visivo (ma spesso anche l'opera d'arte) deve comunicare un significato preciso. L'*iconologia* si occupa dell'interpretazione delle immagini, cioè dello studio dei loro significati simbolici o allegorici: è quindi il punto d'arrivo per uno studio integrale dell'opera d'arte.

Dopo aver creato un repertorio iconografico è infatti necessario attribuire alle varie immagini il loro preciso significato, non sempre leggibile con immediatezza. L'iconologia è infatti lo studio dei significati intrinseci al soggetto, all'immagine, cioè il contenuto storico, sociale, culturale di cui quelle immagini sono espressione.

L'iconologia è scienza più complessa, rispetto all'iconografia, ed esige un alto grado di specializzazione.

Funzione del messaggio

La funzione del messaggio esprime lo scopo per cui, ad esempio, un grafico pubblicitario, un pittore che esegue un ritratto o un architetto che progetta una casa realizzano le loro opere.

Nella sezione dedicata alla comunicazione visiva abbiamo già introdotto i concetti di funzione informativa, emotiva, conativa, estetica ecc. (vedi *pag. 35 e seguenti*)

Le espressioni artistiche dell'arte antica, sia nell'architettura che nella scultura e nella pittura, avevano sempre una precisa funzione, legata quasi sempre alla celebrazione del potere politico, religioso o economico del tempo. Con le avanguardie artistiche del primo Novecento si è interrotta questa logica: spesso l'artista si esprime innanzi tutto per se stesso, anche se non disdegna vendere i propri quadri.

6. IL VALORE SIMBOLICO DI OGGETTI, ANIMALI, PAESAGGI

Le considerazioni svolte nelle pagine precedenti ci consentono di capire come, nella comunicazione visiva, oggetti, animali, paesaggi possano assumere un significato simbolico. La loro immagine, cioè, non solo è una rappresentazione della realtà, ma rimanda ad altri significati, che gli osservatori riconoscono se ne possiedono le chiavi di interpretazione.

Ciò è sempre avvenuto nella storia dell'arte, ma avviene continuamente anche oggi, in particolare, nella comunicazione pubblicitaria.

Cerchiamo di verificare questo importante concetto attraverso alcuni esempi concreti.

L'immagine simbolica nell'arte

A titolo di esempio, vediamo i vari significati simbolici che ha assunto la conchiglia nell'immagine artistica.

Fin dall'antichità la **conchiglia** è stata collegata al simbolismo della nascita e della fecondità. Così nel Rinascimento **Sandro Botticelli** riprende il significato simbolico proprio della cultura classica e rappresenta Venere che nasce dalla conchiglia (*in basso a sinistra*).

Nell'iconografia cristiana, invece, la conchiglia diventa un attributo del pellegrino, assumendo tre distinti significati:
• da una parte la conchiglia diventa simbolo del viaggio per mare in Terra Santa;
• dall'altro richiama la forma dell'orecchio e quindi della parola di Dio, che va ascoltata e seguita;
• da ultimo, evoca il Sacramento del Battesimo che veniva celebrato versando acqua da una conchiglia.

Nell'arte contemporanea la conchiglia assume significati diversi, legati alla cultura attuale. Nell'opera di **Hélio Oiticica** (*in basso a destra*) l'accumulo di conchiglie sempre più sminuzzate verso il fondo allude al consumarsi della materia e al trascorrere inesorabile del tempo.

La statua di un pellegrino medievale diretto verso Santiago de Compostela in Spagna con la conchiglia simbolo del suo villaggio.

Sandro Botticelli, *Nascita di Venere*, 1483. Particolare.

Hélio Oiticica, *Bicchiere di vetro*, 1965-66.

L'immagine simbolica nella comunicazione pubblicitaria

Ciò che avviene nell'arte avviene anche nella comunicazione pubblicitaria: il marchio di una delle più importanti compagnie petrolifere è proprio una conchiglia che rievoca l'origine fossile del petrolio.

Un altro esempio: nel manifesto di **Gavino Sanna** per la propaganda del cibo italiano in America (in basso), vediamo chiaramente degli oggetti "reali": un compasso, un'arancia, un tortellino, una mora e la sezione di una conchiglia della specie Nautilus.

Il loro vero scopo è quello di comunicare un significato simbolico: quello di una sapienza artigianale (della cucina italiana tradizionale) che trasforma la cucina e l'elaborazione dei cibi in un'arte. Per questo il frutto e il tortellino sono esposti come in una galleria d'arte, accanto al compasso (che richiama la geometria e quindi una scienza perfetta) e alla conchiglia (che richiama la natura, che ha dotato l'Italia di un clima ideale).

La conoscenza di questi significati simbolici dell'immagine è così importante che sono nate, a partire dall'Ottocento, due discipline specifiche per studiarli: l'*Iconologia* e l'*Iconografia*.

In appendice a questo tomo (*pagg. 224-230*) viene proposto un repertorio esteso sulle immagini simboliche nell'arte.

I significati simbolici delle immagini artistiche sono molto usati anche nella pubblicità. Tuttavia, oggi, sempre nuovi simboli vengono offerti alla nostra attenzione, e non sempre ci bastano sensibilità e cultura per riuscire a coglierli. Tocca a noi allenarci per comprendere i significati simbolici comunicati dalle immagini in cui oggi siamo immersi (il successo, la bellezza, il potere, il denaro, ecc.) e selezionare i valori trasmessi, senza diventarne vittime inconsapevoli.

Gavino Sanna, manifesto per la campagna di propaganda del cibo italiano in America, 1999.

Il colore

Il colore **azzurro** dà sensazione di spiritualità ed evoca l'idea di infinito;

Il **rosso** evoca la forza e la passione;

Il **giallo** suggerisce eccitazione e dinamismo;

I **toni caldi** e quelli **freddi** danno rispettivamente la sensazione di avanzare o retrocedere, di attrarre o respingere lo spettatore;

I **colori secondari**, il verde, l'arancione e il viola, assumono qualità espressive intermedie ai primari.

Sopra, Linea ondulata libera con accentuazione: posizione orizzontale

Sotto, la stessa linea ondulata accompagnata da linee rette e spezzate, piccoli cerchi e archi.

Le forme geometriche

Il **quadrato** è la forma più stabile e viene associata al colore *rosso*.

Il **triangolo** deriva dalla linea spezzata ed è caratterizzato dall'angolo acuto. E la forma che contiene in sé maggiore tensione e dinamismo ed è collegata al colore *giallo*.

Il **cerchio**, forma pacata e priva di tensione, è associata al colore *azzurro*, perché più di ogni altra forma tende verso la quiete.

La grammatica del vedere

Come la parola (scritta o pronunciata), anche l'immagine può descrivere, raccontare, suggerire emozioni e comportamenti, far sorridere o commuovere. Mentre per il linguaggio parlato o scritto, fornito di grammatica e sintassi, tutto è più rigoroso, esistono varie teorie e diversi metodi di interpretazione del linguaggio visuale, con regole più o meno rigide e codificate, come abbiamo visto con le indicazioni di Kandinskij

È opportuno quindi, all'inizio, limitarsi a poche regole, semplici e chiare, per conseguire la massima obiettività e sicurezza nella descrizione e analisi degli elementi del linguaggio visuale.

Lo studio del visual design e della storia dell'arte, infatti, non possono prescindere dalla loro individuazione, conoscenza e interpretazione, nel contesto delle varie opere di grafica, architettura, scultura, pittura e arti ornamentali. Possiamo suddividere gli elementi del linguaggio visuale in quattro gruppi principali:

1. **Elementi concettuali**
   (segno, punto, linea, superficie, volume)
2. **Elementi visivi**
   (forma, dimensione, colore, texture, luce e ombra)
3. **Elementi compositivi**
   (posizione, direzione, ritmo, peso, simmetria)
4. **Elementi estetici e funzionali**
   (soggetto, funzione, significato)

Questi elementi sono sintetizzati nelle due pagine seguenti, ma saranno ulteriormente approfonditi in apposite lezioni.

1. GLI ELEMENTI CONCETTUALI GEOMETRICI

Si definiscono "concettuali" gli elementi legati all'astrazione geometrica: essi indicano un concetto ma non esistono di per sé. Ad esempio, per visualizzare il punto che corrisponde al vertice di un angolo dobbiamo ricorrere all'intersezione delle semirette che lo determinano. Gli elementi concettuali che consideriamo sono i seguenti:

a. **Punto.** Il punto indica una posizione e non possiede dimensioni (lunghezza o larghezza), non occupa area né spazio, anche se quando lo indichiamo nel disegno occupiamo una porzione del foglio, in relazione allo strumento che usiamo. Indica anche gli estremi di un segmento, i vertici di un poligono, l'intersezione di rette o l'origine di semirette.

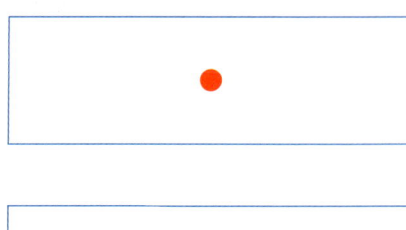

b. **Linea.** Un punto in movimento genera un tracciato lineare. La linea possiede lunghezza, posizione e direzione ma non ha spessore. Rappresenta anche il limite di un piano.

c. **Piano.** È la superficie generata da una linea in movimento, lungo una qualsiasi direzione. Il piano ha lunghezza e larghezza, ma non lo spessore e definisce il limite esterno di un volume.

d. **Volume.** La traccia di un piano in movimento, in qualsiasi direzione, definisce un volume, cioè una porzione di spazio tridimensionale. Nel disegno bidimensionale la rappresentazione dei volumi, ottenuta con le proiezioni ortogonali, l'assonometria o la prospettiva, è evidentemente illusoria.

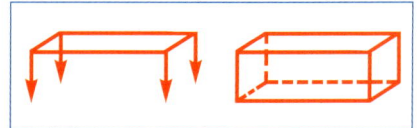

2. ELEMENTI VISUALI

Si definiscono "visuali" gli elementi che balzano ai nostri occhi, quando disegniamo su un foglio, concretizzando gli elementi concettuali: ad esempio, la linea che traccia il contorno di un oggetto ha una lunghezza ma anche una larghezza, in relazione agli strumenti che usiamo. Gli elementi visuali che consideriamo sono quindi i seguenti:

a. **Forma (o sagoma).** La forma (o sagoma, in inglese *shape*) è l'elemento che fornisce alla nostra percezione visiva le modalità di identificazione dell'oggetto che vediamo: così riusciamo, ad esempio, a distinguere un quadrato da un triangolo o da un cerchio.

b. **Dimensione.** Ogni forma ha una certa dimensione, che possiamo descrivere con aggettivi (grande, media, piccola) oppure ricorrendo a misurazione oggettiva. Diremo allora che il quadrato più grande ha il lato di 1,5 cm.

c. **Colore.** Il colore è l'elemento che più facilmente colpisce la nostra percezione visiva: ogni oggetto si distingue dallo sfondo proprio grazie al suo colore.

d. **Texture.** Il termine francese *texture* esprime tutto ciò che si riferisce alla qualità e alle caratteristiche della superficie di un oggetto. La texture può essere liscia o ruvida, nitida o più o meno decorata, in relazione al tatto o alla vista.

e. **Luce e ombra.** La luce è alla base della visione e ci fa distinguere gli oggetti nello spazio, mediante l'ombra e il chiaroscuro.

3. ELEMENTI COMPOSITIVI

In ogni messaggio visuale o opera d'arte, le forme degli oggetti sono collocate dall'autore nel *campo visivo* (che può essere un foglio da disegno, un quadro, la pagina di una rivista, una pietra da incidere o una parete da affrescare) secondo precise motivazioni. È quindi di fondamentale importanza capire come vengono disposti forme ed oggetti e come questi si pongono in relazione tra loro. Gli elementi compositivi e relazionali che consideriamo sono i seguenti:

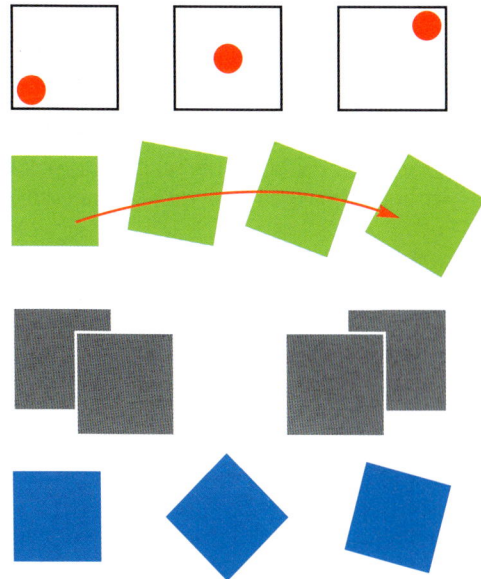

a. Posizione. La posizione di una forma visuale viene percepita in relazione alla struttura del campo visivo in cui è inserita. Forme ripetute possono creare ritmo e simmetria.

b. Direzione. È determinata dal rapporto con l'osservatore e dalle relazioni con gli altri oggetti presenti nel campo visivo.

c. Collocazione spaziale. Ogni oggetto occupa uno spazio, grande o piccolo che sia. La rappresentazione dello spazio può essere bidimensionale o suggerire (ad esempio con la prospettiva) il senso della profondità.

d. Peso. Il peso è inteso in senso psicologico, non fisico: si riferisce all'impressione di leggerezza o gravità che percepiamo dalle forme rappresentate. Il peso attira la nostra attenzione in una certa zona del campo visivo.

4. ELEMENTI ESTETICI E FUNZIONALI

Tutti i messaggio visivi, ma soprattutto le opere d'arte, al di là degli elementi oggettivi della rappresentazione, nascondono significati e funzioni che vanno oltre la conoscenza e l'analisi dei singoli elementi del linguaggio visuale.

Questi aspetti sono tuttavia indispensabili per comprendere pienamente ciò che vediamo e vanno quindi studiati e analizzati. Ricordiamo alcuni elementi estetici e funzionali.

a. Rappresentazione iconografica. Se l'immagine richiama una forma naturale o un oggetto è realistica. È invece stilizzata, o addirittura astratta, quando non vi riconosciamo forme reali. L'*iconografia* si occupa di catalogare repertori di immagini corrispondenti a un soggetto riconoscibile.

b. Significato del messaggio. Il messaggio visivo (ma spesso anche l'opera d'arte) deve comunicare un significato preciso. L'*iconologia* si occupa dell'interpretazione delle immagini, cioè dello studio dei loro significati simbolici o allegorici.

c. Funzione del messaggio. La funzione del messaggio esprime lo scopo per cui, ad esempio, un grafico pubblicitario, un pittore che esegue un ritratto o un architetto che progetta una casa producono i loro disegni.

d. Valori espressivi ed estetici. Dalla conoscenza e dall'analisi dei precedenti elementi si arriva gradualmente ad una sintesi che ci consente di percepire il valore espressivo di un messaggio visuale e di attribuirgli eventuali valori estetici.

IL PUNTO

Ad un semplice contatto con il foglio, uno strumento lascia un piccolo segno: un punto. Il **punto**, dunque, costituisce la più elementare unità visiva, caratterizzata dalla piccola dimensione.

In senso geometrico il punto è un'entità astratta, priva di dimensione. Il punto nel linguaggio visivo è invece concreto: lo vediamo emergere dal fondo, possiamo identificarlo e dargli dimensione e significato.

La forma e la dimensione del punto possono dipendere da diversi fattori:

• dalla *materia* con cui esso è realizzato: può essere un granello di sabbia, un piccolo foro, una pallina di creta collocata su una superficie, o ancora colore solidificato, ecc.;

• dallo *strumento* di cui ci serviamo per realizzarlo: la punta, variamente affilata, della matita, la penna, il pennarello, il pennello, il dito che si immerge nella creta fresca, ecc.;

• dal *supporto*: la carta, la tela, la creta, la plastica, ecc.;

• dalla *pressione* della mano che lo genera.

Nella comunicazione visiva e nelle arti figurative esso può assumere molteplici aspetti, e prestarsi a diversi utilizzi espressivi.

Interessante è il suo uso per addensamento e rarefazione, per cui si possono creare superfici variamente texturizzate, si generano ritmi e configurazioni di immagini.

La semplicità della forma non impedisce, dopo un po' di esercizio, di conseguire notevoli risultati espressivi, in relazione anche agli strumenti e al tipo di supporto impiegati.

Vasilij Kandinskij, *Accento in rosa*,1926. Particolare.
Nelle composizioni astratte il punto costituisce un elemento dinamico della grammatica visiva: qui contribuisce a definire la composizione, presentandosi in varie dimensioni e colori diversi, contrapponendosi energicamente alla solidità della cornice quadrata.

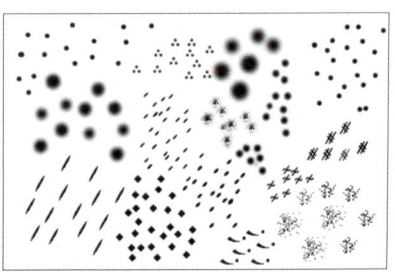

Punti eseguiti con diversi strumenti.

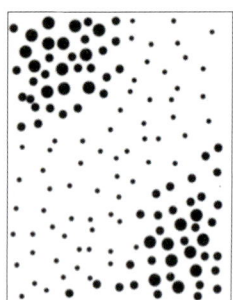

Effetto di addensamento e rarefazione.

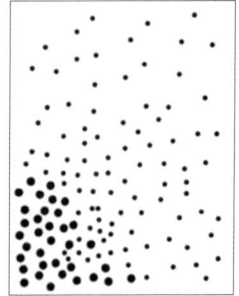

Armando Testa, *Punt e Mes*, 1960, manifesto pubblicitario.
In questa geniale immagine pubblicitaria, il punto non è solo il protagonista grafico della comunicazione, ma conferisce anche il nome al prodotto da propagandare.
Il concetto di punto (di amaro) e mezzo (di dolce) è poi ribadito dalla headline (o slogan).

IL SEGNO

Il segno è l'espressione più immediata per comunicare un pensiero o uno stato d'animo. Può essere una parola, un suono, un gesto, un tratto inciso nella pietra o disegnato sulla carta.

Come entità elementare lo riconosciamo in un puntino nero lasciato sul foglio da una matita, in una macchia di colore su una superficie, ma anche nella scia di un aereo nel cielo, nell'orma del piede sulla sabbia o su un terreno fangoso.

Possiamo distinguere vari tipi di segni:

• **segni grafici**: tracciati su un foglio o incisi sulla pietra, sono parte integrante di una superficie, sulla quale si dispongono come entità isolate o in configurazioni complesse;

• **segni pittorici**: sono quelli realizzati dai pittori, spesso con l'uso esclusivo del colore;

• **segni plastici tridimensionali**: sono i segni in rilievo, fondamentali nella scultura, ma fatti propri anche dai pittori, almeno in certe opere d'arte contemporanea;

• **segni architettonici**: sono presenti nelle facciate o all'interno degli edifici, nell'articolazione dei volumi, in una decorazione continua, nel ritmo delle aperture, e così via.

Nel linguaggio visivo il segno può essere individuato in ciascuno dei singoli elementi che compongono un'immagine.

Ad esempio, osserva il disegno dell'artista olandese **Vincent van Gogh**: quale varietà di segni ha usato e con quale perizia sono accostati, sovrapposti, rapportati tra loro!

Vincent van Gogh, *Paesaggio*, 1888. Penna e inchiostro.

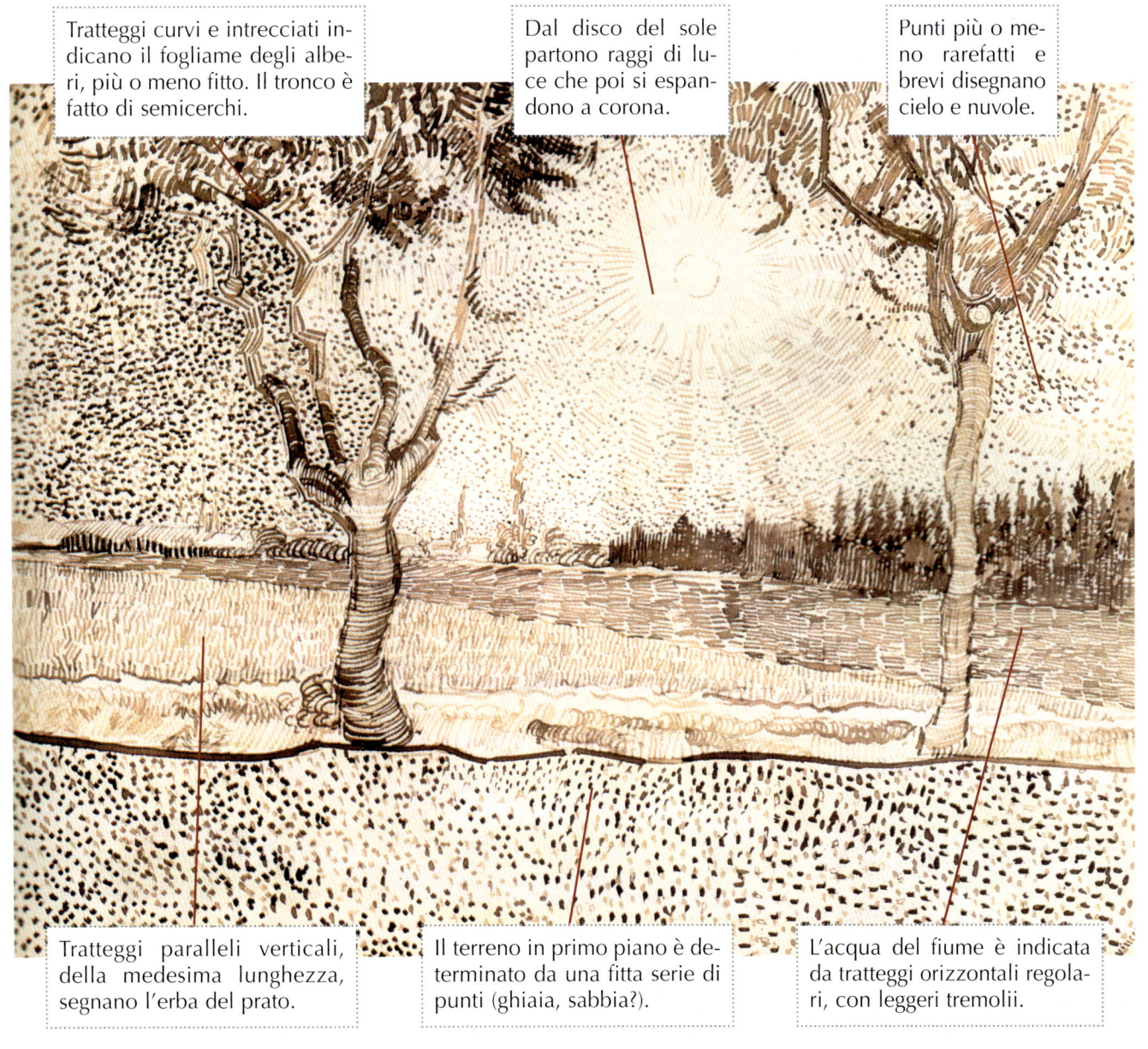

Tratteggi curvi e intrecciati indicano il fogliame degli alberi, più o meno fitto. Il tronco è fatto di semicerchi.

Dal disco del sole partono raggi di luce che poi si espandono a corona.

Punti più o meno rarefatti e brevi disegnano cielo e nuvole.

Tratteggi paralleli verticali, della medesima lunghezza, segnano l'erba del prato.

Il terreno in primo piano è determinato da una fitta serie di punti (ghiaia, sabbia?).

L'acqua del fiume è indicata da tratteggi orizzontali regolari, con leggeri tremolii.

LEGGERE IL PUNTO E IL SEGNO

L'espressività del punto e del segno

Osserva con attenzione le immagini di questa pagina, che esemplificano diversi utilizzi di punti e segni nell'arte e nella comunicazione visuale.

Cerca poi altri esempi, da libri, riviste o in internet, eseguine una breve analisi formale e descrivi quali sensazioni visive generano.

Paul Signac, *Pino a Saint Tropez*, 1909. Olio su tela. Mosca, Museo Puskin.
Signac, con Georges Seurat, è il principale esponente del movimento chiamato *Pointillisme* (Puntinismo), sviluppatosi in Francia verso la fine del XIX secolo, che fa del punto di colore l'elemento fondamentale di ogni composizione pittorica: sarà il nostro occhio che, osservando a una certa distanza, ricomporrà l'immagine dandole significato.

Lucio Fontana, *Concetto spaziale. La fine di Dio*, 1963. Rovereto, MART.
I *Concetti spaziali* di Fontana sono tagli e buchi prodotti sulla tela o su lamiera in modo apparentemente casuale; mantengono tuttavia un sapiente gusto compositivo e generano una riflessione interiore sul rapporto tra oggetto e spazio.

Marchi pubblicitari
Alcuni segni grafici, associati a un prodotto, ne diventano un preciso marchio che li rende riconoscibili anche senza leggere il nome dell'azienda. Accade, come negli esempi, per una marca di abbigliamento sportivo (*sopra*) e per una casa automobilistica (*sotto*).

Tessuto stampato *a pois* su fondo blu
Molto diffuso è l'utilizzo di motivi puntinati (*a pois*) nella stampa dei tessuti: l'addensamento e la rarefazione dei punti, la variazione di scala o una leggera deformazione creano piacevoli motivi ornamentali.

Marc Tobey, *Verso i bianchi*, 1957. Torino, Galleria d'Arte Moderna e Contemporanea.
Un caotico intrecciarsi di gomitoli di linee colorate copre l'intera superficie del quadro, creando un senso di agitazione e confusione, tipica dell'arte gestuale e segnica.

Dopo aver osservato gli esempi di questa pagina esegui una composizione utilizzando solo punti e segni, con tecnica a piacere.

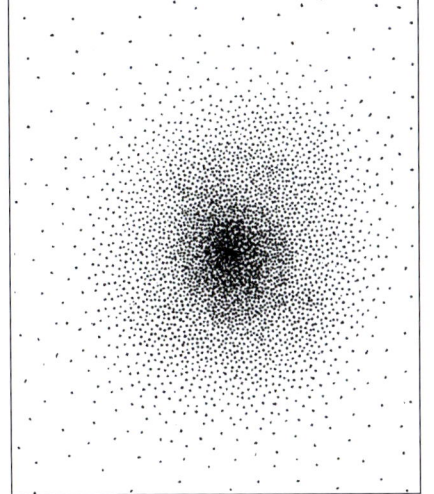

1. Addensamento verso il centro.

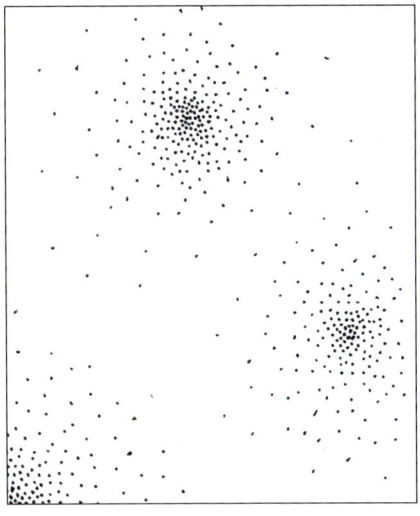

2. Addensamento a nuclei.

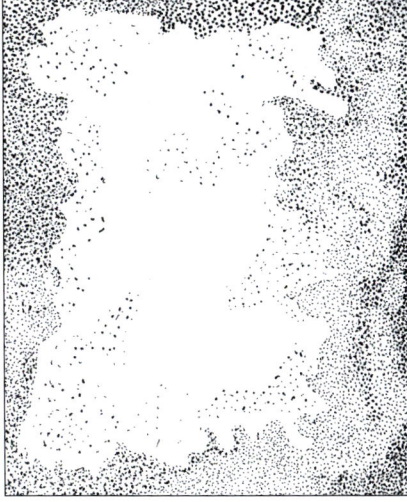

3. Rarefazione verso il centro.

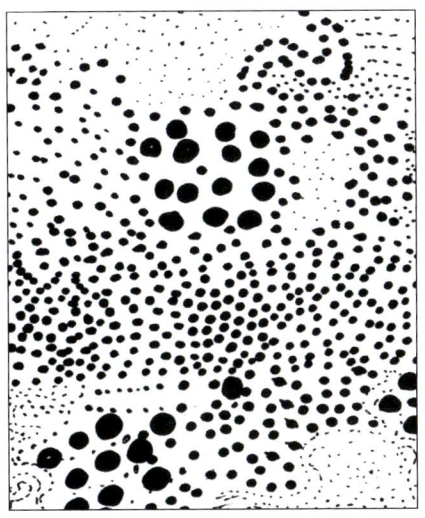

4. Addensamento punti con diverse misure.

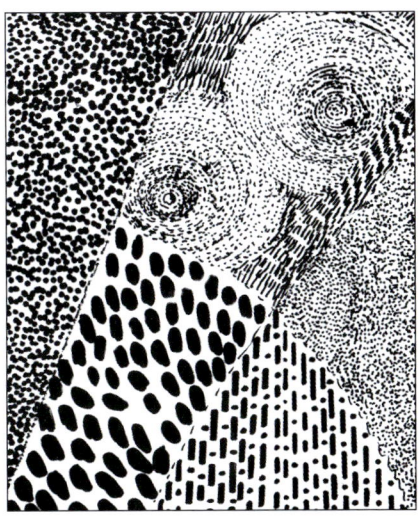

5. Punti e segni accostati.

6. Segni e tratti in composizione figurativa.

7. Andamenti a spirale.

8. Tracce colorate.

9. Effetto rilievo.

LA LINEA

Secondo le regole della geometria, la linea è un insieme di punti. Anche graficamente la linea nasce dal punto: dal punto segnato dalla penna appoggiata sul foglio, prima che questa sia fatta scorrere, e dalla serie di punti che, senza soluzione di continuità, crea tracciati sul foglio.

Concettualmente la linea ha una sola dimensione, la **lunghezza**, e questa è **infinita**. Naturalmente, per rappresentarla graficamente dobbiamo limitarne la lunghezza in segmenti e materializzarne lo spessore.

La linea definisce il contorno delle figure

Mediante la linea, nel disegno, definiamo il contorno delle figure e le separiamo dallo sfondo. È questo il metodo di rappresentazione più spontaneo e immediato, usato spesso anche dai grandi artisti nel disegno monocromatico.

Del resto anche quando il colore domina sull'elemento segnico percepiamo la linea di contorno tra campi cromatici diversi.

Espressività della linea

La linea è alla base della tecnica del disegno e si presta a numerosi utilizzi: schizzi, disegni preparatori, tracciati geometrici e disegni scientifici. Come elemento visuale possiede una precisa **tensione**, è cioè in grado di attirare l'attenzione dell'osservatore per le sue qualità visive.

Si presenta in molteplici forme: ogni linea è caratterizzata anzitutto dallo **spessore** e dall'**andamento direzionale**. Lo spessore dipende dal tipo di strumento utilizzato (matita, penna, pennello, ecc.) e dalla pressione esercitata per tracciarla: la linea quindi può essere *sottile* o *spessa*, a *spessore costante* o *variabile*. L'andamento indica la direzione prevalente e le variabili formali: può essere *retta*, *spezzata* o *mista*, *orizzontale*, *verticale* od *obliqua*, con diversi gradi di inclinazione.

Variando l'articolazione e l'andamento della linea possiamo dare origine a innumerevoli combinazioni: una linea *curva* può essere *ondulata*, con un armonioso e fluido andamento regolare, può avvolgersi a *spirale*, o svilupparsi in anse e *intrecci* imprevedibili e vivaci. Lo spessore più o meno marcato e l'improvviso variare di direzione di una linea può suscitare in chi osserva delle sensazioni contrastanti e, viceversa, quando disegniamo, il nostro particolare stato d'animo può far scaturire un segno ora aggressivo e deciso, ora dolce e fluido, ora nervoso e incerto.

Nel disegno di **Pablo Picasso** (1869-1954) (*sopra*), la linea definisce perfettamente il contorno dell'immagine mentre, nel disegno di **Henri Matisse** (1869-1954) (*sotto*), la linea non si limita a contornare la figura, ma crea anche un senso di fluidità compositiva e di solenne movimento.

Esempi della potenzialità espressive della linea.

Tranquillità

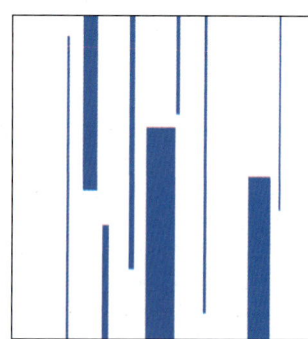

Elevazione

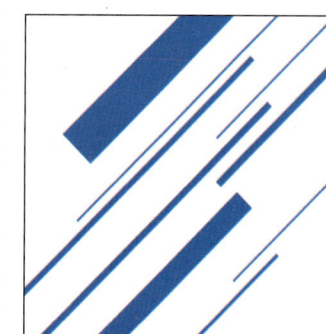

Slancio diagonale

Dinamismo fluido

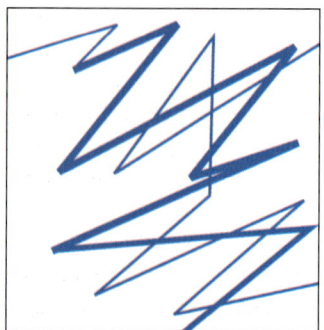

Aggressività

Agitazione

A sinistra:
Maurice Denis,
Gli alberi verdi, 1893.
Olio su tela, 46,3x42,8 cm.
Parigi, Museo d'Orsay.
Nel dipinto prevale lo slan-
cio verticale dei tronchi, i
quali sono contornati da
una netta linea nera.

A destra:
Giovanni Michelucci,
*Torre campanaria della
chiesa di Longarone*, 1966,
schizzo progettuale.
La linea della scala si
avvolge a spirale intorno
alla torre, conferendo ritmo
ascensionale.

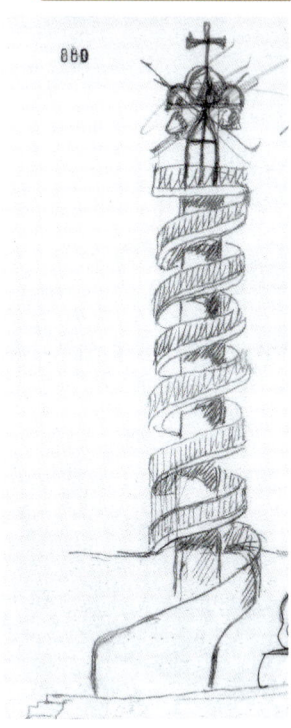

La linea organizza il campo visivo

Nel disegnare un soggetto realistico, ad esempio un ritratto, un paesaggio o una natura morta, possiamo iniziare con uno schizzo semplificato, a semplici tratti lineari, per definire la posizione, le proporzioni degli oggetti e la struttura compositiva dell'insieme. Inoltre il ricorso a studi preliminari eseguiti con tratti lineari sommari è frequente anche nella pittura astratta.

La linea definisce le forme e i volumi

La linea contribuisce anche a definire le forme e i volumi degli oggetti. In questo caso svolge una **funzione strutturale**: ogni linea segue la forma dell'oggetto descritto e ne coglie le variazioni di superficie e di volume, aiutando l'osservatore a meglio comprenderne i significati.

Un ben distribuito sviluppo delle linee e dei tratteggi descrive in dettaglio la forma di ciocche di capelli, il libero fluire dei panneggi di un abito, le delicate nervature di una conchiglia, creando l'impressione realistica del volume.

Quando la linea è decorazione

La linea, sviluppata liberamente sul piano o disposta secondo andamenti modulari, può dare origine a infinite e fantasiose variazioni di forme. Ne troviamo interessanti esempi fin dall'antichità nella decorazione ceramica, nei rilievi dei monumenti architettonici e nell'arte dell'oreficeria.

I motivi ornamentali possono essere ispirati al mondo naturale (come foglie, fiori, conchiglie), o derivare da forme geometriche elementari (il cerchio, il quadrato, il triangolo) e complesse, quali meandri, spirali, ecc.

Gli artisti dello stile *Liberty*, all'inizio del XX secolo, hanno adottato la linea curva come elemento base delle loro composizioni, in pittura, scultura, architettura e arti decorative. Si parlava anche di *stile floreale*, poiché ci si ispirava alle flessuose forme di alberi e fiori, stilizzati secondo armoniosi andamenti lineari.

Nel fumetto la linea viene
utilizzata frequentemente
per sottolineare il movimento ed indicarne la direzione.

La linea indica il movimento

L'elemento lineare è per lo più dinamico: percepiamo come linea il solco scavato dal faticoso movimento di un aratro o il lampo saettante tracciato da un fulmine. E ancora, mediante la linea possiamo dare l'idea della velocità nell'azione illustrata in un fumetto.

La linea concretizza il gesto dell'artista

La linea si presta a rappresentare l'immediata concretizzazione del gesto.

Gli esponenti dell'arte segnica e gestuale, **Pollock** e **de Kooning** in America, **Mathieu**, **Wols**, **Tobey** in Europa, hanno affidato il valore espressivo delle loro opere a linee, tracce di colore e segni derivati da impulsi istintivi, immediati e comunque non premeditati.

LEGGERE LA LINEA

Osserva con attenzione le immagini di questa pagina, che esemplificano diversi utilizzi della linea nell'arte e nella comunicazione visiva. Cerca poi altri esempi, da libri, riviste o in internet.

Di questi esegui una breve analisi formale e descrivi quali sensazioni visive generano.

Nelle *xilografie*, molto usate dagli Espressionisti, l'elemento lineare è ridotto all'essenzialità, e definisce le figure con tratti decisi. Possiamo osservarne un esempio in questo *Lago nel parco* di **Herich Heckel**, del 1914.

L'uomo-linea del disegnatore **Osvaldo Cavandoli**, uno degli antichi eroi del programma televisivo italiano *Carosello*. Atteggiamenti e stati d'animo sono espressi in modo semplice, seppur molto efficace, mediante un tratto continuo di contorno che si anima.

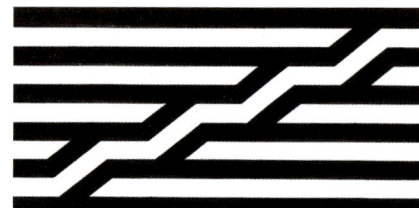

Nel logo del *Centre Georges Pompidou*, museo parigino progettato da **R. Piano** e **R. Rogers** e detto anche *Beaubourg*, le linee parallele indicano i piani dell'edificio, mentre la spezzata diagonale indica il sistema delle scale mobili di accesso.

Nelle sculture di **Alexander Calder** dedicate ai personaggi del circo (1927-1930), di cui è riprodotto un disegno preliminare, la linea, in filo di ferro, segna il contorno delle figure e nello stesso tempo fa emergere il dinamismo dell'azione.

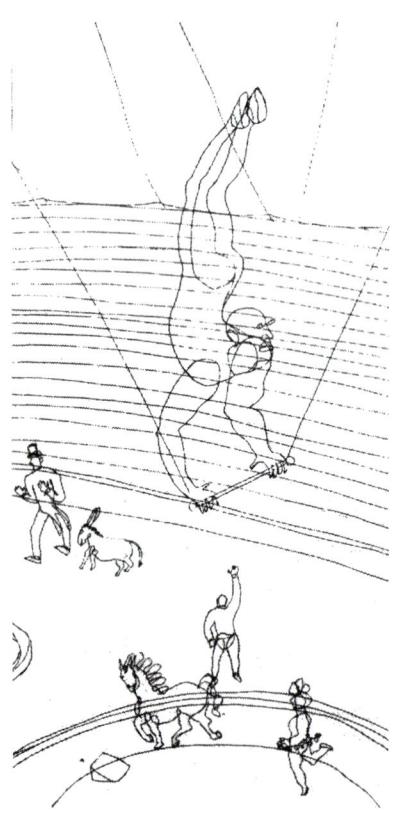

Nella *Ballerina* di **Walter Crane**, la linea non solo indica il movimento, ma assume anche una valenza decorativa, tipica dello stile *Liberty*.

Questa poltroncina in legno curvato, opera dell'architetto finlandese **Alvar Aalto**, esemplifica l'uso della linea nel design.

Osserva le immagini di questa pagina, che propongono diversi utilizzi della linea, in semplici rielaborazioni scolastiche.

Prendendo spunto da questi esempi, esegui analoghe composizioni utilizzando la tecnica che preferisci.

1. Linea come contorno, alla maniera dell'artista spagnolo Juan Mirò.

2. Tratteggi lineari direzionali, che suggeriscono il movimento.

3. Tratteggi paralleli variamente inclinati e accostati, creando effetti di volume.

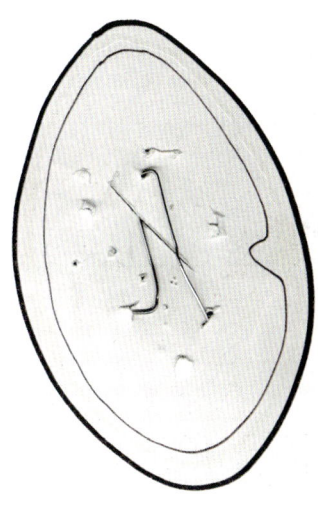

4. Linea come contorno, con inserimento di elementi metallici filiformi.

5. Linee con andamento orizzontale, a spessore variabile: suggeriscono la venatura del legno.

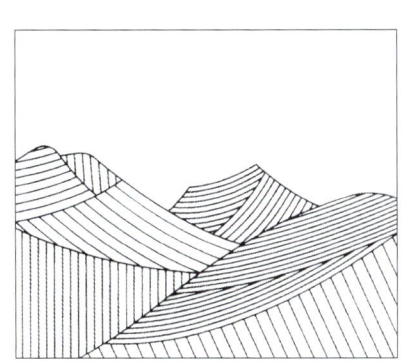

6. Tratteggi paralleli: colline o dune sabbiose.

7. Linee ondulate e capricciose per un mare agitato.

8. Andamenti convulsi per un vulcano in eruzione.

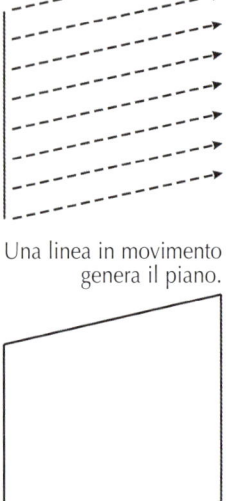

Una linea in movimento genera il piano.

L. Mies van Der Rohe, Veduta interna di una *Sala del Padiglione tedesco dell'Esposizione Internazionale di Barcellona del 1929* (ricostruito nel 1986). Tutta la costruzione è basata su sottili piani perpendicolari tra loro.

IL PIANO

Il piano è la superficie generata da una linea in movimento, lungo una qualsiasi direzione. Il piano ha quindi due dimensioni, *lunghezza* e *larghezza*, ma non lo spessore.

Geometricamente il piano è infinito, ma lo possiamo delineare mediante linee di contorno, che generano sul piano forme poligonali (triangoli, quadrati, cerchi). Come faccia di un poliedro, può anche definire il limite esterno di un volume.

Sono piani il pavimento, il soffitto e le pareti di una stanza e la facciata di un edificio, è piano il foglio su cui scrivi e disegni e il banco su cui appoggi libri e quaderni. Sono piani gli schermi di computer e televisore, la tela del pittore e la lavagna dell'aula.

Il limite del piano definisce spesso anche il cosiddetto ***campo visivo***, cioè la superficie omogenea entro cui avviene la composizione delle immagini.

Nelle Proiezioni Ortogonali i piani (orizzontale, verticale e laterale) definiscono le viste principali di un oggetto e servono per le rappresentazioni grafiche di un progetto.

Essendo bidimensionale, il piano ha costretto gli artisti ad inventare tutta una serie di artifici per la rappresentazione tridimensionale dei volumi e dello spazio, fino all'invenzione della ***prospettiva***.

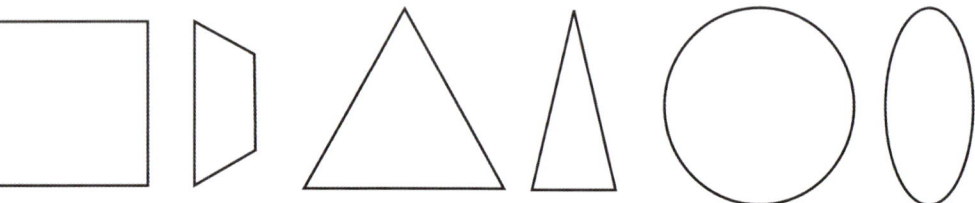

Nelle figure geometriche piane la forma è la caratteristica primaria del piano: è costituita dal contorno (o *perimetro*) lineare che definisce la porzione di piano. La vera forma del piano la possiamo osservare solo nella vista frontale, come nelle proiezioni ortogonali.

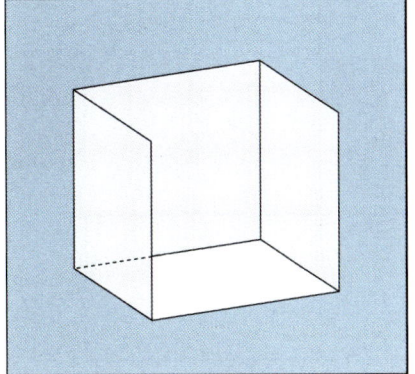 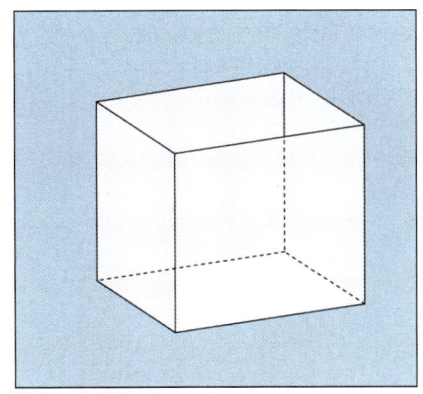 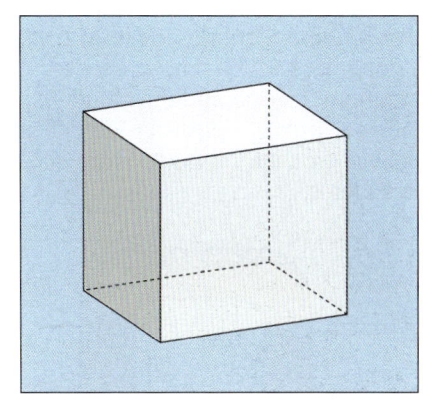

In questa progressione, possiamo osservare come il piano definisca i confini di un volume: il piano è quindi un elemento determinante nella progettazione architettonica.

IL VOLUME

La traccia di un **piano in movimento**, in qualsiasi direzione, **definisce un volume**, cioè una porzione di spazio tridimensionale che possiede *lunghezza*, *larghezza* e *profondità*.

Ogni volume solido ha quindi una precisa collocazione nello spazio ed è definito da punti (i *vertici*), da linee (gli *spigoli*) e da superfici piane (*facce*) variamente disposte.

Il **volume** può essere **chiuso**, cioè pieno, oppure **aperto**, semplicemente definito da piani.

In campo artistico, il volume è tipico della scultura e dell'architettura, mentre nel disegno bidimensionale la rappresentazione dei volumi, ottenuta con le proiezioni ortogonali, l'assonometria o la prospettiva, è evidentemente illusoria.

Ogni oggetto tridimensionale possiede volume e può essere osservato da punti di vista diversi: il senso compiuto di una scultura, ad esempio, si può cogliere solo girando intorno ad essa e guardando con attenzione i diversi effetti espressivi che si percepiscono da varie angolature d'osservazione.

Lo stesso vale per l'architettura: passeggiare all'interno di un edifico, sotto la navata di una chiesa, o salire su uno scalone di un palazzo è certo molto meglio che osservare una fotografia, per quanto ben realizzata, o guardare un documentario in televisione: la percezione è decisamente diversa, poiché avviene da molteplici direzioni e sollecita tutti i nostri sensi.

La rappresentazione dei volumi nello spazio, negli aspetti geometrici della prospettiva, nei contrasti di luce-ombra e negli effetti cromatici è approfondita in altre lezioni di questo volume (*vedi pag. 110 e seguenti*).

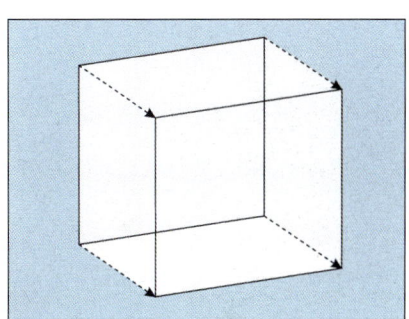

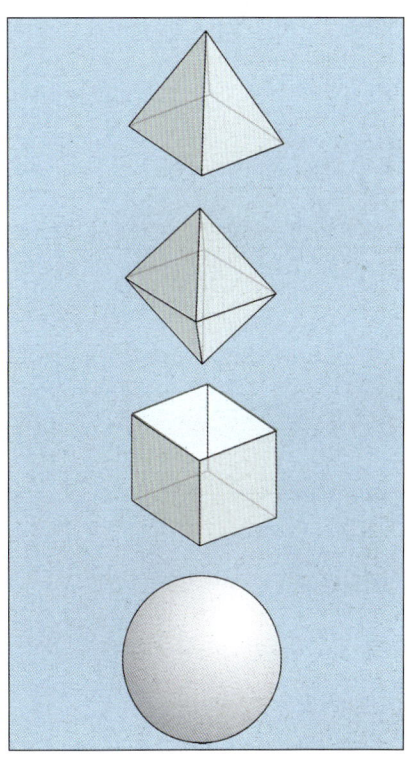

Il *packaging*: dallo sviluppo dei solidi all'arte della confezione

I solidi geometrici più comuni sono composti da un certo numero di poligoni regolari (triangoli equilateri, quadrati, esagoni, pentagoni ecc.) che, appositamente assemblati, ricreano il volume corrispondente.

Ad esempio, è sufficiente disegnare, attaccate fra loro, le basi e le facce di un prisma e poi ritagliare, piegare e incollare i lembi di collegamento per ottenere il solido richiesto.
Per rendere il solido adatto al *packaging*, cioè farlo diventare un contenitore, dobbiamo prevedere il modo più opportuno per lasciare un lato da aprire e chiudere. Osserva le immagini di questa pagina, prova a costruire alcuni semplici poliedri e successivamente progetta un contenitore che si possa agevolmente aprire e chiudere.

Dal piano al volume: le sculture di Jean Arp

Jean Arp (o Hans Arp, alla tedesca; 1887-1966), dadaista e poi surrealista, per le sue opere partiva quasi sempre da una forma bidimensionale, astratta e frastagliata come un frattale, e poi le alzava per accumulazione, oppure le faceva idealmente ruotare nello spazio fino a creare sculture dai contorni fluidi e dall'aspetto biomorfo, simili a forme viventi quali cellule od organismi acquatici.

Raccontano i biografi che una volta, stanco di un dipinto su carta non particolarmente riuscito, lo stracciò lasciandone cadere i pezzi sul pavimento. Tornato più tardi nell'atelier, fu stupito nel vedere la composizione creatasi per terra: *"Possedevano tutto quanto il potere espressivo che per giorni e giorni avevo tentato inutilmente di raggiungere…".*

La casualità rimarrà per Arp una fonte di invenzione, benché molte delle sue opere siano invero state accuratamente progettate.

Il passaggio dal bidimensionale al 3D si può realizzare anche partendo da una figura piana ripetuta variandone la posizione e la direzione. Osserva gi esempi di questa pagina e realizza qualche esperimento usando cartoncino rigido su un supporto piano di compensato.

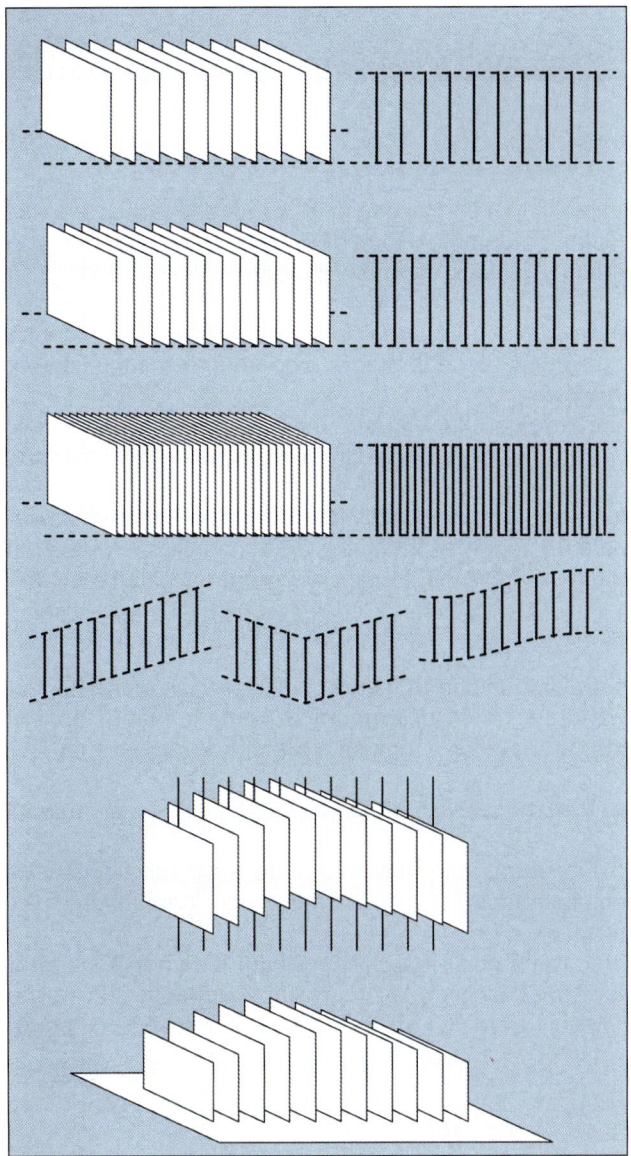

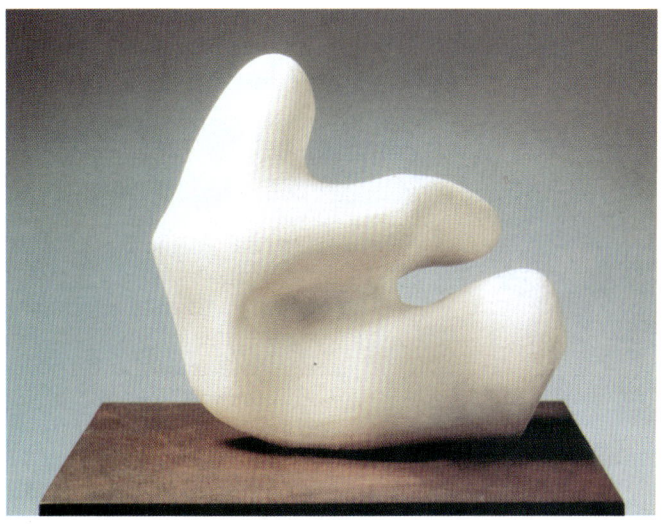

Pechino, *Polo intermodale Xizhimen*, Progetto **AREP**. Forme fantasiose per la città del futuro.

LA FORMA

La forma (figura o sagoma, in inglese *shape*) è l'insieme di elementi che forniscono alla nostra esperienza percettiva le modalità di identificazione dell'oggetto che vediamo: così riusciamo, ad esempio, a distinguere un quadrato da un triangolo o da un cerchio.

Le immagini che ci circondano sono infinite per numero e per varietà di forme: possiamo distinguere, ad esempio, **forme naturali** e forme **artificiali** (costruite dall'uomo); forme **geometriche** (delimitate da segmenti e curve secondo precisi rapporti matematici) e forme **libere**; **forme semplici** e **forme complesse**.

Tra le forme geometriche più semplici ricordiamo quelle indicate da **Kandinskij** come forme base, perché da esse derivano le altre: esse sono il *triangolo equilatero*, il *quadrato* e il *cerchio* (*vedi pagg. 82-84*).

Supporto della forma è la **struttura**, che possiamo individuare mediante la corretta sovrapposizione di griglie lineari, fissate da norme geometriche e da modalità percettive: in tal modo si evidenziano le simmetrie, le suddivisioni e i rapporti proporzionali tra le parti.

Le forme della natura

Forme geometriche elementari si trovano anche in natura: nella maggior parte dei casi, comunque, le forme naturali (siano esse di origine organica, come le piante, oppure inorganica, come le rocce) ci appaiono irregolari, confuse e difficili da capire e rappresentare.

Tuttavia *"Anche nel caos* - diceva Albert Einstein - *possiamo trovare delle leggi ancora sconosciute"*.

Diversi artisti contemporanei si sono ispirati alle forme naturali, soprattutto dopo l'invenzione dei microscopio (ottico ed elettronico), che ha svelato mondi infinitamente piccoli e decisamente suggestivi per forme e colori.

Ad esempio, secondo alcuni critici, molti degli acquerelli di **Paul Klee** non sono altro che la rappresentazione della vita al microscopio. Anche **Vasilij Kandinskij**, per le sue composizioni astratte, si ispirò ad amebe, crostacei, diatomee e ad altri esseri che popolano il mondo della biologia.

Particolare ingrandito al microscopio di un'ala di farfalla.

Foto al microscopio elettronico di alghe diatomee.

LA DIMENSIONE

Ogni forma possiede una certa dimensione, solitamente descritta mediante aggettivi (grande, media, piccola) oppure ricorrendo a misurazione oggettiva.

Ad esempio, si dice: " Questo quadrato ha il lato di 3 cm".

La dimensione di un oggetto costituisce un importante elemento percettivo, quanto la forma: possiamo avere oggetti simili, che hanno la stessa forma ma dimensioni diverse. Per valutare le dimensioni effettive di un oggetto, abbiamo bisogno di confrontarlo visivamente con un altro di cui conosciamo le esatte dimensioni.

Gli artisti (soprattutto quelli della Pop Art) e i grafici pubblicitari si sono spesso serviti dell'alterazione delle dimensioni di un oggetto, proprio per attirare la nostra attenzione.

Paul Klee, *Fioritura*, 1934.

Pubblicità di un'acqua minerale.

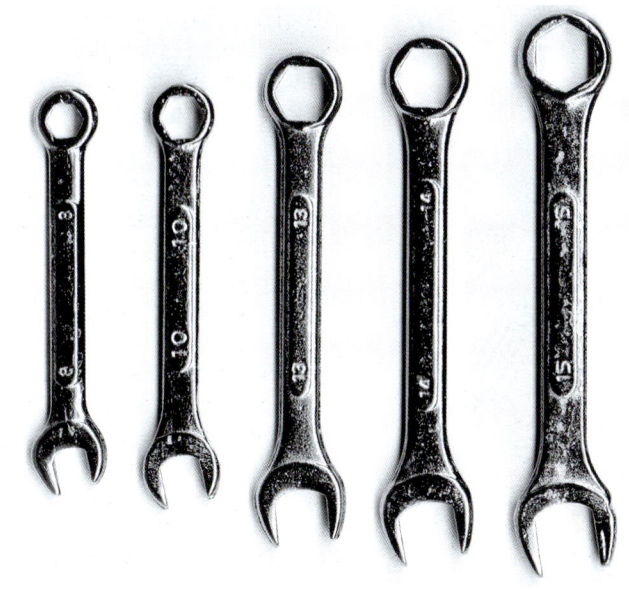

Serie di chiavi inglesi,
simili per forma
ma con dimensioni
diverse.

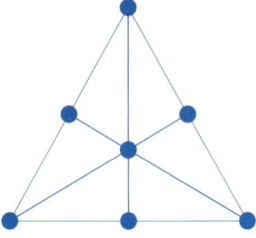

Struttura portante.

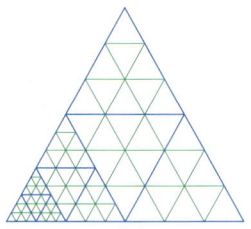

Struttura modulare.

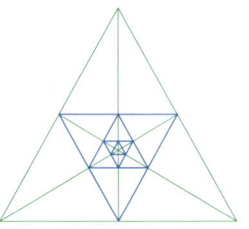

Struttura proiettiva.

IL TRIANGOLO EQUILATERO

Il triangolo equilatero è un poligono formato da tre lati uguali e avente tre angoli uguali di 60°. La forma del triangolo equilatero contiene in sé, secondo Kandinskij, un alto grado di tensione e dinamismo, dovuto ai tre vertici acuti.

La nostra attenzione si concentra sui nodi costituiti dai vertici, nei quali convergono i lati e da cui partono le mediane.

La sua **struttura portante** è infatti costituita dai *lati* e dalle *mediane*, che coincidono con le *bisettrici* degli *angoli* e con le *altezze*, e si intersecano in un punto centrale (*baricentro*).

Si possono comporre forme derivate dal triangolo partendo dalla sua **struttura modulare**, basata su un triangolo più piccolo.

Possiamo individuarne anche la **struttura proiettiva**, che traccia le linee di tensione spaziale all'interno della figura, facendo partire da ogni nodo delle frecce indirizzate verso gli altri nodi estremi.

Il triangolo equilatero non è molto frequente in natura, se non celato entro strutture più complesse. Ne troviamo qualche esempio nel mondo minerale e vegetale: osserva, a proposito, la struttura del trifoglio.

L'unione di sei triangoli equilateri, coincidenti in un vertice, dà origine all'esagono, la cui composizione modulare è un'ulteriore derivazione di quella del triangolo.

Il triangolo come simbolo

Il triangolo esprime significati simbolici legati al numero tre. Con varianti riferite ai diversi sistemi di pensiero, la forma equilatera (equilibrio di forze positive e negative) rappresenta l'armonia, la proporzione, il principio divino, la vita. La sua trasformazione esprime perdita dell'equilibrio.

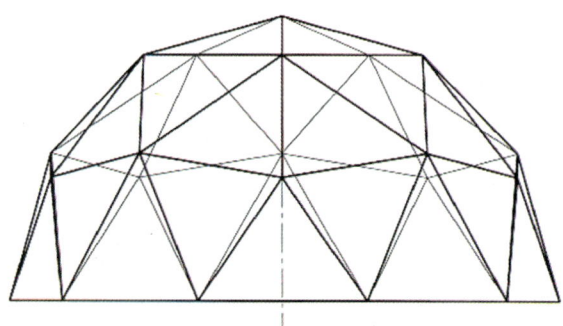

Cupola geodetica di **R.B. Fuller**, basata sull'assemblaggio di elementi triangolari. *A sinistra*: Schema compositivo spaziale.

Esempi di uso grafico del triangolo equilatero: segnaletica stradale e marchi di fabbrica.

Sul triangolo erano incentrati i simboli dei quattro elementi della natura nell'antichità: *fuoco, aria, acqua, terra*.

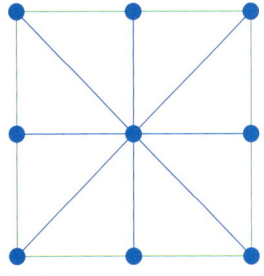

Struttura portante.

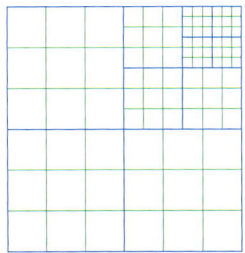

Struttura modulare.

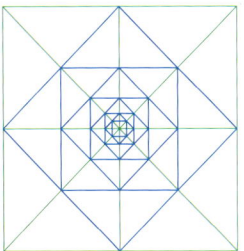

Struttura proiettiva.

IL QUADRATO

Il quadrato è un poligono regolare formato da quattro lati uguali, con quattro angoli retti: comunica un senso solidità, stabilità ed equilibrio.

La sua **struttura portante** è formata dai *lati*, dalle due *diagonali*, dalle due *mediane* e dai *nodi* determinati dai quattro vertici, dai punti medi dei lati e dal *baricentro*. La sua **struttura modulare** si ottiene tracciando linee parallele ai lati ed equidistanti tra loro, fino a formare quadrati sempre più piccoli. La **struttura proiettiva** si ottiene unendo ciascun nodo della struttura portante con un altro, direttamente raggiungibile, senza dover scavalcare altri nodi. Su queste strutture si possono costruire infinite composizioni geometriche.

Il quadrato come forma simbolica

Il quadrato è una delle figure più ricorrenti nel linguaggio dei simboli, assieme al cerchio e alla croce. Ancorato sui quattro lati, è associato all'idea di stasi e consente l'orientamento nello spazio. Ad esso, in società sedentarie, poteva associarsi l'idea del recinto, della casa, del paese: quadrato è, infatti, l'impianto razionale di molte città romane e del *castrum* (accampamento o cittadella fortificata).

Quadrata è la forma di molte città immaginarie, come la Gerusalemme Celeste descritta da San Giovanni nell'*Apocalisse*, in cui è espresso il principio della perfezione raggiunta.

Come simbolo terreno è posto in contrapposizione al cerchio, simbolo celeste: tale è il significato da attribuire ai templi a base quadrata, la cui struttura a gradoni rappresenta la montagna cosmica. In architettura la pianta quadrata è utilizzata per costruzioni religiose e ad uso civile, grazie alle sue potenzialità compositive.

I quadrati di Albers

Il pittore tedesco **Josef Albers** (1888-1976) studiò a fondo gli aspetti compositivi e percettivi delle forme geometriche.

Nella folta serie di opere *Omaggio al quadrato,* realizzate a partire dal 1957 (*a lato*) i quadrati non sono organizzati attorno allo stesso centro, ma leggermente spostati. La composizione pertanto non è statica, ma assume un effetto di tensione dinamica, con compressione verso il basso e dilatazione verso l'alto. Questo effetto, ulteriormente evidenziato dall'accostamento dei colori, risulta sottoposto al controllo di princìpi geometrici che ne garantiscono la stabilità e il bilanciamento dei pesi. Si consideri, ad esempio, la coincidenza degli assi di simmetria verticali.

I quadrati di Mondrian

Nelle opere dell'olandese **Piet Mondrian** (1872-1944), realizzate intorno al 1920 e basate sulla figura dei quadrati, si realizza un perfetto bilanciamento di forze e direzioni. Linee orizzontali e verticali, perpendicolari fra loro, determinano una distribuzione omogenea degli elementi quadrilateri, equilibrati con l'uso di colori puri.

Questo bilanciamento perfetto esprime il superamento dei dati materiali (il peso, la direzione, la tensione, la gravità) per arrivare alla pura astrazione. Per Mondrian l'arte deve appagare lo spirito, che anela alla quiete, e tale condizione *"diviene plasticamente visibile grazie all'armonia dei rapporti"* (di posizione, di proporzione, di colore).

Kazimir Malevič,
Quadrato nero su fondo bianco, 1915.
Per il suprematismo russo, di cui Malevič (1879-1935) è il principale teorizzatore, l'arte deve abbandonare qualsiasi intento mimetico o naturalistico, per far scaturire la sua espressività da *"forme pure"*.

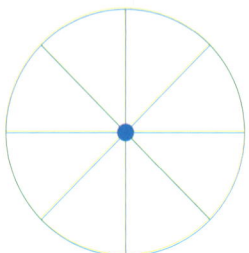

Struttura portante.

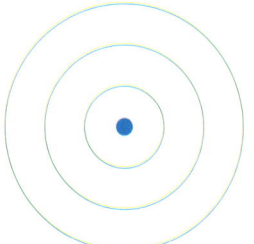

Struttura modulare.

IL CERCHIO

Il cerchio è da sempre considerato figura perfetta, per l'assenza di elementi di discontinuità. La sua linea perimetrale (*circonferenza*) non ha né inizio né fine, e i suoi punti sono tutti equidistanti dal centro. Geometricamente può essere assimilato ad un poligono con un numero infinito di lati.

La sua **struttura portante** è determinata dagli *infiniti raggi* che si diramano dal centro verso la circonferenza, di cui possiamo considerare gli otto che corrispondono alla struttura del quadrato circoscritto. La **struttura modulare** è invece dettata dalla infinita serie di *circonferenze concentriche*, cioè la serie di figure sottomultiple, parallele alla circonferenza di partenza.

La **struttura proiettiva** è suggerita dagli infiniti raggi che partono dalla circonferenza e si dirigono verso il centro, o dalle corde che uniscono punti qualsiasi della circonferenza.

Per le sue caratteristiche il cerchio è associato all'idea di movimento, dando l'idea di ruota, ma anche allo spazio chiuso che delimita l'area di molte città, progettate su pianta radiale.

Particolare della volta del *Battistero* di Parma, sec. XII-XIII.

Il cerchio come simbolo

Simbolo celeste, il cerchio è da sempre legato ai concetti di perfezione, di unità e di spiritualità. Esso non ha un inizio né una fine, né un orientamento definito: per questo, in molte religioni, è rappresentazione simbolica di ciò che è intangibile e assoluto, dunque della divinità. Hanno forma circolare città ideali e leggendarie, quale Atlantide, che il filosofo greco Platone descrisse come un sistema di anelli concentrici di terra e d'acqua.

Se il quadrato implica il concetto di spazio, il cerchio è la figura base del tempo (in particolare la sua evoluzione in spirale). È dunque associato al concetto di eternità, espresso, nel mondo classico, come un serpente che si morde la coda chiudendosi in forma circolare.

La presenza di raggi interni trasforma il cerchio in ruota, conferendogli un effetto di dinamicità che viene riferito al mondo del divenire, della creazione, della continua trasformazione.

Nel repertorio figurativo di tutte le civiltà antiche il cerchio rappresenta la volta celeste, il Sole e la Luna.

Kazimir Malevič, *Il Cerchio nero*, 1913.

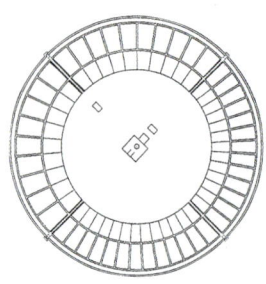

Baghdad, *Schema della città del califfo H-Mansur*, 762 d.C.

IL COLORE

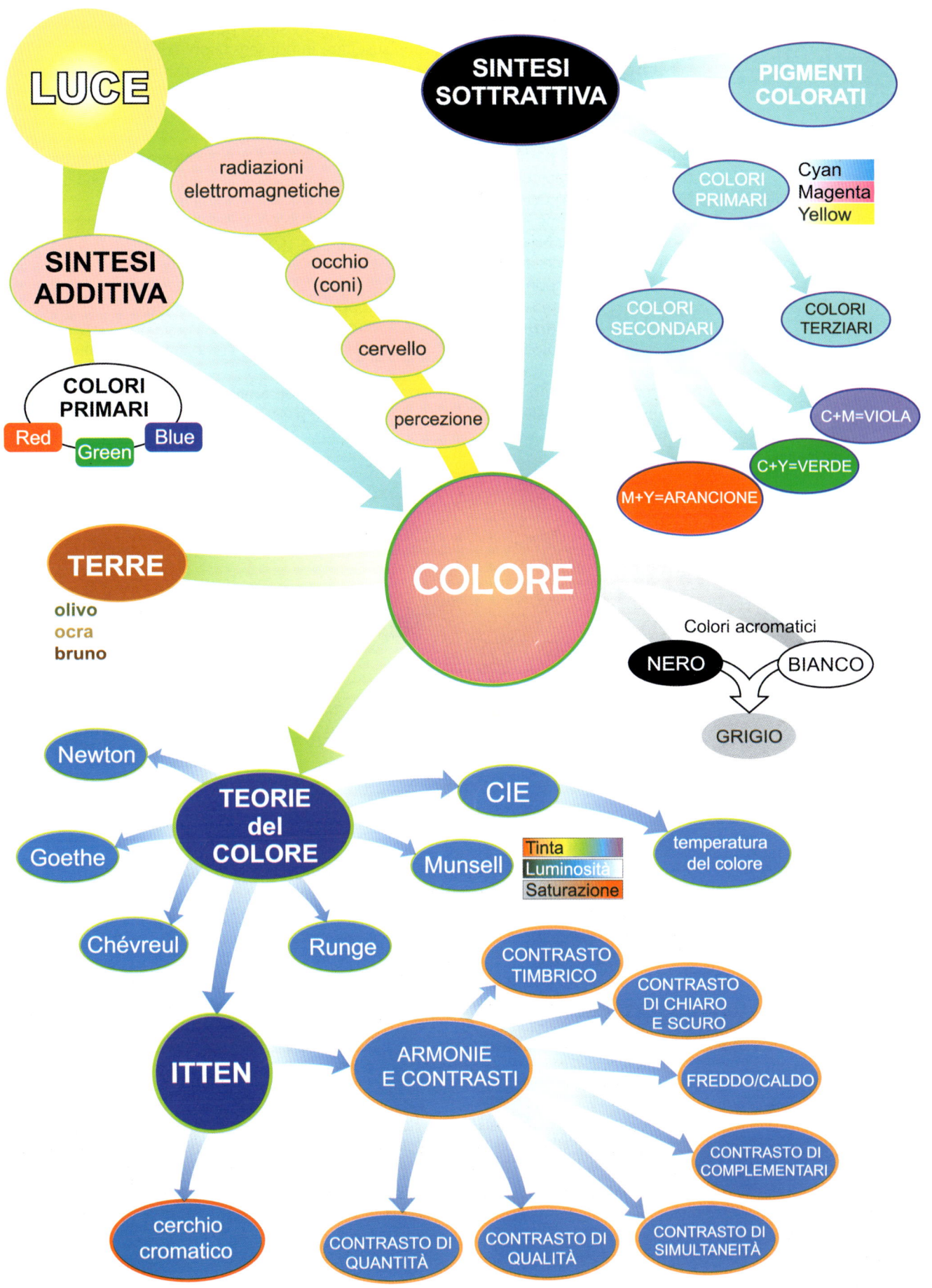

IL COLORE E LE SUE CARATTERISTICHE

La struttura del colore: l'esperimento di Newton

Il colore è un prezioso elemento del linguaggio visuale, poiché anche da solo è in grado di fornire numerose informazioni e suscitare in noi sensazioni ed emozioni.

Normalmente si pensa che l'uso del colore, nell'espressione artistica e nella comunicazione visiva, sia un problema di estro e di gusto personale.

In realtà, la mancata conoscenza delle teorie del colore produce solitamente una tavolozza sporca o caotica, con accostamenti poco equilibrati.

Bisogna quindi partire dalla conoscenza del colore come struttura, analizzandolo anzitutto come fatto percettivo, poiché i colori si propongono alla nostra percezione già strutturati in un modo definito.

Osserviamo come avviene la scomposizione naturale della luce, secondo l'esperimento eseguito da **Isaac Newton** nel 1666.

Un fascio di luce solare passa da una fessura orizzontale fino a incontrare un prisma.

La luce si scompone: una parte prosegue rettilinea e mantiene le sembianze della luce diretta; le altre parti sono raggi di luce sottoposta a *rifrazione* nell'interno del prisma e costituiscono lo *spettro luminoso* che si proietta su uno schermo. Possiamo osservare che la successione dei colori é la seguente: rosso, arancio, giallo, verde, azzurro (o blu), indaco, violetto.

In natura possiamo osservare lo spettro visibile, con lunghezze d'onda separate, nel fenomeno dell'arcobaleno, quando la luce del sole passa attraverso le gocce di pioggia dopo un temporale.

Schema della rifrazione della luce solare, secondo l'esperimento di Newton.

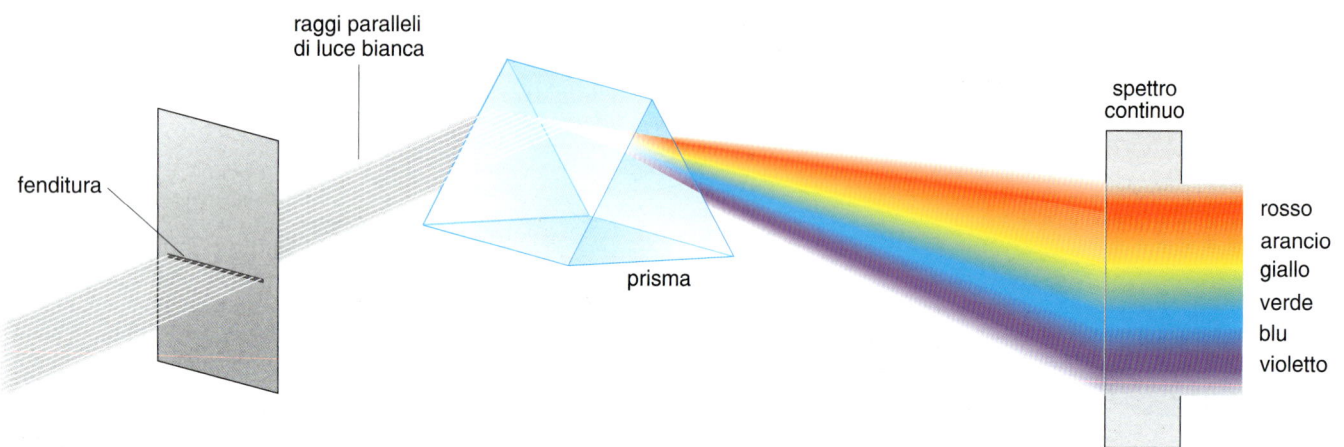

raggi paralleli
di luce bianca

spettro
continuo

fenditura

prisma

rosso
arancio
giallo
verde
blu
violetto

Il colore è luce

Schema delle lunghezze d'onda delle radiazioni elettromagnetiche, con in evidenza lo spettro visibile, la cui lunghezza d'onda va da circa 400 a 750 nanometri (miliardesimi di metro).

Siamo in grado quindi di affermare, senza incertezze, che *il colore è luce*.

La luce è una forma di energia radiante, che propaga onde che colpiscono gli oggetti e si riflettono sulla loro superficie per poi essere catturate dai nostri occhi. L'occhio umano non riesce a percepire tutte le onde di energia radiante, ma solo una piccola parte, chiamata *spettro visibile*.

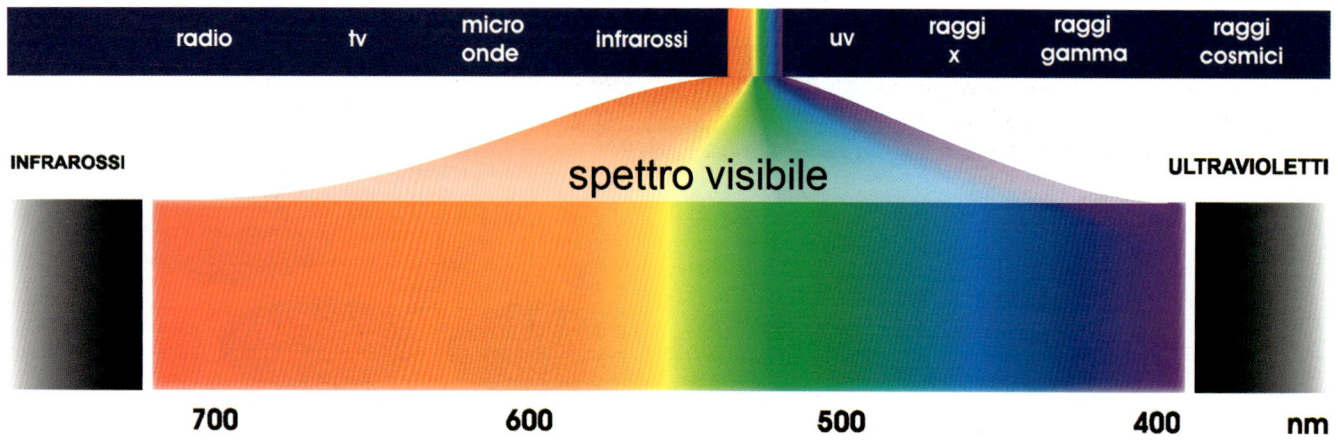

| radio | tv | micro onde | infrarossi | uv | raggi x | raggi gamma | raggi cosmici |

INFRAROSSI

spettro visibile

ULTRAVIOLETTI

700   600   500   400   nm

Perché vediamo i colori

Percepiamo il colore perché la superficie di un oggetto illuminato assorbe alcune radiazioni e ne riflette altre che colpiscono l'occhio.

La retina, all'interno dell'occhio, è formata da una complessa struttura nervosa, e contiene ricettori sensibili alla luce (detti *coni* e *bastoncelli*), che sono responsabili della trasformazione degli impulsi di luce in impulsi nervosi. In particolare, i **coni** sono responsabili della ***percezione del colore***.

La percezione del colore dipende anche da altri fattori fisici (ad esempio dalla capacità visiva di chi guarda, dalle condizioni di illuminazione e dal tipo di superficie riflettente dell'oggetto) e culturali, cioè dalla nostra esperienza nell'osservare i colori.

I colori primari della luce

Newton individuò sette colori, ma osservò che la lunghezza d'onda visibile dell'intero spettro poteva essere suddivisa in tre bande di colore predominanti. Queste bande corrispondevano ai colori **Rosso**, **Verde** e **Blu** (**RGB** = *Red, Green, Blue*), che furono definiti come colori primari della luce.

La ragione per cui vengono chiamati ***primari*** è dovuta al fatto che, attraverso una loro adeguata combinazione, è possibile creare tutti i colori dell'arcobaleno (cioè l'intero spettro visibile), come riuscì a dimostrare, nel 1860, il medico inglese **Thomas Young**.

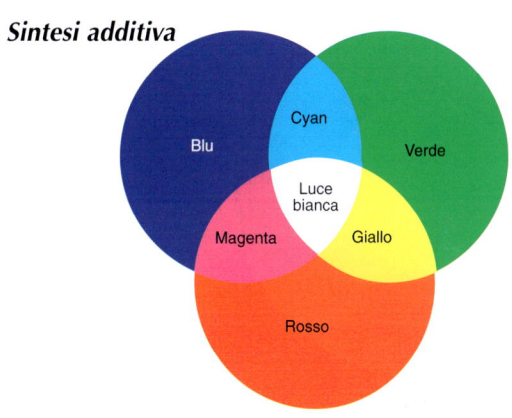

Sintesi additiva

I colori della luce e la sintesi additiva

Osservando con attenzione uno schermo televisivo a colori o il monitor di un computer, ci accorgiamo che la sensazione del colore è generata dall'emissione diretta di radiazioni luminose e dall'accostamento di tre puntini con i colori primari della luce, il Rosso, il Verde e il Blu. Da questi, per ***sintesi additiva***, si formano, attraverso innumerevoli combinazioni, gli altri colori, fino al bianco: l'occhio umano può percepire anche milioni di diverse combinazioni.

I pigmenti colorati e la sintesi sottrattiva

Se invece osserviamo il quadro di **Paul Cézanne** (o una sua riproduzione a stampa), ci rendiamo conto che un colore si forma per "sottrazione", cioè per assorbimento, da parte del pigmento o dell'inchiostro colorato, di una parte della radiazione luminosa: avviene, cioè, una ***sintesi sottrattiva***, per cui la parte di radiazione riflessa, che giunge all'occhio, produce la percezione di quel colore.

Nel caso della sintesi sottrattiva, i colori primari sono il **Blu ciano** (*Cyan*), il **Rosso Magenta** (*Magenta*) e il **Giallo** (*Yellow*), perché sono i soli che, mescolati tra loro, possono generare tutti gli altri colori, fino al **Nero** (*Black*).

Paul Cézanne, *La montagne Sainte-Victoire*, 1885-1887.

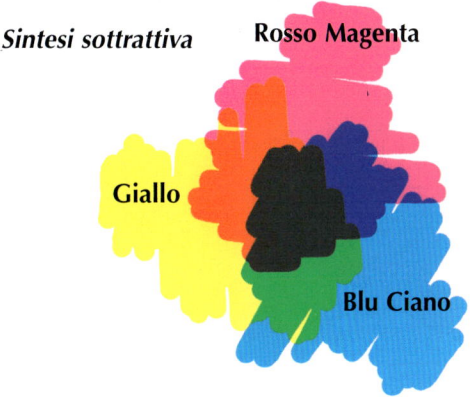

Sintesi sottrattiva

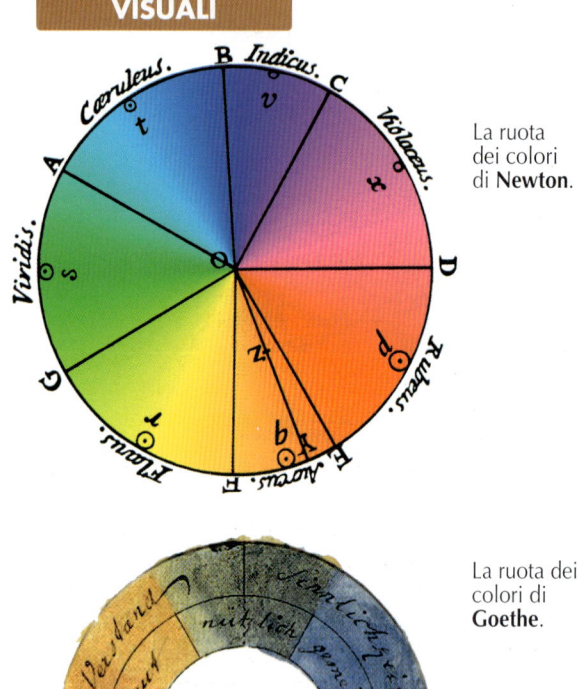

La ruota dei colori di **Newton**.

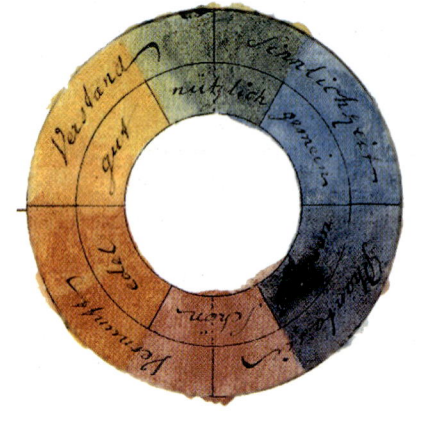

La ruota dei colori di **Goethe**.

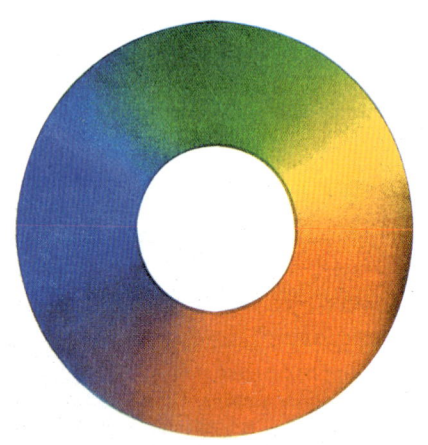

Il cerchio cromatico di **Chevreul**.

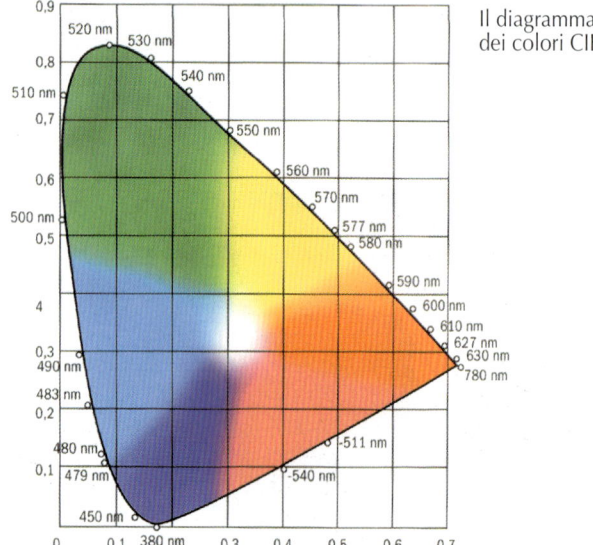

Il diagramma dei colori CIE.

LE TEORIE DEL COLORE

Ruote di luce

Secondo la teoria di **Isaac Newton** (1643-1727) la luce solare bianca è composta non solo dai tre colori primari (Red, Green, Blue) ma contiene anche il giallo, l'arancione e il viola, che egli suddivise in due colori, indaco e violetto, per analogia con la musica, facendo corrispondere, in modo alquanto arbitrario, ad ogni colore una nota musicale.

Nell'arcobaleno, il verde si colloca nitidamente fra il giallo e il ciano e l'arancione tra il giallo e il rosso. Ma il viola (miscela di magenta e ciano) si trova oltre il ciano, all'estremità opposta al magenta: venne così spontanea a Newton l'idea di unire le estremità dello spettro fino a formare un *cerchio*: una ruota di colori. Così il rosso-magenta si raccorda al viola mediante un colore intermedio che non appartiene allo spettro solare. La ruota servirà agli studiosi successivi ad organizzare in modo simmetrico i colori e agli artisti come modello di riferimento teorico.

Johann Wolfgang Goethe (1749-1832), studiò il colore dal punto di vista psicologico e fisiologico, osservando il fenomeno delle ombre colorate e realizzando una ruota dei colori in cui visualizza, ad esempio, le leggi dei colori complementari: nella sua ruota, infatti, la coppie armoniche di colori sono situate una di fronte all'altra.

Una delle ruote di colori più diffuse fu quella del chimico francese **Michel-Eugène Chevreul**, basata non su settori colorati ma su morbide gradazioni da un colore al successivo.

L'equivoco tra *sintesi additiva* (della luce) e *sintesi sottrattiva* (tra pigmenti colorati) fu dissipato solo nel 1855 da **James Clerk Maxwell**, che utilizzò dischi rotanti, con settori dipinti con i tre colori primari additivi, che facevano percepire all'osservatore un colore grigio argenteo acromatico.

Il modello basato sulla ruota dei colori fu sviluppato da numerosi altri studiosi, in particolare da **Johannes Itten**, come vedremo nelle pagine successive.

La versione più recente non si basa su alcuna teoria, ma su di un modello sperimentale, non ha più una forma simmetrica ma è irregolare (sembra quasi una campana o una lingua), però contiene maggiori informazioni: è il diagramma dei colori realizzato dalla CIE (*Commission Internationale de l'Eclairage*, in francese) nel 1931, detto anche **curva cromatica CIE**. Tre luci colorate standard generano lo spazio cromatico di tutti i colori visibili (triangolo cromatico).

Il diagramma di cromaticità è bidimensionale: al centro c'è il bianco e lungo la parte curva del perimetro sono collocati, in senso antiorario, i colori saturi dello spettro luminoso: rosso, giallo, verde, blu, viola. Il diagramma rappresenta quindi le *tinte* (lungo il perimetro) e le *saturazioni* (dal perimetro verso il centro). I colori interni sono infatti generati dalla sintesi additiva dei vari raggi: qualsiasi colore che si trovi lungo un segmento che unisce due punti del bordo può essere ottenuto mescolando quei colori dello spettro. Quando il segmento attraversa la zona bianca al centro significa che con i due colori periferici si può ottenere il bianco.

Ogni colore del diagramma può inoltre avere una diversa *luminosità* (per esempio un certo verde esiste anche in una versione più scura) e quindi al diagramma va aggiunta una terza dimensione.

La terza dimensione del colore

La sfera dei colori di **Runge**.

Dalle ruote di colore e dallo stesso diagramma CIE restano inevitabilmente esclusi vari colori, come il marrone, il rosa ecc. perché questi vengono generati da variazioni di luminosità: ciò dimostra che l'universo dei colori è di fatto tridimensionale.

Il primo parametro del colore, rappresentato dal diagramma CIE, è la **tinta** (*hue*, in inglese), cioè il colore vero e proprio, determinato dalla lunghezza d'onda dominante che lo identifica.

Il secondo parametro, pure rappresentato nel diagramma CIE, è la cosiddetta **saturazione** (*saturation*, in inglese), che va definita anche con la pienezza o intensità, e si riferisce al grado in cui il colore puro è mescolato ad altri che ne riducono la purezza: ad esempio, il rosso, con un po' di bianco perde in saturazione e diventa rosa e, se un colore ha saturazione pari a zero diventa grigiastro.

Il terzo parametro del colore, non presente nel diagramma CIE, è la **luminosità** (o **chiarezza** o **tono**, *brightness* in inglese), che dipende dalla quantità di luce riflessa dall'oggetto e può considerarsi come il grado di chiaro o di scuro di un colore.

Dalle ruote bidimensionali, già all'inizio del XIX secolo, si era passati a modelli tridimensionali, come la sfera cromatica del tedesco **Philipp Otto Runge**, che colloca i colori puri primari e secondari all'equatore: verso un polo i colori diventano sempre più chiari, verso l'altro più scuri. Il polo superiore risulta completamente bianco e quello inferiore nero.

Ma dove si colloca il grigio? Come è possibile visualizzare ciò che accade all'interno della sfera, se consideriamo solo la sua superficie?

A partire dal 1905, con successive modificazioni, l'insegnante e pittore americano **Albert Munsell** riuscì a proporre un modello, a forma di albero, che rispondeva a queste esigenze, come un diagramma CIE portato a tre dimensioni.

Schema grafico dell'albero di **Munsell**.

A partire dalla circonferenza centrale e **verso l'alto**, i colori vengono progressivamente **mescolati al bianco**, guadagnando luminosità.

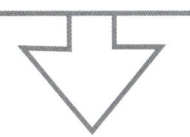

A partire dalla circonferenza centrale e **verso il basso**, i colori vengono progressivamente **mescolati al nero**, perdendo di luminosità.

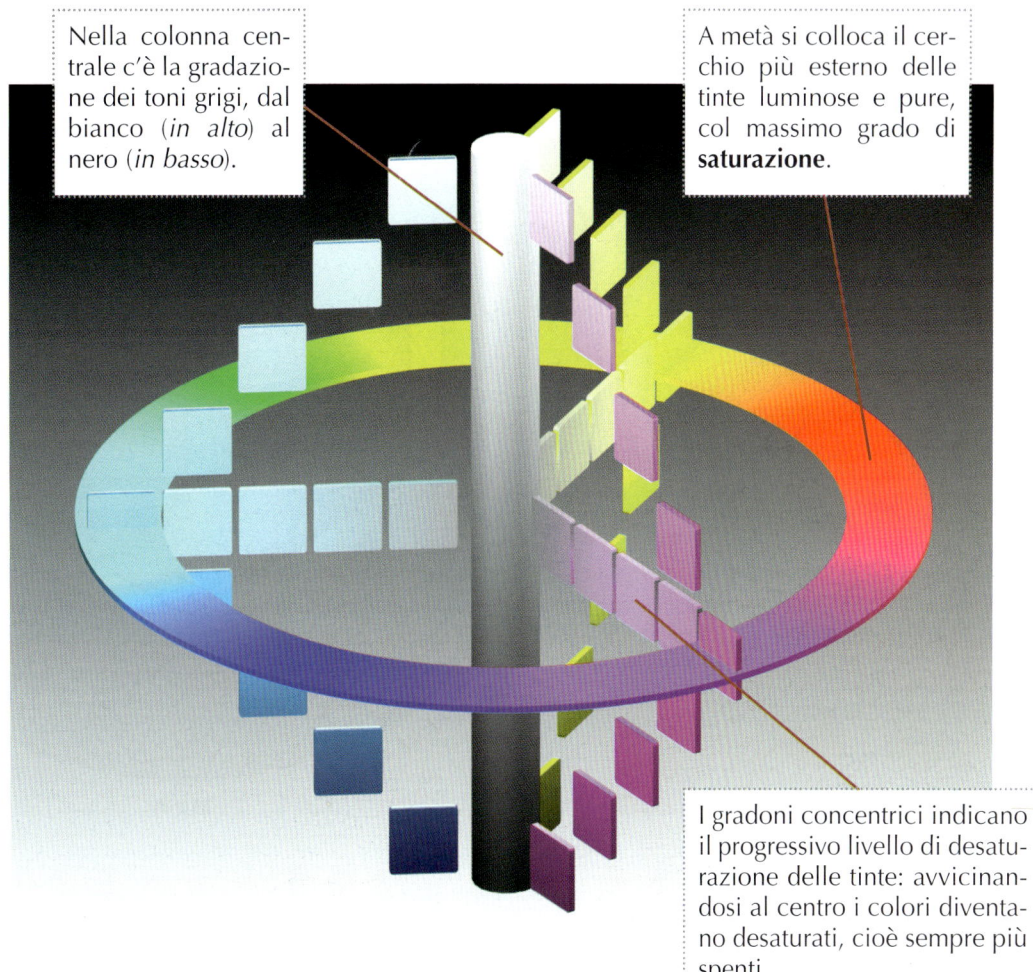

Nella colonna centrale c'è la gradazione dei toni grigi, dal bianco (*in alto*) al nero (*in basso*).

A metà si colloca il cerchio più esterno delle tinte luminose e pure, col massimo grado di **saturazione**.

I gradoni concentrici indicano il progressivo livello di desaturazione delle tinte: avvicinandosi al centro i colori diventano desaturati, cioè sempre più spenti.

Johannes Itten.

L'ARTE DEL COLORE, DI JOHANNES ITTEN

Johannes Itten insegnò teoria del colore alla Bauhaus di Weimar tra il 1919 e il 1923 e qui sviluppò le sue indagini che furono poi riassunte e pubblicate, nel 1961, nel testo *L'arte del colore* che ancora oggi è di riferimento, per quanto per certi aspetti superato.

Il suo cerchio cromatico, ad esempio, ci aiuta a classificare i colori, perché evidenzia la progressione dai primari verso i secondari e i terziari, e le reciproche relazioni.

Il triangolo equilatero posto al centro (*vedi disegno in basso*) contiene i tre **colori primari**: **giallo cadmio**, **rosso magenta** e **blu cyan** (o **ciano**).

La mescolanza dei primari a due a due, in parti uguali, determina i **colori secondari**: l'**arancione** è ottenuto mescolando *rosso e giallo*, il **verde** mescolando *giallo e blu*, il **viola** mescolando *blu e rosso* e sono collocati nei triangoli corrispondenti, fino a formare un esagono.

Componendo poi in misure uguali un primario con un suo secondario, si ottengono 6 colori intermedi, detti **terziari**.

Nello schema di Itten, il cerchio esterno è quindi composto dai tre primari, i tre secondari e i sei terziari. In esso i colori si susseguono secondo l'ordine dell'arcobaleno e dello spettro visivo e si dispongono simmetricamente le sequenze dei **colori caldi** (generati dal rosso) e dei **colori freddi** (generati dal blu cyan).

Inoltre, costituiscono una coppia di **colori complementari** due colori collocati in posizione diametralmente opposta (es. giallo-viola): accostati tra loro generano il massimo contrasto cromatico.

Infine, disponendo in linea retta i colori del cerchio di Itten, otteniamo una sequenza che rispetta abbastanza fedelmente quella dello spettro solare (*presentato a pag. 86*).

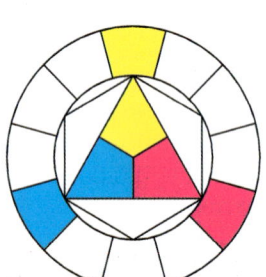

Colori primari

Colori secondari

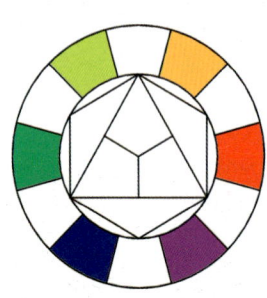

Colori terziari

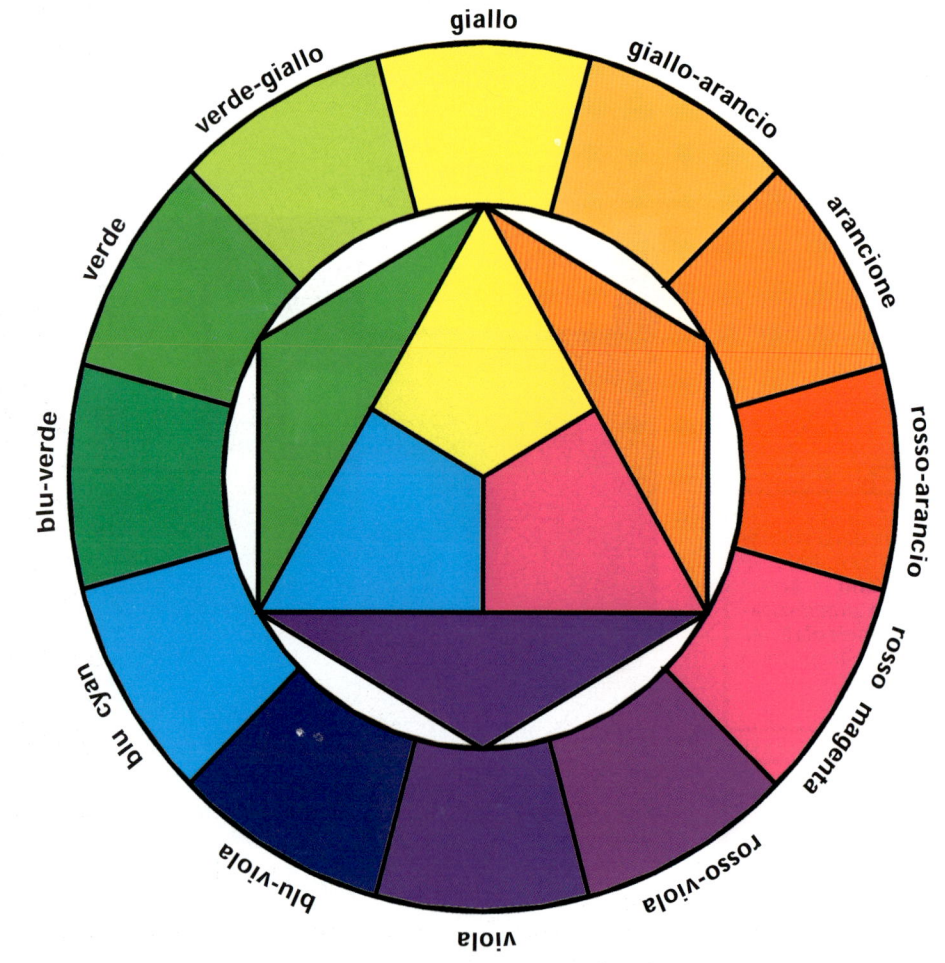

COLORI FREDDI   **COLORI CALDI**

COLORE E NON COLORE

Il bianco, il nero e il grigio

Il **bianco** e il **nero** sono detti *colori acromatici*, cioè privi di colore. Essi non sono presenti nel cerchio cromatico di Itten e non possono essere ottenuti attraverso la mescolanza di altri pigmenti.

Nella sintesi additiva (*vedi pag. 87*), il bianco è dato dalla somma di tutti i colori che formano lo spettro della luce (che, appunto, ci appare bianca); il nero corrisponde alla mancanza di colori: nessun oggetto, in assenza di luce, è colorato.

Bianco e nero svolgono, comunque, un ruolo importante nella comunicazione visiva, in relazione tra loro e con tutti gli altri colori. Il loro accostamento produce il massimo contrasto tonale; essi si rafforzano reciprocamente, raggiungendo un notevole livello percettivo.

Uniti ad altri colori, in percentuali diverse, determinano mescolanze monocromatiche, variandone anche la tonalità, indebolendoli. Così il rosa, ottenuto da rosso e bianco, è più chiaro del rosso stesso, e l'azzurro è più chiaro del blu oltremare, ma, rispetto a questi, presentano una forza cromatica minore.

Il nero invece diminuisce la luminosità dei colori, rendendoli più scuri e spenti. I *colori neutri* corrispondono alla gamma di **grigi** ottenuti attraverso la mescolanza di bianco e nero, in proporzioni diverse. Gradazioni monocrome di grigi offrono un elevato grado di leggibilità: possono essere usate per rendere effetti di volume e di profondità.

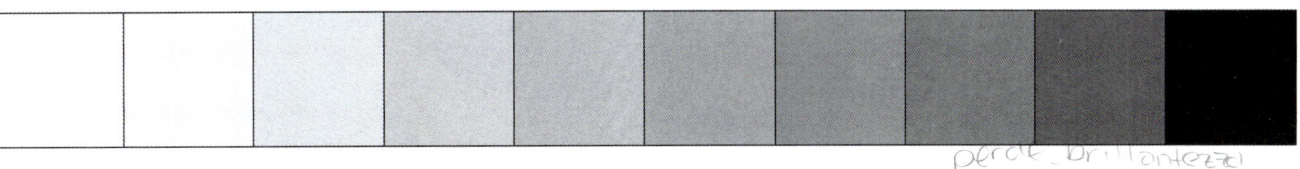

I grigi colorati

Mescolando due complementari e variandone gradualmente le relative quantità, si producono colori opachi, perché impoveriti dei colori originari: sono i *grigi colorati*.

Ad esempio, aggiungendo verde al magenta e magenta al verde, si passa ad una varietà di rossi-grigiastri sempre più neutri e opachi, fino a giungere al quasi nero, quando le quantità dei due colori sono eguali.

Con buona approssimazione, se mescoliamo i colori complementari con equilibrio e gusto, possiamo disporre di un ampio repertorio di grigi colorati da utilizzare a fini espressivi, soprattutto per le ombre.

Le terre

Le terre sono colori derivati da sostanze minerali naturali. È possibile ricavarli anche **mescolando tra loro i tre secondari**.

Si ottengono, così, tre terre fondamentali, dette *primari terrosi*:
- mescolando *viola e arancio*, si ottiene il **rosso cupo** o **bruno**;
- mescolando *arancio e verde*, avremo il **giallo ocra**, o citrino;
- mescolando *verde e viola* otteniamo il **verde oliva**.

Questi colori sono caldi, a differenza dei grigi colorati, ottenuti mescolando due complementari.

bruno

ocra

oliva

Composizioni con colori primari, secondari, terziari

Dopo aver osservato le immagini di questa pagina, esegui alcune composizioni, su base geometrica, utilizzando accostamenti di colori primari, primari e secondari, primari, secondari e terziari, colori caldi e freddi, grigio e terre. Puoi usare pastelli, tempere o acquerelli.

Composizione con colori primari e secondari.

Composizione con colori primari e secondari.

Alighiero Boetti, composizione con colori caldi e freddi.

Composizione con colori primari, secondari e terziari.

Il contrasto di colori puri è accentuato quando l'irradiazione reciproca è bloccata dal rafforzamento dei margini con linee nere di separazione.

ARMONIE E CONTRASTI DI COLORE SECONDO ITTEN

Accostamenti di colori

Proseguendo secondo l'insegnamento di Johannes Itten, verifichiamo come l'accostamento dei colori determina nell'osservatore diversi effetti percettivi ed emotivi: colori affini tra loro possono generare effetti di pacatezza e armonia; abbiamo esaltazione cromatica se i colori sono invece contrastanti tra loro.

Nel primo caso, i colori possono essere affini per chiarezza, luminosità o tonalità; sono invece contrastanti quando i valori cromatici sono molto differenti o addirittura opposti.

Itten ha individuato **sette tipi di contrasto**, che gli artisti usano, più o meno consapevolmente, per determinare differenti effetti percettivi ed espressivi:

1. contrasto di colori puri;
2. contrasto di chiaro e scuro;
3. contrasto di freddo e caldo;
4. contrasto dei complementari;
5. contrasto di simultaneità;
6. contrasto di qualità;
7. contrasto di quantità.

1. Contrasto timbrico di colori puri

Questo effetto di contrasto è determinato dall'accostamento di tre o più colori saturi. L'effetto di maggiore vivacità si ottiene con l'accostamento dei tre colori primari, che sono nettamente distinti e irradiano reciprocamente la propria luminosità, attenuando il contrasto.

In generale, il contrasto è accentuato quando l'irradiazione reciproca è bloccata, ad esempio dal rafforzamento dei margini con linee nere di separazione o dall'emergere di campi cromatici da un fondo scuro. L'effetto allora sarà chiassoso, energico e deciso. L'accostamento di colori secondari o loro derivati determina invece effetti di contrasto progressivamente più attenuati.

Il contrasto dei colori puri è frequente nell'arte popolare, in particolare quella sud-americana, ma troviamo contrasti di colori puri nelle decorazioni medievali, e nell'arte delle vetrate, in particolare quelle gotiche. L'arte moderna ha proposto squisiti contrasti di colori puri con **Matisse**, e con l'Espressionismo tedesco del *Blaue Reiter*, in particolare con **Kandinskij**, **Marc**, **Macke**.

I pittori di *De Stjil*, e sopra tutti **Mondrian**, hanno creato tutte le loro opere sulla base di questo contrasto, ottenuto per lo più tramite i tre colori primari.

Sopra a destra: **Franz Marc**, *Cavallo blu*, 1911.

A lato: **Mondrian**, *Grande Composizione A con nero, rosso, giallo e blu*, 1920. Olio su tela 91,5x92. Roma, Galleria d'Arte Moderna.

Rembrandt, *Gesù guarisce i malati*, detta *La Stampa dei Cento Fiorini*, 1648 circa.

Caravaggio, *Incredulità di San Tommaso*, 1600-1601. Olio su tela, 107x146 cm. Potsdam-Sanssouci, Stiftung Schlösser und Gärten.

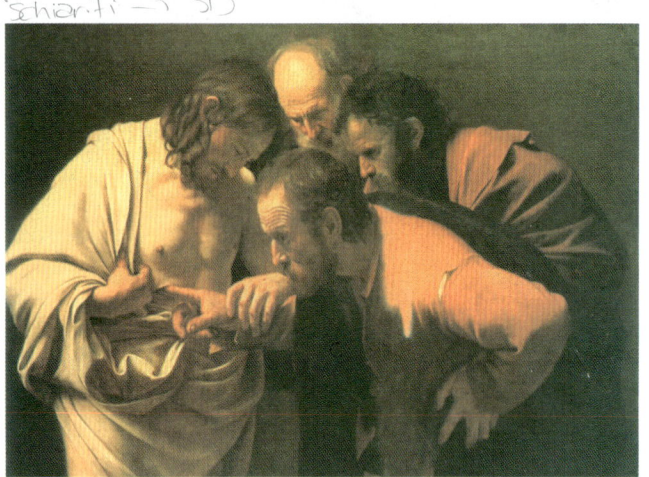

2. Contrasto di chiaro e di scuro

Il bianco, il nero, il grigio

I valori di chiaro e di scuro si trovano nelle direzioni opposte della scala tonale, realizzata mescolando un colore con quantità crescenti di bianco o di nero.

Infatti, si ha un evidente contrasto di chiaro e scuro con la gamma dei grigi nella direzione verticale dell'albero di Munsell, che va dal bianco al nero (*vedi pag. 89*). Possiamo osservare questo contrasto nei disegni a matita e nelle stampe monocromatiche, basate sul chiaroscuro.

Anche il cinematografo, prima dell'avvento del colore, e la fotografia in bianco e nero trovano nel contrasto di chiaro e scuro e nelle dimensioni spaziali del bianco e del nero, una forte espressività luminosa.

Accordi chiaroscurali di colori diversi

Al di là del bianco e del nero, seppur con minor evidenza, ogni colore presenta innumerevoli gradazioni determinate dal diverso grado di oscurità o di chiarezza. Si parla infatti di *pittura tonale* quando l'artista usa un colore prevalente, giocando opportunamente sui suoi toni chiari e scuri.

Lo studio del cosiddetto chiaroscuro costituisce poi un momento importante, perché su di esso si basano moltissime opere della storia dell'arte e della comunicazione visiva, basti pensare alle acqueforti di Rembrandt, al gioco di luci e oscurità di Caravaggio fino ai disegni di Seurat.

3. Contrasto di freddo e caldo

Operiamo sul cerchio cromatico, tracciando un asse verticale che va dal giallo al viola, e l'asse orizzontale che va dal rosso-arancio al blu-verde. Questi due assi determinano due polarità: l'asse verticale, la polarità del chiaro-scuro; l'asse orizzontale quella del freddo-caldo.

Si considerano **colori caldi**, per associazione con la luce del Sole e con il fuoco, il rosso vermiglione o cinabro, i gialli, i bruni e l'arancione.

I **colori freddi**, così detti perché associati alla luce lunare e all'acqua, sono il verde-azzurro, il viola tenue e le tonalità dei blu.

Il colore più caldo è il rosso-arancio, chiamato rosso saturno, e il colore più freddo è il blu-verde, o ossido di manganese.

Rosso-arancio e blu-verde insieme neutralizzano l'effetto calorico reciproco, e potenziano l'effetto luminoso, essendo esattamente complementari. Se però il rosso-arancio prevale per quantità sul blu-verde, l'effetto luminoso ha un'accentuazione calda; viceversa, se prevale il blu-verde, l'effetto luminoso ha un'accentuazione fredda.

Uno stesso colore, poi, può assumere diverse qualità a seconda della sua composizione: il grigio appare freddo quando è composto da bianco e nero, caldo quando è composto da rosso, giallo, blu e bianco, o da quest'ultimo mescolato con una coppia di complementari.

Il verde può apparire più caldo o più freddo in base alla quantità di giallo o di blu che contiene, ed alla sua vicinanza ad altri colori, rispettivamente freddi o caldi.

Molti artisti hanno improntato le loro opere su tonalità, accostamenti e contrasti tra colori caldi e colori freddi.

4. Contrasto di colori complementari

Le coppie di colori complementari, la cui somma dà il grigio, sono costituite da un secondario e dal primario estraneo alla sua formazione: giallo e viola, rosso e verde, blu ciano e arancione.

Il viola, colore secondario, non è un derivato del giallo. Analogamente, il verde non è derivato del rosso, e l'arancio non può essere ottenuto da mescolanze con il blu.

Questi colori sono fra loro complementari, od opposti, anche per la posizione diametralmente opposta che occupano nel cerchio cromatico.

L'accostamento di due colori complementari determina un forte effetto di contrasto, che ne accentua l'intensità.

Henri Matisse, *I pesci rossi*, 1912. Esemplare applicazione del contrasto di colori complementari (rosso-verde).

Claude Monet, *Il Parlamento di Londra*, 1904. L'uso del contrasto caldo e freddo crea le figure e dà espressività all'immagine.

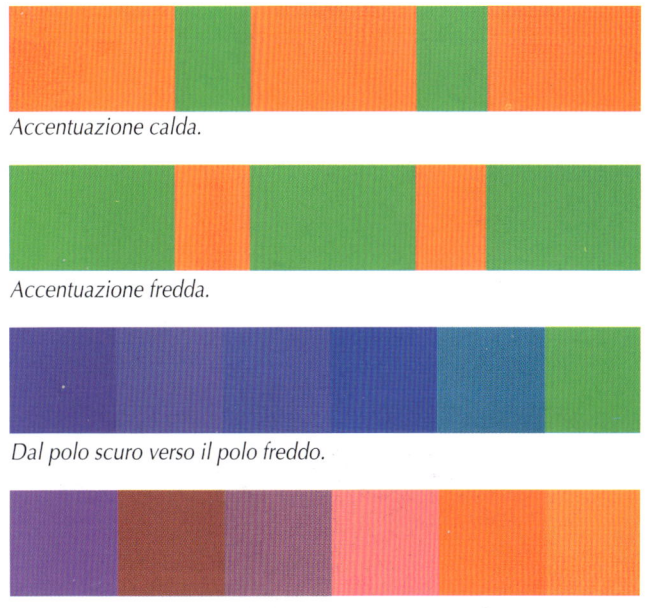

Accentuazione calda.

Accentuazione fredda.

Dal polo scuro verso il polo freddo.

Dal polo scuro verso il polo caldo.

5. Contrasto di simultaneità

Nel 1839 il chimico francese **Michel Eugène Chevreul** scoprì il fenomeno che definì del "*contrasto simultaneo*" dei colori. Secondo questo principio, l'intensità luminosa e il tono dei colori sono percepiti in maniera diversa in relazione al campo cromatico in cui sono inseriti.

È la logica conseguenza del contrasto dei complementari, che si crea non per presenza ma per assenza del complementare.

Il nostro occhio, sottoposto ad un dato colore, esige simultaneamente la presenza del suo complementare, e non ricevendolo se lo rappresenta da sé: in ultima analisi, ogni colore produce simultaneamente il proprio complementare, per una legge analoga a quella statica dell'azione e reazione, al fine di ottenere l'equilibrio, cioè una condizione di armonia cromatica.

Ciò determina anche uno stato di tensione ai margini delle figure, che vengono esaltati in caso di colori molto diversi fra loro.

Se osserviamo attentamente un colore puro, dopo qualche istante nelle zone circostanti si percepisce il suo complementare.

Effetti di contrasto sono dovuti anche al confronto tra aree cromatiche dal diverso grado di luminosità, che si valorizzano, quindi, a vicenda.

Un esperimento molto significativo in questo senso è quello di tingere sei quadrati uguali con un colore: giallo, arancio, rosso, verde, blu, viola, lasciando al centro di ciascuno un quadratino che tingeremo di grigio. Se osserviamo ogni quadratino grigio intensamente, dopo un'osservazione lunga, ravvicinata, effettuata con luce obliqua e socchiudendo gli occhi, vedremo che il quadratino grigio osservato assume il riflesso del colore complementare al colore del fondo circostante.

6. Contrasto di qualità o di luminosità

Si determina un contrasto di qualità mediante l'accostamento di colori con diverso grado di luminosità. In base a questo parametro i colori possono essere saturi o desaturati, cioè offuscati, opachi, spenti.

La mescolanza di un colore con altre tinte può determinare innumerevoli variazioni di saturazione. Anche la mescolanza di un colore saturo con bianco, nero o grigio permette di schiarire o di scurire il colore di partenza, pur implicando sempre una perdita di purezza e luminosità.

L'accostamento di un colore ad alto grado di saturazione con un altro molto opaco produce una accentuazione del contrasto di qualità, esaltando le caratteristiche luminose del primo.

Henri Matisse, *La lezione di piano,* 1917. Esempio di applicazione del contrasto di qualità.

Il significato simbolico del colore varia in contesti culturali differenti, e muta col tempo anche all'interno di una stessa società o civiltà: per noi occidentali, ad esempio, il nero è il colore del lutto, mentre in Giappone è il bianco, esattamente il contrario.

Quando il colore esprime un messaggio

Tutti noi, anche senza rendercene conto, comunichiamo un messaggio e, nello stesso tempo, esprimiamo i nostri sentimenti servendoci del colore degli oggetti: un mazzo di rose rosse, il fiocco azzurro per la nascita di un bambino, il nero e il viola per il lutto o la maglia azzurra per la nostra squadra nazionale.

Nella vita quotidiana il colore ha una grande importanza perché serve a comunicare diversi messaggi e situazioni, utilizzando norme e codici che sono ormai di uso internazionale. Ciò si verifica, ad esempio, nel campo dell'urbanistica, nella segnaletica stradale, negli impianti tecnologici, nelle indicazioni per la sicurezza ecc.

La psicologia del colore

È stato ormai verificato scientificamente che i vari colori suscitano negli esseri viventi sensazioni ed emozioni anche molto forti.

Passare le ore del giorno in ambienti colorati, anziché bianchi o grigiastri, genera sovente uno stato d'animo più ottimista.

A loro volta, i colori esprimono sovente la personalità di chi li sceglie, quando li usa nell'abito che indossa o nella tinteggiatura della casa in cui abita.

Anche Kandinskij (*vedi pag. 64*), attribuiva ai vari colori la capacità di suscitare sentimenti: ad esempio, l'azzurro dà sensazione di spiritualità, calma e tranquillità; il rosso evoca la forza e la passione, suscitando agitazione.

Osserva come si vestono gli uomini d'affari, i militari, i ragazzi che vanno in discoteca o al pub, gli sportivi e gli uomini politici: non trovi che la varietà di colori possa indicare, sostanzialmente, anche la loro personalità?

Le reazioni psicologiche al colore

Nella tabella *sotto* sono schematicamente riassunte le sensazioni che, secondo le più recenti teorie psicologiche, sono determinate dai vari colori.

C'è una comprensibile ed evidente diversità di reazione tra i colori caldi e i colori freddi.

Il nero e il bianco costituiscono un caso specifico e complesso in quanto la loro valenza dipende fortemente dal contesto in cui sono utilizzati.

COLORI FREDDI	ISPIRANO UN SENSO DI...
VERDE	pace, serenità, tranquillità, riposo, quiete, freschezza, autostima
BLU	calma, tenerezza, armonia, malinconia, serenità, soddisfazione, quiete
VIOLA	stabilità, dignità, tristezza, misticismo

COLORI CALDI	ISPIRANO UN SENSO DI...
ROSSO	energia, eccitazione, calore, passione, azione, gioia, sicurezza
ARANCIONE	gioia, vivacità, esuberanza, espansione
GIALLO	gioia, vitalità, ispirazione, calore, libertà, autonomia

COLORI ACROMATICI	ISPIRANO UN SENSO DI...
NERO	tristezza, potere, ostilità, forza
BIANCO	freddezza, purezza, pulizia, giovinezza

LEGGERE IL COLORE

Ogni artista utilizza una certa varietà di colori, accostandoli e mescolandoli opportunamente, in relazione a quanto vuole esprimere.

Osserviamo con attenzione le opere rappresentate in queste pagine, scelte per la loro particolare valenza cromatica, ma anche altre riprodotte in diverse sezioni del testo.

Proviamo ad analizzarle proprio dal punto di vista dell'uso del colore: alcune sono ricchissime di varietà cromatiche; in altre i colori sono pochi o addirittura tendono al monocromo.

In alcune i colori vibrano di luce; in altre le tinte sono più spente, cupe, quasi tenebrose.

In alcune il colore sottolinea le forme e fa risaltare i personaggi; in altre viene steso in modo apparentemente casuale e vediamo solo macchie colorate.

In alcune l'equilibrio dei colori esprime armonia, serenità; in altre l'accostamento dei colori è disarmonico, crea disagio.

In alcune il colore è steso con la massima cura e precisione; in altre il gesto violento dell'artista si esprime mediante grumi di colore spremuto dal tubetto o fatto colare sulla tela...

Ma che cosa ne dicono i pittori?

William Turner, *Esequie in mare*, 1842.

"Egli cominciò versando tinta fresca sulla carta fino che fu saturata, la strappò, la graffiò, la raspò, con gran frenesia, e tutto fu caos, ma lentamente, come per magia, la bella nave con tutti gli squisiti dettagli venne alla luce [...]" Ruskin, a proposito di William Turner.

Eugène Delacroix, *Cavalli uscenti dal mare*, 1860.

"Sarebbe una buona cosa stabilire, incominciando, la scala dei valori di un quadro con un oggetto chiaro, il cui tono fosse preso esattamente dal vero: un fazzoletto, una stoffa, ecc." Eugène Delacroix.

Paul Cézanne, *Ragazzo con il gilet rosso*, 1893-95.

"Il disegno e il colore non sono distinti. Il disegno esiste nella misura in cui il colore è realmente dipinto. Più i colori armonizzano l'uno con l'altro e più il disegno è definito." Paul Cézanne.

Piet Mondrian, *Composizione in giallo, rosso e blu*, 1929.

"Nei suoi dipinti più tardi Mondrian si limitò a colori elementari, giallo, rosso, blu, bianco e nero. Ciascuno di questi colori ha un carattere ben preciso e un peso particolare, la loro posizione nel quadro, e così il loro orizzontalismo o verticalismo hanno un peso determinante [...]" Johannes Itten a proposito di Piet Mondrian.

Henri Matisse, *Donna con cappello*, 1905.

"In pittura, i colori hanno il loro potere e la loro eloquenza solo se usati allo stato puro, quando lo smalto e la purezza non ne sono alterati o attenuati da mescolanze: il blu e il giallo che formano un verde devono essere accostati e non mescolati." Henri Matisse.

Vincent van Gogh, *Interno di caffè di notte*, 1888.

"Ho tentato di esprimere le terribili passioni dell'umanità mediante il rosso e il verde. La stanza è di colore rosso sangue e arancione, con al centro un biliardo verde; ci sono poi quattro lampade di color giallo-limone che irraggiano una luminosità arancio e verde. In ogni direzione c'è contrasto tra i rossi e i verdi più estremi [...]" Vincent van Gogh

Il colore nella comunicazione visiva e nel design

Pubblicità e colore

Quasi tutti i messaggi visivi traggono forza ed efficacia, in buona parte, dall'uso del colore.

Nella pubblicità, ad esempio, il colore attira l'attenzione del consumatore per valorizzare il prodotto: come resistere e non afferrare una di quelle belle scatole colorate allineate ordinatamente sugli scaffali di un supermercato?

L'immagine pubblicitaria, ancor più di quella pittorica, deve richiamare l'attenzione sul messaggio che vuol comunicare mediante un preciso codice linguistico e simbolico, in cui il colore ha grande importanza, proprio per le sue implicazioni psicologiche.

Il colore nel design

Anche negli oggetti di produzione industriale il colore rappresenta un elemento di grande importanza.

Dalla tendenza originaria ad unificare i prodotti industriali, mimetizzandoli quasi con colori spenti e neutri, oggi siamo passati a prodotti dalla superficie levigata e coloratissima, che allietano la casa e sono immediatamente riconoscibili.

Pensiamo, ad esempio, al *personal computer*, un tempo grigia scatola anonima ed ora elegante contenitore dai colori più vari.

Nel caso di elementi d'arredo o di macchine utensili, la scelta e l'accostamento di colori è da studiare con grande cura.

Ettore Sottsass, mobile *Carlton*, 1981. Produzione Memphis. Mobili con forme originali, colori e texture vivaci entrano nelle nostre case, rallegrando gli ambienti.

AUTOVERIFICHE DI CONOSCENZA E DI ABILITÀ

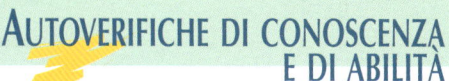

Lettura e analisi del colore

Osserva l'opera di **Lorenzo Lotto**, *Nozze mistiche di Santa Caterina*, conservata presso l'Accademia Carrara di Bergamo: vi possiamo trovare, riassunti, alcuni dei principi fondamentali che regolano la comprensione e l'uso del colore nell'arte e, più in generale, nella comunicazione visiva. Scegli un'immagine a tuo piacimento, posizionala al centro di un foglio da disegno ed esegui un esercizio analogo.

Blu ciano, ***rosso magenta*** e ***giallo*** sono i ***colori primari*** da cui derivano tutti gli altri.

Rosso e arancione, accostati, sembrano meno intensi, perché sono simili tra loro.

Blu e arancione, accostati, si esaltano a vicenda perchè sono ***colori*** tra loro ***complementari***.

Verde, arancione e viola sono i ***colori secondari***.

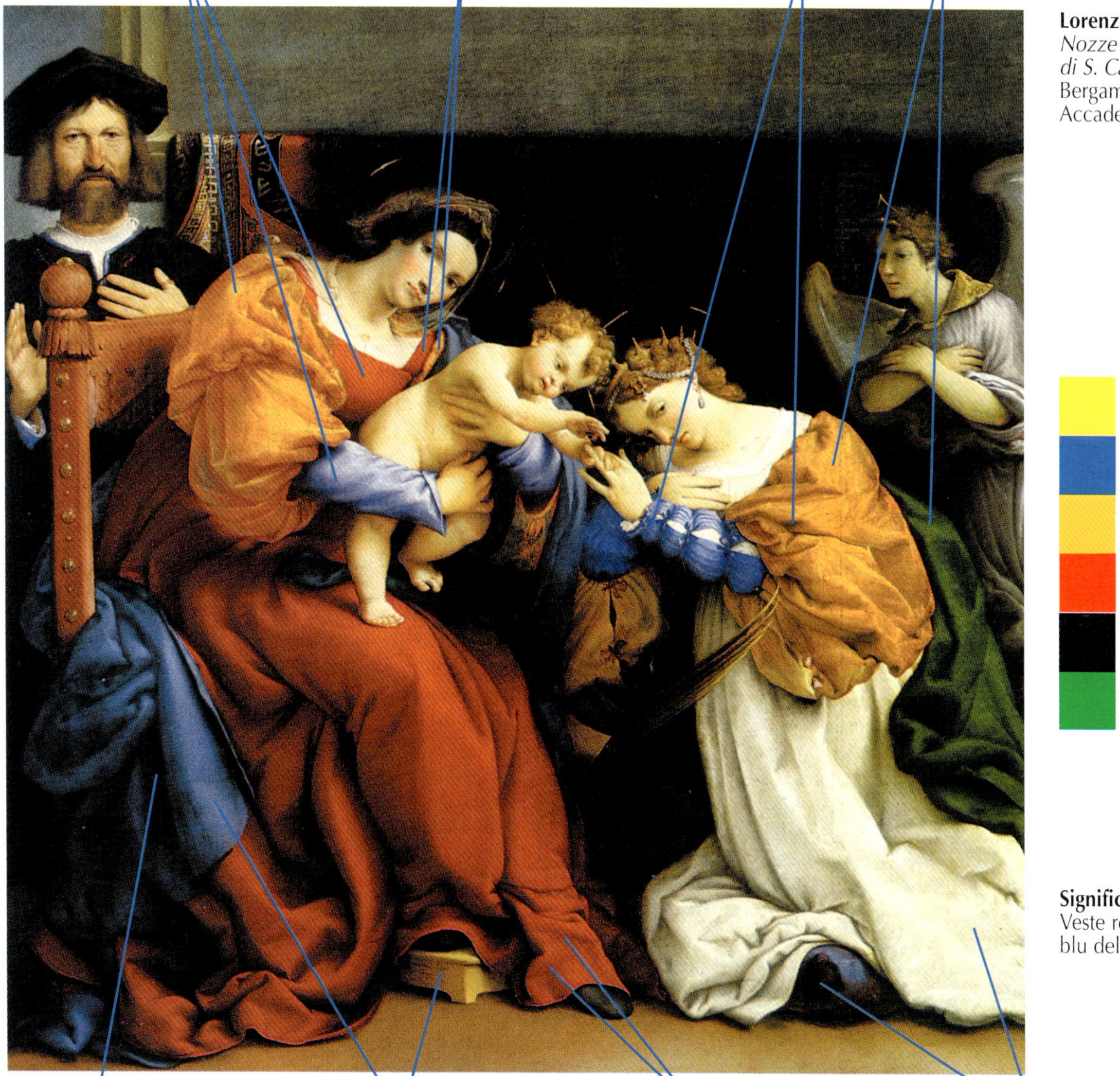

Lorenzo Lotto, *Nozze mistiche di S. Caterina*. Bergamo, Accademia Carrara.

Palette dei colori usati nell'opera.

Significato simbolico: Veste rossa e manto blu della Madonna...

Nell'abito e nel mantello si osservano variazioni di colore (rosso e blu): sono ***variazioni tonali***.

I colori vicini al rosso, al giallo e all'arancione sono detti ***colori caldi***; quelli vicini al verde e al blu sono ***colori freddi***.

I ***colori*** delle figure in primo piano sono molto ***saturi***, cioé luminosi e puri; sullo sfondo il colore è scuro, insaturo.

Il ***bianco*** e il ***nero*** sono considerati colori acromatici: si possono presentare, mescolati tra loro, in gradazioni di ***grigio***.

1. Le gradazioni tonali

Osserva, nell'esempio, la gradazione tonale del colore verde. Disegna una serie di 11 quadrati (lato 3 cm); usando le tempere, riempi i quadrati con la gradazione tonale di una tinta a tua scelta: colloca il colore puro, spremuto dal tubetto e diluito con poca acqua, nel quadrato centrale, il nero nel primo quadrato a sinistra e il bianco nell'ultimo a destra. Riempi gli altri quadrati con la gradazione di colore, ottenuta aggiungendo in quantità crescente il bianco e il nero al colore puro, usando magari due pennelli diversi.

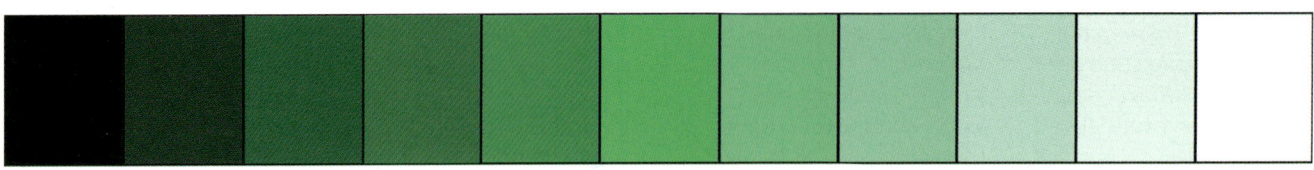

NERO **COLORE PURO** **BIANCO**

2. La saturazione dei colori

I colori saturi possono facilmente essere desaturati aggiungendo, ad esempio, il colore complementare. Quando un colore perde la sua saturazione, però, non è più possibile ripristinarne la purezza.

Dopo aver osservato l'esempio (realizzato con il giallo), scegli un colore puro e aggiungi, progressivamente, piccole quantità del suo complementare (in questo caso il viola), fino ad ottenere un grigio spento.

Ripeti l'esercizio con gli stessi colori, ma invertendo il primo con il secondo; puoi osservare che le aggiunte successive, a parità di quantità, non producono il medesimo effetto desaturante: questo avviene perché le tinte hanno diversa luminosità intrinseca. Ad esempio, per creare il verde, è opportuno aggiungere al giallo una piccola quantità di blu e non viceversa!

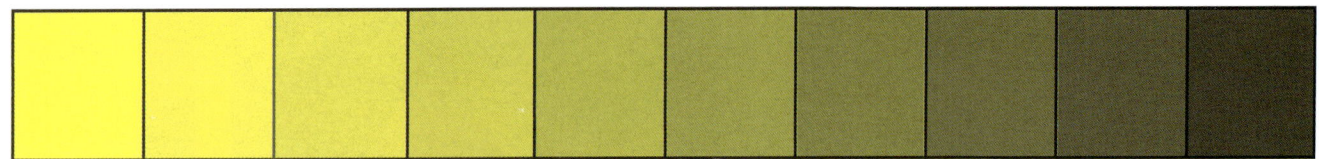

3. Gradazioni all'acquerello

L'artista tedesco **Paul Klee** ha realizzato numerosi lavori ad acquerello su carta, utilizzando in modo esemplare le gradazioni di tono e le variazioni di saturazione di un colore.

Nell'esempio, puoi osservare una serie di rettangoli con gradazioni di tono e saturazione del colore blu, dal blu scuro (quasi nero) all'azzurro pallido (quasi bianco).

I colori sono in prevalenza freddi, con l'unica eccezione di un cerchio arancione, che contrasta con tutto il resto, dando senso alla composizione.

Inoltre, alle forme in prevalenza rettangolari (fredde) si contrappone il cerchio arancione (caldo).

Seguendo uno schema compositivo analogo, prova a creare una composizione con gradazioni dello stesso colore.

Paul Klee, *Il messaggero dell'autunno*. Acquerello.

PORTFOLIO

IL COLORE NELLA CITTÀ

1. Le architetture colorate di Luis Barragán

"Bellezza, ispirazione, magia, incantesimo, ed anche serenità, mistero, silenzio, privacy, stupore. Tutte queste cose hanno trovato un focolare amoroso nella mia anima".

Luis Barragán nacque a Guadalajara (Messico) nel 1902 e morì nel 1988. Per lui il colore svolge una funzione molto importante, perché crea atmosfere a volte calde e avvolgenti, a volte rarefatte e spirituali, come puoi osservare nelle immagini di questa pagina. Altre architetture, antiche e moderne, in diverse zone del mondo, affidano al colore gran parte del loro valore espressivo. Prova ad osservare il colore degli edifici della tua città, oppure cerca alcune immagini di edifici colorati ed analizzane eventuali affinità o divergenze.

Luis Barragán, *Casa Gilardi*, 1975. Il corridoio giallo.

Luis Barragán, **Casa Egerstrom**, 1966. La piscina.

2. I "wall drawings" di Sol LeWitt

L'opera dell'artista americano **Sol LeWitt** (1928) ha origine da forme geometriche semplici: cerchi, quadrati, triangoli rettangoli e altre più complesse derivate da queste. Il suo metodo di lavoro riduce i disegni e le sculture all'essenza dell'astrazione geometrica. In particolare, nei suoi *"wall drawings"*, disegni murali dai colori vivaci, egli restituisce vitalità agli ambienti: grandi cerchi, rettangoli e quadrati, strisce colorate che ondeggiando ampliano a dismisura lo spazio esprimendo energia e voglia di vivere. Non potrebbero essere un'idea per un mural su qualche grigio muro della scuola o del vostro quartiere, al di là degli immancabili, quanto discutibili, interventi dei *writers*?

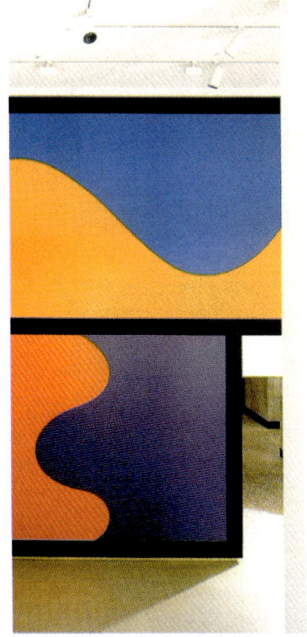

SUPERFICIE E TEXTURE

Ogni oggetto, grande o piccolo, possiede una sua superficie, riconoscibile anche per la specificità della sua **texture**. Il termine *"texture"* è francese e significa letteralmente *"struttura, trama di un tessuto"*. Nel linguaggio visivo la *texture* è una trama di punti, di linee o forme omogenea e regolare al punto da apparire come unitaria.

Essa è dunque composta da segni organizzati in diversi modi: accostati, intrecciati, ripetuti, disposti a caso o ritmicamente. La texture può essere liscia o ruvida, nitida o più o meno decorata, in relazione al tatto o alla vista.

Texture naturali e texture geometriche

La natura offre numerosi tipici esempi di *texture*, caratterizzati dalla presenza di elementi uguali o assai simili, anche se aggregati in modo casuale: la corteccia di un albero, il mare increspato da piccole onde, la superficie ruvida ma regolare della buccia di un'arancia. Queste *texture* sono *di tipo organico o naturale*.

Le *texture di tipo geometrico* sono invece generate da segni ed elementi geometrici, accostati in modo da formare reticoli omogenei. Possiamo trovare una grande ricchezza di texture geometriche sia nelle superfici naturali sia in quelle artificiali.

Nella **pittura**, soprattutto nella pittura contemporanea, la superficie texturizzata coincide molto spesso con il segno dell'artista, ed è quindi un importante mezzo espressivo. La pennellata, il colpo di spatola, il segno lasciato dalla matita colorata, danno origine a superfici diversamente caratterizzate: fitte tracce uniformi, macchie larghe e irregolari, elementi ripetuti secondo un principio seriale, in cui il valore espressivo è strettamente legato alla scelta del mezzo tecnico.

Anche nella **scultura**, il segno è diretta emanazione del gesto dell'artista, che può incidere la pietra, il marmo, il legno, o apporvi nuova materia, come negli assemblaggi polimaterici o nella lavorazione della creta.

In **architettura**, la qualità della superficie è determinata generalmente dai materiali, o da elementi segnici che ne evidenziano la struttura o l'impianto formale (ripetizione di finestre, di colonne, di pannelli di rivestimento, ecc.). In alcuni casi è proprio la texture l'elemento che più caratterizza l'edificio: il *bugnato* del rinascimentale *Palazzo dei Diamanti* a Ferrara, ad esempio, con la trama ordinata di elementi lapidei in rilievo, è certamente l'elemento più rappresentativo dell'edificio.

A destra, dall'alto: texture naturali ottenute fotografando parti di pelle ingrandita al microscopio, lamiera metallica, steccato in legno, fogliame, pavimento piastrellato.

Particolare della facciata del *Palazzo dei Diamanti* a Ferrara.

LEGGERE LA TEXTURE

1. Abaco di texture

Osserva gli esempi qui riportati; disegna alcuni quadrati di 10 cm di lato e riempine la superficie con texture (geometriche e non), a matita, penna o pennarello.

2. Tappezzerie e texture naturali

L'idea di texture è ben rappresentata dal rivestimento delle pareti con tappezzerie di carta o di stoffa. Recupera immagini da un catalogo e prova a "rivestire" graficamente le pareti di una stanza o di un'aula.
Nella prima immagine puoi osservare un disegno per stoffa da tappezzeria, realizzato da **William Morris** nel 1883.
Le altre sono texture naturali.

LUCE E OMBRA

La luce e le cose

La luce ha il potere di svelare gli oggetti del mondo naturale, di dare loro definizione, sfiorandone la superficie e delineandone le forme. Per questa ragione gli studiosi medievali le attribuivano un potere divino: un alone luminoso, un raggio di sole o la brillantezza dell'oro indicavano la presenza di Dio. *spirituale, spazio divino*

Fu a partire dal XV secolo, con il Rinascimento, che la luce fu considerata non più come evento soprannaturale, ma come mezzo per indagare e descrivere la realtà. Il pittore toscano **Cennino Cennini** (1370-1440), autore del celebre *libro dell'Arte*, suggeriva già nel 1390: *"Analizza accuratamente la luce, scopri da dove viene; seguila, altrimenti la tua opera sarà piana "*.

La qualità indagatrice della luce si accentuò ulteriormente in età barocca, quando fu impiegata in violente e drammatiche contrapposizioni di chiaro e scuro.

La luce si distribuisce sugli oggetti, modulando la propria intensità in relazione alle caratteristiche ed alle variazioni di superficie, suggerendo la tridimensionalità degli oggetti stessi.

La luce è anche un indicatore di profondità spaziale, poiché tende a sfumare e a farsi più vibratile in lontananza: essa dunque aiuta a definire anche la posizione degli oggetti nello spazio.

La percezione delle radiazioni luminose
in lontananza - colori più chiara, desaturano i colore

Il mutare della qualità e della quantità della luce può provocare percezioni diverse dello stesso oggetto. La **luce** infatti può essere **naturale** o **artificiale**, in relazione al tipo di fonte luminosa, e può variare parecchio per intensità (pensiamo al giorno e alla notte o ad una lampada con reostato regolatore).

Se l'oggetto è molto illuminato, aumenta anche la luce riflessa, per cui ci appare più vicino rispetto ad un altro meno illuminato, per effetto del fenomeno dell'irradiazione.

L'illuminazione

A seconda dell'intensità, della qualità e della posizione della fonte luminosa, varia il rapporto tra luce e ombra in ogni oggetto.

In modo analogo varia anche la nostra percezione del suo volume. possiamo descrivere la natura dell'illuminazione di un oggetto in riferimento alla provenienza della luce. Si possono quindi individuare le seguenti condizioni: **luce diffusa**, **luce frontale**, **luce laterale**, **controluce** che possiamo osservare nelle illustrazioni di queste pagine.

Luce frontale. La sorgente luminosa è posta presso l'osservatore o alle sue spalle; l'ombra si forma dietro l'oggetto e il volume di questo tende ad appiattirsi, in quanto risulta attenuato il contrasto nella progressione dei valori chiaroscurali;

Luce laterale o incidente. Sull'oggetto si formano, a destra o a sinistra, evidenti zone d'ombra che accentuano concavità e sporgenze, e mettono in risalto la qualità materica della superficie. Quando la fonte luminosa è collocata in modo da determinare accentuazioni marcate dell'ombra, si è in presenza di luce radente. *in ambito espressivo → suspense, inquie...*

Luce diffusa. Corrisponde alla condizione migliore per l'osservazione delle cose nello spazio. È generata dall'illuminazione naturale del sole quando non è diretta, ovvero è filtrata dalla nebbia o da uno strato di nubi; può essere ottenuta artificialmente attraverso l'utilizzo di filtri o l'impiego contemporaneo ed equilibrato di più sorgenti luminose. La forma dell'oggetto illuminato non ha rilievo marcato, e le sue ombre sono sfumate. Questa condizione corrisponde spesso ad un'intensità luminosa attenuata.

niente volume

Controluce. L'oggetto è posto tra la sorgente luminosa e l'osservatore. Ne scorgiamo nettamente i profili, ma non riusciamo a leggerne la superficie. L'ombra è uniforme ed i volumi si appiattiscono.

volume

Le ombre

Le ombre si formano nella parte dell'oggetto che non è investita dalla luce e sono definite dalla **direzione della luce** (da destra, da sinistra, frontale, ecc.) e dall'**inclinazione** dei raggi (dall'alto, dal basso, ecc.).

In relazione alla loro natura le ombre possono essere di diverso tipo:

– **ombre proprie**, che coprono una parte della superficie dell'oggetto, quella meno illuminata;

– **ombre portate**, che l'oggetto illuminato proietta su un altro oggetto o sul piano d'appoggio. L'ombra portata è utile per comprendere le relazioni spaziali e compositive tra gli elementi di un insieme.

– **ombre autoportate**, cioè quelle che l'oggetto, per la sua forma particolare, proietta su alcune parti di se stesso.

LUCE DA DESTRA

Ombre proprie

Ombre portate

Ombre autoportate

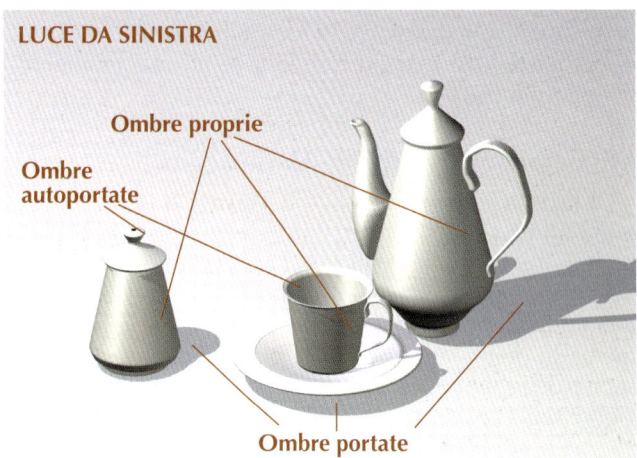

LUCE DA SINISTRA

Ombre proprie

Ombre autoportate

Ombre portate

La teoria delle ombre

La geometria descrittiva si occupa di descrivere esattamette l'andamento delle ombre nelle rappresentazioni grafiche (Proiezioni ortogonali, Assonometrie e Prospettiva) secondo una più generale **teoria delle ombre**.

Il metodo più semplice, qui visualizzato, riguarda le ombre in assonometria: ipotizzando la sorgente di luce all'infinito, si scelgono l'inclinazione dei raggi luminosi (indicata con la lettera r) e la direzione r' della luce. È sufficiente poi mandare dai punti caratteristici degli oggetti (spigoli e vertici) linee parallele all'inclinazione e alla direzione: queste, incontrandosi sul piano, determinano il punto di proiezione dell'ombra portata. Se un oggetto è vicino ad un altro (come il parallelepipedo a destra del cono) la proiezione dell'ombra portata finisce non sul piano ma sull'oggetto.

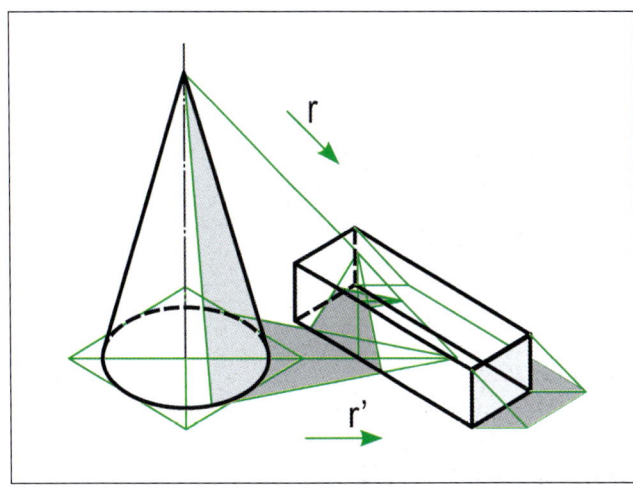

LEGGERE LUCI E OMBRE

La luce ha sempre avuto grande importanza nelle opere di pittori, scultori e architetti. Alcuni artisti si sono dedicati in modo particolare allo studio degli effetti luminosi, tanto che il loro stile inconfondibile è legato in buona parte all'uso della luce. Vediamone alcuni.

Antonello da Messina

Nel dipinto di **Antonello da Messina** (1340-1479) rappresentante la *Vergine annunziata*, la luce si distribuisce nel quadro con un artificio. Essa proviene da sinistra e dall'alto ed illumina, in maniera diretta, il viso della Vergine; una parte della luce giunge però riflessa sul volto mediante il piano a noi invisibile del leggio, come si può osservare anche dai giochi di luce sulle mani. L'immagine acquista così maggiore solidità e un rafforzamento della forma plastica.

Michelangelo Merisi da Caravaggio

La luce radente nei quadri di **Caravaggio** (1571-1610) porta ad una sintesi estrema: il forte contrasto di luce e ombra, infatti, pone in rilievo i caratteri emergenti degli oggetti e dei personaggi, lasciando talora nel buio, indeterminata, ampia parte della scena. In tal modo aumenta la drammaticità della rappresentazione e la plasticità delle figure, i cui volumi sembrano emerge con vigore dalle tenebre.

Antonello da Messina, *Vergine annunziata*, 1470-75. Olio su tavola, 46x34 cm. Palermo, Galleria Nazionale.

Caravaggio, *Flagellazione di Cristo*, 1607-1608. Olio su tela, 286x213 cm. Napoli, Museo e Gallerie Nazionali di Capodimonte.

Jan Vermeer, *La pesatrice di perle*, 1665 circa. Olio su tela, 42x35,5 cm. Washinghton, National Gallery of Art.

Jan Vermeer

Per il pittore olandese **Jan Vermeer** (1632-1675) la luce è il principale strumento di indagine della realtà: essa proviene sempre da una finestra posta sulla sinistra dell'osservatore e appare con improvvisi contrasti sugli oggetti immersi nella penombra della stanza, investe ogni cosa, disegna ogni dettaglio, sembra frugare negli angoli più segreti. È una luce resa con colori chiari e luminosi, che prende corpo mediante un sottile pulviscolo sospeso nell'aria.

Nell'esempio raffigurato, anche la profondità dello spazio è resa mediante la luce. Questa aumenta progressivamente verso la figura femminile: in primo piano a sinistra, immerse nell'ombra, aprono la scena un drappo blu ripiegato e il tavolo, mentre la donna è investita da una luce diretta, esaltata dal bianco del velo sul capo e dei bordi della giacca. La luce dà nitidezza alle immagini e sembra quasi immobilizzare la scena.

Particolare attenzione merita la raffigurazione delle perle: sulla loro superficie l'artista ha saputo rendere i riflessi in modo così sapiente da farci percepire la consistenza dell'oggetto prezioso.

Giuseppe Pellizza da Volpedo

La processione fu uno dei primi quadri divisionisti di **Pellizza da Volpedo** (1868-1907) e fu oggetto di una lunga elaborazione. Esso presenta una ricca varietà di soluzioni luminose: il lungo tratto in ombra in primo piano, con il riflesso di fronde d'alberi traforate dai raggi del sole, la soleggiata strada di campagna su cui avanzano le donne in doppia fila. Gli abiti, nel loro biancore, offrono ampia possibilità di riflettere la luce colorata. Risaltano le vibrazioni luminose delle piante e delle siepi che delimitano la strada, chiudendo quasi a triangolo la composizione. La luce, più che la materialità e il volume dei corpi, suggerisce qui un senso di sottile misticismo ed è strumento per rappresentare un'atmosfera rarefatta e sospesa.

Giuseppe Pellizza da Volpedo, *La processione*, 1892-95. Olio su tela, 84x155 cm. Milano, Museo della Scienza e della Tecnica.

Dan Flavin

Dan Flavin (New York 1933-1996) si è soprattutto concentrato sui fenomeni luminosi generati da tubi al neon. Flavin ha usato il tubo al neon come fosse un segno, ma ne ha anche utilizzato la luce come fosse un colore. In questo senso egli ha sovente "dipinto" interi ambienti: è il caso della Chiesa Rossa di Milano, progettata da Giovanni Muzio (1893-1982) negli anni Trenta del XX secolo, secondo uno schema tradizionale cruciforme. Flavin ha progettato per questo spazio un sistema di colorazioni luminose che rispetta le simbologie cristiane: azzurro per la volta, luogo che allude alla serenità del paradiso; giallo oro per il retro dell'altare, luogo dell'apparizione e della gloria divina; violetto per le zone che ricordano la Passione di Cristo.

Dan Flavin, *allestimento luminoso permanente per Santa Maria in Chiesa Rossa*. Milano, 1995.

PER CAPIRE LE OMBRE COLORATE

La sequenza illustra cosa avviene illuminando un oggetto, posto su un piano di colore bianco, con luci colorate provenienti da direzioni diverse e usando rispettivamente una sola fonte luminosa, usandone due e poi tre contemporaneamente. Vengono impiegati tre faretti di colore rosso (Red), verde (Green) e blu (Blue), i colori fondamentali della luce (*vedi pagg. 86 e 87*). I fasci luminosi si sovrappongono parzialmente creando ombre sul piano. Di che colore sono le ombre? Possiamo eseguire l'esperimento, in camera oscura, usando comuni faretti colorati, utilizzati in genere per il teatro.

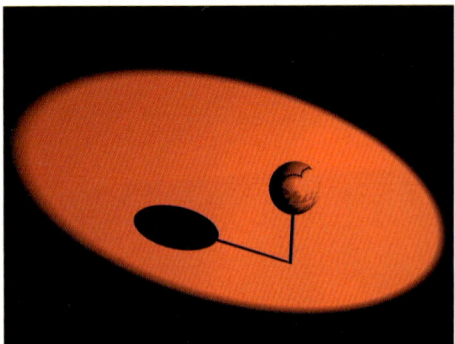

1. L'oggetto è illuminato con la sola luce **rossa** (**R**)

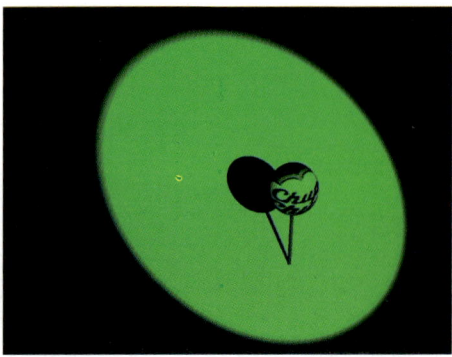

2. L'oggetto è illuminato con la sola luce **verde** (**G**)

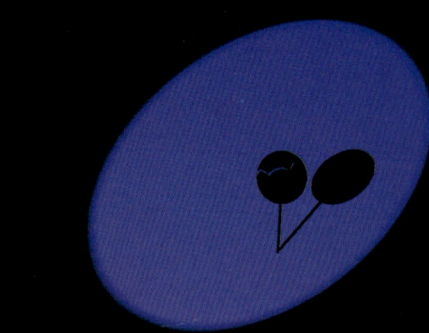

3. L'oggetto è illuminato con la sola luce **blu** (**B**)

4. L'oggetto è illuminato con le luci **rossa e verde** (**R+G**)

5. L'oggetto è illuminato con le luci **verde e blu** (**G+B**)

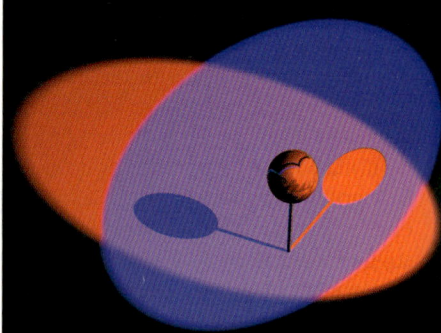

6. L'oggetto è illuminato con le luci **rossa e blu** (**R+B**)

7. L'oggetto è illuminato con le tre luci **rossa**, **verde e blu** (**R+G+B**)

Nelle prime tre figure le ombre sono nere infatti le zone d'ombra non riflettono alcuna radiazione luminosa.

Nelle tre figure seguenti le ombre appaiono colorate perché le zone d'ombra riflettono la luce non schermata dall'oggetto.

Nella *fig. 4*, ad esempio, l'ombra al centro è rossa, perché è generata dal faretto verde quindi il piano non riflette la luce verde bensì quella rossa che arriva da un'altra direzione.

Nella *fig. 7* la zona bianca è l'area di sovrapposizione di tutti e tre i fasci di luce colorata: le sovrapposizioni parziali di rosso e verde creano il *giallo*, quelle di rosso e blu creano il *magenta* e quelle di verde e blu creano il **ciano** (che sono i colori della sintesi sottrattiva).

Le ombre create dall'oggetto illuminato in questo caso sono il risultato della rispettiva combinazione di due luci colorate:

$$R+G=Y \qquad R+B=M \qquad G+B=C$$

TRA LUCE E OMBRA: IL CHIAROSCURO

Il principale metodo grafico e pittorico con il quale luce ed ombra danno il senso del volume, pur nella rappresentazione sul piano del foglio o del quadro, si chiama *chiaroscuro*: con questo metodo, soprattutto nelle opere *monocromatiche* (a un solo colore), l'artista fa emergere la figura dall'ombra con diverse gradazioni di luce, espresse da tonalità molto scure (*l'ombra*) fino al bianco (*le zone più illuminate*).

In mezzo, innumerevoli sfumature di luce sono date dai valori chiaroscurali: la presenza di profondi contrasti e improvvisi bagliori può dare all'immagine grande forza espressiva.

Usando il chiaroscuro, sono proprio i *gradienti di luminosità*, cioè i differenti stadi nel passaggio tra la luce e l'ombra, a comunicare il senso del volume degli oggetti e la loro collocazione nello spazio.

Il chiaroscuro si può ottenere con varie tecniche e modalità; può essere **sfumato**, cioè realizzato con progressive sfumature, reso con varie combinazioni e **intrecci di linee**, tratteggi e accostamenti di **punti più o meno fitti**; può essere generato dalla **granulosità della carta** e dalla rugosità dei supporti in genere, realizzato a **mezzatinta** o a **macchia**, con nette separazioni di chiaro e di scuro.

Mescolando bianco e nero in proporzioni progressive, si possono ottenere innumerevoli passaggi di luci ed ombre. Ognuna di queste sfumature è conosciuta come *tono della gradazione del grigio*.

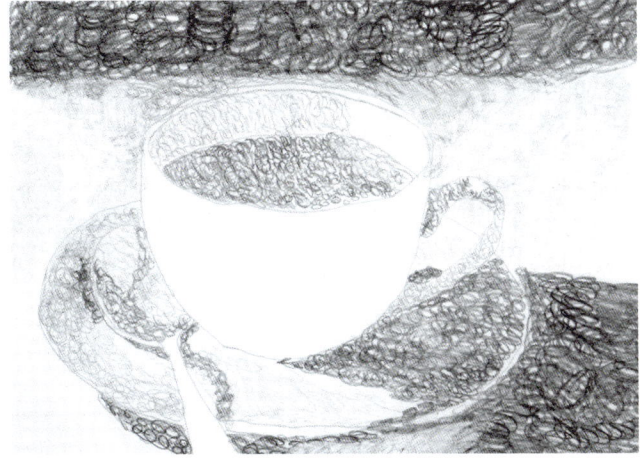

Esempi di rielaborazione in chiaroscuro su una tazzina di caffé.

Lettura e analisi di luci e ombre in un dipinto

Osserva l'opera di **Georges de La Tour**, *San Giuseppe falegname*, conservata presso il Museo del Louvre a Parigi: vi possiamo trovare, riassunti, alcuni dei principi fondamentali che regolano la comprensione e l'uso della luce e delle ombre in pittura e, più in generale, nella comunicazione visiva. Scegli un'immagine a tuo piacimento, posizionala al centro di un foglio da disegno ed esegui un esercizio di lettura analogo.

Georges de La Tour, *San Giuseppe falegname*, 1640 ca. Olio su tela, 137x101 cm. Parigi, Museo del Louvre.

Dal fitto **buio dello sfondo** emergono i profili delle due figure raffrontate: *San Giuseppe* che lavora nella sua bottega di falegname e il *bambin Gesù* che gli fa luce.

La **luce** proviene dal centro della composizione, emanata dalla tremolante fiamma di una candela tenuta in mano dal Bambino. Essa **illumina direttamente** il volto del fanciullo, la fronte del vecchio, la sua spalla sinistra e il braccio.

Le **ombre** sono nette e profonde: sono **ombre proprie** quelle che si formano, ad esempio, sul braccio di Giuseppe; sono **ombre portate** quelle che si proiettano sul corpo di Giuseppe e sulla veste di Gesù.

La mano del Bambino fa da schermo per l'osservatore, ponendosi **in controluce**: le dita sembrano quasi trasparenti e traslucide, per effetto della luminescenza diffusa.

Veduta di un cascinale della pianura emiliana.
I solchi lasciati dall'aratura, pur paralleli tra loro, sembrano convergere verso la cascina.

LA PERCEZIONE E L'OSSERVAZIONE DELLO SPAZIO

La percezione e l'osservazione dello spazio

L'occhio umano percepisce e comprende lo spazio mediante due differenti modalità di **visione**: **stereoscopica** e **cinestetica**.

• **Visione stereoscopica**: poiché osserviamo con due occhi, noi operiamo continuamente un processo di adattamento reciproco tra le cose che vediamo, al fine di percepire un'unica immagine tridimensionale. Questo processo visuale ci consente di cogliere le distanze e le dimensioni degli oggetti.

• **Visione cinestetica**: nel vedere una superficie bidimensionale, ad esempio la facciata di una casa, noi intuiamo che dietro di essa esiste uno spazio: così, basta vedere le parti separate di un oggetto, o anche una di esse, per comprenderlo nel suo insieme e ricomporlo in modo unitario nel cervello.

Tutta la nostra esperienza si colloca all'interno dello spazio: in esso viviamo, viaggiamo, corriamo, utilizziamo gli oggetti, puri volumi anch'essi collocati nello spazio. Le montagne, gli alberi, le case, tutto ciò che vediamo ci aiuta a comprendere lo spazio, delimitandolo: il mare e i piatti paesaggi desertici fanno da limite orizzontale, così come le pareti di una stanza o un'alta scogliera lo delimitano verticalmente.

Tra i diversi tipi di spazio, riconosciamo con facilità i seguenti:

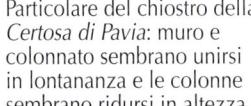

Particolare del chiostro della *Certosa di Pavia*: muro e colonnato sembrano unirsi in lontananza e le colonne sembrano ridursi in altezza.

1. Lo **spazio aperto naturale** ci offre la visione di un paesaggio che giunge fino al cielo, alle montagne lontane, all'orizzonte. Esso può essere dunque virtualmente infinito. Leggiamo uno spazio aperto soprattutto mediante la luce che lo inonda, facendo variare l'intensità e i toni dei colori a seconda delle distanze. I piani di profondità più lontani, ad esempio, tendono ad essere più chiari e sfumati.

   Osservando con attenzione ambienti chiusi e spazi aperti, noteremo precisi indicatori di profondità spaziale, che dobbiamo essere in grado di rappresentare anche graficamente, con una certa approssimazione alla nostra realtà visiva.

2. Lo **spazio naturale e urbanizzato di media profondità**: pensiamo alla città, in cui palazzi, muri, e ancora automobili, biciclette, uomini in movimento delimitano lo sguardo; pensiamo anche allo spazio della natura non modificata dall'uomo, come una radura o l'interno di un bosco fitto di alberi. Dentro la città gli stimoli visivi che ci fanno percepire lo spazio sono molteplici: la veduta prospettica di un viale fa sì che distinguiamo gli edifici più vicini, perché più grandi e più ricchi di particolari; scorgiamo il mutare dei colori di un semaforo, la segnaletica stradale, distinguiamo gli oggetti nelle vetrine, i manifesti pubblicitari, le scritte sui muri.

3. Lo **spazio interno dell'architettura**, chiuso da pareti, articolato da scale, definito dalla presenza di oggetti di arredamento. Muovendoci dentro la scuola o in casa percepiamo la distanza tra noi e le pareti, gli oggetti, i mobili, la loro collocazione e l'ingombro.

LA RAFFIGURAZIONE DELLO SPAZIO NELLE TRE DIMENSIONI: LA PROSPETTIVA INTUITIVA

Con un po' di esercizio d'osservazione, possiamo individuare nell'ambiente che ci circonda alcune costanti percettive che, trasformate in segni grafici elementari, consentono di rappresentare lo spazio prospettico in modo intuitivo ma abbastanza vicino alla realtà e senza essere sottomessi alle ferree regole della Geometria descrittiva. Osserva l'immagine di questa pagina, che è la fotografia di un lungo porticato della città di Sabbioneta, e gli schemi relativi, che evidenziano alcuni 'trucchi del mestiere' per la rappresentazione intuitiva della prospettiva centrale.

centrale

Sabbioneta (Mantova).

1. Il porticato sembra restringersi in lontananza e le linee convergono in un punto di fuga (F.) posto sulla linea di orizzonte (L.O.).

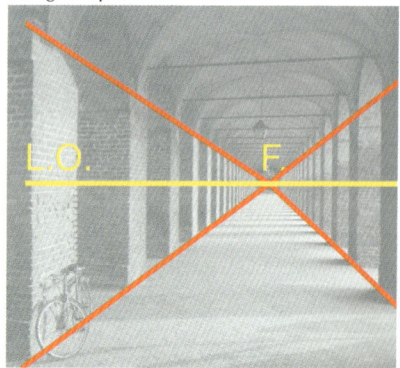

2. La stessa persona appare sempre più piccola, man mano che si allontana.

linee verticali rimangono verticali

3. Le linee verticali degli spigoli si mantengono parallele, ma si riducono progressivamente in altezza.

4. Le linee orizzontali dei tiranti e del pavimento si mantengono parallele, ma si riducono progressivamente in larghezza.

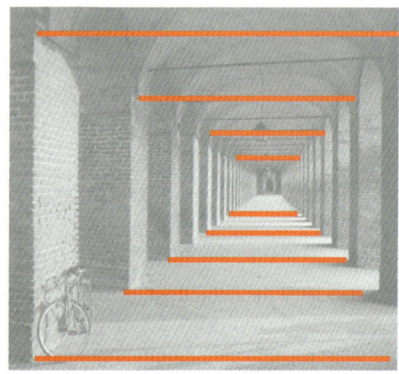

5. I rettangoli tra i pilastri diventano dei trapezi sempre più piccoli e ravvicinati tra loro in lontananza.

LA RAPPRESENTAZIONE PROSPETTICA DELLO SPAZIO

Dispositivo prospettico di **Leon Battista Alberti**, con la piramide dei raggi visivi.

Masolino, *Guarigione dello storpio e Resurrezione di Tabita*, 1425 circa. Firenze, Cappella Brancacci.

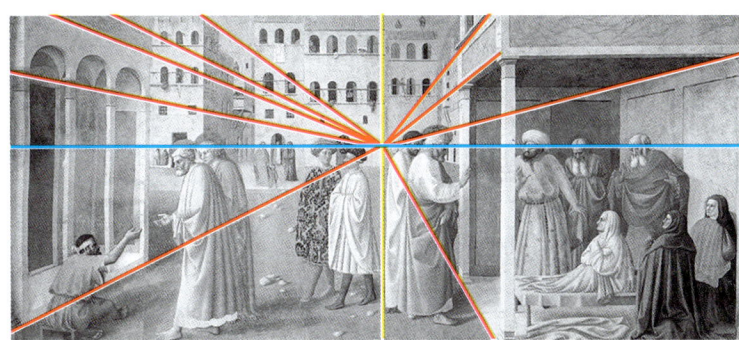

Schema prospettico.

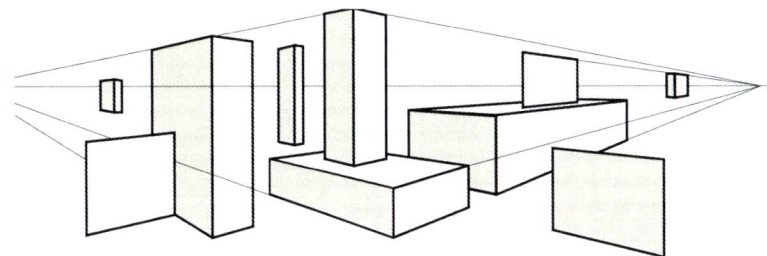

La prospettiva geometrica

La prospettiva è un metodo di rappresentazione grafica e pittorica che crea l'illusione di profondità spaziale (*tridimensionale*) su una superficie piana (*bidimensionale*).

Osserviamo un gruppo di linee parallele che si allontanano da noi in linea retta, come le rotaie della ferrovia, un colonnato, un filare di alberi o i margini di una strada rettilinea: notiamo che esse sembrano restringersi in lontananza, fino a convergere idealmente in un punto: è il loro *punto di fuga*.

Come calcolare la progressiva riduzione di misura degli oggetti in lontananza? **Leon Battista Alberti** descrive nel '400 una piramide di raggi che vanno dall'occhio dell'osservatore agli oggetti. Nel modello prospettico teorizzato da Alberti, i raggi incontrano gli oggetti consentendoci di individuarne i vertici e gli spigoli.

Ipotizziamo che i raggi intersechino uno schermo trasparente, che funge da piano immaginario. Su questo schermo, definito **quadro**, si forma l'immagine del pavimento in prospettiva. Le linee che si sviluppano in profondità, in realtà parallele fra loro, sul quadro prospettico convergono in un punto, il **punto di fuga** o *punto principale*. Questo è sempre posto di fronte all'occhio dell'osservatore.

La prospettiva centrale

In età rinascimentale, la **prospettiva centrale**, con un **solo punto di fuga**, è stata considerata il mezzo più adatto a rappresentare la realtà naturale. Questo sistema pone al centro l'uomo, che osserva il mondo dal suo punto di vista.

Nell'affresco della *Guarigione dello storpio*, del 1425, **Masolino** ha collocato il punto di fuga al centro, in fondo alla piazza: qui convergono le linee parallele delle cornici degli edifici, come evidenziato dallo schema. L'altezza dell'orizzonte è poco sopra la metà, come se anche noi fossimo presenti alla scena, ma guardando leggermente dal basso, poiché l'affresco è collocato nella parte superiore della parete destra della Cappella Brancacci, in Santa Maria del Carmine a Firenze.

La prospettiva accidentale

La **prospettiva accidentale** (o **angolare**) si differenzia da quella centrale perché presenta **due punti di fuga** delle linee di profondità.

L'osservatore si colloca, dunque, non più frontalmente, ma obliquamente alla scena e gli oggetti sono disposti con le facce non parallele al quadro prospettico. La veduta accidentale introduce nuovi elementi espressivi nell'arte: essa rifiuta infatti la centralità dell'osservazione, dilatando lo spazio.

Lettura e analisi dello spazio prospettico

Osserva l'opera di **Paolo Uccello**, Il *miracolo dell'ostia profanata*, conservata nella Galleria Nazionale delle Marche ad Urbino: vi possiamo trovare, riassunti, alcuni dei principi fondamentali che regolano la comprensione e l'uso della prospettiva in pittura e, più in generale, nella comunicazione visiva. Scegli un'immagine a tuo piacimento, posizionala al centro di un foglio da disegno ed esegui un esercizio di lettura analogo a quello proposto.

Nella prospettiva, l'**osservatore** si colloca a distanza finita rispetto al quadro di proiezione: nell'esempio di questa pagina è posto al centro, di fronte alla stanza in cui si svolge l'azione. L'altezza del punto di vista determina la posizione dell'**orizzonte**.

Le rette perpendicolari al quadro prospettico convergono, cioè si uniscono, nel **punto di fuga**, posto sull'orizzonte: osserva dove confluiscono le linee delle travi del soffitto e delle piastrelle del pavimento.

Le **altezze degli oggetti** si mantengono verticali, ma diminuiscono progressivamente avvicinandosi al punto di fuga: osserva gli stipiti della porta e la cornice della finestra.

Le **rette orizzontali**, parallele al quadro prospettico, si mantengono tali: osserva le orizzontali del pavimento, del bancone, l'anta della finestra e le linee della parete di fondo.

Paolo Uccello, Il *miracolo dell'ostia profanata*, 1465-69. Tempera su tavola, 33x58,5 cm. Urbino, Galleria Nazionale delle Marche.

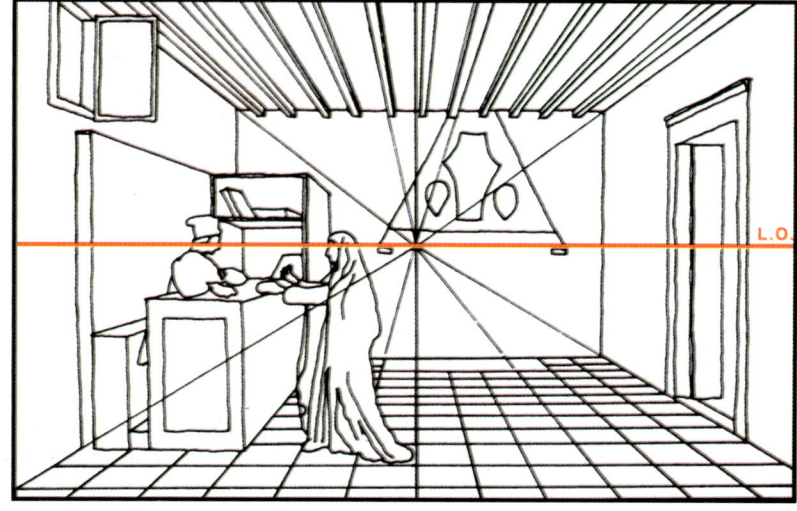

LA COMPOSIZIONE

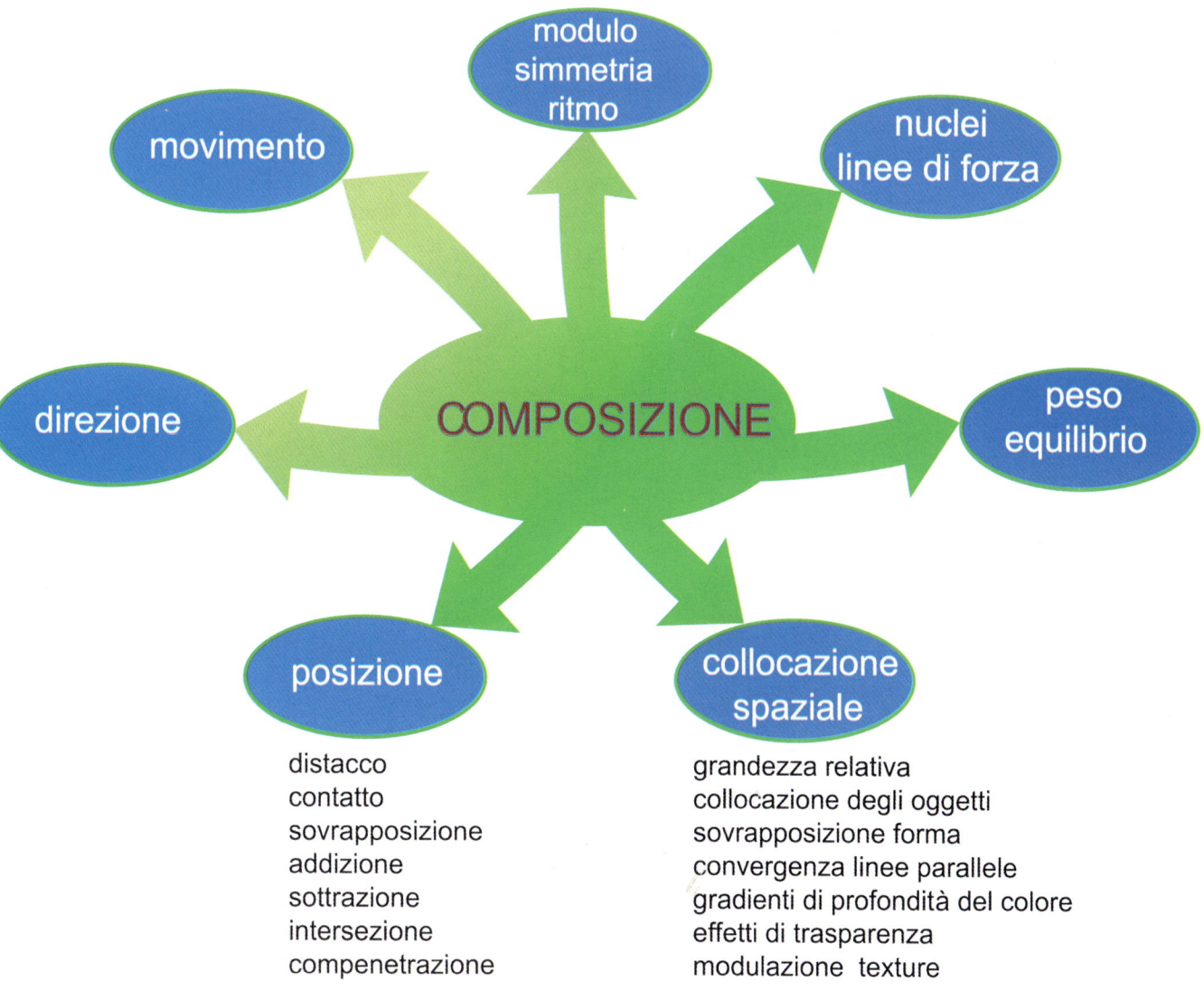

distacco
contatto
sovrapposizione
addizione
sottrazione
intersezione
compenetrazione

grandezza relativa
collocazione degli oggetti
sovrapposizione forma
convergenza linee parallele
gradienti di profondità del colore
effetti di trasparenza
modulazione texture

Le regole della composizione

Comporre significa risolvere un problema di suddivisione del campo visivo nei suoi valori strutturali ed espressivi: la **composizione** è infatti *l'organizzazione intenzionale degli elementi del linguaggio visuale e plastico* dentro l'opera.

Come per scrivere un testo componiamo frasi seguendo precise regole grammaticali e sintattiche, così per creare la composizione visiva, accostiamo segni, forme, colori, ponendoli in relazione tra loro mediante le regole della grammatica visiva. Nasce così un messaggio visivo, con precisi valori strutturali ed espressivi, suggeriti in gran parte dalla composizione.

Un'opera d'arte (un dipinto, un bassorilievo, un edificio) è proprio il risultato felice della giusta composizione degli elementi dei linguaggio visuale: il punto, la linea, la forma, la superficie, il volume, lo spazio, la luce, il colore, ecc.

Diverse sono le regole della composizione visiva che vengono applicate dall'autore secondo il suo gusto estetico, la sua cultura, il messaggio che vuole dare: sono la **simmetria** (e l'asimmetria), il **modulo** e il **ritmo**, il **peso** e l'**equilibrio visivo**, la **direzione dinamica** e il **movimento**, la **struttura geometrica**. Possiamo, in ogni opera, analizzare questi fattori singolarmente o nell'insieme.

Pieter Bruegel il Vecchio, *Battaglia tra la Quaresima e il Carnevale*, 1559. Olio su tavola, 118x164,5 cm. Vienna, Kunsthistorisches Museum.

LA SCELTA COMPOSITIVA

Tutti abbiamo osservato, qualche volta, un fiorista disporre dei fiori in un vaso: ne toglie uno, ne mette un altro, li ragguppa per colore, taglia qualche foglia di troppo o accorcia i gambi; infine mette il mazzo, in bella posa, a centro tavola o in vetrina. Oppure un commesso, che sistema i manichini, con i relativi abiti, nella vetrina di un negozio: alza un braccio, allarga una gamba, ruota e sposta finché non ricrea una situazione soddisfacente.

Un artista lavora, più o meno, allo stesso modo: dispone colori, linee, forme e figure finché non ottiene l'effetto voluto, cioè la **composizione** dell'immagine.

Osserva le immagini di queste pagine. La prima, opera di un pittore olandese del XVI secolo, **Pieter Bruegel il Vecchio** (1526 ca.-1569), rappresenta una festa di Carnevale: la composizione è complessa perché non c'è una figura centrale, ma è caratterizzata piuttosto da un brulichio di personaggi e situazioni. Il nostro sguardo è portato a spostarsi da un dettaglio all'altro; linee, forme, colori e figure sono disposti in modo apparentemente disordinato. In realtà non c'è alcuna incoerenza in quest'opera, poiché l'artista riesce a trasmettere pienamente il senso della festa e dell'allegria un po' folle del Carnevale.

La seconda immagine è il ritratto fotografico di una celebre attrice, *Marlene Dietrich*, eseguito dal fotografo inglese **Cecil Beaton** (1904-1980). In questo caso la composizione è semplicissima: il viso dell'attrice, con una mano sulla guancia, emerge dall'ombra dello sfondo, mentre in primo piano biancheggia una splendida orchidea, che ben accompagna la bellezza raffinata e diafana della donna. La composizione è calma e serena: il bianco e nero, inoltre, semplificano ulteriormente la lettura dell'immagine.

Quale delle due composizioni è più riuscita? Il problema non esiste, poiché entrambi gli artisti hanno raggiunto il loro scopo: Bruegel rende molto bene l'esplosione di vita e di gioia della festa con i colori e il movimento, mentre il fotografo interpreta il carattere misterioso della diva, con un sapiente gioco di luci e ombre e l'inserimento del fiore in primo piano.

Questi sono solo due esempi di composizione dell'immagine, ma possono bastare per farci accostare con la dovuta attenzione a questo importante argomento.

Cecil Beaton, *Marlene Dietrich*, 1932.

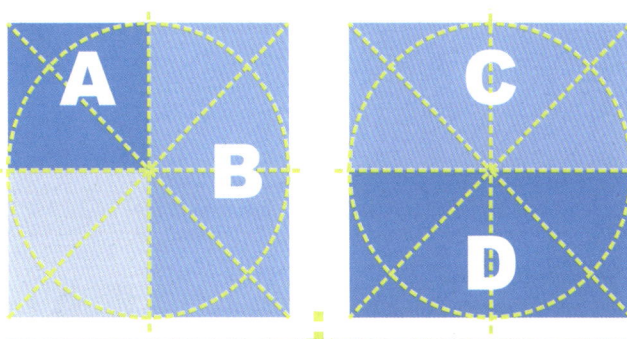

Davanti all'immagine

Delle innumerevoli immagini che ci passano sotto gli occhi nel corso di una giornata, ben poche rimangono impresse nella nostra memoria, poiché la maggior parte di esse sono banali e stereotipate. Che cos'è allora che ci fa soffermare davanti a un'immagine, e la rende ai nostri occhi originale e significativa?

Ebbene, quasi tutti gli elementi del linguaggio visivo possono influire, ma il fattore più importante è quello che comunemente si definisce composizione dell'immagine. In questa *Unità di apprendimento* poniamo la nostra attenzione sui fattori che riguardano l'**organizzazione formale** degli elementi dell'immagine.

La posizione degli elementi nell'immagine

Quando osserviamo un'immagine, si stabiliscono spontaneamente relazioni di posizione degli elementi, nel piano e nello spazio (nel caso di scultura o architettura), secondo uno schema geometrico "nascosto" che corrisponde al nostro senso di orientamento spaziale.

In particolare, per descrivere sommariamente la posizione degli elementi di un'immagine è sufficiente ricorrere ad un semplice schema, basato sulla struttura portante del quadrato (*vedi pag. 83*) da sovrapporre al campo visivo.

Diremo quindi che una figura si trova in alto, in basso, al centro, a destra o a sinistra dell'asse verticale; sopra o sotto l'asse orizzontale; inscritta in un cerchio; in direzione coincidente con la diagonale ecc. Nell'osservazione, inoltre, prevalgono alcune condizioni di tipo culturale che portano a privilegiare determinati punti di vista:

A. all'inizio dell'osservazione, il nostro occhio tende a partire dall'angolo in alto a sinistra del quadro e andare dall'alto verso il basso;

B. vediamo con maggior facilità ciò che è situato a destra nel quadro (per i destrorsi);

C. la parte superiore del quadro sembra più grande e prevale sulla parte bassa: l'alto viene associato al cielo, alla spiritualità;

D. la parte bassa ci sembra più piccola e viene associata alla terra, al peso, all'umiltà.

Nelle pagine seguenti vi sono approfondimenti ed esempi sul valore della posizione nella comunicazione visiva.

Raffaello Sanzio, *Il sogno del cavaliere*, 1504. Olio su tavola, 17x17 cm. Londra, National Gallery.
La struttura compositiva ha l'asse di simmetria coincidente con l'albero al centro; le figure femminili si bilanciano in perfetto equilibrio.

LA POSIZIONE

La disposizione delle forme nel campo visivo è uno degli elementi più importanti della composizione. Essa consiste nel collocare e mettere in relazione tra loro le figure.

Al proposito, possiamo individuare alcune semplici regole, per certi aspetti simili a quelle degli insiemi logico-matematici:

1. distacco

2. contatto

3. sovrapposizione

4. addizione

5. sottrazione

6. intersezione

7. compenetrazione

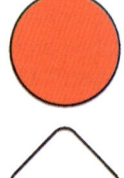

1. Distacco

Le forme possono essere tra loro separate, distanti o vicine; è il caso delle mani di Dio e Adamo, raffigurate da **Michelangelo** nella *Creazione dell'uomo,* nella Cappella Sistina a Roma.

2. Contatto

Le figure sono talmente vicine da creare un contatto tra loro; è ciò che avviene nelle pietre sovrapposte del *dolmen* di Bisceglie, in Puglia.

3. Sovrapposizione

Le forme si sovrappongono, con effetti di *opacità* (quando una nasconde l'altra) o *trasparenza* (quando vediamo anche la forma che sta dietro).

La sovrapposizione determina indici di profondità, perché ci fa capire che la figura che sta davanti è più vicina a chi guarda. Osserva un esempio di sovrapposizione opaca nei volti della copertina di un disco e di trasparenza nella proiezione a luce polarizzata di **Bruno Munari**.

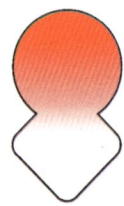

4. Addizione

Le forme si sommano tra loro e le percepiamo come un'unica nuova forma più grande. Nei punti di unione la linea di contorno delle figure tende a sparire, come osserviamo nella scultura *Il bacio* di **Costantin Brancusi**.

forme si fondono perdono contorni

Costantin Brancusi, *Il bacio,* 1912 circa. Pietra, altezza 23 cm. Philadelphia, Museo d'A

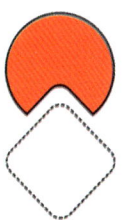

5. Sottrazione

Da una forma se ne sottrae un'altra, asportando una parte della forma originaria. Si crea così anche una forma in negativo, come osserviamo nell'inquietante opera di **René Magritte**.

6. Intersezione

Si definisce intersezione la parte comune ottenuta mediante l'addizione di due forme. L'intersezione è una forma nuova, più piccola e non somigliante alle forme originarie; è quanto possiamo osservare nei giochi di colore di alcune composizioni surreali di **Juan Miró**.

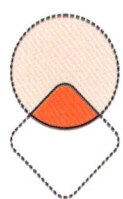

7. Compenetrazione

Avviene quando una forma attraversa l'altra, creando un risultato composito, come vediamo nel tavolino dell'architetto e designer olandese **Gerrit Rietveld**: semplici piani geometrici si incastrano in perfetto equilibrio.

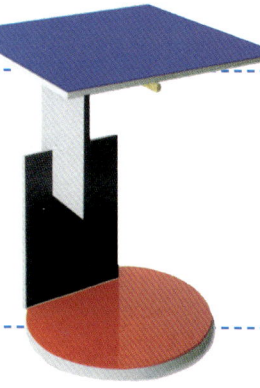

LA DIREZIONE

La direzione delle figure dipende da come queste si relazionano con l'osservatore, ma anche dalla cornice del quadro (o del campo visivo) e dal rapporto con le forme più vicine.

In molte composizioni, sia figurative che astratte, si nota immediatamente la direzione prevalente che l'artista vuole farci percorrere con lo sguardo e con il pensiero.

Ciò può avvenire in vari modi, ad esempio modificando le dimensioni delle figure, deformandone leggermente e progressivamente l'aspetto o conferendo alla composizione un forte senso di dinamicità.

André Derain, *Imbarcazioni sulla Senna*, 1906. Parigi, Museo Nazionale d'Arte Moderna. La direzione delle barche, dal basso a destra verso l'alto a sinistra, caratterizza in modo deciso la composizione.

Claude Lorrain, *Il giudizio di Paride*, 1645. Olio su tela, 112x150 cm. Washington, National Gallery of Art.

Sotto, particolare dello stesso quadro.

LA COLLOCAZIONE SPAZIALE

Lo spazio dell'immagine non è certo lo spazio della realtà: i segni e le figure, bidimensionali, possiedono una spazialità nel senso che, collocati in un certo modo, suggeriscono una determinata idea di spazio. I problemi dello spazio sono problemi di orientamento, direzione, distanza: sono cioè problemi di profondità.

Gli indicatori spaziali della profondità, secondo quanto suggeriscono le leggi della percezione visiva, sono i seguenti:
1. grandezza relativa;
2. sovrapposizione delle forme;
3. prospettiva lineare, con la convergenza di linee parallele
4. gradienti di profondità del colore (i colori interagiscono tra loro);
5. intensità e modulazione della texture di superficie (il "pieno" ci sembra più vicino del "vuoto");
6. collocazione degli oggetti in primo piano nella parte inferiore del quadro, presso la linea di terra.

Quasi tutti questi **indici di profondità** (schematizzati *sotto* ed esemplificati alla *pagina seguente*) sono di facile comprensione. Un discorso particolare merita il **gradiente di profondità del colore**, cioè il graduale e progressivo variare di intensità del chiaroscuro, del colore o della texture. In un paesaggio, ad esempio, i piani più lontani avranno minor intensità cromatica e la tendenza a toni più freddi e sfumati (la cosiddetta *prospettiva aerea*), mentre il colore caldo (ad esempio il rosso) tende ad "avvicinarsi" rispetto a uno freddo (come il blu o il verde).

1. Grandezza relativa

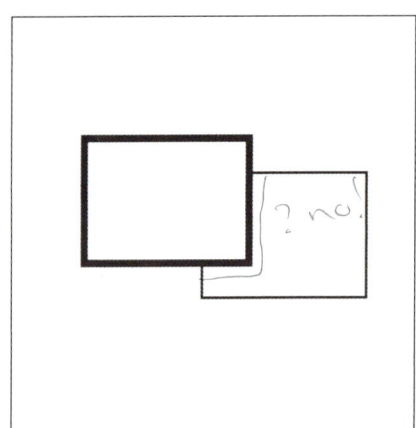

2. Sovrapposizione delle forme

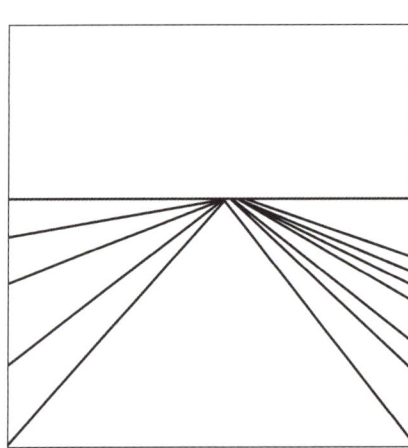

3. Effetto prospettico

4. Interazione del colore

5. Intensità texture (vuoto-pieno)

6. Vicinanza alla Linea di Terra.

1. Grandezza relativa

2. Sovrapposizione delle forme

4. Interazione del colore

3. Effetto prospettico

5. Intensità texture (vuoto-pieno)

6. Vicinanza alla Linea di Terra.

L.O.

L.T.

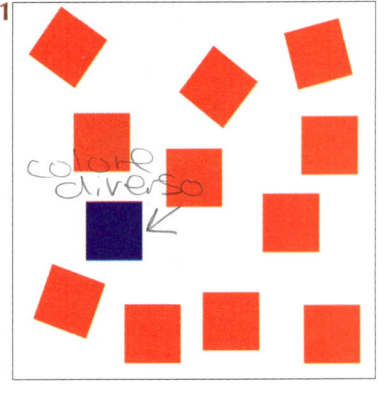

colore diverso

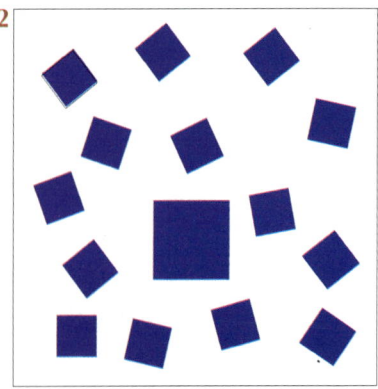

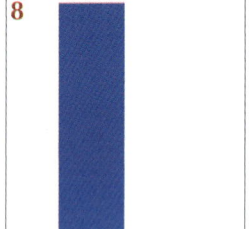

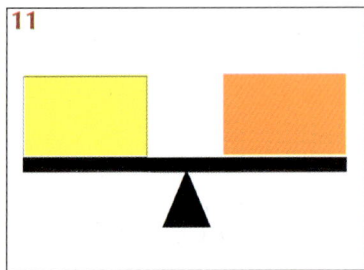

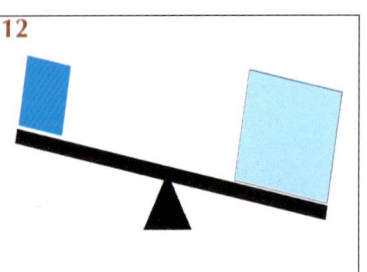

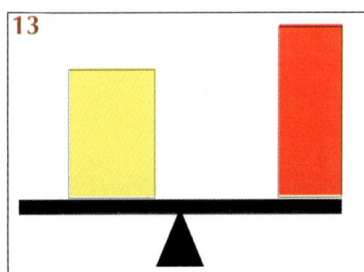

IL PESO E L'EQUILIBRIO

Nella comunicazione visiva il peso è inteso in senso percettivo e psicologico, non certo in senso fisico. Per l'esattezza, si riferisce all'impressione di leggerezza o gravità che riceviamo dalla composizione delle forme nel campo visivo.

Il peso richiama anche il problema dell'equilibrio delle masse, un vero e proprio bilanciamento delle figure, studiato per attirare l'attenzione al centro della composizione, oppure per spezzare questo equilibrio e creare maggior dinamicità.

Gli elementi in gioco, a questo proposito, sono la forma delle figure, la dimensione, la posizione e il colore, come già evidenziato dalle **leggi della Gestalt** sulla percezione visiva (*pag. 15 e seguenti*).

Osservando, ad esempio, gli *schemi a lato*, possiamo fare alcune osservazioni per ciascuna figura:

1. il peso visivo è determinato dal **colore** blu del quadrato, che predomina sugli altri rossi;
2. in questo caso è la **dimensione** del quadrato più grande che attira la nostra attenzione;
3. qui è da notare la particolare **posizione** del quadrato che diventa rombo;
4. in questo caso è la differenza di forma (cerchio anziché quadrato) che sposta il peso al centro.

Per quanto riguarda l'**equilibrio compositivo**, le figure 5-10 sintetizzano le varie possibilità:

5. equilibrio perfettamente statico;
6. situazione di forte squilibrio;
7. tensione orizzontale;
8. slancio e tensione verticale;
9. equilibrio instabile;
10. tensione direzionale verso destra.

Per l'equilibrio, è possibile applicare anche le leggi della fisica, posizionando le forme su una bilancia. Avremo allora:

11. forme e dimensioni uguali, in perfetto equilibrio;
12. peso maggiore verso destra;
13. equilibrio dettato dalla collocazione delle figure (diverse per dimensione) rispetto al perno della bilancia, cioè all'asse di simmetria centrale del campo visivo;
14. squilibrio dovuto all'inserimento di un punto forte (il rettangolo verde) nella parte destra.

Questi schemi trovano senso quando li riconosciamo all'interno delle varie immagini: opere d'arte, fotografie, pubblicità, come proposto alla *pagina seguente*.

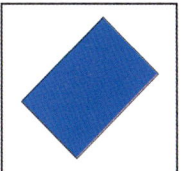

Situazione di forte squilibrio.

Equilibrio instabile.

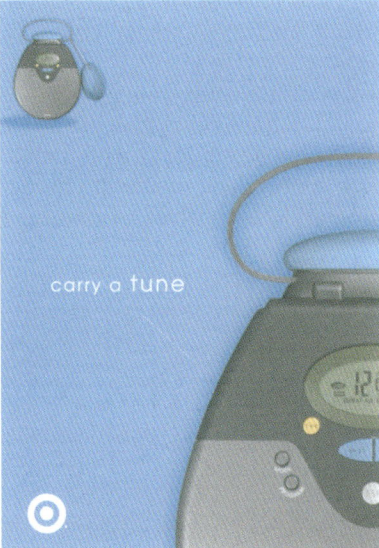

Peso maggiore verso destra.

Slancio e tensione verticale.

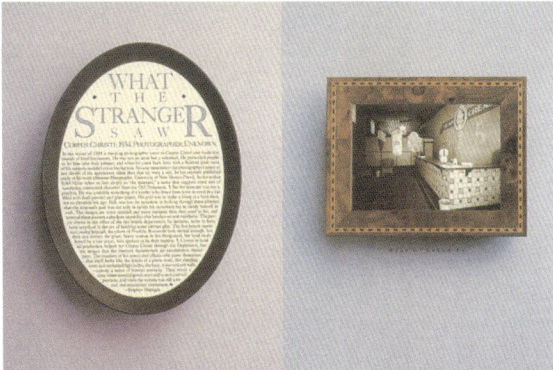

Equilibrio tra figure diverse.

Tensione orizzontale.

NUCLEI E LINEE DI FORZA

All'interno del campo visivo si creano quasi spontaneamente nuclei o raggruppamenti di figure e forme, oppure si impongono linee di forza prevalenti, più o meno evidenti, in relazione al formato della cornice e ai contenuti dell'immagine.

Nell'opera *Musica* di **Matisse**, ad esempio, sono ben evidenti i nuclei della composizione, determinati dai cinque personaggi ben distinti e separati tra loro, disposti in un prato in leggera pendenza e in posizioni diverse per dare il giusto equilibrio alla composizione.

Analizzando l'immagine di *San Pietro*, dipinta da **El Greco**, **Johannes Itten** ha realizzato, su un quaderno di appunti, uno schema della struttura geometrica portante dell'opera, inserendola in un rettangolo, con in bella evidenza le linee di forza che evidenziano gli andamenti della composizione.

Inoltre, usando un tratteggio più o meno fitto, ha differenziato le zone chiare da quelle scure, poiché il chiaroscuro è uno degli elementi che determinano il peso visivo.

Henry Matisse,
La musica,1909-10.
Olio su tela, 260x391 cm.
San Pietroburgo,
Museo dell'Ermitage.

El Greco, *San Pietro*,1603, olio su tela. Madrid, Escorial.
Al centro possiamo osservare un disegno di **Johannes Itten**, con l'analisi della struttura geometrica e del chiaroscuro dell'opera, ottenuto ricalcando l'immagine da un libro, con l'uso della carta da lucido.

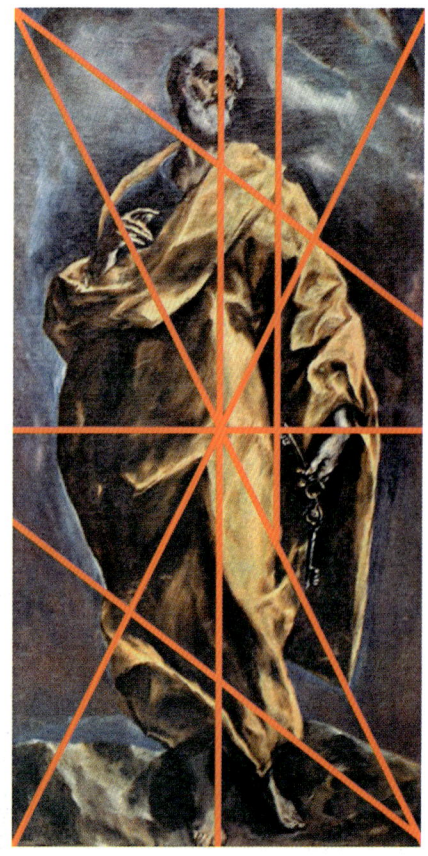

Guido Reni, Davide e Golia.

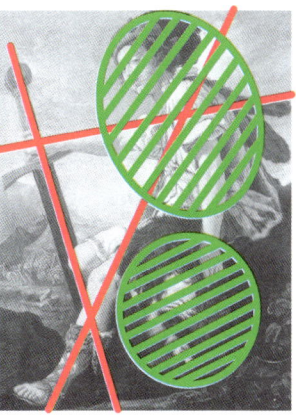

Henri Matisse, Natura morta.

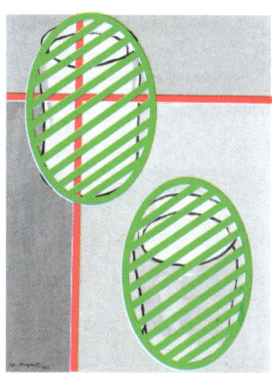

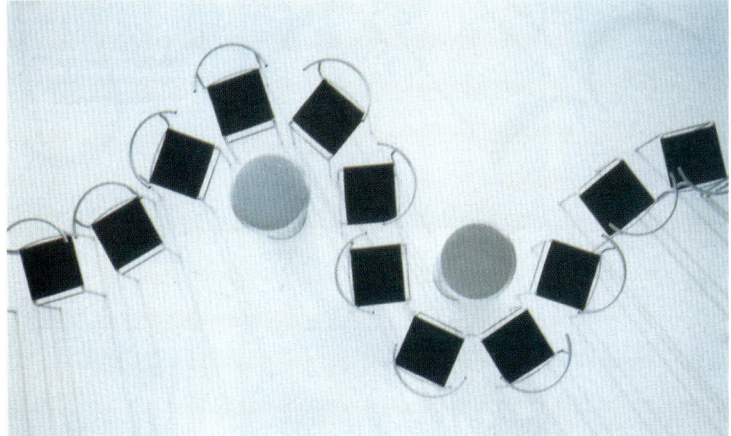

Pubblicità di un'azienda che produce mobili.

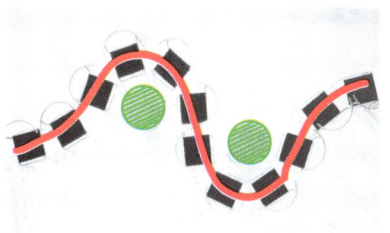

Pubblicità di pasta alimentare.

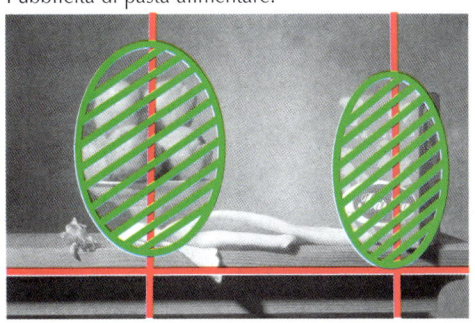

L'ESPRESSIVITÀ DELLA COMPOSIZIONE

Anche la composizione possiede forte valenza espressiva ed emotiva. Scegliendo una certa struttura compositiva, l'artista può trasmettere un senso di equilibrio e armonia, oppure di violenza e di disagio, al di là della riconoscibilità delle immagini e della scelta di forme e colori.

Modellizzando la composizione attraverso uno schema, possiamo compiere alcune osservazioni.

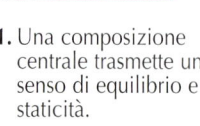

1. Una composizione centrale trasmette un senso di equilibrio e staticità.

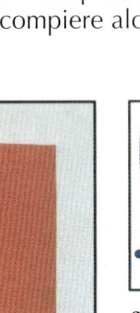

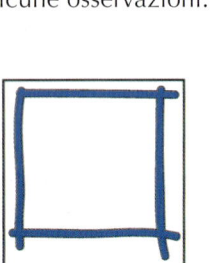

2. Se la figura occupa, in prevalenza, il perimetro del quadro dà un senso di espansione, di ampiezza quasi oppressiva.

3. La diagonale determin[a] dinamismo e instabilit[à] ascensionale (dal bass[o] a sinistra verso l'alto a destra) e viceversa.

4. La composizione radiale denota importanza e attrae verso il centro.

5. Se il nucleo visivo è nella parte inferiore si ha un senso di pesantezza.

6. Viceversa, se il nucleo visivo è collocato in alto trasmette un senso di leggerezza, agilità, volo.

7. La collocazione latera[le] crea squilibrio visivo.

al centro lei
sarebbe troppo statica

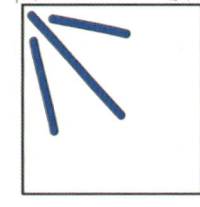

8. Se la composizione è in prevalenza angolata, si ha un senso di direzionalità e movimento, come di un'andata o un ritorno.

9. La composizione simm[e]trica dà un senso di n[eu]tralità ed equilibrio, m[a] spesso è scarsamente espressiva.

toulouse lautrec

IL MOVIMENTO: STATICITÀ E DINAMISMO

In genere, nella composizione visiva, viene spontaneo associare alla prevalenza di un **andamento orizzontale** l'idea di **calma e staticità**, ad un **andamento verticale** l'idea di **equilibrio ascensionale** e ad **andamenti diagonali** o **irregolari** e contorti il senso di **movimento**.

Infatti, certe forme possono suggerire un effetto di **movimento** e indirizzare la nostra attenzione verso determinate direzioni. Ciò dipende dalla loro posizione e da alcuni elementi visivi, che, attraverso la nostra esperienza, colleghiamo al moto: per esempio, se una nave lascia una scia sull'acqua ipotizziamo che stia navigando.

Anche la **direzione dello sguardo** del personaggio di un ritratto, ad esempio, può suggerire all'osservatore un'irresistibile direzione visiva.

Analogamente, alcuni oggetti in **posizione obliqua** suggeriscono l'idea di una direzione o di un movimento (almeno potenziale), dato che deviano dalla posizione di riposo, cioè da quella verticale (ad esempio, per una bottiglia) oppure orizzontale (ad esempio, per un aereo).

Un altro interessante indicatore del movimento è la linea curva o a spirale: nella scultura barocca, ad esempio, la torsione esasperata dei corpi conferisce grande dinamicità alla forma compositiva.

In alto: **Luigi Russolo**, *La rivolta*, 1913. Olio su tela, 104x140cm. L'artista, esponente del Futurismo, visualizza con chiarezza l'incedere della folla in rivolta che, come una freccia, avanza verso sinistra e si incunea nello spazio, creando un moto ad ondate successive. Le linee spezzate sovrapposte evidenziano lo schema compositivo, dettato dall'idea di movimento.

Sopra: il dinamismo di un cavallo al trotto è evidenziato, dal fotografo, mediante una leggera sfocatura dello sfondo, delle zampe del cavallo e della ruota del sulky.

Étienne-Jules Marey, *Volo di gabbiani* 1887. Bronzo. Museo di Beaune. Questa curiosa scultura in bronzo materializza in immagini successive il movimento del volo di un uccello.

Immagine dal fumetto *The rocketeer* di **Dave Steavens**. L'eroe è immobile o in movimento? Da cosa lo si capisce?

SIMMETRIA E ASIMMETRIA

Il senso dell'ordine: la simmetria

Osserviamo l'immagine frontale di un'automobile e proviamo a dividerla esattamente in due parti mediante una linea verticale (asse).

Piegando le due parti lungo la linea e sovrapponendole, possiamo verificare che esse corrispondono perfettamente: è il caso più tipico di **simmetria assiale**.

Si ha **simmetria** in un oggetto, in una struttura o in un insieme di forme, quando gli elementi che li compongono si dispongono in esatta corrispondenza (per dimensione, collocazione o forma) rispetto a un punto, a un asse o a un piano.

La simmetria comunica il senso dell'ordine, per cui, anche a livello psicologico, essa ci sembra "buona", ci mette a nostro agio. Il termine **simmetria** deriva dal greco *"symmetria"*, che significava *ben commisurato, ben proporzionato* e che veniva usato sia in senso morale sia in senso geometrico e spaziale. Aristotele si riferisce, con questo termine, al giusto fine a cui dovrebbero tendere gli uomini virtuosi nelle loro azioni: la simmetria, infatti, ci educa all'ordine, alla regolarità.

Secondo la matematica, le operazioni di simmetria sono quelle trasformazioni che lasciano immutato un oggetto nello spazio. Nel piano i quattro movimenti rigidi che permettono di muovere una figura senza alterarne le dimensioni sono la **traslazione**, la **riflessione** rispetto ad un asse, la **glissoriflessione**, che è una **riflessione con scorrimento**, e la **rotazione** rispetto ad un punto.

Simmetria speculare di una farfalla: il mondo naturale presenta numerose forme di simmetria, facilmente individuabili.

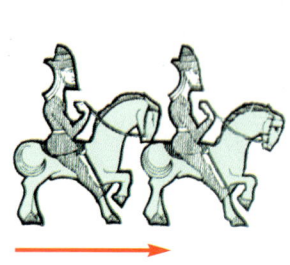
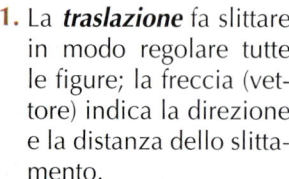

1. La **traslazione** fa slittare in modo regolare tutte le figure; la freccia (vettore) indica la direzione e la distanza dello slittamento.

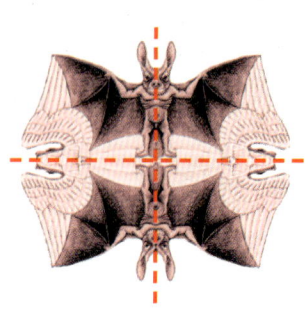

2. La **riflessione** trasforma le figure in immagini speculari rispetto ad una retta, l'asse di riflessione. Qui si evidenzia una duplice riflessione, rispetto ad un asse orizzontale e ad uno verticale.

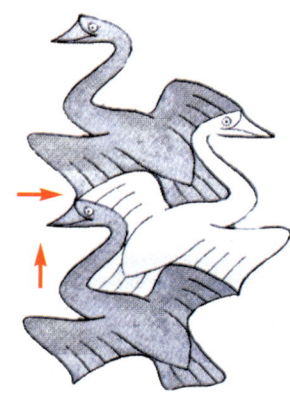

3. La **simmetria di scorrimento** è una trasformazione in due gradi: una traslazione lungo un vettore viene seguita da una riflessione attorno ad un asse, parallelo alla figura.

4. La **rotazione** fa girare le figure attorno ad un punto fisso, il centro di rotazione: in questo caso, una lucertola ruota di 90° rispetto all'altra.

Georges Seurat, *La parata del circo*, 1888. Olio su tela,
100x150 cm. New York, Metropolitan Museum.

La composizione dell'opera di Seurat è basata sulla sezione aurea. Infatti, tracciando la diagonale dall'alto a sinistra fino in basso a destra, si intercetta il lato del quadrato in corrispondenza della balconata orizzontale.
Altri rettangoli aurei, più piccoli, si possono individuare a destra della verticale presso il musicista, che è esattamente al centro della composizione, mentre le altre figure sono collocate in punti nodali o lungo linee strategiche.

La regola dei terzi, in fotografia

Nella fotografia, soprattutto quella di paesaggio, vige la regola di dividere idealmente *in tre parti* il campo visivo (cioè il fotogramma, che misura 24x36 mm per le pellicole reflex) mediante linee strutturali, sulle quali collocare i punti di maggior interesse della composizione.

In tal modo, pur non raggiungendo l'armonia della sezione aurea, la fotografia comunica un senso di ordine e di equilibrio, che l'osservatore percepisce come un elemento di valore estetico per l'immagine.

Ciò vale, naturalmente, anche per i messaggi visivi della pubblicità.

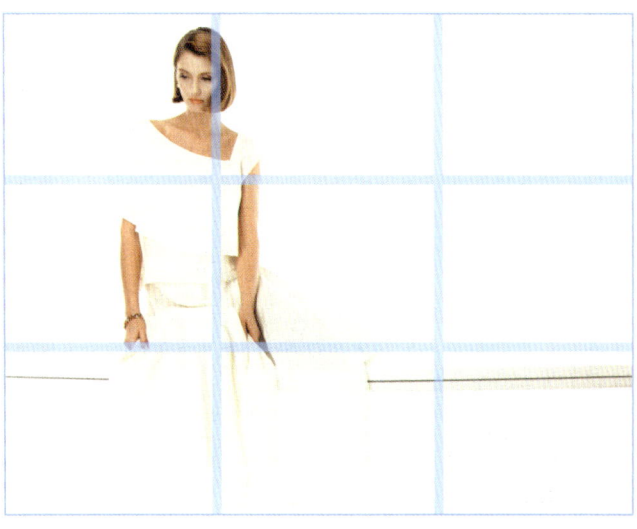

LEGGERE LA COMPOSIZIONE

L'Assunzione della Vergine di Tiziano

La straordinaria pala d'altare dell'*Assunta* è impostata da Tiziano su tre registri sovrapposti: in quello superiore si colloca la figura di Dio; al centro è posta Maria, in piedi sulle nuvole e attorniata dagli angeli festanti; in basso si trovano gli apostoli che assistono all'evento con esibito stupore.

Forme e dimensioni	Colore e texture

L'insieme dei fattori indicati costituisce la struttura compositiva, da evidenziare mediante schemi grafici.

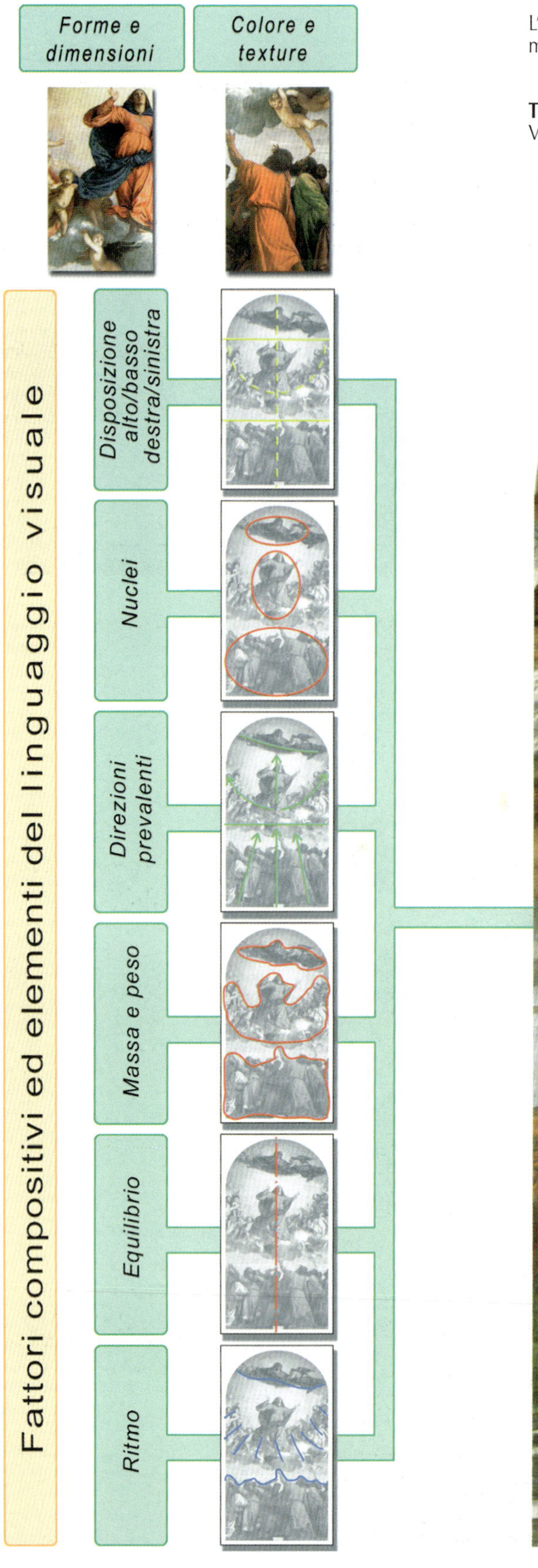

Tiziano, *Assunzione della Vergine*, 1516-18. Olio su tavola, 690x360 cm. Venezia, Chiesa di Santa Maria Gloriosa dei Frari.

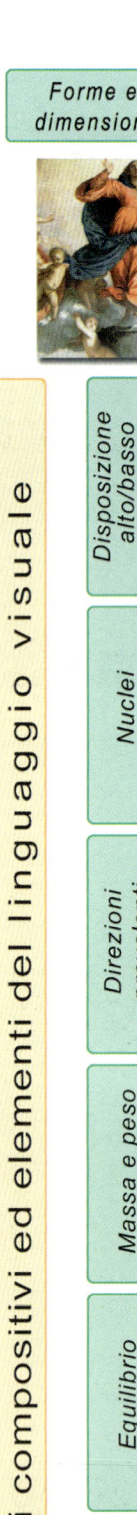

Fattori compositivi ed elementi del linguaggio visuale

Disposizione alto/basso destra/sinistra

Nuclei

Direzioni prevalenti

Massa e peso

Equilibrio

Ritmo

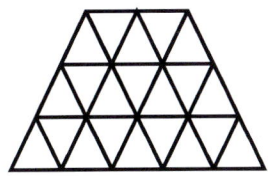

Esempio di
composizione modulare

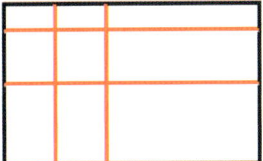

Esempio di
divisione armonica

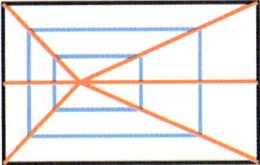

Possibile organizzazione
delle direzioni prospettiche

Struttura compositiva dell'opera

In relazione ai fattori compositivi predominanti, possiamo sovrapporre diverse strutture geometriche all'opera: alcune determinano varie zone, altre indicano i piani di profondità, altre segnano ritmi o la presenza di moduli ripetuti, ecc. Riportiamo a lato tre schemi di riferimento, utili a individuare l'organizzazione complessiva di un'opera:

- composizione modulare;
- divisione armonica;
- direzioni prospettiche.

Valori espressivi dell'opera

Le immediate, spontanee emozioni trasmesse da quest'opera non dipendono esclusivamente dal suo tema, ma anche da:

- qualità del disegno, dei materiali e della tecnica utilizzata dall'artista;
- grandi dimensioni del quadro: le figure sono a grandezza naturale;
- qualità espressive degli elementi del linguaggio visuale, cioè linee morbide ed avvolgenti, colori saturi, caldi e luminosi, senso ascensionale dello spazio, luce radiosa della divinità;
- forte prospettiva dal basso;
- struttura compositiva gerarchica (dall'alto verso il basso) che rafforza il significato religioso del quadro.

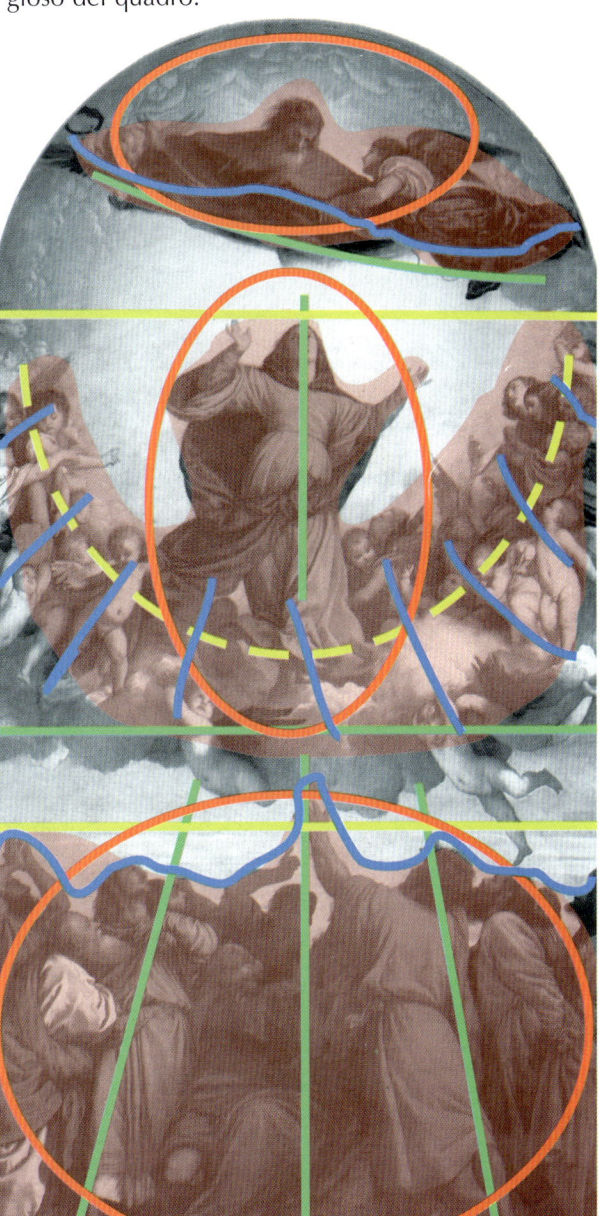

NELLA PARTE ALTA
spiritualità, dinamismo,
vibrazione di luce, festosità

NELL'INSIEME
grandiosità, spettacolarità,
dinamismo, equilibrio delle
masse, varietà di personaggi

NELLA PARTE BASSA
movimento, stupore, equilibrio
delle masse, varietà nella
disposizione dei personaggi

Modello generale di analisi compositiva delle immagini nelle arti visive

1. Analisi degli elementi compositivi di un'immagine

Gli aspetti compositivi, insieme a quelli del colore, sono sicuramente i più importanti nell'ambito della lettura e analisi di un'immagine. È quindi opportuno esercitarsi ripetutamente su immagini di varia tipologia e provenienza (opere d'arte, fotografie, pubblicità, illustrazioni), in modo da sviluppare un'adeguata proprietà di linguaggio. In questa pagina puoi osservare due esempi di analisi dell'immagine svolta in relazione agli elementi compositivi. Prova ad eseguire un'analoga lettura utilizzando un'altra immagine presente in questo libro.

A. Pittura

La **simmetria assiale** è ben evidente nel dipinto: l'asse corrisponde alla posizione della Madonna col Bambino.

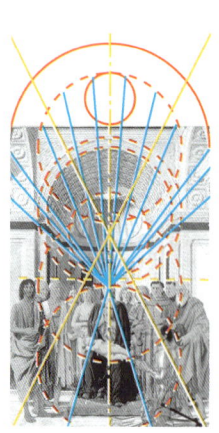

Un **modulo** decorativo (un fiore a 5 petali inserito in un quadrato) viene ripetuto nella volta dell'abside.

La **struttura geometrica** è chiara e armonica: il centro della composizione e il punto di fuga prospettico sono posti in corrispondenza del volto di Maria.

La composizione è **statica**: i gruppi di santi, disposti ad emiciclo, sono in perfetto equilibrio; il **peso** visivo è verso il basso, dove c'è il gruppo di persone.

Un cenno di **dinamismo** è dato dalla posizione del Bambino e dalla collocazione del donatore, Federico II di Montefeltro, posto in ginocchio.

Piero della Francesca, *Madonna col bambino, angeli e Santi (pala di Montefeltro)*, 1472, 248x170 cm. Milano, Pinacoteca di Brera.

B. Fotografia

La composizione è in perfetto **equilibrio**, grazie alla **simmetria orizzontale** (segnata dal profilo del mare a metà immagine) e a quella **radiale** delle pale del mulino, collocato al centro dell'immagine.

Il **ritmo** è segnato dalle pale del mulino e dallo zig zag dei **moduli** regolari delle saline.

Il **peso** visivo è concentrato al centro, in corrispondenza della figura del mulino, e aumenta verso il basso, dove si disegnano le saline.

La composizione è statica: solo il riverbero del sole sull'acqua crea un leggero senso di **movimento**.

Franco Fontana, *Sicilia*, 1992.

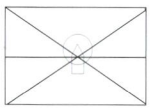 La struttura geometrica evidenzia la posizione centrale del mulino.

U.A. 5 — LE TECNICHE DELL'ARTE

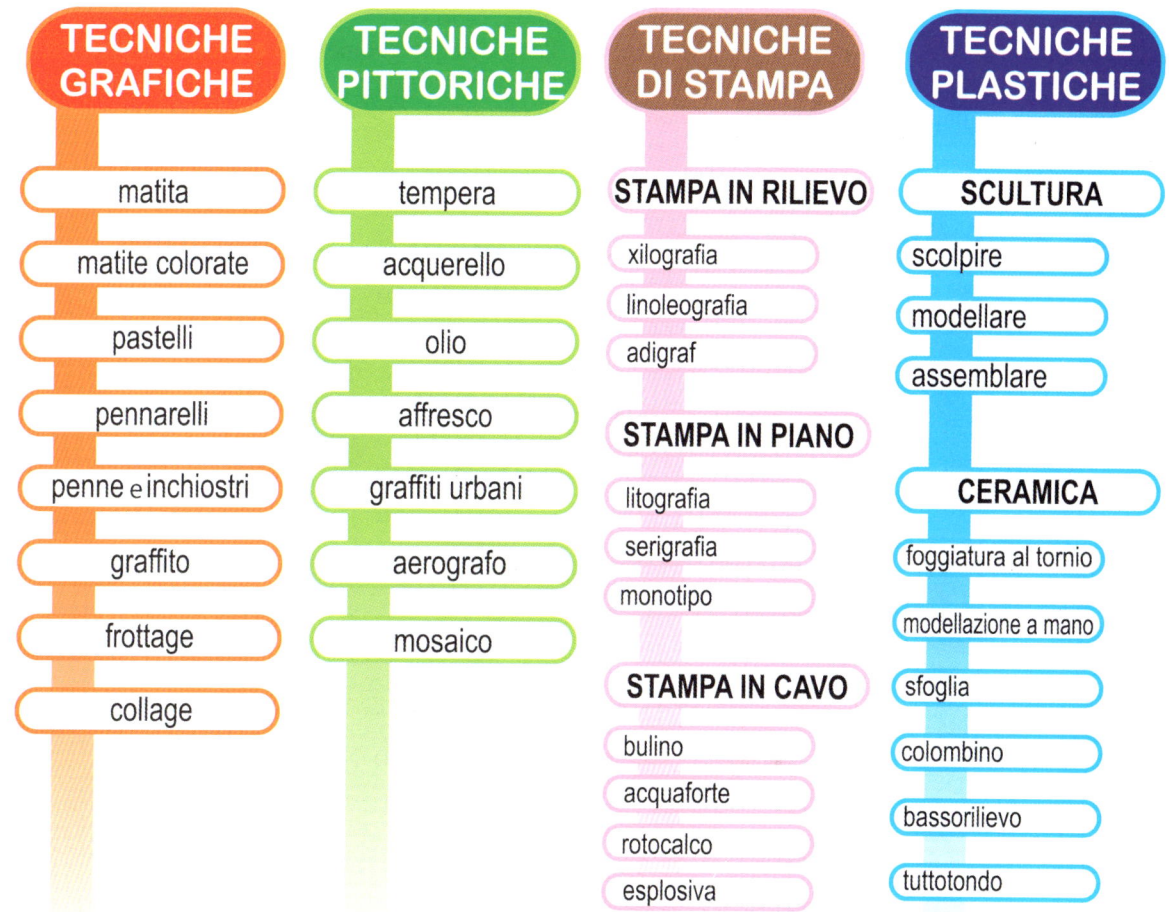

TECNICHE GRAFICHE
- matita
- matite colorate
- pastelli
- pennarelli
- penne e inchiostri
- graffito
- frottage
- collage

TECNICHE PITTORICHE
- tempera
- acquerello
- olio
- affresco
- graffiti urbani
- aerografo
- mosaico

TECNICHE DI STAMPA

STAMPA IN RILIEVO
- xilografia
- linoleografia
- adigraf

STAMPA IN PIANO
- litografia
- serigrafia
- monotipo

STAMPA IN CAVO
- bulino
- acquaforte
- rotocalco
- esplosiva

TECNICHE PLASTICHE

SCULTURA
- scolpire
- modellare
- assemblare

CERAMICA
- foggiatura al tornio
- modellazione a mano
- sfoglia
- colombino
- bassorilievo
- tuttotondo

GLOSSARIO DEI TERMINI TECNICI

Ogni tecnica esige strumenti e materiali propri ed una terminologia specifica. Esistono però alcuni termini ricorrenti, da conoscere e memorizzare. Ti sarà quindi utile consultare questo piccolo dizionario.

Abbozzo Forma iniziale di un'opera, già in grado di suggerirne l'aspetto definitivo.

Andamento (lineare) Modo e direzione in cui vengono tracciate delle linee (rette, spezzate, curve).

Campitura Superficie omogenea di colore o texture.

Chiaroscuro Modellazione delle forme attraverso il disegno o il colore, per mettere in evidenza le ombre e le luci.

Contrasto Accostamento di elementi diversi (grafici, cromatici, forme, materiali, ecc.) in modo da determinare un risalto reciproco.

Gradazione tonale Passaggio progressivo di luminosità o di intensità di uno stesso colore.

Modellatura o **foggiatura** Procedimento del *dar forma* ad un materiale, partendo dal suo stato grezzo.

Ombreggiatura Rappresentazione delle ombre degli oggetti sul piano pittorico, in modo da rendere l'effetto dello spazio e del volume; si realizza con il chiaroscuro, il tratteggio, lo sfumato.

Plastico (effetto) Percezione della tridimensionalità, propria della scultura. In pittura o nelle arti grafiche si ottiene attraverso il chiaroscuro.

Puntinato Tecnica di riempimento di una superficie mediante l'accostamento, più o meno fitto, di punti.

Sgrossatura Fase iniziale del procedimento scultoreo, ottenuta generalmente con lo scalpello.

Sovrapposizione Stesura successiva di strati di colore. In relazione alle tecniche utilizzate si ottiene miscelazione, trasparenza, velatura o copertura dello strato sottostante.

Sfumato Passaggio graduale da un tono all'altro di colore, o tra zone a diverso grado di luminosità.

Tratteggio Accostamento di linee parallele o incrociate tra loro. Può determinare campiture omogenee o effetti di gradazione tonale.

Velatura Stesura di un colore su un altro già asciutto, in modo da lasciarlo trasparire.

MATITA

La **matita** è costituita da una **mina**, composta da un impasto di argilla e grafite, racchiusa entro un involucro cilindrico in legno. Strofinata su un foglio di carta, la mina lascia un segno di colore grigio o nero, in relazione alla sua *durezza* e alla consistenza del foglio, che può essere liscio o ruvido.

Il disegno a matita è ideale per la sua rapidità, per la facilità di correzione e le possibilità espressive.

Fino al XVI secolo gli artisti utilizzavano, per disegnare, la **punta d'argento**, la **mina a piombo** (su pergamena), la **sanguigna** (impasto di argilla ferrosa dal colore rossastro)

oppure il **carboncino**, dal grosso e morbido tratto.

Modalità d'uso e possibilità espressive

Le mine sono presenti in diverse gradazioni, dalla **8B** alla **9H**, che definiscono le caratteristiche del segno. Questo risulta sempre più morbido e pastoso procedendo nella serie delle B, chiaro e netto utilizzando le mine più dure della serie H.

Per il **disegno geometrico e tecnico** si preferisce la matita a pulsante, un corpo di metallo o plastica da cui la mina fuoriesce premendo un pulsante a molla.

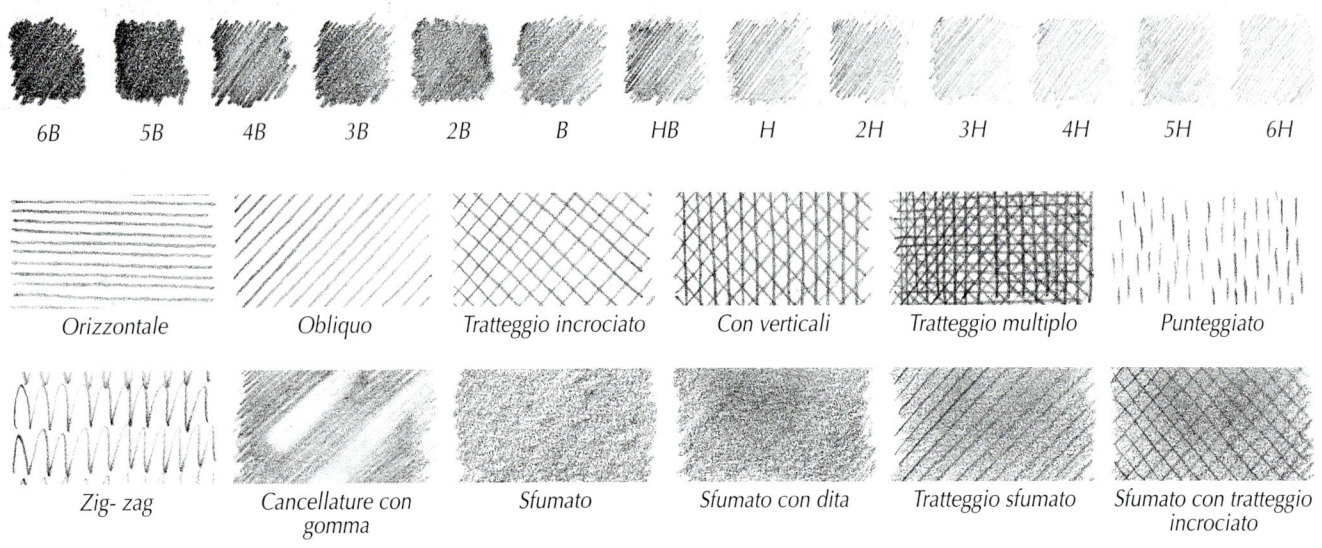

6B   5B   4B   3B   2B   B   HB   H   2H   3H   4H   5H   6H

Orizzontale   Obliquo   Tratteggio incrociato   Con verticali   Tratteggio multiplo   Punteggiato

Zig- zag   Cancellature con gomma   Sfumato   Sfumato con dita   Tratteggio sfumato   Sfumato con tratteggio incrociato

Nel *Ritratto di ignoto* di **Jean Clouet** (1535 circa), il contorno e i tratti principali del volto sono segnati da una morbida linea continua. Tratteggi leggeri individuano le parti in ombra; segni paralleli o diversamente incrociati definiscono il copricapo e la massa compatta dei capelli. Con la sanguigna l'artista ha reso l'effetto dell'incarnato, mentre piccole cancellature evidenziano le parti in luce.

Nei due studi a matita realizzati da **Georges Seurat** nel 1884, preparatori dell'opera *La grande jatte*, sono riconoscibili le potenzialità espressive di questa tecnica: la *Giovane donna con ombrello*, a destra, si delinea come una massa scura sul fondo quasi intatto della carta; la *Bambina bianca*, al contrario, sembra emergere dall'ombra. L'effetto è ottenuto lasciando bianca una parte del foglio, o attraverso opportune cancellature. La matita è molto tenera, su supporto ruvido.

MATITE COLORATE

Le matite colorate (da non confondere con i pastelli), rappresentano un mezzo artistico relativamente recente, di facile utilizzo ed elevata versatilità. Come nel caso della matita a grafite, un sottile cilindro, composto da materie coloranti impastate con acqua e sostanze agglutinanti, viene inserito entro un involucro cavo.

Il loro utilizzo ha sostituito progressivamente quello delle tradizionali tecniche del carboncino o della sanguigna, in cui gli effetti coloristici erano affidati prevalentemente alla ricchezza dei toni chiaroscurali, arricchiti da tocchi di bianco o di gesso.

Modalità d'uso e possibilità espressive

Le matite colorate offrono la possibilità di ottenere splendidi effetti cromatici, mantenendo la rapidità e la facilità del gesto tecnico.

In relazione al loro grado di morbidezza, esse consentono effetti espressivi altamente differenziati: campiture omogenee e coprenti, sovrapposizioni o morbide sfumature, volta a volta vicine agli effetti del carboncino, del pastello, dell'acquerello. In molti casi, infatti, esse sono diluibili con acqua, tanto da poter essere utilizzate come matite per dipingere.

     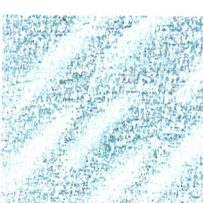

Tratti paralleli orizzontali | Gradazione di toni, ottenuta aumentando la pressione | Sovrapposizione di un colore chiaro su uno scuro | Tratteggio incrociato | Texture ottenuta con tratteggi in diverse direzioni | Cancellatura parziale con colpi di gomma

Pressione del dito sul pigmento macinato | Campitura mediante sovrapposizione di tratteggi leggeri | Matita acquerellabile e matita a tratto: quattro diverse soluzioni espressive.

David Hockney, *Celia con le maniche a quadri*, 1973.

Il risultato realistico è ottenuto, in questo ritratto, attraverso un utilizzo differenziato del mezzo grafico: il volto è disegnato con sfumature leggere; occhi e bocca sono invece tracciati con segni più incisivi. I capelli sono definiti da tratteggi e andamenti curvilinei eseguiti con almeno tre colori diversi, diversamente addensati.

Luigi Russolo, *senza titolo*, 1912. Il pittore futurista Russolo ha accentuato l'effetto di spazialità dato dal disegno in prospettiva (linee convergenti) attraverso la gradazione dei toni di blu.

PASTELLI

I pastelli sono bastoncini a sezione circolare o quadrata, composti di pigmenti colorati finemente macinati e mescolati in acqua con argilla e gomma arabica. Possono essere più o meno duri e contenere sostanze a base di **cera** o **olio**.

Questa tecnica ebbe larga diffusione in particolare a partire dal XVIII secolo, quando si affermò la moda del *ritratto a pastello*, caratterizzato da atmosfere eleganti e rarefatte, trovando poi spazio, nel XIX secolo, nell'ambito della *pittura impressionista* e *simbolista*.

Modalità d'uso e possibilità espressive

I colori non sono mescolabili tra loro ma, sovrapposti in successive stesure, consentono di ottenere atmosfere leggere e sfumate.

Vanno però distinti i *pastelli ad olio* dai *pastelli a cera*: i primi, più morbidi, sono adatti a realizzare campiture compatte, lucide e pastose. Utilizzati su supporti colorati, consentono effetti di particolare vivacità e brillantezza. I pastelli a cera sono meno compatti, quindi si sgranano con facilità se usati su una superficie ruvida.

Completato il disegno, è necessario fissare il colore o proteggerne la superficie con un vetro.

PASTELLI A OLIO

| Gradazione ottenuta aumentando la pressione | Tratteggi incrociati | Sovrapposizione parziale di colori complementari | Macchie ottenute esercitando diverse pressioni | Asporto con raschietto |

PASTELLI A CERA

| Passaggio graduale tra colori vicini | Tratteggi incrociati | Macchie | Unico colore con diverse intensità | Asporto con raschietto su strati di colori sovrapposti |

Odilon Redon, *Fiori*, 1890 circa.
Redon ha sfruttato il colore del supporto, accostando e sovrapponendo toni contrastanti. Grazie alle trasparenze consentite dal pastello, i fiori sembrano svanire in figure vaporose e leggere, con effetti cari alla sensibilità simbolista.

Edgar Degas, *Ballerine dietro le quinte*, 1897 circa.
La volontà di cogliere con immediatezza immagini appartenenti alla realtà del proprio tempo ha spinto il pittore impressionista Edgar Degas ad utilizzare ampiamente il pastello: questa tecnica, infatti, gli consentiva sovrapposizioni di colore in grado di rendere la vibrazione della luce sui corpi; la velocità del tratto grafico, inoltre, determina efficaci effetti di movimento.

PENNE E INCHIOSTRI

La penna con inchiostro di china è lo strumento ideale per tracciare un disegno nitido e preciso. Un tempo si usavano penne d'oca o di bambù, poi cannucce con pennini di varia forma: oggi si usano moderne penne per il disegno artistico (tipo graphos) o tecnico (tipo rapidograph).

L'inchiostro di china è nero e brillante: asciugando lascia una superficie compatta. Non è cancellabile; al limite si gratta leggermente la superficie con una lametta.

Per la grafica sono molto usati inchiostri colorati trasparenti (ecoline), piuttosto costosi: sono diluibili in acqua e si possono combinare tra loro per ottenere effetti acquerellati.

La penna a sfera (o biro) può sostituire, in alcune applicazioni, la penna a china.

Modalità d'uso e possibilità espressive

La penna con pennino consente di realizzare un segno variabile a seconda della forma e dello spessore della punta, del movimento e della pressione della mano.

Il rapidograph traccia linee uniformi, di spessore variabile in relazione alla dimensione della punta, anche sottilissime (diam. 0,1 mm.).

L'inchiostro di china consente comunque effetti originali, se usato a pennello, a spruzzo, per sgocciolamento, su carta bagnata ecc.

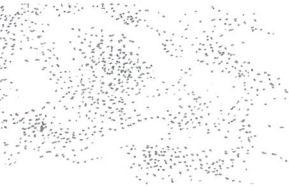

Puntinato

Tratteggio

Andamenti lineari

Texture a maglia, linee, tratti

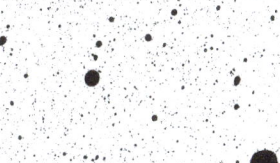

Inchiostro soffiato

Inchiostro spruzzato

Sfumatura con diluzione con acqua

Stesura a pennello su carta asciutta

Vincent van Gogh ha realizzato molti disegni a china, in particolare vedute di soggetti naturali o urbani. Questa tecnica gli consentiva di realizzare con evidenza ed immediatezza le diverse parti del paesaggio, attraverso una fitta texturizzazione della superficie.
Nell'opera a lato (*Arles, campi di grano*, 1888) i segni, ora sottili ora spessi, sono tracciati con punte di diversa dimensione. Un fitto puntinato caratterizza il cielo; soffici segni ondulati indicano il fumo delle ciminiere. Tratteggi ad andamento diverso, più fitti in lontananza e più ariosi in primo piano, descrivono i campi durante la mietitura e i covoni di grano. Brevi segni paralleli individuano i tetti delle case, contrastando con la superficie chiara dei muri.

PENNARELLI

Prodotti solo di recente, i pennarelli sono costituiti da un **involucro di plastica** che contiene un feltro **imbevuto di colore**. La punta, di solito in nylon, può essere di varia forma e dimensione.

I colori, luminosi e vivaci, si possono sovrapporre ma non mescolare: non è possibile quindi ottenere particolari sfumature o effetti di trasparenza, né cancellare.

I pennarelli sono utilissimi per eseguire disegni di rapida esecuzione e di efficacia comunicativa, quali studi e bozzetti per la **grafica pubblicitaria**, per l'**architettura** e l'**illustrazione** in genere.

Le sostanze coloranti, però, tendono a scolorire nel tempo, soprattutto se il disegno viene esposto alla luce.

Modalità d'uso e possibilità espressive

I pennarelli a punta grossa si chiamano anche *marker*, quelli a punta sottile *stilo*, perché il loro segno è simile a quello tracciato da una penna. I pennarelli del tipo *Uniposca* hanno inchiostri coprenti, indelebili e resistenti alla luce.

I diversi tipi di punte esistenti in commercio presentano caratteristiche tecniche diverse: puoi osservare di seguito alcuni degli effetti che si possono ottenere.

1. **Punta conica** fine, a larghezza costante, adatta per contorni e tratteggi

2. **Punta ad ogiva**, che dà buona precisione e varietà di spessore al segno

3. **Punta smussata**, piatta e larga, con notevole varietà di segno

4. **Punta lunga**, come un pennello

 PUNTINATO

 TRATTEGGIO

 SFUMATURE CON ACQUA

Federico Fellini, *Gelsomina*, pennarelli su carta.

Bozzetto di moda: il tratto continuo è tracciato con punta sottile, le pieghe dell'abito con un grosso marker. Le sfumature che danno rilievo alla figura sono ottenute con svelte stesure.

ACQUERELLI

L'acquerello è la **pittura della trasparenza**: i colori, mescolati a gomma arabica e sciolti nell'acqua, vengono stesi con rapidi colpi di pennello morbido (in pelo di martora). Dopo la stesura asciugano rapidamente. Sovrapponendo velature di colore sul foglio ancora bagnato si ottengono toni delicati e trasparenti, con effetti di particolare luminosità. Il colore si schiarisce con acqua e non con il bianco, come avviene invece per le tempere. La tecnica dell'acquerello è molto antica, e già conosciuta in Oriente. In Europa fu impiegata nel Cinquecento da artisti come **Leonardo** e **Dürer**, che la utilizzarono per studi di figure umane o di paesaggio; essa ebbe però ampia diffusione soprattutto nel XVIII secolo, grazie ai pittori paesaggisti inglesi (**Constable**, **Turner**), e poi in età romantica. In epoca moderna fu usato, con risultati del tutto originali, da molti pittori dell'avanguardia: ricordiamo tra tutti **Emil Nolde** e **Paul Klee** (*vedi pag. 106*).

Modalità d'uso e possibilità espressive

Dopo avere realizzato un leggero schizzo a matita si stendono i colori, con rapidità e precisione. L'acquerello non ammette cancellature, quindi non sono possibili ripensamenti o correzioni: per questo è importante, prima di iniziare il lavoro, osservare e sperimentare le diverse possibilità tecniche ed espressive.

Il colore va steso su carta spessa, ruvida o semiruvida; è consigliabile inumidirla e lasciarla asciugare prima dell'utilizzo, per evitare ondulazioni durante l'esecuzione del lavoro ed un eccessivo assorbimento dei colori.

Le gradazioni di tono si realizzano anche per sgocciolatura del colore sul foglio, lasciato asciugare senza interventi ulteriori.

Campitura uniforme, realizzata con pennellate rapide	Sovrapposizione di due colori: blu cobalto + rosso	Sovrapposizione di due colori: giallo + azzurro	Gradazione di tono per successive velature	Espansione del colore su fondo umido	Effetto di bagnato su bagnato

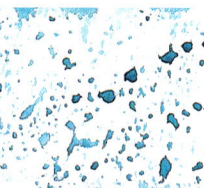

Espansione del colore su carta molto bagnata	Colore diffuso con una spugna	Colori fatti colare e fluire liberamente sul foglio	Macchie simmetriche casuali, su foglio piegato in due	Superficie acquerellata, smerigliata con carta vetrata	Superficie trattata a base di cera e poi acquerellata

John Singer Sargent, *Scuola di San Rocco*, 1903.

TEMPERE

La tecnica della tempera fu diffusamente utilizzata in età medievale. I pigmenti, ricavati da **terre colorate**, venivano mescolati con tuorlo d'**uovo e sostanze collanti** (animali o vegetali) e sciolti in acqua. Si ottenevano colori intensi e dall'elevato valore coprente, rapidi nell'essiccare.

I supporti per la tempera erano, in prevalenza, tavole di legno preparate con uno strato di gesso (*imprimitura*) o superfici murarie.

A partire dalla fine del XIV secolo la tecnica della tempera fu progressivamente sostituita dai colori ad olio, caratterizzati da maggior lucentezza e da originali effetti di trasparenza.

Versione moderna della tempera sono i colori **acrilici**, costituiti da pigmenti legati in una resina sintetica: si sciolgono in acqua e asciugano velocemente; consentono stesure di colore brillanti ed uniformi e resistono alle intemperie, per cui sono adatti anche per **pitture murali**.

Modalità d'uso e possibilità espressive

Acrilici e tempera sono costosi e poco adatti ad un uso scolastico: il termine "tempere" viene genericamente utilizzato anche per indicare un tipo di colori più economici, i colori a **guazzo** (dal francese *gouache*). Simile all'acquarello, il guazzo ha colori mescolati al bianco opaco (*biacca*), per cui risultano più corposi e coprenti.

Si possono utilizzare vari tipi di supporti: cartoncino, tela, tavola di compensato; i pennelli possono avere punta piatta o tonda e sono disponibili in diverse misure, in rapporto al tipo di segno da tracciare (campiture per sfondi, dettagli, sfumature ecc.)

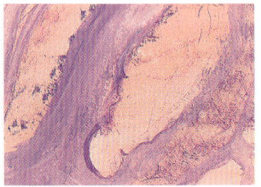

Effetto di marmorizzazione ottenuto con pennello asciutto

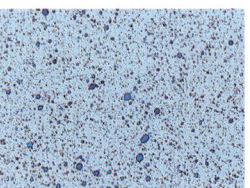

Spruzzo su colore bagnato

Superficie lavorata col profilo di una moneta

Tempera su masonite ricoperta di sabbia e vinavil

Tempera su tavola rivestita di gesso non liscio

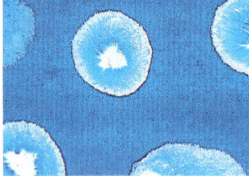

Gocce di bianco su colore bagnato

Quattro studi a gouache di **Sonia Delaunay**.

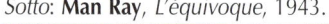

Due esempi di gouache su carta.

A sinistra: **Marc Chagall**, *Bella con il violino*, 1914.

Sotto: **Man Ray**, *L'équivoque*, 1943.

COLORI A OLIO

La tecnica della pittura con i colori ad olio è sicuramente quella più diffusa. I colori sono costituiti da **pigmenti macinati** e **mescolati ad olio di lino**, di **noce o di papavero**, con eventuale aggiunta di trementina per aumentarne la trasparenza. La stesura avviene su **tavola** o, più di frequente, su **tela**, mediante pennelli di setola o di pelo di bue di varie dimensioni, piatti o tondi, ma anche con spatole e altri attrezzi.

Introdotta dai *pittori fiamminghi*, questa tecnica si è diffusa rapidamente in tutta Europa a partire dal XV secolo, prendendo il posto della pittura a tempera. La possibilità di stendere il colore per velature successive permette infatti di realizzare effetti di morbidezza e di trasparenza che le tecniche tradizionali non consentivano. Inoltre, poiché i colori a olio asciugano in un tempo piuttosto lungo, l'artista può intervenire con più facilità per correzioni o ripensamenti.

Modalità d'uso e possibilità espressive

I colori ad olio sono contenuti in tubetti e vanno disposti su una tavolozza di legno; possono essere usati puri o diluiti: l'olio, esposto all'aria, essicca lentamente, formando una pellicola solida ed elastica che funge da strato protettivo per il dipinto. I supporti più adatti sono la tela, il cartone telato, il compensato, preparati in superficie con una leggera *imprimitura* in gesso. Terminato il lavoro bisogna pulire perfettamente tavolozza e pennelli con acquaragia.

È possibile sperimentare diverse tecniche di stesura del colore e realizzare differenti soluzioni espressive: osserviamo alcuni esempi nei particolari che seguono.

Gradazione del rosso, per successiva aggiunta di colore bianco.

Olio, pastello e carboncino su cartone, particolare da **Toulouse-Lautrec**.

Olio su tavola, particolare da **Toulouse-Lautrec**.

Olio su tela, particolare da **Edgar Degas**.

Olio su tela, particolare da **Franco Prayer**.

Olio su cartone, particolare da **Robert Wilson**.

Maurice de Vlaminck, pittore francese appartenente al movimento *fauve*, realizza una pittura di forte contrasto cromatico. Egli accosta rapide ed energiche pennellate, dense di colore, senza preoccuparsi se traspare la grana della tela sottostante, o se si formano grumi sulla sua superficie.
L'artista ha operato senza disegno preparatorio: egli non ha ricercato effetti sfumati, né ha realizzato passaggi graduali di tono, ma ha dato forma al paesaggio attraverso l'aggregazione di macchie di colore: queste assumono un particolare risalto timbrico grazie alla caratteristica brillantezza dei colori ad olio.

AFFRESCO E PITTURA MURALE

La pittura a *fresco* o *affresco*, consiste nello stendere il colore (derivato da terre minerali) sulla parete ricoperta da uno strato o più strati di **intonaco ancora umido**: con l'evaporazione dell'acqua il colore viene assorbito dalla calce e si mescola ad essa fino a consolidare in una superficie solida e liscia.

Usata fin dall'antichità, questa tecnica ha trovato grande sviluppo a partire dal Medioevo, sostituendo il mosaico nella decorazione di chiese e palazzi nella narrazione di storie sacre, storiche e mitologiche.

Oggi si preferisce dipingere su muro asciutto con i colori acrilici (tecnica del **murale**) oppure spruzzare il colore con bombolette spray e vernici sintetiche (*spray art* o tecnica dei *graffiti urbani*).

Realizzare un affresco: il procedimento tradizionale

a. Si prepara la parete con un leggero scalpello, quindi la si lava per eliminare la polvere e altri residui.

b. Si stende l'intonaco a più strati, fino a formare una superficie perfettamente liscia: l'ultimo strato (tonachino), fresco, deve essere dipinto in giornata.

c. Il disegno, preparato su cartone bucherellato, va trasferito con il sistema dello spolvero, eseguito con polvere rossa.

d. Si comincia a stendere abbondanti mani di colore per lo sfondo, quindi si passa alla definizione delle figure, delineandone i contorni.

e. Vengono aggiunti gli effetti di luce su toni chiari; le ombre vengono rinforzate con toni più scuri.

Come trasferire il disegno sulla parete

Uno dei problemi principali della pittura murale è quello di riportare sulla grande superficie della parete lo schizzo in scala ridotta. Si tratta di una fase importante, perché dal suo esito dipende la correttezza delle proporzioni rispetto a quelle realizzate dall'artista nei disegni preparatori.

Di seguito sono riportati i principali metodi seguiti per la sua realizzazione.

1. Quadrettatura. Si sovrappone un reticolo al disegno e lo si riporta sulla parete, ingrandito. Si procede quindi alla realizzazione del disegno sul muro seguendone le linee quadrato per quadrato, fino a completarlo.

2. Incisione. Si realizza il disegno a grandezza reale (*cartone*); si stende quindi il cartone sull'intonaco umido e si seguono i contorni del disegno con una punta di metallo, fino ad inciderli sulla superficie muraria ancora tenera.

3. Ricalco a spolvero. Si sovrappone alla parete il cartone, bucherellato lungo le linee del disegno; successivamente lo si strofina con un fazzoletto riempito di polvere rossa, finché sull'intonaco rimane la traccia del disegno.

4. Proiezione. Si proietta il disegno sul muro con l'*episcopio*, oppure se ne proietta l'immagine in diapositiva o con il videoproiettore, arretrando fino a raggiungere le dimensioni volute. Si ripassano quindi i contorni con carboncino.

1. Quadrettatura

2. Incisione

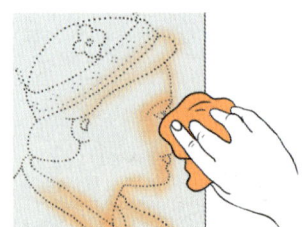

3. Ricalco a spolvero

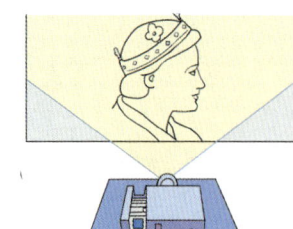

4. Proiezione

Michelangelo Buonarroti, *Diluvio Universale*, particolare della volta della Cappella Sistina a Roma, 1508-1514.

In questo particolare si possono individuare le tracce lineari e puntinate dello **spolvero**, che traspare sotto la pittura. Si osservino il profilo del viso, il contorno dell'orecchio e i vari punti lungo i capelli: è la traccia precisa, preparata accuratamente su cartone forato, che il pittore riportava sull'intonaco fresco. Questo doveva essere dipinto nell'arco della giornata, prima che, asciugando, l'intonaco facesse presa e indurisse.

PITTURA A SPRUZZO E GRAFFITI URBANI

La tecnica a spruzzo è antichissima: si pensi che già in età paleolitica venivano utilizzate a questo scopo ossa cave e pigmenti ricavati da terre e minerali.

Oggi questa tecnica può essere realizzata con i mezzi più diversi, ottenendo svariati ed originalissimi risultati: da semplici cannucce a bombolette spray, fino ai sofisticati strumenti professionali usati, ad esempio, nella grafica pubblicitaria.

Aerografo e pittura a spruzzo

L'aerografo è una specie di pistola a spruzzo, messa in funzione da un piccolo compressore d'aria e fornita di uno stantuffo, premendo il quale si distribuisce il colore (*inchiostri colorati*) sulla superficie del foglio. La variazione della pressione consente di dosare la quantità di colore, fino ad ottenere sfumature, trasparenze o completa copertura della zona (sopra, un'immagine dalla resa estremamente realistica, realizzata da **Giuseppe Bottoli**).

Questa tecnica, molto usata nella **grafica pubblicitaria**, esige grande abilità. È importante progettare in precedenza le varie fasi di lavoro: per delimitare con esattezza i di-

versi campi cromatici, così come per ottenere effetti di sfumatura, sovrapposizione o contrasto, bisogna infatti procedere volta per volta alla **mascheratura** delle zone del foglio che non devono ricevere il colore.

Di più facile applicazione la tecnica dello **spruzzo a bocca**, che può essere sperimentata utilizzando apposite cannucce o vaporizzatori. Anche in questo caso è importante imparare a dosare correttamente la quantità di inchiostro, per ottenere gli effetti voluti, e procedere correttamente alla mascheratura delle zone del foglio che volta per volta non sono interessate alla stesura del colore.

I graffiti urbani

I graffiti urbani rappresentano una nuova tecnica di pittura murale. Nati come forma di protesta individuale e sociale, hanno trovato diffusione soprattutto nelle periferie delle grandi città; se eseguiti con competenza tecnica e seguendo un progetto grafico, possono diventare espressione artistica a tutti gli effetti.

Keith Haring è stato il primo esponente di questa tendenza, che iniziò, da ragazzo, dipingendo le pareti ed i vagoni della metropolitana di New York: oggi le sue opere sono esposte nei principali musei d'arte moderna (a lato, particolare del *Murale della Chiesa di sant'Antonio*, Pisa, giugno 1989).

I graffiti urbani si eseguono spruzzando vernici sintetiche da bombolette spray. Si possono realizzare semplici scritte ma anche suggestive pitture murali con effetti tridimensionali, accostando zone di colori vivaci e contrastanti, spesso abilmente sfumati.

I tappini delle bombolette spray, disponibili in commercio in vari colori, sono intercambiabili, consentendo di variare forma e grado di definizione del segno in relazione alle esigenze espressive.

Dondi, *Children of the Grave Again*, Part 3, 1980. New York.

Facciata del Palazzo dei Cavalieri, Pisa, 1562.

GRAFFITO, FROTTAGE E GRATTAGE

1. Il *graffito* è un'**incisione**, eseguita **con uno strumento appuntito**, su una qualsiasi superficie, in modo da lasciare una traccia, più o meno profonda, che formi un disegno.

Era usato dagli uomini del Paleolitico e del Neolitico, che incidevano rocce e pareti di caverne per motivi magici e religiosi e impiegato nell'antichità per realizzare scritture su tavolette di cera o di argilla. Greci ed Etruschi se ne servirono per decorare vasi e suppellettili.

A partire dal Medioevo, questa tecnica venne utilizzata per decorare facciate di edifici: graffiando la tinteggiatura in superficie veniva messo in luce l'intonaco sottostante, fino a creare complessi motivi ornamentali, fregi, decorazioni e scritte.

La tecnica del graffito può essere sperimentata con facilità su carta o su gesso, facilmente scalfibile. Il *graffito su carta* può essere realizzato principalmente in due modi.

• Si realizza il soggetto su carta spessa, colorandolo in modo da saturare perfettamente la superficie del foglio. Alcune parti, ad esempio i contorni delle figure, vanno lasciate bianche. Il foglio va quindi interamente rivestito di nero o di un colore scuro. Si procede infine alla raschiatura: possono essere utilizzati pennini, punte di compasso, raschietti, coltelli non troppo affilati, lamette e altri strumenti.

• Si procede rivestendo interamente la superficie del foglio con uno strato compatto di uno o più colori; a questo va sovrapposto un secondo rivestimento, con un colore più scuro. Si procede quindi asportando parti limitate dello strato superficiale, in modo che le figure emergano per contrasto con i colori sottostanti. Interessante, in questo caso, la realizzazione di texture con andamenti lineari, segni, macchie, tratteggi paralleli o incrociati ecc.

Gli strati di colore possono essere stesi con **tempera**, **inchiostro di china**, **pastelli a cera** o **a olio**.

2. Il termine francese *frottage* significa, letteralmente, *stofinamento*. Questa tecnica consiste nel passare **matite** o **pastelli morbidi** sopra un foglio di carta sovrapposto ad una superficie non perfettamente liscia ma variamente texturizzata: premendo sul foglio, la texture viene riportata sulla carta, quasi per ricalco, creando immagini a volte suggestive.

Il primo artista a servirsi di tale tecnica è stato **Max Ernst**, in molte opere a carattere surreale: il frottage, infatti, ben si presta a rendere sfondi e personaggi di fantasia (in basso a sinistra, *Frottage*, 1924, realizzato a matita).

Qualsiasi superficie ruvida è adatta al frottage: carta vetrata, legno grezzo, masonite, linoleum, reti metalliche, tessuti a trama grossa, vetro stampato o retinato, ecc. La carta deve essere sottile, per evidenziare meglio la texture sottostante; variando la pressione, si possono ottenere effetti tonali.

Questa tecnica è usata anche dagli archeologi, per riportare su carta lucida tracce di scrittura o disegni da frammenti di argilla o di pietra.

3. Il *grattage* (letteralmente *raschiamento*) è il procedimento inverso al frottage: consiste nell'asportare, tramite una spatola, il colore a olio steso su una tela appoggiata ad una superficie ruvida. In tal modo le forme in rilievo restano più chiare, creando texture sorprendenti (in basso a destra, un particolare da Max Ernst, *La foresta di lische di pesce*, 1927).

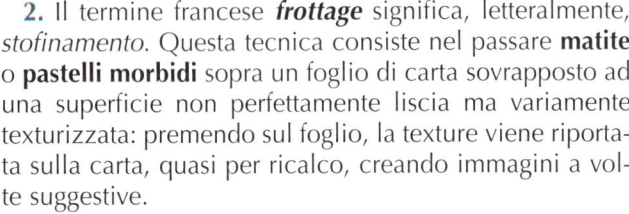
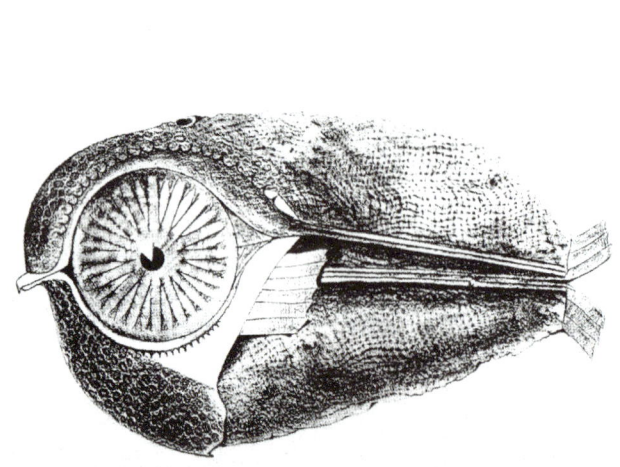

MOSAICO E COLLAGE

Comporre un *mosaico* significa incollare su una superficie tanti piccoli elementi quadrati (*tessere*) di pietra o di vetro colorato, in modo da formare una figura o un motivo ornamentale.

Già i Romani usavano questa tecnica per rivestire pavimenti e pareti di ville e terme; la massima diffusione in Italia si ebbe però in età medievale, soprattutto nelle aree soggette all'influenza dell'arte bizantina: splendidi mosaici rivestono, ad esempio, le basiliche di *Ravenna* (fotografia *a fianco*), la *Basilica di San Marco a Venezia*, il *Duomo di Monreale*, in Sicilia.

Verso la fine del XIX secolo la tecnica trovò nuova diffusione nell'*Art Nouveau*, per i suoi splendidi effetti coloristici e decorativi. Fu proprio grazie all'uso della linea morbida e alla vivida policromia delle coperture a mosaico che l'architetto spagnolo **Antoni Gaudí** riuscì a fare delle grotte, dei parapetti e delle fontane del parco *Güell* a Barcellona (fotografia *a fianco*) un labirinto di meraviglia e di magia.

Modalità d'uso e possibilità espressive

In commercio si trovano **tessere** già pronte di vari colori e diversi materiali; si possono comunque utilizzare **carta colorata**, sottili strati di **DAS**, **sassolini** o frammenti di **ceramica**.

Per realizzare un **mosaico con ciottoli o tessere in materiali solidi**, è importante utilizzare **cartoncino rigido** o **tavola di legno**. Alcune tessere devono essere sagomate, utilizzando una apposita piccola tenaglia. Le tessere vanno poi disposte, con una pinzetta, sulla base di un disegno precedentemente tracciato a matita, possibilmente partendo da un angolo. La **colla vinilica** va stesa su piccole zone, da completare gradualmente. Gli **spazi tra le tessere** vanno **sigillati con stucco** o malta.

Il termine francese *collage* significa *incollare*, cioè applicare ritagli di carta (*papier collé*), stoffa, frammenti di materiali vari su una superficie. Tali composizioni, completate con figure disegnate o colorate, vennero introdotte agli inizi del XX secolo, per opera soprattutto dei pittori cubisti, espressionisti, futuristi, dadaisti.

Nel 1945 **Alberto Burri** cominciò ad eseguire composizioni con sacchi di juta, tessuti e lamine metalliche: da allora l'idea del collage si è estesa agli **assemblaggi polimaterici**, in cui si passa con facilità dalla pittura alla scultura, dalle due alle tre dimensioni.

Modalità d'uso e possibilità espressive

Il **supporto** base per il collage deve essere un cartoncino rigido; per assemblaggi polimaterici è più adatta una tavoletta di legno. Oltre alle **carte colorate** disponibili in commercio, si possono usare carte dei più diversi tipi, che rendono disponibile una gamma più ampia di tinte e di texture.

Per **assemblaggi polimaterici** si può ricorrere a pezzi di stoffa, di tappezzeria e moquette, materiali plastici, piallacci di legno, lamine metalliche ecc.

Per realizzare assemblaggi è adatta la colla liquida ad essiccazione rapida (tipo UHU).

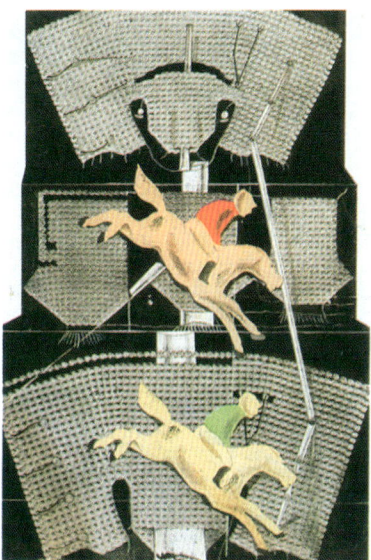

Max Ernst,
Dada Degas,
1920-1921.

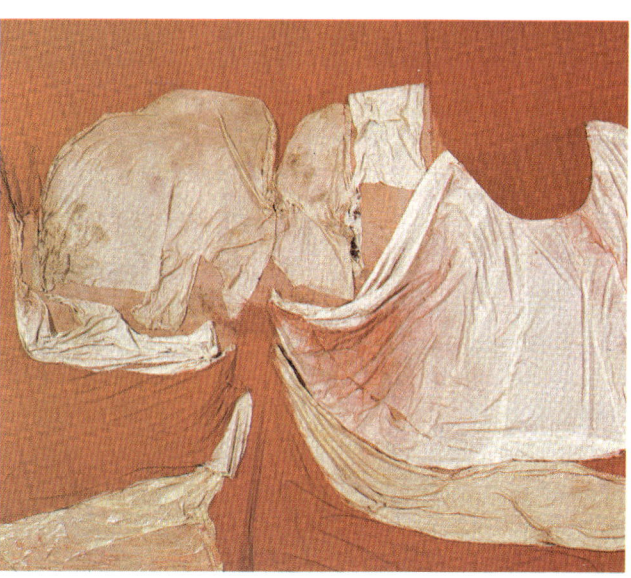

Alberto Burri,
Rosso, 1956.
Composizione
con stoffa,
carta e vinavil
su tela.

TECNICHE DI STAMPA

Stampare significa **riportare su una superficie un'immagine**, partendo da una **matrice**, in modo da ottenerne parecchie copie uguali e speculari. A seconda dei vari sistemi, avremo **stampe** da matrici **in rilievo**, **in piano** e **in cavo**.

Diversi sono gli effetti visivi e cromatici che si possono ottenere: tutti i metodi hanno però in comune la possibilità della **riproducibilità**, che consente di ampliare la diffusione delle immagini e **delle opere d'arte**.

Alcune tecniche di stampa sono antichissime, altre introdotte dalla recente tecnologia elettronica. Si può stampare su carta ma anche su tessuto, con matrici di *legno* o di *metallo*: di seguito sono classificati i principali metodi.

Giorgio Morandi, *Natura morta con caffettiera*, 1933. Acquaforte.

STAMPA IN RILIEVO

**XILOGRAFIA
STAMPA TIPOGRAFICA
LINOLEOGRAFIA**

La stampa in rilievo si realizza incidendo l'immagine su una superficie piana. Vengono lasciate a rilievo le parti corrispondenti alle figure, incavate le parti che non devono ricevere inchiostro. Segue la stesura dell'inchiostro sulla matrice incisa e il trasferimento dell'immagine, attraverso una apposita pressa, sul foglio.

La **stampa tipografica**, inventata da Johann Gütenberg nel 1456, usa caratteri incisi nel piombo.

Nella **xilografia** la matrice è di legno, mentre la **linoleografia** è realizzata su una matrice, appunto, di linoleum.

STAMPA IN PIANO

**LITOGRAFIA
SERIGRAFIA
OFFSET**

Nella stampa in piano la riproduzione avviene per trasferimento dell'immagine da una matrice piana a un'altra superficie.

La **litografia** sfrutta il principio della incompatibilità tra la sostanza grassa con cui il disegno viene tracciato su una pietra e l'acqua usata per il lavaggio. Il sistema, perfezionato, è oggi chiamato **off-set** e viene usato per la stampa di pubblicazioni in genere.

In piano è anche la **serigrafia**, che utilizza per la stampa un telaio in seta.

STAMPA IN CAVO

**ACQUAFORTE
ACQUATINTA
ROTOCALCO**

Nella stampa in cavo le immagini vengono incise, con appositi strumenti, su una lastra di metallo; l'inchiostro da stampa viene così depositato negli incavi e poi impresso sulla carta per pressione.

Le tecniche di incisione, utilizzate per stampe d'arte, si differenziano in base agli strumenti ed ai procedimenti utilizzati: **bulino**, **puntasecca**, **acquaforte** o **acquatinta**.

Con il sistema a **rotocalco** sono stampati ancor oggi molti giornali e riviste.

Matrici per caratteri da stampa.

Andy Warhol, *Liz #6*, 1963. Serigrafia.

Salvator Rosa, *Giovane pensierosa che cammina*, 1650 circa. Acquaforte e puntasecca.

1. Stampa in rilievo

Il più antico metodo di stampa è la *xilografia*. Usato in Giappone e Cina già nel VII secolo, fu introdotto in Europa nel XV secolo e adattato per la stampa su tessuti. Nei secoli successivi la tecnica xilografica cadde in disuso, fino a quando, alla fine del XIX secolo, venne riscoperta da Postimpressionisti ed Espressionisti, che ne apprezzavano la nitidezza del segno e la forza dei contrasti.

La matrice di stampa è costituita da una tavoletta in legno duro (dal greco *xilon*, legno) sulla quale si incide il disegno, lasciando in rilievo i contorni e le zone che si vogliono riprodurre e scavando il resto con appositi strumenti, detti sgorbie.

Con un rullo si stende l'inchiostro sulla matrice e vi si appoggia la carta; esercitando una forte ed omogenea pressione; sul foglio resterà impressa specularmene l'immagine realizzata sul legno.

Le stampe a colori sono realizzate con matrici diverse; gli inchiostri colorati vengono impressi sul foglio con stampe successive.

2. Stampa in piano

La *litografia* (dal greco *lythos*, pietra) consiste nel disegnare su una lastra di pietra calcarea ben levigata, usando un materiale grasso (inchiostro o matita); la pietra viene quindi bagnata con acqua e successivamente inchiostrata con un rullo. L'inchiostro utilizzato contiene a sua volta una sostanza grassa che aderisce alle parti disegnate e non a quelle bagnate. La stampa avviene con una pressa litografica. È possibile anche eseguire litografie a colori, mediante più passaggi su diverse pietre e con diversi colori, ma la traccia della matita grassa si consuma e non consente un numero elevato di copie.

Questa tecnica ha trovato ampia diffusione a partire dalla fine del XIX secolo, in particolare per la realizzazione di manifesti pubblicitari, locandine per spettacoli, ecc. (*vedi foto a lato*).

Nel moderno metodo *off-set* una lamina di metallo (*zinco* o *alluminio*) sostituisce la pietra.

Per la *serigrafia* si usa un telaio di tessuto finissimo (*seta* o *nylon*) ricoperto da un disegno realizzato con gomma liquida o con un procedimento fotografico: l'inchiostro, distribuito con una speciale paletta (*racla*) passa solo dove non trova lo strato impermeabilizzante.

3. Stampa in cavo

La base per la stampa in cavo è costituita da una **matrice di metallo**, solitamente rame (*calcografia*, dal greco *kalkos*, rame), ma anche zinco, alluminio o acciaio. Sulla superficie metallica il disegno può essere inciso in modo diretto o indiretto.

a. Metodo di incisione diretta

L'artista incide direttamente con strumenti appuntiti: il **bulino** (uno strumento con punta d'acciaio e manico di legno che consente tratteggi con solchi nitidi) o la **puntasecca** (il cui stilo, in acciaio o con punta di diamante, va usato solo perpendicolarmente alla superficie e determina solchi esatti e sottili). La lastra viene quindi inchiostrata e stampata.

b. Metodo di incisione indiretta

L'artista incide il disegno su una lastra di rame ricoperta da uno strato di vernice a base di cera; la punta d'acciaio penetra fino a scoprire la lastra. Questa viene poi immersa nella **morsura**, una soluzione di acqua e acido nitrico, che intacca le parti non protette dalla vernice. La qualità dell'opera dipende dalla capacità dell'artista di controllare esattamente la fase di immersione nell'acido, ricoprendo via via le parti che egli ritiene abbiano raggiunto un giusto livello di corrosione.

Con questo sistema si eseguono l'**acquatinta** e l'**acquaforte**, con la quale si ottengono effetti più sgranati e sfumati.

Vasilij Kandinskij, *Lirico*, 1912.

Henri de Toulouse-Lautrec, *Ambassadeurs: Aristide Bruant*, 1892.

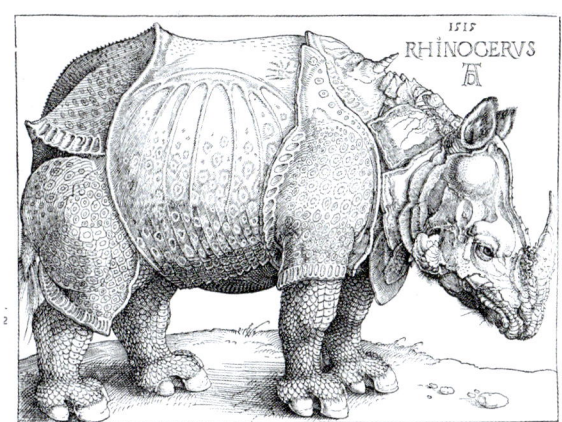

Albrecht Dürer, *Rhinocerus*, 1515. Bulino.

SCULTURA

Con il termine scultura si indicano quelle espressioni artistiche che privilegiano l'uso di **volumi e forme tridimensionali**, anziché la forma bidimensionale tipica del disegno e della pittura.

Diverse sono le possibili forme espressive: **scolpire** significa, generalmente, ricavare una *forma definita da un materiale grezzo* (legno, pietra, metallo); **modellare** significa invece *plasmare materiali teneri* (argilla, gesso, cera) che assumono forme volute.

Nel Novecento è stata introdotta la pratica di **assemblare** volumi tridimensionali *polimaterici*, in cui cioè vengono accostati oggetti e materiali diversi in libere composizioni, astratte o figurative.

La storia della scultura ha origini antichissime; le innumerevoli testimonianze presenti in ogni parte del mondo, confermano la presenza di tecniche e di linguaggi espressivi diversi e di grande originalità.

Analizziamo i principali metodi.

SCOLPIRE

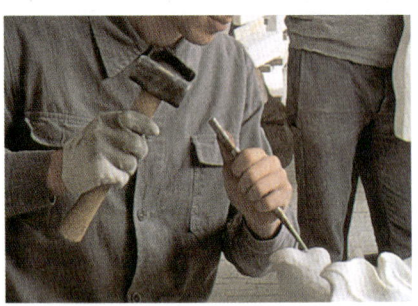

Scolpire significa togliere progressivamente del materiale da un blocco solido, fino a definire la forma voluta.

MODELLARE

Modellare significa plasmare materiale tenero, fino a dargli forma. Questa tecnica consente di togliere e di aggiungere.

ASSEMBLARE

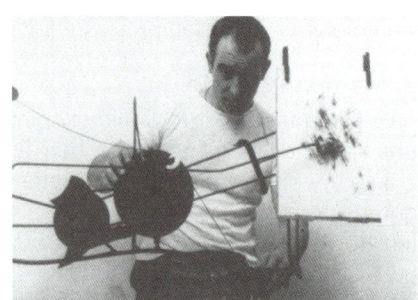

Assemblare significa comporre materiali e oggetti diversi, creando nuove e originali forme.

SCULTURA IN GESSO E SBALZO SU RAME

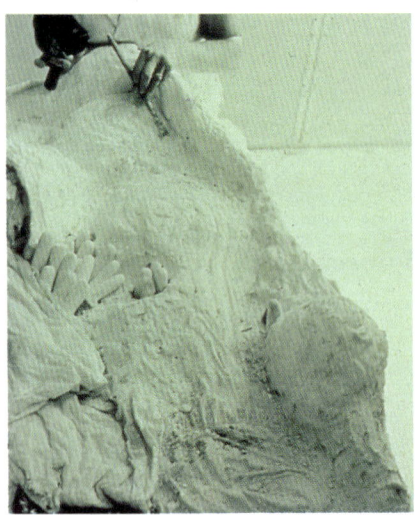

La tecnica della scultura è praticabile su gesso, materiale solido ma facilmente scalfibile. Più complessa la lavorazione dei metalli, per i quali si può realizzare lo sbalzo su lastre di rame.

MODELLAZIONE IN GESSO E CARTAPESTA

Possiamo sperimentare la modellazione con gesso e cartapesta, lavorando con calchi e modelli anche in creta.

Nel modellato con procedimento additivo, invece, si aggiunge progressivamente materiale alla forma. Per questa tecnica rimandiamo alla specifica tecnica della **ceramica**.

ASSEMBLAGGI POLIMATERICI E SCULTURE DI CARTA

L'assemblaggio di materiali e oggetti diversi è una tecnica divertente e facile da sperimentare.

Consente la creazione di forme fantasiose e imprevedibili, ricche di colore e di effetti dinamici.

1. Scolpire

Per scolpire si incide su un blocco di pietra, legno o gesso, con uno strumento appuntito, percosso tramite colpi di martello. Il materiale in eccesso viene così asportato secondo un procedimento progressivo, dando forma al soggetto desiderato.

In base al tipo di materiale, si usano strumenti diversi, che offrono ampie possibilità espressive.

Una prima classificazione viene fatta in relazione alle caratteristiche plastiche delle forme. Vengono così individuate sculture:

1. ad **altorilievo**, se le figure sono appoggiate ad una superficie ma emergono da essa quasi completamente;

2. a **bassorilievo**, quando le figure si staccano solo in parte dalla superficie del fondo, creando comunque giochi di luce e ombre;

3. a **bassorilievo stiacciato** (o **schiacciato**), quando il bassorilievo è appena accennato, per cui si ottengono effetti quasi pittorici;

4. a **tuttotondo**, quando la statua è isolata nello spazio o può comunque essere osservata da ogni punto di vista.

1. ALTORILIEVO

2. BASSORILIEVO

1. Nicola Pisano, *Adorazione dei Magi*, particolare del Pulpito del Duomo di Pisa, 1302-1310.
2. *Lastra con pavone*, VIII secolo. Particolare.

3. STIACCIATO

3. Donatello, *San Giorgio uccide il drago*, 1417. Particolare.

4. TUTTOTONDO

Esempio di scultura a tuttotondo in bronzo.
Il bronzo è una lega costituita da rame e stagno. Può assumere tonalità diverse in base alle tecniche di fusione o alle condizioni atmosferiche.
È caratterizzato dalla lucentezza delle superfici su cui scivola la luce.

Alberto Giacometti, *Donna cucchiaio*, 1926. Bronzo.

La tecnica scultorea è evidente grazie al non finito: alcune parti sono appena sbozzate, in altre il marmo è quasi grezzo, con grossi segni di scalpello in evidenza. In altre parti la superficie è perfettamente levigata.

Michelangelo Buonarroti, *San Matteo*, 1505 circa, Marmo. Particolare.

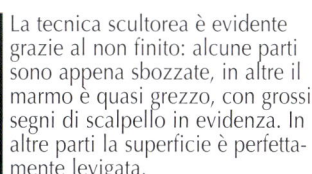

I capelli e le pieghe degli abiti, derivano da nette linee incise in andamenti regolari. Nelle opere in legno, lo scultore deve tener conto dell'andamento naturale delle venature.

Maestà Battlò, legno policromo, metà XII sec. Particolare.

2. Modellare

Modellare significa plasmare del materiale malleabile fino a conferirgli la forma desiderata. Si possono plasmare l'*argilla*, il *gesso*, la *plastilina*, la *cera*, la *carta bagnata* ecc.

Trattiamo a parte la modellazione dell'argilla per la produzione della ceramica: qui osserviamo la tecnica e le possibilità espressive del gesso e della cartapesta.

Per le sue caratteristiche di plasmabilità ed economicità, il **gesso** è stato usato fin dall'antichità per preparare *modelli di sculture* o per eseguire *decorazioni in rilievo*, sotto forma di **stucco**; sotto forma di **scagliola** viene usato per decorazioni piane, ad esempio per imitare il marmo.

Lo stucco si ottiene mescolando acqua, gesso e altri materiali (polvere di marmo, sabbia); solidifica rapidamente e può essere applicato a strutture metalliche (*anime*) per ottenere opere a tutto tondo: questa tecnica è stata particolarmente utilizzata in età barocca, per decorazioni interne di fantasioso effetto scenografico (foto *qui sotto a destra*). Purtroppo il materiale è tenero e, attaccato dall'umidità, può perdere consistenza e sbriciolarsi.

Le opere in gesso sono conservate in *gipsoteche* (dal greco *gypsos*, gesso) famosa è quella di Possagno, ove sono conservate le copie in gesso delle sculture del **Canova**.

Il *calco in gesso* è la copia fedele della statua, o il suo modello originale. In questo caso il calco viene ricavato dalla figura modellata in argilla: su questa viene steso del gesso, in due fasi distinte, in modo da poter separare le due metà (*valve*). Una volta asciugato il gesso, viene rimossa la creta dal suo interno: si ottiene così una matrice che porta impressa in negativo la forma da realizzare.
I punti rappresentano i riferimenti da riportare sul blocco di marmo, lavorato poi da abili scultori per realizzare l'opera definitiva.
A lato, **Antonio Canova**, *Le tre Grazie*, modello originale in gesso, 1813. Particolare.

3. Assemblare

Assemblare significa collegare tra loro pezzi di oggetti e materiali diversi in modo da creare una nuova struttura tridimensionale, che assume un significato autonomo.

L'uso di accostare materiali diversi sulla superficie della tela risale all'inizio del XX secolo, quando gli artisti di avanguardia si divertivano a provocare il gusto del pubblico e della critica tradizionalista.

Gli artisti Dada e Surrealisti eseguirono assemblaggi tridimensionali estrosi e ironici al tempo stesso, utilizzando oggetti d'uso comune, frammenti di materiali ormai in disuso o, ancora, capovolgendo, attraverso interventi minimi ma geniali, la funzione di un oggetto conosciuto.

Legno, ferro, cartone, cemento, vetro, pietra, materie plastiche, pezzi di motore e di circuiti elettronici, sfruttati per il loro effetto visivo, cromatico e plastico, forniscono anche oggi la possibilità di eseguire assemblaggi di ogni genere; tale pratica è ormai acquisita nella produzione artistica contemporanea, divenendo in molti casi tema centrale della sperimentazione di molti artisti: citiamo, tra tutti, gli esponenti della cosiddetta Arte Povera.

Pablo Picasso, *Mandolino e clarinetto*, 1911-1913.

Jean Tinguely, *Baluba n. 3*, 1961. Assemblaggio di materiali di recupero con motorino.

2. Dipingere con il computer

Sono disponibili numerosi programmi di grafica pittorica per eseguire semplici disegni a mano libera: dal semplicissimo **Paint**, contenuto in *Windows*, ad altri, più professionali, che presentano innumerevoli possibilità espressive.

Oltre a disegnare tratti lineari, rette, curve e spezzate, sono disponibili anche forme libere o geometriche, con le quali comporre la traccia del disegno. È naturalmente possibile modificare i colori e cancellare errori, o intervenire su disegni preesistenti.

La variazione di forme e colori di un'immagine data è consentita da speciali filtri predisposti dal programma, controllabili dall'operatore.

I programmi più potenti mettono a disposizione strumenti che consentono effetti vicini alle tecniche tradizionali (acquerello, pittura a olio, aerografo ecc.) o a particolari stili espressivi (puntinista o impressionista, ad esempio), con la possibilità di sperimentare innumerevoli e originali combinazioni.

3. Progettare e modellare con il computer

A. Grafica professionale e CAD

Esiste oggi un'ampia scelta di programmi di progettazione grafica e tridimensionale, adatti alle esigenze di *illustratori*, *grafici pubblicitari*, *progettisti d'architettura*, *ingegneri meccanici* e *designer*: l'uso di questi programmi, veloci e di grande qualità tecnica, consente di realizzare soluzioni complesse con estrema precisione, diminuendo drasticamente i tempi di progettazione e i materiali impiegati. Bastano pochi comandi per modificare una figura, ridimensionare un pezzo, cambiare colori, quote e ambientazione.

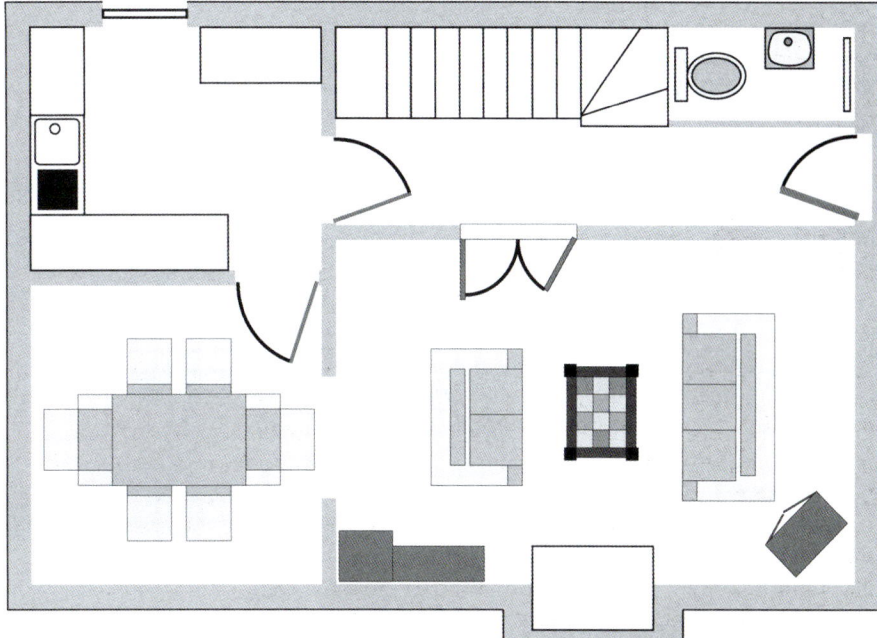

Disegnato il progetto, la stampante (o il plotter) restituiranno con precisione l'immagine.

Tra i programmi di grafica vettoriale più usati ricordiamo **Corel Draw**, **Illustrator** e **Free Hand**; tra i programmi di CAD (*Computer Aided Design*) il più diffuso è certamente **Autocad**.

B. Modellazione 3D

Con i programmi di modellazione solida tridimensionale, il progettista dispone di numerosi strumenti che gli permettono di creare direttamente forme tridimensionali e di modificarne l'aspetto con appositi comandi (*operazioni booleane*, *nurbs*, ecc.), svincolandolo dalla necessità di "ragionare" preventivamente "a due dimensioni".

Tra i software più recenti ricordiamo **3D Studio Max**, di non facile utilizzo ma dalle elevate potenzialità.

4. Frattali, stereogrammi, morphing

La computer grafica, orientata a una costante evoluzione, propone con frequenza nuovi sistemi di trattamento dell'immagine, nonché strumenti di supporto al disegno e alla trasformazione dei testi visivi.

Analizziamo di seguito alcune possibilità.

A. Le immagini frattali

I frattali sono configurazioni complesse ottenute applicando in modo ricorsivo una regola semplice su un'immagine di partenza (fig. 2). Il computer compie queste operazioni in modo velocissimo, fino a creare immagini dinamiche e fantastiche, dai contorni frastagliati e dai colori sorprendenti.

Gli insiemi frattali più conosciuti sono quelli di **Mandelbrot** e **Julia**: partendo da formule matematiche diverse, si può dare origine a paesaggi *virtuali*, cioè perfettamente verosimili, ma inesistenti in natura.

B. Gli stereogrammi

Lo stereogramma consiste nella rappresentazione di una configurazione tridimensionale, "nascosta" all'interno di una sequenza di immagini astratte e a due dimensioni.

La visione degli stereogrammi è legata a precisi meccanismi di percezione visiva e insieme ad aspetti psicologici; la realtà fisica, infatti, appare ai nostri occhi *secondo i principi che ci sono familiari, cioè nel modo in cui abbiamo imparato a vedere il mondo*. Possiamo percepire uno stereogramma avvicinandoci molto allo schermo del computer fino quasi a toccarlo, in modo da sfuocare l'immagine, per poi allontanarci lentamente da esso, mantenendo la sfocatura, fino a quando non appare l'immagine tridimensionale. Per individuarli sulla pagina del libro bisogna focalizzare lo sguardo su un punto lontano; quindi, mantenendo la messa a fuoco su quel punto, introduciamo lo stereogramma tra quel punto e i nostri occhi: l'immagine apparirà sfuocata finché, muovendola lentamente avanti e indietro, non apparirà nitida e volumetrica. Osserva la *figura 3*.

C. Morphing

Questo procedimento, consistente nella graduale trasformazione di un'immagine in un'altra, corrisponde ad uno dei più antichi effetti speciali usati nel cinema. Oggi si ricorre a speciali programmi per rendere più efficaci e spettacolari queste soluzioni.

Alcuni programmi, semplificati, possono risultare facilmente utilizzabili: è sufficiente definire le due immagini, di partenza e di arrivo, stabilire alcuni punti caratteristici, da far coincidere nelle due sequenze estreme, e fissare il numero di fotogrammi intermedi. Il computer si occuperà di gestire l'intero processo.

4. Esempio di morphing.

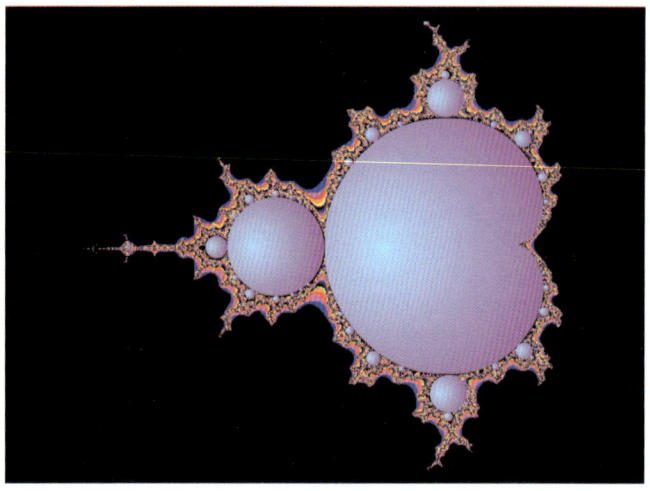

1. Frattale della serie di Mandelbrot.

2. Formazione grafica di un frattale. ***Curva di Koch.*** Un triangolo equilatero con lato pari a 9 o a un suo multiplo, si trasforma progressivamente in un fiocco di neve, attraverso un principio di ricorsività.

3. Stereogramma. Frapponendo la figura tra i nostri occhi e un punto lontano sul quale si è posizionato lo sguardo, emergerà dalla geometria astratta l'immagine di un uccelli in volo.

COME LEGGERE OPERE D'ARTE E IMMAGINI

Leggere un'opera d'arte (pittura, scultura, architettura, design), un'immagine fissa (fotografia, pubblicità, grafica) o in movimento (video, cinema, animazione) è l'obiettivo finale di tutto il percorso teorico e operativo che abbiamo fin qui condotto: la conoscenza degli elementi generali della comunicazione; gli elementi del linguaggio visuale e, in particolare, del colore e della composizione; la conoscenza del valore simbolico delle immagini, quindi, del loro significato iconografico e iconologico; il rapporto tra arte e società.

I diversi metodi di approccio all'osservazione e analisi di un'immagine o di un'opera d'arte, infatti, tengono conto di tutti questi elementi oppure ne privilegiano uno in particolare. Possiamo, così, distinguere:

1. un *approccio formale/compositivo*, basato sugli aspetti della forma e sugli elementi del linguaggio visivo;
2. un *approccio iconografico/iconologico*, che ci guida alla descrizione del soggetto e alla ricerca del significato più profondo dell'immagine;
3. un *approccio storico/sociologico*, che propone di studiare i rapporti che intercorrono tra l'opera d'arte e il periodo storico e sociale in cui essa è stata realizzata.

Un'ulteriore sintesi di queste modalità di approccio ci porta ad una **lettura completa e organica**, per quanto sintetica ed essenziale, di qualunque immagine e di qualsiasi opera d'arte. In questo lavoro, risulta assai efficace ricorrere all'uso di schemi grafici, con funzione metalinguistica: sovrapposti all'immagine (una fotocopia o uno schizzo dell'opera) servono per indicare con immediatezza gli aspetti legati agli elementi del linguaggio visivo (andamenti lineari, linee di forza, simmetria, peso visivo, colore, ecc.).

Nelle pagine seguenti si propongono alcuni esempi di schede di lettura e analisi di opere di architettura, pittura, scultura, design, fotografia, pubblicità e video: partendo da uno schema di base analogo per le varie tipologie, avremo risultati che, di volta in volta, privilegiano un approccio metodologico rispetto agli altri, in relazione alla sensibilità personale e alle evenienze suggerite dall'opera stessa.

Avremo quindi schede di lettura in cui prevalgono aspetti legati alla composizione e agli elementi del linguaggio visuale (*vedi pagg. 182-185, 200-201 e 206*), altre in cui è forse più interessante l'approccio iconografico e iconologico (*pagg. 194-195 e 210*), altre in cui l'analisi privilegia gli aspetti storici e sociologici (*pagg. 180-181, 196-197, 202-203, 213-214*).

A livello scolastico è importante curare anche l'aspetto formale dell'impaginazione e della presentazione grafica della scheda di lettura e analisi dell'immagine, proprio come se fosse la scheda per un immaginario catalogo di una mostra o di un museo. Un'impaginazione curata e ordinata, sintetica ma esauriente, senza eccessi di verbosità e con l'aiuto di schemi grafici, aiuta ancor meglio a comprendere e ad apprezzare l'immagine e l'opera considerata.

Michelangelo, volta della *Cappella Sistina*, particolare.

1. L'ARCHITETTURA: FORMA, SPAZIO, ORDINE

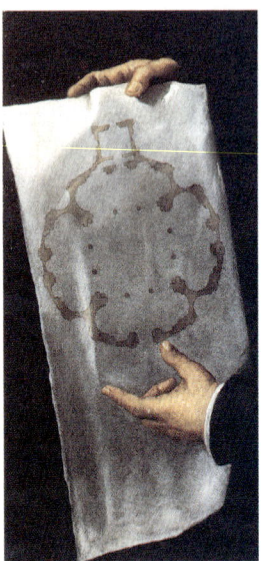

Tiziano, *Ritratto di Giulio Romano*, 1536 circa. Particolare. Olio su tela, 102x87 cm. Mantova, Collezioni provinciali.

Lo spazio è un elemento concettuale che non si concretizza finché non è delimitato: le dimensioni, l'apertura o la chiusura, le qualità della luce dello spazio visibile dipendono infatti dalle forme che lo definiscono e lo configurano.

Quando lo spazio vissuto dall'uomo viene da lui disegnato, modificato, chiuso, composto, aperto, secondo precise scelte formali e un efficace ordine compositivo, allora possiamo parlare di architettura.

L'architettura del passato, ma anche l'architettura in cui trascorriamo la nostra vita quotidiana, risponde a determinati principi compositivi, che la rendono funzionale alle nostre attività, ma tiene conto anche di esigenze ed intenzionalità estetiche e, in certi casi, di motivazioni di tipo culturale, religioso e simbolico.

Per comprendere l'architettura e saperla apprezzare dobbiamo imparare ad analizzarla obiettivamente, per essere coscienti delle sensazioni che provoca e apprezzarne le qualità progettuali e i significati storici e culturali.

Il linguaggio dell'architettura

Numerosi sono gli elementi artistici e tecnici che entrano in gioco nella progettazione e costruzione di un'architettura, fino a formularne un preciso linguaggio. La buona riuscita di un edificio dipende da come questi elementi sono rapportati fra loro, per arrivare alla soluzione del problema cui l'edificio deve rispondere. Ricordiamo alcuni degli elementi più importanti.

1. Spazio, struttura, chiusura

Lo spazio va organizzato secondo relazioni tra gli ambienti, rapporti gerarchici e funzionali: significa definire forma, scala e proporzione degli ambienti, la qualità delle superfici, la distribuzione della luce. Rapporti tra vuoto e pieno, tra interno ed esterno.

2. Contesto ambientale

Scelta del luogo e caratteristiche dell'ambiente circostante; clima e temperatura.

3. Organizzazione dei percorsi

La particolarità dell'architettura è quella di potervi entrare, seguire un percorso, passare da un ambiente all'altro, soffermarsi ad osservare particolari costruttivi. Esiste quindi un preciso rapporto tra lo spazio, il movimento e il tempo.

4. Aspetti tecnologici

Sono essenziali per la vivibilità dell'architettura, anche se non sempre evidenti. Ricordiamo le tipologie delle strutture portanti e di copertura, le modalità di tamponamento delle pareti, le tecniche per garantire la salubrità degli ambienti, gli impianti e gli accessori tecnici.

5. Aspetti funzionali, estetici, culturali e simbolici

Alcune architetture sono poco funzionali, anche se esteticamente apprezzabili e significative sul piano storico e culturale. La funzionalità è chiaramente più importante per l'architettura moderna: gli edifici in cui viviamo devono garantire agevoli modalità di accesso e di uscita, facilità di percorrenza e di sosta negli ambienti, clima ideale per lo svolgimento delle varie attività. Inoltre vanno considerate le qualità della luce, dei colori, le texture della facciata, e la cura per i dettagli e le finiture, che contribuiscono ad accrescere l'aspetto estetico dell'edificio. Non di rado poi un edificio, col passare del tempo, acquisisce valore simbolico per motivi religiosi, politici e sociali, in ogni parte del mondo.

Tutti questi elementi, presi sia singolarmente sia in relazione tra loro, sono da riconoscere, comprendere e da tenere in considerazione per una corretta lettura e analisi di un edificio (antico o moderno che sia) in modo da poterne fornire in ultimo anche una valutazione motivata.

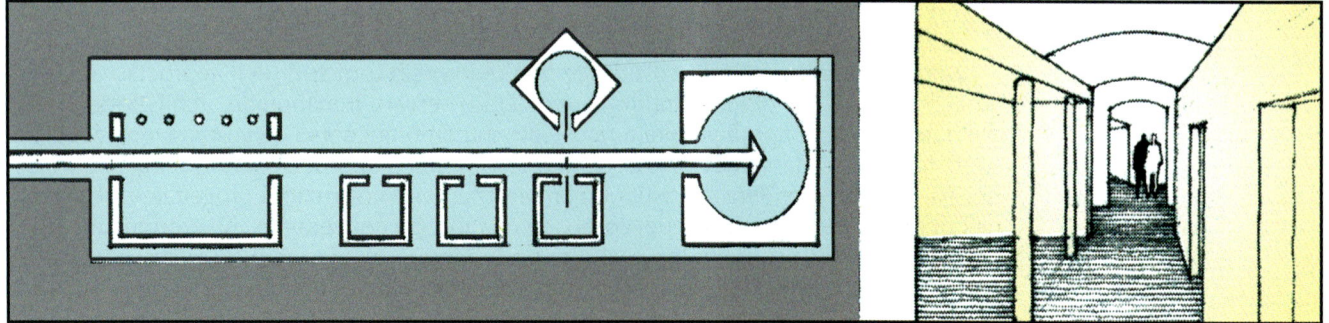

4. Rapporto percorso/spazio

Oltre alle varianti di itinerario in piano, spesso lungo il tragitto ci si imbatte in spigoli o deviazioni imposte da muri, ostacoli vari, stanze a fondo cieco, varianti più o meno obbligate. Pensate, ad esempio, al percorso di una mostra o di un museo. Anche la scelta e la collocazione di questi elementi contribuisce a incrementare la qualità dello spazio architettonico.

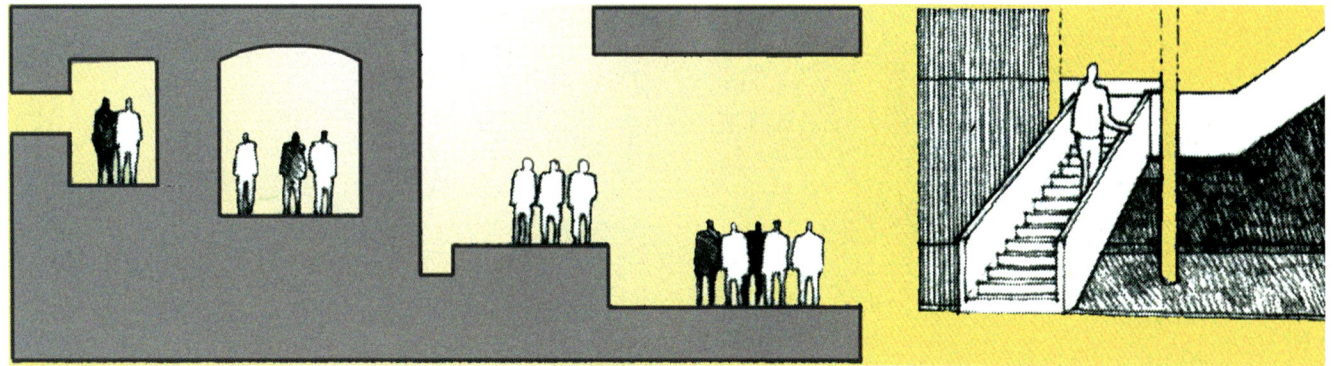

5. Forme degli spazi di passaggio

I percorsi possono essere organizzati in corridoi o gallerie, in piano o con scale e rampe, balconi e terrazze, portici e loggiati, stanze e saloni. La corretta collocazione di questi elementi suscita talora piacevoli emozioni nel visitatore e lo fa sentire a proprio agio, oppure viceversa, incute un senso di disagio e oppressione, fino alla claustrofobia.

Le aperture: porte e finestre

Gli spazi chiusi e coperti hanno bisogno di luce e aria, per la loro vivibilità. Ecco quindi le necessarie aperture: porte, finestre, balconi, abbaini ecc.

Nel disegnare le facciate degli edifici, gli architetti usano questi elementi per dare senso alla composizione, creando ritmi, simmetrie, equilibrio, oppure limitando al massimo le aperture o deformandole in una composizione più originale, asimmetrica ed imprevedibile.

La forma e le dimensioni di porte e finestre hanno subito notevoli evoluzioni nel corso della storia, connotando in più occasioni un preciso stile architettonico.

Non si tratta quindi solo di una scelta legata alla tecnologia e ai materiali, ma anche di una scelta stilistica. In questa pagina possiamo osservare alcune tipologie di porte di epoche diverse.

LE TIPOLOGIE DELL'ARCHITETTURA

La tipologia di un edificio costituisce uno dei possibili metodi dell'approccio all'architettura, come punto di vista preliminare da cui osservare il manufatto architettonico.

Numerosi sono i tipi di architettura che incontriamo nel corso della storia e nei vari Paesi del mondo: le classificazioni possono essere varie e l'approccio per tipologia può essere utile per comprendere la vastità e complessità delle costruzioni progettate e realizzate dall'uomo. In questa pagina puoi osservare una mappa concettuale che propone un inizio di classificazione per funzione e che può comunque essere ampliata ulteriormente approfondendo l'analisi delle numerose varianti tipologiche dell'architettura.

SCHEDA DI LETTURA E ANALISI DI UN EDIFICIO

Le considerazioni espresse nelle pagine precedenti, in riferimento allo spazio architettonico e alle costruzioni, trovano diretta e logica applicazione nell'osservazione, analisi e lettura di un edificio. Pur distinguendo le epoche storiche e le specificità dei singoli edifici, è comunque opportuno predisporre una scheda da seguire, sintetica ma quanto più possibile completa, per il rilevamento delle notizie storiche e dei dati tecnici relativi all'edificio. In questa pagina puoi trovarne un modello, eventualmente da integrare, modificare, ampliare. Nelle pagine successive potrai osservarne alcune dirette applicazioni.

A. DATI PRELIMINARI

Nome dell'edificio
L'edificio può avere una precisa denominazione oppure essere stato chiamato in modo diverso in vari periodi storici o in relazione ai diversi proprietari.

Architetto
È un'opera autografa o è stata attribuita dai critici d'arte e dagli storici? Se l'edificio è antico, l'attribuzione può essere incerta. L'autore poi può aver avuto degli aiuti. Se l'edificio è recente, talvolta si distingue l'ideatore del complesso dal progettista delle strutture.

Committente
Può essere un privato cittadino, un'azienda, lo Stato, la Chiesa, ecc.

Collocazione, conteso ambientale e clima
Bisogna indicare il luogo in cui si trova l'edificio, magari con qualche informazione sull'ambiente circostante. Interessante è anche il riferimento al clima, che condiziona spesso la scelta delle modalità e dei materiali di costruzione, come anche la forma dell'edificio (pensiamo alle aperture e al tetto).

Datazione
Anno di inizio e di fine della costruzione: alcuni edifici sono stati costruiti e modificati nel corso di molti anni (se non addirittura secoli). Di altri non abbiamo documentazione, per cui la data è approssimata.

Materiali e tecniche di costruzione
In relazione al periodo storico, la struttura può essere di legno, mattoni, pietra, acciaio, cemento. Le diverse tecnologie usano anche abbinare i materiali in strutture miste. Eventualmente da segnalare anche lo stato di conservazione.

Dimensioni
Le grandi dimensioni di un edificio possono testimoniare la sua importanza, soprattutto quando sono simbolo del potere politico o religioso. Alcuni edifici, pur fondamentali nella storia dell'architettura, sono invece di dimensioni assai limitate.

Tipo di edificio
Identificazione della destinazione d'uso dell'insieme e delle parti. Casa o tempio, castello o villa, monastero o edificio termale… La tipologia può essere legata alla funzione: a pag. 178 puoi osservare un'ipotesi di classificazione delle diverse tipologie.

B. DESCRIZIONE FORMALE DELL'EDIFICIO

Si descrivono le parti più evidenti, sia esterne sia interne. Proponiamo alcuni esempi.

– Modalità della composizione volumetrica (è semplice o complessa, presenta un ordine geometrico o è un aggregato di volumi?).

– Analisi della planimetria (è semplice o articolata, organizzata lungo assi di simmetria o asimmetrica, ortogonale o radiale, aperta verso l'esterno o chiusa entro il suo perimetro?).

– Analisi della facciata (semplice o complessa, organizzata in modo simmetrico o asimmetrico, divisa in parti o uniforme, prevalgono le masse piene o i vuoti, è piana, frastagliata o curva, presenta parti rientranti o sporgenti?).

– Trattamento delle texture di superficie (sono lisce e appiattite, arrotondate o spigolose, solcate, scanalate, grezze, levigate e lucide, porose, rugose, a bugnato?).

– Elementi strutturali e sistema costruttivo: colonne, pilastri, travi o archi (sistema trilitico, archivoltato, a telaio?).

– Sistemi di tamponamento: murature, pannelli di legno, vetro o plastica.

– Sistemi di copertura: tetto (in legno, laterizio, pietra, cemento armato? A spioventi, piano, a volta, a cupola, a capriate, a carena di nave?).

– Organizzazione dello spazio: distribuzione degli spazi e dimensioni e disposizione delle stanze.

– Organizzazione dei percorsi: modalità di approccio all'edificio, ingressi, finestre ecc.

– Caratteri stilistici: sono usati ordini classici più o meno ortodossi? Molti edifici si collocano all'interno di una precisa corrente artistica, altri sono più eclettici, magari presentano una commistione o una sovrapposizione di stili.

C. ELEMENTI DEL LINGUAGGIO VISIVO

Segno, punto e linea, superfici e texture, volumi e spazio, colore (monocromo o policromo?), luci e ombre, composizione (modulo e ritmo, simmetria o asimmetria) sono elementi quasi sempre presenti e ben visibili nelle architetture.

D. VALORI ESPRESSIVI E SIMBOLICI

Ogni edificio mostra, in genere, il proprio carattere funzionale, ma spesso siamo colpiti dall'espressività architettonica, cioè da come forme, colori, materiali, decorazioni sono assemblati tra loro. Molti edifici introducono elementi di novità, rispetto ai precedenti, sotto l'aspetto tipologico, morfologico e stilistico: quali differenze lo caratterizzano e come si possono spiegare?

Inoltre, alcune costruzioni hanno anche valore simbolico, come certi monumenti, obelischi, torri, e il simbolo talvolta prevale anche sulla funzionalità.

Interessante è anche stabilire quali relazioni possono esistere tra l'opera considerata e altri edifici, vicini e lontani, nel tempo e nello spazio.

Infine, si può chiudere esprimendo proprie e motivate valutazioni personali.

Paestum, il tempio di Hera II (a sinistra) e il tempio di Hera I (detto la Basilica) a destra.

A. DATI PRELIMINARI

Nome dell'edificio: Tempio di Hera II, detto anche tempio di Poseidone (Nettuno).

Architetto: sconosciuto.

Committente: sconosciuto.

Collocazione, contesto ambientale e clima: nel centro della città di Paestum (o Poseidonia), situata in una pianura presso Salerno; il clima è mediterraneo.

Datazione: intorno al 460 a.C.

Materiali e tecniche di costruzione: basamento e struttura in pietra calcarea, che con il tempo ha assunto una tonalità dorata; tetto (andato perduto) originariamente in legno con tegole di laterizio. Lo stato di conservazione è buono: probabilmente è il tempio dorico arcaico meglio conservato al mondo.

Dimensioni: 49 m x 20,5 m circa.

Tipo di edificio: tempio dedicato al culto di Hera.

B. DESCRIZIONE FORMALE DELL'EDIFICIO

Il volume è un semplice parallelepipedo ben proporzionato, perfettamente simmetrico, con un timpano triangolare a suggerire l'inclinazione del tetto.

La planimetria è rettangolare. Su un basamento di tre gradini si eleva una peristasi di ordine dorico con sei colonne sulla fronte e quattordici sui lati lunghi. Le colonne, alquanto tozze, presentano ventiquattro scanalature e un leggero rigonfiamento lungo il fusto; esse sorreggono un architrave sopra il quale si trova il fregio, composto di triglifi e metope non decorate. Anche il frontone era privo di decorazione plastica. La cella, con *pronao in antis* e *opistodomo*, è divisa in tre navate da due file di colonne in doppio ordine.

Lo stile è assimilabile al dorico arcaico, con alcuni adattamenti tipici dei templi edificati in Magna Grecia.

Lo spazio è armonioso e regolare, scandito dal ritmo delle colonne, imponente ma non oppressivo. I percorsi sono dettati dall'allineamento delle colonne e dalla collocazione delle celle per il culto.

C. ELEMENTI DEL LINGUAGGIO VISIVO

Prevalgono andamenti lineari verticali delle colonne, che creano un suggestivo ritmo visivo. Nell'insieme si percepiscono immediatamente armonia e simmetria, equilibrio e giuste proporzioni, grazie anche all'ottimo stato di conservazione. Il colore della pietra è tenue: certamente un tempo era ravvivato da colorazioni vivaci, nelle parti decorative e plastiche.

D. VALORI ESPRESSIVI E SIMBOLICI

Insieme agli altri templi della città si è creato un complesso monumentale di assoluto valore storico e archeologico. Non a caso il sito è stato nominato dall'Unesco a far parte dei luoghi considerati *Patrimonio dell'umanità*, da conoscere, ammirare e salvaguardare.

Veduta aerea dei due templi e di una parte della città di Paestum.

SCHEDA DI LETTURA E ANALISI DI UN'OPERA PITTORICA

TITOLO COMUNEMENTE ADOTTATO ED EVENTUALI ALTRI (specificarne le ragioni): ....

A. DATI PRELIMINARI

Autore: è un'opera autografa; realizzata con aiuti; momentaneamente attribuita? Nel Medioevo, ad esempio, l'autore restava anonimo, confondendosi con il lavoro della sua bottega.

Committente e destinazione d'uso: un privato cittadino, un'azienda, un sovrano, la Chiesa?

Datazione: anno di inizio? anno di termine? decennio? secolo? Possiamo indicare data di inizio e di completamento (se non coincidono).

Collocazione: attuale e, se diversa, originale. La maggior parte delle opere oggi si trova nei Musei, quindi con collocazione diversa dall'originale. Molte opere hanno avuto diversi proprietari e collocazioni anche molto distanti tra loro.

Materiali e tecniche: mosaico, affresco, tempera, olio su tavola o su tela o su pietra, acquerello. Eventualmente, quando possibile, indicare lo stato di conservazione.

Dimensioni: in cm. Dalla riproduzione fotografica, ovviamente, non si riescono a cogliere le esatte dimensioni, e ciò può creare un certo smarrimento quando ci troviamo di fronte all'opera reale.

B. DESCRIZIONE ICONOGRAFICA, DENOTAZIONE E CONNOTAZIONE

1. Il **soggetto** (e il genere): l'opera raffigura un paesaggio, una natura morta, un ritratto o una scena mitologica, storica, religiosa? È una composizione astratta? In alcuni casi il titolo ci può aiutare nella giusta identificazione.

2. **Descrizione degli elementi raffigurati (denotazione e iconografia)**
   Dopo aver identificato il soggetto si procede ad una descrizione analitica: si illustra ogni elemento della composizione, iniziando da quelli principali, posti in una posizione privilegiata, o comunque posti in evidenza per dimensione o colore.

3. **Significato degli elementi raffigurati (connotazione e iconologia)**
   Bisogna precisare se sono elementi della realtà fisica, appartenenti ad una determinata religione o credo, riconoscibili o ignoti, fantastici o appartenenti all'esperienza sensibile, simbolici, allegorici, metaforici, realistici.

C. DESCRIZIONE FORMALE, SECONDO GLI ELEMENTI DEL LINGUAGGIO VISUALE

1. **Uso e funzione di segno, punto, linea:** sono evidenti segni particolari? Alcuni segni sono tipici di un certo artista, fanno parte del suo stile; sono ben visibili punti, tratteggi e segni grafici; sono radi o addensati; con dimensioni diverse? Servono per definire luci e ombre? La linea è presente o assente; frequente; ha un ruolo importante nella definizione della forma; è decorativa; marcata o leggera; sottile o ampia; continua o discontinua; armonica; spezzata, curva, mista, frastagliata?

2. **Superficie e texture:** la qualità della superficie è determinata dai materiali, dalle tecniche e dal segno espressivo dell'artista. La superficie può essere liscia, levigata, più o meno luminosa od opaca, avere effetti di texturizzazione ritmici o casuali, più o meno evidenti.

3. **Colore:** il colore è steso per campiture omogenee? Con pennellate distinte, regolari, irregolari, ordinate, disordinate, controllate, parallele, incrociate, ampie, brevi, larghe, sottili?
   È monocromo o policromo; naturalistico o artificiale; simbolico; è convenzionale; complessivamente chiaro o scuro; presenta colori luminosi e saturi o spenti e sbiaditi; presenta forti o tenui contrasti; vi sono colori molto diversi e vi è un colore dominante? È timbrico o tonale? Si accostano colori freddi o caldi, complementari o no?

4. **Luci e ombre:** l'illuminazione è interna o esterna; diretta e concentrata o tenue e diffusa; intensa o bassa; zenitale o obliqua? Le ombre sono evidenti o leggere e sfumate? È presente il chiaroscuro; è tenue o marcato; è grossolano o raffinato; è drammatico; conferisce tridimensionalità ai corpi; è tale da compromettere la visibilità di alcune parti dell'immagine?

5. **Volume e spazio:** è presente la percezione dello spazio e da cosa deriva? Si può individuare il senso della profondità spaziale? È bidimensionale; determina una profondità illusoria; si organizza secondo una prospettiva, coerente o meno?

6. **Composizione:** è paratattica o sintattica; simmetrica o asimmetrica; semplificata; geometrica; stilizzata; deformata; astratta? La struttura della composizione è ortogonale, obliqua, radiale; insiste su assi di simmetria; simmetrica o asimmetrica; insiste su un punto, centrale o marginale; contiene una cornice interna; si apre verso l'esterno; conferisce un effetto dinamico o statico; determina un ritmo costante o meno? Sono evidenti linee di forza e direzioni prevalenti? Il peso è equilibrato o sbilanciato? Prevalgono masse distinte?

D. VALORI ESPRESSIVI E FORMALI (CONSIDERAZIONI DI SINTESI)

Bisogna specificare quali aspetti originali presenta l'opera, rispetto ai precedenti e ai contemporanei, sotto l'aspetto tecnico, iconografico, stilistico. Stabilire poi quali relazioni ci sono fra l'opera considerata e altri prodotti culturali (letteratura, musica, teatro ecc.), prossimi e lontani. Concludi con brevi ma motivate valutazioni personali.

LETTURA E ANALISI DI UNA PITTURA RINASCIMENTALE:
CONSEGNA DELLE CHIAVI A SAN PIETRO DI PERUGINO

TITOLO: *Consegna delle chiavi a San Pietro*, detto anche *Conturbatio Iesu Christi legislatoris* per l'iscrizione sovrastante.

A. DATI PRELIMINARI

Autore: Pietro Vannucci, detto il Perugino (Città della Pieve 1448 circa - Fontignano 1523). Si formò in Umbria e poi a Firenze nella bottega del Verrocchio, accanto a Botticelli e Leonardo, ma derivò da Piero della Francesca l'interesse per gli spazi ampi, la capacità di accordare figure e paesaggi, l'attenzione per i colori chiari.

Committente e destinazione d'uso: Papa Sisto IV, per celebrare l'importanza del papato.

Datazione: 1481-1482.

Collocazione: Roma, Vaticano, Cappella Sistina.

Materiali e tecniche: Affresco, stato di conservazione eccellente, dopo i recenti restauri.

Dimensioni: 335x550 cm

Presunto autoritratto
di Perugino.

B. DESCRIZIONE ICONOGRAFICA, DENOTAZIONE E CONNOTAZIONE

Domina la scena in primo piano l'episodio della consegna a Pietro, inginocchiato davanti a Cristo e tra due ali di personaggi (apostoli ed altri seguaci), delle "chiavi del regno dei cieli" (Matteo 16, 13-20) (*denotazione*). Le chiavi sono il simbolo della sovranità e quindi del conferimento dei poteri al primo papa, vicario di Cristo in terra (*connotazione*). Dietro la scena principale si apre un'ariosa piazza, con pavimento in marmo rosato. Sullo sfondo si erge il Tempio di Gerusalemme, rappresentato in forme rinascimentali come una costruzione ottagonale a cupola, ai lati del quale sono disposti simmetricamente due archi trionfali che ricordano quello di Costantino a Roma. In secondo piano sono rappresentati altri due episodi evangelici: a sinistra il pagamento del tributo (Matteo 17, 24-27) e a destra la tentata lapidazione di Cristo (Giovanni 8, 31-59; 10, 31-39), a cui si riferisce l'iscrizione soprastante (*"Conturbatio Iesu Christi legislatoris"*). Sullo sfondo un dolce paesaggio collinare con alcuni alberi stilizzati. Nel personaggio con il berretto nero e una folta capigliatura scura, il quinto da destra, si suole riconoscere il Perugino stesso.

Pagamento del tributo.

Tentata lapidazione di Cristo.

C. DESCRIZIONE FORMALE, SECONDO GLI ELEMENTI DEL LINGUAGGIO VISIVO

In primo piano prevale un andamento lineare morbido ed ondulato, generato dalla posizione delle teste dei personaggi e dal fluire dei panneggi delle eleganti vesti. Le linee si fanno poi rette e convergenti prospetticamente verso il punto di fuga. La superficie è molto curata e dettagliata: possiamo notare texture nella cupola del tempio e ritmi modulari della decorazione degli archi di trionfo e nei quadrati della piazza, che in prospettiva diventano parallelogrammi. Il colore è raffinato, ricco e diversificato. Prevalgono colori luminosi e saturi, in primo piano, più sfumati ed evanescenti sullo sfondo. I colori sono vari ma accostati in modo armonico ed equilibrato, contribuendo a conferire un senso di ordine e simmetria alla composizione.

La luce è naturale, in esterno, e diffusa, proveniente da sinistra con forte inclinazione. Le ombre sono quindi leggere e circoscritte ai personaggi. Il paesaggio dello sfondo, al tramonto, è immerso in una particolare dolcezza di luce, costante nell'arte di Perugino. Il volume è dettato dalle sfumature di colore e dalle ombre; lo spazio è suggerito dalla collocazione e dalle dimensioni dei personaggi, ma soprattutto da un eccellente esempio di impianto a prospettiva centrale, con l'orizzonte appena sopra la metà e il punto di fuga al centro della porta del tempio. La composizione è rigorosamente simmetrica, con asse verticale esattamente al centro. La struttura è ortogonale, con le linee della piazza (linee di forza) che convergono verso il punto di fuga centrale. L'effetto è assolutamente statico, per sottolineare la solennità del momento. Un cenno di movimento è suggerito dall'episodio della tentata lapidazione di Cristo, collocato in secondo piano. Il peso visivo è assolutamente equilibrato, con masse di figure ben distribuite.

D. VALORI ESPRESSIVI E FORMALI (CONSIDERAZIONI DI SINTESI)

L'affresco costituisce uno dei vertici artistici del ciclo della Sistina ed è considerato il capolavoro del Perugino. La sua pittura, che pur spesso cede al sentimentalismo per la costante ricerca di dolcezza dei tratti, di calma, armonia e simmetria, si è rivelata essenziale per la formazione di Raffaello.

Arco di trionfo.

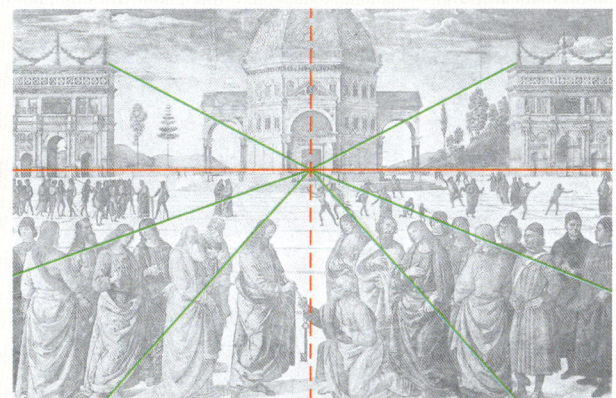

Perugino, *La consegna delle chiavi a San Pietro*, 1482. Affresco, 3,35x5,50 m. Roma, Cappella Sistina.

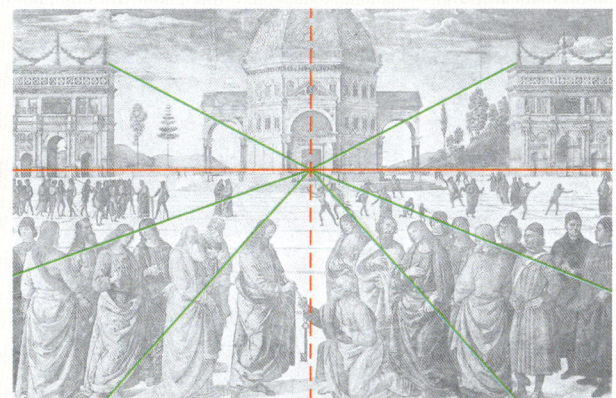

Schema compositivo: simmetria assiale.

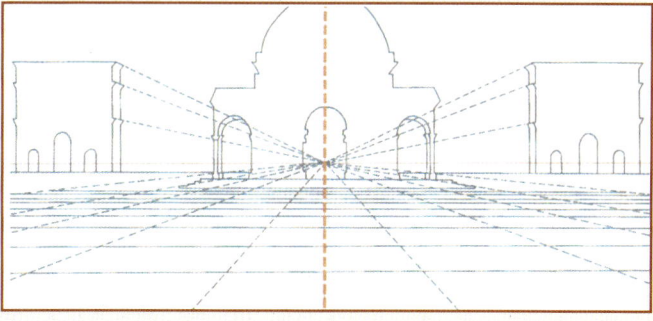

Schema prospettico/spaziale: prospettiva centrale.

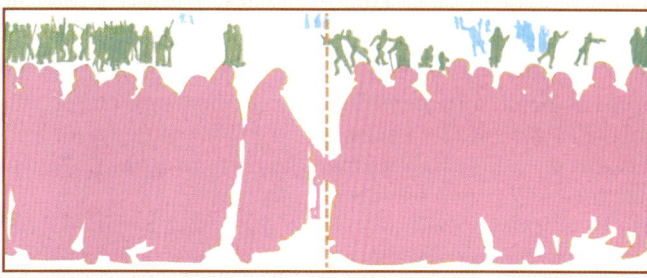

Schema della collocazione spaziale e dimensionale delle figure.

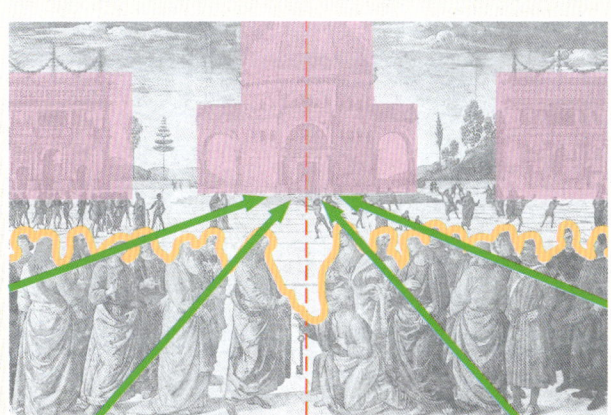

Masse (in perfetto equilibrio) ed andamenti lineari.

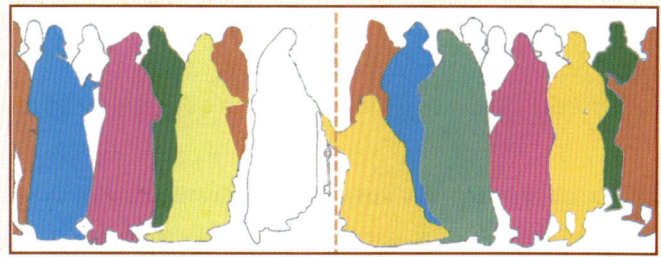

Schema della distribuzione dei colori: equilibrio e armonia.

LETTURA E ANALISI DI UNA PITTURA MODERNA: GUERNICA DI PICASSO

TITOLO: *Guernica*

A. DATI PRELIMINARI

Autore: Pablo Ruiz Picasso (Malaga 1881 - Mougins 1973), pittore spagnolo, a Parigi dal 1900, fondatore del Cubismo.

Committente e destinazione d'uso: Governo repubblicano spagnolo, per l'Expo di Parigi del 1937.

Datazione: 1 maggio - 4 giugno 1937 a Parigi.

Collocazione: dopo l'Expo di Parigi, questa enorme tela viaggiò parecchio, allo scopo di raccogliere fondi destinati ai profughi spagnoli della guerra civile, per poi finire a Londra, New York e infine a Madrid, prima al Prado e oggi al Museo Nacional Centro de Arte Reina Sofia.

Materiali e tecniche: olio su tela, in ottimo stato di conservazione, nonostante gli spostamenti.

Dimensioni: 776,6 x 349,3 cm.

B. DESCRIZIONE ICONOGRAFICA, DENOTAZIONE E CONNOTAZIONE

1. **Il soggetto:** l'opera si ispira al bombardamento che distrusse la cittadina basca di Guernica il 26 aprile 1937, compiuto dall'aviazione tedesca durante la guerra civile (1936-1939), in appoggio al generale Franco contro il governo repubblicano. Il genere potrebbe essere quello storico, ma il quadro è poi diventato un simbolo degli orrori della guerra. L'evento comunque non è descritto in modo naturalistico: pochi segni indicano un incendio e qualche breccia nei muri. Si distinguono alcune drammatiche figure: un toro, donne e uomini in fuga, un cavallo che si contorce alla luce di una lampadina.

2. **Descrizione degli elementi raffigurati (denotazione e iconografia)**
   Gli elementi dominanti sono, da sinistra:
   - una madre che urla al cielo il suo strazio, stringendo con il braccio destro il figlioletto morto il cui capo è rovesciato all'indietro: il corpo fasciato e inarcato è totalmente abbandonato tra le braccia materne. La mano sinistra della madre è tesa e se ne vede tutto il palmo allargato. Il viso della donna è rovesciato all'indietro, la bocca drammaticamente spalancata come in un grido senza fine;
   - sotto tale figura vi sono un braccio e una mano appartenenti a un uomo, steso, mortalmente colpito, che sembra una statua spezzata;
   - dietro la madre c'è un toro ferito, con gli occhi spalancati, le narici dilatate e la bocca aperta tra orrore e furore;
   - verso il centro c'è un cavallo che si contorce per le ferite, figura fondamentale del dipinto, illuminato dall'alto da una lampada domestica che scende dal soffitto, e dal lato destro da un lume a petrolio retto in mano da una donna che si sporge da una finestra; della donna si intravedono un braccio, una mano e il volto; un'altra donna è quasi in ginocchio, come se stesse per cadere durante la fuga;
   - a destra, infine, un'altra donna urlante tra le fiamme leva le braccia al cielo, travolta dalle macerie del bombardamento.

3. **Significato degli elementi raffigurati (connotazione e iconologia)**
   La madre col bambino ricorda la prima Pietà di Michelangelo; il toro è il simbolo della Spagna ferita dalla guerra civile: è un'immagine molto usata dall'artista anche in altre opere; la donna a destra, con le braccia alzate, ricorda nella posizione la Maddalena di molte crocifissioni, dove il dolore si manifesta in modo spettacolare.

C. DESCRIZIONE FORMALE, SECONDO GLI ELEMENTI DEL LINGUAGGIO VISUALE

Sono evidenti andamenti lineari molto marcati, che segnano il contorno delle figure; piccoli tratti verticali segnano il mantello del cavallo. La superficie è variamente texturizzata, con forme piatte e semplificate.

I colori sono limitati a tonalità di grigio, di nero, di bianco spesso sfumato verso tonalità leggermente rosate; verde e azzurro-grigio anch'essi appena accennati.

Luci e ombre si contrastano in un drammatico bianco e nero, rischiarato dalle fiamme, dalla lampada e dal lume a petrolio. Lo spazio è compresso, privo di prospettiva, frammentato e quasi snaturato (modalità tipica del cubismo).

La composizione, accuratamente concepita dopo quasi 100 studi e numerose varianti, è divisa in parti (quasi come i polittici medievali e molti quadri storici): gli elementi che compaiono ritmicamente in alto (toro, cavallo, donna con lume e donna tra le fiamme) sono come isolati da una linea verticale che li inquadra. A tale divisione si sovrappone una forma triangolare centrale, con vertice in alto, in corrispondenza della mano che regge il lume a petrolio: il gruppo di figure è di colore chiaro (illuminate dalle lampade).

La rappresentazione è fortemente dinamica, con linee di forza che attraversano il dipinto, quasi spingendo le figure verso sinistra.

D. VALORI ESPRESSIVI E FORMALI (CONSIDERAZIONI DI SINTESI)

Picasso ha creato con questo monumentale dipinto il più drammatico trionfo della morte che si conosca nella storia della pittura, con il preciso intento di scuotere le coscienze indifferenti portandole a vivere la tragedia universale della guerra. Il quadro dunque si trasforma in una allegoria del dolore in ogni sua forma fisica e morale.

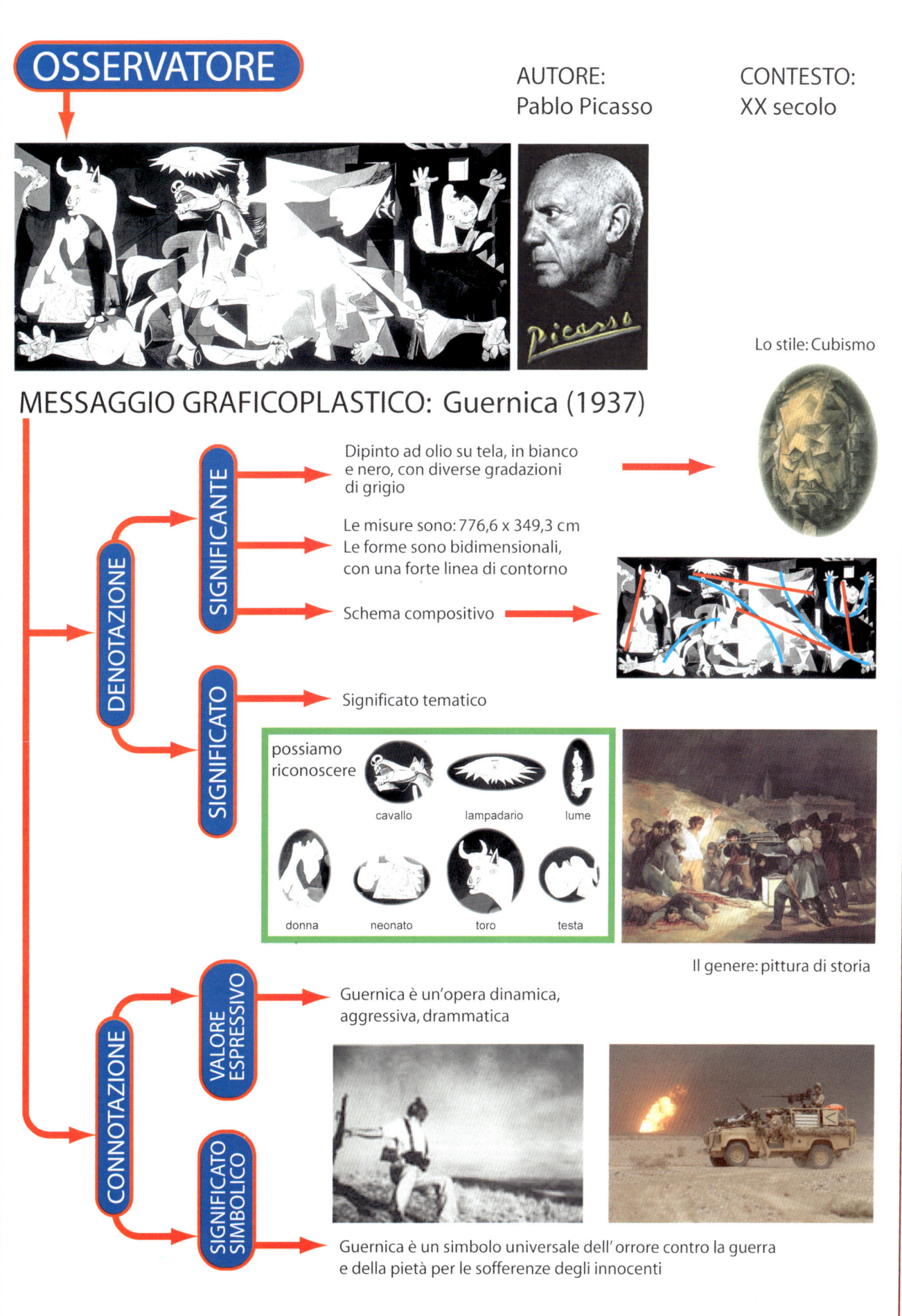

OSSERVATORE

AUTORE:
Pablo Picasso

CONTESTO:
XX secolo

Lo stile: Cubismo

MESSAGGIO GRAFICOPLASTICO: Guernica (1937)

DENOTAZIONE

SIGNIFICANTE

Dipinto ad olio su tela, in bianco e nero, con diverse gradazioni di grigio

Le misure sono: 776,6 x 349,3 cm
Le forme sono bidimensionali, con una forte linea di contorno

Schema compositivo

SIGNIFICATO

Significato tematico

possiamo riconoscere

cavallo · lampadario · lume
donna · neonato · toro · testa

Il genere: pittura di storia

CONNOTAZIONE

VALORE ESPRESSIVO

Guernica è un'opera dinamica, aggressiva, drammatica

SIGNIFICATO SIMBOLICO

Guernica è un simbolo universale dell'orrore contro la guerra e della pietà per le sofferenze degli innocenti

3. LA SCULTURA

Scolpire, modellare, assemblare

Nell'ambito della creazione artistica, l'attività specifica della scultura consiste nel creare figure, forme e oggetti tridimensionali, solidi e più o meno consistenti, che occupano una certa porzione di spazio. Le **sculture sono caratterizzate da massa**, cioè da volumi delimitati da andamenti lineari e da piani variamente disposti, e dalla qualità del **modellato**, cioè del modo in cui la superficie della scultura si comporta al variare della luce.

Fin dall'antichità l'uomo ha sentito la necessità di creare forme tridimensionali per celebrare la divinità, magari scheggiando la radice di un albero o ricavando da una roccia un idolo dalle forme rudimentali. Ciò avvenne perché la scultura è l'espressione artistica più vicina alla realtà, proprio per il suo carattere tridimensionale, con la studiata articolazione di volumi plastici nello spazio e la volontà dell'artista di infondere vita alla materia inerte. Secondo i maestri del Rinascimento, infatti, lo scultore aveva il compito di liberare il materiale superfluo da un blocco di pietra o di legno fino ad ottenere la forma desiderata. Si tratta quindi, anzitutto, di un'operazione concettuale e creativa e solo in un secondo tempo di abile realizzazione tecnica: da qui la difficoltà maggiore che si incontra nel praticare quest'arte.

Nel modellare materiale tenero (cera, argilla, gesso) si procede invece per aggregazione, aggiungendo materiale, come il pittore aggiunge i colori sulla tela. Il risultato può essere fine a se stesso, oppure anche inteso come tappa intermedia del processo creativo, che porta poi a realizzare la scultura in pietra o in metallo, fornendo un modello in scala ridotta. Come per un dipinto possiamo trovare parecchi disegni preparatori, così anche per la scultura esistono numerosi modelli, prima della realizzazione finale.

Con le avanguardie del XX secolo il processo tradizionale della scultura è stato affiancato da altre modalità, come l'**assemblaggio dadaista** e, successivamente, dalle **installazioni ambientali**.

Il processo creativo della scultura è comunque agevolato da numerose possibilità tecniche (scolpire, modellare, assemblare) illustrate nelle pagine 160-162 di questo volume, da una grande varietà di materiali, teneri o durissimi, a disposizione dello scultore.

Luoghi e funzioni della scultura

Possiamo classificare le sculture in base alla tecnica, alla collocazione, alla funzione e destinazione d'uso, ai materiali usati, alla consistenza del rilievo (alto, basso, stiacciato), dei volumi o del modellato.

Solitamente, le statue vengono realizzate perché siano collocate in un determinato luogo e con una precisa funzione, non soltanto decorativa e ornamentale.

Oggi ammiriamo le opere di scultura nei musei, ma ne possiamo osservare alcune collocate anche in altri ambienti, ad esempio in una chiesa, all'ingresso di un palazzo o al centro di una piazza. Per una sua corretta fruizione, l'artista deve pensare anzitutto alla distanza fisica tra spettatore e scultura, soprattutto quando è possibile girarle intorno.

Se ad esempio una scultura è collocata in alto, sulla guglia di un campanile o su un piedistallo, l'artista deve tener conto della deformazione prospettica della vista dal basso, apportando opportune correzioni ottiche magari curando meno i dettagli (che non si notano) ma accorciando l'altezza della statua, che diversamente apparirebbe troppo allungata.

Se invece abbiamo un oggetto di oreficeria (un portafrutta o una saliera) da posare sulla tavola di una sala da pranzo, allora l'artista deve curare in modo particolare i dettagli e gli elementi decorativi e ornamentali.

Abbiamo poi *sculture monumentali*, legate all'architettura, come i rilievi di un portale gotico o il baldacchino di San Pietro del Bernini.

La maggior parte delle sculture rappresenta figure umane: troviamo ideali di bellezza e armonia nella raffigurazione delle divinità greche, oppure realistici ritratti di nobili romani, ma anche mistiche figure di sante in estasi nelle chiese barocche e ancora figure deformi, lacerate o stilizzate nella scultura moderna. Il corpo umano, comunque, rappresenta un soggetto privilegiato, fin dalla preistoria, e il canone di proporzione proposto dai greci ha dominato per secoli interi, a più riprese, il mondo della scultura.

Temi, iconografia e iconologia della scultura

Come la pittura, possiamo classificare anche la scultura per temi, generi e valori simbolici. I temi sono praticamente gli stessi: scene mitologiche o storiche, episodi dalla Bibbia, dai Vangeli o da altre opere poetiche o letterarie, celebrazione di personaggi storici, decorazioni e ornamenti. Per quanto riguarda i generi, abbiamo sculture:

1. Religiose e votive;
2. Ritratti a figura intera o a mezzobusto;
3. Monumenti equestri e monumenti funebri;
4. Festoni, fregi ed ornamenti in rilievo.

Uno studio a parte meriterebbero l'**oreficeria** e la **glittica**, cioè l'arte di intagliare e incidere pietre dure e pietre preziose per ricavarne *cammei* (rilievo di basso spessore a due colori, basato sulla diversità degli strati di colore della pietra o altro materiale) ed altri oggetti pregiati.

SCHEDA DI LETTURA E ANALISI DI UN'OPERA SCULTOREA

TITOLO COMUNEMENTE ADOTTATO ED EVENTUALI ALTRI (specificarne le ragioni): ....

A. DATI PRELIMINARI

Autore: è un'opera autografa; realizzata con aiuti; momentaneamente attribuita?

Committente e destinazione d'uso: un privato cittadino, un sovrano, lo Stato, la Chiesa?

Datazione: anno di inizio; anno di termine; decennio; secolo? Possiamo indicare data di inizio e di completamento (se non coincidono).

Collocazione: attuale e, se diversa, originale. La maggior parte delle sculture oggi si trova nei Musei, quindi con collocazione diversa dall'originale. Molte opere hanno avuto diversi proprietari e collocazioni anche molto distanti tra loro.

Materiali e tecniche: scolpire, modellare, assemblare: quale tecnica è stata usata? Il tuttotondo, il rilievo, la fusione, il ready-made (oggetto pronto), la performance o l'installazione 3D? E quali materiali (marmo, bronzo, creta, legno, ecc.)? Eventualmente, quando possibile, indicare lo stato di conservazione.

Dimensioni: in cm (altezza, larghezza, profondità). Dalla riproduzione fotografica, ovviamente, non si riescono a cogliere le esatte dimensioni, e ciò può creare un certo smarrimento quando ci troviamo di fronte all'opera reale.

B. DESCRIZIONE ICONOGRAFICA, DENOTAZIONE E CONNOTAZIONE

1. Il **soggetto** (e il genere): l'opera raffigura un personaggio storico (più o meno famoso) o una scena mitologica o religiosa? È una composizione astratta? In alcuni casi il titolo ci può aiutare nella giusta identificazione.
2. **Descrizione degli elementi raffigurati (denotazione e iconografia)**
   Dopo aver identificato il soggetto si procede ad una descrizione analitica: si illustra ogni elemento della composizione, iniziando da quelli principali, posti in una posizione privilegiata, o comunque posti in evidenza per dimensione o collocazione.
3. **Significato degli elementi raffigurati (connotazione e iconologia)**
   Bisogna precisare se sono elementi della realtà fisica, appartenenti ad una determinata religione o credo, riconoscibili o ignoti, fantastici o appartenenti all'esperienza sensibile, simbolici, allegorici, metaforici, realistici o puramente ornamentali e decorativi.

C. DESCRIZIONE FORMALE, SECONDO GLI ELEMENTI DEL LINGUAGGIO VISUALE

1. **Uso e funzione di segno, punto, linea:** sono evidenti segni particolari? Alcuni segni sono tipici di un certo artista, fanno parte del suo stile; sono ben visibili punti, segni, graffi e colpi di scalpello? Sono radi o addensati? Con dimensioni diverse? Servono per definire luci e ombre? La linea è presente o assente? Ha un ruolo importante nella definizione della forma; è decorativa; marcata o leggera; sottile o ampia; continua o discontinua; armonica; spezzata, curva, mista, frastagliata, ecc.?
2. **Superficie e texture:** la qualità della superficie è determinata dai materiali, dalle tecniche e dal segno espressivo dell'artista. La superficie può essere liscia, levigata, più o meno luminosa od opaca, appiattita oppure ondulata, solcata e scanalata, spigolosa e frastagliata; può presentare effetti di texturizzazione ritmici o casuali, più o meno evidenti.
3. **Modellato e chiaroscuro:** anticamente le statue erano colorate con tinte vivacissime. Oggi noi vediamo quasi sempre il bianco luminoso del marmo o il verde dorato del bronzo. In questi casi conviene considerare le qualità del modellato e le caratteristiche del chiaroscuro che si forma sull'opera: è tenue o marcato; grossolano o raffinato; morbido o drammatico? Contribuisce a definire la tridimensionalità dell'opera?
4. **Volume e spazio:** è presente la percezione della profondità e da cosa deriva? È accentuata o minima; determina una profondità illusoria; si organizza secondo una prospettiva o si staglia su uno sfondo piano?
5. **Composizione:** è paratattica (con accostamenti quasi casuali di forme e figure) o sintattica (con elementi in stretto rapporto tra loro); simmetrica o asimmetrica; semplificata; geometrica? È stilizzata; deformata; astratta? La struttura della composizione è ortogonale, obliqua, radiale; insiste su assi di simmetria; conferisce un effetto dinamico o statico; determina un ritmo costante o meno? Sono evidenti linee di forza e direzioni prevalenti? Il peso è equilibrato o sbilanciato; prevalgono i vuoti o i pieni? Prevalgono masse distinte?

D. VALORI ESPRESSIVI E FORMALI (CONSIDERAZIONI DI SINTESI)

Bisogna specificare quali aspetti originali presenta l'opera rispetto ai precedenti e ai contemporanei, sotto l'aspetto tecnico, iconografico, stilistico. Stabilire poi quali relazioni ci sono fra l'opera considerata e altri prodotti culturali (letteratura, musica, teatro ecc.), prossimi e lontani.
Concludi con brevi ma motivate valutazioni personali.

Lettura e analisi di una scultura rinascimentale: Il ratto delle Sabine di Giambologna

TITOLO COMUNEMENTE ADOTTATO: *Il ratto delle Sabine*, anche se il nome fu assegnato solo dopo la realizzazione dell'opera.

A. Dati preliminari

Autore: Jean de Boulogne, detto Giambologna (1529-1608), artista di origine fiamminga, seguace di Michelangelo, che trovò fortuna in Italia nel periodo del Manierismo.

Datazione: 1579 -1583

Collocazione: Firenze, Loggia dei Lanzi in Piazza della Signoria.

Materiali e tecniche: scultura in marmo, recentemente restaurata.

Dimensioni: 410 cm di altezza.

B. Descrizione iconografica, denotazione e connotazione

1. **Il soggetto:** l'opera raffigura un episodio leggendario della storia di Roma, che narra come per ovviare alla scarsità di donne, Romolo invitò a una festa il popolo dei Sabini e, con l'aiuto dei suoi compagni, ne rapì alcune ragazze, con l'intenzione di costituire nuove famiglie per la città appena fondata.

2. **Descrizione degli elementi raffigurati (denotazione e iconografia)**
   È un gruppo di tre personaggi: un uomo inginocchiato, con la mano sul volto in segno di sorpresa e sottomesso a un altro uomo, in piedi, che afferra una donna spaventata che tenta invano di divincolarsi dalla ferrea presa.

3. **Significato degli elementi raffigurati (connotazione e iconologia)**
   Il gruppo rappresenta la furbizia e l'abile sfrontatezza dei primi romani, impegnati nell'opera di conquista del territorio laziale. Non è una scena violenta, quanto piuttosto un esercizio di stile e di abilità tecnica nella raffigurazione del corpo umano, disposto in posizioni innaturali quanto scenografiche.

C. Descrizione formale, secondo gli elementi del linguaggio visuale

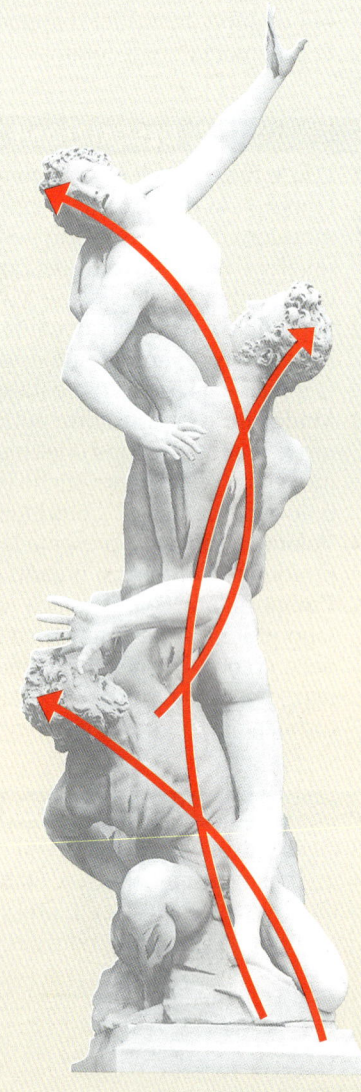

1. **Uso e funzione di segno, punto, linea:** la disposizione dei corpi avviluppati suggerisce un dinamico andamento lineare a serpentina, quasi a spirale. Non sono evidenti segni o puntinati particolari.

2. **Superficie e texture:** la superficie è perfettamente levigata, luminosa (dopo la pulitura e il restauro), dolcemente ondulata, con particolari effetti di texturizzazione per definire i capelli dei personaggi.

3. **Modellato e chiaroscuro:** la luce pervade tutto il gruppo marmoreo e il chiaroscuro mette in risalto il senso di dinamismo, perché l'ombra si addensa là dove i corpi muscolosi accentuano il movimento con l'articolazione di braccia e gambe, in una continua variazione dei rapporti tra luce e ombra.

4. **Volume e spazio:** il senso del volume è determinato dalle masse dei tre corpi, sovrapposti tra loro ma in posizioni divergenti e contrapposte; le figure sono aperte verso l'esterno e il loro moto pluridirezionale accentua la molteplicità dei punti di vista, particolarmente affascinanti se li percepiamo girando intorno alla scultura.

5. **Composizione:** è decisamente sintattica, con le tre figure in stretto rapporto tra loro, disposte a serpentina, cioè avvolte una sull'altra. Tale impostazione crea una serie di rimandi visivi, che si conclude in alto, nella mano della donna, ideale vertice di una piramide. L'artista ha usato blocchi di pietra diversi, incastrandoli perfettamente tra loro, rinunciando all'unicità del blocco. Nel complesso la composizione è equilibrata anche se asimmetrica ed estremamente dinamica: il peso dell'uomo inginocchiato a terra bilancia il precario equilibrio della donna che si divincola e l'uomo in piedi è saldamente appoggiato al terreno. Nell'insieme prevale decisamente il senso di pieno, pur se le tre masse sono distinte.

D. Valori espressivi e formali (considerazioni di sintesi)

La rinuncia alla simmetria e il senso di instabilità, carattere anticlassico, rimandano alla statuaria ellenistica (vedi ad esempio il *Laocoonte*), mentre la teatralità dell'opera anticipa i principi dell'arte barocca.

La scultura del Quattrocento richiedeva l'osservazione frontale e statica: ora il ruolo dell'osservatore muta decisamente, in quanto chi guarda diviene protagonista, muovendosi intorno alla statua a 360°, ammirandola da diversi punti di vista.

Giambologna, *Il ratto delle Sabine*, 1579-1583, Firenze, Loggia dei Lanzi.

Questo gruppo di tre figure, costruito con movimento vorticoso, illustra in modo evidente il nuovo ideale della scultura a *vedute multiple*. Le torsioni dei corpi, la ricchezza del movimento, l'incrociarsi e il sovrapporsi degli arti, invitano quasi inconsapevolmente l'osservatore a girare intorno all'opera.

Arrivato a Roma a 20 anni, l'artista conobbe e si ispirò certamente a **Michelangelo**, pur nelle differenze stilistiche; lasciò numerosi bozzetti e modelli in terracotta o cera delle sue opere, in cui dimostra lo studio attento di progettazione e l'intensità della preparazione per le sue sculture. Non sempre, infatti, realizzava personalmente le opere in marmo: probabilmente impiegava qualche tipo di trasferimento meccanico dal modello in scala 1:1 alla scultura finita.

In molti casi le sculture erano composte di pezzi separati, modalità che il **Vasari** criticava come "*rattoppamento da ciabattini*" e apostrofava come "*cosa vilissima e brutta*", ma che diventerà abituale in periodo barocco, ad esempio nelle sculture di **Bernini**.

La scultura *Il ratto delle Sabine* fotografata da tre punti di vista differenti, prima e dopo il restauro.

LETTURA E ANALISI DI UNA SCULTURA MODERNA: FORME UNICHE NELLA CONTINUITÀ DELLO SPAZIO DI BOCCIONI

TITOLO COMUNEMENTE ADOTTATO: *Forme uniche nella continuità dello spazio.*

A. DATI PRELIMINARI

Autore: Umberto Boccioni.

Data di realizzazione: 1913.

Dimensioni: Altezza 110 cm.

Tecnica e materiali: Fusione in bronzo.

Collocazione: Milano, Galleria d'Arte Contemporanea.

B. DESCRIZIONE ICONOGRAFICA, DENOTAZIONE E CONNOTAZIONE

Si tratta di un'opera figurativa, in quanto riconosciamo il soggetto, una figura umana senza braccia; tuttavia i particolari sono resi in modo essenziale e appaiono deformati. L'artista studia il movimento di un uomo che cammina con passo veloce, quasi che questo sia originato da un unico scatto vitale.

C. DESCRIZIONE FORMALE, SECONDO GLI ELEMENTI DEL LINGUAGGIO VISUALE

Il segno è dinamico, sottolineato da linee nette, tracciate dal movimento. Avvolgendo ogni parte dell'opera, poi, esse ne disegnano i volumi, a loro volta nitidi. Prevalgono gli andamenti curvilinei: li scorgiamo anche nelle superfici, levigate e ondeggianti, che accolgono un evidente chiaroscuro.

La luce, evidenziando le superfici ricurve, scandisce i volumi e mette in evidenza il movimento della figura. È proprio il movimento a definire lo spazio, che si misura nell'apertura del passo e nell'ondeggiare della figura.

La composizione è impostata su linee oblique, calibrate in modo da suggerire rimandi tra le varie parti in cui è suddiviso il corpo. Al suo interno, le zone illuminate si dispongono in un assetto equilibrato. Si percepiscono zone aperte, "vuoti", intervallati da zone in evidenza, rese mediante aspri riflessi della luce.

D. VALORI ESPRESSIVI E FORMALI (CONSIDERAZIONI DI SINTESI)

Esaltando gli effetti dinamici della figura, Boccioni toglie alla scultura il ruolo prevalentemente celebrativo avuto nell'Ottocento, il suo carattere di statico monumentalismo.

Il tema del movimento dei corpi nello spazio è stato affrontato dagli artisti fin dall'Ottocento, utilizzando in particolare lo strumento della fotografia, che riesce a fissare le fasi del moto in diversi fotogrammi.

Boccioni supera la frammentazione delle immagini, esprimendo il movimento nel suo effetto di sintesi, in una visione simultanea. In questo modo l'osservatore è spinto a percepire le forme non come entità inanimate, ma in continuo divenire. Esprimendo il moto, la forma si compenetra con l'ambiente circostante.

Foto di moda.

Man Ray, *Ritratto di Jean Cocteau*, 1922.

Christopher Broadbent, *Natura morta con zucca.*

3. Reportage giornalistico di attualità

Prima dell'avvento della televisione e di Internet, solo i servizi fotografici di giornali e riviste diffondevano immagini di guerre e disastri naturali, di sport e spettacolo, di nozze regali e miseria umana. La fotografia continua ancora a svolgere questo ruolo di documentazione, ben integrata con gli altri mezzi di comunicazione.

4. Pubblicità e moda

Dalle patinate riviste di alta moda e dai vistosi manifesti pubblicitari, sofisticate immagini ci seducono con i loro vivaci colori e la loro bellezza.

5. Natura morta (Still life)

Molto usato nella pubblicità di prodotti commerciali (cataloghi, manifesti), questo genere di fotografia offre spesso risultati estetici esemplari, per l'equilibrio compositivo e il nitore dell'immagine.

6. Fotografia scientifica

È un genere tecnicamente all'avanguardia, utilissimo in medicina, astronomia, chimica e biologia. Alcune foto al microscopio rivelano armonie di forme e colori stupefacenti, da far invidia a molte pitture astratte.

7. Fotografia creativo-sperimentale

Molti sono i trattamenti non tradizionali dei materiali fotografici. Pensiamo alle elaborazioni in camera oscura, ai fotomontaggi (oggi eseguiti al computer), alla combinazione di tecniche di ripresa e lavorazione diverse, all'intervento creativo su foto già realizzate.

TITOLO: *Roma, Eur.*

A. DATI PRELIMINARI

Autore: Luigi Ghirri (Fellegara, Reggio Emilia, 1943 - Roncocesi, Reggio Emilia, 1992).

Committente e destinazione d'uso: libero professionista, l'artista collaborò con numerose istituzioni e riviste, soprattutto su progetti finalizzati all'architettura e al paesaggio italiano.

Datazione: 1982

Materiali e tecniche: stampa fotografica a colori da un negativo 6x6 cm.

Dimensioni: il formato consente stampe di dimensioni variabili, secondo le esigenze.

Genere: fotografia di paesaggio.

B. DENOTAZIONE ICONOGRAFICA

L'immagine mostra una statua di spalle, inquadrata entro un arco. Sullo sfondo edifici moderni e un cielo con alcune nuvole

C. CONNOTAZIONE

L'immagine rievoca la fredda imponenza di edifici monumentali in un quartiere di Roma progettato per l'Expo del 1942, a celebrazione del Fascismo, mai tenutasi a causa della guerra.

D. DESCRIZIONE FORMALE

L'arco in primo piano inquadra la statua come se fosse una quinta teatrale.

Prevale decisamente l'impianto spaziale a prospettiva centrale, con orizzonte piuttosto basso, simmetria assiale ben evidente, appena alterata dagli edifici sullo sfondo e dalla luce che proviene da destra in alto, segnando ombre nette sull'arco, la statua e il pavimento.

La luminosità del cielo crea quasi un effetto di controluce, bilanciato dalla massa degli edifici e dalla profondità di campo.

Prevalgono colori freddi e sfumati, caratteristici di molte opere di Ghirri.

E. VALORI ESPRESSIVI E FORMALI

L'autore fotografa un ambiente architettonico moderno con il gusto dell'archeologo, in una composizione quasi irreale, sospesa nel tempo. Sa cogliere il contrasto tra l'ambiente urbano reale e vissuto e lo statico silenzio di edifici celebrativi e monumentali che comunicano un senso di disagio e freddezza.

Luigi Ghiri è considerato, in assoluto, uno dei migliori interpreti della fotografia di paesaggio, soprattutto per le vedute segnate dall'assenza dell'uomo, che assumono una valenza rievocativa di certe pitture metafisiche.

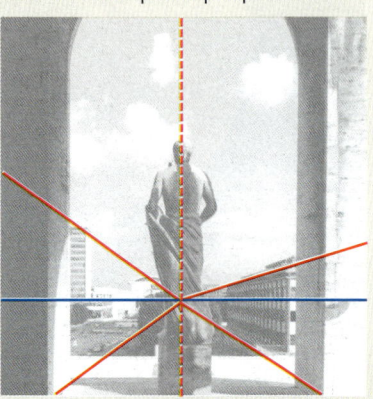

Schema dell'impianto prospettico.

6. L'IMMAGINE PUBBLICITARIA

Pubblicità e comunicazione

La pubblicità costituisce una delle più vaste e diffuse forme di comunicazione di cui l'uomo oggi si avvale. Non solo: essa è anche una delle forme più efficaci, proprio perché il suo fine è innanzi tutto quello di **comunicare** e **persuadere**.

Per pubblicizzare un prodotto, le immagini devono essere altamente informative. Il massimo di informazione è fornito da quel segnale che, per la sua novità e imprevedibilità, ci procura il grado più elevato di sorpresa: proprio in questo aspetto consiste il fascino dell'immagine pubblicitaria, nel fatto che si rinnova continuamente.

La comunicazione pubblicitaria è forse l'unica forma di arte visuale che oggi viene a contatto con vastissimi e diversificati strati di pubblico; l'unica che può influenzare direttamente gruppi di persone (il suo target) attraverso gli schermi televisivi, le pagine dei quotidiani e delle riviste, i manifesti sulle facciate di case e palazzi.

Dobbiamo perciò imparare ad osservare ed analizzare con senso critico le varie immagini pubblicitarie, per operare scelte consapevoli e motivate, in modo da educare il nostro gusto.

LA PUBBLICITÀ NELL'ARTE

La pubblicità ha avuto origine molto tempo fa, quando si cominciò a sentire la necessità di sviluppare le attività commerciali e di incrementare le vendite dei manufatti. Tra le prime espressioni pubblicitarie possono essere annoverati gli annunci scritti sui muri delle case romane di Pompei, che invitavano a votare per questo o per quel candidato.

Nel Medioevo la pubblicità era prevalentemente verbale, in quanto affidata a banditori e araldi che diffondevano i messaggi in paesi e città. Successivamente si passò a forme di pubblicità murale e, molto tempo dopo, a quella sulla carta stampata.

Nell'Ottocento, in seguito allo sviluppo industriale e alla maggior disponibilità di beni di consumo, le inserzioni pubblicitarie comparvero sempre più spesso su giornali e riviste.

Con il perfezionarsi delle tecniche di stampa si diffuse anche l'affissione murale di splendidi manifesti colorati, alcuni dei quali erano delle vere e proprie opere d'arte: basti pensare a quelli del pittore francese **Henry de Toulouse-Lautrec** e del futurista italiano **Fortunato Depero**, di **Leonetto Cappiello** e **Marcello Dudovich**.

A partire dal secondo Dopoguerra la pubblicità ha assunto grande importanza e, con il diffondersi di altri mezzi di comunicazione, ha sviluppato nuovi sistemi e tecniche.

In Italia il boom economico degli anni Sessanta è stato scandito da una serie di realizzazioni pubblicitarie di grande creatività e impatto visivo. Molti slogan, manifesti e caroselli televisivi realizzati in quegli anni sono ancor oggi apprezzati, studiati e presi come modello.

Oggi la pubblicità è diventata un fenomeno complesso e diffuso, che offre possibilità di lavoro a molte figure professionali, diversificate e specializzate.

Sopra: **Leonetto Cappiello**, manifesto pubblicitario.
Sotto: **Henry de Toulouse-Lautrec**, *Il balletto di Mademoiselle Églantine*, 1896. Litografia, 61,7x80,4 cm. Londra, Victoria and Albert Museum.

ELEMENTI TECNICI DI UNA PUBBLICITÀ

Logotipo e/o Marchio
Consentono di rendere individuabili le aziende produttrici di ciò che viene pubblicizzato.

Headline
È la frase di apertura; deve essere breve, semplice, originale e durare nel tempo; non contenere aggettivi esagerati. Di solito ha un rilievo tipografico particolare.

Visual
È la parte iconico/visiva: può essere costituita da una fotografia o da un'illustrazione. Può essere l'unico elemento della pagina, senza headline e body copy, accompagnato solo dal marchio. Ha la funzione di attirare l'attenzione del consumatore, sintetizzare visivamente il contenuto del messaggio e facilitare la memorizzazione.

PURINA

Il segreto si chiama ONE.

Un sistema immunitario forte è essenziale per una vita lunga e sana.

Ecco perché tutti i prodotti Purina ONE contengono un esclusivo complesso antiossidante per rinforzare il sistema immunitario del tuo cane in ogni fase della sua vita.

Grazie alla sua formula, Purina ONE gli garantisce un'ottima condizione fisica e lo mantiene in salute.

Giorno dopo giorno, anno dopo anno.

Per il benessere del tuo cane, la differenza si chiama ONE.

Quanti segreti per vivere a lungo?

ONE.

PURINA ONE
ADULT POLLO & RISO

Purina ONE
Salute visibile oggi e domani

Lead in (occhiello)
Solitamente collocato nella parte superiore della pagina pubblicitaria. Funge da completamento dell'headline spiegando, sempre in modo sintetico, quanto viene annunciato dallo slogan.

Body copy (testo)
È la parte che, una volta catturata l'attenzione dell'osservatore, fornisce indicazioni più specifiche riguardo al prodotto per sollecitarne l'acquisto.

Pack shot
È la fotografia del prodotto. Consente di memorizzarlo quindi di riconoscerlo, una volta che ci si rechi nei punti vendita presso i quali è distribuito.

Pay off
È la frase che conclude un annuncio stampa e deve chiaramente essere in linea con il senso di ciò che si vuole comunicare.

Il linguaggio della pubblicità

La pubblicità presenta molteplici forme, spesso coordinate tra loro da un'accorta campagna di propaganda. Soffermiamo qui la nostra attenzione sulla pubblicità stampata, che è composta da due elementi fondamentali: il testo e l'immagine.

Il testo è costituito solitamente da:

1. un'apertura (o *headline*), posta in alto o in basso e scritta con caratteri ben visibili, per richiamare l'attenzione sul prodotto e presentarlo in breve;
2. una parte centrale, più lunga e in caratteri più piccoli, che contiene il testo esplicativo sulle caratteristiche del prodotto o del servizio reclamizzato;
3. uno slogan, cioè una frase breve ed incisiva che spesso coincide con l'*headline*, studiata in modo tale da essere facilmente ricordata.

Nel testo pubblicitario non sempre sono presenti le tre parti: spesso ci si affida solo allo slogan o magari semplicemente all'immagine e al nome del prodotto.

L'immagine pubblicitaria

L'immagine assume una funzione molto importante, spesso decisiva. In molti casi ci soffermiamo su un messaggio pubblicitario proprio perché attratti da un'immagine particolarmente efficace. Tale scopo può essere raggiunto mediante scelte diverse: accostamenti visivi audaci e provocatori, foto di personaggi famosi dello spettacolo o dello sport, immagini suggestive e raffinate.

Pubblicità e comunicazione visiva: le figure retoriche

Per evidenziare un determinato messaggio, uno dei sistemi più frequenti è quello di applicare anche all'immagine le figure retoriche verbali, abbondantemente usate nei testi, con doppi sensi e giochi di parole. Tra le figure retoriche più diffuse ricordiamo:

- la **metafora** ("Luca è una tigre");
- la **similitudine** ("Quel ragazzo corre come un treno");
- la **metonimia** ("Ho visto il dolore nei suoi occhi", al posto di "lacrime");
- l'**ossimoro** ("dolcezza amara");
- la **sineddocche** ("la città ha paura" al posto di "la gente della città ha paura");
- la **litote** ("non brilla certo per intelligenza" per dire che è tonto);

Per questo si vedano le *pagine 48 e seguenti* sulla comunicazione visiva.

Scheda di lettura e analisi dell'immagine pubblicitaria

Osserva anzitutto il messaggio per un paio di minuti, facendo scorrere l'occhio su ogni parte, leggendo l'eventuale testo scritto, senza sforzarti nel trovare subito significati particolari. Esegui poi una prima analisi a **livello descrittivo**, appuntando ciò che riguarda la collocazione del testo e della parte visiva e l'uso degli elementi del linguaggio visuale. Successivamente procedi ad un'analisi a **livello referenziale**, in cui verificare l'eventuale situazione narrativa e funzionale, in relazione al *target* (destinatari del messaggio). Concludi poi, a **livello interpretativo**, individuando eventuali schemi ricorrenti, e con una personale *valutazione* sull'efficacia del messaggio. Ti proponiamo quelle che potrebbero essere le voci generali di una scheda di analisi di un messaggio pubblicitario (pagina di rivista o manifesto pubblicitario).

A. Dati preliminari

Prodotto pubblicizzato: prodotto o servizio.

Testata di giornale/rivista: se è una pagina pubblicitaria, ma può essere un manifesto in affissione su muro o pannello.

Data: data dell'osservazione o della pubblicazione sulla rivista.

Posizione e dimensioni: la posizione (all'interno del giornale o sul muro) e le dimensioni testimoniano l'importanza e l'impegno economico della campagna pubblicitaria.

Autore (Agenzia): raramente il titolare è identificabile, poiché la pubblicità, oggi, è quasi sempre lavoro in equipe; tuttavia talvolta il nome dell'agenzia pubblicitaria viene riportato, magari stampato in piccolo.

B. Analisi del processo di comunicazione

- Indica e descrivi mittente, destinatario, canale, contesto, messaggio, codice e contatto.
- Collocazione e delimitazione dell'eventuale testo.
- Descrivi la forma del testo (tipo e dimensione dei font) e la parte visiva (foto a colori, disegno, fumetto?).
- Descrivi gli elementi grafici: cornici, riquadri, sfondi; eventuali elementi di connessione, marchio, *brand*, *packshot*.
- Indica gli elementi verbali: *headline, body copy, baseline* (testo posto sotto il *visual*), *pay off*.
- L'immagine è realistica, fantasiosa, paradossale, provocatoria?
- Sono presenti elementi di retorica visuale (metafore, similitudini, prosopopee, iperboli…)?
- Qual è il genere del messaggio? Comico, drammatico, emotivo, sensuale? È basato su momenti di vita quotidiana, su una dimostrazione di qualità, sull'informazione tecnologica, su un gioco di parole, un doppio senso, un indovinello?
- Indica come sono usati gli elementi del linguaggio visuale: punti, linee e texture; colore (armonie e contrasti); luce/ombre; volumi e spazio prospettico; composizione (masse, peso ed equilibrio visivo, simmetria/asimmetria, linee di forza e direzioni prevalenti, stasi o movimento ecc.).
- Realizza uno o più schemi, anche in scala ridotta, per evidenziare con maggior immediatezza le modalità di impiego degli elementi del linguaggio visuale.

C. Analisi narrativa e funzionale

- Osservare gli elementi della scena: personaggio che usa il prodotto, il prodotto stesso, l'ambiente, l'abbigliamento, l'arredo; ciò che si trova in primo piano e ciò che si vede sullo sfondo…
- È presente una chiara struttura narrativa nel messaggio? Quale?
- Nell'immagine è presente il produttore, un *testimonial* famoso, il consumatore, un esperto, il prodotto stesso? Altri prodotti a confronto?
- Quali sono le strategie di comunicazione? Quali sono gli obiettivi del messaggio?

D. Interpretezione e valutazione

- Puoi individuare uno schema ricorrente, già utilizzato in altre pubblicità dello stesso prodotto o per altri prodotti? È del tutto nuovo e originale per te?
- Indica eventuali temi ricorrenti (tempo libero e divertimento, affermazione personale e successo, richiamo sensuale e sessuale, prestigio e ricchezza, qualità del prodotto e bontà gastronomica, unicità e innovazione tecnologica ecc.
- Quali effetti produce il messaggio? Fornisce solo informazioni o suggerisce comportamenti, atteggiamenti, valori culturali e sociali?
- Esprimi un giudizio motivato sulla rispondenza tra strategie pubblicitarie ed effetti del messaggio, in termini di suggestione, efficacia, qualità della produzione visiva.

LETTURA E ANALISI DI UN MANIFESTO PUBBLICITARIO: CAMPAGNA *GRANDI MAGAZZINI MELE* DI DUDOVICH

Prodotto pubblicizzato: abbigliamento per signora (azienda Fratelli Mele).

Testata di giornale/rivista: manifesto per affissione nei Grandi Magazzini Mele di Napoli.

Data: 1910

Posizione e dimensioni: la posizione (all'interno del giornale o sul muro) e le dimensioni testimoniano l'importanza e l'impegno economico della campagna pubblicitaria.

Autore: Marcello Dudovich (Trieste 1878 - Milano 1962), cartellonista, illustratore, decoratore e pittore.

Il manifesto fa parte di una serie che Dudovich realizzò tra il 1907 e il 1914 per i Grandi Magazzini dei Fratelli Mele di Napoli, specializzati in abbigliamento di lusso per signora.

Una figura femminile, elegantemente vestita, sale in macchina (o in carrozza?), aiutata da un ossequioso *chauffeur*, e accompagnata da un delizioso piccolo cane chihuahua. Una scritta indica la ditta e i prodotti.

Composizione piramidale, colori freddi, direzione prevalente segnata dallo sguardo della signora verso il cagnolino.

Il testo è tipicamente in stile Liberty, imperante all'epoca della Belle Époque, con caratteri arrotondati, fregi e svolazzi floreali.

Le tinte sono piatte, i volumi appena accennati mediante la sovrapposizione delle figure; non esistono ombre; il senso del movimento è delicatamente abbozzato.

I manifesti per i Fratelli Mele rappresentano in assoluto le invenzioni più originali e felici di Marcello Dudovich. Il successo fu enorme, a testimonianza dell'efficacia comunicativa del messaggio, oltre che delle abilità tecniche dell'autore.

7. L'IMMAGINE IN MOVIMENTO

Cinema e televisione sono basati su una serie di immagini fisse che, opportunamente proiettate alla velocità di 24 fotogrammi al secondo, danno al nostro occhio la sensazione del movimento.

L'analisi delle immagini cinematografiche e televisive, quindi, mantiene le stesse prerogative rispetto all'analisi delle immagini fisse, ma vi aggiunge alcune riflessioni legate al movimento e al montaggio.

I movimenti di macchina

La cosa più interessante e coinvolgente, per comunicare il senso del movimento, sono proprio i movimenti di macchina. Osserviamone alcuni.

• *Panoramica:* da destra a sinistra (e viceversa) e dall'alto in basso (e viceversa); la macchina da presa ruota intorno al proprio asse (verticale o orizzontale) scoprendo man mano, più o meno velocemente, l'ambiente in cui si svolge l'azione;

• *Carrellata:* la macchina da presa, posta su un carrello, si sposta in avanti (o indietro) e verso destra (o verso sinistra), accompagnando magari gli attori in una romantica passeggiata o in un folle inseguimento.

• *Dolly:* la camera è montata su una gru, libera di muoversi rapidamente nello spazio, con suggestive inquadrature dall'alto e dal basso.

• *Steady-cam:* movimento libero ed arbitrario nello spazio, poiché la camera non è fissa su un treppiede ma collocata su un'impalcatura equilibrata, solidale alla spalla dell'operatore, che cammina per il set seguendo gli attori. È spesso usata per le riprese di film d'azione e di videoclip musicali.

In alcuni casi la macchina non si sposta dalla posizione originaria, ma si avvicina (o si allontana) al soggetto mediante lo *zoom*, un sistema di variazione dell'ottica dell'obiettivo di ripresa: dal grandangolo (28 mm circa) che allarga il panorama, al teleobiettivo (200 mm e più) che avvicina mostrando i dettagli.

Il montaggio

Lo spettacolo cinematografico e televisivo si affida in modo particolare al ritmo della narrazione e alla concatenazione delle varie scene: questo compito è affidato al *montaggio*, cioè l'assemblaggio delle varie inquadrature in scene, delle scene in sequenze e delle sequenze nella struttura del film (come avviene per i capitoli di un romanzo). Solitamente si ricorre a uno *storyboard* preliminare, una specie di fumetto in cui sono disegnate, schematicamente, le varie scene, con le indicazioni necessarie per le riprese. Gli spezzoni di pellicola (o i nastri) con le riprese vengono poi numerati e messi in ordine. Alla fine del film si procede al montaggio (*editing*, cioè taglio delle scene per il video) con l'aggiunta di parlato, musica e rumori. Il montaggio può essere fluido e sequenziale, di tipo narrativo, con stacchi violenti o morbide dissolvenze, libero e arbitrario (presentando magari *flash-back*, cioè ritorni al passato); è proprio il montaggio che determina, in buona parte, lo *stile* del film (commerciale, d'autore, sperimentale ecc.).

Analizzare una sequenza cinematografica o televisiva

Con l'aiuto del videoregistratore, prepara una sequenza cinematografica (tratta da un film qualsiasi) o un clip televisivo (spot pubblicitario o videoclip musicale) che abbia breve durata (3 o 4 minuti) e senso compiuto. Dopo averla rivista con attenzione per qualche volta, cerca di evidenziare le sue componenti principali.

• L'azione: che cosa succede in questa sequenza? In quale luogo si svolge?

• I personaggi: chi sono i personaggi principali?

• I dialoghi: scrivi le battute pronunciate dai personaggi. Senza i dialoghi si riuscirebbe lo stesso a capire di che cosa si tratta?

• Ti sembra che le immagini, le scenografie e i costumi siano curati o che prevalga l'interesse per l'azione?

• La colonna sonora: indica la presenza o meno di rumori di fondo e di musica. Ti sembrano funzionali allo svolgimento dell'azione?

Osserva le immagini, prese singolarmente e nel loro fluire.

• Noti una prevalenza di primi piani (immagini ravvicinate) o di campi lunghi (paesaggi, vedute di città, ecc.)?

• La permanenza della stessa immagine sullo schermo è breve o lunga (almeno 3 secondi)?

• Ci sono frequenti cambiamenti di inquadratura (spostamento della macchina da presa) e di scena (cambio di ambiente) o l'azione si svolge sempre nello stesso ambiente?

• Osservi movimenti di macchina o l'inquadratura è fissa?

• Sono presenti interventi di post-produzione (effetti speciali, scenografie al computer, personaggi digitali)?

• Sapresti esprimere un giudizio motivato di gradimento, anche in riferimento ad altri programmi analoghi?

SCHEMA DI ORDINE ARCHITETTONICO E MODANATURE

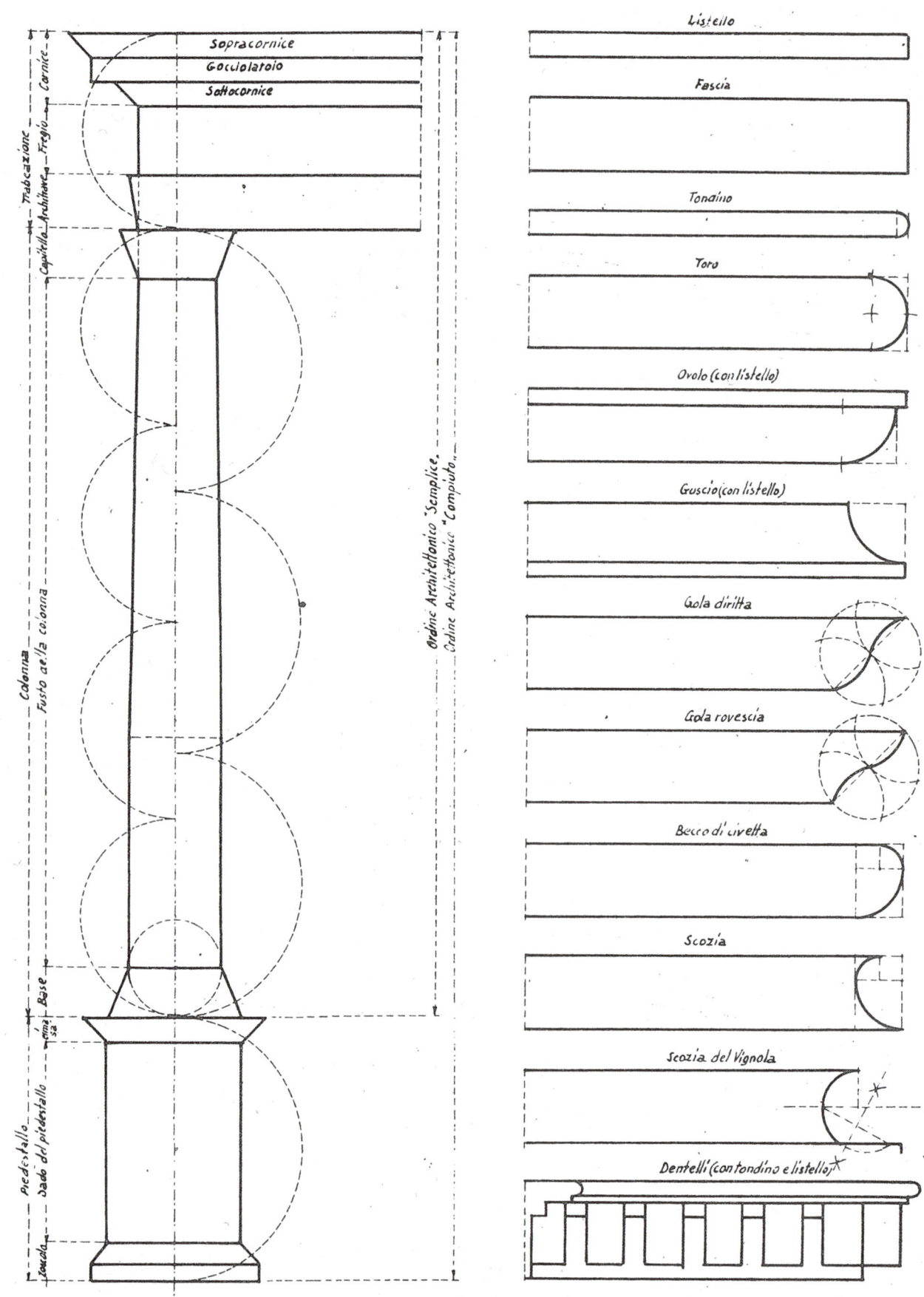

ORDINI ARCHITETTONICI: COMPOSITO

SISTEMA TRILITICO E ARCO

Legenda:

- **A. Imbarcamento**
- **B. Raddrizzatore**
- **C. Disassamento**
- **D. Muro di spalla**
- **E. Contrafforte**
- **F. Puntellamento**
- **G. Tirante**

- **a. carico**
- **b. spinta**
- **c. forza trasversale**

architrave
piedritto
a
A
B
D
b
c

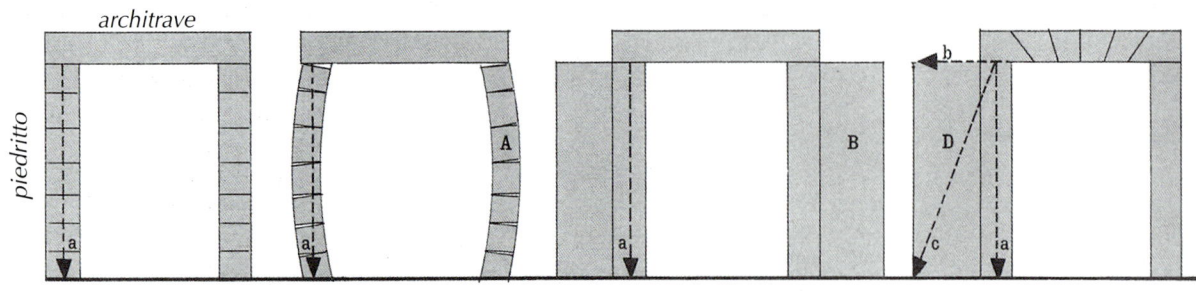

1. Schema del sistema trilitico e suo comportamento strutturale.

archivolto
b
c
a
C
chiave
dell'arco
imposta
dell'arco
piedritto
D
E

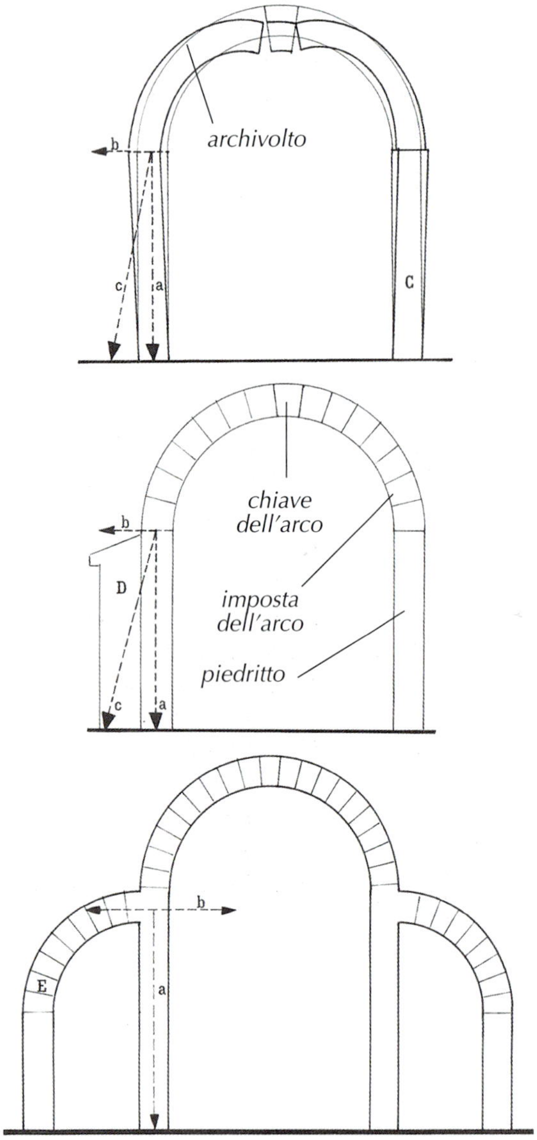

2. Schema del sistema arcuato e suo comportamento strutturale.

b
G
D
c
a
F

3. Schema delll'organizzazione e del comportamento strutturale del sistema ad arco acuto.

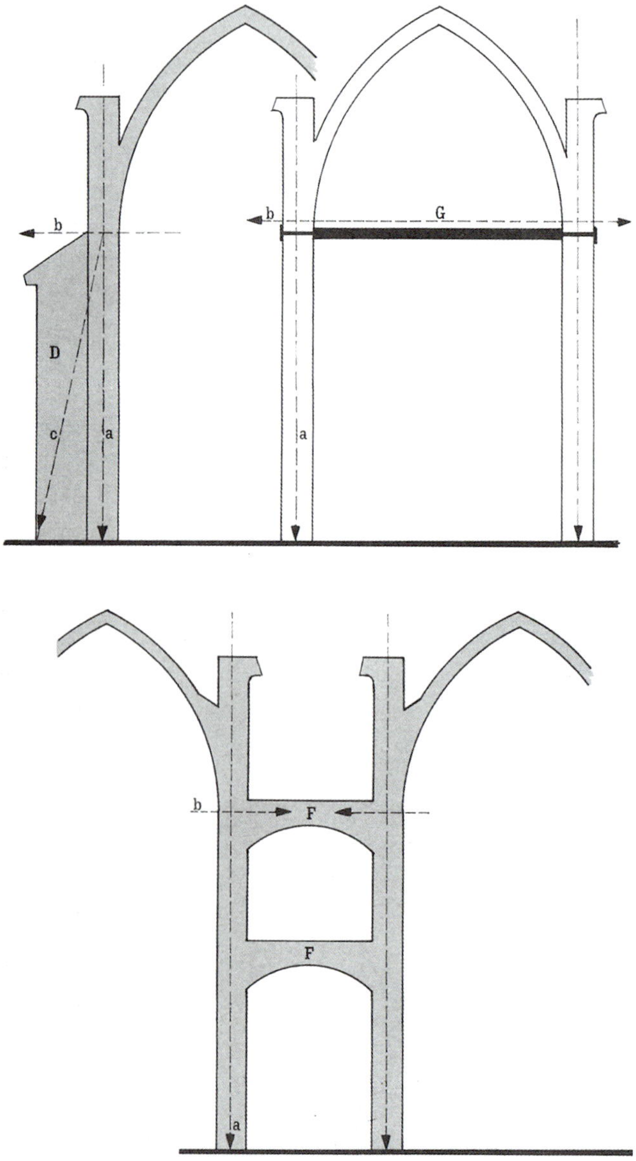

L'ARCO NELLA STORIA

ARCHI A TUTTO SESTO

1. A semicerchio (arco romano)
2. A semicerchio allungato
3. Ribassato o scemo
4. A ferro di cavallo
5. Moresco
6. A cesto (o a sesto) (policentrico)
7. A sesto ribassato
8. Ellittico
9. A parabola
10. Trilobato
11. Triplice
12. A falso cesto
13. A spalla
14. Veneziano
15. Fiorentino
16. A tutto sesto con piedritti

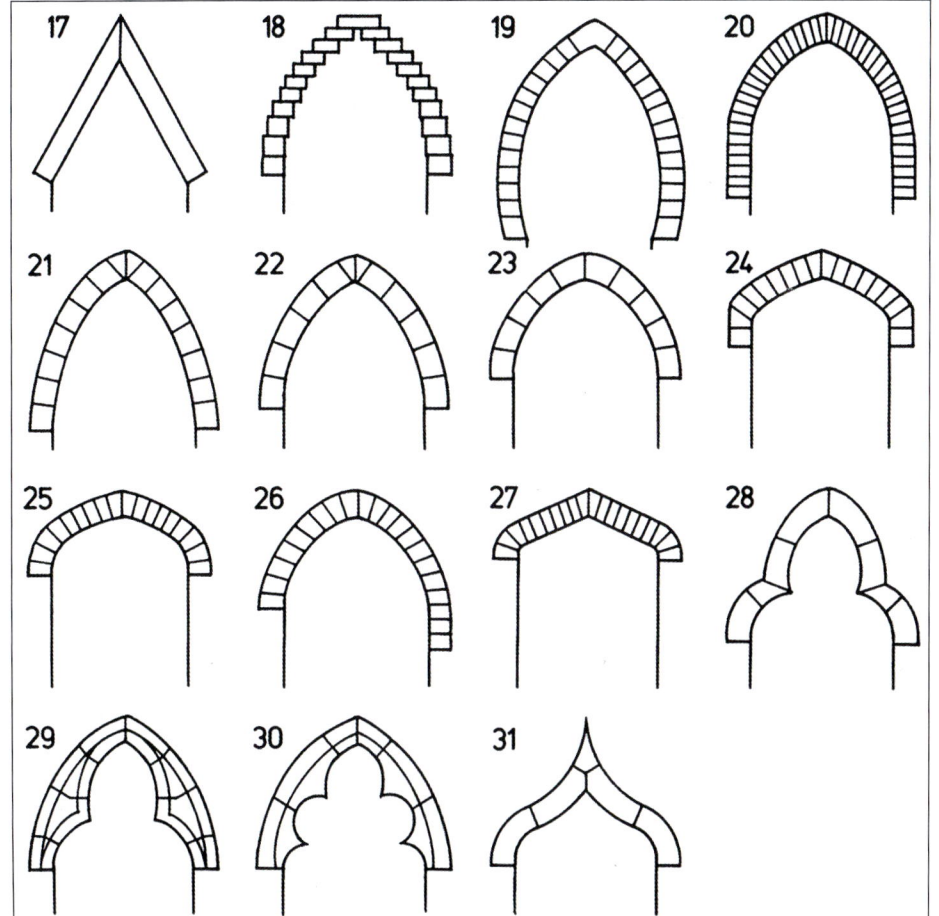

ARCHI A SESTO ACUTO

17. Triangolare
18. Con aggetto (falso arco)
19. A ferro di cavallo
20. Moresco a ferro di cavallo
21. A lancetta
22. Equilatero
23. Ribassato
24. Pseudo arco Tudor
25. Arco Tudor
26. Con un sol fianco (rampante)
27. Arco Tudor ribassato
28. A tre centri
29. Triplice
30. A punta
31. Inflesso (a schiena d'asino)

PIANTE, FRUTTI, ANIMALI, OGGETTI E FIGURE SIMBOLICHE

AGNELLO ◄ Simbolo di Cristo nel suo ruolo sacrificale. Si identifica, in particolare, con l'innocenza e la mitezza.

ALBERO ◄ Ha le radici infisse nella terra ma è rivolto verso il cielo: è quindi rappresentazione dell'unione tra vita terrena e divina. È anche simbolo della croce e della rinascita.

ACQUA ◄ Sorgente di vita in molti miti delle origini, può essere anche fonte di distruzione; in questo senso, rappresenta anche l'elemento che purifica e porta a nuova vita (dal Diluvio Universale al rito del Battesimo).

AQUILA ◄ Espressione di regalità, rappresenta la forza vittoriosa sul male; in epoca cristiana simboleggia l'azione purificatrice del Battesimo. È anche attributo dell'Evangelista Giovanni.

ASINO ◄ In Palestina e nei territori mediorientali è espressione di nobiltà. La cultura greca gli attribuì in seguito il significato negativo di ignoranza e cocciutaggine.

AUREOLA ◄ Cerchio luminoso sopra il capo dei santi. Già nelle culture asiatiche e in età tardoantica è rappresentazione di sacralità.

BALENA ◄ Può assumere il significato negativo di inganno e perdizione o quello positivo di iniziazione e rinascita.

BILANCIA ◄ Simbolo della giustizia e del retto comportamento; in molte religioni, tra cui quella cristiana, è attributo del Supremo Giudice nell'atto di pesare le anime.

BUE ◄ In qualità di animale addomesticato, è simbolo di forza pacifica e di servitù paziente.

CAPRO ◄ Animale sacrificale, indica i peccatori. È spesso presente nella rappresentazione del giudizio finale, quale simbolo dei dannati in opposizione all'agnello, simbolo dei giusti.

CADUCEO ◄ Attributo di Ermes-Mercurio, messaggero degli dei; è associato al principio dell'equilibrio tra elementi o principi opposti. Consiste, infatti, in un bastone cui sono attorcigliati simmetricamente due serpenti, simboli di polarità positiva e negativa.

CANE ◄ Espressione di fedeltà e vigilanza. Nella mitologia può essere guardiano dell'aldilà (Cerbero).

CAVERNA ◄ Rappresenta il luogo di contatto con forze misteriose. In questo senso è carica di pericoli, dai quali si può uscire in seguito a prove, secondo un percorso collegato al principio di purificazione o di rinascita. È anche luogo in cui si nascondono tesori.

CEDRO ◄ Per la durezza dell'albero da cui ha origine, è simbolo di incorruttibilità.

CENTAURO ◄ Essere con corpo di cavallo e busto umano, rappresenta la duplice natura dell'uomo, animale e divina. Può dunque assumere significato positivo di dominio sugli istinti o, al contrario, d'abbandono ad essi.

CERVO ◄ Nel Cristianesimo rappresenta l'anima nella ricerca della purificazione spirituale.

CHIAVE ◄ In antichità simbolo di potere, può assumere il significato di conoscenza.

CHIMERA ◄ Essere mostruoso con sembianze di leone, capra e serpente. Fin dall'antichità rappresenta le forze spaventose della terra e del mare.

CHIOCCIOLA ◄ Simbolo lunare e di rigenerazione stagionale; può rappresentare anche la Resurrezione di Cristo.

CIGNO ◄ Immagine della purezza e simbolo del Redentore sulla croce. Nel Medioevo assume anche il significato negativo dell'ipocrisia.

CILIEGIA ◄ Per il suo colore rosso, è simbolo del sacrificio e della passione.

CIVETTA ◄ Uccello notturno, che vede nel buio; per questo nell'antica Grecia era simbolo di conoscenza razionale, attributo della dea Atena. Solo in tempi recenti ha assunto il significato negativo di malaugurio.

COLOMBA ◄ È simbolo di pace, mitezza e amore. Già attributo di Venere, nell'iconografia cristiana è rappresentazione dello Spirito Santo.

CONCHIGLIA ◄ Fin dall'antichità è collegata al simbolismo della nascita e della fecondità. Nell'iconografia cristiana è attributo dei pellegrini, sia perché allude al viaggio per mare verso la Terra Santa, sia perché richiama la forma dell'orecchio e quindi della parola di Dio.

CONIGLIO-LEPRE ◄ In quanto animali inermi, rappresentano la fiducia in Dio. Posto ai piedi di Maria, di colore bianco, il coniglio indica la sconfitta delle vanità terrene. Nell'antichità era simbolo di fecondità.

CORALLO ◄ Generato, secondo il mito greco, dal sangue di Medusa, funge da amuleto per allontanare le forze del male.

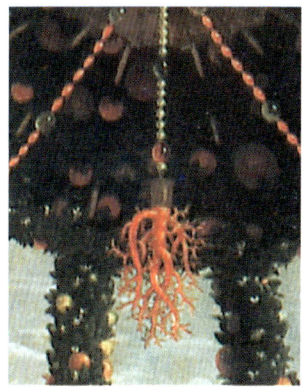

CORNUCOPIA ◄ Vaso a forma di corno adornato di fiori, da cui sgorgano frutti e altri doni; nell'iconografia classica è simbolo di abbondanza.

DELFINO ◄ Associato presso i Greci a Poseidone, dio del mare, nella religione etrusca trasporta le anime nell'aldilà. È dunque anche simbolo di cambiamento; per questo, nell'iconografia cristiana, talvolta rappresenta Gesù Salvatore.

DRAGO ◄ Animale fantastico, con sembianze di rettile alato, presente nell'immaginario di molti popoli. Nell'iconografia cristiana è simbolo di Lucifero e del caos originale. Nelle culture orientali è invece legato alla fertilità e alla rinascita della natura. In Cina è simbolo dell'Imperatore.

EDERA ◄ In quanto sempreverde, rappresenta l'immortalità dell'anima dopo la morte del corpo.

ERMELLINO ◄ Per il suo bianco pelo rappresenta l'innocenza, la purezza morale e, di conseguenza, la giustizia. Per questo è spesso associato a insegne regali o ecclesiastiche.

FARFALLA ◄ Rappresenta l'anima umana. Per la sua bellezza, leggerezza e fragilità, può anche essere associata alla inconsistenza delle gioie passeggere.

FENICE ◄ Uccello simile all'airone, in grado di rigenerarsi dalle proprie ceneri. È simbolo di immortalità e resurrezione, di rinascita ciclica.

FIORE ◄ Simbolo di giovinezza, di innocenza e di energia vitale. Può rappresentare la caducità delle bellezze terrene. Ogni fiore è collegato ad una specifica simbologia.

FIUME ◄ Lo scorrere delle acque è legato al concetto di rinnovamento e di morte e a quello di purificazione. In molti miti originari uno o più fiumi sono posti a delimitazione del mondo.

FUOCO ◄ Elemento dalla duplice valenza, in quanto riscalda e illumina, ma può portare distruzione. Simbolo positivo del focolare domestico presso i Romani, per la religione cristiana rappresenta lo Spirito Santo o, al contrario, la punizione divina dell'inferno.

GIARDINO ◄ Circondato da mura e ben curato, è simbolo della Vergine Maria. Può anche raffigurare il Paradiso.

GIGLIO ◄ Attributo di molti santi, indica purezza. Nel *Discorso della montagna*, contenuto nel Vangelo, i gigli del campo sono indicati come esempi della fede in Dio.

GRIFONE ◄ Creatura fantastica con corpo di leone e testa ed ali di aquila, domina terra e aria. È anche simbolo dell'unione di forza e saggezza. Per questa dualità può alludere alla duplice natura, divina e umana, di Cristo.

LABIRINTO ◄ Rappresentazione del lungo e difficile cammino da percorrere per giungere a un obiettivo, spesso con valore iniziatico.

LEONE ◄ Simbolo dell'Evangelista Marco, rappresenta la forza e la potenza ed è spesso collocato a difesa di luoghi sacri. Può essere anche immagine negativa della forza selvaggia.

LIBRO ◄ Custodisce la sapienza rivelata, è quindi simbolo fondamentale per molte religioni, in quanto ne rappresenta la dottrina. Indica anche saggezza.

LUNA ◄ Simbolo presente in culture antichissime e associato alla figura femminile. La luce riflessa e il suo continuo mutare hanno dato origine a molteplici leggende e simbologie.

LIUTO ◄ Se rappresentato con le corde rotte è simbolo di morte.

MANDORLA ◄ L'aureola a forma di mandorla che ospita le immagini di Gesù o di Maria rappresenta la gloria celeste. La simbologia è legata al guscio durissimo che protegge il frutto.

MANDORLO ◄ Tra i primi alberi a fiorire, è simbolo di vigilanza.

MELA ◄ Simbolo della tentazione e del peccato originale. La mela in mano al Bambino Gesù indica che Egli prende su di sé i peccati del mondo. La simbologia deriva dalla duplicità del termine *malum*, che significa sia "melo" che "male".

MELAGRANA ◄ Nelle culture antiche la melagrana dischiusa è simbolo dell'abbondanza e della fecondità; nel Cristianesimo il rosso succo diviene simbolo del martirio e i semi dell'unità della Chiesa.

NOCE ◄ Per la durezza del suo guscio che difende il frutto, è rappresentazione simbolica di corpo e anima. Ad essa sono paragonate le Sacre Scritture, in quanto difendono un contenuto prezioso.

NODO ◄ Presenta significati diversi, connessi allo sciogliere o al legare.
Nell'iconografia cristiana è spesso simbolo di unione nella comunità.

OCCHIO ◄ Associato alla luce, rappresenta la conoscenza spirituale. L'occhio entro un triangolo, o circondato da raggi luminosi, è il simbolo cristiano della Trinità e dell'onnipresenza divina.

OLIVO ◄ Nell'antichità greca, collegato alla dea Atena, fu simbolo di vittoria; nell'antica Roma divenne emblema della dea della pace. In ambito cristiano è collegato anche all'olio che placa, purifica e nutre.

PALMA ◄ Ritenuta sacra fin dall'antichità, rappresenta l'ascesa e la vittoria.
Un suo ramo è simbolo di martirio e di eternità.

PASTORE ◄ Nell'uomo che custodisce e guida il suo gregge è rappresentato Cristo che protegge e guida i fedeli.

PAVONE ◄ Poiché ogni primavera rigenera le sue penne, indica rinascita e immortalità. Per la sua altera bellezza può essere assunto a simbolo di vanità e superbia.

PECORA ◄ Innocente e inerme di fronte al nemico, rappresenta l'umanità, facile vittima di seduzione.

PEGASO ◄ Cavallo alato, sorto, secondo la mitologia greca, dal collo mozzato di Medusa.

Rappresenta l'ispirazione poetica, unione della vitalità del cavallo e della spiritualità degli uccelli.

PELLICANO ◄ Secondo una leggenda questo animale, beccandosi il petto, dona il proprio sangue ai figli, riportandoli alla vita. È dunque allusione all'Eucarestia e al sacrificio di Cristo, e simbolo dell'amore incondizionato dei genitori per i propri figli.

PERA ◄ Nell'iconografia cristiana rappresenta l'umanità che discende da Eva.

PERLA ◄ Simbolo lunare e femminile, per la sua forma sferica è associata all'idea della perfezione. Poiché si trova racchiusa nella dura conchiglia, è allusione alla conoscenza e alla verità.

PESCE ◄ Simbolo di Cristo e dell'Eucarestia, derivante dalla parola greca *ichthus* (pesce), acrostico della frase "Gesù Cristo, Figlio di Dio, Salvatore". Nella tradizione orientale rappresenta, a volte, le forze del male.

PIETRE PREZIOSE ◄ Possiedono innumerevoli significati, anche collegati al simbolismo astrologico. Poiché mostrano la loro bellezza solo se lavorate, indicano la necessità di purificazione. I cristalli sono simboli di Maria e rappresentano la virtù.

RUOTA ◄ È simbolo del cosmo ed espressione di luce. Può essere anche ruota della fortuna, che allude alla ciclicità della vita.

SERPENTE ◄ Ha assunto nelle diverse culture significati spesso contrapposti.
Nell'iconografia cristiana è emblema delle forze demoniache, dell'astuzia e dell'inganno.
Rappresentato nell'atto di mordersi la coda, quindi in forma circolare, diviene simbolo di eternità.

SERPENTE PIUMATO ◄ Unione di serpente e uccello, nelle culture precolombiane è simbolo del dio Quetzakcoatl e rappresenta l'unione tra cielo e terra.

SFINGE ◄ Essere con corpo di leone e testa umana, può rappresentare l'ottusità, che solo l'intelletto può sconfiggere, o l'enigma insondabile.

SIBILLA ◄ Profetessa dell'antichità in grado di comunicare con il divino e di diffondere la sua parola agli uomini. Per questo è strumento di rivelazione.

SOLE ◄ In molte religioni è associato alla divinità; nell'iconografia cristiana è simbolo di resurrezione e di immortalità.

SPECCHIO ◄ Può significare vanità (come nel mito classico di Narciso), ma anche conoscenza di se stessi.
È inoltre simbolo mariano.

SPIRALE ◄ Rappresentazione del cambiamento, del nascere e del morire delle cose.

STRADA ◄ Simbolo di destino e fortuna.

UCCELLO ◄ Simbolo dell'anima umana. Poiché vola in alto, indica il desiderio di staccarsi dalla vita terrena ed avvicinarsi alla sfera spirituale.

UNICORNO (o LIOCORNO) ◄ Animale fantastico rappresentato generalmente come un cervo bianco con criniera di cavallo e un corno a spirale sulla fronte.
Presente nella simbologia antica e medievale, indica purezza, spiritualità e forza.

UOVO ◄ Simbolo di nascita, creazione (totalità racchiusa in un guscio) e resurrezione (risveglio primaverile della fertilità naturale).

UVA e VITE ◄ Simboli eucaristici, rappresentano il sangue di Cristo.
Alludono inoltre al lavoro dell'uomo come partecipazione al cammino spirituale. I tralci indicano la Chiesa universale.

ZUCCA ◄ Attributo dei pellegrini (che vi conservavano l'acqua) e simbolo di resurrezione.

I NUMERI

Fin dall'antichità i numeri hanno assunto un significato simbolico, legato alla comprensione dei principi che regolano l'universo. Secondo il filosofo Pitagora, ogni forma può essere espressa attraverso numeri, che rappresentano il principio originario da cui tutto ha avuto origine e nel quale risiede l'essenza di ogni cosa.

UNO ◄ Simbolo dell'unità, e quindi dell'essenza divina. Indica anche principio e fine del mondo.

DUE ◄ Ricorda la duplice natura, divina e umana, di Cristo. Secondo la concezione filosofica cinese del Taoismo indica il principio dello *yin* e dello *yang*, basato sull'unità armonica tra elementi opposti.

TRE ◄ Indica la Trinità, e in quanto tale è simbolo di perfezione. Allude anche ai tre figli di Noè, da cui ebbero origine tutti i popoli, alle tre virtù teologali, alle tre età dell'uomo, alle tre potenze dell'anima umana (intelligenza, volontà, memoria).

QUATTRO ◄ Simbolo di ciò che è terreno: secondo la *Bibbia*, quattro sono le regioni del mondo, i venti, i fiumi che percorrono la terra; inoltre quattro sono gli elementi (acqua, fuoco, aria, terra), le stagioni, i cavalieri dell'Apocalisse; quattro i profeti maggiori, i padri della Chiesa, le virtù cardinali.

SETTE ◄ Fin dall'antichità è importante per il suo significato astrologico.
Può indicare l'unione della componente spirituale (associata al numero tre) con quella terrena (quattro). Sulla sua simbologia è fondato l'intero libro dell'*Apocalisse*.
Legata al numero sette è anche l'opposizione tra i vizi capitali e le virtù.

OTTO ◄ Simbolo battesimale e di resurrezione. Otto sono i lati dei battisteri, otto le beatitudini.

DIECI ◄ Denota perfezione e completezza. Indica il decalogo della legge di Dio.

UNDICI ◄ In quanto trasgressione del numero dieci, indicante la legge, significa peccato.
Undici sono gli apostoli riuniti attorno a Gesù dopo il tradimento di Giuda.

DODICI ◄ Multiplo di tre e di quattro, indica la sintesi tra spirituale e terreno (presso molte civiltà è la sintesi tra maschile e femminile). Dodici sono gli apostoli, i mesi dell'anno e i segni dello zodiaco.

Sopra: I quattro elementi e i dodici segni dello zodiaco, da **Barthélemy l'Anglais**, miniatura da *Le Livre des propriétés des choses*, XV sec. Parigi, Biblioteca Nazionale di Francia.

A sinistra: **Hieronymus Bosch**, *I sette peccati capitali*, 1480. Olio su tavola, 120x150 cm. Madrid, Museo del Prado. Particolare.

RICONOSCERE I SANTI NELL'ARTE CRISTIANA

ANDREA APOSTOLO ◄ È rappresentato come un vecchio con la barba bianca che porta una croce a X, in riferimento al suo martirio.

ANNA ◄ Madre di Maria. Indossa un abito rosso, simbolo dell'amore, e un mantello verde, simbolo di rinascita della primavera.

ANTONIO DA PADOVA ◄ Reca il giglio, simbolo di fede.

BENEDETTO ◄ È riconoscibile per l'abito monacale e la tonsura.

CATERINA D'ALESSANDRIA ◄ È riconoscibile per la ruota e la palma, simboli del martirio; porta un anello, riferimento al suo matrimonio mistico con Cristo. Veste ricchi abiti, che rammentano le sue origini regali.

CATERINA DA SIENA ◄ Suo attributo è il giglio.

FRANCESCO D'ASSISI ◄ Porta il saio e la cintura a tre nodi, simboli dei voti di povertà, castità e obbedienza. È riconoscibile anche per le stigmate.

GABRIELE ◄ Angelo dell'Annunciazione, porge a Maria un giglio.

GEROLAMO ◄ Dottore della Chiesa, può essere rappresentato nei rossi abiti cardinalizi e con il bastone pastorale, in meditazione nel suo studio, o seminudo come eremita penitente. Lo accompagna un leone, a cui, secondo la leggenda, tolse la spina da una zampa.

GIACOMO ◄ È associato alla conchiglia, attributo dei pellegrini.

GIORGIO ◄ Nobile eroe guerriero vincitore sul drago, creatura del male. Viene raffigurato in armatura su un cavallo bianco; sul suo scudo e sulla sua bandiera è raffigurata una croce.

GIOVANNI BATTISTA ◄ Messaggero di Cristo, predicò nel deserto: è poveramente vestito di pelli e porta in mano una croce, spesso di canna.

GIUSEPPE ◄ I suoi attributi sono il giglio, gli arnesi da falegname e il bastone fiorito.

LORENZO ◄ È raffigurato con la graticola con cui fu martirizzato.

LUCIA ◄ Mostra su un vassoio gli occhi, simbolo, secondo la leggenda, del suo martirio.

MICHELE ◄ Arcangelo, cacciò Lucifero dal Paradiso. È quindi raffigurato in armatura, accompagnato da Satana o da un drago sui quali è vincitore.

PIETRO ◄ Apostolo e primo Pontefice, ha come simbolo le chiavi.

SEBASTIANO ◄ È rappresentato trafitto da frecce, segni del suo martirio.

STEFANO ◄ Primo martire. Suo attributo sono le pietre, con le quali subì il sacrificio.

A destra:
Vincenzo Foppa,
Martirio di San Sebastiano,
1487-1489 circa.
Affresco staccato e trasportato su tela,
268x173 cm. Milano,
Pinacoteca di Brera.

Sotto:
Spinello Aretino,
I quattro Evangelisti, 1387.
Affresco sulla volta della sagrestia di San Miniato al Monte, Firenze.

I QUATTRO EVANGELISTI

LUCA ◄ Patrono dei pittori; suo attributo è il bue.

GIOVANNI EVANGELISTA ◄ Apostolo, suo simbolo è l'aquila. Ha in mano il libro del Vangelo o un rotolo di pergamena. Talvolta ha un calice con serpente e un paiolo.

MARCO ◄ È accompagnato da un leone alato.

MATTEO ◄ Apostolo, scrisse il primo Vangelo. È accompagnato da un angelo che lo aiuta a scrivere.

RICONOSCERE LE DIVINITÀ DELLA MITOLOGIA CLASSICA

APOLLO ◄ Dio Sole, patrono delle arti ed in particolare della musica, è rappresentato come un giovane con la testa coronata di alloro che conduce un carro a quattro cavalli. Suo attributo è anche la lira.

BACCO (DIONISO) ◄ Dio del vino e dell'ebbrezza, ma anche del teatro, compare coronato di grappoli d'uva e di foglie di vite.

CUPIDO (EROS) ◄ Dio dell'amore, raffigurato come fanciullo alato, spesso con gli occhi bendati, con arco e frecce.

DIANA (ARTEMIDE) ◄ Dea cacciatrice, è accompagnata da un cervo o da cani.

GIUNONE (ERA) ◄ Moglie di Giove, protettrice della mater-nità. L'accompagna un pavone.

GIOVE (ZEUS) ◄ Massima divinità dell'Olimpo. I suoi attributi sono l'aquila e il fulmine.

MARTE (ARES) ◄ Dio della guerra. È rappresentato in armatura, spesso in compagnia di Venere.

MERCURIO (HERMES) ◄ Dio dei viaggiatori e del commercio e messaggero degli dei. Porta sandali alati, un cappello e un caduceo con due serpenti.

MINERVA (ATENA) ◄ Possiede una duplice simbologia, come dea della saggezza e protettrice delle arti e come divinità guerriera. È accompagnata da una civetta e spesso armata di egida, elmo e lancia.

NETTUNO (POSEIDONE) ◄ Dio del mare. È armato di un tridente.

SATURNO (CRONOS) ◄ Dio dell'agricoltura e del tempo, porta una falce.

VENERE (AFRODITE) ◄ Dea della bellezza e dell'amore. I suoi attributi sono la colomba o il cigno.

VULCANO (EFESTO) ◄ Dio del fuoco. È rappresentato come un fabbro ed è zoppo.

A destra: Copia romana del II sec. d.C. dell'*Athena Parthenos* di **Fidia**.

Sotto: **Andrea Mantegna**, *Il Parnaso*, 1497. Tempera su tela, 160x192 cm. Parigi, Museo del Louvre.

LE DIVINITÀ DEL PARNASO

Il dipinto è una **allegoria**, cioè la rappresentazione di un concetto astratto attraverso la concatenazione di figure, ognuna portatrice di un preciso significato. Il *Parnaso* è il monte sacro alle muse; la scena, popolata di numerosi personaggi mitologici, è la visualizzazione del concetto di Armonia, derivata dall'unione degli opposti, rappresentati da *Venere*, dea dell'amore, e *Marte*, dio della guerra.

VULCANO ◄ Consorte di VENERE, è all'ingresso della sua fucina, dove si scorgono gli arnesi da fabbro, ed indica con rabbia gli amanti.

VENERE E MARTE ◄ Marte è riconoscibile per l'armatura e la lancia; sono seguiti da CUPIDO, armato di frecce ed arco. La loro unione rappresenta l'armonia.

ORFEO ◄ Musicista e poeta, è rappresentato mentre suona la lira. Secondo la mitologia, tutte le creature erano incantate dalle sue armoniose melodie e lo seguivano.

MERCURIO ◄ È raffigurato con elmo, calzari alati e caduceo. Secondo la mitologia, ha protetto l'amore di MARTE e VENERE. Rappresentato accanto a PEGASO, incarna la sapienza immortale.

LE NOVE MUSE ◄ Divinità protettrici delle arti e delle scienze danzano in cerchio. Ad esse si riferiscono le montagne che crollano, a causa di eruzioni vulcaniche determinate dal loro canto. Vi pone fine PEGASO, il mitico cavallo alato, protettore dell'ispirazione poetica.

I TEMI ICONOGRAFICI DELLE OPERE ARTISTICHE

 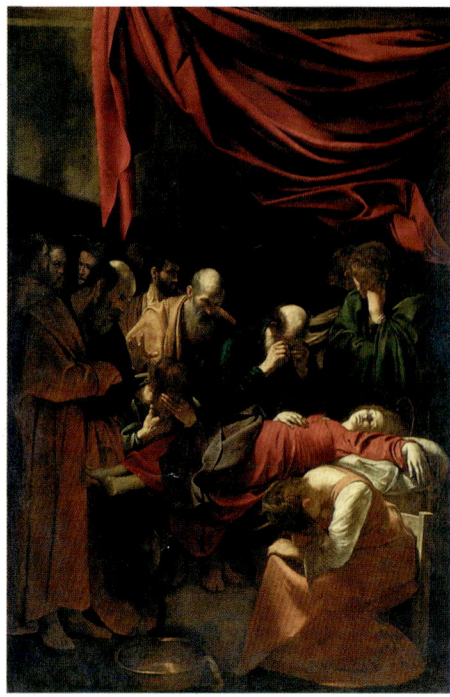 

ADORAZIONE DEI MAGI ◄ Rappresentazione dei Magi nell'atto di rendere omaggio a Gesù appena nato, alla capanna o alla grotta di Betlemme. Assistono all'evento Maria, San Giuseppe e spesso anche i pastori.

ADORAZIONE DEI PASTORI ◄ Rappresentazione dei pastori alla grotta di Betlemme, venuti a salutare Gesù appena nato.

ANNUNCIAZIONE ◄ Raffigura l'Arcangelo Gabriele che annuncia a Maria l'imminente maternità.

ASSUNZIONE ◄ Si rappresenta la Vergine mentre, circondata dagli angeli, ascende al cielo.

AUTORITRATTO ◄ Ritratto che l'artista fa di se stesso, disegnato, dipinto o scolpito utilizzando uno o più specchi.

CENACOLO ◄ Rappresentazione di banchetti descritti nei testi biblici o evangelici; nell'Ultima Cena, o Cenacolo, viene raffigurato Gesù con gli Apostoli nell'atto di istituire l'Eucarestia. Spesso è collocato nel refettorio di un convento.

COMPIANTO SUL CRISTO ◄ Raffigurazione di Cristo morto, appena deposto dalla croce, circondato da Maria, San Giovanni e altre figure di dolenti.

CROCIFISSIONE ◄ Dipinto o scultura raffigurante Cristo sulla croce. Nel *Christus patiens* è raffigurato Gesù sofferente; nel *Christus triumphans* Gesù ha gli occhi aperti, perché vincitore sulla morte.

CAPRICCIO ◄ Piccolo dipinto che rappresenta scene o vedute, immaginate dall'artista, con rovine o elementi di fantasia. Genere diffuso nel XVIII secolo.

PANTOCRATORE (CRISTO) ◄ Raffigurazione di Cristo come "colui che domina su ogni cosa". Immagine solitamente musiva che esprime la solenne maestosità del Cristo nel punto più sacro della Chiesa, il catino absidale.

DEPOSIZIONE DALLA CROCE ◄ Rappresentazione di Cristo mentre viene tolto dalla croce, circondato da Maria con le pie donne e San Giovanni, spesso accompagnati da Nicodemo e Giuseppe d'Arimatea.

DORMITIO VIRGINIS ◄ Rappresenta la morte di Maria.

GENERE (pittura di) ◄ Pittura a tema popolare o con scene di vita quotidiana. È frequente nei secoli XVII e XVIII.

GIUDIZIO UNIVERSALE ◄ Rappresentazione di Gesù che, in cielo, giudica e divide le anime degne del Paradiso da quelle destinate all'Inferno.

MADONNA DELLA MISERICORDIA ◄ Raffigura Maria che accoglie i poveri e gli emarginati sotto il suo manto.

MAESTÀ ◄ Immagine, frequente nel Medioevo, della Divinità (la Trinità, Cristo o la Vergine col Bambino) in trono e vista frontalmente.

NATIVITÀ ◄ Rappresentazione della nascita di Gesù, nella grotta, con Maria, Giuseppe e i pastori.

NATURA MORTA ◄ Rappresentazione di soggetti inanimati, come suppellettili e oggetti domestici, cacciagione, fiori, frutti, strumenti musicali. È frequente a partire dal XVII secolo.

PAESAGGIO ◄ Genere pittorico in cui sono rappresentati ambienti naturali. Indica anche lo sfondo di composizioni con altro soggetto.

PIETÀ ◄ Immagine di Maria che tiene sulle ginocchia Cristo morto, dopo la deposizione dalla croce.

QUADRO STORICO ◄ Dipinto con scene riferite a precisi episodi civili o patriottici.

RESURREZIONE ◄ Immagine di Cristo che risorge dopo la morte. Spesso si scorge il sepolcro con la pietra rimossa.

RITRATTO ◄ Rappresentazione del volto o della figura di un personaggio (a mezzo busto o a figura intera) di cui sia riconoscibile l'identità.

SACRA CONVERSAZIONE ◄ Raffigura la Madonna in trono con il Bambino, attorniata da Santi e, talvolta, dai committenti.

SACRA FAMIGLIA ◄ Rappresentazione di Gesù, bambino o fanciullo, con Maria e Giuseppe.

VEDUTA ◄ Rappresentazione particolareggiata di un paesaggio naturale o urbano. Genere diffuso nel XVIII secolo.

VISITAZIONE ◄ Visita di Maria Vergine alla cugina Elisabetta quando seppe che questa era incinta di Giovanni il Battista.

In alto, a sinistra: **Michel Erhart**, *Madonna della Misericordia di Ratisbona*, 1480-90 ca. Legno policromo, altezza 135 cm. Berlino, Museo Statale di Cultura Prussiana.

Al centro: **Caravaggio**, *La morte della Vergine*, 1606. Olio su tela, 369 x 245 cm. Parigi, Museo del Louvre.

A destra: **Pontormo**, *Visitazione*, 1528-1529 ca. Olio su tavola, 202x156 cm. Carmignano (FI), Pieve di San Michele.

GLOSSARIO DEI PRINCIPALI TERMINI ARTISTICI

A

Abaco
(Dal greco *abax*, tavoletta). Parte superiore del capitello delle colonne, in forma di parallelepipedo a base quadrata o di prisma, che sorregge l'architrave o gli archi. Già utilizzato nell'antico Egitto, ebbe notevole sviluppo nell'architettura orientale e quindi negli ordini dell'architettura greco-romana. In età tardo-antica la sua evoluzione diede origine al pulvino (v.) e all'abaco di grandi dimensioni, entrambi elementi tipici dell'architettura bizantina. Interessanti varianti sono offerte dai pilastri polistili di età gotica e dall'abaco diagonale barocco.

Abbazia
Monastero retto da un abate. Il termine può anche definire la sola chiesa abbaziale. Si definì tipologicamente dal VI-VII secolo, quando la regola di San Benedetto introdusse nei monasteri il lavoro manuale (e quindi la necessità di ambienti per la conservazione e la lavorazione dei prodotti della terra). L'esigenza di esportare la tipologia abbaziale in realtà territoriali diverse determinò la definizione di caratteri distributivi e stilistici costanti.

Abside
Struttura terminale di edifici, avente pianta semicircolare o poligonale, coperta da volta a quarto di sfera (catino) e visibile dall'esterno mediante una sporgenza. Già presente nell'architettura protostorica (ad esempio nei monumenti megalitici di Malta) e in quella greca preclassica, fu frequente in età romana e soprattutto nelle chiese cristiane, dove conclude la navata centrale e a volte quelle laterali.

Acànto
Motivo ornamentale che imita le foglie dell'omonima pianta. Fu utilizzato nel capitello corinzio e composito, o nelle decorazioni scultoree di fregi e cornici.

Acquaforte
(dal latino *aqua fortis*, acido nitrico). Procedimento di stampa che comporta l'uso di una lastra metallica spalmata di vernice grassa, inattaccabile dall'acido. Dopo aver inciso lo strato di vernice, la lastra viene immersa nell'acido nitrico diluito con acqua, che corrode il metallo solo nelle zone scoperte. Asportata la vernice, la lastra viene quindi inchiostrata e stampata mediante il torchio. L'acquaforte presenta un carattere grafico e spiccatamente lineare.

Acquarello (o Acquerello)
Tecnica di pittura che prevede l'uso di colori stemperati in acqua, a scarsa capacità coprente. Produce effetti lievi e luminosi, in tonalità chiare. Analogo a procedimenti già conosciuti nelle antiche civiltà orientali, venne utilizzato in età medievale nell'illustrazione dei codici miniati e in genere nella realizzazione di disegni e studi preparatori.

Acquatinta
Tecnica di stampa ottenuta da una lastra metallica intaccata dall'acido mediante stadi successivi. Ne deriva una superficie granulosa e diseguale, che produce effetti sfumati e chiaroscurali. È utilizzata anche per la preparazione di basi per acquaforte.

Acropoli
Parte alta della città ellenica, e per estensione di quella antica. Detto anche di rocca, in genere fortificata, abitata o meno. Presso i Greci in età classica era il centro religioso della città.

Acrotèrio
Elemento decorativo del frontone di un edificio templare, costituito in origine (VII sec. a.C.) da un elemento fittile in bassorilievo, quindi da una statua su piedestallo.

Affresco
Tecnica pittorica murale antichissima, che consiste nel dipingere sull'intonaco ancora 'fresco'. Sul muro vengono stesi due strati di intonaco: sul primo, rustico, detto arriccio, il pittore traccia il disegno preparatorio (sinòpia); su questo è steso il piano definitivo, che occorre dipingere entro la giornata.

Agorà
Piazza principale della città greca; generalmente porticata, era circondata dai principali edifici pubblici. Fu adibita a luogo di mercato, di riunione della cittadinanza, alle celebrazioni sacre.

Altare
Struttura per la celebrazione dei sacrifici. Negli edifici religiosi cristiani era realizzato dapprima in legno, quindi in pietra o marmo.

Altorilievo
Rilievo scultoreo a forte sporgenza dal piano di fondo. Può avvicinarsi sensibilmente al tuttotondo, nel qual caso presenta, là dove esiste un retro delle figure, il sottosquadro.

Ambòne
Elemento architettonico posto nelle chiese, rialzato su colonne o su basamento e delimitato per lo più da parapetti; vi si accede da una o più scale. Utilizzato per la lettura dei testi sacri, è collocato entro il presbiterio, a differenza del pulpito, posto generalmente nella navata centrale.

Ambulacro
Sorta di corridoio all'aperto o coperto, del tipo a portico. Nelle chiese cristiane si sviluppa intorno al presbiterio (v.).

Anamòrfosi
Deformazione dell'immagine dipinta, che può essere vista in modo corretto da un solo punto di osservazione, prospetticamente decentrato. Fu sperimentata nel XVI secolo (Leonardo, Paolo Uccello), quindi frequentemente utilizzata nell'arte figurativa barocca e settecentesca.

Antefissa
Elemento decorativo fittile o in pietra, posto a conclusione dello spiovente del tetto in edifici greci, etruschi, italici e romani.

Arabesco
Elemento decorativo a disegni geometrici o floreali intrecciati e stilizzati. Fu in uso nell'arte tardo-romana, nell'arte bizantina e in quella barbarica. Celebri sono i motivi ad arabesco della cultura figurativa araba.

Arazzo
Tessuto eseguito a mano su telaio, arricchito da motivi decorativi, destinato a ricoprire le pareti. Già noto nell'Antico Oriente e nel mondo classico, risale nella forma moderna all'XI secolo. Prende nome dalla città di Arras, nella Francia settentrionale, un tempo grosso centro di produzione.

Arcata
In una struttura architettonica, l'insieme dell'arco e dello spazio che esso contiene; detto anche di successione di archi. Frequente nell'architettura civile romana (per esempio negli acquedotti) e in quella rinascimentale. Le arcate cieche sono in risalto su parete continua.

Architrave
Elemento architettonico orizzontale, poggiante su colonne o pilastri. È elemento costitutivo del sistema trilitico.

Arco
Struttura architettonica curvilinea composta di conci in pietra o mattoni addossati fra loro, poggianti alle estremità su sostegni (piedritti). La fascia frontale esterna dell'arco è detta archivolto. Per estensione, porta monumentale in forma di arco (arco di trionfo).

Arcosolio
(Dal latino *arcum*, arco, e *solium*, tomba). Nicchia ad arco (o anche architravata) frequentemente situata nelle catacombe, dove veniva collocato il sarcofago. Era sovente decorato o affrescato.

Assonometria
Metodo grafico che consente di rappresentare elementi tridimensionali sul piano, raffigurandone contemporaneamente tre superfici ortogonali tra loro. Fu teorizzato da G. Monge alla fine del Settecento. La si può considerare una "prospettiva isometrica", in cui i raggi visuali sono paralleli tra loro, come scaturiti da una distanza infinita.

Atrio
Ambiente d'ingresso di edificio civile o religioso; può essere o meno coperto. Deriva dall'*atrium* della domus romana, luogo centrale da cui si accedeva alle diverse stanze.

Attico
Parte dell'arco di trionfo collocata sopra il cornicione. Per estensione, ultimo piano di un edificio, separato da un cornicione, spesso a terrazzo.

Balaustra
Elemento architettonico formato da colonnine (balaustri) reggenti un davanzale. Nelle chiese è usata per delimitare gli ambienti destinati al clero; nell'architettura civile è utilizzata nelle scalinate e nei balconi.

Baldacchino
Elemento di copertura in stoffa, retto da aste o colonne. Per estensione, in architettura, coronamento di edicole e cibori (v.).

Basamento
Nell'ordine architettonico elemento che sostiene la colonna e la sua base. È costituito da un dado (v.) posto su modanature e chiuso in alto da una cornice. Detto anche di parte inferiore di un edificio, che vi funge da base.

Basilica
Nell'architettura romana, edificio a destinazione civile a pianta rettangolare e diviso in 3 o 5 navate da colonne. Da questa è derivato l'edificio sacro del rito cristiano, che ne riprende la distribuzione interna. Per estensione, il termine suole indicare la chiesa cristiana, anche non pienamente coerente con la tipologia di origine.

Bassorilievo
Scultura a rilievo, le cui figure sono poco sporgenti dal fondo. Gli effetti di profondità spaziale sono generalmente resi attraverso particolari soluzioni prospettiche.

Bastione
Sistema difensivo costituito da un terrapieno, con mura fortificate a scarpata. Conosciuto dai Greci e dagli Arabi, fu teorizzato ed ampiamente utilizzato nel Cinquecento.

Battistero
Edificio cristiano destinato al rito del battesimo, collocato presso le basiliche paleocristiane e romaniche. Successivamente fu utilizzato più per motivi monumentali che funzionali. Ha pianta centrale (circolare o quadrata, più spesso ottagonale), con copertura generalmente a cupola.

Bìfora
Finestra a due luci, divisa da una colonnetta o da un pilastrino.

Bugnato
Rivestimento murario usato per decorare gli edifici; formato da bugne (pietre sporgenti dal muro), si distingue in liscio, rustico e a punta di diamante.

Bulíno
Strumento appuntito in acciaio, usato dagli incisori o dagli orefici per incidere il metallo.

Calco
Impronta ottenuta attraverso pressione o colatura di una materia molle quale gesso, cera o argilla sul modello da realizzare. Da questo, una volta solidificato, si ottiene la copia.

Càmera ottica
Strumento costituito da un piccolo vano con sistema di specchi, che permette di riflettere le immagini in dimensione ridotta su un piano di carta o di vetro; su questo l'artista può poggiare un foglio e ricalcare a disegno i contorni del soggetto prescelto.

Campata
Spazio compreso tra elementi portanti successivi (pilastri, colonne, ecc.). Anche spazio individuato da quattro pilastri che sostengono una volta a crociera.

Canone
Regola, norma. Sistema di proporzioni tra le varie parti di un'opera.

Canòpo
Vaso in bronzo o terracotta, in uso presso gli Egizi e gli Etruschi, contenente le ceneri del defunto. Imita la figura umana nelle anse a forma di braccia e nel coperchio a forma di testa.

Capitello
Elemento architettonico che conclude un sostegno verticale (colonna, pilastro, parasta), raccordandolo con l'architrave o con l'arco. Assume forme diverse; in generale vi si sviluppa fortemente l'elemento figurativo.

Cappella
Piccolo ambiente di culto, indipendente o parte di edificio più grande. Già frequente in età paleocristiana come edificio singolo a pianta centrale, è in uso entro organismi chiesastici a partire dall'età medievale.

Capriata
Struttura ad impianto triangolare, generalmente in legno a vista, più raramente in ferro, destinata a sorreggere il tetto di un edificio.

Carboncino
Asticciola di carbone usata per disegnare. Per estensione, il disegno eseguito con tale tecnica.

Cariàtide
Statua femminile usata al posto della colonna come sostegno di trabeazioni, cornici, logge o balconi. Originariamente ebbe funzione votiva.

Cartone
Disegno preparatorio per affreschi, arazzi, mosaici, di dimensioni uguali a quelle dell'opera.

Cassettoni
Incavi decorativi dei soffitti e delle volte, di forma quadrata o poligonale. Motivo già presente nell'architettura romana, è derivato dall'incrocio delle travi in legno.

Cattedra episcopale
Seggio per lo più in marmo o legno, variamente ornato o decorato, posto nel vano presbiteriale, riservato al vescovo nelle funzioni religiose. Fino al sec. XI era posto dietro l'altare, al centro dell'abside.

Càvea
Gradinata ad emiciclo del teatro romano, suddivisa in più settori da ambulacri (v.).

Cella
La parte chiusa del tempio pagano, dove si custodiva l'immagine del dio cui l'edificio era dedicato. A pianta rettangolare nel tempio ellenico, era tripartita in quello etrusco-italico. Riferito all'età medievale, il termine indica la piccola stanza dei monaci nei conventi o nelle abbazie.

Cèntina
Parte incurvata dell'arco o della volta. Struttura lignea ricurva che sostiene l'arco o la volta durante la costruzione.

Ceramica
(Dal greco *keramos*, argilla). Arte di fabbricare oggetti modellati con terra (argilla, caolino), poi cotta in forni. Generalmente il termine si riferisce ai soli manufatti, che fin dalle età arcaiche venivano decorati prima della cottura: oggetti destinati ad uso diverso, statue, elementi decorativi (antefisse, formelle). Fin dalle antiche civiltà egizia e mesopotamica formelle di ceramica invetriata vennero utilizzate a scopo decorativo.

Cesellatura
Lavorazione a cesello (strumento d'acciaio appuntito, ma non tagliente) su di una superficie metallica.

Chiostro
Cortile dei monasteri, circondato da portici. È generalmente spazio centrale del complesso monastico, fiancheggiante la chiesa ed elemento di distribuzione dei vari locali. La parte scoperta è sovente adibita a giardino, con vasca o fontana centrale.

Cibòrio
Edicola posta sull'altare maggiore delle basiliche cristiane, composta da quattro colonne e copertura a quattro spioventi. Per estensione, tabernacolo.

Cloisonné (smalto)
Tecnica di lavorazione dello smalto, in cui le varie parti sono delimitate da lamine metalliche.

Collage
Tecnica pittorica che prevede l'uso di materiali diversi, per colore e consistenza, quali carta colorata e piccoli oggetti.

Colonna
Elemento architettonico di sostegno, a sezione circolare. È composta da tre elementi: la base, generalmente a forma di disco o di plinto, che raccorda la colonna al basamento (non è presente nell'ordine dorico); il fusto, liscio o scanalato, che può assumere un rigonfiamento al centro (*èntasis*); il capitello. Nata con funzione portante, assunse in età romana anche ruolo decorativo (specialmente come semicolonna addossata al muro o al pilastro). Può svolgere funzione votiva o celebrativa, come nell'architettura romana: in questo caso assume grandi dimensioni ed è arricchita da scene scolpite in rilievo sul fusto.

Compendiario, stile
Stile pittorico in cui l'immagine è resa nelle sue parti essenziali, mediante pennellate veloci e macchie di colore, senza definire i contorni e i dettagli.

Composito
Ordine architettonico usato dai Romani, che fonde ed elabora gli elementi degli ordini ionico e corinzio. Ignorato da Vitruvio, fu descritto, per quanto riguarda il capitello, da L.B. Alberti nel Rinascimento, quindi da S. Serlio e A. Palladio.

Contrafforte
Sostegno esterno degli edifici, con funzione di rinforzo o di controspinta; può avere forma di pilastro addossato (come in età romanica) o di arco rampante (come in età gotica).

Corinzio
Ordine architettonico greco caratterizzato dal capitello a foglie d'acànto, fregio continuo e colonna scanalata con base. Fu considerato da Vitruvio una variante dell'ordine ionico, cui si avvicina, in un periodo iniziale, nella base e nella trabeazione. Nato alla fine del V sec. a.C., si diffuse nell'architettura ellenistica e, con varianti, in quella romana.

Cornice
Elemento architettonico sporgente, posto a coronamento di una superficie o di una fascia decorativa. Può concludere un piedistallo, l'imposta di un arco, la parte di facciata corrispondente ad un piano (marcapiano), o l'intera facciata (cornicione).

Coro
Nella chiesa cristiana, parte della navata principale posta dietro l'altare maggiore, destinata ai cantori o ai monaci. Più tardi, il termine passò a definire gli stalli lignei, sempre più finemente decorati e intarsiati, sui quali sedevano i cantori.

Costolone
Elemento portante di una volta o di una cupola, in aggetto rispetto alla superficie interna o esterna di queste (v. nervatura).

Cripta
Ambiente sotterraneo (dal greco *kryptós*, nascosto, quindi dal latino *crypta*, sotterraneo). Nelle catacombe erano così chiamate le cappelle più grandi. Nelle chiese cristiane vi si conservano generalmente le reliquie dei martiri. È posta nella zona del presbiterio, che spesso si eleva su di essa, lasciandone intravvedere l'interno.

Croce greca
Pianta di edificio sacro a bracci uguali che si intersecano. Più frequente nell'architettura sacra bizantina, che valorizza la pianta centrale.

Croce latina
Pianta di edificio cristiano con bracci di misura diversa, intersecantesi perpendicolarmente. Se il braccio corto (transetto) si appone all'apice di quello longitudinale, è detta a T o a croce commissa; se lo attraversa a circa 2/3 della sua lunghezza, è detta a croce immissa.

Cròmlech
Complesso architettonico del periodo megalitico composto da pietre lavorate verticali, disposte a cerchio e sormontate da architravi.

Cupola
Copertura di un vano, ottenuta virtualmente dalla rotazione di una curva intorno ad un asse verticale. Può avere forma semisferica, acuta o ribassata. Si distingue dalla pseudocupola, frequente nel Mediterraneo protostorico, composta da filari concentrici e sovrapposti di pietre o mattoni. La cupola ebbe notevole sviluppo a partire dall'architettura romana, con l'utilizzo del cemento. Interessante l'uso di costoloni di rinforzo, per lo più collegati ai lati della base poligonale.

Cùspide
Elemento architettonico triangolare, usato come coronamento di portali, di facciate o di parti di esse.

<hr>

D

Deambulatorio
Sorta di corridoio che percorre internamente gli edifici a pianta centrale; negli edifici a sviluppo longitudinale prolunga le navate perimetrando il coro e seguendo l'andamento semicircolare o semipoligonale delle absidi. È collegato allo spazio interno attraverso arcate.

Dìttico
(Dal greco *dìptykos*, piegato in due). Insieme composto da due tavolette in legno o avorio, scolpite o dipinte, unite da cerniere. Dai sec. XIV-XV è esteso alle opere di pittura o di scultura anche di grandi dimensioni, composte da due parti accostate e formanti un complesso unitario sotto il profilo stilistico e descrittivo.

Dòlmen
Costruzione megalitica costituita da due pietre infisse nel terreno, sormontate da una terza, orizzontale.

Domus
Vocabolo latino che indica l'abitazione signorile unifamiliare. Suo carattere fondamentale è l'unicità sotto l'aspetto funzionale e fondiario. È chiusa all'esterno, se si eccettua il vano di entrata e una o due botteghe sul fronte, ed ha come elemento distintivo il *peristylium*, cortile interno porticato (a volte ripetuto), sul quale si affacciano i vani di abitazione.

Dorico ordine
Ordine architettonico greco caratterizzato da colonne a scanalature a spigolo vivo, poggianti direttamente sul basamento (o stilòbate), dal capitello suddiviso in àbaco ed echìno, e dal fregio composto da triglifi e mètope. Ebbe origine nel VII sec. a.C., forse derivato da prototipi in legno. Caratterizza la maggior parte della produzione templare nelle colonie della Magna Grecia.

Dripping
Tecnica pittorica consistente nel disporre il colore senza pennello, facendolo gocciolare direttamente sulla tela.

Dròmos
Nell'architettura greca arcaica, corridoio (anche con gradini) di accesso ad una tomba sotterranea (per es. la *tholos* micenea).

<hr>

E

Echìno
Parte del capitello dorico a forma di anello schiacciato posto tra il fusto della colonna e l'abaco.

Edìcola
(Piccola casa, dal latino *aedes*, casa). Piccola costruzione con prospetto a somiglianza di tempietto classico (con timpano e colonne); per estensione, vano inserito entro la muratura di un edificio, inquadrato architettonicamente, contenente un'immagine sacra.

Emicìclo
Costruzione architettonica a pianta semicircolare. Detto in particolare della parte del teatro destinata al pubblico.

Encausto
Tecnica pittorica di origine greca e romana che utilizza colori misti a cera spalmati a caldo. Applicata su legno o tela, ma anche su muro, trovò rinnovato impiego a partire dal XVIII secolo.

Esèdra
Spazio architettonico semicircolare o rettangolare aperto su un lato. Frequente nell'architettura romana, sia pubblica (spazio colonnato, frequente nelle terme), che privata (elemento posto a conclusione del peristilio nelle domus).

Estradosso
La parte esterna dell'arco che ne segue il profilo.

Euritmia
Secondo Vitruvio, è una delle sei categorie che costituiscono l'architettura. Può essere definita la distribuzione armonica tra le parti di una composizione.

Exùltet
Pergamena miniata a rotolo, contenente testi di canti e di preghiere riferiti alla liturgia pasquale. Veniva srotolata dal pulpito, cosicché il fedele potesse vederne le illustrazioni.

<hr>

F

Facciata
Parete esterna dell'edificio, corrispondente ad un lato del suo perimetro. Generalmente si riferisce al fronte in cui è collocato l'ingresso principale.

Fàscio (pilastro a)
Pilastro tipico dell'architettura gotica, cui sono addossate più colonne e/o semicolonne.

Festone
Motivo ornamentale classico costituito da una fascia di foglie, fiori e frutta retti da nastri e putti.

Filigrana
Tecnica di lavorazione dei metalli preziosi consistente nell'intreccio di fili d'oro e d'argento.

Formella
Tavoletta dipinta o scolpita applicata con funzione decorativa su muri o soffitti.

Fòrnice
(dal lat. *fornix*, arco, volta). Apertura dell'arco monumentale o di porte urbane.

Foro
La piazza più importante della città romana, centro della vita pubblica, su cui prospettavano o insistevano edifici civili e religiosi.

Fregio
Elemento della trabeazione del tempio classico, posto tra l'architrave e la cornice. Per estensione, qualunque parte decorata, a rilievo o meno, di un edificio.

Frontone
Nell'architettura classica, struttura triangolare o, più raramente, ad arco ribassato, posta a coronamento del tempio. In genere, completamento superiore della facciata di un edificio religioso o civile.

Fusione
Lavorazione di materiale fuso, generalmente metallo (in particolare rame, bronzo e ottone), o resine poliestere, che colato in stampi o secondo la tecnica della cera persa, permette di ottenere una scultura.

Fusto
La parte della colonna composta da una struttura cilindrica, formata da blocchi regolari e sovrapposti di pietra (rocchi)

G

Galleria
Passaggio coperto a corridoio o loggia. Con il termine si indica anche un museo di arti figurative.

Girale
Elemento decorativo, di origine romana, formato da motivi vegetali avvolti a spirale.

Glìttica
Arte della lavorazione delle pietre dure.

Graffito
Disegno ottenuto incidendo con una punta dura una superficie (muro, pietra, intonaco, ceramica, metallo). Frequente fu il suo utilizzo per la decorazione di palazzi in età rinascimentale.

Greca
Motivo decorativo stilizzato, composto da linee spezzate ad angolo retto, in successione regolare.

Grisàille
Tinta grigio-bruna o nera utilizzata dai maestri vetrai del medioevo per realizzare il disegno o dare chiaroscuro alle immagini.

Guazzo (o gouache)
Tecnica pittorica che prevede l'uso di colori mescolati ad acqua, colla e biacca. Si differenzia dall'acquerello per il suo carattere coprente e, per questo, tendenzialmente opaco. Fu utilizzato a partire dalla fine del XIV secolo.

Guglia
Elemento decorativo a forma di cono o di piramide molto allungata, tipico dell'architettura gotica, posto al culmine di strutture architettoniche verticali.

H

Haiku
Ideogramma utilizzato nella figurazione giapponese, che raffigura una breve composizione poetica. È tracciato con rapidità e senza ripensamenti, e presenta perciò carattere sintetico.

Hortus
Spazio recintato, adibito a giardino. Si trovava generalmente nel retro della domus, poi sostituito dal peristylium. Nel Medioevo divenne un motivo iconografico (*hortus conclusus*), raffigurante un giardino recintato, lussureggiante e generalmente arricchito della presenza di figure sacre (Madonna col Bambino, santi).

I

Icòna
Immagine sacra dell'arte bizantina e orientale, spesso dipinta su tavola. È iconica ogni cultura basata sull'immagine. Per il significato nell'ambito della semantica, v. segno.

Iconòstasi
Struttura architettonica diffusa nelle prime chiese cristiane, soprattutto in oriente, che divide la navata centrale dal presbiterio. È composta da una transenna in marmo sorretta da colonne e ornata da statue e immagini sacre.

Imposta
Il piano di appoggio della volta dell'arco sul piedritto (v.).

Incisione
Tecnica di stampa, di probabile origine orientale (in Cina fu usata dal VI sec. d.C.). Consiste nell'incidere un disegno su una lastra metallica, di legno o di altro materiale, allo scopo di stamparlo su un foglio. La riproduzione a stampa si ottiene per pressione di carta o altro materiale sulla matrice inchiostrata. Tra le tecniche di disegno in cavo: acquaforte, acquatinta, bulino, punta secca.

Intaglio
Lavorazione di materiali diversi, legno, metallo, pietra, pietre dure, ad incisione o a rilievo.

Intarsio
Applicazione ad incastro di materiali diversi o di diverso colore su di una superficie precedentemente intagliata secondo un disegno preordinato.

Intercolumnio
Spazio tra due colonne. Negli ordini architettonici classici, specialmente in base alle teorizzazioni degli architetti del Rinascimento, le sue misure seguono determinate leggi proporzionali.

Intonaco
Strato di rivestimento steso uniformemente sul muro, anche per prepararlo all'affresco. Si costituisce di legante (calce, cemento, gesso) e di inerte (sabbia, pozzolana).

Intradosso
Superficie concava, interna dell'arco o delle volte. Per estensione, parte sottostante dell'architrave nel sistema trilitico.

Ionico (ordine)
Ordine architettonico greco, caratterizzato da colonne con leggere scanalature, capitello con volute laterali e fregio continuo. Nato nella Ionia nel VII sec. a.C., si diffuse a partire dal VI sec. a.C. nelle isole dell'Egeo, in Asia Minore e in Attica.

Ipogèo
Edificio scavato nella roccia o nel terreno; generalmente destinato a sepoltura, può essere anche adibito ad abitazione o a luogo di culto.

Ipòstilo
Ambiente il cui soffitto è retto da colonne o pilastri distribuiti in modo uniforme. Tale disposizione è frequente, nell'antichità, nell'architettura egizia e in minor misura in quella greca; dal X secolo d.C. ebbe interessante sviluppo nell'architettura sacra araba.

Isòdomo
Muro costituito da filari di pietre o mattoni di uguale altezza, disposti in modo che i giunti siano alternati.

Isometria
Metodo di rappresentazione grafica che descrive un elemento spaziale riproducendone le lunghezze, senza alterarne i rapporti dimensionali.

K

Kakemòno
Rotolo dipinto di carta o seta, tipico dell'arte giapponese, da appendere alla parete.

Kòilon
Gradinata del teatro greco dove sedevano gli spettatori.

Kòre
(Pl. *kòrai*). Statua greca d'età arcaica raffigurante una fanciulla vestita.

Koúros
(Pl. *koúroi*). Statua greca d'età arcaica che rappresenta un giovane nudo.

L

Lacca
Densa vernice derivata dalla linfa dell'albero della lacca (diffuso in Estremo Oriente, dove nacque e si sviluppò la tecnica), usata

soprattutto per la decorazione dei mobili. Ha aspetto lucido, è impermeabile e molto resistente.

Lanterna

Elemento architettonico a pianta poligonale o circolare posto a sommità della cupola, dalle cui aperture laterali penetra la luce all'interno.

Laterizio

(dal latino *later*, mattone). Materiale edile ottenuto attraverso un processo di indurimento, naturale o artificiale, dell'argilla. Già nel IV millennio era diffuso l'utilizzo di argilla cotta al sole. Celebri per varietà e qualità furono i laterizi romani, cotti in fornaci.

Lesèna

Elemento architettonico con funzione decorativa, costituito da un semipilastro o semicolonna adagiato al muro, spesso completo di base e capitello.

Libro d'ore

Libro di preghiere per laici, manoscritto e spesso arricchito da disegni miniati.

Litografia

Procedimento di stampa in cui l'immagine è disegnata su una lastra di pietra o metallo. Si basa sul principio che una sostanza grassa attira sostanze analoghe e respinge, invece, l'acqua. La grana fine della pietra, o del metallo lavorato, trattiene il disegno, realizzato con materiale grasso. Nelle parti scoperte, la lastra assorbe l'acqua di lavaggio, e respinge l'inchiostro litografico, spalmato in una successiva fase, che si fissa soltanto sulle parti disegnate. La litografia odierna, sia quella commerciale che quella artistica, utilizza lastre flessibili di zinco o di alluminio.

Loggia

Elemento architettonico composto da un porticato con balaustra, autonomo o facente parte di un edificio monumentale.

Lunetta

Parte di una parete limitata in alto da un arco.

M

Maiolica

Ceramica tenera realizzata con pasta porosa a base di argilla, e rivestita con smalto a base di stagno. Celebre fu nel Rinascimento la sua lavorazione nella città di Faenza, da cui trae origine il sinonimo francese di *faïence*.

Mastàba

Monumento sepolcrale egizio a forma di tronco di piramide, utilizzato soprattutto nel III millennio a.C..

Mastio (o maschio)

Torre principale di una fortezza; per estensione, fortezza.

Matroneo

Nelle basiliche cristiane, zona riservata alle donne, costituita da una galleria ricavata sopra ciascuna navata laterale e aperta su quella centrale.

Mausolèo

Monumento funerario di grandi dimensioni. Così detto in riferimento a quello fatto erigere dal re Mausolo di Alicarnasso.

Medaglia

Disco in metallo talvolta pregiato che reca impresse figure e scritte. Ha intenti celebrativi o commemorativi.

Mègaron

Nella reggia micenea, e poi nelle case greche arcaiche, sala rettangolare che costituiva l'ambiente centrale, dove generalmente era posto il focolare.

Menhír

Monumento dell'età megalitica, costituito da una lunga pietra conficcata verticalmente nel terreno.

Mensola

Elemento architettonico sporgente da un muro, utilizzato come sotegno di travi o cornici.

Merlo

Elemento in muratura con funzione difensiva, collocato in sequenza regolare a coronamento degli edifici in età medievale o rinascimentale. Sc ha profilo superiore rettilineo è detto guelfo; se è a coda di rondone, è detto ghibellino.

Mètopa

Elemento decorativo del fregio dorico, alternato al triglifo. Realizzata in materiale fittile, in pietra o in marmo, ha forma di lastra quadrangolare, ed è spesso decorata con rilievi.

Mihràb

Nicchia scavata nel muro interno della moschea, orientata verso la città sacra di La Mecca.

Minareto

Torre alta ed esile, da cui i fedeli islamici vengono chiamati alla preghiera. Ebbe origine intorno alla fine del VII secolo d.C..

Miniatura

(Dal latino *minio*, colore rosso cinabro). Tecnica pittorica all'acquarello o a guazzo (v.) usata per decorare o illustrare libri o pergamene. Di origine orientale, ha avuto particolare fioritura in Europa tra il XIII e il XIV sec. Per estensione, ogni dipinto di piccolo formato.

Modanatura

Elemento decorativo in rilievo che orna un elemento architettonico.

Mòdulo

Unità di misura assunta convenzionalmente per stabilire i criteri di proporzionalità di un'opera.

Monòfora

Finestra con un'unica apertura.

Monogramma

Intreccio o sovrapposizione delle iniziali o di alcune lettere di un nome, utilizzate come simbolo del nome stesso.

Mosaico

Tecnica consistente nell'accostamento di piccoli elementi in pietra, marmo o pasta vitrea colorata (detti tessere), disposti in modo da comporre figure. Il mosaico pavimentale può essere composto da elementi marmorei o lapidei (*opus tessellatum*) o smaltati (*opus vermiculatum*); il mosaico parietale consta di tessere in marmo o pietre di varia forma (*opus sectile*) o di tessere in pasta vitrea (*opus musivum*). Di origine asiatica, trovò ampia diffusione in Grecia e presso i Romani, soprattutto come rivestimento pavimentale; nel mondo cristiano, utilizzato come rivestimento di pareti e volte, per i suoi particolari caratteri di luminosità assunse valore simbolico.

N

Nàos

Cella del tempio greco dove era collocata la statua della divinità.

Nartèce

Portico largamente usato nelle chiese paleocristiane. Se esterno all'edificio, si chiama esonartece, se interno, endonartece.

Navata

Ciascuno degli spazi interni della basilica romana e cristiana, individuati da file di colonne o pilastri.

Nervatura

Elemento architettonico corrispondente alle linee di raccordo tra le volte, che scarica le spinte e le controspinte della struttura.

Nicchia

Incavo ricavato nello spessore del muro, frequentemente a forma di semicilindro sormontato da un quarto di sfera.

Niello

Tecnica usata nell'oreficeria, consistente nell'inserire una pasta di colore nero composta di stagno, argento, zolfo e rame (il niello) negli incavi incisi a bulino su una superficie metallica.

Ninfèo

(Dal greco *nymphàion*, consacrato alle ninfe). Costruzione frequente in età romana, dotata spesso di àbside e nicchie, con vasca centrale. Il termine passò a individuare, nel Rinascimento, qualsiasi luogo chiuso con fontana.

Nuràghe

Costruzione di origine megalitica a tronco di cono composta di massi in pietra sovrapposti, caratteristica delle zone costiere della Sardegna.

O

Obelisco

Pilastro celebrativo tipico dell'arte egizia, poi etìope; monolitico di forma allungata, restringentesi verso l'alto, ha sezione quadrangolare e punta piramidale. Poggia su una base quadrata con gradini. Importato a

Roma in età imperiale, fu variamente utilizzato nel Rinascimento.

Offset
Procedimento di stampa che consente di riprodurre in serie immagini poste su lastra. Sfrutta il principio della litografia, basato sulla distinzione tra i grassi e l'acqua: nella stampa le parti umide restano bianche, quelle inchiostrate assorbono il colore. Differisce pertanto dalla tipografia, che si avvale di parti in rilievo. Le lastre possono essere realizzate in alluminio, (materiale più diffuso), zinco, plastica, rame e carta.

Ogiva
Costolone diagonale della volta a crociera dell'architettura gotica. È detto ogivale l'arco a sesto acuto.

Ombreggiatura
In pittura e nel disegno, tecnica di chiaroscuro che suggerisce il rilievo.

Opus
Tecnica di opera muraria o pavimentale. Si fa generalmente riferimento alle distinzioni di età romana, estese poi a tutta l'edilizia antica:
- *opus caementicium*: ottenuta dall'impasto di sassi e malta;
- *opus incertum*: ottenuta con pietre di formato diverso;
- *opus latericium*: costituita da mattoni di forma uguale legati con malta di calce e sabbia;
- *opus mixtum*: alterna strati di mattoni con altri di pietra;
- *opus quadratum*: composta da blocchi di pietra squadrati, legati con malta;
- *opus poligonale*: generalmente utilizzata per le mura urbane, è formata da blocchi di pietra in poligoni irregolari, disposti a secco;
- *opus reticulatum*: composta da blocchi di pietra regolari, a forma di prisma, disposti diagonalmente;
- *opus sectile*: decorazione pavimentale o parietale a tarsie marmoree, talvolta con disegni di elevato valore estetico.

Oratorio
Cappella privata di palazzo o di convento. Generalmente in edificio isolato, venne talvolta disposto entro le mura dei castelli medievali. Ebbe particolare fortuna in età barocca.

Orchestra
Nel teatro greco, lo spazio tra la càvea e il proscenio, dove agivano il coro e i danzatori.

Ordine architettonico
Sistema architettonico costituito da un insieme di regole stilistiche e proporzionali, in modo da essere unitario sotto l'aspetto del linguaggio e della forma. Originati dalla cultura greca (ordine dorico, ionico, corinzio), gli ordini furono poi codificati e rielaborati in età romana, fino alle definitive sistematizzazioni teoriche di età rinascimentale e barocca.

Orditura
(Dal latino *ordiri*, tessere una trama).

Superficie composta da elementi lineari posti a reticolo, che sostengono un solaio o la copertura di un tetto.

P

Padiglione
Costruzione architettonica isolata, che sorge all'interno di un parco o di un giardino.

Pagoda
Tempio sacro buddista, generalmente a pianta quadrata in India, a più piani con logge e tetto ricurvo in Cina.

Pala
Dipinto o rilievo di soggetto sacro collocato sopra l'altare.

Palcoscenico
Parte del teatro dove avviene la rappresentazione e dove si collocano i servizi annessi all'azione scenica. Il palcoscenico moderno ha ricevuto impulso al rinnovamento dal Total Theater di Gropius, sperimentato al Bauhaus, che sposta il palcoscenico al centro del teatro e lo rende mobile ed attivo.

Papiro
Pianta da cui gli Egizi ricavavano fogli per scrivere. La sua parte interna veniva tagliata in strisce sottili, quindi sovrapposte, bagnate e pressate. Per estensione, foglio ottenuto dalla lavorazione della pianta omonima.

Parasta
Pilastro incassato nella parete ma da questa leggermente sporgente, avente funzione portante.

Pastello
Tecnica pittorica che prevede l'uso di matite di pasta grassa, duttile e coprente. Viene generalmente utilizzato per rendere campiture piene, a zone cromatiche vivaci e brillanti.

Pàtio
Cortile interno circondato da logge e da portici, a somiglianza del *peristylium* della domus romana. Fu introdotto in Europa dagli Arabi, attraverso la Spagna.

Peduccio
Pietra sporgente, a forma di mensola o di capitello, che regge l'imposta di un arco o di una volta.

Pennacchio
Elemento architettonico a forma di triangolo sferico posto tra la base circolare della cupola e il sottostante edificio a base quadrangolare.
Parte di muratura compresa tra l'estradosso di due archi affiancati.

Peplo
Abito femminile in uso nell'antica Grecia, formato da un drappo di lana passato sotto il braccio destro e fermato sulla spalla sinistra con una fibbia.

Pergamo
v. pulpito

Peristilio
Colonnato, o genericamente porticato con

colonne, che si sviluppa intorno a un edificio o ad uno spazio aperto delimitato (ad es. nella domus romana).

Pianta
Rappresentazione grafica di un'architettura sul piano orizzontale.

Piedestallo
Struttura idonea a reggere una colonna, una statua o un obelisco.

Piedritto
Elemento architettonico verticale posto tra il capitello e l'arco.

Pieve
Termine medievale che indica una piccola chiesa di campagna.

Pigmento
Sostanza colorante, naturale o artificiale, che amalgamata con leganti è usata come base per la realizzazione di colori.

Pilastro
Elemento architettonico di sostegno per archi, volte e architravi, generalmente a pianta quadrata o quadrangolare. Con l'introduzione del cemento armato è aumentato sensibilmente il suo uso, in quanto vi si concentra in maniera puntiforme la spinta dei carichi, rendendo superfluo il muro portante. Tra le principali tipologie, il pilastro cruciforme (quadrangolare, con quattro semicolonne addossate ai lati) e a fascio (o polìstilo, cui si addossano semicolonne o lesene a sostegno delle nervature che corrono sulle strutture sorrette).

Pinacoteca
Museo o semplice raccolta destinati all'esposizione di opere di pittura.

Pinnacolo
Piccola guglia a forma di piramide o di cono.

Piombatura
Tecnica utilizzata per unire gli elementi di una vetrata con liste di piombo.

Piramide
Edificio sepolcrale dell'antico Egitto di forma piramidale, utilizzato nel periodo tra la III e la XVII dinastia. Contiene una o più stanze funerarie con ambienti annessi, collegate da corridoi. Nelle civiltà precolombiane è a gradoni, percorsa sui quattro lati da una gradinata. Sulla sommità, piatta, si ergeva un tempio.

Piramide visiva
Piramide virtuale costituita dai raggi che collegano i punti di un oggetto al punto di vista (il vertice della piramide), fissando l'immagine su un piano teorico trasparente (il quadro). La prospettiva dell'oggetto raffigurato è determinata dall'intersezione del piano pittorico con la piramide.

Pirografia
Tecnica di incisione che consiste nel lavorare con una punta metallica arroventata su materiali diversi, quali pelle, cartone o legno.

Placcatura
Rivestimento di un metallo povero con un altro di maggior pregio.

Plinto
Parte del piedestallo della colonna poggiante sul basamento. Estensivamente, il termine designa ogni elemento con funzione di basamento. Nelle moderne costruzioni in cemento armato, il plinto è una struttura parallelepipeda di fondazione.

Pòdio
Basamento elevato di un edificio. Noto è il podio degli edifici templari etruschi e romani.

Polìfora
Finestra a più aperture divise da colonnette o pilastrini

Polimaterica
Opera figurativa eseguita con materiali di diversa natura.

Polìstilo (pilastro)
v. fascio (pilastro a).

Polìttico
Dipinto o rilievo composto da più pannelli. Se i pannelli sono tre (trittico), i laterali possono essere richiusi (portelle).

Ponderazione
Nella statuaria, equilibrio della distribuzione del peso della figura umana. In scultura si fa riferimento soprattutto alla ponderazione di Policlèto, che esaltò la corrispondenza inversa tra le parti di una figura (chiasma).

Porcellana
Ceramica di origine cinese, realizzata con argille pregiate, quarzo e feldspato, a pasta bianca e dura, con rivestimento lucido.

Portale
Ingresso monumentale di un edificio.

Portante
Struttura architettonica atta a sostenere una spinta o un peso.

Portico
Galleria aperta con un colonnato, posta generalmente al pianterreno di un edificio.

Predella
Parte inferiore, dipinta o scolpita, di una pala d'altare o di un polittico, di cui può seguire la suddivisione in più parti. In genere, pedana lignea sottostante un mobile.

Presbiterio
Detto anche coro o sacrarium, è la zona della chiesa che circonda l'altare maggiore, riservata al clero. Può essere recintato ed elevato sulla cripta.

Proiezione
(Dal latino proicere, gettare in avanti) Nella geometria descrittiva, operazione grafica consistente nel congiungere con raggi proiettanti i punti dell'oggetto che si intende descrivere con il centro di proiezione (da cui partono i raggi proiettanti) e con la stessa figura che si ottiene sul piano che riceve la proiezione. Se il centro di proiezione è all'infinito, i raggi proiettanti sono paralleli e la proiezione è detta ortogonale; negli altri casi la proiezione è detta prospettica o centrale.

Prònao
Nel tempio greco, l'atrio con colonne antistante al naos. Per estensione, portico che precede un edificio monumentale.

Propilèi
Ingresso monumentale con porticato di edifici o luoghi monumentali, quali aree sacre, palazzi, piazze. Il termine si riferisce ad impianti realizzati nell'antichità, o in età moderna nel caso di progetti classicisti.

Prospettiva
In generale, la visione "prospettica" corrisponde al modo di vedere la realtà da parte dell'uomo. Nella geometria descrittiva, è la tecnica di rappresentazione di una figura tridimensionale o dello spazio in generale su una superficie bidimensionale, mediante un punto di vista e un punto di fuga o di concorso: il primo corrisponde alla posizione dell'occhio di chi osserva, il secondo alla convergenza in profondità delle linee parallele tra loro. La rappresentazione prospettica è stata utilizzata nelle arti figurative, in forma intuitiva, già in età greca e romana. Gli artisti non utilizzavano il punto di fuga o di concorso, ma generalmente un asse, cui fare convergere le linee in profondità (asse di fuga).
Il pensiero simbolico del Medioevo non favorì l'uso di rappresentazioni naturalistiche come la prospettiva (giungendo persino, nella figurazione bizantina, a definire una prospettiva inversa, con le linee convergenti non in profondità, ma in un piano vicino all'osservatore). All'inizio del Quattrocento, a Firenze, F. Brunelleschi, e successivamente L.B. Alberti e P. della Francesca definirono con rigore le leggi geometriche prospettiche. Dopo le 'forzature' barocche e settecentesche per alterare l'effetto di profondità a fini espressivi, in età contemporanea si tende a non utilizzare la prospettiva come strumento di mimesi della realtà, ma solo come elemento utile a riflettere sul concetto di spazio.
Se la geometria descrittiva e proiettiva si occupano della prospettiva lineare (in cui il punto di convergenza delle linee proiettive, detto di fuga o di concorso, è posto sulla linea di orizzonte, all'altezza degli occhi dello spettatore), la pittura conosce anche la prospettiva aerea teorizzata da Leonardo nel Rinascimento (non le regole geometriche, ma la densità del colore 'descrive' lo spazio) e la prospettiva cromatica, generalmente utilizzata dai pittori veneti del Rinascimento (la profondità spaziale è resa mediante accostamento di toni dello stesso colore e di colori diversi).

Prospetto
Disegno architettonico che raffigura una parete esterna di un edificio, misurata in proiezione ortogonale.

Pròtiro
Locale d'accesso della casa romana. Nelle chiese romaniche, piccolo atrio di accesso posto davanti al portale, costituito da due colonne che sorreggono una volta.

Pùlpito (o pergamo)
Elemento architettonico rialzato riservato all'oratore, collocato nella navata centrale della chiesa. Ha forma quadrata o poligonale, raramente circolare.

Pulvìno
Elemento architettonico di origine bizantina, posto tra il capitello e l'imposta dell'arco. Ha forma di piramide tronca rovesciata, ed è spesso decorato a rilievo.

Puntasecca
Tecnica di stampa che consiste nell'eseguire l'incisione direttamente sulla lastra in metallo (generalmente rame).

Q

Quadratura
Fondale scenografico dipinto su di una parete con lo scopo di dare l'effetto di una prospettiva architettonica reale. Fu molto utilizzato nel teatro dal Rinascimento ai secoli XVIII-XIX.

Quadriportico
Nelle basiliche paleocristiane, e più raramente in quelle protoromaniche, portico che si sviluppa sui quattro lati del cortile antistante la facciata. In origine vi sostavano i catecumeni, in attesa di ricevere il battesimo.

Quadro
Il termine fu utilizzato da L. B. Alberti per definire il piano trasparente che, fungendo da piano di sezione della piramide visiva (v.), fissa i punti di passaggio dei raggi visivi. Sul quadro pertanto si proiettano le immagini prospettiche.

R

Radialità
Principio compositivo utilizzato nella grafica e nella progettazione architettonica e urbanistica, che tende a mettere in relazione le varie parti rispetto a un centro. La radialità pertanto non si riferisce soltanto a configurazioni ad impianto centrale, come per es. i poligoni regolari, quanto agli organismi in cui la relazione tra il centro e gli altri elementi diviene l'aspetto predominante della composizione.

Radiali (cappelle)
Cappelle collocate a raggiera attorno all'abside delle chiese romaniche e gotiche.

Rampante (arco)
Arco dell'architettura gotica che collega dall'esterno il pilastro perimetrale della navata minore con il muro o la continuazione di un pilastro della navata centrale, e serve a sorreggere la spinta che questa opera sul pilastro.

Restauro
Insieme degli interventi tecnici finalizzati alla conservazione o al recupero di un'opera d'arte. Le sue modalità dipendono da parametri di tipo storico-filologico, e sono condizionate da precise scelte teoriche.

Rilievo
Attività volta alla misurazione di presenze sul territorio, di opere di architettura o di sue parti, o di elementi o opere di arte figurativa. La qualità del rilievo dipende dal

numero, dalla qualità e dalla correttezza delle informazioni raccolte.

Detto anche di opera di scultura in cui le figure emergono dal fondo piano. Se esse sporgono in modo notevole, è detto altorilievo, se la sporgenza non supera la metà della profondità delle figure, è detto bassorilievo.

Rinzaffo
La prima mano di intonaco stesa sul muro destinato ad essere dipinto ad affresco.

Rosone
Finestra circolare posta al centro della facciata delle chiese romaniche e più spesso gotiche, ornata di cornice e raggi, e/o di vetrata dipinta.

S

Sala capitolare
Sala di riunione del collegio di una comunità monastica. Generalmente si affacciava sul chiostro del convento.

Saliente
La linea obliqua che segue il profilo della facciata di una chiesa, in corrispondenza della navata.

Sanguigna
Pastello composto di un'argilla ferruginosa color rosso scuro; per estensione il disegno con esso ottenuto.

Sarcòfago
Cassone funerario in legno, pietra o altro materiale, spesso scolpito.

Sbalzo
Tecnica con cui si modellano figure su lastre metalliche, con ceselli, mediante pressione sul rovescio delle lastre stesse.

Scanalatura
Solco rettilineo che orna gli elementi architettonici, quali ad es. il fusto delle colonne negli ordini classici.

Scena
Termine che deriva dalla *skenè* greca, edificio rettangolare posto sul fondo del basamento che formava il palcoscenico. Come nei teatri antichi, anche in quelli moderni il termine designa le parti architettoniche fisse in cui viene ambientata l'azione.

Schematizzazione
Riduzione in forma essenziale, tramite disegno, di una figura o composizione di figure.

Schizzo
Abbozzo rapido e sintetico, a matita o ad inchiostro, mediante il quale l'autore traccia le idee preliminari di un'intervento artistico o di progettazione di qualsiasi natura. Può avere un valore espressivo autonomo, soprattutto a partire dal '700.

Schola cantorum
Nelle chiese paleocristiane, spazio antistante l'altare, talvolta transennato, riservato ai cantori. Dall'età romanica è trasferito nell'area del coro (v.).

Segno
Indizio (grafico, sonoro, visivo, olfattivo, ecc.) da cui si possono trarre informazioni. Relativamente al suo rapporto con il significato, è stato classificato in:
- segno-icona, se assomiglia all'oggetto reale (ad esempio un ritratto);
- indice, se è un indizio dell'oggetto (ad esempio, il suono di una campana suggerisce la presenza di una chiesa);
- simbolo, se il suo rapporto con l'oggetto reale è basato su forme convenzionali (ad esempio, il cartello stradale prescrive il comportamento da seguire).

Serigrafia
Procedimento di stampa in piano basato sull'uso di un telaio di seta o nylon, reso impermeabile nelle zone non stampanti; l'inchiostro viene quindi fatto passare tra le maglie del tessuto rimaste libere.

Sesto
Curvatura dell'arco e della volta. Più frequentemente è a tutto sesto (se di forma semicircolare), ribassato o acuto.

Sezione
Rappresentazione grafica che evidenzia l'interno di un edificio, ottenuta tagliandolo idealmente mediante un piano verticale o orizzontale (in tal caso si visualizza la pianta).

Sguancio
Superficie obliqua del muro che contorna portali e finestre.

Sigillo
Strumento in metallo o in pietra recante sulla superficie, inciso o in rilievo, un disegno che rimarrà segnato in negativo su cera lacca, carta o altro materiale.

Sikkàra
Torre in pietra, spesso decorata a rilievo o con statue, che si erge sopra la cella dedicata alla divinità nei templi indiani.

Simmetria
Nella comunicazione visiva, corrispondenza delle parti di una composizione rispetto ad uno o più assi, o ad un piano. Più generalmente, indica il rapporto tra le parti e il tutto.

Sinòpia
Disegno preparatorio per l'affresco in terra rossa eseguito sull'arriccio. È poi coperto con l'ultimo strato di intonaco, su cui viene dipinto l'affresco.

Smalto
Pasta vitrea colorata che viene applicata a fuoco sui metalli. Vernice oleosa opaca con cui si rivestono le ceramiche.

Spicchio
Porzione della volta o della cupola delimitata dalle nervature, a forma di triangolo sferico.

Spiovente
Falda inclinata del tetto, coperta di pietre o tegole.

Spolvero
Procedimento esecutivo dell'affresco, tramite il quale il disegno su cartone viene riportato

sul muro. Consiste nel far passare della polvere di carbone in piccoli fori praticati sul cartone, che seguono le linee del disegno.

Stadio
Edificio destinato alle competizioni sportive. Nell'antica Grecia e nel mondo romano, essendo utilizzato per le gare di corsa, aveva forma allungata. Quello romano, era concluso su un lato da un semicerchio ed era diviso al centro da una spina, che divideva i percorsi.

Stallo
Sedile ampio e riccamente lavorato (ad intaglio o intarsio), generalmente in legno. È frequente nel coro delle basiliche cristiane, ripetuto in più file.

Stampa
Procedimento di riproduzione di un disegno, viene ottenuta per impressione da una matrice (detta anche stampo) inchiostrata. Il disegno può essere realizzato in rilievo, in cavo o in piano. Si dice anche della riproduzione stessa.

Stele
Lastra marmorea con iscrizioni e rilievi posta con fini celebrativi o commemorativi su un luogo, a memoria di un evento.

Stemma
Emblema araldico, spesso usato a fini decorativi.

Stiacciato (o schiacciato)
Rilievo a bassissima sporgenza, usato nel Rinascimento, in cui l'effetto di profondità è ottenuto attraverso particolari accorgimenti applicati al disegno prospettico.

Stilòbate
Piano superiore del basamento del tempio greco, su cui sono collocate le colonne (detto anche crepidòma).

Stilòforo
Scultura realizzata per sostenere elementi architettonici, generalmente colonne.

Stipite
Sostegno laterale del vano di una porta o di una finestra.

Stòa
Portico rettangolare aperto tipico dell'architettura greca classica.

Strappo
Procedimento tramite il quale l'affresco viene trasferito dal supporto originale ad un altro.

Stucco
Materiale a base di gesso e calce, facilmente modellabile, spesso usato per la decorazione degli interni; può essere dipinto o dorato.

T

Tabernacolo
Piccola struttura a forma di tempietto, posta sull'altare, dove vengono conservate le particole consacrate.

Detto anche di edicola posta lungo la strada, contenente un'immagine sacra.

Tablìnum
Nella casa romana, la stanza situata oltre l'atrio, dove si conservavano le memorie familiari e in cui venivano accolti gli ospiti.

Tamburo
Struttura architettonica a base circolare o poligonale, sulla quale viene eretta la cupola.

Teatro
Edificio di origine greca usato per la rappresentazione di spettacoli. Si componeva di una zona semicircolare (platea) a gradoni, destinata al pubblico, di uno spazio generalmente circolare (orchestra) destinato al coro, di una zona praticabile, su cui agivano gli attori, e di una scena architettonica fissa.

Telamone
Statua raffigurante la figura umana maschile, con funzione di sostegno di strutture architettoniche.

Telèro
Tela dipinta di grandi dimensioni. Il termine generalmente indica i grandi dipinti eseguiti a Venezia tra il XV e il XVII secolo.

Tempera
Tecnica pittorica che prevede l'uso di colori diluiti in acqua e fissati per mezzo di sostanze diverse (uovo, colla, latte, lattice di fico, gomma, cera, ecc.).

Terme
Complesso di edifici per bagni pubblici, in uso nel mondo greco e particolarmente in età romana imperiale. In quest'ultimo periodo si arricchiscono di nuove funzioni, annettendo palestre, biblioteche e luoghi di riunione. Il nucleo termale si compone di *calidarium*, *frigidarium* e *tepidarium*, distinti in base alla temperatura dell'acqua e all'utilizzo.

Terracotta
Argilla lavorata a mano e cotta al sole o in forni.

Tèssere
I singoli framenti in pietra, marmo o pasta vitrea che compongono il mosaico.

Thòlos
Costruzione funeraria a pianta circolare coperta da una volta a cupola o a pseudocupola, raggiungibile mediante un corridoio, tipica dell'architettura micenea. Per estensione, nelle età antiche successive, il termine designa ambienti a pianta centrale, coperti da cupola, a destinazione civile o religiosa.

Tibùrio
Copertura esterna di una cupola, di forma cubica o poligonale. È spesso aperta in finestre e coperta da un tetto a spioventi.

Timpano
Zona superiore della facciata di un edificio generalmente di stile classico, avente forma triangolare. Spesso ospita rilievi.

Ting
Vaso cinese da cerimonia, per lo più dotato di manici.

Toro
Modanatura a sezione semicircolare posta in genere alla base di una colonna.

Tòrtile (colonna)
Colonna con scanalatura a spirale attorno al fusto.

Tòtem
Nell'arte primitiva e nelle culture etnologiche, scultura lignea di idolo, rappresentazione degli antenati, spesso legata al culto dei morti. Può essere isolato o parte decorativa di edifici.

Trabeazione
L'insieme degli elementi orizzontali sovrastanti colonne e pilastri. Negli ordini greci si compone di architrave, fregio e cornice.

Traforo
Tecnica per mezzo della quale vengono intagliati, con trapano o altri strumenti, legno, pietra o lamine metalliche.

Transenna
Lastra lavorata, generalmente in pietra o marmo, usata per separare spazi interni o esterni.

Transetto
Nelle chiese cristiane, navata trasversale che interseca quelle longitudinali (V. croce latina).

Tribuna
Nella basilica romana, spazio riservato ai giudici; in quella cristiana, alle autorità clericali. Per estensione, l'area del presbiterio e dell'abside della chiesa.

Triclìnio
Nella casa romana, sala da pranzo.

Trìfora
Finestra a tre luci divisa da colonnette o pilastrini.

Triglifo
Elemento decorativo tipico dell'ordine dorico, costituito da una lastra di marmo o pietra di forma parallelepipeda percorsa da tre scanalature.

Trìttico
Dipinto o rilievo composto di tre parti principali unite fra loro.

Tùmulo (tomba a)
Tomba etrusca parzialmente scavata nel terreno, da cui emerge la copertura a calotta o conica.

Tuscanico (ordine)
Ordine architettonico di origine etrusca, caratterizzato da colonna liscia, capitello simile a quello ionico e dall'echino schiacciato.

U

Urna
Recipiente di varia forma ed utilizzo. In particolare destinato a raccogliere le ceneri del defunto dopo la cremazione.

V

Vascolare
Relativo alla lavorazione (fabbricazione e decorazione) dei vasi.

Vela
Volta a forma di triangolo sferico poggiante su di un edificio a pianta quadrata. Anche spicchio di volta a crociera.

Vetrata
Chiusura in vetro di un'apertura su muro. Può essere composta da un insieme di tasselli di vetro, di vario colore e dimensione, uniti da un'intelaiatura metallica (generalmente in piombo).

Volta
Struttura architettonica ad arco che copre un edificio o parte di esso.

Voluta
Elemento decorativo ad andamento curvilineo e/o spiraliforme. Caratteristica del capitello ionico e composto, può anche raccordare le parti della facciata di una chiesa.

X

Xilografia
Tecnica di stampa che prevede l'uso di una tavoletta di legno incisa e inchiostrata sulle parti in rilievo

Z

Ziggurat (o ziqqurat)
Nell'architettura mesopotamica, alta torre in mattoni, per lo più a gradoni, avente sulla sommità un santuario e percorsa da una lunga scala.

Zoccolo
Elemento architettonico che funge da basamento di una struttura di sostegno. Parte sporgente di un muro alla base di un edificio.

INDICE DEI NOMI